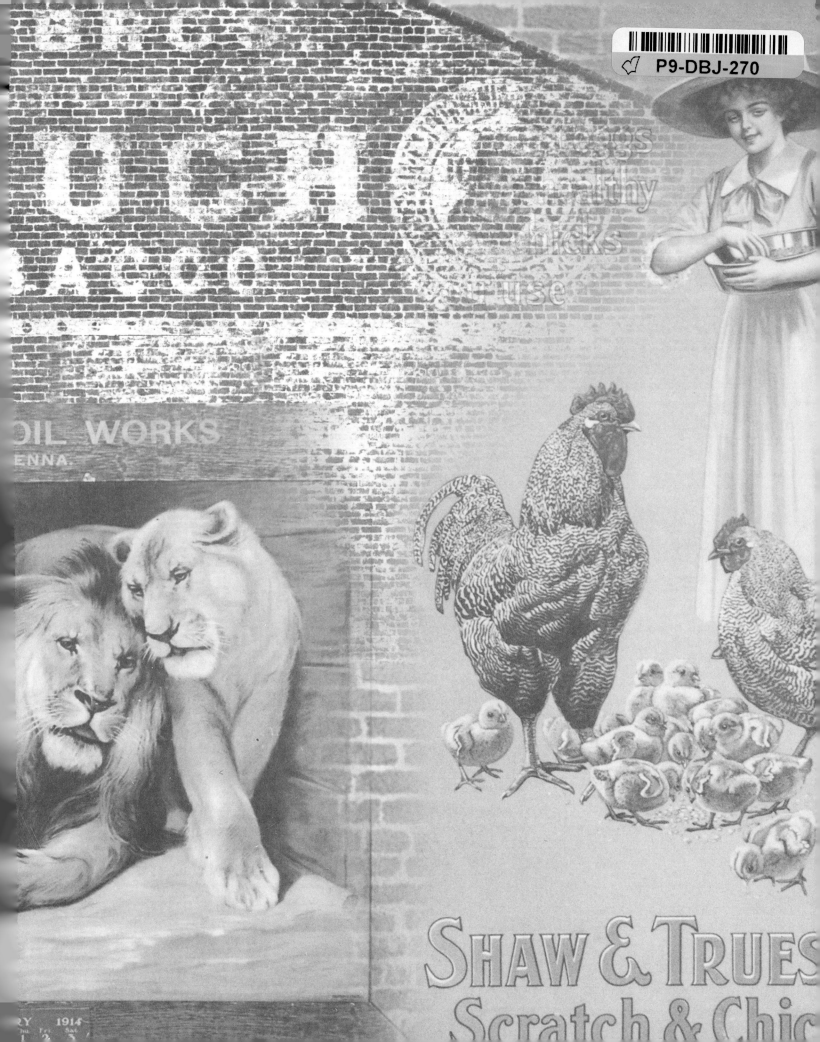

ANTIQUE & CONTEMPORARY
Advertising
MEMORABILIA
Identification & Value Guide

BACO=CURO

CURES

TOBACCO   HABIT

B. J. Summers

cb

COLLECTOR BOOKS
A Division of Schroeder Publishing Co., Inc.

Dedication:
This book is dedicated to a couple of great copy editors Cherry
Pyron and Laurie Swick. Thanks for all the hard work.

Front cover:
Baco-Curo Advertising, $425.00 (B);
Geo. Goodman 1 gal. jug, $155.00;
Coca-Cola Sprite Boy Advertising, $275.00;
Champion Advertising Thermometer, $75.00;
Carll Advertising Calendar, $675.00.

Cover design by Beth Summers

Book design by Mary Ann Hudson

COLLECTOR BOOKS
P.O. Box 3009
Paducah, Kentucky 42002-3009

www.collectorbooks.com

The current values in this book should be used only as a guide. They are not
intended to set prices, which vary from one section of the country to
another. Auction prices as well as dealer prices vary greatly and are affected
by condition as well as demand. Neither the author nor the publisher
assumes responsibility for any losses that might be incurred as a result of
consulting this guide.

Searching For A Publisher?

We are always looking for people knowledgeable within their fields. If you feel
that there is a real need for a book on your collectible subject and have a
large comprehensive collection, contact Collector Books.

Acknowledgments

Many thanks to the following for their valuable contributions, either by supplying photographs or allowing their collectibles to be photographed:

Past Tyme Pleasures, 2491 San Ramon Valley Blvd., #1, 925-484-6442, e-mail: pasttyme@excite.com
Steve and Donna Howard produce several yearly advertising absentee auctions with a great colorful catalog and complete item descriptions. Call for a catalog or check them out at www.pasttyme.com.

Farmer's Daughter Antiques, 6330 Cairo Rd., Paducah, KY 42001, 270-444-7619
Bill and Jane Miller have one of the neatest shops you'll ever find. The mix of advertising (Bill's specialty), and primitives (Jane's specialty) is a winning combination in everyone's book. Their shop is easily located just a mile off 1-24 at Exit 3. You can't miss the big barn — stop by and talk to one of the friendliest couples in the antique world.

Richard Opfer Auctioneering, Inc., 1919 Greenspring Drive, Timonium, MD 21093, 410-252-5035
Richard Opfer Auctioneering, Inc. provides a great variety of antique and collectibles auctions. Give his friendly staff a call for his next auction catalog.

Charlie's Antique Mall, 303 Main St., P.O. Box 196, Hazel, KY 42049, 270-492-8175
Located in the historic antique community of Hazel, Ky., on Main St., this place has it all. The manager, Ray Gough, has some great dealers with a wide variety of antiques and collectibles and some of the friendliest help you'll find . This border town mall can keep even the pickiest collector busy for the better part of a day.

Wm. Morford, RD #2, Cazenovia, NY 13035, 315-662-7625
Wm. Morford has been operating one of the country's better cataloged phone auction businesses for several years. He doesn't list reproductions or repairs that are deceptive in nature. In each catalog is usually a section with items that are for immediate sale. Try out this site and tell him how you got his name and address.

Eric Reinfeld, 87 Seventh Avenue, Brooklyn, NY 11217, 718-783-2313
An avid Whistle and Coca-Cola collector all wrapped into one. Give Eric a call if you're interested in selling or buying advertising relating to these two categories.

Rare Bird Antique Mall, 212 South Main St., Goodlettsville, TN 37072, 615-851-2635
If you find yourself in the greater Nashville, Tenn., area, stop by this collector's paradise. Jon and Joan Wright have assembled a great cast of dealers who run the gamut of collectible merchandise. Step back to an era when the general store was the place to be, and be prepared to invest some well-spent time.

Buffalo Bay Auction Co., 5244 Quam Circle, Rogers, MN 55374, 612-428-8879
A great catalog auction with a good variety of advertising fare. If advertising is your cup of tea, you'll enjoy browsing their catalog with its excellent quality photographs and descriptions.

Twin Lakes Antique Mall, Hwy. 641 North, Gilbertsville, KY, 270-362-2218
Located conveniently in the heartland beside beautiful Kentucky Lake, this new mall is great. Ed and Dee Hanes run a super clean mall in this vacation land with a good selection of general line antiques and collectibles. You'll find a better than average selection of gas collectibles (Ed's hobby).

Antiques, Cards and Collectibles, 203 Broadway, Paducah, KY 42001, 270-443-9797
Right on the river in the historic Michael Hardware building, Ray Pelley has three floors filled with antiques and collectibles. Easy to find just off the loop in downtown Paducah. If you need help, Ray, Donna, and Emma are always ready with information and a smile.

Creatures of Habit, 406 Broadway, Paducah, KY 42001, 270-442-2923
A touch of the unusual is the first thing you'll notice when you walk into Natalya and Jack's shop. With an ample supply of out-of-the-ordinary advertising, this is a "must stop" when in the area. Good merchandise and plenty of friendly help are a winning combination.

Collectors Auction Services, Route 2, Box 431, Oakwood Drive, Oil City, PA 16301, 814-677-6070
Mark and Sherry run a great cataloged advertising auction service. With at least two very strong auctions a year, you'll find a fantastic variety of advertising and gas collectibles. Their catalogs are second to none and provide a great reference source. Make sure to give them a call and get involved in their next auction.

The Illinois Antique Center, 308 S.W. Commercial, Peoria, IL 61602, 309-673-3354
Overlooking the river in downtown Peoria, this huge warehouse has been remodeled by Dan and Kim and now has a wonderful selection of antiques and collectibles. Always a great source of advertising signs, statues, and memorabilia. You'll find an ample supple of smiling faces and help here. Plan on spending the better part of a day.

Gary Metz's Muddy River Trading Company, P.O. Box 18185, Roanoke, VA 24014, 540-982-3886
Gary probably produces one of the best advertising auctions in this country. While his emphasis is primarily on Coca-Cola and other soda products, he certainly isn't limited to those fields. Gary is probably one of the nicest people you'll ever meet. Give him a call and send for his next catalog to open up a whole new level of collecting.

Pleasant Hill Antique Mall and Tea Room, 315 South Pleasant Hill Rd., East Peoria, IL 61611, 309-694-4040
Bob Johnson and all the friendly staff at this mall welcome you for a day of shopping. And it'll take that long to work your way through all the quality antiques and collectibles at this mall. When you get tired, stop and enjoy a rest at the tea room where you can get some of the best home cooked food found anywhere. All in all, a great place to shop for your favorite antiques.

Michael and Deborah Summers, Paducah, KY 42001
My brother and sister-in-law are avid collectors and have been invaluable in helping compile information for this book. Mike and I have spent many days chasing down treasures at auctions.

Bill and Helen Mitchell, 226 Arendall St., Henderson, TN 38340, 731-989-9302
Bill and Helen have assembled a great variety of advertising with special emphasis on Coca-Cola, and they are always searching for new finds. So if you have anything that fits the bill, give them a call or drop them a letter.

Patrick's Collectibles, 612 Roxanne Dr., Antioch, TN 37013, 615-833-4621
If you happen to be around Nashville, Tenn., during the monthly flea market at the state fairgrounds, be certain to look for Mike and Julie Patrick. They have some of the sharpest advertising pieces you'll ever hope to find. And if Coca-Cola is your field, you won't be able to walk away from the great restored drink machines. Make sure to look them up, you certainly won't be sorry.

John and Vicki Mahan, 1407 N. 4th St., Murray, KY 42071, 270-753-4330
John's specialty is porcelain signs, but like most collectors, he's certainly not limited to signs. He's always looking to buy, sell, or trade, so give him a call.

Chief Paduke Antiques Mall, 300 S. 3rd St., Paducah, KY 42003, 270-442-6799
This full-to-overflowing mall is located in an old railroad depot in downtown Paducah with plenty of general line advertising including good Coke pieces, plus a good selection of furniture. Stop by and see Charley or Carolyn if you're in this area.

Autopia Advertising Auctions, 19937 N.E. 154th St. Bldg. C2, Woodinville, WA 98072, 425-883-7653
Autopia produces great mail, phone, and fax auctions. The catalogs are second to none, with great clear photos and very detailed product descriptions. Their auctions contain a complete line of advertising collectibles, so call them for a catalog.

Introduction

In this busy and fast-paced world, most of us are looking for a way to recapture a slower, simpler time. And usually we are willing to pay almost any price for those memories. One easy way to do this is to surround ourselves with the past. Advertising is a magical art form to that end. It offers collectibles as numerous as the sands on the beach. And yet there is an affordable niche that almost everyone can fit into comfortably. This book will hopefully help both the beginning as well as the advanced collector.

Entries are listed alphabetically, using either the company name or recognizable product name. A brief description of the advertising piece is next. The condition is noted as follows: NOS-New Old Stock; M-Mint; NM-Near Mint; Exc-Excellent; VG-Very Good; G-Good; F-Fair; P-Poor. Also in parentheses after the price is a code that will tell you how I arrived at the listed price. If you see a (B), then you know that the price quoted is an actual paid price at auction (please remember that some auction prices can be artificially high due to two determined bidders, and likewise low due to a lack of interest at that particular sale); (D) denotes a retail price placed on an object by a dealer, which may or may not have sold. (C) refers to a value placed by a collector. With many photos you will see a photo credit that indicates the origin of the item. The listed price may or may not have originated from that source.

It is my purpose to report market values, not to set prices. A well-educated collector is always one step ahead of the collecting crowd.

Enjoy.

Year	Patent #	Year	Patent #	Year	Patent #	Year	Patent #	Year	Patent #
1836	1	1866	51,784	1896	552,502	1926	1,568,040	1956	2,728,913
1837	110	1867	60,658	1897	574,369	1927	1,612,700	1957	2,775,762
1838	546	1868	72,959	1898	596,467	1928	1,654,521	1958	2,818,567
1839	1,061	1869	85,503	1899	616,871	1929	1,696,897	1959	2,866,973
1840	1,465	1870	98,460	1900	640,167	1930	1,742,181	1960	2,919,443
1841	1,923	1871	110,617	1901	664,827	1931	1,787,424	1961	2,966,681
1842	2,413	1872	122,304	1902	690,385	1932	1,839,190	1962	3,015,103
1843	2,901	1873	134,504	1903	71 7,521	1933	1,892,663	1963	3,070,801
1844	3,395	1874	146,120	1904	748,567	1934	1,941,449	1964	3,116,487
1845	3,873	1875	158,350	1905	778,834	1935	1,985,878	1965	3,163,865
1846	4,348	1876	171,641	1906	808,618	1936	2,026,516	1966	3,226,729
1847	4,914	1877	185,813	1907	839,799	1937	2,066,309	1967	3,295,143
1848	5,409	1878	198,733	1908	875,679	1938	2,104,004	1968	3,360,800
1849	5,993	1879	211,078	1909	908,436	1939	2,142,080	1969	3,419,907
1850	6,981	1880	223,211	1910	945,010	1940	2,185,170	1970	3,487,470
1851	7,865	1881	236,137	1911	980,178	1941	2,227,418	1971	3,551,909
1852	8,622	1882	251,685	1912	1,013,095	1942	2,268,540	1972	3,631,539
1853	9,512	1883	269,820	1913	1,049,326	1943	2,307,007	1973	3,707,729
1854	10,358	1884	291,016	1914	1,083,267	1944	2,338,081	1974	3,781,914
1855	12,117	1885	310,163	1915	1,123,212	1945	2,366,154	1975	3,858,241
1856	14,009	1886	333,494	1916	1,166,419	1946	2,391,856	1976	3,930,271
1857	16,324	1887	355,291	1917	1,210,389	1947	2,413,675	1977	4,000,520
1858	19,010	1888	375,720	1918	1,251,458	1948	2,433,824	1978	4,065,812
1859	22,477	1889	395,305	1919	1,290,027	1949	2,457,797	1979	4,131,952
1860	26,642	1890	418,665	1920	1,326,899	1950	2,492,944	1980	4,180,867
1861	31,005	1891	443,987	1921	1,364,063	1951	2,536,016	1981	4,242,757
1862	34,045	1892	466,315	1922	1,401,948	1952	2,580,379		
1863	37,266	1893	488,976	1923	1,440,362	1953	2,624,046		
1864	41,047	1894	511,744	1924	1,478,996	1954	2,664,562		
1865	45,685	1895	531,619	1925	1,521,590	1955	2,698,434		

A.A. Godkin Chemist, brass sign for drug store, 72" x 9", EX, $275.00 (B). *Courtesy of Riverview Antique Mall*

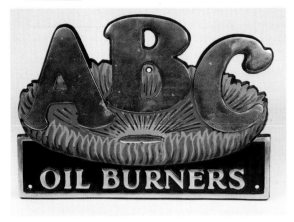

ABC Oil Burners, die cast metal sign, 11" x 8", EX, $135.00 (C).

AC Aircraft Products Servicenter, metal sign, 17¾" x 24¼", VG, $200.00 (B). *Courtesy of Collectors Auction Services*

Ace of Drinks, die cut cardboard advertising, framed and matted, 8" x 11⅞", VG, $50.00 (B).

Acme Cowboy Boots, neon sign, neon on painted metal, 20¼" x 12½", NM, $750.00 (B).

A.A. Godkin Chemist, brass sign for drug store, 72" x 9", F . . . .$95.00 (C)

A & P, very early die cut cardboard of kids in a wheelbarrow being pushed by a man, "going to the Great Atlantic and Pacific Tea Company," double-sided, 5½" x 8½", 1884, EX . . . .$75.00 (C)

A & P, wooden tea bin with slanted lid and A & P logo in front and lid in old red paint, EX . . . .$210.00 (B)

Abbott's Bitters, painted wood advertising thermometer, 5⅛" x 21", VG . . . .$255.00 (D)

A-B-C Bohemian Beer, early celluloid advertising sign from the American Brewing Company, St. Louis, MO, 9" x 6½", EX . . . .$395.00 (D)

A.B.C. Chewing Gum, featuring artwork of the A.B.C. bathing girl on the beach, with product message at bottom, 13" x 28", EX . . . .$250.00 (C)

A.B.C. Gum, advertising poster in frame, graphics of girl at beach in early bathing attire, Canadian, 13" x 28", EX . . . .$135.00 (C)

ABC Oil Burners, die cast metal sign, 11" x 8", NM . . . .$150.00 (B)

A.C. Huff Music Store...High Grade Pianos, round metal tip tray with artwork of pretty woman in tray center, 4⅛" dia., EX . . . .$90.00 (B)

Acme Brand Coffee, American Stores Co., tin litho with embossed slip lid, graphics of polka dot banner around bottom, 1-lb., EX . . . .$84.00 (B)

Acme Cycle Co., pocket catalog 1894, 6¾" x 4⅝", EX, $12.00 (B).

AC Oil Filter, one-sided metal sign, 10" x 30", VG, $280.00 (B). *Courtesy of Collectors Auction Services*

Abram Clark Cigars, countertop advertising sign, cardboard easel back, 9" x 12¼", G, $90.00 (B). *Courtesy of Collectors Auction Services*

Adams' Honey Chewing Gum, tin, 9" x 5⅜" x 1", VG, $100.00 (B). *Courtesy of Collectors Auction Services*

Adams' Red Rose Pure Chewing Gum, single-sided paper advertising, 12¾" x 6¼", G, $325.00 (B). *Courtesy of Collectors Auction Services*

Acme Cowboy Boots, neon sign, neon on painted metal, 20¼" x 12½", VG . . . .$300.00 (C)

Acme, neon cowboy boot display sign, 20¼" x 12½", EX . . . .$525.00 (C)

Acme Paints, double-sided sign porcelain with paint can in center, 14½" x 20", EX . . . .$75.00 (D)

Acme Quality Paints, double-sided porcelain advertising sign with image of paint can, 14⅝" x 20", EX .$275.00 (C)

Acme Quality Paints, porcelain sign featuring artwork of paint can on front, 14½" x 20", G . . . .$75.00 (C)

AC Oil Filter Service, double-sided tin flange advertising sign, 13½" x 11¾", 1940s, EX . . . .$425.00 (C)

AC Spark Plugs, metal sign advertising AC method of cleaning, with artwork of donkey in bath tub, cost 5¢, vertical rectangle, black & yellow, G . . . .$95.00 (D)

AC Spark Plugs, self-framing tin advertising sign with graphics of spark plug, NOS, 8¾" x 17⅞", 1941, NM . . . .$195.00 (C)

Action Advertising Clock Co., salesman's sample of advertising item with flip cards to left of neon clock, 24" x 7" x 12½", 1950s, EX . . . .$275.00 (B)

Adams' Tutti-Frutti Gum, paperboard sign with graphics of young girl 8¼" x 12½", 1910, EX, **$275.00 (C).** *Courtesy of Buffalo Bay Auction Co.*

Admiral Cigarettes, sign, paper litho of scantily clad woman on board ship at lookout, 16" x 22½", EX, **$150.00 (B).** *Courtesy of Buffalo Bay Auction Co.*

Admiration Cigars...Mild and Mellow To The Last Inch, advertising sign, 11" x 15", 1930s, EX, **$475.00 (B).** *Courtesy of Muddy River Trading Co./Gary Metz*

Amoco Battery Cable Service, embossed tin die cut sign, 17" x 10", NOS, EX, **$175.00 (C).** *Courtesy of Autopia Advertising Auctions*

Aeroshell Lubricating Oil Stocked Here, one-sided die cut porcelain sign, 38" x 19¾", VG, **$3,000.00 (B).** *Courtesy of Collectors Auction Services*

Adam Forepaugh & Sells Bros., Big United Shows, poster featuring circus activity on front, 17½" x 13", EX . . . . . **$55.00 (C)**

Adam Forepaugh & Sells Circus, advertising poster with graphics of circus scene, 17½" x 13", VG . . . . **$155.00 (D)**

Adams' California Fruit Chewing Gum, counter display by H.D. Beach Co., graphics of gum packs, 6¾" x 4¾" x 6", 1917, EX . . . . **$575.00 (C)**

Adams' Chewing Gum, box with advertising photos in center of both sides, 7½" x 1" x 9", EX . . . . **$90.00 (B)**

Adams' Gum Sweet Rubber Tolo Chewing Gum, tin with lift-off lid, made to hold 200 pieces of gum, colors still strong on cover, stork in lower right, 4½" x 4⅝" x 1", EX . . . . **$1,100.00 (B)**

Adams' Pepsin Gum, counter top cardboard die cut advertising display in the form of a young girl with advertising on her back, 2¼" x 5", NM . . . . **$195.00 (C)**

Adams' Pepsin Gum, tin store bin with hinge top, graphics of product messages on all sides and lid, 7" x 6" x 5", EX . . . . **$330.00 (B)**

A. Hussey & Co., tin litho match holder, die cut, good graphics, "while others think we work," 7" H, VG, **$1,500.00** (C).

Courtesy of Richard Opfer Auctioneering, Inc.

Alexander poster, "The man who knows," 28¼" x 42", red, black & white litho, EX, **$85.00** (D).

Alka-Seltzer, tin litho store display, 7" x 12" x 9¾", VG, **$95.00** (C).

Alliance Coffee/For Coffee Contentment Serve Alliance Coffee, with man in chef's wear tipping a cup of coffee, die cut cardboard, 1910, 12½" x 16⅛", NM, **$325.00** (C).

Allyn & Blanchard Co., tin litho match holder, 7" H, EX, **$320.00** (B).

Adams' Pepsin Tutti-Frutti Gum, store counter display box, 6⅜" x 5¼" x 4¼", EX . . . .**$125.00** (C)

Adams' Spearmint, countertop gum display unit, 6½" x 4¾" x 6", EX . . . .**$230.00** (B)

Adams' Sweet Fern Chewing Gum, two-piece cardboard box with artwork of small girl, 4¾" x 8⅝" x 1⅜", EX . . . .**$130.00** (B)

Adams' Tutti-Frutti Chewing Gum, product box with graphics of Miss Lillian Russell on front, EX .**$220.00** (B)

Adams' Tutti-Frutti Gum, paper board sign with graphics of young girl, 8¼" x 12½", 1910, EX . . . .**$275.00** (C)

Admiral Cigarettes, sign, paper litho of scantily clad woman on board ship at look-out, 16" x 22½", EX . . . .**$150.00** (B)

Admiration Cigars...Mild and Mellow To The Last Inch, advertising sign, 11" x 15", 1930s, EX . . . . .**$475.00** (B)

Admiration Cigars, three-dimensional plaster advertising sign of moon-faced cigar smoker, EX . . . . .**$1,400.00** (B)

American Airlines, light-up clock with metal body and glass face and cover, with artwork of trademark AA in center of clock, 15" dia., VG, **$230.00 (B).** *Courtesy of Collectors Auction Services*

American Beauty Coffee, grinder with original tin cup and cast iron bottom, 4¼" x 3¼" x 12", EX, **$425.00 (C).**

Courtesy of Buffalo Bay Auction Co.

American Eagle Fire Insurance Company, New York, painted tin sign with wood frame, 20½" x 26½", NM, **$875.00 (D).**

American Clean Cutter, tobacco cutter, rare design and difficult to find, G, **$295.00 (D).**

Courtesy of Chief Paduke Antiques Mall

American Express Co. Agency, raised lettering, heavy porcelain sign, 18½" x 16½", EX, **$1,550.00 (B).** *Courtesy of Wm. Morford Investment Grade Collectibles*

Admiration miniatures, tin litho advertising sign, with easel back display stand, 5¾" x 7½", EX ....**$275.00 (C)**

Advance-Rumely Power Farming Machinery, cardboard advertising sign with graphics of farming scenes and machinery, 15" x 21", EX ....**$210.00 (B)**

Advo Peanut Butter, tin litho container with pry lid, to be used as a measuring cup when empty, 12 oz., EX ....**$120.00 (B)**

Aetna Automobile Insurance, painted tin sign, 24" x 12", black lettering on orange, F ....**$75.00 (C)**

Aetna Gas Globe, wide glass body with two lens, 13½", EX ....**$2,785.00 (B)**

A.F. Movitt Prescription Druggist, die cut cardboard calendar from Chicago, IL, with artwork of young girl with flowers, 11½" x 17", EX ....**$181.00 (B)**

Agent Quaker Tea, flange porcelain ad sign, foreign item, 18" x 9½", VG ....**$375.00 (B)**

A. Hussey & Co., tin litho match holder, die cut, good graphics, "while others think we work," 7" H, EX ....**$1,550.00 (B)**

Aircraft Oats, container with litho of birds and circling airplane, 1 lb. 4 oz., EX ....**$183.00 (B)**

Airline Flexible Flyer, salesman's sample, wood and metal sled, 23" x 9", EX ....**$750.00 (B)**

American Express Money Orders Sold Here, porcelain flange sign, 16" x 13", white lettering on blue background, EX, **$225.00 (D)**. *Courtesy of Riverview Antique Mall*

American Hat Works Co. Inc., porcelain advertising sign, 40¼" L, VG, **$355.00 (C)**.

American Ingot Iron Road Culverts, embossed painted metal sign, 20" x 5½", white lettering on blue, NM, **$110.00 (D)**. *Courtesy of Riverview Antique Mall*

American Insurance Company, Newark, N.J., single-sided porcelain sign, 20" x 14", VG, **$155.00 (B)**. *Courtesy of Collectors Auction Services*

American Negro Exposition/Chicago Coliseum, framed, 7-color screened print, 1940, EX, **$175.00 (D)**. *Courtesy of Creatures of Habit*

AJJA Tobacco, advertising sign with graphics of older gent and younger man enjoying a smoke, self-framing porcelain sign, "T.P. Bruxeles 359-254-1951," 21½" x 25½", EX . .**$275.00 (B)**

Akron Brewing Co., Akron, Ohio, litho decal of factory scene on wood, 1930s, 36" x 24", NM . . . .**$210.00 (B)**

Akron Brewing Co., Akron, Ohio, tin litho advertising for White Rock Beer, 33" x 24¾", VG . . . .**$560.00 (B)**

Akron Oats Co. Mother's Oats, advertising sign with youngster in pajamas holding a bowl of the product, 15½" x 21", EX . . . .**$40.00 (B)**

Alabama National AA Motor Club, die cut double-sided porcelain advertising sign, 23⅝" x 16¼", NM . .**$225.00 (C)**

Aladdin...The Wonderful Coffee, tin litho can with artwork of Aladdin lamp in center of product message, 3-lb., EX . . . .**$170.00 (B)**

Alberta Government Telephones...Use Long Distance, flange porcelain sign with graphics of old candlestick phone in center, 19" x 18½", G . . . .**$400.00 (B)**

Albert Pick Co. Chicago Cigar, trade stimulator in oak case, 14" x 22" x 5½", 1895, EX . . . .**$625.00 (B)**

American Stores Co., advertising sign, entitled "The Younger Generation," 14¼" X 18¼", NM, $115.00 (C).

Amoco, single-sided cardboard poster, 61" x 28", VG, $100.00 (B).

Andes Stoves & Ranges, match safe and strikes, 4⅝" x 6¼", G, $155.00 (B).

Amstel, light, on tap, neon, three colors, EX, $120.00 (D). *Courtesy of Pleasant Hill Antique Mall & Tea Room/Bob Johnson*

Andy Pepsodent, die cut cardboard depicting Andy holding a tube of Pepsodent, "Oh! Sho-Sho-Pepsodent! Check an' DOUBLE CHECK," 21" x 54½", 1930s, VG, $825.00 (B). *Courtesy of Collectors Auction Services*

Alemite Gas-Co-Lator, counter top advertising unit that shows how your gas is filtered as you drive, 16¾" x 19½" x 4¼", VG . . . .$425.00 (B)

Alexander Humbolt Cigar, embossed heavy paper advertising sign with image of Humbolt, 24" x 18", VG . . . . . .$385.00 (B)

Alexander poster, "The man who knows," 28¼" x 42", red, black & white litho, G . . . .$45.00 (C)

Al G. Barnes Wild Animal, paper circus poster with artwork of tiger riding a horse, reprint, 13½" x 19", VG $20.00 (B)

Alice Foote Coffee, lithographed tin container with screw-on lid and graphics of silhouette lady bust on front, 4" x 6", EX . . . .$55.00 (B)

Alka Seltzer, advertising counter top display box, has advertising on all sides, 25¼" x 6¼" x 6¼", EX . .$25.00 (D)

Alka Seltzer, die cut cardboard "Speedy" advertising sign with easel back for counter display, 21¾" x 39¾", EX . . . .$235.00 (C)

Alka-Seltzer...effervescent analgesic alkalizing tablets, paper linen display box, 25¼" x 6¼" x 6¼", EX . .$20.00 (D)

Anheuser-Busch, framed paper advertising, "The Father of Waters," 19" x 13¼", EX, $80.00 (B).

Apache Trail Cigars, rare tin litho, with great graphics of Indian on horseback, good strong colors, 5¾" H, EX, $875.00 (B). *Courtesy of Richard Opfer Auctioneering, Inc.*

Arbuckles' Ground Coffee..."It smells good Daddy," embossed tin sign featuring artwork of man with paper and girl with cup of coffee, 27" x 11", EX, $475.00 (B). *Courtesy of Muddy River Trading Co./Gary Metz*

Arm & Hammer Soda, framed cardboard litho advertising sign, copyright 1908 by Church & Dwight Co., signed by Robin Snipe, 14½" x 11½", EX, $95.00 (C).

Alka-Seltzer...Headache Upset Stomach, dial-type thermometer with graphics of "Speedy," 12" dia., EX . . . . . $375.00 (B)

Alka-Seltzer, metal store display, 12" x 9½", G $55.00 (D)

Alka Seltzer, painted metal counter top display with lithos of boxes on front cover, 12" x 9½", EX . . . . . . $75.00 (C)

Allcock's Plasters, paper advertising sign featuring two girls sitting on dock with feet dangling near the water, one with a plaster on her back, 11¼" x 28", 1884, EX . . . . $195.00 (C)

Allens Red Tame Cherry, chalkware figure of girl with apron, 26" T, VG . . . . $775.00 (C)

Alliance Coffee, die cut cardboard advertising sign with graphics of elderly man in chef's hat and coat holding a cup of coffee, 12½" x 16⅛", 1910, EX . . . . . $250.00 (D)

Alliance Coffee/For Coffee Contentment Serve Alliance Coffee, with man in chef's wear tipping a cup of coffee, die cut cardboard, 1910, 12½" x 16⅛", G . . . . . . $95.00 (C)

Allied Mutual Casualty Company "Protected Car," embossed convex tin advertising license plate attachment, NOS, 4⅛", EX . . . . $195.00 (C)

Allied Van Lines...Nation Wide Movers, Buddy L pull-type toy truck, 30" long, VG . . . . $350.00 (C)

All Jersey Milk, aluminum die cut painted license plate attachment with cow graphics, 9⅞" x 5⅝", NM . . . . $135.00 (C)

Allstate Battery Check, dial-type advertising thermometer with graphics of battery at top of face, 16" dia., EX . . . . $175.00 (C)

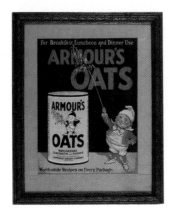

Armour's Oats, Worthwhile Recipes on Every Package, with graphics of young boy holding oats and a package of product on front, 21" x 26¾", VG, $85.00 (B). *Courtesy of Collectors Auction Services*

Armour's Star Products, advertising wall mirror, graphics of butcher with bacon and ham, 18" x 33", G, $175.00 (C).

Aromints...for the breath, felt advertising pennant with graphics of a roll of the products, 28" long, 1912, excellent $175.00 (C). *Courtesy of Autopia Advertising Auctions*

Arrow Beer, matchless body, framed cardboard sign, 22" x 34", EX, $250.00 (B). *Courtesy of Muddy River Trading Co./Gary Metz*

Arrow Coffee, container from Atwood Co., Minneapolis, Mn., with graphics of Indian with bow drawn, 1-lb., excellent $1,125.00 (B). *Courtesy of Buffalo Bay Auction Co.*

Allstate, fire extinguisher can in unused condition, 2¾" x 4¾, EX . . . .$55.00 (C)

Allyn & Blanchard Co., tin litho match holder, 7" H, G . . . .$100.00 (C)

Alonso Rejas...Clear Havana, Made at Key West, Fla., advertising tray with early Vienna-type advertising of woman in center, 10" dia., EX . . . .$400.00 (B)

Alta Crest Certified Milk, embossed tin over cardboard advertising sign designed to be either string hung or used on counter with easel back, 11⅜" x 6⅜", EX .$150.00 (C)

Amalie...Pennsylvania Motor Oil, dial-type scale thermometer, metal body with glass front, 9" dia., EX . . . . .$85.00 (C)

Amalie...Pennsylvania Motor Oil, light-up clock, metal body with glass face, 15" dia., EX . . . .$235.00 (C)

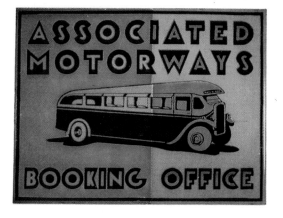

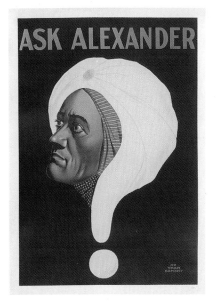

Ask Alexander, paper litho advertising poster, 30½" x 44½", 1920s, EX, $325.00 (B).

Associated Motorways Booking Office, double-sided porcelain advertising sign, 23¼" x 18", VG, $1,600.00 (B). *Courtesy of Collectors Auction Services*

Ath-Lo-Pho-Ros Rheumatism and Neuralgia Remedy, three-piece window display, 20¼" x 18¾", NM, $275.00 (B).

Atlantic White Lead Dutch Boy, paint string holder double-sided sign with the boy in the swing, heavy metal construction, 14" x 26", 1925, EX, $5,200.00 (B). *Courtesy of Buffalo Bay Auction Co.*

Ambrosia Tobacco, store counter top cutter 16" x 9", VG . . . .$190.00 (B)

American Ace Tea, paper litho on cardboard with pry lid, graphics of pilot on one side and airplane on other side, 4-oz., EX . . . .$140.00 (B)

American Airline, light-up clock with metal body and glass face and cover, with artwork of trademark AA in center of clock, 15" dia., NM . . . .$495.00 (C)

American Bakeries Company, bronze building plate, 26" x 15", EX . . . .$75.00 (B)

American Beauty Coffee, grinder with original tin cup and cast iron bottom, 4¼" x 3¼" x 12", EX . . . . .$425.00 (C)

American Blend, tin litho pocket container, 3⅛" x 4⅜" x ⅞", EX . . . .$1,450.00 (B)

American Brakeblok, reverse glass light-up advertising clock, 15" dia., EX . . . .$375.00 (D)

American Can Company..., gift to 1907 National Canner's Convention, tin litho paperweight thermometer shaped like canning tin, NM . . . .$350.00 (B)

American Clean Cutter, tobacco cutter, rare design and difficult to find, G . . . .$295.00 (D)

American cloth sleeve patch, 3" x 2⅜", EX . . .$10.00 (C)

American Eagle Fire Insurance Company, New York, painted tin sign with wood frame, 20½" x 26½", NM . . . . .$875.00 (D)

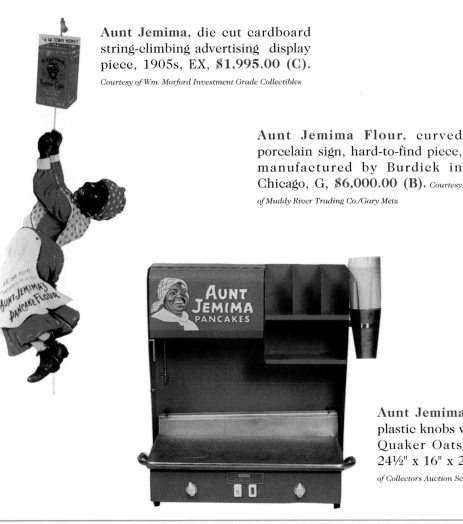

Aunt Jemima, die cut cardboard string-climbing advertising display piece, 1905s, EX, **$1,995.00 (C)**.
Courtesy of Wm. Morford Investment Grade Collectibles

Aunt Jemima Flour, curved porcelain sign, hard-to-find piece, manufactured by Burdick in Chicago, G, **$6,000.00 (B)**. *Courtesy of Muddy River Trading Co./Gary Metz*

Aunt Jemima pancake grill, metal with plastic knobs with Aunt Jemima decal, "The Quaker Oats Company, Chicago, ILL," 24½" x 16" x 26", VG, **$2,800.00 (B)**. *Courtesy of Collectors Auction Services*

American Eagle, one-piece cardboard shot shell box, 2½" x 2½" x 2½", EX . . . .**$55.00 (C)**

American Eagle Shot Shells, one-piece cardboard box with eagle logo on front, EX . . . .**$35.00 (B)**

American Entertainment Co., paper litho advertising poster, "Marvelous Moving Pictures and Illustrated Songs," 20½" x 30½", VG . . . .**$125.00 (C)**

American Entertainment, paper litho advertising poster, litho by Hennegan & Co., Cincinnati, 30" x 30½", EX . . . .**$25.00 (B)**

American Express Co. Agency, raised lettering, heavy porcelain sign, 18½" x 16½", EX . . . . **$1,550.00 (B)**

American Express Money Order, cardboard advertising sign, "To send money...anywhere at anytime...for any purpose," 13" x 17", 1921, VG . . . .**$50.00 (B)**

American Express Money Orders Sold Here, porcelain flange sign, 16" x 13", white lettering on blue background, EX . . . .**$225.00 (D)**

American Express, painted metal double-sided flange advertising sign with graphics of trademark logo in center, promoting their credit cards, 18¾" x 23¾", G .**$50.00 (B)**

American Express Travelers Cheques accepted here, one-sided porcelain sign, 10" x 4½", VG . . . .**$90.00 (B)**

American Hat Works Co. Inc., porcelain advertising sign, 40¼" L, EX . . . .**$375.00 (B)**

American Ingot Iron Road Culverts, embossed painted metal sign, 20" x 5½", white lettering on blue, EX . . . . . .**$85.00 (D)**

American Lady, coffee tin litho container with graphics of pretty young lady on front and back, 5½" x 9½", G . . . .**$140.00 (B)**

Authorized Gulf Dealer, porcelain advertising sign, 1930s, 40" x 9", VG, $145.00 (C).

Authorized De Laval Dealer, on metal arm, G, $350.00 (B). *Courtesy of Riverview Antique Mall*

Auto Hotel, light-up glass globe, rare item, 16" dia., G, $350.00 (B).

Automobile Needs, paper poster, 23½" x 37", $80.00 (B).

Avon Brilliant Polish for Boots and Leggings, single-sided tin advertising sign with graphics of product can in center, 3" x 8", G, $65.00 (B).

American Line...Philadelphia, Liverpool, Queenstown, advertising pocket mirror with graphics of steamship, 1¾" dia., NM . . . .$25.00 (B).

American Motor Hotel Association/Member, porcelain sign with sunburst in center containing AMHA initials, 1951, 20" x 25", EX . . . .$225.00 (D)

American Navy, plug tobacco, framed tin litho hanging advertising sign with the American Navy tin tobacco tag, "For delicious lasting taste," 16" x 3¼", VG . .$130.00 (B)

American Negro Exposition/Chicago Coliseum, framed, 7-color screened print, 1940, NM . . . .$350.00 (C)

American Pale Beer, uncut labels, full sheet, framed, 8¼" x 12", EX . . . .$95.00 (C)

American Powder Mills, one-pound tin powder container with goose scene, 4" x 1¼" x 5¾", EX . . . .$95.00 (C)

American Seal Paint, calendar with graphics depicting Uncle Sam and Spanish-American War heroes, 1899, 13" x 21", NM . . . .$334.00 (B)

American Standard...Heating-Air Conditioning, plastic light-up clock, 15" dia., EX . . . .$135.00 (C)

American Standard Lager Brew Co., reverse painted glass advertising sign showing eagle on branches, 56¼" x 36½", VG . . . .$850.00 (B)

American Stores Co., advertising sign, entitled "The Younger Generation," 14¼" x 18¼", EX . . . . . .$90.00 (D)

American Sunrise Lard, tin with litho of village and Indians, 8-lb., EX . . . .$430.00 (B)

American Sunrise Pure Lard, lithographed tin container from the American Packing Company with graphics of Indian scene, 12½" x 14¼", G . . . .$25.00 (D)

American Telephone and Telegraph and Associated Companies, Public Telephone, porcelain flange sign with Bell System bell in center, 20" x 20", EX . . . .$255.00 (C)

American Tobacco Co., framed paper litho advertising Omar Turkish Blend Cigarettes with graphics of father and son enjoying a smoke together, 18¼" x 25", VG . . . .$405.00 (B)

Amoco, winter lubricants, cloth service station banner, featuring silhouette artwork of car driving up hill in winter weather, 37½" x 35", G . . . .$125.00 (C)

Amos & Andy Longfellow Cigar Box, wood box with paper litho inside lid advertisement, embossed lettering on sides, 9" x 7" x 2½", EX . . . .$150.00 (B)

Amos and Andy, wooden cigar box, 50 count, EX . .$40.00 (B)

Amos N Andy, cardboard litho candy box, 8½" x 11¾", VG . . . .$100.00 (B)

Amos N Andy, compact with graphics of Amos N Andy advertisment on lid, metal and plastic, 2" x 2", EX . . . .$425.00 (B)

Amrhein's Bread...Ask for...It's fresher, painted metal door push, 26" x 3", red, white on blue, EX . . .$65.00 (D)

Amstel light, on tap, neon, three colors, NM .$135.00 (D)

Anastasia, paper movie poster with graphics of Yul Brynner and Ingrid Bergman, 26½" x 41", VG . . . . .$15.00 (B)

Anchor Buggy Co., cloth advertisment with graphics of buggy, 38" x 64", G . . . .$675.00 (B)

Andrew D. White...Mild and Satisfying, cigar tip tray, 4¼" dia., F . . . .$35.00 (B)

Andrews Shoe Repair, light-up advertising globe, 15" dia., G . . . .$225.00 (B)

Andy Gump Biscuits, die cut paper advertising display for window use for the Loose-Wiles Biscuit Co., Sunshine Bakery, 11" x 12", EX . . . .$350.00 (B)

Andy Pepsodent, die cut cardboard depicting Andy holding a tube of Pepsodent, "Oh! Sho-Sho-Pepsodent! Check an' DOUBLE CHECK", 21" x 54½", 1930s, VG . . . .$825.00 (B)

Angelus Marshmallow, advertising pocket mirror with cherub image promoting product, 1¾" x 3½", EX . . . .$70.00 (B)

Angelus Marshmallow, celluloid advertising tape measure with graphics of product box on side, 1½" dia., EX $75.00 (B)

Angelus Marshmallows, die cut easel back cardboard sign in likeness of small angel holding box of product, 5½" x 11¾", EX . . . .$875.00 (B)

Anheuser-Busch Brewing Association Faust Beer, tin lithographed advertising sign with pretty girl holding drum with product advertising, 21½" x 36", VG . .$1,650.00 (B)

Anheuser-Busch Budweiser, embossed cardboard advertising sign, 16" x 11", EX . . . .$95.00 (B)

Anheuser-Busch Budweiser Girl, self-framing tin lithographed advertising sign with pretty young girl holding a bottle and glass of the product, 25½" x 37½", VG . . . .$1,650.00 (B)

Anheuser-Busch Custer, advertising sign in original wood frame with embossed Busch plaque at the top center of the frame, earliest variation of this advertising piece, 44½" x 35", 1897, EX . . . .$560.00 (B)

Anheuser-Busch 5¢, stoneware dispenser by Cardley & Hayes, NY, good strong lettering and color, 1919, NM . . . .$125.00 (B)

Anheuser-Busch Ginger Ale, advertising pocket mirror with celluloid front that has A-B logo, St. Louis, MO, 2¾", EX . . . .$80.00 (B)

Anheuser-Busch Inc. Calendar, advertising Budweiser Beer with artwork of beer bottle and glass of beer on serving tray, tin over cardboard with hanging chain, 12" x 22½", VG . . . .$225.00 (B)

Anheuser-Busch, lighter shaped like a finger candle, pewter, 6½" x 5½", NM . . . .$45.00 (B)

Anheuser-Busch, paper litho advertising poster with graphics of pretty woman in risque dress holding an eagle in one hand and a bowl of roses in the other hand, 26½" x 36½", VG . . . .$1,025.00 (B)

Anheuser-Busch, paper litho advertising sign, "The Father of the Waters," from an original by Oscar Berninghaus, 16" x 7½", NM . . . .$90.00 (B)

Anheuser-Busch, paper litho, "Attack on an Emigrant Train," 15" x 7½", EX . . . .$85.00 (B)

Anheuser-Busch, print of Custer's Last Fight, in wood frame, 46" x 36", 1896, EX . . . .$395.00 (C)

Anheuser-Busch, rare metal ice scraper, "Have you made the Budweiser Beer test?," 3¾" x 3", 1930s, EX . . . .$100.00 (C)

Anheuser-Busch, self-contained tin over cardboard advertising sign, with graphics of doctor with medical bag walking toward house, 12⅝" x 7⅝", EX . . . .$35.00 (C)

Anheuser-Busch, self-framing tin litho of the St. Louis World's Fair with train dining car scene, 22¼" x 28¼", 1904, EX . . . .$475.00 (B)

Anker-Holth, cream separator, porcelain advertising sign, "We use the...," 14" x 10", EX . . . .$95.00 (C)

Anteek Beer, back bar statue in the shape of serving man, 22½" T, EX . . . .$400.00 (D)

Anteek Beer, composition back bar statue in likeness of bartender with product name on apron, 22" T, EX . . . .$275.00 (D)

Antikamnia Tablets...two every three hours...insomnia & nervousness, metal tip tray with graphics of woman seated in chair in tray center, 4¾", EX . . . .$100.00 (B)

Antisepticon Gum, sign, cardboard litho advertising sign featuring artwork of woman on cover, 6⅜" x 10⅝", EX . . . .$1,150.00 (B)

Apache Trail, cigar oval-shaped tin with graphics of Indian on horseback, hard-to-find item, EX . . . . .$1,500.00 (C)

Apache Trail Cigar, tin with great graphics of Indian on horseback, NM . . . .$2,065.00 (B)

Apache Trail Cigars, rare tin litho, with great graphics of Indian on horseback, good strong colors, 5¾" H, EX . . . .$875.00 (B)

Apollinaris, "The Queen of Table Waters," paper sign in frame and mat, "Pretty Polly...The Queen of the Turf," art of horse and handler, 22½" x 27½", G . . . .$34.00 (B)

Apollinaris..."The Queen of Table Waters," rectangular metal tip tray with artwork of woman with glass of product, 6" tall, EX . . . .$60.00 (B)

Arbuckles' Ground Coffee..."It smells Good, Daddy," embossed tin sign featuring artwork of man with paper and girl with cup of coffee, 27" x 11", EX . . . .$475.00 (B)

Arden Dairy Golden Valley Cheese, die cut masonite advertisng sign in likeness of product package, 26½" x 12", EX . . . .$225.00 (C)

Arden Dairy Hat Badge, 4¼" x 1½", EX . . . .$225.00 (C)

Arden Dairy, oval porcelain advertising sign with graphics of delivery boy carrying a rack with various products and holding a bottle of milk, 14" x 24", NM . . . .$1,900.00 (B)

Arden Ice Cream, bevel edge masonite advertising sign, 12" x 7¼", EX . . . .$200.00 (C)

Arden Ice Cream, oval porcelain advertising sign, 48" x 36", 1959, NM . . . .$425.00 (C)

Argood Cigar, liberty tin, "handmade 5¢ cigar," 5½" x 5", EX . . . .$95.00 (C)

Argo, oversized counter top display box in likeness of consumer size package, 9½" x 5⅜" x 18", EX . . . .$135.00 (C)

Arm & Hammer, paperboard advertising sign promoting Arm & Hammer Soda, 14¼" x 11", 1910s, EX . .$225.00 (C)

Arm & Hammer Soda, framed cardboard litho advertising sign, copyright 1908 by Church & Dwight Co., signed by Robin Snipe, 14½" x 11½", G . . . .$70.00 (D)

Arm & Hammer Soda, trading card display with graphics of crow on limb, 11¾" x 14¾", VG . . . .$95.00 (B)

Armour Franks, embossed tin advertising sign with graphics of young boy eating a hot dog, 15" x 12", EX . . . .$235.00 (B)

Armour Franks, tin embossed advertising sign with graphics of young man and a hot dog, 15¼" x 11½", EX . . .$180.00 (B)

Armour's...Drink...Veribest Root Beer, milk glass dispenser, NM . . . .$1,210.00 (B)

Armour's Oats, Worthwhile Recipes on Every Package, with graphics of young boy holding oats and a package of product on front, 21" x 26¾", VG . . . .$85.00 (B)

Armour's Old Black Joe Fertilizer, embossed tin self-framing advertising sign depicting a man playing a banjo, 36" x 17½", VG . . . .$210.00 (B)

Armour's Star Ham, painted tin on cardboard with graphics of ham & eggs on plate beside freshly cut ham, 19" x 13¼", VG . . . .$65.00 (B)

Armour's Star Hams and Bacon, early embossed tin advertising sign with graphics of lady purchasing a ham from a young boy in a meat shop, litho by Meek and Beach Co., 21½" x 27½", 1901, VG . . . .$475.00 (B)

Armour's Star Ham, tin over cardboard with graphics of ham and eggs, 19" x 13", G . . . .$500.00 (C)

Armour Star, self-framed tin litho of "The Ham What Am and Bacon Too," 13" x 37½", VG . . . .$500.00 (B)

Aromints...for the breath, felt advertising pennant with graphics of a roll of the products, 28" long, 1912, EX . . .$175.00 (C)

Arrow Beer, matchless body, framed cardboard sign, 22" x 34", EX . . . .$250.00 (B)

Arrow Coffee, container from Atwood Co., Minneapolis, Mn., with graphics of Indian with bow drawn, 1- lb., EX . . . .$1,125.00 (B)

Arrow Coffee, metal container with slip lid by the American Can Co., with graphics of Indian on front with bow drawn, 1-lb., NM . . . .$750.00 (B)

Arrow Loaded Paper Shells, two-piece cardboard box, EX . . . .$85.00 (B)

Artificial Portland, cement porcelain single-sided advertising sign with graphics of cannon, 13¾", VG .$50.00 (B)

Ashland Kerosene globe, wide hull body with two glass lens, speed lettering on Ashland, 13½" dia., EX . . . .$550.00 (B)

"A Sur-Shot," vet tin with large capsules for "Bot and Worm remover," 3½" x 5" x 2½", EX . . . .$60.00 (B)

Ath-Lo-Pho-Ros Rheumatism and Neuralgia Remedy, three-piece window display, 20¼" x 18¾", NM . . . . . .$275.00 (B)

Atlantic Bulk Plant, porcelain double-sided dealer sign, 35" x 27", F . . . .$35.00 (B)

Atlantic Dutch Boy, painter sign, features the boy sitting on a shelf with a paint brush, 20¾" x 35", 1906, EX . . . .$150.00 (B)

Atlantic, Pure White Lead Paint, framed poster featuring artwork of Dutch boy with paint bucket and brush sitting on shelf, 20¾" x 35", EX . . . .$165.00 (C)

Atlantic White Lead Dutch Boy Paint, string holder double-sided sign with the boy in the swing, heavy metal construction, 14" x 26", 1925, EX . . . .$5,200.00 (B)

Atlas Assurance Co. Limited of London...Established 1808, one-sided porcelain advertising sign with graphics of man holding the world, 17¾" x 11¾", G . . .$180.00 (B)

ATSC Transmission Conditioner, dial-type advertising thermometer, 12" dia., EX . . . .$135.00 (C)

Augustiner Beer, advertising sign, painted tin, 19⅞" x 13¾", EX . . . .$65.00 (C)

Augustiner Beer, properly aged, painted tin sign, 20" x 13¾", EX . . . .$45.00 (C)

Aultman Miller, advertising calendar depicting farm machinery, 6" x 8½", 1881, EX . . . .$325.00 (B)

Aunt Jemima, advertising flour sack with image of Aunt Jemima on front, 25-lb., EX . . . .$85.00 (C)

Aunt Jemima, Breakfast Club scale from "Old Kentucky Home, Belknap Hdw. & Mfg. Co., Louisville, Ky.," has cardboard face of Aunt Jemima on scale, 6¼" x 8¼" x 8", VG . . . .$350.00 (B)

Aunt Jemima Buckwheat Pancakes, electric advertising clock with cardboard face that has graphics of Aunt Jemima, plastic body, 7½" x 7", VG . . . .$500.00 (B)

Aunt Jemima Cooking and Salad Oil, paper panel from 5-gal. tin, Quaker Oats Co., framed, 8" x 13", EX . .$58.00 (B)

Aunt Jemima, die cut cardboard stand-up with Aunt Jemima holding a hot plate of pancakes, "self rising and ready mixed," 12½" x 20", G . . . .$375.00 (B)

Aunt Jemima, die cut cardboard advertising string-climbing display piece, 1905s, EX . . . .$1,995.00 (C)

Aunt Jemima, die cut cardboard string climber, this was a premium toy with the product box and Aunt Jemima on a string, marked Germany, 6" x 13¼" Jemima, 2¼" x 4" box, 1905, NM . . . .$3,050.00 (B)

Aunt Jemima Flour, curved porcelain sign, hard-to-find piece, manufactured by Burdick in Chicago, NM . . . .$7,500.00 (D)

Aunt Jemima, pancake cardboard box with graphics of Aunt Jemima on front, will hold 24 packages of product, 13" x 9" x 13¾", VG . . . .$100.00 (B)

Aunt Jemima, pancake grill, metal with plastic knobs with Aunt Jemima decal, "The Quaker Oats Company, Chicago, ILL," 24½" x 16" x 26", G . . . .$1,100.00 (C)

Aunt Jemima Pancakes, cloth banner with graphics of Aunt Jemima and a plate of pancakes, 58" x 34", EX . .$500.00 (B)

Aunt Jemima, souvenir bell, wood and metal in original box, "Memphis Tenn" on apron, "Made by Hollander Novelty Co., Baton Rouge, La.," 4" H, 1941, VG .$125.00 (D)

Aunt Jemima Uncle Moses uncut doll, double-sided, 10" x 33", 1915, EX . . . .$80.00 **(B)**

Aunt Nellie's Coffee, tin litho key-wound container, 1-lb., EX . . . .$266.00 **(B)**

Austie's Brown Beauty Tobacco, tin with litho of mammy, 8½" x 5¾" x 5½", VG . . . .$620.00 **(B)**

Authorized Buick Service, porcelain dealer sign, single-sided, 42" dia., EX . . . .$600.00 **(B)**

Authorized Gulf Dealer, porcelain advertising sign, 1930s, 40" x 9", G . . . .$130.00 **(B)**

Authorized United Motors Service, wood advertising thermometer with trademark graphics at top, glass scale, 4" x 15", G . . . .$120.00 **(B)**

Auto-Lite, authorized electric motometer owen dyneto service, porcelain sign, 35¾" x 25½", EX . . . .$175.00 **(C)**

Autolite Batteries, self-framing tin sign, 18" x 60", VG . . . .$100.00 **(B)**

Auto-Lite Spark Plugs...Don't Miss, easel back cardboard advertising sign in likeness of billboard, NOS in original envelope, with graphics of spark plug, 21⅝" x 14", EX . . . .$235.00 **(D)**

Auto-Lite Spark Plugs, heavy cardboard die cut advertising counter top display with Rita Hayward in a grass skirt, 11¼" X 14" X 5¾", VG . . . .$170.00 **(B)**

Auto-Lite Spark Plugs...Ignition Engineered, two-sided painted metal flange sign, 19" x 12", VG . . . .$135.00 **(B)**

Automatic Electric Washer Co., Newton, IA, paperweight with artwork of pretty girl inside, EX . . . .$55.00 **(B)**

Avalon Cigarettes, You'd Never Guess They Cost Less, with artwork of woman in hat in center and message at bottom, paper on cardboard, 20" x 30", EX . . .$65.00 **(D)**

A.W. Kerr, advertising paper and cardboard calendar with paper tear sheet at bottom, from Hurricane, WI, featuring graphics of small girl carrying a woven basket, 6" x 9½", 1907, EX . . . .$75.00 **(D)**

Ayers Cathartic, large cardboard store advertising sign with graphics of old doctor treating young child, 7¼" x 12½", EX . . . .$325.00 **(D)**

Ayer's Cathartic Pills, cardboard die cut litho advertising depicting an older black man with a black girl on his knee and a boy kneeling beside him, 7½" x 12½", VG . . . . .$500.00 **(B)**

Ayers Sarsaparilla, cardboard die cut advertising figures shown holding a bottle of the product, easel back, 12" T, EX . . . .$50.00 **(B)**

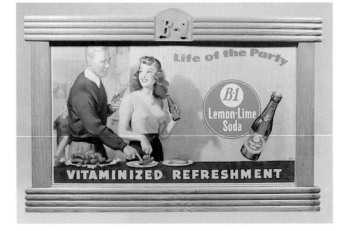

B-1 Lemon-Lime Soda, poster in its original wood frame with B-1 logo at top center, EX, **$240.00 (B).**

Courtesy of Muddy River Trading Co./Gary Metz

Babbitt's Soap Powder, cardboard litho trade card with graphics of Uncle Sam and gold miners, 5½" x 4", EX, **$110.00 (B).**

Courtesy of Past Tyme Pleasures

Baco-Curo, embossed die cut cardboard advertising sign, cures the tobacco habit, 9½" dia., NM, **$425.00 (B).** *Courtesy of Past Tyme Pleasures*

Babbitt's Soap Powder, cardboard litho trade card with graphics of Uncle Sam and gold miners, 5½" x 4", F . . . .**$45.00 (C)**

Babe Ruth Gum, glass store counter top change receiver, 4¼" x 2" x 6¼", EX . . . .**$80.00 (B)**

Baby Ruth...Curtiss...Candy and Gum, tape dispenser, porcelain with paper labels, 10½" x 2", EX . . .**$50.00 (D)**

Baby Ruth, porcelain tape dispenser with paper product label, 10½" x 2", VG . . . .**$45.00 (D)**

Bachanan & Lyall's Tobacco, advertising sign promoting Neptune tobacco, 11½" x 15½", VG . . . .**$55.00 (C)**

Baco-Curo, embossed die cut cardboard advertising sign, cures the tobacco habit, 9½" dia., P . . . .**$75.00 (C)**

Bagdad Coffee, pail, bail handle with good strong colors, 7½" x 9", EX . . . .**$250.00 (C)**

Bagdad Short Cut Smoking, paper on cardboard with graphics of man holding vertical pocket tin, 1909, 20" x 30", EX . . . .**$233.00 (B)**

Bagdad Tobacco, ceramic humidor with graphics of Bagdad on front, 5" x 6½", EX . . . .**$120.00 (B)**

Badger Mutual Fire Insurance, cast iron paperweight in the shape of a badger, 1937, EX . . . .**$65.00 (C)**

Bagley & Co.'s Fast Mail, tobacco can with paper label with graphics of train, large slip lid, 5" x 5½", 1910s, EX . . . .**$395.00 (D)**

Ballantine Beer, ask the man for..., light-up advertising clock, 15" x 15", EX, **$120.00 (D)**.

Baker's Breakfast Cocoa...Walter Baker & Co. Ltd., Dorchester, Mass., round metal tip tray with great graphics of farm house and woman with tray of product, 6" dia., EX, **$190.00 (B)**.

Bandage Increvable "Baudou," tire sign, single-sided, foreign graphics of mermaid holding a tire, G, **$1,500.00 (C)**.

Bagley's Clam Bake, tobacco string hanger, die cut cardboard of old clammer holding tobacco package, 8" x 6¼", EX . . . .$135.00 (C)

Bagley's Old Colony Mixture, John J. Bagley Co., Detroit, Mich., tin litho vertical pocket tin with artwork of woman wearing bonnet, 2" x 3" x ¾", EX . $575.00 (B)

Bagley's Sweet Tips Smoking, tin litho vertical pocket container, EX . . . .$65.00 (B)

Bailey's Pure Rye, round metal tip tray with product bottle and shot glass on tray center, "Used medicinally & socially," 4¼" dia., EX . . . .$140.00 (B)

Baker's Breakfast Cocoa...Walter Baker & Co. Ltd., Dorchester, Mass., round metal tip tray with great graphics of farm house and woman with tray of product, 6" dia., EX . . . .$190.00 (B)

Baker's Coconut, advertising tin litho give-away item with graphics of coconut cake on front, 2½" x 6¼", VG . . . . $95.00 (D)

Baker's Delight Baking Powder Barrel, wood barrel with paper label with trademark mammy with large pan of biscuits, 12½" x 16¾", VG . . . . $275.00 (C)

Baker's Delight Baking Powder Barrel, wooden with handle on lid and paper label, 12½" x 16¾", EX .$150.00 (B)

Bendix Sales and Service, double-sided flange sign, 18" x 18", VG, **$230.00 (B)**.

Banner Milk, It Tastes Better, one-sided porcelain sign, 24" x 14", VG, **$70.00 (B)**.

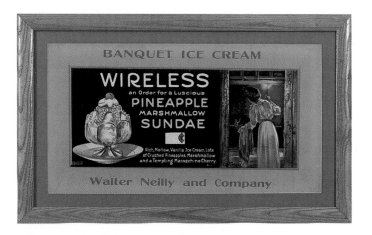

Banquet Ice Cream, cardboard advertisement, 30½" x 18¾", VG, **$325.00 (C)**.

Barber Pole, porcelain pole, 6" x 29", red, white & blue, VG, **$255.00 (C)**.

Baker's Delight Baking Powder, tin litho pail depicting mammy with rolls in pan, 12¼" dia. x 14½", VG . . . . **$330.00 (B)**

Bakers Nursery Talcum Powder, tin with litho of stork and babies, 2¼" x 6" x 1¼", EX . . . .**$85.00 (C)**

Bald Eagle Whiskey, serving tin litho tray with graphics of woman and cherub, 13⅝" x 16⅝", 1890s, EX **$235.00 (C)**

Balkan Cigarette, box with graphics of women in Turkish dress, 6¼" x 2⅞" x 1⅛", VG . . . . **$45.00 (C)**

Balkan Sobranie Turkish Cigarettes...Handmade of the finest Yenidje Tobacco, cigarette box with great artwork of tobacco on animal-drawn wagons, 6¼" x 7⅞" x 1⅛", EX . . . .**$35.00 (D)**

Ballantine Beer, ask the man for..., light-up advertising clock, 15" x 15", G . . . .**$95.00 (D)**

Ballantine XXX Ale, tin sign, 70" x 22", VG . .**$125.00 (B)**

Ballard Ice Cream, metal serving tray with graphics of young woman enjoying ice cream at a table, 13" dia., EX .**$155.00 (C)**

Ball Brand Shoes, easel back cardboard sign with graphics of young boy and shoe with message, 1949, 29" x 20", EX . . . .**$50.00 (B)**

Baltimore American Ale & Beer 10¢, painted tin sign, 35¾" x 18", G . . . .**$85.00 (C)**

Baltimore American Beer, painted advertising sign, 35¾" x 18", EX . . . .**$105.00 (D)**

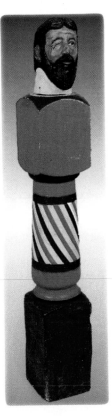

Barber Pole, wooden with carved face at top, 8" x 8" x 55", VG, **$950.00 (B).** *Courtesy of Collectors Auction Services*

Barber Shop, advertising sign, three-piece sign consisting of heavy milk glass globe, center cast iron bracket, and bottom milk glass stripe pole, 11½" x 31", **$1,100.00 (B).** *Courtesy of Wm. Morford Investment Grade Collectibles*

Barber Shop, light-up porcelain pole with glass cylinder and top globe, 13" x 87", EX, **$3,000.00 (B).** *Courtesy of Collectors Aution Services*

Bancroft Tennis Racquets, celluloid over cardboard advertising sign with graphics of tennis racquet from Whitehead & Hoag, 6" x 9", EX . . . .$400.00 (B)

Banjo Tobacco, paper label from David Dunlop at Petersburg, Va., U.S.A., featuring older black gentleman playing a banjo, 12½" x 2" x 6¼", 1880s, EX . . . .$125.00 (B)

Banjo Tobacco, stone litho by A. Moen Co., David Dunlop Tobacco Co., Petersburg, Va., with graphics of black man playing the banjo while a couple of black women dance, 12¾" x 6½", 1880s, EX . . . .$375.00 (D)

Banner Buggies, stone litho paper advertising sign with image of pretty young woman that has buggy advertising info on sash button, 1900s, EX . . . .$335.00 (B)

Barbarossa Premium Beer, embossed paper hanging tavern sign, artwork of Merlin and elves in cameo, 10½" x 13½", NM . . . .$50.00 (B)

Barber Greene, metal toy grain loader, 6½" x 12", green, EX . . . .$225.00 (C)

Barber Pole, porcelain pole, 6" x 29", red, white & blue, EX . . . .$275.00 (B)

Barber Pole, wooden with carved face at top, 8" x 8" x 55", VG . . . .$950.00 (B)

Barber Shop, advertising sign, three-piece sign consisting of heavy milk glass globe, center cast iron bracket, and bottom milk glass stripe pole, 11½" x 31", EX . .$1,100.00 (B)

Barber Shop, two-sided porcelain flange sign, 24" x 12", red, white & blue, NM, **$190.00 (B).** *Courtesy of Muddy River Trading Co./Gary Metz*

Barq's...It's Good Ice Cold...Gas...Oil, embossed tin "tacker" style sign with message blanks for price info, 11¼" x 35⅜", VG, **$500.00 (B).** *Courtesy of Autopia Advertising Auctions*

Barq's Root Beer, embossed tin advertising sign by Donaldson Art Sign Co., Covington, KY, with graphics of bottle in spotlight, 35½" x 19½", EX, **$110.00 (B).** *Courtesy of Buffalo Bay Auction Co.*

Barney Oldfield, heavy paper blotter, "Boedeker Brothers, Higginsville, MO," 6" x 3¼", **$100.00 (B).**

Barber Shop, curved single-sided porcelain pole sign, 15½" x 24", VG . . . .**$250.00 (B)**

Barber Shop, double-sided flange sign simple advertising "Barber Shop," 20" x 24", EX . . . .**$235.00 (B)**

Barber Shop, light-up pole, milk glass cylinder with red stripe, light green porcelain holder, 11" x 26", VG . . . . .**$425.00 (B)**

Barber Shop, milk glass advertising globe with fired-on lettering, 9½" x 9½" x 12", VG . . . .**$750.00 (B)**

Barber Shop Milwaukee Sentinel News, single-sided porcelain advertising sign, 48" x 10", G . . . . .**$225.00 (B)**

Barber Shop, two-sided porcelain flange sign, 24" x 12", red, white & blue, G . . . .**$110.00 (C)**

Bar-B-Q Rolled Oats, paper on tin with slip lid, 7-oz., EX . . . .**$225.00 (C)**

Barclay's Ale, advertising sign with graphics of man holding a large glass of ale, 14" x 21", EX . . . .**$60.00 (B)**

Barclay's Lager, tin litho advertising sign with artwork of man with glass of product, 1910, 14" x 21", EX . .**$75.00 (B)**

Bardahl Try It, die cut advertising sign with likeness of the Bardahl man with a case of the product, 10" x 10", EX . . . .**$175.00 (C)**

Barnsdall Be Square, gas globe, one-piece, etched with trademark logo in center, 16½" h, G . . . . .**$1,700.00 (B)**

Barnsdall Dependable Products, double-sided porcelain sign, 47½" x 47½", VG, **$250.00 (B).** *Courtesy of Collectors Auction Services*

Barq's, tin over cardboard sign, "Drink Barq's it's good," featuring artwork of sandwich and bottle of Barq's, 11" x 14", EX, **$150.00 (B).**

Courtesy of Muddy River Trading Co./Gary Metz

Bartels Beer, painted metal sign, 18" dia., EX, **$150.00 (C).**

Barns-Dall, Be Square To Your Engine, porcelain pump sign with "B square" logo in center and message around edges, 3" dia., EX . . . .$150.00 (C)

Barnsdall B Square Motor Oil, porcelain double-sided advertising dealer sign, 29⅜" dia., F . . . .$275.00 (B)

Barnsdall Monamotor Oil, tin sign in original wood sign, 18" x 72", 1920s, NM . . . .$375.00 (C)

Barnsdall Super-Gas, three-piece milk glass pump globe, 15½" x 16½", EX . . . .$500.00 (B)

Barnum and Bailey's Greatest Show on Earth, advertising poster with graphics of a clown bowing, 25" x 17", VG . . . .$25.00 (D)

Barnum & Bailey, paper litho circus poster with graphics of lion's head with bare teeth exposed promoting "greatest show on earth," 16¾" x 24½", EX . . . .$75.00 (B)

Barq's...Drink...It's Good, tin double-sided flange advertising sign, 21½" x 14", NM . . . .$350.00 (C)

Barq's...It's Good Ice Cold...Gas...Oil, embossed tin "tacker" style sign with message blanks for price info., 11¼" x 35⅜", VG . . . .$500.00 (B)

Barq's, metal advertising menu board, with "Drink Barq's It's Good" in message space over menu space, 19" x 27", EX . . . .$65.00 (D)

Barq's Root Beer, embossed tin advertising sign by Donaldson Art Sign Co., Covington, KY, with graphics of bottle in spotlight, 35½" x 19½", EX . . . .$110.00 (B)

Bartels Brewing Co., cone-shaped ashtray, 4⅝" x 4", G, $600.00 (B).

Bartholomy Brewing Co., cardboard advertising sign with graphics of pretty lady holding grain, 29" x 40", VG, $625.00 (B).

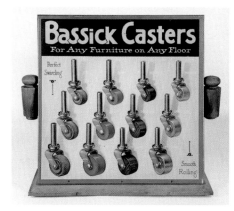

Bassick Casters, wooden display, metal and wood construction with casters on front, 13" W x 12¾" x 4¾" D, NM, $45.00 (C).

Barq's, tin over cardboard sign, "Drink Barq's it's good," featuring artwork of sandwich and bottle of Barq's, 11" x 14", G . . . .$75.00 (C)

Barrus Mustard, wood store display box with paper litho label on lid with product information, 21" x 10½" x 5", VG . . . .$120.00 (B)

Barteldes Seed Co., unopened tin with T-N-T popcorn, EX . . . .$85.00 (B)

Bartels Beer, painted metal sign, 18" dia., G . .$125.00 (D)

Bartels Beer, tin self-framing advertising sign, 18½" dia., VG . . . .$75.00 (B)

Bartels Lager, Ale & Porter, Syracuse, NY, with artwork of man with large tankard of product, 4⅛" dia., EX . . . .$100.00 (B)

Bartholomy Ale, tip tray with image of pretty young lady, 4¼" dia., VG . . . .$140.00 (B)

Bartholomy B…Beers, Ales & Porter…in Kegs & Bottles, round metal tip tray with artwork of woman on large bird, 4¼" dia., EX . . . .$110.00 (B)

Baseball Centennial, painted tin license plate attachment celebrating the 100th anniversary of baseball, 3½" x 4⅝", EX . . . .$275.00 (C)

Bass Ale, for men, celluloid over tin advertising sign with easel back, 7" x 9", EX . . . .$55.00 (C)

Bayer Aspirin, Does Not Depress The Heart, trifold cardboard litho, 42⅝" x 33¾", G, **$160.00 (B).**

Beacon Shoes...Lighthouse on Rock, with product name beaming out from light source, composition construction, 6¼" x 10½", NM, **$95.00 (C).** *Courtesy of Creatures of Habit*

Belar Cigars, self-framing tin advertising sign, 9⅞", VG, **$45.00, (B).**

Belga Vander Elst, self-framing porcelain foreign advertising sign, 18½" x 27½", G, **$325.00 (B).** *Courtesy of Collectors Auction Services*

Belle Plains Candy Kitchen, framed embossed die cut calendar, 1916, EX, **$110.00 (B).**

Bass Ale, tap handle, features fox hunt scene, EX . .**$25.00 (D)**

Bassick Casters, wooden display, metal and wood construction with casters on front, 13" W x 12¾" x 4¾" D, EX . . . .**$30.00 (B)**

Baum's Wonderful Polish, die cut cardboard advertising sign with great graphics of vintage auto with top down, being driven by a lady with scarf blowing in the wind, NOS, 9¼" x 10⅜", NM . . . .**$195.00 (C)**

Bausch and Lomb Optical, cardboard sign with finish to look like canvas with graphics of vintage-dressed folks looking through a hand-held telescope, 17" x 21½", VG . . . .**$75.00 (C)**

Baxters 5¢ Cigar, self-framing embossed tin advertising sign with graphics of drum in center, "beats all...how good they are," 9½" x 13¾", VG . . . .**$80.00 (B)**

Bayerson Oil Works, calendar with artwork of two lions, at bottom on original frame is message, 1914, EX .**$75.00 (D)**

B-B Dairy Feeds, Poultry Feeds, metal ad sign from Buffalo, N.Y., 24" x 12", EX . . . .**$40.00 (B)**

B.B. French Corsets, cardboard advertising sign with graphics of product in use on mannequin, 15" x 10", 1875s, NM . . . .**$195.00 (C)**

Beacon Oil, double-sided porcelain advertising sign, overall image of fan blade design, 30" dia., EX . . . .**$875.00 (B)**

Berry Brothers Varnishes, When You See Varnishes and Hard Oil Finish, painted tin sign with embossed lettering, The Tuscaro Adv. Co., Coshocton, Ohio, 27½" x 19½", G, **$165.00 (C).**

Bennett's Metal Polish, tin litho match holder, with artwork of metal polish can on front, 5"H, VG, **$355.00 (C).**

Courtesy of Richard Opfer Auctioneering Inc.

Betsy Ross 5¢ Cigar, advertisement, self-framed tin sign, 20" x 24", VG, **$595.00 (C).**

Beacon Shoes...Lighthouse on Rock, with product name beaming out from light source, composition construction, 6¼" x 10½", EX . . . .**$75.00 (D)**

Beacon Shoes, reverse painted glass in wood frame, 14⅜" x 20½", EX . . . .**$125.00 (C)**

Beacon Shoes, There Are None Better, reverse painted glass advertising with lighthouse logo in center, 14½" x 20½", EX . . . .**$125.00 (D)**

Beacon Tires, painted metal double-sided flange sign with graphics of lighthouse inside tire, "low mileage cost," 17" x 24¼", VG . . . .**$3,250.00 (B)**

Bear Wheel Alignment...Wheel Balancing, die cut metal advertising sign in likeness of bear holding message board, 36" x 54½", G . . . .**$425.00 (B)**

Beauty Shop, light-up one-piece milk glass ad globe with etched lettering, 11" x 12½", VG . . . .**$425.00 (B)**

Beaver Coal, composition paperweight in shape of lump of coal, 3" x 5½" x 4¾", EX . . . .**$50.00 (B)**

Beck's Bottled Beer, round metal tip tray with artwork of eagle on red, white, and blue shield in center of tray, 4⅛" dia., G . . . .**$140.00 (B)**

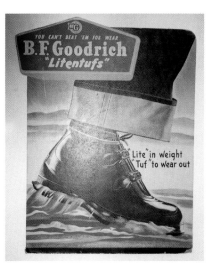

Beverly Farms Milk, glass and metal light-up advertising Pam clock, 15" dia. VG, **$50.00 (B).**

B.F. Goodrich, "Litentufs," Lite in weight, tuf to wear out, cardboard sign, with artwork of rubber footwear, 14" x 19½", EX, **$35.00 (D).** *Courtesy of Pleasant Hill Antique Mall & Tea Room/Bob Johnson*

Bickmore, Easy-Shave Cream, die cut cardboard, featuring artwork of man applying product to shaving brush, 13" x 21", NM, **$50.00 (C).**

Bickmore's Gall Cure, three-panel die cut cardboard display sign with great images of horses and people and other period scenes, 41" x 33¼", NM, **$375.00 (C).** *Courtesy of Autopia Advertising Auctions*

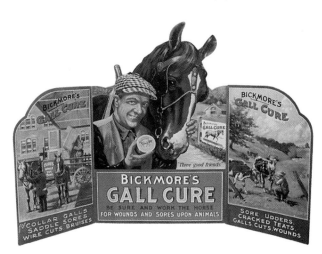

Bee Brand Playing Cards, store counter display boxes, graphics in likeness of regular decks of playing cards, 8¼" x 6" x 12", EX . . . .$300.00 (B)

Beech-Nut Brand Chewing Gum, mechanical valentine card, 7" x 5", EX . . . .$75.00 (C)

Beech-Nut Brand Coffee, key-wound tin litho container with graphics of product leaf in oval on front, 1-lb., EX . . . .$65.00 (D)

Beech-Nut, cardboard litho advertising with artwork of gum package, "It costs you no more...to enjoy Beech-Nut...the Quality Gum," in original wood frame, 46½" x 22½", VG . . . .$95.00 (B)

Beech-Nut Chewing Tobacco, porcelain advertising sign with graphics of product at left, 22" x 10½", EX$95.00 (D)

Beech-Nut Chewing Tobacco, porcelain sign with artwork of product packaging at left of sign, 22" x 10½", F . .$55.00 (D)

Beech-Nut, cigar tin with graphics of beech nut on tree, 50 count, 1920s, EX . . . .$45.00 (C)

Beech-Nut Coffee, tin with key-wound top, 1-lb., F . .$12.00 (D)

Beech-Nut, metal counter top store display bin with graphics of Beech Nut package on lift lid, "Quality made it famous," 9¾" x 8" x 9", EX . . . .$195.00 (B)

Big Ben, tobacco tin, featuring artwork of horse on front of tin, Brown Williamson Tobacco Co., rare piece, 1-lb., VG, **$75.00 (D).** *Courtesy of Chief Paduke Antiques Mall*

Big Ben, vertical pocket tin with graphics of Big Ben clock tower on front, "Roll Cut" marked, unusual, EX, **$1,100.00 (B).** *Courtesy of Buffalo Bay Auction Co.*

Big Boy, single-sided cardboard advertising sign, 14" x 22", G, **$40.00 (B).**

Big Giant Cola, embossed tin advertising sign, 23½" x 11½", G, **$45.00 (B).**

Beech-Nut Spearmint Gum, 3-D cardboard store advertising display, in shape of gum container, 15" x 4¼" x 4¼", EX . . . .$55.00 (B)

Beechum's Pills, advertising die cut easel back advertising display in the form of a young boy, 2¼" x 5¼" NM . . . .$195.00 (C)

Beefeater Gin, backbar display statue, 8½" x 17", EX . . . .$95.00 (D)

Beefeater Gin...The imported One, wood and composition back bar statue, 8½" x 17", EX . . . .$95.00 (D)

Beeman's Pepsin Chewing Gum, embossed die cut cardboard advertising sign with graphics of young woman in low-cut dress, 13½" x 17¾", NM . . . . $325.00 (D)

Beeman's Pepsin Chewing Gum, trade card with graphics of woman sitting on a product box, 3½" x 5½", EX . . . .$30.00 (B)

Beeman's Pepsin Gum, advertising card with sleeping baby that wakes up when held to light, hard-to-find item, 3¼" x 5", EX . . . .$95.00 (C)

Beeman's Pepsin Gum, advertising pocket mirror, EX . . . .$160.00 (B)

Beeman's Pepsin Gum, tin strip advertising sign with graphics of gum package, 17½" x 2½", EX . . .$275.00 (B)

Belar Cigars, self-framing tin litho sign with images of product and message in center, 10" x 7½", NM $150.00 (C)

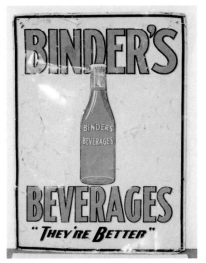

Binder's Beverages...they're better, painted metal sign with bottle in center of message, 20" x 28", orange & black on white, fair, $50.00 (D). *Courtesy of Patrick's Antiques*

Birchola, ceramic dispenser decorated with cascading leaves and metal pump at top, 14" tall, 1910, EX, $1,850.00 (B). *Courtesy of Buffalo Bay Auction Co.*

Bit-O-Honey, embossed tin sign, great graphics, 20" x 9", EX, $650.00 (B). *Courtesy of Muddy River Trading Co./Gary Metz*

Belar Cigars, self-framing tin litho advertising sign with easel back for counter display, graphics of product on sign, 10" x 7½", EX . . . .$40.00 (B)

Bell Brand Chocolates & Bon Bons, tin litho advertising sign with graphics of cherubs around a center bell, EX . .$355.00 (B)

Belle Plains Candy Kitchen, framed embossed die cut calendar, 1916, EX . . . .$110.00 (B)

Bell Ethyl Gas Globe, plastic body with two glass lens, 13½" dia., VG . . . .$475.00 (B)

Bell System, die cut porcelain flange sign with message part of sign in die cut circle, 16¼" x 14", EX .$155.00 (C)

Bell System, double-sided porcelain advertising sign for Southwestern Bell Telephone with logo Bell System bell in center, these normally hung at pay phone locations, 11" x 11", 1950s, EX . . . .$180.00 (B)

Bell System, Public Telephone, double-sided porcelain sign with arrow pointing to pay station, 12½" x 5½", EX . . . .$180.00 (B)

Bell System, Public Telephone, flange porcelain sign featuring the bell in the center, 18" x 18", EX . . .$95.00 (C)

Bell System, Public Telephone, square double-sided porcelain advertising sign, 18" x 18", EX . . . . .$55.00 (B)

Belzile Ice Cream, double-sided metal sign with graphics of ice cream cone, 22" x 28", VG . . . .$100.00 (B)

Black Cat Shoe Dressing, tin wind-up clock with graphics of black cat, 17½" x 23½", G, $900.00 (B).

Black-Draught a Good laxative, double-sided metal flange sign, 12" x 6½", G, $100.00 (B).

Black Kow, single-sided embossed tin advertising sign, 23¾" x 11¾", G, $80.00 (B).

Bemgal Shirts, paper litho advertising sign with graphics of tiger, litho by Colortype, NY, 8¼" x 11", EX . . . . $110.00 (B)

Bendix Radio, light-up advertising clock, cardboard body with glass face and cover, Telechron Inc., Ashland Mass., U.S.A., C.A.P., Product of Bendix Aviation Corporation, 15" dia., VG . . . . $200.00 (B)

Ben-Hur Coffee, key-wound tin litho container with graphics of horse-drawn chariot on front, 10½" x 11½", EX . . . . $240.00 (B)

Ben Hur Rye Whiskey, reverse glass advertising sign for saloon with top hanging chain, 10" x 4⅛", EX . . . $210.00 (B)

Bennett Coffee Tin, litho container with small lid, graphics of company headquarters , 7" x 7" x 11", EX . . . $100.00 (B)

Bennett's Metal Polish, tin litho match holder, with artwork of metal polish can on front, 5"H, G . . . $325.00 (B)

Berghoff Beer, tin on cardboard advertising sign with graphics of bird dogs in snowy field, 21" x 13", EX . . . . $120.00 (B)

Berghoff Beer, tin over cardboard advertising sign with graphics of hunting dogs in the field, string hung, 21" x 13", VG . . . . $95.00 (C)

Berry Brothers, advertising celluloid pocket mirror from White-head & Hoag with graphics of young boy with wagon advertising Berry Bros. varnishes, 2¾" x 1¾", EX . . . . $135.00 (C)

Berry Brothers Toy Wagon, advertising pocket mirror, graphics depicting youngsters with wagon and dog, 2" dia., EX . . . . $126.00 (B)

Berry Brothers Varnishes, pocket advertising mirror with image of young boy pulling wagon, 2¾" x 1¾", G . . $150.00 (B)

Berry Brothers Varnishes, When You See Varnishes and Hard Oil Finish, painted tin sign with embossed lettering, The Tuscaro Adv. Co., Coshocton, Ohio, 27½" x 19½", F . . . . $150.00 (D)

Berwind Briquets, single-sided tin sign, "Why go south? Burn Berwind Briquets," 20" x 14", VG . . . . . $75.00 (B)

Beta Beer, round light-up advertising sign, 17" dia., VG . . . . $150.00 (B)

Blatz at Local Prices, skater statue, EX, $135.00 (C). *Courtesy of B.J. Summers*

Blanke's Coffee, tin litho store bin with great graphics of horseback rider on front, 24¾" H, EX, $600.00 (B). *Courtesy of Richard Opfer Auctioneering Inc.*

Blatz Beer, light-up back bar figure; when lit, bars behind man appear to move, VG, $145.00 (D).

Courtesy of Pleasant Hill Antique Mall & Tea Room/Bob Johnson

Bethelem Extra Fancy Rio Coffee, John Bird Co., Maine, store bin, Three Cow logo at top left inside star, 1900s, 10" x 17", G . . . .$155.00 (B)

Betsy Ross Coffee, tin litho container from the Akron Grocery Co., 4" dia. x 6", EX . . . .$50.00 (B)

Betsy Ross 5¢ Cigar, advertisement, self-framed tin sign, 20" x 24", G . . . .$500.00 (C)

Betsy's Best Flour, Bake and See Why, paper litho on cardboard with graphics of product bag to left of message, 38½" x 21½", EX . . . .$150.00 (B)

Bettendorf Steel Gear Wagon, metal tip tray with graphics of wagon in center of tray, additional product info below wagon image, 4⅞", EX . . . .$275.00 (B)

Betty Rose, Coats and Suits, painted wood sign, with cut-out lettering, 24" x 5¼", EX . . . .$65.00 (D)

Between the Acts Cigar, paper litho by Donaldson Bros., NY, of young girl in early dress and bonnet, 12½" x 29", 1880s, VG . . . .$1,800.00 (C)

"Between The Acts," Trihos. Hall Tobacco Co., NY, paper litho advertising, graphics of young girl with bouquet of roses, 1910, 16" x 25", G . . . .$165.00 (B)

B.F. Goodrich, "Litentufs," Lite in weight, tuf to wear out, cardboard sign, with artwork of rubber footwear, 14" x 19½", NM . . . .$65.00 (D)

B.F. Gravely's Plug Cut Tobacco, tin with litho of turban-wearing person, 6½" x 3¼", EX . . . .$75.00 (C)

Blatz bottle and can man, Milwaukee's Finest Beer, back bar advertising statue, VG, $135.00 (D). *Courtesy of B.J. Summers*

Blatz, man at keg, We serve the finest people everyday, At Local Prices, light-up back bar statue, VG, $125.00 (D). *Courtesy of B.J. Summers*

Blue Coral Treatment, litho on canvas, 93" x 34½", VG, $95.00 (B).

B.H. Voskamp's Sons, paper litho advertising importers and wholesale grocers with graphics of a couple of kids on dock, 21" x 26", EX . . . .$1,500.00 (B)

Bickmore, Easy-Shave Cream, die cut cardboard, featuring artwork of man applying product to shaving brush, 13" x 21", EX . . . .$25.00 (C)

Bickmore, Easy-Shave Cream, die cut litho advertising sign with graphics of man spreading the product on his shaving brush, 21" x 31", VG . . . .$35.00 (C)

Bickmore Gall Salve, advertising cardboard poster with graphics of horses crossing a mountain pass, "for all wounds and sores on animals," 32" x 20", EX . .$60.00 (B)

Bickmore Gall Salve, counter display box, originally held gall salve tins, 8" x 5½" x 2½", EX . . . .$85.00 (C)

Bickmore Gall Salve, paper advertising sign, "For all wounds and sores on animals," 34" x 21½", EX . . . .$95.00 (C)

Bickmore's Gall Cure, three-panel die cut cardboard display sign with great images of horses and people and other period scenes, 41" x 33¼", NM . . . .$375.00 (C)

Bidu...We Serve Ice Cold, embossed tin sign with graphics of caballero on donkey, 16" x 16", NM . . . .$125.00 (B)

Big Ben, tobacco tin, featuring artwork of horse on front of tin, Brown Williamson Tobacco Co., rare piece, 1-lb., G . . . .$65.00 (D)

Big Ben, vertical pocket tin container with graphics of the tower of Big Ben on front and back, pipe and cigarette tobacco, G . . . .$130.00 (B)

Blue Parrot Coffee, tin with great colors and artwork of parrot on limb, extremely rare piece, 6" H, EX, **$5,000.00 (B).** *Courtesy of Richard Opfer Auctioneering Inc.*

Blue Ribbon Bourbon, framed oleograph of cabin beside stream, 48" x 38", near mint, **$600.00 (D).**

Blue Ridge Bus Lines, etched glass sign, 21½" x 18½", G, **$160.00 (B).** *Courtesy of Collectors Auction Services*

Big Ben, vertical pocket tin with graphics of Big Ben clock tower on front, "Roll Cut" marked, unusual, P . . . .**$125.00 (B)**

Big Ben, vertical pocket tin with the usual version "Pipe and Cigarette," EX . . . .**$950.00 (B)**

Big Boy..., Pale Dry in green bottles only 5¢, embossed tin advertising sign, 19" x 9", EX . . . .**$88.00 (B)**

Big Chief, wooden cigar box with great graphics of horses and Indians on inside lid, 50 ct., EX . . . .**$55.00 (B)**

Big Mac, tin litho coffee container with key-wound lid, 1-lb., EX . . . .**$145.00 (C)**

Big Snap Cigar Box, wood construction with paper litho on inside lid showing a black man with a cigar, 5" x 4½" x 1½", VG . . . .**$350.00 (B)**

Big West Oil Co of Montana Zippo, pocket lighter, NOS, 1¼" x 2¼", NM . . . .**$125.00 (C)**

Bobolink Silk Hose, original art work, vinyl layering on cardboard, 25¼" x 37¼", EX, $100.00 (B). *Courtesy of Collectors Auction Services*

Bock Beer, paper ad, framed, copyright 1925, near mint, $375.00 (D). *Courtesy of Affordable Antiques/Oliver Johnson*

Booster Cigar, paper advertising sign with fantastic graphics of man smoking a cigar while his lady adjusts her stocking, "High Grade Cigar Manufacturers...Stirton & Dyer...London, Canada, 1910, NM, $1,775.00 (C). *Courtesy of Buffalo Bay Auction Co.*

Booker T. Motel, Colored, single-sided advertising sign from Humboldt, Tenn., 24" x 15½", G, $900.00 (B). *Courtesy of Collectors Auction Services*

Billings-Chapin, die cut cardboard, moving sign with worker and customer that move in agreement with each other, 32" x 29", VG . . . .$475.00 (C)

Biltrite, advertising door push promoting rubber heels and non-slip soles, 32" x 3", VG . . . .$140.00 (B)

Biltrite Shoes, litho on cardboard sign with graphics of shoe cobbler working on a shoe, "Get Longer Wear by Shoe Repair," 21½" x 32½", EX . . . .$30.00 (B)

Binder's Beverages...they're better, painted metal sign with bottle in center of message, 20" x 28", orange & black on white, F . . . .$50.00 (D)

Bing Crosby Ice Cream, wax cardboard container featuring artwork of Bing Crosby on front, NOS, pint, NM . . . .$25.00 (C)

Birchola, ceramic dispenser decorated with cascading leaves and metal pump at top, 14" tall, 1910, EX $1,850.00 (B)

Bird Brand Steel Cut Coffee, tin litho with small canister top, graphics of colorful bird on perch, G . . . . .$97.00 (B)

Bireley's...For real fruit taste...drink..., one-sided tin advertising sign with raised field showing fruit, 36" x 15", 1949, VG . . . .$175.00 (B)

Bireley's, painted metal sign, "Drink Bireley's non-carbonated beverages," 28" x 10", 1950s, EX . . . . . .$25.00 (C)

Bireley's, tin advertising thermometer with tilted bottle, "Drink Bireley's non-carbonated beverages," 4½" x 15¾", 1950s, EX . . . .$155.00 (B)

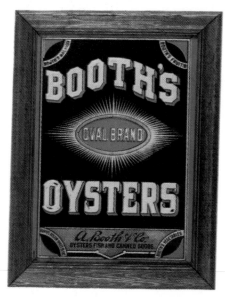

Booth's Oysters, embossed tin ad sign in wood frame, A. Booth & Co. Oysters, Fish and Canned Goods, 30" x 22", EX, **$325.00 (B).** *Courtesy of Collectors Auction Services*

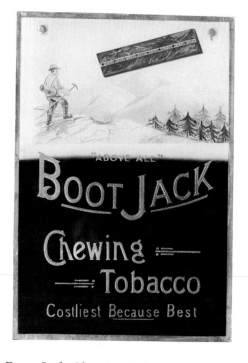

Boot Jack Chewing Tobacco, Costliest Because Best, reverse painted glass sign with beveled edges and original chain, 1900s, 8" x 12", EX, **$550.00 (B).** *Courtesy of Muddy River Trading Co./Gary Metz*

Borax Extract of Soap, for washing everything, painted metal sign, 24" x 7", G, **$65.00 (D).** *Courtesy of Riverview Antique Mall*

Bishop's Move Tobacco, tin litho container with graphics of chessboard and players, 3¼" x 2¼" x 1", EX . . . . . $40.00 (B)

Bissell's Carpet Sweeper, floor display unit, 23" x 59", F . . . . $55.00 (B)

Bit-O-Honey, embossed tin sign, great graphics, 20" x 9", EX . . . . $650.00 (B)

Blackbird Red Pepper, paper on cardboard with graphics of red-winged blackbird on front label, 1½ - oz., EX . . . . $75.00 (C)

Black Caps, tin advertising sign, cure for Gonorrhoea Gleet in two to five days, the Safety Remedy Co., Canton, Ohio, 7" x 10", 1900, EX . . . . $48.00 (B)

Black Cat Stove and Shoe Polish, celluloid and metal bill hook, celluloid button has graphics of black cat in center, 2¼" dia., NM . . . . $138.00 (B)

Black-Hawk Coffee, tin container with paper label showing Indian bust on front, slip-lid, from The Black Hawk Coffee and Spice Co., Waterloo, IA, 1-lb., EX . . . . $375.00 (B)

Black Label Beer, die cut cardboard in image of man carrying case of product, three-dimensional, 110" x 23", NM . . . . $75.00 (D)

Black Patti's Troubadours, paper litho poster, "Lloyd G. Gibbs...The Black Jean DeReike," 21" x 31", 1954, VG . . . .$75.00 (B)

Borax Extract of Soap, single-sided tin sign, 24" x 7", VG, **$95.00** (B).

Borden's Elsie and Elmer, ceramic S & P, 2⅜" x 4", VG, **$90.00 (B)**.

Borden's Elsie, porcelain neon advertising sign, VG, **$1,700.00 (B)**.

Black Pete Toffee Tin, 6½" x 4" x 9½", G . . . . . **$55.00 (C)**

Black Rose Tea, die cut cardboard in the shape of a young girl wearing a bonnet, holding an advertising poster for the product, 7½" x 16", EX . . . . **$155.00 (B)**

Black Sheep 5¢ Cigar...A Sanitary Package for 25¢, tin litho cigar container, 3¼" x 5½" x ¾", EX . . . . . **$275.00 (B)**

Black Spots Cigar, wooden box with paper litho advertising inside and outside, graphics of three boys eyeballing a watermelon, 15" x 4½" x 5", VG . . . . **$975.00 (C)**

Black Spots, wooden cigar box with inside label showing three black youngsters about to devour a watermelon, 250 ct., VG . . . . **$230.00 (B)**

Blackwells Durham Tobacco Co., Julie Carrs Tobacco, litho tin container for cut plug product, 1½" x 4½" x 3¼", EX . . . .**$300.00 (B)**

Blake's Tea, blue & white stoneware pot with pouring spout and graphics of Grant cabin, EX . . . . . .**$190.00 (B)**

Blanke's Coffee, tin litho store bin with great graphics of horseback rider on front, 24¾" H, EX . . . . . .**$600.00 (B)**

Blanke's, curved front metal counter store bin with lift slant lid, message promoting product on front and sides, 15½" x 18" x 25", VG . . . .**$475.00 (C)**

Blanke's Grants Cabin, tin litho tea container, graphics of cabin on label, with hinge lid, 5" x 3¼" x 2¾", 1910, EX . . . .**$155.00 (C)**

Borden's Fine Dairy Products, light-up advertising clock by Pam, 15" dia., G, **$210.00 (B).**
Courtesy of Collectors Auction Services

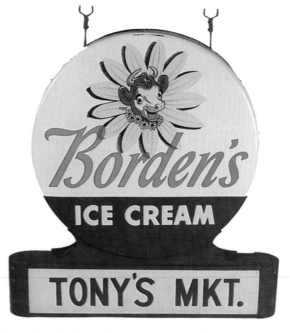

Borden's Ice Cream sign, double-sided embossed tin, "Tony's Mkt.," 51" x 56" x 9", VG, **$675.00 (B).**

Borden's Milk, sign with graphics of young girl, supposedly the Bordens' daughter, advertising Eagle Brand milk, 13½" x 16", NM, **$425.00 (C).** *Courtesy of Buffalo Bay Auction Co.*

Blatz, alto-plaster ad sign of F. Scott Fitzgerald in German pub, Blatz Old Heidelberg, 1933, 42¾" x 27¾", EX . . . .**$175.00 (B)**

Blatz at Local Prices, skater statue, G . . . .**$95.00 (C)**

Blatz Beer, light-up back bar figure; when lit, bars behind man appear to move, G . . . .**$125.00 (D)**

Blatz...Blatz, can (barrel) man holding mug of beer, metal and plastic bar statue, 6½" x 10½", EX . . . . . .**$125.00 (D)**

Blatz bottle and can man, Milwaukee's Finest Beer, back bar advertising statue, G . . . .**$100.00 (C)**

Blatz, bottle man holding mug of beer with one hand and advertising pennant in other hand, plastic and glass construction, 6¾" x 15½", EX . . . .**$125.00 (D)**

Blatz, man at keg, We Serve The Finest People Everyday, At Local Prices, light-up back bar statue, G . . . .**$95.00 (C)**

Blatz, Milwaukee's most exquisite beer, tin over cardboard with embossed figures, 10½" x 13¾", EX . . . .**$165.00 (B)**

Blatz...Old Heidelberg...better because it's ester aged, metal serving tray, 13¼" x 10½", G . . . .**$105.00 (D)**

Blatz Pilsner Beer, die cut easel back cardboard store advertising sign in shape of bottle of product, 1947, 7" x 27", NM . . . .**$25.00 (B)**

Bordens Trucks, one-sided tin plant sign, 24" x 12", G, $160.00 (B).

Bowers Windproof Lighter, countertop die cut cardboard easel back display card with lighters, G, $20.00 (B).

Boulevard Coffee, Henry Horner & Co., Chicago, Ill., paper label on cardboard container, street scene graphics, 1-lb., EX, $325.00 (C) *Courtesy of Buffalo Bay Auction Co.*

Boylan's Birch Beers, double-sided metal flange signs, new, 18" x 13", EX, $37.00 (B).
Courtesy of Collectors Auction Services

Blend 150, coffee tin, key-wound, 1-lb., EX . .$75.00 (C)

Bliss Coffee, key-wound tin, 1-lb., F . . . .$15.00 (D)

BL Tobacco, sign, porcelain with circle in square, 15" sq., EX . . . .$250.00 (C)

Blue and Scarlet, tin litho lunch pail from Booker Tobacco Co., Richmond, VA, with top wire handle, blue, scarlet, and gold, G . . . .$125.00 (B)

Blue Bonnet Coffee, key-wound tin litho container with graphics of woman in blue hat on front, 1-lb., EX .$348.00 (B)

Blue Bonnet Coffee, tin litho can with artwork of red-haired woman wearing blue hat, key-wound lid, 1-lb., EX . . . .$1,700.00 (B)

Blue Buckle Work Garments...Strong for work...Overalls Pants Shirts, one-sided porcelain sign, 13" x 4½", G . . . .$115.00 (B)

Blue Crown Spark Plugs, store display, has plug on top of electrical display that fires when button on box is pushed, never used, 9" x 8¾" x 5", NM . . . .$210.00 (B)

Blue Flame Coffee, lithographed tin container, 10-lb., VG . . . .$55.00 (B)

Blue Parrot Coffee, tin with great colors and artwork of parrot on limb, extremely rare piece, 6" H, EX . . . . .$5,000.00 (B)

Blue Ribbon Bourbon, framed oleograph of cabin beside stream, 48" x 38", EX . . . .$550.00 (D)

Boy Scout, paper litho poster, "We, too have a job to do," 19¾" x 29½", VG, $325.00 (C).

Brach's Candy, stand-up rabbit advertising prop with hat pegs, 48" H, NM, $35.00 (C).

Brattleboro Steam Laundry, thermometer on painted wood, 9¼" x 18", VG, $410.00 (C).

Courtesy of Riverview Antique Mall

Blue Ribbon, coffee cardboard litho advertising with graphics of caravan traveling down road to meet ship, 26" x 19", VG . . . .$650.00 (C)

Blue Ribbon Coffee, silk screen on paperboard advertising sign with graphics of natives carrying beans to the ships in the harbor, 26" x 19", 1906, EX . . . .$120.00 (B)

Blue Ribbon Malt Extract, cardboard string hanger, "America's Biggest Seller," 10½" x 13½", EX . . . .$150.00 (C)

Blue Ribbon, spice tin litho with graphics of tropical scene on label, Peoria, IL, 1-oz., EX . . . .$65.00 (C)

Blue Twins Cigar, paper litho over wood cigar box, "Factory No. 815 9th District, State of Penna." with graphics of of boys dancing with boxes of twin cigars, 9" x 5¼" x 2¾", VG . . . .$350.00 (B)

Blu-J Brooms, double-sided die cut string-hanging advertising sign with likeness of bird on broom, 4" x 10½", EX . . . .$95.00 (C)

Board of Trade Tobacco, store counter top display wood box with paper labels and a glass window on front side, from Power & Stuart Tobacco Co., 12½" x 12½" x 10½", EX . . . .$165.00 (B)

Bob White Baking Powder, paper litho over tin can, never opened, with artwork of bobwhite quail on front, 2⅛" x 3¼", NM . . . .$200.00 (B)

Bob White, tobacco tin, great litho of quail on front and hunting scene on back, 4" L, G . . . .$160.00 (B)

Bock Beer Hangers from Donaldson Litho Co., Newport, Ky., retail trade generic sign, graphics of serving girl with tray of product, 18½" x 26½", NM . . . .$330.00 (B)

Bock Beer, paper ad, framed, copyright 1925, EX . . . .$300.00 (B)

Bock beer sign, paper hanger sign with metal strip by Donaldson Litho Co., graphics of old gent wearing apron enjoying a glass of beer, 19" x 30", 1900s, EX . . . . . .$160.00 (B)

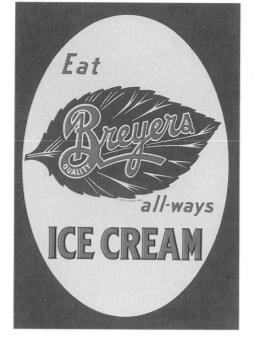

Braun's Town Talk Bread, one-sided tin self-framing embossed sign, 35½" x 23½", G, **$70.00 (B)**.

Briggs & Stratton, Authorized Service-Parts, light-up advertising sign with clock and illusion wheel for the "easy-spin starting," 38" x 10" x 4½", EX, **$395.00 (C)**. *Courtesy of Autopia Advertising Auctions*

Breyers all-ways ice cream, double-sided porcelain advertising sign, NOS, 20" x 28", VG, **$505.00 (B)**.

Bold Cigars, the National Smoke, framed paper advertising sign with graphics of battleships, 21" x 27", EX ...**$185.00 (B)**

Bonded Pennzoil Dealer, rainbow-shaped double-sided porcelain advertising sign, originally was used over the oval curb sign, 29½" x 3½", 1930s, NM .....**$325.00 (C)**

Bond Street Pipe Tobacco, Philip Morris & Co, New York, London, tin, EX ....**$35.00 (D)**

B-1 Lemon-Lime Soda, poster in its original wood frame with B-1 logo at top center, G ....**$75.00 (D)**

B-1 Lemon-Lime Soda, single-sided die cut tin advertising sign in shape of bottle, 1940s, VG ....**$80.00 (B)**

Booker T. Motel, Colored, single-sided advertising sign from Humboldt, Tenn., 24" x 15½", F .....**$125.00 (C)**

Booster Cigar, paper advertising sign with fantastic graphics of man smoking a cigar while his lady adjusts her stocking, "High Grade Cigar Manufacturers...Stirton & Dyer...London Canada, 1910, NM ....**$1,775.00 (C)**

Booth's Compound Derma Talcum, cardboard container with paper label containing graphics of frolicking cherubs, 2¼" x 4⅛" x 1¾", EX ....**$400.00 (B)**

Booth's Oysters, embossed tin ad sign in wood frame, A. Booth & Co. Oysters, Fish and Canned Goods, 30" x 22", EX ....**$325.00 (B)**

Boot Jack Chewing Tobacco, Costliest Because Best, reverse painted glass sign with beveled edges and original chain, 1900s, 8" x 12", EX ....**$550.00 (B)**

Borax, early porcelain advertising sign, "Welcome ask for Borax Soap," 36" x 6", EX ....**$295.00 (C)**

Borax Extract of Soap, for washing everything, painted metal sign, 24" x 7", G ....**$65.00 (D)**

Borden's "Elsie" logo sign, embossed tin, NOS, 17½" x 17½", NM ....**$250.00 (C)**

Borden's Elsie, self-framed embossed advertising sign with the image of Elsie in the famous daisy collar, 17½" x17½", EX ....**$140.00 (B)**

Brookfield Rye, self-framing tin litho advertising sign with scantily clad woman holding a bottle of the product, "made famous by public favor," 23" x 33", EX, **$925.00 (C).** *Courtesy of Wm. Morford Investment Grade Collectibles*

Brother Jonathan, store chewing tobacco counter tin with graphics of Brother Jonathan sitting in a tobacco patch, from F.F. Adams Tobacco Co., Milwaukee, 8¼" x 12", EX, **$895.00 (C).** *Courtesy of Wm. Morford Investment Grade Collectibles*

Brooklyn Varnish Co., embossed tin sign, foreign, in wood frame, 17½" x 12", VG, **$50.00 (B).**

Borden's Ice Cream, calendar with Boy Scout promotion at top of tear sheet and Elsie on both sides of sheets, 16" x 33", 1945, EX . . . .**$175.00 (C)**

Borden's Ice Cream, flange double-sided painted metal advertising sign, with graphics of Elsie the Cow in the left side of the sign, 24" x 15", EX .**$350.00 (C)**

Borden's Ice Cream, tin advertising sign with TM Elsie graphics, 24" x 12", NM . . . . **$175.00 (C)**

Borden's Instant Coffee, jar with screw top, featuring paper label, 5-oz., EX . . . .**$7.00 (D)**

Borden's, light-up advertising clock with likeness of Elsie in center of clock, 20½" dia., G . . . .**$155.00 (B)**

Borden's Milk, sign with graphics of young girl, supposedly the Bordens' daughter, advertising Eagle Brand milk, 13½" x 16," NM . . . .**$425.00 (C)**

Borden's Richer Malted Milk, metal can and lid, 6" x 8½", EX . . . .**$110.00 (B)**

Borden's...The Malted Milk In The Square Package, round metal tip tray with artwork of woman with product package, 4½" dia., EX . . . .**$230.00 (B)**

Born Steel Range, tin litho match holder with great graphics of early kitchen range, "Oven Heats In 10 Minutes," 5" H, G . . . .**$380.00 (B)**

Brown's-Oyl For Fords, single-sided embossed tin sign, 13¼" x 20", G, $325.00 (B).

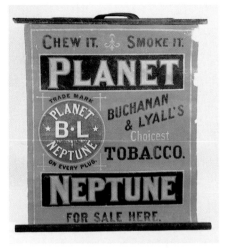

Buchanan & Lyall's Planet Neptune Chewing Tobacco, cloth scroll, pat. June 12, 1877, 11½" x 15½", fair, $25.00 (C).

Budweiser, cardboard poster "Attack on the Overland Stage 1860," 41" x 28½", G, $110.00 (B).

Bossy Brand Cigar, oil lamp with graphics of cow on globe, "Buy The Incomparable...Look for the star...on every cigar," with handle on oil holder, 4" x 5" x 7½", EX . . . .$800.00 (B)

Boston Fish Co., metal tip tray with image of young woman, from the Mpls. Grocer, 305 Hennepin Avenue, 4¼" dia., EX . . . .$120.00 (B)

Boston Garter, wood store display, 9¾" x 14" x 5¾", VG . . . .$160.00 (B)

Boston Tire & Rubber Co...Automobile, Bicycle, and Carriage Tires, round metal tip tray with artwork of pretty girl with bouquet of flowers, 4¼" dia., G . . . .$200.00 (B)

Boulevard Coffee, Henry Horner & Co., Chicago, IL, paper label on cardboard container, street scene graphics, 1-lb., EX . . . .$325.00 (C)

Bouquet Roasted Coffee, Tracy & Co., Syracuse, NY, paper litho on tin with slip lid, 1-lb., NM . . . . .$60.00 (B)

Bowey's...Hot Chocolate Powder, tin litho container with small canister lid, graphics of hot chocolate being served, 7" x 10", NM . . . .$70.00 (B)

Bowl of Roses Pipe Mixture, tin vertical litho tobacco pocket tin with artwork of man smoking pipe in front of fireplace, 3" x 4⅜" x ⅞", EX . . . .$325.00 (B)

Boyce Moto Meter, litho on wood, "Know the heat of your motor and prevent costly repairs," 19" x 13", VG . $850.00 (B)

Budweiser Clydesdales, cardboard poster, 47½" x 20", VG, $50.00 (B).

Budweiser Clydesdales, plastic advertising clock, 36" x 20" x 7", F, $160.00 (B).

Budweiser Draught Beer, art deco styling with eagle logo holders for reverse painted glass message bar, 18½" x 3" x 9½", EX, $386.00 (B). *Courtesy of Buffalo Bay Auction Co.*

B.P.O. Elks, 45th Annual Reunion Grand Lodge, July 1909, Los Angeles, California, round metal tip tray with artwork of large moose in tray center, 4⅛" dia., G . . . .$25.00 (B)

Brabo Coffee, tin litho with screw lid, Geo Rasmussen Co., Chicago, Ill., 1-lb., EX . . . .$135.00 (C)

Brach's Candy, stand-up rabbit advertising prop with hat pegs, 48" H, EX . . . .$25.00 (C)

Brach's Swing, Swing's the thing, two-part candy box with graphics of majorette twirling baton, 1930s, 9" x 9" x 1½", EX . . . .$31.00 (B)

Brandy Wine, Seminole Flavor Co., Chattanooga, TN, paper sign with artwork of woman riding on eagle, 1939, 22" dia., NM . . . .$75.00 (B)

Brandy Wine Soda, cardboard advertising sign with graphics of woman riding on eagle, 22" dia., EX . . .$195.00 (C)

Brattleboro Steam Laundry, thermometer on painted wood, 9¼" x 18", G . . . .$350.00 (D)

Breakfast Call Coffee, tin container with small lid, 6" x 9", EX . . . .$75.00 (C)

Breakfast Call Coffee, tin litho coffee can, Independence Coffee Co., Denver, Colo., 4⅛" x 5⅞", EX . . . .$60.00 (B)

Breck, light-up advertising clock with image of the Breck girl in the message space above the clock, plastic and metal, 13" x 25" x 3¾", VG . . . .$125.00 (C)

Budweiser Draught Beer, light-up sign featuring pair of hunting dogs, VG, **$120.00 (C).** *Courtesy of Pleasant Hill Antique Mall & Tea Room/Bob Johnson*

Budweiser Draught, light-up advertising sign displaying the team in front of a frosty mug of beer, 16½" dia., NM, **$85.00 (C).** *Courtesy of B.J. Summers*

Budweiser, framed lithograph of Custer's last fight, Anheuser-Busch, St. Louis, Missouri, U.S.A., 44" x 34", NM, **$375.00 (C).**

Breyers Ice Cream, double-sided top hanging porcelain advertising sign promoting "Sodas," 36" x 27", VG . . . .**$600.00 (B)**

Bridgeman Ice Cream, double-sided porcelain sign, 36" x 24", EX . . . .**$375.00 (C)**

Briggs & Stratton Authorized Service-Parts, light-up advertising sign with clock and illusion wheel for the "easy-spin starting," 38" x 10" x 4½", EX . . . .**$395.00 (C)**

Bright Globe Range, round metal tip tray with graphics of product on tray center, 4⅛" dia., EX . . . .**$160.00 (B)**

Brilliant, tobacco mixture tin, Weisert Bros. Tobacco, St. Louis, MO, 4½" x 2¾" x 1¾", EX . . . .**$85.00 (C)**

Bristol Fishing Rods, calendar with graphics of couple fishing from a canoe, with metal bands on top and bottom, 16" x 31", 1918, EX . . . .**$275.00 (C)**

British Navy Chewing Tobacco...Strictly Union Made, cardboard advertising sign with graphics of swimming sailors, Canadian product, 9" x 18", EX . . . . . .**$69.00 (B)**

Bromo-Seltzer for Headaches, embossed tin advertising sign, 20" x 9", NM . . . .**$65.00 (B)**

Brooke Bond, dividend tea porcelain advertising sign, 30" x 20", NM . . . .**$100.00 (B)**

Brookfield Rye, self-framing tin litho advertisng sign with scantily clad woman holding a bottle of the product, "made famous by public favor," 23" x 33", F . . . .**$275.00 (C)**

Brookside Quick Cook Oats, container with graphics of winding brook, 3-lb., EX . . . .**$175.00 (C)**

Brotherhood Tobacco, advertising lunch tin, EX . .**$225.00 (C)**

Budweiser, King of Beers, light-up with hitch at bottom, 9½" x 14¾", NM, **$40.00 (D).**
Courtesy of B.J. Summers

Buffalo Bill's Wild West Show, paper litho advertising poster with graphics of Buffalo Bill on horse, 22½" x 35", EX, **$1,600.00 (B).** *Courtesy of Collectors Auction Services*

Buick, Bangor, Mich., embossed tin dealer sign, 1920s, 19½" x 13½", VG, **$235.00 (C).**
Courtesy of Muddy River Trading Co./Gary Metz

Brother Jonathan, store chewing tobacco counter tin with graphics of Brother Jonathan sitting in a tobacco patch, from F.F. Adams Tobacco Co., Milwaukee, 8¼" x 12", EX . . . .**$895.00 (C)**

Brown Betty Coffee, pry-lid container with graphics of woman with flower in hair, 3-lb., EX . . . . . . **$195.00 (B)**

Brown Collegian Cut, clothing advertising pocket mirror, 1¾" dia., EX . . . . **$425.00 (B)**

Browning, laminated cardboard advertising sign with crossed long guns, 9¼" x 9½", EX . . . .**$35.00 (D)**

Brown's Worm Lozenges, cardboard standing advertising sign for medicine, 10⅞" x 13⅞", EX . . . .**$400.00 (B)**

Brucks Beer-Ale, embossed tin countertop advertising sign, "over 85 years continous brewing," in shape of horse shoe, 11½" x 11¼", EX . . . .**$115.00 (B)**

Brunswick Cocoanut, tin with small lip and graphics of woman on front, 3¼" x 3¼" x 6¼", VG . . . .**$45.00 (C)**

Bubble Up Drink, double-sided disc tin advertising sign, 14" dia., 1940s, EX . . . .**$175.00 (C)**

Bubble Up, menu board with message over black board area, self-framing with rolled edge, 19" x 30", NM . . . .**$75.00 (D)**

Bubble Up, one-sided tin advertising sign, "Drink...," 27¼" x 12⅜", 1920s, F . . . .**$50.00 (B)**

Buick 1915 pennant, one-sided felt, 28½" x 11", VG, $275.00 (C).

Buick Service, double-sided metal sign, 18" dia., G, $220.00 (B).

Bull Dog Cut Plug, die cut tin litho match striker, deluxe straight leaf finest bright burley tobacco, great graphics of dog "won't bite," 6¾"H, EX, $1,800.00 (B). *Courtesy of Richard Opfer Auctioneering Inc.*

Buck Cigar, die cut metal advertising sign in shape of deer head, "King of the Range," with embossed lettering, 10¼" x 12¼", EX . . . .$750.00 (B)

Buckeye Beer, self-framing embossed tin sign, "on draught here," 13½" x 2¾", EX . . . .$70.00 (B)

Buckeye Cultivators, metal double-sided flange advertising sign, "We Sell Buckeye Cultivators," 18½" x 9", VG . . . .$45.00 (B)

Buckingham Cut Plug Smoking Tobacco, trial-size pocket tin, with recessed lid, EX . . . .$155.00 (B)

Buckingham Cut Plug Tobacco, lithographed tin container, 5" x 5", EX . . . .$40.00 (B)

Buckingham Cut Plug Tobacco, pocket package, John J. Bagley Co., EX . . . .$95.00 (B)

Buckingham, paper tobacco container, unopened with tax stamp, EX . . . .$125.00 (C)

Buckingham, tobacco pocket tin, EX . . . . . .$150.00 (C)

Buckingham, vertical pocket tin, "Bright Cut Plug" with full tax stamp, EX . . . .$65.00 (B)

Buddha Talcum, Lingering Oriental Fragrance, tin litho container with artwork of Buddha image on front, 16-oz., NM . . . .$30.00 (B)

Bud's Union 76, ceramic salt & pepper set, 3½" tall, EX . . . .$250.00 (C)

Bull Durham, advertising poster in original stamped frame from the American Tobacco Co. with scene of bull fighter in arena, 1909, EX, $1,600.00 (B). *Courtesy of Buffalo Bay Auction Co.*

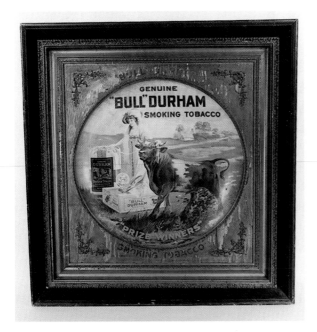

Bull Durham, Genuine Smoking Tobacco, round tin with original wood frame, rare item, 36" x 38", EX, $2,300.00 (C).

Bull Durham, litho sign on textured paper, framed under glass, 23¼" x 29¼", EX, $500.00 (B).

Budweiser Beer, light-up cash register light and sign, 10¼" x 8¼", EX . . . .$45.00 (D)

Budweiser Beer Tray, litho of St. Louis in the '70s, 17½" x 12¾", 1914, VG . . . .$90.00 (B)

Budweiser Draught Beer, art deco styling with eagle logo holders for reverse painted glass message bar, 18½" x 3" x 9½", EX . . . .$386.00 (B)

Budweiser Draught Beer, light-up sign featuring pair of hunting dogs, G . . . .$95.00 (D)

Budweiser Draught, light-up advertising sign displaying the team in front of a frosty mug of beer, 16½" dia., EX . . . .$55.00 (C)

Budweiser, electric grandfather watch, plastic for indoor use only, Mfg. Everbrite Electric Signs, Milwaukee, WI, 15½" dia., VG . . . .$50.00 (B)

Budweiser...Enjoy DuBois...DuBois Brewing Co., DuBois, PA, metal back with glass front light-up clock, 15" dia., EX . . . .$225.00 (D)

Budweiser, framed lithograph of Custer's last fight, Anheuser Busch, St. Louis, Missouri, U.S.A., 44" x 34", EX . . . .$325.00 (D)

Budweiser Girl, cardboard advertisement showing a pretty girl holding a bottle of the product, 20½" x 35", G . . . .$600.00 (B)

Bull Durham Standard Smoking Tobacco, composition bull with embossed lettering, 22"W x 17¾"H x 7½"D, EX, $1,800.00 (C).

Bull Frog Shoe Polish, tin litho advertising sign with likeness of frog, double-sided, 17¾" x 13", G, $4,000.00 (B). *Courtesy of Richard Opfer Auctioneering Inc.*

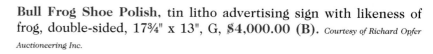

Buell's Coffee, tin, litho of lady enjoying the product, 4½" x 6", G, $160.00 (B).

Budweiser/King of Beers, light-up wall sign with plastic convex cover, 15" x 20", EX . . . .$95.00 (C)

Budweiser, King of Beers, light-up with hitch at bottom, 9½" x 14¾", EX . . . .$25.00 (C)

Budweiser, nickel silver pitcher from Wallace Bros. with script "The Budweiser" on the side, 9¼" H, NM . .$60.00 (B)

Budweiser on draught, light-up advertising globe with fired-on lettering and graphics, from the Solar Electric Co., Chicago, 12" dia. x 12½" H, VG . . . .$675.00 (C)

Budweiser, serving tray with steamboat and wharf scene, 17½" x 13", 1914, EX . . . .$100.00 (B)

Budweiser, take home, painted metal door push bar; this is in fairly bad shape, but they aren't very common, P . .$25.00 (D)

Budweiser...The New..You've waited 7 years for this...served everywhere, paper litho mounted on cardboard with mug in hand graphics, 1920s, 21" x 11", G . . . .$41.00 (B)

Buffalo Bill Saddle Soap, with graphics of Buffalo Bill sitting on his horse, 1½" x 5", EX . . . .$725.00 (B)

Buffalo Bill's Wild West Show book, by McLaughlin Bros, with stone litho graphics on front and back covers, 1887, EX . . . .$126.00 (B)

Buffalo Bill's Wild West Show, paper litho advertising poster with graphics of Buffalo Bill on horse, 22½" x 35", EX . . . .$1,600.00 (B)

Buffalo Brand Peanut Butter, tin litho pail, 1-lb., EX . . . .$175.00 (B)

Bunny Bread, self-framing embossed tin sign with graphics of trademark, 27½" x 12", G, **$325.00 (B)**.

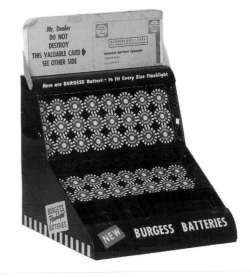

Burgess Batteries, painted metal counter display stand, 10¾" x 14¾", G, **$30.00 (B)**.

Burr-Oak, tobacco cutter, Harry Eeissinger Tobacco Co., Louisville, Ky., EX, **$225.00 (D)**. *Courtesy of Chief Paduke Antiques Mall*

Buffalo Club Rye Whiskey, tin litho advertising sign from Chas W. Shonk Co., with graphics of buffalo head in center cameo, 23½" x 34", VG . . . .**$475.00 (B)**

Buick, Bangor, Mich., embossed tin dealer sign, 1920s, 19½" x 13½", G . . . .**$210.00 (B)**

Buick, die cut cloisonne award clock in image of radiator, 4" x 5½", EX . . . .**$550.00 (C)**

Buick...Motor Cars, vertical porcelain thermometer with dealer address at bottom, 1915, 7¼" x 27", white on blue, EX . . . .**$300.00 (C)**

BullBrand Feeds...Maritime Milling Co., Inc., Buffalo, NY..., metal tip tray with artwork of bull on tray center, 6⅝" L, EX . . . .**$75.00 (B)**

Bull Durham, advertising poster in original stamped frame from the American Tobacco Co. with scene of bull fighter in arena, 1909, EX . . . .**$1,600.00 (B)**

Bull Durham, "Blackwell's Bull Durham smoking tobacco," with man at window, 24" x 31", 1880s, EX . . . .**$595.00 (C)**

Bull Durham...1 oz. bag 5¢, embossed tin litho sign, strong colors with artwork of bull in center, 8½" x 12", EX . . . .**$1,400.00 (B)**

Bull Durham Smoking Tobacco, double-sided cardboard litho advertising with graphics of sweethearts on fence with product pouch hanging off to side, 9" x 11¾", VG . . . .**$795.00 (B)**

Busch...Beer, western scene, light-up clock, 15" x 15", EX, $75.00 (D).

Buss Auto Fuses, Why Be Helpless, tin advertising sign, featuring man in front of older period car in head-lights of oncoming car, 8½" x 7½", VG, $65.00 (C).

Buss Clear Window Fuses, metal display with great graphics, 1920s, 18¼" x 13¼" x 5", EX, $110.00 (B).

Bull Durham, vintage cardboard litho store counter display unit with graphics of trademark bull, 8" x 5¼" x 12", EX . . . . $550.00 (B)

Bull Frog Shoe Polish, tin litho advertising sign with likeness of frog, double-sided, 17¾" x 13", G . .$4,000.00 (B)

Bull Frog Shoe Polish, tin litho container, 2¾" dia., EX . . . .$98.00 (B)

Bull's Eye Beer, porcelain advertising sign, with graphics of bull's eye target in center, 18" x 18", EX . .$320.00 (B)

Bull's Eye Beer, porcelain sign from Golden West Brewing Co., Oakland, California, 18" sq., EX . . . . . . $325.00 (C)

Bulova, tin litho advertising clock, 15" x 15", NM . $155.00 (C)

Bunker Hill Brewery, pin back, "Oh Be Jolly" with graphics of owl, Owl Musty, 1¼", EX . . . .$75.00 (CN)

Bunte Marshmallow, tin with graphics of youngster in front of large tin of product, 12½" x 9½", EX . . . .$200.00 (B)

Bunte Rabida Dark Caramels, two-piece cardboard candy box with factory scenes on both sides, 7½" x 11" x 3½", EX . . . .$25.00 (B)

Burger Beer, counter top light-up advertising sign, 10" x 10" x 2½", NM . . . .$135.00 (C)

Burger Beer, electric clock with tin litho face promoting Burger Beer, 18½" x 3" x 14½", VG . . . .$65.00 (B)

Buster Brown and Tige, silk-screened, cloth mounted on die cut wood block advertisment, 24" x 20", EX, $350.00 (B).

Buster Brown Bread, double-sided metal die cut hanging sign featuring Buster and Tige, 18" x 13½", EX, $5,600.00 (B). *Courtesy of Wm. Morford Investment Grade Collectibles*

Burma Cola...It's different...It's better, oval embossed tin advertising sign, designed to be string hung, 13½" x 9½", NM . . . .$125.00 (B)

Bursley's Coffee, tin litho key-wound container, 1-lb., EX . . . .$30.00 (B)

Busch...Beer, western scene, light-up clock, 15" x 15", G . . . .$55.00 (C)

Busch, bill hook with message button advertising the Busch Shoe Repair Co., Wichita, 2" x 7¾", EX . . . . . .$145.00 (C)

Buscho, prohibition, tin litho advertising sign, "A non-intoxicating cereal beverage...serve cold," 10" x 7", EX . . . .$95.00 (B)

Busch, paper advertising sign with top and bottom metal strips, John B. Busch Brewing Co., images of vintage people eating at table, 15½" x 19½", 1910s, NM . .$220.00 (B)

Buss Auto Fuses, Why Be Helpless, tin advertising sign, featuring man in front of older period car in headlights of oncoming car, 8½" x 7½", EX . . . .$75.00 (C)

Buss Clear Window Fuses, metal display with great graphics, 1920s, 18¼" x 13¼" x 5", EX . . . . .$110.00 (B)

Buss, fuse cabinet, "Why be helpless," 6½" x 3½" x 8", 1920s, EX . . . .$85.00 (B)

Buster Brown and Tige, round shoe store throw rug with their image on the face, 54" dia., EX . . . .$315.00 (B)

Buster Brown, light-up advertising clock featuring artwork of Buster Brown and Tige from the Pam Clock Co., has metal body with glass cover and face, 15" dia., VG, **$925.00 (B).** *Courtesy of Collectors Auction Services*

Buster Brown, light-up advertising clock from the Pam Clock Co. with metal body and glass face and cover, 15" dia., VG, **$500.00 (B).** *Courtesy of Collectors Auction Services*

Buster Brown, plastic and metal light-up advertising sign, 14½" x 6¼", VG, **$205.00 (B).**

Buster Brown Bread, double-sided metal die cut hanging sign featuring Buster and Tige, 18" x 13½", EX **$5,600.00 (B)**

Buster Brown, double-sided tin litho with image of Buster holding shoe "Buster Brown shoes...Get them here," 15" x 23½", G . . . .**$1,000.00 (B)**

Buster Brown, embossed plaster advertising plaque featuring likeness of Buster and Tige, 12" x 12", EX . .**$275.00 (C)**

Buster Brown Head air tank inflator, fits on the head of air or helium tank, 20" x 21" x 24", EX . . . . .**$125.00 (B)**

Buster Brown, light-up advertising clock featuring artwork of Buster Brown and Tige from the Pam Clock Co., has metal body with glass cover and face, 15" dia., F . . . .**$375.00 (C)**

Buster Brown, light-up advertising clock from the Pam Clock Co. with metal body and glass face and cover, 15" dia., VG . . . .**$500.00 (B)**

Buster Brown, paper advertising sign with graphics of Buster and Tige, easel back, 14" x 14", EX . . . .**$95.00 (D)**

Buster Brown, plate with image of Buster and Tige, 7½", VG . . . .**$30.00 (B)**

Buster Brown, poster, cloth backed, featuring animal impersonator George Ali, 27" x 40⅞", EX . . . .**$75.00 (C)**

Buster Brown Shoe Company, calendar with image of Buster and Tige in center of monthly pages and underwater scene at top, 8½" x 19", NM . . . .**$40.00 (B)**

Butterfly Quality Bread, door push, porcelain on aluminum, frame, 1930s, VG, **$195.00 (C)**.

Butter-Nut Bread, embossed tin bread sign, 13¾" x 5⅞", G, **$120.00 (B)**.

Butter Krust Bread, die cut porcelain advertising sign, 1930s, 14" x 18½", EX, **$2,100.00 (B)**.

Courtesy of Muddy River Trading Co./Gary Metz

Buster Brown Shoes, advertising plate, 5½" dia., NM . . . . **$150.00 (C)**

Buster Brown Shoes, bandana, 1940s, EX . . .**$75.00 (C)**

Buster Brown Shoes, bas-relief plaster advertising sign with Buster Brown and Tige, 1940s, 17" round, NM . .**$320.00 (B)**

Buster Brown Shoes, neon advertising sign with images of Buster and Tige, 54" x 55", EX . . . .**$1,400.00 (B)**

Buster Brown, two-piece die cut tin advertising Buster and Tige, Tige 19" x 21", Buster 22" x 32½", G . . . .**$950.00 (B)**

Butter Eggs K.C. Baking Powder, cardboard litho advertising poster with rotating price wheels to change the product price, 14" x 11", VG . . . . **$50.00 (B)**

Butterfly Quality Bread, door push, porcelain on aluminum, frame, 1930s, G . . . . **$170.00 (B)**

Butter Krust Bread, die cut porcelain advertising sign, 1930s, 14" x 18½", EX . . . . **$2,100.00 (B)**

Butter-Nut Bread, door push, porcelain, G . .**$175.00 (B)**

Butter-Nut specially mellowed coffee, "The Delicious Coffee," with key-wound top, Paxton and Gallagher Co., Omaha, Nebraska, 1-lb., EX . . . .**$20.00 (D)**

California Poppy Brand Oranges, box end label with litho by Dickman Jones, San Francisco, graphics of poppies in bloom, 10½" x 11", 1890s, EX, **$525.00 (B).** *Courtesy of Past Tyme Pleasures*

Campbell's Soup, cardboard litho trolley card, 20½" x 12", VG, **$80.00 (B).**

Campbell's Soup, porcelain thermometer, features facsimile of tomato soup can with dial-type thermometer in center of can, great graphics, 7"W x 12"H x 1¼"D, NM, **$2,100.00 (B).** *Courtesy of Muddy River Trading Co./Gary Metz*

Caddy Label, tobacco advertising sign with graphics of King Neptune riding on giant shell with naked mermaids, from David Dunlop, Virginia, 1880s, EX . . . .**$140.00 (B)**

Cadillac Service, plastic clock with Cadillac logo in center, 12" dia., EX . . . .**$175.00 (D)**

Cafe Empire Blend Coffee, tin litho can, 4⅜"x 5½", EX . . . .**$70.00 (B)**

California Dairy Industries Association, double-sided porcelain sign with good, strong graphics of cow and an award ribbon, 25" x 22", EX . . . .**$425.00 (C)**

California Fruit Gum, raised finish die cut cardboard advertising sign featuring graphics of youngsters about to kiss, 10" x 13½", EX . . . .**$450.00 (B)**

California Nugget Chop Cut Pipe Tobacco, flat pocket container, 2¾" x 4½" x ¾", EX . . . .**$75.00 (C)**

California Peanut Co., tin litho pail container with graphics of whimsical comic characters all around pail, 3¼" x 3¾", EX . . . .**$175.00 (C)**

California Perfume Co., baby talc in tin litho container with graphics of youngsters playing, 1¾" x 4½", EX . . . .**$275.00 (B)**

California Poppy Brand Oranges, box end label with litho by Dickman Jones, San Francisco, graphics of poppies in bloom, 10½" x 11", 1890s, EX . . . .**$525.00 (B)**

Cali-Orange Syrup Dispenser, with frosted globe on reverse painted base with product decal on front and reverse side, EX . . . .**$290.00 (B)**

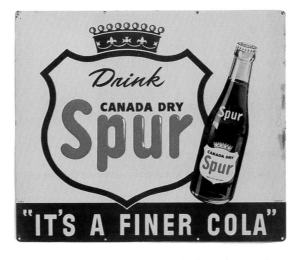

Canada Dry Spur, one-sided embossed tin advertising sign, 26" x 22½", G, $135.00 (B).

Campbell's "Vegetable Soup," curved porcelain pole-mounted sign, 13" x 22½", scarce item, VG, $4,450.00 (B).

Canada Dry, The Best Drink of All, die cut cardboard counter top display with easel back, 15½" x 28", VG, $25.00 (B). *Courtesy of Collectors Auction Services*

Canadian National Telegraph and Cable Office, porcelain flange sign, NM, $395.00 (D). *Courtesy of Riverview Antique Mall*

Calotabs for Biliousness, wood scale advertising thermometer, promoting the cure for biliousness torpidity, 4" x 15⅛", VG . . . .$80.00 (B)

Calso Supreme Gasoline, die cut porcelain pump sign, 11" x 13¾", NM . . . .$550.00 (B)

Calso Supreme Gasoline, one-sided porcelain pump sign with die cut chevrons at bottom, 11" x 13¾", VG . . . .$250.00 (C)

Calumet Calendar, give-away with "Weekly Kitchen Reminders" pocket with the Calumet Boy and product tin, 9½" x 15½", EX . . . .$45.00 (D)

Calumet Baking Powder, wooden advertising thermometer with image of product container at top of scale, 6" x 22", 1920s, VG . . . .$275.00 (B)

Calvert Whiskey, electric light-up bubble clock, "Clear Heads Choose Calvert" with graphics of owl in center, Telechron, NM . . . .$130.00 (B)

Cambridge Coffee Whole Bean, tin litho can, 3½" x 7¼", EX . . . .$210.00 (B)

Camel Cigarettes Sold Here, porcelain flange sign, 12" x 18", yellow on red, G . . . .$85.00 (D)

Camels, die cut cardboard advertising poster with image of man in tuxedo and woman enjoying a cigarette, 32" x 29½", VG . . . .$75.00 (B)

Camels, die cut paper advertising sign with likeness of young lady in swim suit, "Camels Cool Mild," 5¼" x 14¾", 1954, EX . . . .$35.00 (B)

Canadian Northern Express, double-sided porcelain advertising sign, 26" x 14", G, $850.00 (C).

Careystone Asbestos Shingles, painted embossed metal sign, 29" x 11½",VG, $55.00 (D). *Courtesy of Riverview Antique Mall*

Carborundum/Aloxite Grinding Wheels, canvas litho with image of workman holding a chisel in workshop, and images of products at bottom, NOS, 28" x 40", NM, $165.00 (D). *Courtesy of Autopia Advertising Auctions*

Camel, Smoke...Cigarettes, painted metal sign, with facsimile of product package in spotlight at bottom of sign, 12" x 18", yellow on red, G . . . .$45.00 (D)

Cameron & Cameron, tobacco company, square corner Louisiana Perique tobacco tin, from Richmond, VA, 3½" x 2½" x 1½", EX . . . .$160.00 (B)

Campbell & Co.'s Ale, paper advertising sign with wood frame, 28½" x 22⅝", EX . . . .$55.00 (D)

Campbell & Co.'s Edinburgh Ales, framed advertising sign, 28½" x 55½", EX . . . .$35.00 (C)

Campbell Brand Coffee, tin litho pail with wire handles, graphics of camels on desert, 4-lb., EX . . . . .$75.00 (B)

Campbell Kids, cast iron bank, 4¼" x 3¼" x 2", 1900s, EX . . . .$175.00 (C)

Campbell's Coffee, can with bail type handle with desert scene with camels and men, from Bloomington, IL, 4-lb., EX . . . .$75.00 (B)

Campbell's, soup advertising pocket mirror with graphics of soup can on front, 1¾" x 2¾", EX . . . . . .$225.00 (C)

Campbell's Soup, porcelain thermometer, features facsimile of tomato soup can with dial-type thermometer in center of can, great graphics, 7"W x 12"H x 1¼"D, NM . .$2,100.00 (B)

Campbell's Soup, potholder, with Campbell's kids on surface, G . . . .$15.00 (D)

Campbell's Soup...Ready In a Jiffy, tin advertising sign, graphics of Campbell's kid, 17½" x 11½", EX . .$175.00 (C)

Campfire Marshmallows..., the original food, round tin container with lid, G . . . .$15.00 (D)

Campfire Marshmallow, tin, great graphics of campfire scene, 8" x 2¼", EX . . . .$95.00 (C)

Canada Dry, light-up advertising clock, Pam Clock Co., 15½" x 15½", VG . . . .$95.00 (B)

Canada Dry Beverages, porcelain advertising sign with logo at left of message, 24" x 7", NM . . . .$135.00 (B)

Carnation Ice Cream, single-sided die cut porcelain advertising sign, 22" x 23", VG, $550.00 (B). *Courtesy of Collectors Auction Services*

Carter the Great, framed cardboard poster by the Otis Lithograph Co., Cleveland, Ohio, made in U.S.A/4630-M, 42" x 78", EX, $500.00 (B).

Canada Dry, cardboard advertising sign, with graphics of ginger ale and club soda bottles, 28" x 34", VG ..$35.00 (D)

Canada Dry...Drink, tin double-sided flange sign with image of shield logo, 17½" x 14½", EX .....$160.00 (B)

Canada Dry Ginger Ale, tin litho friction advertising truck by Rasko with graphics of product on side of delivery style truck, 1950s, NM ....$225.00 (C)

Canada Dry, The best of them all, with artwork of bottle in hand, embossed door push, EX ....$100.00 (B)

Canada Dry, toy delivery truck with graphics of Canada Dry cases on side, 8" x 3" x 5", EX ....$135.00 (C)

Canadian Club 5¢ Cigar, cardboard ad sign with graphics of man with product, 21" x 13½", NM ......$50.00 (B)

Canadian National Telegraph and Cable Office, porcelain flange sign, EX ....$365.00 (D)

Candee brand, salesman sample of rubber high top boots, 5¼" x 3" x 1", NM ....$125.00 (C)

Candee Rubbers, hanging cardboard sign with graphics of puppy being chased by young girl, 10½" x 12½", NM ....$85.00 (B)

Candee Shoes, hanging cardboard advertising sign from McCord Rubber Co., Chicago, Ill., graphics of kids playing with kittens, 1910s, 10" x 12½", EX ....$165.00 (B)

C & F Motor Sales...Dodge and Plymouth, advertising paper calendar with scouts in church scene over tear sheets, 16" x 33", 1954, EX ....$45.00 (B)

Castle Hall Cigar, self-framing tin advertising sign, 37½" x 13", VG, $185.00 (B).

Case, cast iron advertising eagle, 57½" tall, VG, $2,600.00 (C).

Castle Gate Coal, porcelain one-sided sign with strong colors, "The Main Highway to Fuel Satisfaction," 30" x 12", EX, $375.00 (C).

Candy Bros., Fruit Juice Tablets, Always Fresh, tin litho advertising serving tray with artwork of bottles of product, 13¾" x 16¾", EX . . . .$925.00 (B)

Canoe Club, "Once You Try It-You'll Always Buy It," cardboard advertising sign in metal frame, 30" x 14", VG . . . .$65.00 (B)

Canuck 28 gauge, black powder shell box, 3¼" x 3¼" x 2½", EX . . . .$95.00 (C)

Capital Brand, coffee container with wooden knob bail handle from the Atwood Co., 10-lb., EX . . . . .$200.00 (B)

Carborundum/Aloxite Grinding Wheels, canvas litho with image of workman holding a chisel in workshop, and images of products at bottom, NOS, 28" x 40", NM . . . .$165.00 (D)

Carborundum Brand Sharpening Stones, canvas litho advertising banner with image of three men sharpening different implements, NOS, 28" x 40", NM . . .$150.00 (C)

Cardinal Beer...The Beer with the Real Hop Flavor, round metal tip tray with graphics of red-haired woman with bouquet of flowers, 4⅛" dia., EX . . . . . .$110.00 (B)

Cardui, advertising fan, with graphics of woman on couch on front side, product messages on reverse side, wooden handle, EX . . . .$7.00 (D)

Careystone Asbestos Shingles, painted embossed metal sign, 29" x 11½", EX . . . .$65.00 (D)

Carlsberg...calling for, foreign porcelain advertising sign with a glass of beer with a full head of foam, G . . . . . .$75.00 (C)

Cat-Tex Soles, light-up reverse painted advertising clock with image of cat on cover, "We rebuild shoes, like new at less than 1/2 new cost," 14½" dia., EX, $620.00 (B). *Courtesy of Buffalo Bay Auction Co.*

Centlivre's Nickel Plate Beer, litho advertising poster with graphics of dining car scene, in period frame, 26¾" x 31", NM, $500.00 (C). *Courtesy of Autopia Advertising Auctions*

Carmacks Barber Shop, give-away premium combination wrench and screwdriver, NM . . . .$35.00 (C)

Carmen Condom, early tin litho with great graphic of pin-up girl with fan and shawl, good strong colors, 1⅝" x ⅝", EX . . . .$170.00 (B)

Carnation Cigars, tin with paper label that contains graphics of carnation flower, from League Cigar Co., 25 ct., EX . . . .$70.00 (B)

Carnation Fresh Milk, porcelain die cut advertising sign with graphics of milk bottle, 22" x 23", EX . . .$275.00 (C)

Carnation Gum...Chew Dorne's, "Taste the Smell," tin litho tip tray with artwork of carnations, 4⅜" dia., EX . . . .$475.00 (B)

Carnation Gum, tin litho tip tray advertising Carnation Chewing Gum with graphics of carnations, 4¼" dia., EX . . . .$210.00 (B)

Carnation Ice Cream, die cut painted hat badge with graphics of ice cream sundae in center, 2" x 2", NM . . . .$775.00 (B)

Carnation Ice Cream, single-sided die cut porcelain advertising sign, 22" x 23", VG . . . .$550.00 (B)

Carnation Malted Milk, milk glass container with metal lid and fired-on lettering, 6½" dia. x 8½", EX . . . .$210.00 (B)

Carnation Milk, die cut cardboard advertising sign with graphics of milk bottle in center, "Carnation fresh Milk," 24" x 24", EX . . . .$325.00 (C)

Carnation Milk, paper litho advertising with graphics of Perry Triplets, 36¾" x 22½", VG . . . .$550.00 (B)

Carter Carburetor, light-up advertising piece of iron construction with product name on milk glass globe, 13½" x 27½", red, EX . . . .$575.00 (C)

Carter's Alma Infants Underwear, die cut cardboard easel back store advertising sign with image of young child over message, 14" x 15½", EX . . . .$423.00 (B)

Carter's Infants Underwear, cardboard easel back die cut advertising sign with artwork of infant over message, 14" x 16", EX . . . .$220.00 (B)

Carter's Infants Underwear, cardboard easel back store advertising sign with young child playing with tin climbing monkey, 14½" x 18¾", EX . . . .$400.00 (B)

Carter's Inky Racer, box with original bottle and instructions, graphics of black runner on front, 3" x 3" x 1", EX . . . .$55.00 (C)

Centlivre Brewing Co., framed paper advertising poster with graphics of brewery in Fort Wayne, Ind., 42" x 29", G, $645.00 (B).

Ceresota Flour match safe, die cut tin, 2½" x 5½", VG, $275.00 (B).

Ceresota, prize bread flour, tin litho match holder, featuring graphics of young boy cutting loaf of bread, 5" H, G, $330.00 (B). *Courtesy of Richard Opfer Auctioneering, Inc.*

Carter's Union Suits for Boys, cardboard die cut easel back store advertising sign featuring young boy with scooter, 14" x 15½", NM . . . .$341.00 (B)

Carter's Union Suits for Girls, easel back die cut cardboard sign with graphics of young girl writing on blackboard, 1910, 15" x 14", NM . . . .$645.00 (B)

Carter the Great, framed cardboard poster by the Otis Lithograph Co., Cleveland, Ohio, made in U.S.A/4630-M, 42" x 78", EX . . . .$500.00 (B)

Casarets, paper litho advertising sign, candy cathartic, Best for the Bowels, 41" x 28", VG . . . .$335.00 (B)

Case, cast iron advertising eagle, 57½" tall, G . .$1,975.00 (C)

Case Neon, light-up dealer ad sign made from two porcelain signs with metal housing and neon letters, 12½" x 20" x 72", VG . . . .$805.00 (B)

Casewell's National Crest Coffee, key-wound tin litho container, 1-lb., EX . . . .$30.00 (B)

Castle Hall Cigar, D.S. Erb & Co., self-framing tin litho ad sign, 37½" x 13", EX . . . .$220.00 (B)

Castrol, advertising thermometer with graphics of woman with quart of product, 8¼" x 6", EX . . . .$60.00 (B)

Castrol, die cut tin sign, 18" x 23½", VG . . . . .$75.00 (B)

Castrol Motor Oil, self-framing porcelain scale type advertising thermometer, 9" x 30", VG . . . . . .$175.00 (B)

Champion Spark Plugs, die cut cardboard advertising sign in image of vintage race car driver with oversized spark plug, 14½" x 6", EX, **$675.00 (C).**

Courtesy of Autopia Advertising Auction

Charles Denby Cigar, die cut cardboard stand-up depicting a black boy drummer advertising the product, 17" x 29½", 1899, VG, **$1,800.00 (B).** *Courtesy of Collectors Auction Services*

Champion Spark Plug, steering wheel advertising clock, 11½" dia., **$345.00 (B).**

Caswell's Coffee, tin litho container with graphics of woman in cameo center, 3-lb., EX . . . .**$135.00 (C)**

Caterpillar, metal watch fob, picture of dozer on one side and earth scraper on reverse, EX . . . .**$25.00 (C)**

Cattaraugus Knife, die cut cardboard advertisement by the Cattaraugus Cutlery Co., Little Valley, N.Y., 12" x 15", EX . . . .**$90.00 (B)**

Cattaraugus Knife, die cut cardboard advertising with graphics of woodworker sharpening his Cattaraugus knife, Niagara Litho Co., 12¼" x 15¼", G . . . .**$110.00 (B)**

Cat-Tex Soles, advertising light-up clock with image of black cat in center, 14" dia., F . . . .**$135.00 (C)**

Cat-Tex Soles, light-up reverse painted advertising clock with image of cat on cover, "We rebuild shoes, like new at less than ½ new cost," 14½" dia., G . . . .**$275.00 (C)**

C.D. Kenny Co., coffee pail with wire handle containing Hanover Brand fresh Roasted Coffee, 3-lb. container, EX . . . .**$995.00 (D)**

Celluloid Starch...Mail Trade Marks to...Premium Dept. Philadelphia, cardboard advertising sign with graphics of young girl ironing, 14" x 12½", EX . . . .**$100.00 (B)**

Centlivre's Nickel Plate Beer, litho advertising poster with graphics of dining car scene, in period frame, 26¾" x 31", NM . . . .**$500.00 (C)**

Charlex Razor Display, celluloid and metal, 26½" closed, VG, $650.00 (B). *Courtesy of Collectors Auction Services*

Cheerio, It's Lewie's Refreshing Beverages I Want, tin over cardboard sign, featuring artwork of man holding bottles of Cheerio, 11" x 8", G, $35.00 (B).
Courtesy of Muddy River Trading Co./Gary Metz

Chero-Cola, Drink...There's none so good, painted metal sign with sunburst and bottle to left side of sign, good, $70.00 (D). *Courtesy of Pleasant Hill Antique Mall & Tea Room/Bob Johnson*

Centlivre Tonic, cardboard advertising sign, "Builds up the system, gives strength and enjoyment to life...for sale here," with graphics of serving worker with hospital attire, from Fort Wayne, Ind. Brewing Co., 22" x 12", EX . . $350.00 (C)

Central Brewing Co., Highest Grades of Pure Lager, Ales & Porter, round metal tip tray with artwork of horse in center of tray, 4½" dia., EX . . . .$150.00 (B)

Central Union tobacco pail, lunchbox-size with wire handle on lid, 7" x 4½" x 4¼", EX . . . .$175.00 (C)

Ceresota Flour, advertising pinback, 1½" dia., EX . .$50.00 (B)

Ceresota Flour, match holder, barrel-style with image of young boy on top of barrel, with original box, 3" x 6", NM . . . .$500.00 (B)

Ceresota Flour, match holder, bread box-style, image of young boy sitting on stool on top of product, 3" x 6", NM . . . .$230.00 (B)

Ceresota, "Prize Bread Flour of the World," advertising match holder in likeness of Ceresota boy on barrel, 2¼" x 5½", EX . . . .$725.00 (C)

Ceresota, prize bread flour, tin litho match holder, featuring graphics of young boy cutting loaf of bread, 5" H, EX . . . .$375.00 (C)

Cer-ola...A Triumph in Soft Drinks...Made by Kolb at Bay City, Mich., hanging cardboard Prohibition advertising sign, 11" x 17", EX . . . .$75.00 (C)

Chero-Cola In The Twist Bottle, paper advertising, 24" x 18½", VG, $525.00 (C).

Chero-Cola Ice Cold Served Here, single-sided cardboard sign, graphics of ballplayer, 12" x 18", VG, $290.00 (B).

Champagne Velvet Beer, tin litho over cardboard with graphics of man in stream fishing, 19½" x 14½", VG . . . .$160.00 (B)

Champion...dependable...Spark Plug Service, double-sided flange advertising sign, NOS, 18" x 12", '50s, NM . . . .$155.00 (C)

Champion Implements Calendar, with graphics of products and tear sheets at bottom, heavy paperboard, 3½" x 6¼", 1902, NM . . . .$195.00 (B)

Champion Spark Plugs...Cost Less...More Power, embossed tin advertising sign with graphics of spark plug, 14¾" x 5⅜", NM . . . .$595.00 (C)

Champion Spark Plugs, die cut cardboard advertising sign in image of vintage race car driver with oversized spark plug, 14½" x 6", EX . . . .$675.00 (C)

Champion Spark Plugs, porcelain single-sided advertising sign with graphics of spark plug in center, 30" x 14", G . . . .$110.00 (B)

Champion Spark Plugs, reverse glass advertising sign with graphics of spark plug, 10¼" x 13¼", EX . . . .$295.00 (D)

Champlain Horse Nails, litho on paper board advertising calendar with graphics of horse and rider with bottom tear sheets, 11" x 14", 1888, VG . . . .$275.00 (B)

Champlin Distributor Motor Oils, single-sided tin sign with wood frame on blank side, 59" x 29½", VG . . .$135.00 (B)

Champlin Refining Co., cardboard advertising with graphics of old man winter blowing cold wind on vintage touring car, 58½" x 28½", VG . . . .$650.00 (B)

Chappell's Ice Cream, celluloid fountain menu with graphics of ice cream on front, 5" x 7¼", 1920s, NM . . . .$125.00 (C)

Chappell's Milk, metal and plastic light-up clock, 16" x 16", gold, red and yellow, EX . . . .$165.00 (C)

Chariots, condom tin with artwork of racing chariot on cover, 2⅛" x 1⅝" x ¼", EX . . . .$180.00 (B)

Charles Denby Cigar, die cut cardboard advertising, black boy in bellman's uniform with a box of the product, "Dese Denby's sho tastes different from ordinary cigars," 12¼" H, VG . . . .$250.00 (B)

Cherry-Cheer, Drink...It's Good, hanging cardboard sign, great graphics, 1920s, 7" x 11", EX, **$210.00 (B)**. *Courtesy of Muddy River Trading Co./Gary Metz*

Cherry Smash, Our Nation's Beverage, cardboard bottle topper, 1920s, EX, **$70.00 (B)**. *Courtesy of Muddy River Trading Co./Gary Metz*

Chevrolet Advance Design Trucks, paper poster, 50" x 38½", G, **$150.00 (C)**.

Charles Denby Cigar, diecut cardboard stand-up depicting a black boy drummer advertising the product, 17" x 29½", 1899, VG . . . .**$1,800.00 (B)**

Charles Denby...Where cigars are Made...Evansville, Ind., oval metal tip tray with graphics of factory in tray center, 6", EX . . . .**$30.00 (B)**

Charles The Great Cigars, tin litho advertising sign with artwork of a full box of the product, EX . . . . .**$220.00 (B)**

Charles W. Cranshaw/Atlantic, sterling and enamel spoon with black man on handle, EX . . . .**$375.00 (B)**

Chas. D. Kaier Co. Ltd...Mahanoy City, Pa., round metal tip tray with product bottle in center of tray, 4⅛" dia., EX . . . .**$55.00 (B)**

Chase & Sanborn choice quality coffee, with small lid, 7¼" x 9¼", 4-lb., EX . . . .**$175.00 (C)**

Chase and Sanborn Drip Grind Coffee, tin, key-wound lid, 1-lb., F . . . .**$15.00 (D)**

Chase & Sanborn's Coffee, sample size with original mailer box and letter from company, 2" T, EX . . .**$100.00 (B)**

Chase & Sanborn, tin litho counter top store coffee bin promoting "Standard Java," 13" x 13" x 21", EX . . .**$295.00 (D)**

Chase & Sanborn, tin store bin with embossed lettering "Old Gov't Java" on front with litho birds, flowers, and stems, 1880s, 13" x 14" x 19", G . . . .**$420.00 (B)**

Chas. P. Shipley Saddlery Co., premium clothes brush in original box, 7" x 2" x 1½", EX . . . .**$30.00 (B)**

Chateau Quebec, a cool mellow pipe tobacco, round tin, F . . . .**$23.00 (D)**

Chattanooga & St. Louis, spittoon with raised lettering, made of cast iron and porcelain, EX . . . .**$225.00 (C)**

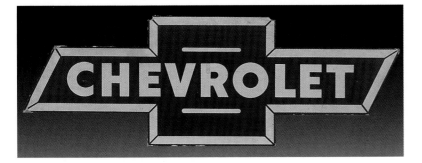

Chevrolet "Bow Tie," die cut cardboard sign, 30" x 10¾", $80.00 (B).

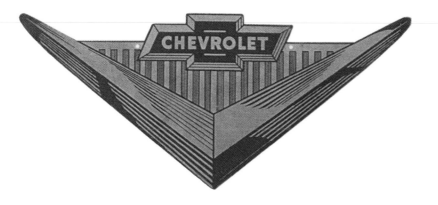

Chevrolet, die cut masonite chain-hung emblem sign, 21" x 9½", 1950s, EX, $350.00 (C).

Chevrolet Guardian Maintenance, paper poster, 17" x 44", EX, $105.00 (B).

Checkers, cough drops, tin litho match safe with striker on base, 3" x 1½" x ¼", EX . . . .$40.00 (B)

Checker Taxi, hanging cardboard advertising sign promoting the Checker Taxi Service with graphics of vintage car, 11" x 7", 1920s, EX . . . .$125.00 (C)

Cheerio Coffee, key-wound tin litho coffee can with artwork of singing bird, 5" x 4", G . . . .$190.00 (B)

Cheerio, It's Lewie's Refreshing Beverages I Want, tin over cardboard sign, featuring artwork of man holding bottles of Cheerio, 11" x 8", G . . . .$35.00 (B)

Cheer Up Beverages, embossed painted tin license plate attachment, 6" x 6¼", EX . . . .$155.00 (C)

Cheer Up, Drink..., glass with message in spotlight, EX . . . .$30.00 (B)

Chef Baking Powder, paper label on cardboard container with pry lid, Montreal, 3" x 4½", EX . . . .$175.00 (C)

Chef Coffee, tin litho key-wound can with artwork of chef on front, rare piece, Lee & Cady, Detroit, 1-lb., EX . .$500.00 (B)

Chero-Cola, Drink...There's none so good, painted metal sign, with sunburst and bottle to left side of sign, G . . . . .$70.00 (D)

Cherry Blossom Shoe Polish, tin advertising sign with image of three kittens in shoes, 17¾" x 27¾", NM . . . . .$195.00 (C)

Cherry Blossoms, tin litho die cut bottle topper with images of youngsters on each side, 11½" X 6¼", 1920s, EX . . . .$495.00 (D)

Cherry Brand, advertising celluloid and metal mirror with message promoting "Fine Chocolates and Bon Bons" and ornate gold handle and frame, 2" x 4", VG . . . .$90.00 (B)

Cherry-Cheer, Drink...It's Good, hanging cardboard sign, great graphics, 1920s, 7" x 11", EX . . . .$210.00 (B)

Chevrolet Impala, cardboard advertising poster, 34½" x 20½", VG, **$35.00 (B)**.

Chevrolet Super Service, advertising clock, 15⅛" x 15⅛", VG, **$310.00 (B)**.

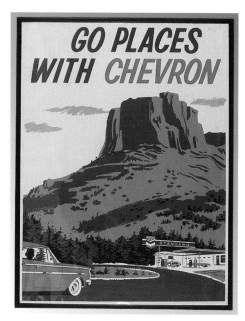

Chevron, framed paper poster, 43" x 57", VG, **$125.00 (C)**.

Cherry Smash, advertising cardboard sign with reverse glass decals over the cardboard in oval frame, 10" x 12", NM . . . .**$345.00 (C)**

Cherry Smash, Our Nation's Beverage, cardboard bottle topper, 1920s, EX . . . .**$70.00 (B)**

Chesterfield, Buy...Here, die cut metal painted flange sign with product package die cut at top of sign, 12" x 15", EX . . . .**$55.00 (D)**

Chesterfield, Buy...Here, metal die cut flange sign with artwork of product packages under message, 11¾" x 16½", EX . . . .**$45.00 (D)**

Chesterfield, cardboard advertising sign with graphics of George Burns and Gracie Allen working around a radio microphone, 22" x 21", 1940s, EX . . . .**$325.00 (C)**

Chesterfield Cigarette, advertising thermometer with embossing and self framing, 5¾" x 13½", VG . .**$110.00 (B)**

Chesterfield, cigarette cardboard sign featuring Betty Grable, 21" x 22", EX . . . .**$125.00 (C)**

Chesterfield Cigarettes...They Satisfy..., metal tip tray with product image in center of tray, 6½" L, F .**$45.00 (B)**

Chesterfield, flat fifties, hinged cigarette tin, G . .**$15.00 (D)**

Chesterfield, heavy cardboard advertising sign with band leaders Fred Waring and Henry James, 21" x 11", VG . . . .**$85.00 (D)**

Chesterfield, heavy paper banner with graphics of cigarette packages, 42" x 19", VG . . . .**$165.00 (D)**

Chew STAG Tobacco, cutter, EX, $140.00 (D). *Courtesy of Chief Paduke Antiques Mall*

Chicago Kahn Bros., tin clothing display, 17" x 14" x 11", VG, $80.00 (B).

Chief garden tractors & implements, double-sided painted metal flange sign with graphics of Indian, 17⅝" x 13⅜", G, $95.00 (B).

Chesterfield, painted metal double-sided flange advertising sign with graphics of cigarette packages, 11¾" x 16½", EX . . . .$75.00 (C)

Chesterfield, paper advertising sign with graphics of woman opening a pack of cigarettes, 18" x 24", EX . . . .$85.00 (C)

Chest-O-Silver, oats box with litho of treasure chest, from Keokok, LA, 2-lb. 10-oz., EX . . . .$60.00 (B)

Chevrolet, die cut masonite chain-hung emblem sign, 21" x 9½", 1950s, EX . . . .$350.00 (C)

Chevrolet, die cut metal bow tie sign, 20½" x 7", VG . . . .$450.00 (B)

Chevrolet Motor Cars, calendar with great graphics of early touring car in front of house with large porch, 1920, F . . . .$175.00 (C)

Chevron, painted tin sign, 7¼" dia., EX . . . . .$100.00 (C)

Chevron Supreme Gasoline, cloth sleeve patch, 2¾" dia., G . . . .$10.00 (C)

Chew STAG Tobacco, cutter, EX . . . .$140.00 (D)

Chickencock Whiskey tin, key-wound container from Distillers Corp. Limited with graphics of brewery on reverse, rooster on front panel, scarce item, 4¼" x 3" x 7½", 1931, EX . . . .$350.00 (C)

Chiclets, countertop tin litho container, "Help Yourself," featuring your favorite flavor, EX . . . .$115.00 (B)

Chief Oshkosh, wooden cigar box with graphics of Indian on inside cover wearing top hat, 1916, 50-count, EX . . . .$70.00 (B)

Chief Watta Pop, countertop display, shaped like an Indian head in full war bonnet with locations for the pops immediately behind the bonnet, 8½" x 5" x 9½", NM . . . .$850.00 (B)

Chief Watta Pop, plaster lollipop store counter top display in the likeness of Indian chief with headdress made of lollipops, EX . . . .$474.00 (B)

Chief Watta Pop lollipop holder, molded plaster Indian head holds 17 lollipops, VG, $370.00 (B).

Cities Service Koolmotor, The Perfect Pennsylvania Oil, double-sided tin sign, both sides shown, 20¾" x 12", VG, $550.00 (B).

Chocolate Honey Dairy Drink, paper advertising sign with graphics of young black girl, 7" x 18", 1940s, EX . .$65.00 (C)

Chocolate Sundae, die cut embossed tin advertising sign in likeness of sundae, 15" x 24", NM . . . .$275.00 (C)

Christian Feigenspan Brewing Co., metal serving tray with artwork of woman with red ribbon in hair, 13¼" dia., EX . . . .$75.00 (D)

Christmas Plum Pudding Sundae, paper advertising poster with graphics of Santa Claus examining a sundae, 20¾" x 9", EX . . . .$140.00 (B)

Chrysler, MoPar Parts, metal painted flange sign, 23¾" x 16¾", black, orange on yellow, EX . . . .$215.00 (D)

Chum's...Scranton Distributing Co., round metal tip tray with graphics of man in tux seated at table with product and large dog, 4⅛" dia., EX . . . .$375.00 (B)

Cinderella Ice Cream, cardboard advertising sign with graphics of youngster sitting on steps eating ice cream, 13⅞" x 10⅝", VG . . . .$175.00 (C)

Cinderella Ice Cream, Tickles Your Tummy, Henderson Creamery Co. Inc., cardboard sign with artwork of young child sitting on steps with bowl of product, 14" x 10½", G . . . .$95.00 (D)

Citgo, cloth sleeve patch, 2⅜" sq., EX . . . .$10.00 (C)

Cities Service Kold Pruf, double-sided die cut cardboard countertop display sign with the pigeon holding a thermometer, 11½" x 18", NM . . . .$275.00 (C)

Cities Service National Charge Cards Accepted Here, metal flange double-sided sign, 20" x 12", EX $175.00 (C)

Cities Service Oils, die cut double-sided porcelain advertising sign, 23¾" x 23¾", EX . . . .$350.00 (B)

Cities Service, light-up advertising clock from the Pam Clock Co., New Rochelle, NY, with the trademark 3-leaf clover in center, 15" dia., VG, $425.00 (B). *Courtesy of Collectors Auction Services*

Clabber Girl Baking Powder, single-sided embossed sign, 34" x 11¾", G, $60.00 (B).

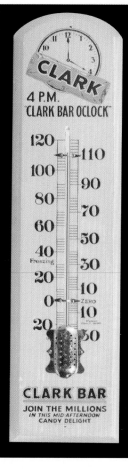

Clark Bar, Clark Bar, join the millions, wooden thermometer, 1920s, 5½" x 21½", NM, $1,550.00 (B). *Courtesy of Muddy River Trading Co./Gary Metz*

Cities Service Oils...Koolmotor gas globe, narrow glass hull body with glass lens with trademark cloverleaf design, 13½" dia., VG . . . . $800.00 (B)

Cities Service, light-up advertising clock from the Pam Clock Co., New Rochelle, NY, with the trademark 3-leaf clover in center, 15" dia., VG . . . . $425.00 (B)

Citizen's Coal Company...Our Modern Coal Pocket Insures Clean Coal, round metal tip tray with artwork of head shot of deer with large rack in center, 4¼" dia., EX . . . . $30.00 (B)

City National, cigar tin with full slip lid, "Mild and pleasing...quality supreme," 50-count, EX . . . . $75.00 (C)

City of Ardmore, one-sided porcelain sign with graphics of oil derrick and a large bull, 16" x 10½", VG $275.00 (B)

Clabber Girl Baking Powder, double-sided tin advertising sign, "The Double-Acting Baking Powder," 34" x 11½", G . . . . $40.00 (B)

Clark & Host, My Favorite Coffee, Milwaukee, tin container with paper label with graphics of youngster in lap of older gentleman, 5½" x 9½", EX . . . . $115.00 (C)

Clark Bar, Clark Bar, join the millions, wooden thermometer, 1920s, 5½" x 21½", NM . . . . $1,550.00 (B)

Clark's Teaberry Gum, That mountain tea flavor, sign, 11¾" x 8¾", EX, $350.00 (B).

Cleo Cola, cardboard cut-out sign with graphics of pretty girl with the product, art deco likeness, 25" x 26", 1939, G, $300.00 (B).

Courtesy of Muddy River Trading Co./Gary Metz

Cleveland and Buffalo...The Great Ship Seeandbee...C&B Line, oval metal tip tray with graphics of ship at sea, 6¼"L, VG, $350.00 (C).

Clark Bar...4 p.m. Clark Bar, wooden thermometer with image of product at top of scale, 1920s, 5¼" x 19", F ....$125.00 (B)

Clark Bar, thermometer, painted wood, with bar clock figure at top, 19" H, G ....$325.00 (B)

Clark's Honest Square, two-piece candy box with artwork of elves making candy, 110" x 11" x 2½", EX ..$28.00 (B)

Clarks Mile End spool cotton, paper litho advertising sign depicting man in cotton field with bag around his neck and spool of the product in other hand, 18½" x 24", EX ....$600.00 (B)

Clark's, spool thread, wood box with paper litho of kids playing Blind Man's Bluff, 4¼" x 3¼" x 1½", 1920s, VG ....$85.00 (D)

Clark's Super Motor Oil, double-sided porcelain advertisig sign with image of oil pouring from an upturned can, 30" dia., EX ....$1,050.00 (B)

Clark's Teaberry Gum, That mountain tea flavor, sign, 11¾" x 8¾", EX ....$350.00 (B)

Clark's Thread Sign, on heavy cardboard with graphics of young girl with her dog promoting Clark's Spool Cotton thread, 12⅝" x 17⅝", EX ....$325.00 (D)

Clark's Zagnut...A Real Treat, display case decal featuring product bar both wrapped and unwrapped, 9" x 5", EX ....$30.00 (B)

Class Cigars, tin from the Cordove Cigar Co. with graphics of peacock on both sides and most of the 1909 stamp left, 50-count, VG ....$30.00 (B)

Climax The Black Shells, shot shells box, paper litho over cardboard, 4⅛" x 4⅛" x 2½", G, **$55.00 (C)**.

CLIX, Clix Always Clicks, Smooth Shaving, barber shop three-dimensional razor blade display, barber pole lights up, 17½" x 26", NM, **$375.00 (D)**. *Courtesy of Rare Bird Antique Mall/Jon & Joan Wright*

Cloverbloom Butter cottage, cardboard die cut store display with usual dairy scenes, 31¼" x 16¼", NM, **$210.00 (B)**. *Courtesy of Autopia Advertising Auctions*

Clauss Shears, die cut advertisement featuring likeness of woman holding an enlarged pair of shears, with "Clauss/Freemont,O" on shears, 20" x 51½", EX . .**$25.00 (B)**

Clemak Razor, porcelain flange sign with graphics of man feeling his smooth shave, 12" x 12", EX . . . . .**$800.00 (B)**

Cleo Cola, cardboard cut-out sign with graphics of pretty girl with the product, art deco likeness, 25" x 26", 1939, G . . . .**$300.00 (B)**

Cleo Cola, embossed tin advertising sign with graphics of Cleopatra, 27⅜" x 12½", EX . . . .**$275.00 (C)**

Cleveland and Buffalo...The Great Ship Seeandbee...C&B Line, oval metal tip tray with graphics of ship at sea, 6¼" L, G . . . .**$300.00 (B)**

Clicquot Beverages, embossed tin advertising sign with graphics of Eskimo in center spotlight, 30" x 12", NM . . . .**$100.00 (C)**

Clicquot Club beverages...we recommend, free-standing advertising sign with graphics of Eskimo, 10" x 4¾" x 3", EX . . . .**$75.00 (C)**

Clicquot Club Ginger Ale, advertising calendar with graphics of woman giving the Eskimo Clicquot Club boy a ride on her bicycle, 12" x 24", 1942, NM . . . .**$100.00 (B)**

Clicquot Club Ginger Ale, embossed tin advertising sign with Eskimo image in center, 30" x 12", NM .**$150.00 (B)**

Clicquot Club Soda, calendar with metal strips on top and bottom, graphics of red-haired woman and child, full pad, 1942, NM . . . .**$225.00 (C)**

Clicquot Club Telechron, light-up advertising clock with Eskimo holding product bottle, 15" dia., 1940s, NM . . . .**$525.00 (C)**

Climax-Plug...Chew, litho tip tray with great graphics of flowers, EX . . . .**$50.00 (B)**

J & P Coats' Spool Cotton Is Strong, paper on cardboard advertising, G, 24" x 19", $80.00 (B).

Coca-Cola — and Coke, too, single-sided cardboard litho graphics of woman and daughter at table, 35½" x 55", G, $55.00 (B).

Coca-Cola, aluminum 12-bottle carrier, with embossed lettering on each side, 1940s, VG, $200.00 (D).

Climax-Plug Tobacco, cutter, P. Lorillard Tobacco Co., EX . . . .$140.00 (D)

Climax Thin Plug, P. Lorillard Co., tobacco tin, G . .$40.00 (D)

Clinton and Damascus Steel Safety Pins, Oakville Company, Waterbury, Ct., tip tray, graphics of hand holding product, 4½" x 6", EX . . . .$85.00 (B)

Clinton's Violet Talc, unopened container with image of pretty young woman on front, 2½" x 4", VG . .$100.00 (B)

CLIX, Clix Always Clicks, Smooth Shaving, barber shop three-dimensional razor blade display, barber pole lights up, 17½" x 26", NM . . . .$375.00 (D)

Cloverbloom Butter cottage, cardboard die cut store display with usual dairy scenes, 31¼" x 16¼", NM . . . .$210.00 (B)

Clover Farm Coffee, in tin litho can with key-wound lid, from Cleveland, Ohio, 1-lb., EX . . . .$35.00 (C)

Cloverine Talc, early tin litho can with graphics of woman on front, EX . . . .$300.00 (B)

Cloverleaf Milk...Famous for Purity, metal frame with bubble glass front, 16½" dia., EX . . . .$55.00 (B)

Clown Cigarettes, cast iron product advertising in shape of embossed horseshoe, used to hold papers down at street corner news stands, 6" x 8½" x 2", NM . . . . . .$102.00 (B)

Clown Cigarettes, full unopened pack from Axton Fisher Tobacco Co., Louisville, KY with graphics of clown head on cover, VG . . . .$25.00 (B)

Clown Cigarettes, round dial-type thermometer, "You'll never know how good Clown Cigarettes are till you touch a match to one," G . . . .$225.00 (D)

Coca-Cola bicycle, manufactured by Huffy in 1986 to commemorate the 100th anniversary of Coca-Cola, 26", mint, $895.00 (D).

Coca-Cola...Delicious and Refreshing...at Soda Fountains, embossed cardboard die cut advertising sign with graphics of children being instructed by the rabbit, super rare item, 6½" x 7", 1890s, EX, $16,000.00 (B). *Courtesy of Muddy River Trading Co./Gary Metz*

Club City Brewing Co., advertising with full pad and both top and bottom metal strips, calendar, 16" x 33¼", 1947, VG . . . .$35.00 (B)

Club Lake Coffee, paper litho on tin can with graphics of lake and club house, 3-lb., G . . . .$65.00 (D)

Club 100 count, cardboard box top for ammunition with graphics of hunting scene, 7¾" x 7¾", EX . . .$575.00 (B)

Clyde Beatty and Cole Bros. Circus, paper litho framed poster with graphics of growling lion and tiger, 28½" x 41½", G . . . .$100.00 (B)

Clyde Beatty Cole Bros., combined circus poster with graphics of lion tamer and lion with signature of Roland Butler, 21" x 36½", G . . . .$25.00 (D)

Clyde Beatty Cole Bros., paper litho ad poster promoting the greatest show on earth, 14" x 25", VG . . . .$25.00 (D)

Clyde Beatty Cole Bros., paper litho circus advertising poster with graphics of clown face, 25" x 21", VG . . . . .$25.00 (B)

Clyde Beatty Cole Bros., paper litho circus poster with signature by Roland Butler and image of large tiger on front, 28" x 21", G . . . .$25.00 (B)

Clyde Bros. Circus, paper advertising poster to be in Johnstown on Friday June 3, with artwork of the world's largest chimpanzee, 28" x 50", VG . . . .$20.00 (B)

Coca-Cola, acid etched green glass seltzer bottle, EX . . . .$225.00 (C)

Coca-Cola, aluminum 12-bottle carrier, with embossed lettering on each side, 1940s, EX . . . .$225.00 (D)

Coca-Cola..., bell-shaped pewter glass tumbler with Coca-Cola on shoulder, EX . . . .$350.00 (C)

Coca-Cola bicycle, manufactured by Huffy in 1986 to commemorate the 100th anniversary of Coca-Cola, 26", VG . . . .$700.00 (C)

Coca-Cola..., bobbed hair girl with bottle, metal serving tray, 1927, EX . . . .$825.00 (C)

Coca-Cola, bottle lighter, embossed lettering with Coca-Cola logo on lid, pulls apart in middle for lighter access, 2½" T, EX . . . .$55.00 (D)

Coca-Cola bottle thermometer, die cut tin, 5¼" x 16¾", 1953, EX . . . .$50.00 (B)

Coca-Cola, double bottle thermometer of embossed tin, 1941, 7" x 16", EX. BEWARE: This thermometer has been reproduced, $475.00 (B).

Coca-Cola, double-sided cardboard advertising sign with clown background, 16" x 27", EX, $210.00 (B). *Courtesy of Autopia Advertising Auctions*

Coca-Cola, double-sided tin litho crossing guard with original cast iron embossed base, 30" x 64", EX, $2,600.00 (B).

Coca-Cola, calendar, artwork of Victorian girl at table with fern, 1898, G . . . .$7,500.00 (C)

Coca-Cola, calendar, Elaine seated with parasol holding glass of Coke, with full pad, framed, 1915, EX . . . . .$4,000.00 (C)

Coca-Cola, calendar featuring June Caprice, early star, with glass of Coke, with full pad, although this is an early piece, it is somewhat common, 1918, EX . . . .$375.00 (C)

Coca-Cola, calendar, girl with snow skis, 1947, G . .$295.00 (C)

Coca-Cola, calendar with artwork of Army nurse holding a bottle of Coke, complete with all pads, 1943, EX . . . . .$575.00 (C)

Coca-Cola, calendar with artwork of two women at beach, one with parasol and glass, other sitting with bottle of Coke, no month pad, 1918, EX . . . .$1,250.00 (C)

Coca-Cola, calendar with Betty in bonnet, this is the version with her holding the product, but with message at upper right of picture, 1914, G . . . .$1,800.00 (C)

Coca-Cola, calendar with boy at well with dog, enjoying a bottle of Coke, with partial pad, 1932, EX . . .$725.00 (C)

Coca-Cola, calendar with girl in blue hat with glass of Coke, full calendar pad, framed, 1921, EX .$1,275.00 (C)

Coca-Cola, calendar with woman wearing broad-brimmed hat, partial calendar pads, 1944, G . . . .$300.00 (C)

Coca-Cola, ceramic dispenser with base, bowl, spigot and lid, marked The Wheeling Pottery Co., 1896, 18" tall, EX . . . .$5,200.00 (C)

Coca-Cola, cigar-style tin thermometer, "Drink...Sign of Good Taste," 8½" x 30", 1950s, EX . . . .$400.00 (B)

Coca-Cola, clear flare glass with etched syrup line, Coca-Cola in curve section of 5¢, EX . . . .$700.00 (C)

Coca-Cola...Delicious and Refreshing...at Soda Fountains, embossed cardboard die cut advertising sign with graphics of children being instructed by the rabbit, super rare item, 6½" x 7", 1890s, EX . . . .$16,000.00 (B)

Coca-Cola...Drink Bottled...So Easily Served, leather boudoir clock, bottle-shaped with clock face in center of body, 1910, 3" x 8", G, $1,300.00 (B).

Courtesy of Muddy River Trading Co./Gary Metz

Coca-Cola, Drink, button with curved sides, metal, 12" dia., white lettering on red, NM, $325.00 (C).

Coca-Cola...Delicious Refreshing, wooden thermometer, Coca-Cola 5¢, 1905, 4" x 15", EX . . . .$700.00 (B)

Coca-Cola, die cut metal bottle thermometer, 1933, EX . . . .$300.00 (B)

Coca-Cola, die cut metal bottle thermometer of Dec. 25th, 1923 bottle, 1931, EX . . . .$375.00 (C)

Coca-Cola, double bottle thermometer of embossed tin 1941, 7" x 16", EX. BEWARE: This thermometer has been reproduced, G . . . . $300.00 (C)

Coca-Cola, double-sided cardboard advertising sign with clown background, 16" x 27", EX . . . .$210.00 (B)

Coca-Cola, double-sided die cut porcelain sign, "Arndt Groc," 42" x 50", EX . . . .$675.00 (C)

Coca-Cola, double-sided tin litho crossing guard with original cast iron embossed base, 30" x 64", EX . .$2,600.00 (B)

Coca-Cola...Drink Bottled...So Easily Served, leather boudoir clock, bottle-shaped with clock face in center of body, 1910, 3" x 8", G . . . .$1,300.00 (B)

Coca-Cola, Drink, button with curved sides, metal, 12" dia., white lettering on red, EX . . . .$300.00 (C)

Coca-Cola, Drink..., Cavalier 6-case master, wet box, red with white lettering, G . . . .$695.00 (D)

Coca-Cola...Drink Coca-Cola In Bottles, mirror with thermometer at upper left, with silhouette girl panel at bottom, 1939, 10" x 14", EX . . . .$850.00 (B)

Coca-Cola, Drink...Delicious and Refreshing, cowboy cardboard, in original wood frame, good graphics, EX . . . .$1,150.00 (B)

Coca-Cola...Drink...Delicious and Refreshing, oval Betty serving tray, 1914, EX . . . .$300.00 (C)

Coca-Cola...Drink...Delicious and Refreshing, oval metal serving tray with the Hamilton King Coca-Cola Girl holding a glass of Coke, 1913, EX . . . .$325.00 (C)

Coca-Cola...Drink...Delicious and Refreshing, paper bottle topper of woman in yellow scarf with umbrella, 1927, EX . . . .$2,000.00 (B)

Coca-Cola, Drink..., die cut porcelain script sign with copyright in tail of first C, EX . . . .$750.00 (C)

Coca-Cola...Drink Coca-Cola In Bottles, mirror with thermometer at upper left, with silhouette girl panel at bottom, 1939, 10" x 14", VG, $400.00 (C).

Coca-Cola, Drink...Delicious and Refreshing, cowboy, cardboard, in original wood frame, good graphics, EX, $1,150.00 (B). *Courtesy of Muddy River Trading Co./Gary Metz*

Coca-Cola, drink dispenser, Vendo # 23, restored, 1940s – 1950s, NM . . . .$1,295.00 (D)

Coca-Cola...Drink, double-sided porcelain advertising sign, 52½" x 35½", G . . . .$130.00 (B)

Coca-Cola, Drink..., 50th anniversary poster featuring two girls sitting on product banner holding bottles of Coke, 1936, 27" x 47", EX . . . .$1,850.00 (C)

Coca-Cola...Drink 5¢, glass change receiver with reverse glass lettering, 1904, 6" dia., G . . . .$320.00 (B)

Coca-Cola...Drink... Have a Coke, adjustable paper visor, G . . . .$5.00 (D)

Coca-Cola...Drink...Have a Coke, cooler radio, 1950s, EX . . . .$675.00 (C)

Coca-Cola...Drink...Ice Cold, double-sided sidewalk sign on legs, graphics of fishtail sign over bottle, 22½" x 24" x 33", EX . . . .$350.00 (B)

Coca-Cola...Drink...Ice Cold, fountain dispenser, white on red, EX . . . .$725.00 (D)

Coca-Cola...Drink...Ice Cold, green Vernonware bowl, 1930s, EX . . . .$450.00 (C)

Coca-Cola...Drink...Ice Cold, miniature music box shaped as a box cooler, plays "Let me call you sweetheart," 1950s, EX . . . .$150.00 (C)

Coca-Cola...Drink...Ice Cold, small crystal radio in shape of radio cooler, 1950s, EX . . . .$250.00 (C)

Coca-Cola...Drink... Ice Cold, Westinghouse 10-case master dry box with a hinged lid that opens side to side instead of front to back, embossed, restored, 1950s, 45⅛" x 36" H x 30½" D, white on red, EX . . . . . .$1,850.00 (D)

Coca-Cola...Drink...in bottles, new molded plastic cooler in the shape of drink machine, 22½" x 35" X 12", red, EX . . . .$275.00 (D)

Coca-Cola, drink dispenser, Vendo #23, restored, 1940s – 1950s, NM, **$1,295.00 (D)**.
Courtesy of Affordable Antiques

Coca-Cola...Drink...ice cold, fountain dispenser, white on red, NM, **$795.00 (D)**. *Courtesy of Patrick's Collectibles*

Coca-Cola...Drink, In Bottles, small dual chute machine with four bottle stacks inside that alternately dispense the product, will only use 6½-oz. bottle, 1950s, 25" W x 58" H x 15" D, white logo on red front, G . . . .$1,500.00 (D)

Coca-Cola...Drink, In Bottles, successor to the table-top 27, much sought after for home use because of their compact size, restored, 1950s, 25½" W x 52" H x 17½" D, white on red, EX . . . .$1,800.00 (C)

Coca-Cola...Drink...in Bottles, waxed cardboard container, used both as popcorn container and ice bucket, 5T3 Lily Nestrite tub, EX . . . .$25.00 (D)

Coca-Cola...Drink in bottles, wood framed clock with message spotlighted in center of face, 1940s, 16" x 16", G . . . .$195.00 (C)

Coca-Cola, Drink..., iron frame is 24" dia. with a 16" metal button on one side and a 10" button on reverse side, EX . . . .$875.00 (C)

Coca-Cola...Drink, Knowles china sandwich plate with bottle and glass in center, EX . . . .$250.00 (C)

Coca-Cola, Drink..., masonite with bottle in spotlight at bottom of diamond, made by Evans-Glenn Co., Marietta, GA, Made In USA, 12-46, 1946, 48" x 48", G . .$695.00 (D)

Coca-Cola...Drink, metal cargo truck with working headlights and taillights, 1950s, red, yellow, and white, EX . . . .$375.00 (C)

Coca-Cola...Drink, painted metal "curb service" serving tray, 1927, EX . . . .$1,000.00 (C)

Coca-Cola...Drink, painted metal self-framing sign with couple at right of message, 1940s, 33½" x 12", EX . .$500.00 (D)

Coca-Cola...Drink, Refreshment right out of the bottle, cardboard poster, 1940s, G . . . .$700.00 (D)

Coca-Cola...Drink, reverse glass advertising sign, 21" x 11", 1939, NM . . . .$1,500.00 (C)

Coca-Cola...Drink, syrup bottle with metal lid, 1920s, EX . . . .$1,200.00 (C)

Coca-Cola...Drink..., take enough home, adjustable wire carton rack, with message sign at top, EX . . .$165.00 (D)

Coca-Cola...Drink, Vendo 39 with bottle drop at center of door, approx. 80,000 made, restored, '40s – '50s, 27" W x 58" H x 16" W, white on red, NM . . . .$2,995.00 (D)

Coca-Cola, electric light-up clock, aluminum body with glass front, Drink Coca-Cola in red dot center, with original box, Modern Clock Adv. Co., 15" dia., EX . . . .$575.00 (B)

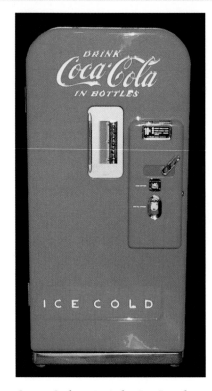

Coca-Cola...Drink, In Bottles, successor to the table-top 27, much sought after for home use because of their compact size, restored, 1950s, 25½" W x 52" H x 17½" D, white on red, NM, **$2,195.00 (D)**. *Courtesy of Patrick's Collectibles*

Coca-Cola...Drink in bottles, wood-framed clock with message spotlighted in center of face, 1940s, 16" x 16", VG, **$215.00 (C)**.

Coca-Cola, Drink..., iron frame is 24" dia. with a 16" metal button on one side and a 10" button on reverse side, G, **$325.00 (C)**.

Coca-Cola, embossed tin bottle thermometer on background plate, 1938, EX . . . .**$275.00 (D)**

Coca-Cola, embossed tin straight-sided advertising bottle with likeness of paper label, 3¼" x 10¼", 1910s, EX . .**$425.00 (C)**

Coca-Cola...**Enjoy big king size...ice cold here**, metal self-framing painted metal sign with fishtail in center and bottle at right, 27¾" x 19¾", red, white, and green, G . . . .**$225.00 (D)**

Coca-Cola...**exposition girl**, oval metal serving tray, 1909, 13½" x 16½", EX . . . .**$2,500.00 (C)**

Coca-Cola, figural bottle cooler door handle, found on newer coolers in stores, 2⅜" x 7⅞" x 1½", NM . . . .**$100.00 (C)**

Coca-Cola...**fishing boy with dog**, metal serving tray, 1931, EX . . . .**$850.00 (C)**

Coca-Cola, Flapper Girl calendar, with partial calendar pad, framed, this particular calendar shows both the bottle and glass, 1929, EX . . . .**$875.00 (C)**

Coca-Cola..., foxskin fur girl with glass of Coke, metal serving tray, 1925, EX . . . .**$375.00 (D)**

Coca-Cola...**Francis Dee**, metal rectangular serving tray, 1933, EX . . . .**$950.00 (B)**

Coca-Cola, frosted glass anniversary cigarette case, 1936, EX . . . .**$500.00 (C)**

Coca-Cola...Drink, painted metal self-framing sign with couple at right of message, 1940s, 33½" x 12", NM, **$595.00 (C)**.

Coca-Cola, Drink..., masonite with bottle in spotlight at bottom of diamond, made by Evans-Glenn Co., Marietta, GA, Made In USA, 12-46, 1946, 48" x 48", G, **$695.00 (D)**.

Coca-Cola...Drink, **Refreshment right out of the bottle**, cardboard poster, 1940s, G, **$700.00 (D)**.

Coca-Cola, girl in bathing suit and hat with beach towel, 1930, EX . . . .**$375.00 (C)**

Coca-Cola, grocery store aisle divider advertising sign, 30" x 13", VG . . . .**$95.00 (B)**

Coca-Cola, hanging metal arrow sign, double-sided with hanging arm, 30" x 21½", 1920s, EX . . . . . .**$875.00 (C)**

Coca-Cola...Have a Coke, metal self-framing sign with spotlight bottle in center, 18" x 54", white and yellow on red, EX . . . .**$325.00 (D)**

Coca-Cola...Have a Coke, plastic and metal door pull, handle shaped like a bottle, 1950s, EX . . . . .**$200.00 (D)**

Coca-Cola, Hilda Clark metal serving tray, 1903, 9¼" dia., EX . . . .**$3,500.00 (C)**

Coca-Cola, Hospitality in your hands, horizontal cardboard poster featuring artwork of woman with serving tray of bottled Coke, 1948, 36" x 20", EX . . . .**$325.00 (C)**

Coca-Cola...ice skater, rectangular metal serving tray featuring artwork of girl in ice skates sitting on log, 1941, EX . . . .**$345.00 (C)**

Coca-Cola...It's the real thing, with dynamic wave contour logo, metal picnic cooler with side handles and metal latching top, 18" x 13" x 16½", white on red, G . . . .**$150.00 (D)**

Coca-Cola...Johnny Weissmuller, metal serving tray. BEWARE: This tray has been reproduced, 1934, EX . . . .**$900.00 (B)**

Coca-Cola...Enjoy big king size...ice cold here, metal self-framing painted metal sign with fishtail in center and bottle at right, 27¾" x 19¾", red, white, and green, VG, $245.00 (C). *Courtesy of Patrick's Collectibles*

Coca-Cola, framed calendar page, 12¾" x 21¼", VG, $35.00 (B).
Courtesy of Collectors Auction Services

Coca-Cola, I'd Love It, cardboard poster, 31¾" x 21¼", G, $100.00 (B).
Courtesy of Collectors Auction Services

Coca-Cola...Have a Coke, metal self-framing sign with spotlight bottle in center, 18" x 54", white and yellow on red, VG, $295.00 (C). *Courtesy of Patrick's Collectibles*

Coca-Cola, Join the friendly circle, horizontal poster with artwork of friends swimming around float with cooler of Cokes, 1955, 36" x 20", EX . . . .$450.00 (C)

Coca-Cola license plate attachment, "Aloysus Purple Flashes...Drink Coca-Cola in Bottles," a great advertising item that was probably developed for a special local interest event, 11" x 4", NM . . . .$295.00 (C)

Coca-Cola, light-up advertising clock, Pam Clock Co., Brooklyn 1 NY, U.S.A., with green outside ring and red center, NOS, 15" dia., EX . . . .$500.00 (B)

Coca-Cola, light-up advertising clock, "things go better with Coke," with logo button in lower right corner, 16" sq., VG . . . .$85.00 (B)

Coca-Cola, light-up advertising clock with advertising message board for billards between product message and clock, 24" x 37½" x 3½", G . . . .$300.00 (B)

Coca-Cola, light-up advertising clock with fishtail logo in center, metal body with glass face and cover, 15¼" sq., VG . . . .$400.00 (B)

Coca-Cola, light-up advertising clock with graphics of girl drinking a Coca-Cola from a bottle in spotlight at bottom, 15" dia., VG . . . .$725.00 (B)

Coca-Cola, light-up advertising clock with message board at bottom, 11" x 12", NM . . . .$185.00 (B)

Coca-Cola, light-up advertising clock with neon around outside of face with spotlight bottle in center above the number 6, 15½" sq., VG . . . .$350.00 (B)

Coca-Cola, light-up advertising clock with reverse painted fishtail "Drink Coca-Cola" in center, 15" x 15", NM . . . .$325.00 (C)

Coca-Cola Lillian Nordica, cardboard advertising sign, 26" x 46", 1905, EX . . . .$4,100.00 (B)

Coca-Cola, **Join the friendly circle,** horizontal poster with artwork of friends swimming around float with cooler of Cokes, 1955, 36" x 20", VG, **$375.00 (C).**

Coca-Cola license plate attachment, "Aloysius Purple Flashes...Drink Coca-Cola in Bottles," a great advertising item that was probably developed for a special local interest event, 11" x 4", NM, **$295.00 (C).** *Courtesy of Buffalo Bay Auction Co.*

Coca-Cola, light-up advertising clock, metal clock with plastic message strip at top, 27" x 18½" x 4½", VG, **$600.00 (B).**

Coca-Cola "Luncheonette," self-framed tin advertising sign with fishtail under message with bottle and diamond can, 59¼" x 23¼", VG . . . .**$360.00 (B)**

Coca-Cola...**Madge Evans,** metal serving tray, 1935, EX . . . .**$325.00 (C)**

Coca-Cola...**menu girl,** metal serving tray, 1950s, EX . . . .**$75.00 (D)**

Coca-Cola, metal serving tray, girl in afternoon, 1938, EX . . . .**$225.00 (C)**

Coca-Cola, metal serving tray, Soda Jerk, 1928, EX . .**$825.00 (C)**

Coca-Cola, metal serving tray with artwork of two girls at early model convertible, 1942, EX . . . .**$375.00 (C)**

Coca-Cola, miniature red 6-pack, EX . . . .**$85.00 (C)**

Coca-Cola, light-up advertising clock, Pam Clock Co., Brooklyn 1 NY, U.S.A with green outside ring and red center, NOS, 15" dia., EX, $500.00 (B). *Courtesy of Collectors Auction Services*

Coca-Cola, light-up advertising clock with message board at bottom, 11" x 12", NM, $185.00 (B). *Courtesy of Autopia Advertising Auctions*

Coca-Cola, molded plastic menu board with football graphics around menu selections, 31½" x 34½", VG . . . .$25.00 (B)

Coca-Cola...Now! 12-oz. cans too!, rack sign with graphics of cans & bottles circling the globe, 10½" x 22", EX . . . .$45.00 (D)

Coca-Cola, oval metal serving tray with "yellow girl," 1920, 13¼" x 16½", EX . . . .$775.00 (C)

Coca-Cola, painted metal tray with artwork of "sailor girl" fishing on dock, Drink...Delicious and Refreshing, 1940, EX . . . .$325.00 (C)

Coca-Cola, paper advertising sign, "Your choice of sizes," 16" x 27", 1960s, EX . . . .$25.00 (B)

Coca-Cola, paper on cardboard advertising poster with graphics of young girl and mother "...and Coke too," 26¾" x 16", 1946, G . . . .$90.00 (B)

Coca-Cola, red-haired girl with yellow scarf, metal serving tray with solid background, 1950 – 1952, EX . .$250.00 (C)

Coca-Cola, rolled edge tin advertising sign with bottle at bottom of tag, "Drink Coca-Cola...Ice Cold," 20" x 28", VG . . . .$225.00 (B)

Coca-Cola, running girl on beach in yellow bathing suit, 1937, EX . . . .$325.00 (C)

Coca-Cola, self-framing painted tin sign with graphics of fishtail sign in center of sign, 27" x 9¼", VG . .$165.00 (B)

Coca-Cola, Serve...Taste treat for the year, paper double-sided store advertising, framed, 1956, EX . . .$125.00 (D)

Coca-Cola, set of four educational "Our America" posters, 32" x 22", 1946, EX . . . .$120.00 (B)

Coca-Cola, single-sided self-framing painted tin advertising sign with graphics of bottle on right of name tag, EX . . . .$190.00 (B)

Coca-Cola, soda fountain attendant cloth hat with "Drink Coca-Cola" patch, NOS, NM . . . .$150.00 (C)

Coca-Cola, Soda Fountain calendar, 1901, G . .$4,500.00 (C)

Coca-Cola, Sold Here...Ice Cold, arrow sign with original hanging arm, 1927, 30" x 21½", red, green, and white, EX . . . .$725.00 (C)

Coca-Cola...So Refreshing, die cut cardboard sign with graphics of young waitress with serving tray of Coca-Cola in glasses, designed to be either string hung or used on counter with the easel back, 17" x 20", VG . .$475.00 (B)

Coca-Cola, Sprite Boy advertising decal featuring Sprite Boy in bottle cap hat beside Coke bottle, 4½" x 8", NM . . . .$15.00 (D)

Coca-Cola, metal-lined menu board with fishtail logo, 19½" x 28", G, $100.00 (B).

Coca-Cola Lillian Nordica, cardboard advertising sign, 26" x 46", 1905, EX, $4,100.00 (B).

Coca-Cola, rolled edge tin advertising sign with bottle at bottom of tag, "Drink Coca-Cola...Ice Cold," 20" x 28", VG, $225.00 (B).

Coca-Cola...Sprite Boy...Take some home today, metal toy cargo truck, 1940s, red and yellow, EX . .**$450.00 (C)**

Coca-Cola "Sprite Boy" Take Some Home Today, paper window advertising sign, NOS, 25" x 10", 1950, NM . . . . **$275.00 (C)**

Coca-Cola...swim suit girl with glass, metal serving tray, fountain sales, 1929, EX . . . .**$425.00 (C)**

Coca-Cola, Take Some Home Today, vertical cardboard poster in original frame, artwork of girl with bottle of product at party, 16" x 27", EX . . . .**$675.00 (C)**

Coca-Cola, Take Some Home Today, wire bottle rack, with metal rack sign at top, G . . . .**$45.00 (D)**

Coca-Cola...things go better with..., painted metal self-framing sign, with message to left of bottle, 35¼" sq., red, white, and green, G . . . .**$275.00 (D)**

Coca-Cola, toy dispenser with original box, 12" x 6" x 9", 1950s, EX . . . .**$60.00 (B)**

Coca-Cola, toy shopping cart, masonite, EX .**$550.00 (C)**

Coca-Cola, waxed cardboard carton case, red on yellow, EX . . . .**$75.00 (D)**

Coca-Cola, Serve...Taste treat for the year, paper double-sided store advertising, framed, 1956, NM, $135.00 (D). *Courtesy of Creatures of Habit*

Coca-Cola, single-sided cardboard WWII poster, 1943, G, $300.00 (B).

Coca-Cola...So Refreshing, die cut cardboard sign with graphics of young waitress with serving tray of Coca-Cola in glasses, designed to be either string hung or used on counter with the easel back, 17" x 20", VG, $475.00 (B).

Courtesy of Muddy River Trading Co./Gary Metz

Coca-Cola... Wherever Ginger Ale, Seltzer or Soda is Good...Coca-Cola is Better–Try It, metal lithographed serving tray of topless woman, 1908, EX . .$4,600.00 (C)

Coca-Cola, whirly bird eight-sided spinning sign, NOS, 1950s, NM . . . .$775.00 (C)

Coca-Cola, woman in evening wear with glass, full pad, framed, 1928, EX . . . .$825.00 (C)

Cochran, paint products, painted metal sign, featuring artwork of paint can man running & spilling paint with message, Made better last longer, 36" x 24", G . . . .$45.00 (D)

Cochran, paint sign, two-sided painted metal, "made better lasts longer," 36" x 24", EX . . . .$45.00 (C)

Co-Ed Dresses Sold here, tin litho advertising sign with graphics of young woman in graduation cap and gown, 12" x 13", VG . . . .$50.00 (B)

Coles Pentrating Liniment...Removes All Aches & Pains, early porcelain advertising sign, 6⅛" x 16", EX . .$575.00 (C)

Colgan's Orange Gum, wood and etched glass display cabinet, 17½" T, G . . . .$1,000.00 (C)

Colgate, die cut advertising sign of Colgate baby holding a tin of Cashmere Bouquet, 8½" x 13½", 1913s, EX . . .$275.00 (C)

Colgate, sample box with soap and talc and die cut booklet on how to use product, 3" x 4" x 1", EX . .$225.00 (C)

Coca-Cola, Sprite Boy, advertising decal featuring Sprite Boy in bottle cap hat beside Coke bottle, 4½" x 8", NM, $25.00 (C).

Coca-Cola, Take Some Home Today, wire bottle rack, with metal rack sign at top, G, $45.00 (D).

Coca-Cola, toy dispenser with original box, 12" x 6" x 9", 1950s, EX, $60.00 (B).

Coca-Cola, waxed cardboard carton case, red on yellow, VG, $50.00 (D).

Colgate's Baby Talc, sample tin litho with graphics of young child on front with screw-on lid, NM . .$137.00 (B)

Colgate's Dactylis Talc Powder, sample tin litho with artwork of young girl on front, NM . . . .$88.00 (B)

Colgate Shaving Cream, advertising sign, wood and paper, 42" x 35½", VG . . . .$325.00 (D)

Colgate's Talc Powder, paperboard advertising sign with image of container in center, 10" x 18", EX . .$120.00 (B)

College Girl Talc, tin litho container with graphics of tennis girl on front, 1¾" x 1¾" x 6", EX . . . .$350.00 (B)

Collins & Co. Axe, advertising sign, embossed tin on cardboard, 20" H, G . . . .$25.00 (C)

Collins Axe, hanging cardboard sign with graphics of axe and globe, "The Best is the Cheapest," 1915, 10" x 20", NM . . . .$51.00 (B)

Collins Baking Co., calendar featuring graphics of girl in bonnet, "Collins Celebrated Bread," 8" x 8", 1909, EX . . . .$25.00 (B)

Collins Baking Co., calendar in diamond configuration with tear sheets at bottom of picture, with message of Collins Celebrated Bread, 1909, 8" x 8", EX . .$55.00 (D)

Coca-Cola... Wherever Ginger Ale, Seltzer or Soda is Good...Coca-Cola is Better–Try It, metal lithographed serving tray of topless woman, 1908, EX, $4,600.00 (C).

Colgan's Orange Gum, wood and etched glass display cabinet, 17½" T, EX, $1,500.00 (B). *Courtesy of Richard Opfer Auctioneering, Inc.*

Colman's Mustard, wooden store display box, "Grand Prix Highest Award, Paris 1900," 1900s, 21"W x 4"H x 12¼"D, F . . . .$20.00 (B)

Colonial Bread...is good, painted metal door push, adjustable, 36" x 3½", EX . . . .$65.00 (D)

Colonial Club Cigars, painted metal double-sided flange advertising sign promoting their 5¢ cigars, 18½" x 8¾", G . . . .$115.00 (B)

Colonial Club 5¢ Cigar, litho on canvas-type paper, featuring artwork of woman in green dress with straw hat, NM . . . .$800.00 (B)

Colonist...Up to the Minute...5¢ Cigar...Save The Bands, cardboard litho with artwork of Minute Man type image, 1900s, 13¼" x 19¾", NM . . . .$223.00 (B)

Col. Sanders, molded plastic advertising sign with graphics of the Colonel, 32½" x 36", F . . . .$50.00 (B)

Colt Firearms Catalogue, with graphics of gun in hand on cover and some of the history of Colts inside along with current models, 10" x 7¼", 1950s, EX . . . . . .$50.00 (B)

Columbia Accredited Dealer, porcelain advertising sign with graphics of record in center, 30" x 20", NM . . . .$575.00 (C)

Columbia Brewing Co., premium clothes brush. "Columbia Brewing Co....Tacoma Wash.," 8" x 2" x 1½", 1900s, EX . . . .$60.00 (B)

Columbia Match Holder, embossed die cut tin wall-hung advertising piece promoting Columbia Flour, in the shape of Miss Liberty, 2¼" x 5½", EX . . . .$1,050.00 (B)

Columbia Records, porcelain advertising sign in shape of record with blue Columbia label, 24" dia., EX . .$450.00 (C)

Columbia Spice, vintage tin litho spice tin with graphics of vintage woman in center cameo from Sutherland & McMillian Co., Pittston, Pa., 2-oz., VG . . . . .$275.00 (A)

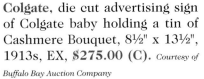

Colgate, die cut advertising sign of Colgate baby holding a tin of Cashmere Bouquet, 8½" x 13½", 1913s, EX, $275.00 (C). *Courtesy of Buffalo Bay Auction Company*

Collins & Co. Axe, advertising sign, embossed tin on cardboard, 20" H, NM, $50.00 (B). *Courtesy of Richard Opfer Auctioneering, Inc.*

Colonial Club 5¢ Cigar, litho on canvas type paper, featuring artwork of woman in green dress with straw hat, NM, $800.00 (B).

Columbus Shock Absorber, authorized dealer, tin flange double-sided advertising sign with graphics of product beside message, 19" x 12½", VG . . . .$165.00 (C)

Combat High Grade 5¢ Cigar, embossed and stamped cardboard advertising sign with image of pretty lady in center, 6" x 10", EX . . . .$295.00 (C)

Comfort Medicated Talc powder, tin litho container with baby face on one side and nurse on back side, 2" x 3⅜", EX . . . .$775.00 (B)

Comfort Talc Powder, tin litho can with artwork of nurse in early uniform, 2" x 3⅜", EX . . . .$600.00 (B)

Commerical Club, maple syrup embossed cardboard advertising sign, 6" x 13", EX . . . .$60.00 (B)

Commonwealth Brand Coffee, Warranted Pure, with litho of White House on front, slip lid, 1-lb., EX . . . .$80.00 (B)

Community brand coffee pail, graphics of large two-story southern mansion, from Baton Rouge, LA, 6¾" x 8", EX . . . .$275.00 (C)

Compeer Snuff, trade card, EX . . . .$145.00 (C)

Comrade, tin litho coffee container, J.A. Folger, Kansas City & S.F., CA, 1-lb., EX . . . .$125.00 (C)

Condition, powder, cardboard box, unopened, contains animal powder that claims to cure almost everything, good graphics of animals, ½" x 2¼" x 7", NM . .$55.00 (C)

Congress Security Tires...Congress Rubber Co., East Palestine, Ohio, double-sided porcelain flange advertising sign, 14¼" x 17", NM . . . .$325.00 (C)

Conkey's Poultry Remedies, wooden scale advertising thermometer, 4" x 15⅛", G . . . .$110.00 (B)

Connolly's Arch Grip Kangaroo Shoes, reverse paint on glass advertising sign with image of kangaroo in upper right corner, 17¼" x 8¼", EX . . . .$95.00 (C)

Conoco Super Motor Oil, license plate sign with graphics of pilgrims, 13½" x 6⅜", EX . . . .$150.00 (C)

Consolidated Biscuit Co., biscuit box, shaped like two-story house, with product message on chimney, cardboard, 1932, 9" x 8½" x 5", EX . . . .$85.00 (B)

Consolidated Ice Company, advertising dresser set with graphics on back of mirror, VG . . . .$95.00 (C)

Colonial Health Guard Ice, single-sided porcelain sign, 21" x 11¾", EX, $400.00 (B).

Columbia Chainless Bicycle, paper advertising poster, 1897, 37½" x 87", VG, $750.00 (B). *Courtesy of Collectors Auction Services*

Consolidated Ice Company, dresser mirror with winter scene on back, EX . . . .$80.00 (B)

Constans Coffee, litho tin container from Minneapolis, Minn., "Constantly Good," 5½" x 9½", VG . . . .$20.00 (B)

Consumer's Beer, ask father, artwork of man with glass of beer, embossed tin sign, from Consumers Brewing Co., Hills Grove, RI, 1940s, 28" x 9¾", EX . . . . . .$225.00 (B)

Consumer's Beer...Ask Father, tin advertising sign with artwork of man with white hair holding glass of product, 27¾" x 9¾", EX . . . .$55.00 (B)

Continental cigar box, wooden, 50-ct., EX . .$125.00 (C)

Continental Cubes, advertising pocket mirror with celluloid back, 2¾" T, EX . . . .$125.00 (C)

Continental Cubes Cigars, litho tin, rare piece, difficult to find, 7½" H, F . . . .$200.00 (B)

Continental Cubes Tobacco, celluloid advertising pocket mirror promoting pipe tobacco with graphics of vintage dressed lady resting on large container of Continental Cubes tobacco, 1¾" x 2¾", EX . . . .$400.00 (B)

Continental Life Insurance Company, metal tip tray, with picture of skyscraper on face, EX . . . .$75.00 (C)

Continental Life Insurance Company...Saint Louis, round metal tip tray with artwork of insurance building in tray center, 4¼" dia., EX . . . .$25.00 (B)

Continental Trailways Bus Depot, porcelain one-sided sign, 36" x 18", white & black on red, EX . . . .$135.00 (C)

Cookie Jar DeLuxe Mellow Mild Modern Cigarettes, cigarette package featuring artwork on cookie jar on front, rare, EX . . . .$15.00 (D)

Cook's Beer, metal over cardboard advertising sign with artwork of woman with long gloves, 1936, 18" x 29", F . . . .$195.00 (D)

Cook's Beer sign, tin over cardboard hanging sign, with graphics of black waiter rushing a bottle of product to his master, "De Boss Sho' Likes His Cook's," 21" x 13", VG . . . .$1,200.00 (B)

Cook's Beer, tin litho advertising sign with graphics of older gent enjoying a glass of the product, 19½" x 27", 1907, EX . . . .$700.00 (B)

Colvert's Milk, one-sided embossed tin advertising sign, 29" x 15", G, $15.00 (B).

Columbia match holder, embossed die cut tin wall-hung advertising piece promoting Columbia Flour, in the shape of Miss Liberty, 2¼" x 5½", EX, $1,050.00 (B). *Courtesy of Wm. Morford Investment Grade Collectibles*

Comfort, litho embossed advertising calendar, promoting yearly subscriptions to Comfort, 5¾" x 11½", VG, $70.00 (B).

Cook's Champagne, tin litho advertising sign with wood-grain look and graphics of product in center oval, 24" x 20½", EX . . . .$110.00 (B)

Coopers Sheep Dipping Powder, single-sided porcelain sign with graphics of trump card, 20" x 30", EX $850.00 (B)

Co-Op Oil Ass'n., license plate attachment, 10" x 4⅝", EX . . . .$135.00 (C)

Coors Malted Milk, from Adolph Coors Company, Golden, Colorado, 25-lb., VG . . . .$56.00 (B)

Copenhagen, tin litho store tobacco dispenser, 3" x 14½", VG . . . .$20.00 (B)

Coppertone, advertising clock with graphics of the Coppertone girl and her dog pulling down her swim suit to expose untanned areas, 36" x 36" x 8", EX .$1,600.00 (B)

Corbin Lock, paper litho advertising sign, 24" x 20", 1890s, VG . . . .$101.00 (B)

Coreco Penn Motor Oil, painted tin strip sign with graphics of oil can at left of message, 21" x 7", EX .$500.00 (B)

Coreco Petroleum Products...Pennsylvania Motor Oils, one-sided porcelain sign advertising "6 quarts of service for the price of 4," 20" x 14", VG . . . .$350.00 (B)

Corona, painted tin die cut bottle sign, 5¼" x 20", EX . . . .$55.00 (D)

Comfort Medicated Talc powder, tin litho container with baby face on one side and nurse on other side, 2" x 3⅜", EX, $775.00 (B). *Courtesy of Wm. Morford Investment Grade Collectibles*

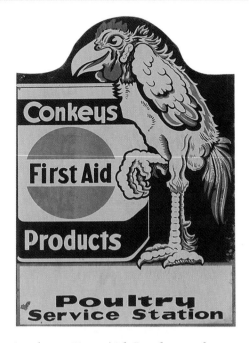

Conkeys First Aid Products, die cut painted metal advertising sign with graphics of old bird beside message, 14" x 20", VG, $150.00 (B). *Courtesy of Collectors Auction Services*

Consumer's Beer, ask father, artwork of man with glass of beer, embossed tin sign, from Consumers Brewing Co., Hills Grove, RI, 1940s, 28" x 9¾", NM, $275.00 (D). *Courtesy of Muddy River Trading Co./Gary Metz*

Cortez Cigars...For Men Of Brains...Made At Key West, metal tip tray, 6⅛" L, G . . . .$60.00 (B)

Corticelli Silk Thread, store display cabinet with pull-out drawer and lift top to show spool storage, graphics of silk worm and other messages on front drawer, unusual item, 20½" x 14½" x 4", EX . . . .$1,300.00 (B)

Corylopsis Talcum Powder Page, tin litho container, with artwork of geisha girl kneeling on front side of container, NM . . . .$193.00 (B)

Cottolene, metal tip tray with graphics of black woman and child picking cotton, 4¼" dia., EX . . . .$70.00 (B)

Cotton State Exposition, Atlanta Ga, match holder, depicts two boys by a bale of cotton sharing a watermelon, 2½" h, VG . . . .$425.00 (B)

Count Casper, die cut cardboard play advertisement, 8¾" x 13¼", 1900s, VG . . . .$95.00 (C)

Country Club Coffee, tin litho key-wound container, 1-lb., EX . . . .$25.00 (B)

Country Club...Smoking or Chewing Kentucky Long Cut, The Scotten Tobacco Co., Detroit, Mich., lunch pail with top-attached metal pail handle, 7" x 4¾" x 4½", EX . . . .$325.00 (B)

Country Club, tall cigar tin with country scenes on three sides, 50-ct., VG . . . .$125.00 (C)

Court House Turmeric, spice, cardboard with paper label, 1½-oz., EX . . . .$45.00 (C)

Co-op Motor Oil, single-sided embossed self-framing tin sign, 20" x 10", VG, $130.00 (B).

Coppertone, advertising clock with graphics of the Coppertone girl and her dog pulling down her swim suit to expose untanned areas, 36" x 36" x 8", EX, $1,600.00 (B). *Courtesy of Collectors Auction Services*

Corn King manure spreaders, paper litho advertising sign, 1908, 20" x 25½", G, $500.00 (B).

Covered Wagon, cardboard cigar box with great graphics of covered wagon scene on inside lid, 50-count, EX . . . .$40.00 (B)

Covington Bros. Co. Wholesale Grocers, Paducah, Ky., tobacco cutter, G . . . .$135.00 (C)

Cowan's Chocolate, paper advertising sign with well-dressed young girl in original "Cowan's" frame, 18" x 25½", EX . . . .$350.00 (B)

Cow Brand Baking Soda, heavy paper litho advertising sign by Church and Dwight Co., 18" x 14½", EX . . .$160.00 (B)

Cow Brand Baking Soda, sample size, unopened, 1¾" x 1" x 2½", EX . . . .$65.00 (C)

Cow-Ease, metal litho product display rack with example sprayer and graphics of man spraying livestock, 21" x 12" x 34", EX . . . .$750.00 (B)

C. Person's Sons Importers and Distillers, Buffalo N.Y. embossed tin litho advertising sign promoting Buffalo Club Rye Whiskey, 23½" x 34", EX . . . .$475.00 (B)

C. Pfeiffer Brewing Co...Detroit, Mich., round metal tip tray, with graphics of product bottle in tray center, 4" dia., EX . . . .$100.00 (B)

C.P.W. Motor Car Enamel, cardboard poster showing man with older model touring car, 17¾" x 21¾", EX . .$195.00 (C)

Corticelli Silk Thread, store display cabinet with pull-out drawer and lift top to show spool storage, graphics of silk worm and other messages on one drawer, unusual item, 20½" x 14½" x 4", EX, **$1,300.00 (B).** *Courtesy of Wm. Morford Investment Grade Collection*

Country Life Tobacco & Cigarettes, paper litho over cardboard advertising sign, British piece, 23" x 14¼", G, **$105.00 (B).**

Covington Bros. Co. Wholesale Grocers, Paducah, Ky., tobacco cutter, G, **$135.00 (C).** *Courtesy of B.J. Summers*

Crazy Cat, animated license plate attachment, die cut tin with tongue and eyes that move with the car's movement, 4¼" x 5⅛", EX . . . . **$135.00 (C)**

Crazy Water Crystals, Just add it to your drinking water, cardboard advertising sign with easel back, 9¾" x 13½", EX . . . .**$55.00 (D)**

Cream Buying Station, Swift & Company, double-sided porcelain sign, 41½" x 14½", white on blue, G . .**$195.00 (D)**

Creamo brand coffee, tin with pry-lid, 1-lb., EX .**$85.00 (C)**

Cream of Wheat, cardboard product box with graphics of waiter with a bowl of Cream of Wheat, 14¼" x 13½", VG . . . .**$50.00 (B)**

Cream of Wheat Rastus Doll, cloth doll framed, 33⅓" x 25", VG . . . .**$110.00 (B)**

Cream Peanut Butter, tin pail with wire bail handle, slip lid, EX . . . .**$85.00 (C)**

Crescent Flour, embossed tin, door push with graphics of sack of flour in center, 3¾" x 9¾", EX . . . . .**$295.00 (B)**

Crescent Macaroni, tin lunch pail with wire handles, G . . . .**$65.00 (D)**

Crescent Peanuts, tin container with top pry-lid, Crescent Nut & Chocolate Co., Philadelphia, PA, EX . . . .**$250.00 (B)**

Crescent Salted Peanuts, pry-lid container with graphics of crescent moon over star, 8½" x 9½", EX .**$125.00 (B)**

C. Person's Sons Importers and Distillers, Buffalo N.Y,. embossed tin litho advertising sign promoting Buffalo Club Rye Whiskey, 23½" x 34", EX, **$475.00 (B)** *Courtesy of Collectors Auction Services*

Crazy Water Crystals, Just add it to your drinking water, cardboard advertising sign with easel back, 9¾" x 13½", EX, **$55.00 (D)**. *Courtesy of Pleasant Hill Antique Mall & Tea Room/Bob Johnson*

Cream Buying Station, Swift & Company, double-sided porcelain sign, 41½" x 14½", white on blue, VG, **$210.00 (C)**. *Courtesy of Riverview Antique Mall*

Cresota Flour, die cut tin litho match holder with likeness of trademark boy slicing bread, 2½" x 5½", EX . . .$400.00 (B)

Cresota Flour...Prize bread of the world, tin die cut litho match holder with unusual vertical match pocket, 5½" x 2⅜", NM . . . .$575.00 (B)

Cresthaven Ice Cream, reverse glass light-up advertising sign, 14" x 6" x 4", EX . . . .$200.00 (B)

Crisco, porcelain advertising sign, die cut in likeness of Crisco can, "For Cooking...Better than Butter," 14" x 20", EX . . . .$4,500.00 (B)

Crispo Lily Sodas...Lily Biscuit Co., Chicago, cracker tin with lid, red and white striped, G . . . .$35.00 (D)

Crosley Radios and Home Appliances, neon advertising sign, metal back with glass front, G . . . .$525.00 (D)

Crown Gold Gasoline, metal advertising sign with graphics of small boy, 20" x 11½", EX . . . .$175.00 (C)

Crown Quality Ice Cream, embossed tin advertising sign in wood frame, Anderson and Patterson Mfgs., Worcester, Mass., 21" x 29", VG . . . .$500.00 (B)

Crubro Apple Butter, cardboard litho trolley car advertisement with graphics of young girl with several geese, 19½" x 12", EX . . . .$75.00 (B)

Crush...ask for a ...natural flavor...natural color, metal, raised lettering strip advertising sign, 26½" x 3½", VG . . . .$60.00 (B)

Crown Quality Ice Cream, embossed tin advertising sign, 18" x 24", G, $155.5 (B).

Crown Quality Ice Cream, embossed tin advertising sign in wood frame, Anderson and Patterson Mfgs., Worcester, Mass., 21" x 29", VG, $500.00 (B). *Courtesy of Collectors Auction Services*

Crystal Club Pale Dry Ginger Ale, painted metal advertising sign with dial-type thermometer located in neck of bottle, 7" x 27", EX, $100.00 (C).

Crush, thermometer, aluminum and plastic dial-type scale with graphics of half-sliced orange above product name in center of dial, 1950s, 12½" dia., NM . . . .$37.00 (B)

Crush...Thirsty...Crush that thirst, painted metal thermometer with Crush cap at top of vertical scale, EX . . . .$45.00 (C)

Crystal Club Pale Dry Ginger Ale, painted metal advertising sign with dial-type thermometer located in neck of bottle, 7" x 27", EX . . . .$100.00 (C)

Cuban Seal, For Satisfaction, cigar tin, G . . . .$35.00 (D)

Cudahy's Diamond "C" Hams, die cut tin litho double-sided flange advertising sign featuring graphics of young woman with a platter of product, hard-to-find item, EX . . . . .$2,800.00 (B)

Cunningham's Ice Cream, The Factory Behind The Products, metal serving tray with graphics of manufacturing factory in center, oval-shaped, 1917, 18½" x 15", EX . . . .$110.00 (B)

Cupid Bouquet, little cigars, flat pocket tin with graphics of cupid in lower right corner, 3½" x 3¼" x ⅜", EX . . . .$55.00 (B)

Cupid Coffee, paper litho on tin container from Excelsior Mills, E.B. Millar Co., Chicago, with graphics, naturally, of Cupid grinding coffee, 1900s, 3¾" x 6¾", EX .$175.00 (B)

Cupples Co., arrow tobacco cutter, EX . . . . .$120.00 (D)

CV Beer, pressed board advertising with graphics of black man drumming, 16½" x 10½", EX . . . .$110.00 (B)

CV...Please Pay When Served, embossed graphic of mother dogs and pups, Terre Haute Brewing Co., 16½" x 10½", EX . . . .$35.00 (B)

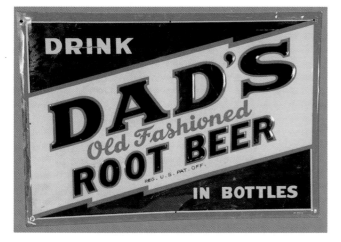

Dad's Old Fashioned Root Beer, painted tin sign, 26¾" x 19", VG, $245.00 (C).

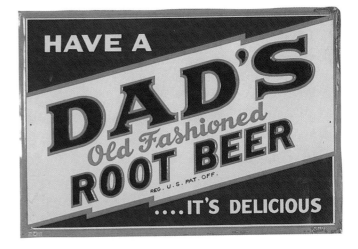

Dad's Root Beer, self-framing embossed tin advertising sign, 27" x 19", G, $160.00 (B).

Dad's Root Beer, self-framing embossed tin bottle cap and blank message sign, 20" x 28", G, $160.00 (B).

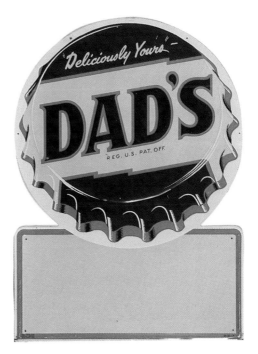

DAB, Imported German Beer, tapper handle, EX . .$25.00 (D)

Dad's Cookie Jar, embossed with "Property of Dad's Cookies," clear pyrex glass store jar, 10½" x 15", VG . . . . . .$165.00 (B)

Dad's Old Fashioned Root Beer, painted tin sign, 26¾" x 19", G . . . .$225.00 (C)

Dad's Root Beer die cut metal sign, likeness of bottle cap, "The old fashioned Root Beer," 20" x 28", EX .$235.00 (C)

Dad's...Root Beer...Diet, bottle cap sign, 29" dia., EX . . . .$85.00 (B)

Dad's tin litho embossed, self-framing advertising sign, "tastes like Root Beer should!," 31" x 12", EX . .$185.00 (B)

Daggett & Ramsdell's, display cabinet with great colorful tin litho front, scarce, 10½" H, EX . . . .$1,300.00 (B)

D. Agostini...Confectionery-Home Made-Ice Cream, paper calendar with metal top and bottom strips, images of American and Italian Lady Liberty, 15½" x 22", EX . .$55.00 (B)

Daily Double Cigars, tin litho container with horse racing scene, 4" x 5¼", EX . . . .$65.00 (C)

Daggett & Ramsdell's, display cabinet with great colorful tin litho front, scarce, 10½" H, EX, $1,300.00 (B). *Courtesy of Richard Opfer Auctioneering, Inc.*

Dairylea Ice Cream, die cut advertising fan with great graphics of cow jumping over the moon, ice cream cone handle, NM, $155.00 (B). *Courtesy of Buffalo Bay Auction Co.*

Dairy Made Ice Cream, you're sure it's pure, serving tray, great graphics of young girl eating ice cream, 10½" x 13½", EX, $325.00 (B). *Courtesy of Muddy River Trading Co./Gary Metz*

Dairy Brand...Ice Cream...New York, vanilla, half-gallon round tin, EX . . . .$20.00 (C)

Dairy Brand, Milk-Ice Cream, light-up sign, metal back with reverse painted glass front, 1950s, 25¾" x 6¾", G . . . .$250.00 (C)

Dairy Brand Roasted Coffee from Foley Bros. Grocery Co., St. Paul, Minn., with farm scene on front cover, with wood knob wire bail handle, 5-lb., EX . . . . . .$650.00 (B)

Dairylea Ice Cream, die cut advertising fan with great graphics of cow jumping over the moon, ice cream cone handle, NM . . . .$155.00 (B)

Dairymen's League, porcelain, one-sided member sign, 14" x 7", G, $40.00 (B).

Dan Patch Cut Plug, Scotten, Dillon Co., Detroit, tin, with graphics of horse and sulky, G, $25.00 (D). *Courtesy of Pleasant Hill Antique Mall & Tea Room/Bob Johnson*

Daisy Brand, One of America's Finest Dairies, light-up reverse painted glass sign, featuring small child on limb with birds singing the praises, 1950s, EX, $325.00 (C).

Courtesy of Michael and Debbie Summers

Dairy Made Ice Cream, embossed tin advertising sign with wood frame, "You're Sure-It's Pure" with graphics of baby with cone, 26" x 35", G . . . .$700.00 (B)

Dairy Made Ice Cream, you're sure it's pure, serving tray, great graphics of young girl eating ice cream, 10½" x 13½", VG . . . .$275.00 (C)

Dairy Made Ice Cream, "You're Sure-It's Pure," tin litho sign with graphics of young boy enjoying some ice cream, 19½" x 28", G . . . .$580.00 (B)

Dairymen's League Member, porcelain member sign, 14" x 7", NM . . . .$95.00 (C)

Daisy Brand, One of America's Finest Dairies, light-up reverse painted glass sign, featuring small child on limb with birds singing the praises, 1950s, EX . . . .$325.00 (C)

Daisy Hair Tonic, advertising sign, "Look your best-it pays," tin litho, 9" sq., 1915, VG . . . .$135.00 (C)

Dale Bros. Coffee, porcelain advertising sign with graphics of friar ready to enjoy a cup of steaming hot coffee, 42" x 14", EX . . . .$675.00 (C)

Damascus Ice Cream, die cut porcelain advertising sign, 1920s, 18" x 17", EX . . . .$1,400.00 (B)

Damascus Milk die cut double-sided porcelain advertising sign in likeness of two bottles of pasteurized milk, complete with hanging arm, 17¾" x 28½", NM .$1,950.00 (C)

Dandro Solvent...for dandruff and beautifying the hair, beveled edge tin over cardboard easel back, featuring product bottle in hand at right of message, 13" x 9", NM . . . .$175.00 (B)

Dandro Solvent, tin over cardboard advertising display with graphics of hand holding product bottle, design to be either string hung or mounted easelback, early tin litho, 13¼" x 9¼", EX . . . .$135.00 (C)

Dandy Cola, Enjoy Life, self-framed embossed tin advertising sign with graphics of Dandy Cola bottle, EX . . . .$150.00 (B)

Daniel Scotten & Co, "Fine Cut Chewing Tobacco," wood barrel with paper litho label with graphics of farmyard dance and young girl with horse, 16" dia. x 21½", VG . .$875.00 (D)

Daniel's Veterinary, advertising cardboard sign promoting their medicines, with graphics of dogs playing cards at round table, 18" x 13½", 1915, EX . . . .$165.00 (C)

Dan Patch Cut Plug, Scotten, Dillon Co., Detroit, tin, with graphics of horse and sulky, G . . . .$25.00 (D)

Deep-Rock Prize Oil, self-framing single-sided embossed tin sign, 27" x 19⅛", G, **$50.00 (B).**

Deering IHC, paper litho calendar featuring graphics of young woman with horse, initials carved into fence post, full calendar pad, 1912, 13¼" x 23¼", NM, **$440.00 (B).** *Courtesy of Buffalo Bay Auction Co.*

John Deere, single-sided porcelain advertising sign with trademark deer, 72" x 24", VG, **$1,050.00 (B).** *Courtesy of Collectors Auction Services*

Darmouth Chocolates...Demand, litho on canvas advertising banner with graphics of elves eating the product, 44" x 16", VG . . . .**$210.00 (B)**

Dauntless Coffee and All Food Products, painted canvas poster with graphics of Roman soldier, Terre Haute, Ind., Mattoon, Ill., 60" x 36", EX . . . .**$375.00 (D)**

David Bradley Mfg. Co., advertising card with graphics of young child with a small dog, 9½" x 7½", EX . .**$30.00 (B)**

Davidson's Bread, "Ask for...They're Different," heavy porcelain strip sign, 16" x 4", EX . . . .**$875.00 (B)**

Davidson's Chocolates & Bon Bons, tin on cardboard advertising sign with graphics of young girl smelling a flower, 13" x 19", EX . . . .**$345.00 (B)**

Dawsonia Toffee, tin with graphics of two black performers on front, slip-on lid, 5¾" x 3¾" x 6½", G . .**$35.00 (C)**

Dayton Cub Tires, die cut easel back cardboard advertising sign in shape of bear cub, 10½" x 20½", G .**$90.00 (B)**

Dayton Tires, light-up advertising clock features trademark triangle in center with horse head, metal body with glass face and cover, 15" dia., VG . . . .**$240.00 (B)**

Dead Shot Smokeless Powder, celluloid pinback with graphics of goose, ⅞" dia., EX . . . .**$60.00 (B)**

Decker Bros. Pianos, heavy paper advertising sign featuring graphics of young girl surrounded by a floral wreath, 1882, EX . . . .**$96.00 (B)**

Dee-Light...Drink, It's Delicious, painted tin sign with artwork of bottle in center, 6" x 17¾", G . . . .**$15.00 (D)**

Dee-Lights advertising painted metal sign with graphics of bottle in center, 6" x 17¾", EX . . . .**$35.00 (D)**

Deep-Rock Gasoline...Motor Oil, double-sided porcelain advertising sign, 32" x 24", VG . . . .**$375.00 (C)**

Deep-Rock Gasoline Oils-Greases, globe, high profile metal body with two glass lenses, 15" dia., G .**$205.00 (B)**

Defense Bonds, this year give a share in America, framed poster with artwork of Santa Claus promoting bonds and stamps, 24" x 30", VG, **$75.00 (C)**.

DeKalb Hybrid Corn, embossed painted tin sign, St. Thomas Metal Signs, Ltd., St. Thomas, Ont., featuring winged corn logo, 19¼" x 13¼", VG, **$155.00 (C)**.

De Laval Cream Separator, Local Agency, double-sided porcelain flange advertising sign, 18" x 26½", VG, **$775.00 (B)**.

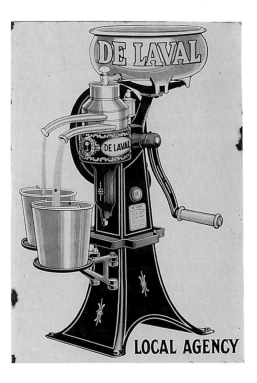

Deerfoot Farm Sausages, cardboard advertising sign with graphics of pig, 15¼" x 11", EX . . . .$93.00 (B)

Deering IHC, paper litho calendar featuring graphics of young woman with horse, initials carved into fence post, full calendar pad, 1912, 13¼" x 23¼", VG . . .$355.00 (C)

Defense Bonds, this year give a share in America, framed poster with artwork of Santa Claus promoting bonds and stamps, 24" x 30", EX . . . .$85.00 (C)

DeKalb, advertising signs, bolted together to form a single double-sided sign with bolted-on wings, 31⅜" x 16", VG . . . .$50.00 (B)

DeKalb Hybrid Corn, embossed painted tin sign, St. Thomas Metal Signs, Ltd., St. Thomas, Ont., featuring winged corn logo, 19¼" x 13¼", EX . . . .$175.00 (B)

De Laval advertising sign featuring a young farm boy and a couple of calves, 11½" x 16", EX . . . .$125.00 (C)

De Laval Cream Separators, die cut tin cow with advertising on back side of cow, 5½" x 3¼", VG, **$120.00 (B).**

De Laval Cream Separator, match holder, die cut tin, 4" x 6⅜", G, **$350.00 (B).**

De Laval, calendar top with the well-known classic lady and cow, advertising the cream separator, EX **$185.00 (C)**

De Laval Cream Separator, advertising calendar with full monthly pad and graphics of young boy and girl, 11⅞" x 23¾", 1916, EX . . . .**$650.00 (B)**

De Laval Cream Separator, die cut tin cow and calf with paper advertising about product, VG . . . .**$175.00 (B)**

De Laval Cream Separator, Jacob Bender, Sutton, Nebr., calendar top with great artwork of young boy with black dog in wagon, 1922, 12" x 19", EX . . . .**$85.00 (B)**

De Laval Cream Separators...The World's Standard, round metal tip tray with graphics of woman and child at product, 4¼" dia., EX . . . .**$140.00 (B)**

De Laval Cream Separators, tin litho advertising sign with great graphics and strong colors, 29½" x 40½", NM . . .**$2,700.00 (B)**

De Laval Cream Separator, tin litho advertising sign with gesso frame, "The De Laval Separator Co., 165 Broadway, New York and 42 Madison St., Chicago," 29½" x 41", VG . . . .**$1,150.00 (B)**

De Laval, die cut tin separator match holder, in shape of product, 4" x 6½", F . . . .**$275.00 (B)**

De Laval, early die cut tin litho hanging match holder in likeness of cream separator beside packaging box, 4" x 6¼", EX . . . .**$575.00 (B)**

De Laval, match holder, die cut in shape of cream separator, 4" x 6¼", EX . . . .**$225.00 (D)**

De Laval, metal tip tray with graphics of cream separator in center by the Savage Manufacturing Co., NY, "Over 750,000 in use," 4¼" dia., VG . . . .**$250.00 (B)**

De Laval Milker, decal on metal, lacquered double-sided sign, 1940s, 4¼" x 20", EX . . . .**$120.00 (B)**

De Laval, salesman's sample calendar for use in selling advertising with prices and info for 1921 on back, graphics of young boy with fish on front, 12" x 18½", 1919, EX . . . .**$350.00 (D)**

De Laval...We use...better farm living, better farm income, painted metal sign, G . . . .**$75.00 (D)**

Delaware Co. Fair...Manchester, Aug. 8-11, die cut embossed tin license plate attachment, 6" x 6¼", EX . . . .**$85.00 (C)**

Delaware Punch...Delicious Anytime, metal advertising clock, 18" x 14", F . . . .**$145.00 (D)**

De Laval Cream Separators, tin litho advertising sign with great graphics and strong colors, 29½" x 40½", NM, $2,700.00 (B). *Courtesy of Richard Opfer Auctioneering, Inc.*

Dentyne-Beeman's Pepsin, countertop gum display with die cut lady on each side of unit, 10" x 3¾" x 7½", 1920s, NM, $3,950.00 (B). *Courtesy of Buffalo Bay Auction Co.*

Delco...Battery Service, United Service Motors, painted metal advertising sign, with battery artwork in upper right corner, 30" x 22", NM, $225.00 (C).

Delco...Battery Service, United Service Motors, painted metal advertising sign, with battery artwork in upper right corner, 30" x 22", EX . . . .$175.00 (C)

Delco...the original equipment battery, two-sided painted advertising sign with graphics of battery in spotlight at lower left corner, 22½" x 18", G . . . .$140.00 (B)

Del Monte Coffee, key-wound container, graphics of natives and plantation around container, 2-lb., EX . . . . .$80.00 (B)

De-Luxe Blue-Ribbon, tin litho condom container with artwork of German shepherd on front cover, 1¾" x 2⅛" x ¼", EX . . . .$725.00 (B)

Denison's Coffee...Ask for, pennant, felt with message, 25", NM . . . .$82.00 (B)

DeNobili Cigar Company, embossed painted tin sign, message of "that different smoke," 3 for 5¢, 19" x 6", EX . . . .$25.00 (D)

Dentyne-Beeman's Pepsin countertop gum display with die cut lady on each side of unit, 10" x 3¾" x 7½", 1920s, NM . . . .$3,950.00 (B)

Derby gas globe, wide glass body with two glass lenses, and graphics of Derby star, 13½" dia., VG . . .$200.00 (B)

Derby Gasoline globe, wide glass body with two lenses, 13½" dia., EX . . . .$375.00 (B)

Desert Brand Java and Mocha Coffee, key-wound container from Browning & Baines, Wash., D.C. with desert scene on front, 1-lb., EX . . . .$130.00 (B)

Denver Sandwich Candy 5¢, single-sided embossed tin sign, 23¾" x 11¾", G, **$70.00 (B)**.

DeSoto Hotel Bath House, metal reflective advertising sign with applied lettering, "Fire Proof, Hot Springs, Ark.," 28" x 20", VG, **$185.00 (C)**. *Courtesy of Riverview Antique Mall*

Devoe Paints & Varnishes, double-sided die cut tin litho advertising sign with graphics of kneeling Indian with painted face beside Devoe Paints, 15" x 26", VG, **$1,900.00 (B)**.

Courtesy of Collectors Auction Services

Desert Gold Tobacco, tin litho container with graphics of horse head in cameo in center, 3-lb., EX . . . .**$550.00 (B)**

DeSoto Dealer Catalog, advertising "America's Smartest Low-priced Car," 11½" x 9", 1938, EX . . . . . .**$50.00 (B)**

DeSoto Hotel Bath House, metal reflective advertising sign with applied lettering, "Fire Proof, Hot Springs, Ark.," 28" x 20", G . . . .**$165.00 (D)**

DeSoto Plymouth Approved Service porcelain die cut dealer sign, 42" dia., 1930s, VG . . . .**$875.00 (B)**

Detroit Brewing Co. Bottled Beer, beveled tin on cardboard advertising sign with graphics of young lady in cameo sipping the product, 13" x 19", 1911, EX . . . .**$205.00 (B)**

Devoe Paints & Varnishes, double-sided die cut tin litho advertising sign with graphics of kneeling Indian with painted face beside Devoe Paints, 15" x 26", VG . . . .**$1,900.00 (B)**

Devotion Coffee, key pry-lid tin litho with graphics of couple ready for devotion, 1-lb., EX . . . .**$109.00 (B)**

DeWitt's Tonic Pills, easel back cardboard store advertising sign with graphics of fish and yellow-slickered fisherman, 13" x 21", G . . . .**$235.00 (B)**

Dexter's Bread, porcelain advertising sign prompting "Don't forget Dexter's Mother's bread," 18" x 24", EX . . . .**$220.00 (B)**

Diamond Dyes, advertising cabinet with tin litho front featuring artwork of the Page in the People's Court, 27" H, EX, **$700.00 (B)**. *Courtesy of Richard Opfer Auctioneering, Inc.*

Diamond Dyes, cabinet with tin litho front of little girl, 20" H, EX, **$1,300.00 (B)**. *Courtesy of Richard Opfer Auctioneering, Inc.*

D. Geisberg Millinery Shop, advertising dish with graphics of Indian on horseback looking at an airplane, 6¼" dia., EX . . . .$55.00 (C)

Diamond Chewing Tobacco, tin litho advertising thermometer, manufactured by Allen & Ellis, Cincinnati, 5" x 10", EX . . . .$400.00 (B)

Diamond Crystal Salt, advertising sign with image of champion cattle, tin litho with thermometer at left of message, 20" x 14½", VG . . . .$80.00 (B)

Diamond D Coffee, Dwinell-Wright Company, New York, N.Y., cardboard container, 1-lb., EX . . . .$25.00 (D)

Diamond Dyes cabinet, good strong graphics of washer woman, 22¼" x 29½" x 9¾", EX . . . . $1,225.00 (B)

Diamond Dyes, advertising cabinet with tin litho front featuring artwork of the Page in the People's Court, 27" H, EX . . . .$700.00 (B)

Diamond Dyes, cabinet with tin litho front of little girl, 20" H, EX . . . .$1,300.00 (B)

Diamond Dyes...Fast Colors...Domestic & Fancy Dyeing, wooden dye cabinet, front door cover has tin litho evolution theme, EX . . . .$850.00 (C)

Diamond Dyes, rare double-sided die cut advertising sign, EX . . . .$1,600.00 (B)

Diamond Dyes, wooden cabinet with embossed tin sign door, "The Standard Package Dyes of the World," EX . . . .$650.00 (B)

Diamond Dyes, wooden display cabinet with embossed tin litho front, great graphics show woman dyeing fabric at table, 29½" H, VG . . . .$1,800.00 (D)

Diamond Dyes, wooden display cabinet, with rare tin litho advertising on front door, by Wells and Hope Co., 30½" H, VG . . . .$1,500.00 (D)

Diamond Dyes, wooden dye cabinet with embossed tin sign on door, "It's easy to dye with...," 23" W x 30" H x 10" D, EX . . . .$775.00 (B)

Diamond Dyes, wooden dye cabinet with the "Evolution" tin litho on door, 1900s, EX . . . .$975.00 (C)

Diamond Dyes, rare double-sided die cut advertising sign, EX, **$1,600.00 (B).**

Courtesy of Wm. Morford Investment Grade Collectibles

Diamond Dyes, wooden cabinet with embossed tin sign door, "The Standard Package Dyes of the World," VG, **$575.00 (C).**

Diamond Dyes, tin display case, 18½" x 15⅝", VG, **$110.00 (B).**

Diamond Dyes, tin cabinet with litho on all sides, 18½" x 16" x 6¼", G . . . .$80.00 (B)

Diamond Match, tin litho container with graphics of family watching father as he uses the new striker, 4½" x 1⅝" x 2¼", VG . . . .$800.00 (B)

Diamond State Brewery, Wilmington, Delaware, tin litho deep dish serving tray with graphics of old man with stein and dog, 12" dia., EX . . . .$35.00 (B)

Dick Custer Cigars..."Holds You Up," litho container with graphics of Custer on front, EX . . . .$741.00 (B)

Diehl Beer, die cut cardboard framed advertising with waiter holding a tray with glasses and bottles of beer, 13" x 19½", VG . . . .$200.00 (B)

Diehl's Bread Sold Here, "It's Thoroughly Baked," porcelain sign, 24" x 12", EX . . . .$185.00 (B)

Diet-Rite Cola...sugar free, self-framing painted metal sign with bottle to left of message, 33" x 12", EX . . .$95.00 (D)

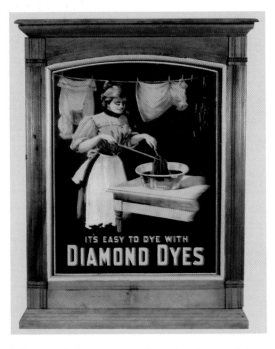

Diamond Dyes, wooden display cabinet with embossed tin litho front, great graphics show woman dyeing fabric at table, 29½" H, EX, **$2,400.00 (B).** *Courtesy of Richard Opfer Auctioneering, Inc.*

Diamond Dyes, wooden display cabinet, with rare tin litho advertising on front door, by Wells and Hope Co., 30½" H, EX, **$2,300.00 (B).** *Courtesy of Richard Opfer Auctioneering, Inc.*

Dill's Foot Powder, tin litho container with image of foot in cameo in center of container, 2½" x 4⅝" x 1⅜", EX . . . .$110.00 (B)

Dilworth's Golden Urn Coffee, tin litho container with screw-on lid, 1-lb., EX . . . .$200.00 (B)

Dimitrino, tobacco tin, super graphics, street scene on one side and carpet scene on other side, 5" x 5" x 1½", EX . . . .$135.00 (C)

Dining Car coffee, tin litho can with key-wound lid, with graphics of black waiter serving the product in railroad dining car, 1-lb., EX . . . .$125.00 (D)

Diplomat Whiskey, "Just Right," tin litho in early gesso frame, "Glasner Barzen Distilling and Importing Co., Kansas City, Mo." with graphics of men seated around table, 50" x 37½", VG . . . .$550.00 (B)

Dixie Gasoline, Oils, Power to Pass, oval double-sided sign on original stand, 24" x 46", F . . . .$450.00 (D)

Dixie Kid Cut Plug, lithographed tin pail with wire handle "He was bred in old Kentucky," 8" x 5½" x 4", VG $400.00 (B)

Dixie 1¢ Bubble Gum, store display box, 7" x 7" x 3", EX . . . .$50.00 (B)

Dixie Queen Pipe Cut, tobacco canister with small top, 4¾" x 6¼", EX . . . .$385.00 (B)

Dixie Salted Nuts Peanuts tin, graphics of young black boy holding peanuts in his mouth, #10 pry lid from Wilkes-Barre Can Co., EX . . . .$350.00 (C)

Dixie Tailoring Co. pocket advertising mirror with graphics of Statue of Liberty, "made to measure clothes," 1¾" x 2¾", EX . . . .$120.00 (B)

Dixon's Stove Polish, advertising sign with group of men gathered around a stove, 6¼" x 5", EX . . . .$85.00 (D)

Dixon's Stove Polish, Lime Kiln Club, trade card with graphics of sales pitch for product, 1886, 5" x 6¼", NM . . . .$50.00 (B)

D.M Ferry & Co., wooden seed box with great paper litho on inside lid, 11½" x 9¾" x 6¾", EX . . . .$350.00 (D)

D.M. Ferry Flower Seeds, countertop display wood box with paper litho label on inside lid, 12" x 7" x 4", NM . . . .$325.00 (B)

Diamond Dyes, wooden dye cabinet with embossed tin sign on door, "It's easy to dye with...," 23" W x 30" H x 10" D, VG, $695.00 (B).

Diet-Rite Cola...sugar free, self-framing painted metal sign with bottle to left of message, 33" x 12", NM, $135.00 (C).

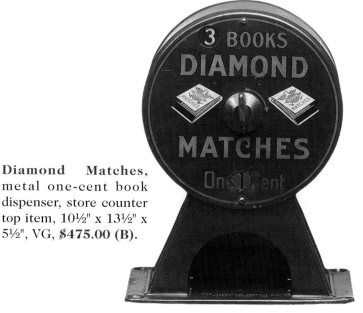

Diamond Edge Tools, advertising sign, embossed single-sided tin, "Hazel Lumber Co., Hazel, Ky.," 27½" x 9¾", VG, $35.00 (B). *Courtesy of Collectors Auction Services*

Diamond Matches, metal one-cent book dispenser, store counter top item, 10½" x 13½" x 5½", VG, $475.00 (B).

Dode Meeks Company, Livestock, advertising calendar with graphics of pretty young woman in center, unusual diamond shape, 11" x 11", 1906, EX ......$140.00 (B)

Dodge Dependable Service, double-sided porcelain dealer sign, 42" dia., EX ....$1,100.00 (C)

Dodge Plymouth Dependable Service...Dodge Trucks, round die cut porcelain dealer sign with arrow in center, 48" dia., 1930s, EX ....$1,600.00 (B)

Dodge...Plymouth, porcelain neon sign, 60" x 28", G ....$1,500.00 (B)

Dodger Beverage, die cut steel sign in shape of bottle, 16" x 65", EX ....$450.00 (C)

Doe-Wah-Jack, calendar with graphics of Indian in hunting scene, with full calendar pad, 10½" x 20¾", 1922, EX ....$360.00 (B)

Doe-Wah-Jack, Round Oak Stove, calendar with full pad of monthly tear sheets, featuring embossed artwork of Indian with peace pipe, 1924, 10½" x 21", EX ......$330.00 (B)

Dog 'n Suds, neon root beer stand advertising sign with graphics of dog with tray with frosty root beer and a hot dog, 8' x 7'6", EX ....$2,100.00 (B)

Dom Dom Benedictine Liqueur, single-sided porcelain advertising sign with graphics of bottle of product, 49" x 39", G ....$150.00 (B)

Domestic, metal litho tip tray, "it stands at the head," 4¼" dia., VG ....$205.00 (B)

District of Columbia Motor Club, safety poster, paper, 17" x 22", G, **$55.00 (C)**.

Dixie Milk, cardboard and paper advertising sign, 14" x 22", G, **$130.00 (B)**.

D.M. Ferry & Co. Standard Onion Seeds, paper litho advertising poster, 1911, 18½" x 30½", G, **$160.00 (B)**.

Domestic Sewing Machine, paper advertising sign, graphics and story line tell how great married life is if you have their product, 14" x 20", EX . . . .**$155.00 (C)**

Domestic Sewing Machine, paper litho advertising sign, "This is the machine that I'll have..." 1890s, 14" x 20", EX . . . .**$121.00 (B)**

Domestic Sew Machines, neon light-up store sign, on metal base, with domestic oil cans, EX . . . . .**$465.00 (D)**

Dominion Ammunition Co., black powder shell box for 28 gauge shotguns, 3¼" x 3¼"x 2½", EX . . . .**$95.00 (C)**

Domino, Smoke... The Mild Cigarette, Let your taste be the judge, framed die cut cardboard advertisement, 34" x 42", EX . . . .**$450.00 (C)**

Domino, The Mild Cigarette, die cut framed heavy cardboard sign, unusual and hard to find, 28" x 44½", EX . . . .**$475.00 (C)**

Donald Duck Beverages, self-framing metal sign with Donald Duck graphics with product message, 28" x 20", EX . . . .**$365.00 (B)**

Donald Duck Chocolate Syrup, tin with graphics of Donald Duck on the front, from the Atlantic Syrup Co., marked Walt Disney Productions, 15-oz., 1950s, NM . .**$120.00 (B)**

Donald Duck Coffee, tin litho container with graphics of Donald Duck on front, from Goyer Coffee Co., Greenville, Miss., 1-lb., VG . . . .**$230.00 (B)**

Donald Duck Cola... Tops for Flavor, die cut paper on cardboard with graphics of bottle cap to left of bottle sitting on ice, duck image on bottle, 22" x 26", EX . . . . . .**$77.00 (B)**

Donald Duck Florida Orange Juice, can with paper label with likeness of Donald Duck looking around juice glass, 1-qt., EX . . . .**$25.00 (B)**

Donald Duck High Grade Pure Coffee, key-wound lid, tin litho with graphics of Donald Duck on front, 1-lb., EX . .**$797.00 (B)**

Donald Duck Oats, paper label cardboard box bearing the image of Donald Duck, 3-lb., VG . . . .**$275.00 (B)**

Donald Duck Soft Drinks, celluloid/tin button advertising sign with graphics of Donald Duck in center, 9" dia., EX . . . .**$275.00 (C)**

Donald Duck Straws, with artwork of Donald Duck, Mickey Mouse, and Pluto on box with clear window to view contents, 3¾" x 8¾", EX . . . .**$45.00 (D)**

Donaldson Litho Company, salesman sample featuring advertising for fair at Newport, Ky., Aug., 5, 6, 7, 8, 1913, great graphics, 1913, 20" x 30", NM . . . .**$290.00 (B)**

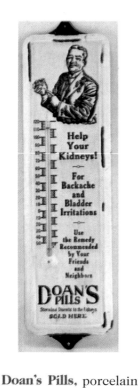

Doan's Pills, porcelain advertising thermometer, 6½" x 24", EX, **$195.00 (B).** *Courtesy of Collectors Auction Services*

Dodge Dependable Service, double-sided porcelain dealer sign, 42" dia., EX, **$1,100.00 (C).** *Courtesy of Autopia Advertising Auctions*

Dodger Beverage, die cut steel sign in shape of bottle, 16" x 65", EX, **$450.00 (C).**

Don Remo, change receiver, reverse glass image with cigar cutter on side, 9½" x 6", EX ....$302.00 (B)

Dortmunder Union, wooden tapper handle, EX ..$25.00 (D)

Double Cola...Drink, die cut tin flange advertising sign, NOS, 18" x 15", 1947, NM ....$575.00 (C)

Double Cola...Drink, Double measure, Double pleasure, metal door push bar, 34" x 4½", red on aluminum, EX ....$135.00 (D)

Double Cola...Drink, Ideal "slider," a great box because of its large capacity and small room, this particular version is painted in the 1940s scheme, restored, 1950s, 37" W x 42" H x 19½" D, yellow and black on red, NM ..$1,895.00 (D)

Double Cola...Drink, menu board with message at top center, 19¾" x 27½", green, white, yellow, and black, EX ....$160.00 (D)

Double Cola, Drink, painted metal flange sign, copyright 1947, The Double Cola Co., Chattanooga, Tenn., 18" x 15", NM ....$325.00 (C)

Double Cola, electric clock with the "Drink Double Cola" in center bull's eye, 12" dia., 1950s, EX .....$155.00 (B)

Double Cola...Enjoy, metal self-framing menu board with message at top center, with burst coming from behind oval logo, 19½" x 28", white lettering on red oval, black, EX ....$125.00 (D)

Double Cola...Make it a Double...or nothing, painted metal thermometer, red & white, G ....$75.00 (C)

Double Cola, painted V-shaped metal wall sign, "Drink Double Cola," 32" x 20", VG ....$275.00 (B)

Double Cola...Swell Drink...We Think, advertising spare tire cover with silkscreen graphics of the Double Cola twins, 27" dia., EX ....$35.00 (B)

Double-Orange, Truly Delightful, round cardboard sign, artwork by Rolf Armstrong, 1920s, 18" dia., EX ...$190.00 (B)

Double Tip, Distributed By Department Sales, Co., New York, NY, condom tin with litho of woman sitting at water's edge, 2¼" x 1⅝", EX ....$750.00 (B)

Domestic Sew Machines, neon light-up store sign, on metal base, with domestic oil cans, NM, **$495.00 (C).**

Courtesy of Riverview Antique Mall

Domino, The Mild Cigarette, die cut framed heavy cardboard sign, unusual and hard to find, 28" x 44½", EX, **$475.00 (C).**

Donaldson Litho Company, salesman sample featuring advertising for fair at Newport, Ky., Aug., 5, 6, 7, 8, 1913, great graphics, 1913, 20" x 30", NM, **$290.00 (B).** *Courtesy of Muddy River Trading Co./Gary Metz*

Douglas Aviation Tested Gasoline, porcelain pump sign, 12" x 12", NM . . . .$675.00 (C)

Douglas Aviation Tested Regular Gasoline, aluminum gas pump sign, 12½" x 18", NM . . . .$675.00 (C)

Douglas Blend Gasoline, embossed aluminum pump sign, 14" x 10", NM . . . .$450.00 (C)

Douglas Premium Gasoline, embossed aluminum pump sign, 10" x 10", G . . . .$125.00 (C)

Dove Brand Meats, tin litho advertising sign with likeness of woman holding doves, for the Roth Meat Packing Co., Cincinnati, 19⅝" x 27¾", EX . . . .$775.00 (C)

Dove Spice, tin with litho of pair of doves on label, Cincinnati, O., 2-oz., EX . . . .$135.00 (C)

Dow and Company, desk top ashtray with graphics of steam roller, 5" x 5½" x 3½", VG . . . .$40.00 (B)

Dr. A.C. Daniels', heavy cardboard sign with artwork of horses in center inset with the message surrounding the artwork, 13⅞" x 19⅝", EX . . . .$650.00 (B)

Dr. A.C. Daniels' Horse and Dog Medicines, wooden sign with wood frame, 30½" x 18¼", G . . . .$400.00 (B)

Dr. A. C. Daniels', tin litho tip advertising tray advertising horse and cattle medicines, with images of horses in center, 4¼" dia., EX . . . .$145.00 (D)

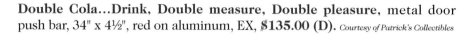

Double Cola...Drink, Double measure, Double pleasure, metal door push bar, 34" x 4½", red on aluminum, EX, **$135.00 (D).** *Courtesy of Patrick's Collectibles*

Double Cola...Drink, menu board with message at top center, 19¾" x 27½", green, white, yellow, and black, NM, **$195.00 (C).**

Double Cola, Drink, painted metal flange sign, copyright 1947, The Double Cola Co., Chattanooga, Tenn., 18" x 15", NM, **$325.00 (C).**

Dr. A.C. Daniels' Veterinary Medicine, wooden advertising thermometer, 5⅝" x 24" x ¾", G . . . .**$300.00 (B)**

Drake's Palmetto Wine, advertising match holder with graphics of goose in flight, 3½" x 4¾", VG . . .**$145.00 (D)**

Drako Coffee, tin litho with slip-on lid, graphics of duck on front label, 1-lb., EX . . . .**$185.00 (C)**

Dr. Collis Brown's Chlorodyne, porcelain advertising sign for their medicine that is good for all sorts of ailments, 14" x 14", EX . . . .**$125.00 (C)**

Dr. Daniels', advertising store card promoting dog medicine with graphics of dogs playing baseball with dogs as spectators in the bleachers, 15" x 12", EX . . .**$175.00 (C)**

Dr. Daniels', advertising store card promoting his line of dog medicine with graphics of dogs playing football, 20" x 14", EX . . . .**$225.00 (C)**

Dr. Daniels', dog and cat remedy, tin cabinet featuring strong graphics of woman and pets, 20" x 14" x 5", EX . . . .**$2,100.00 (C)**

Dr. Daniels', medicine cabinet with tin litho on front with images of Dr. Daniels and his cures, 21½" x 7¾" x 28½", EX . . . .**$1,925.00 (B)**

Dr. Daniels' Veterinary Medicines, wood and tin store cabinet complete with original products, front tin has graphics of Dr. Daniels and some of his medicines, 21½" x 8" x 28¾", VG . . . .**$3,300.00 (B)**

Dr. D. Jaynes Family Medicine, glass advertising sign with wood frame, gold lettering, 21¾" x 21½", EX .**$175.00 (C)**

Dreibus Juanette Chocolates, die cut easel back cardboard store advertising sign with woman in bonnet, 8" x 14", EX . . . .**$47.00 (B)**

Dr. Graves tooth powder, reverse foil on black glass advertising sign. "Dr. E.L. Graves unequaled tooth powder," 12" x 22" x ¼", 1900s, NM . . . .**$495.00 (C)**

Drink City Club, advertising wheel cover from West Union, IA, 28", EX . . . .**$70.00 (B)**

Double Cola, embossed self-framing tin sign with wood backing, 45" x 45", G, **$150.00 (B).**

Double Cola menu board, single-sided self-framing, 20" x 28", VG, **$70.00 (B).**

Double-Orange, Truly Delightful, round cardboard sign, artwork by Rolf Armstrong, 1920s, 18" dia., EX, **$190.00 (B).** *Courtesy of Muddy River Trading Co./Gary Metz*

Dauntless Coffee, Food Products, cardboard litho, 18¾" x 10¾", VG, **$35.00 (B).** *Courtesy of Collectors Auction Services*

Drink Coca-Cola in bottles...Quality you can trust, cardboard advertising poster in original frame, 1950s, VG . . . .**$160.00 (B)**

Dri-Powr, dial advertising thermometer with the dri-powr genie, from the Pam Clock Co., 12" dia., 1958, EX .**$150.00 (B)**

Dr. Jayne's Family Medicines, stone litho advertising sign with graphics of Martha Washington with the original Dr. Jayne's stamped mat and in vintage frame, 16" x 20", 1900s, EX . . . .**$300.00 (B)**

Dr. Kilmers Indian Cough Cure, amber glass container with paper label with graphics of Indian tribe on the move, 2½" x 5½", 1870s, EX . . . .**$95.00 (C)**

Dr. King's, tin litho match holder with graphics of large brick building on front by H.D Beach, 3½" x 5", VG . . . .**$120.00 (B)**

Dr. Miles Nervine, advertising die cut cardboard sign of young girl in early attire holding a bottle of the product, 9" x 21", 1902, EX . . . .**$225.00 (C)**

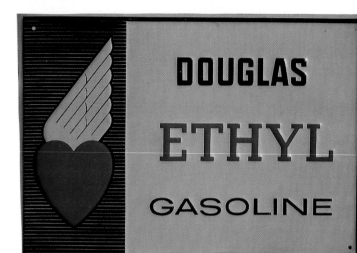

Douglas Ethyl Gasoline, embossed tin sign, 14" x 10", G, $350.00 (B).

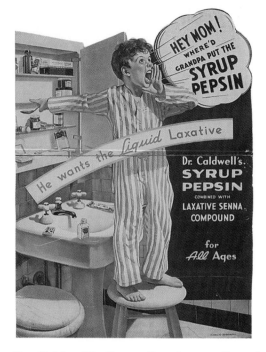

Dr. Caldwell's Syrup Pepsin, cardboard die cut stand-up countertop sign, 27" x 37", G, $125.00 (B).

Dr. A.C. Daniels' Horse and Dog Medicines, wooden sign with wood frame, 30½" x 18¼", G, $400.00 (B).

Dr. Morse's, advertising die cut cardboard sign with easel back promoting Indian Root pill, featuring graphics of Indian in canoe, 19½" x 9½", EX . . . .$225.00 (C)

Dr. Morse's Indian Root Pills, die cut cardboard advertising with easel back, graphics of Indian paddling a canoe, 19½" x 9½", EX . . . .$170.00 (B)

Dr. Morse's Indian Root Pills, tri-fold cardboard die cut countertop advertising with graphics of Indian preparing a meal, 41½" x 27", VG . . . .$550.00 (B)

Dr. Morse's Root Pills, cardboard sign, has great graphics of Indian activities, easel back countertop design, 24½" x 13", EX . . . .$153.00 (B)

Drobish Bros., nickel drop cigar trade stimulator in oak cabinet, 14½" x 19½", 1897, NM . . . .$2,750.00 (D)

Droste's Cocoa, tin container with graphics of Dutch girl on front, 1-lb., VG . . . .$25.00 (C)

Dr. Palmers Almomeal Compound, tin litho container in original box with great art of pretty red-haired woman on front, NM . . . .$25.00 (B)

Dr. Pepper, A lift for life, double-sided cardboard sign in original wood frame, with 10, 2, and 4 o'clock at top, 1950s, 31½" x 19", NM . . . .$400.00 (B)

Dr. Pepper...and Ice Cream, paper ad in original aluminum frame with logo at top, graphics of product in ice, 1950s, 22" x 17", EX . . . .$66.00 (B)

Dr. Pepper, cardboard hanging sign with artwork of clock face 10, 2 & 4 hands, 13" x 13", circa 1920s, VG . . . .$3,100.00 (B)

Dreikorn's Good Bread, single-sided tin sign with rolled lip, 27½" x 16", EX, $90.00 (B).

Dr. Morse's, advertising die cut cardboard sign with easel back promoting Indian Root pill, featuring graphics of Indian in canoe, 19½" x 9½", EX, $225.00. *Courtesy of Buffalo Bay Auction Co.*

Drobish Bros. Nickel, drop cigar trade stimulator in oak cabinet, 14½" x 19½", 1897, EX, $2,000.00. *Courtesy of Past Tyme Pleasures*

Dr. Pepper, clock in the art deco style with reverse painted glass front, electric, rare, 1930s, 22" x 17", G . . . .$2,100.00 (C)

Dr. Pepper...Drink, Frosty Cold, metal thermometer, 10" x 25½", white, red, and black, G . . . .$250.00 (D)

Dr. Pepper, Drink...Good for Life...Drink a bite to eat at 10–2–4, 3" x 3" x 6", NM . . . .$182.00 (B)

Dr. Pepper...Drink Good for life, porcelain sign, 26½" x 10½", EX . . . .$185.00 (D)

Dr. Pepper...Drink...Good For Life, tin litho emergency plate with original paper insert for emergency numbers, 4" x 8", EX . . . .$231.00 (B)

Dr. Pepper...Drink, metal picnic cooler with top wire bail handle, 18" x 12" x 9", white on green, G . . . . .$75.00 (D)

Dr. Pepper...Drink, tin litho advertising sign with chevron under product message, 27¾" x 11¾", NM . . . .$71.00 (B)

Dr. Pepper, embossed tin die cut advertising thermometer with image of bottle and scale in neck of bottle, 5⅛" x 17¼", EX . . . .$325.00 (C)

Dr. Pepper, embossed tin self-framing advertising sign with trademark 10, 2 & 4 dial and image of embossed bottle with dial, 18" x 53½", G . . . .$250.00 (C)

Dr. Pepper...Frosty Cold, metal scale-type advertising thermometer, 9¾" x 25.675", VG . . . .$90.00 (B)

Dr. Pepper, glo glass brand glass sign, "Energy-up Drink Dr. Pepper, Good For Life, Ice Cold," 1930s, 14" x 11", P . . . .$250.00 (D)

Dr. Pepper...good for life, embossed tin litho sign, 19¼" x 7", EX . . . .$375.00 (C)

Dr. Pepper, A lift for life, double-sided cardboard sign in original wood frame, with 10, 2, and 4 o'clock at top, 1950s, 31½" x 19", EX, **$375.00 (C)**. *Courtesy of Muddy River Trading Co./Gary Metz*

Dr. Pepper, cardboard hanging sign with artwork of clock face, hands at 10, 2 & 4, 13" x 13", circa 1920s, VG, **$3,100.00 (B)**. *Courtesy of Muddy River Trading Co./Gary Metz*

Dr. Pepper, clock in the art deco style with reverse painted glass front, electric, rare, 1930s, 22" x 17", EX, **$3,700.00 (B)**.
Courtesy of Muddy River Trading Co./Gary Metz

Dr. Pepper, Good for Life, embossed tin "tacker" style sign, 19½" x 4", 1945, VG . . . .$220.00 (B)

Dr. Pepper Good For Life, tin menu board with embossed bottle at left corner, 17¼" x 23¼", EX . . . . .$225.00 (C)

Dr. Pepper... Good For Life!, wooden bottle carrier with "Loaned Not Sold Deposit Returnable" message on handle, rare and hard to find, 12-package, 15¼" x 5¼" x 9¼", EX . . . .$275.00 (D)

Dr. Pepper... Have a Picnic, New York World's Fair poster with artwork of picnic scene, EX . . . .$30.00 (D)

Dr. Pepper... Hot or Cold, painted metal advertising scale-type thermometer, 8¼" x 27", G . . . .$95.00 (C)

Dr. Pepper... Hot or Cold, painted metal thermometer with Dr. Pepper logo in oval at bottom center, red & white, G . . . .$65.00 (D)

Dr. Pepper Hot or Cold, tin advertising thermometer, NOS, 5⅛" x 26⅝", NM . . . .$275.00 (C)

Dr. Pepper, light-up advertising clock, "Drink Dr. Pepper" banner at bottom, metal body with glass cover and face, 15½" sq., EX . . . .$120.00 (B)

Dr. Pepper, die cut plastic and metal light-up advertising clock, 11½" dia., G, $155.00 (B).

Dr. Pepper...Drink, Frosty Cold, metal thermometer, 10" x 25½", white, red, and black, F, $200.00 (C).

Dr. Pepper...Drink, metal picnic cooler with top wire bail handle, 18" x 12" x 9", white on green, VG, $95.00 (D). *Courtesy of Patrick's Collectibles*

Dr. Pepper, neon advertising clock with metal back and glass face and front, 6" x 21½", VG . . . .$850.00 (B)

Dr. Pepper, paper calendar with artwork of girl in bowling alley holding a bottle of Dr. Pepper, 1961, 16" x 23½", EX . . . .$45.00 (C)

Dr. Pepper, plastic store window advertising, 13" x 9½", EX . . . .$45.00 (C)

Dr. Pepper, porcelain advertising sign with early block background, "Drink Dr. Pepper...good for life," 26½" x 10½", EX . . . .$255.00 (C)

Dr. Pepper, porcelain advertising sign with the 10, 2, 4 image, 10" dia., EX . . . .$185.00 (B)

Dr. Pepper, self-framed porcelain advertising sign, "Drink," 24" x 9¼", VG . . . .$65.00 (B)

Dr. Pepper, Telechron advertising clock with metal body and bubble glass cover, name in center of face in plaid logo, 13½" dia., 1930s, NM . . . .$450.00 (C)

Dr. Pepper, Telechron electric clock with message under hands stem, 1930s, NM . . . .$350.00 (B)

Dr. Pepper...When Hungry, Thirsty or Tired, painted metal thermometer with bottle facsimile at right of scale, 10–2–4 dial at bottom left, G . . . .$65.00 (C)

Dr. Pierce's Favorite Prescription, litho paper advertising sign, in girlhood, womanhood, and motherhood, For Sale Here, great colorful graphics, 11¼" x 48", G . .$1,200.00 (B)

Dr. Pierce's Prescription, decal on window glass, features woman in a flared glass with a glass holder, 1890s, EX . . . .$2,800.00 (D)

Dr. Scholl's, store countertop display glass front metal case with graphics of products that are carried inside, complete with Dr. Scholl's Plant Jr. Massage and Foot Strengthener, 14½" x 10¾" x 23", VG . . . . .$450.00 (B)

Dr. Shoop's Health Coffee, tin litho match safe with great graphics of product package, never used, 3½" x 4⅞", NM . . . .$375.00 (B)

Dr. Pepper, glo glass brand glass sign, "Energy-up Drink Dr. Pepper, Good For Life, Ice Cold," 1930s, 14" x 11", EX, $2,500.00 (B). *Courtesy of Muddy River Trading Co./Gary Metz*

Dr. Pepper, Good for Life, embossed tin "tacker" style sign, 19½" x 4", 1945, VG, $220.00 (B). *Courtesy of Autopia Advertising Auctions*

Dr. Pepper...Good For Life!, wooden bottle carrier with "Loaned Not Sold Deposit Returnable" message on handle, rare and hard to find, 12-package, 15¼" x 5¼" x 9¼", VG, $255.00 (C).

Dr. Siegert's Bitters, tin advertising sign with image of product bottle, framed in vintage frame and under glass, 12" x 16", 1890s, NM . . . .$550.00 (B)

Dr. Stevenson Dentist, light-up advertising sign with original hanging arm, 25" x 14"x 2", 1930s, G . . . . .$60.00 (B)

Dr. Swett's, The Original Root Beer, embossed tin sign, 24" x 9", G . . . .$425.00 (B)

Dr. Townsend's Sarsaparilla, wood advertising thermometer, Brooklyn, NY, 5⅞" x 24", G . . . .$120.00 (B)

Drummond's Horse Shoe, die cut cardboard sign, in frame, 17" x 21", EX . . . .$170.00 (B)

Drummond Tobacco Co., Enterprise Mfg. Co., Philadelphia, Pat. April 13, 1875, EX . . . .$135.00 (D)

Dr. Warner's Health Corset Statue, chalkware statue on plaster base and product displayed around statue, patented Feb.,13,1877, copyright 1886, Hennecke & Co., Milwaukee, Wis., base 72" tall, statue 28" tall, 1880s, EX . . . .$5,500.00 (C)

Dr. White's Cough Drops...extremely pleasant, tin litho with hinged top container for product, hard-to-find item, 3½" x 2¼" x ¾", EX . . . .$600.00 (B)

Dry-Kold Refrigerator Company, porcelain sign, 22" x 11¾", EX . . . .$225.00 (C)

Dr. Pepper...I'd Give A Month's Pay For A..., cardboard poster in wood frame, WWII era, 28½" x 18½", EX, $350.00 (B).

Dr. Pepper, Telechron electric clock with message under hands stem, 1930s NM, $350.00 (B). *Courtesy of Muddy River Trading Co./Gary Metz*

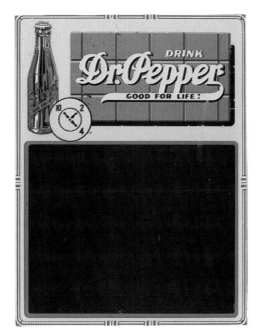

Dr. Pepper, tin over cardboard menu board, 17" x 23", VG, $155.00 (B).

Du Bois Beer, light-up advertising sign with curved glass front panel, Du Bois Brewing Co., Du Bois, Pa., 11" x 9¾", EX . . . .$175.00 (C)

Du Bois Budweiser, advertising sign, painted tin, 6" x 4", EX . . . .$35.00 (D)

Du Bois Budweiser beer, light-up sign, metal back with curved glass front, 11" x 9¾", EX . . . .$175.00 (C)

Du Bois Budweiser, light-up electric advertising clock, 15" dia., EX . . . .$325.00 (C)

Du Bois Expert Beer, self-framing tin sign, wood backed, "Ask for – Du Bois Expert Beer," 70" x 35½", EX . . . . .$100.00 (B)

Ducky Dubble, advertising paper over cardboard sign with graphics of popsicle, 18½" x 8", 1956, EX$135.00 (C)

Duke Beer, electric light-up advertising clock, diamond-shaped, 15¼" sq., EX . . . .$75.00 (C)

Duke of York Cigarettes, tin litho curved charger with graphics of the Duke in the center, rare item, 16" dia., EX . . . .$525.00 (B)

Dr. Pierce's Favorite Prescription, litho paper advertising sign, in girlhood, womanhood, and motherhood, For Sale Here, great colorful graphics, 11¼" x 48", G, **$1,200.00 (B).**

Courtesy of Richard Opfer Auctioneering, Inc.

Dr. Pierce's Prescription, decal on window glass, features woman in a flared glass with a glass holder, 1890s, G, **$2,400.00 (B).** *Courtesy of Muddy River Trading Co./Gary Metz*

Duke's Cameo, cigarette package, W. Duke & Sons, EX . . . .$110.00 (B)

Duke's Mixture, hard-to-find porcelain door push, "the roll of fame," with graphics of tobacco pouring from bag into man's hand, 5¼" x 8", EX . . . .$425.00 (B)

Duke's Mixture, paper litho advertising poster with graphics of black men and an old buggy, 22½" x 20", VG . . . .$425.00 (B)

Duke's Mixture, paper litho poster with graphics of men and buggy with black men "For de lawd ! Dis mus be what date nigger ment when he said he'd float de stock," 22½" x 20", VG . . . .$475.00 (B)

Duke's Mixture, paper litho with graphics of four black men in a buggy while the mule stands behind the buggy, 22½" x 20", VG . . . .$300.00 (B)

Duke's Mixture, sign, heavy porcelain with raised metal surface, Belt Enamel Co., featuring artwork of product, drawstring bag, 8¾" x 12", EX . . . .$525.00 (B)

Duke's Mixture, sign with graphics of blacks in a vehicle out of control going down a hill, 17" x 14", EX$145.00 (B)

Duke's tobacco mixture, advertising poster, 20" x 29¾", 1913, EX . . . .$75.00 (D)

Duluth Flour Sack, with graphics of black chef holding a platter of bread, 11" x 16", EX . . . .$55.00 (B)

Duluth Imperial Flour, tin lithograph with beveled edge and graphics of black chef holding the finished product hot from a bakers pan, hard-to-find piece, 18" x 25", EX . . . .$800.00 (B)

Duluth Imperial Flour, tin sign with graphics of baker using product, 18" x 25", VG . . . .$2,200.00 (C)

Dunham's Cocoanut, die cut paper advertising with graphics of lady with cake, 1915, 13" x 11", NM$84.00 (B)

Du Pont Authorized Agency, die cut porcelain double-sided advertising sign, 16" x 17¾", NM . . . . .$395.00 (C)

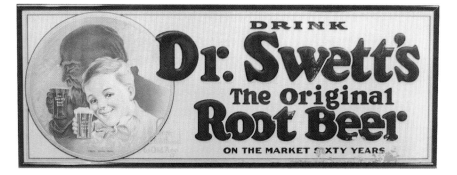

Dr. Swett's, The Original Root Beer, embossed tin sign, 24" x 9", G, $425.00 (B). *Courtesy of Muddy River Trading Co./Gary Metz*

Drummond's Horse Shoe, die cut cardboard sign, in frame, 17" x 21", VG, $155.00 (C).

Drugs, neon sign with neon border, 31½" x 10", VG, $75.00 (B).

Du Pont Auto Polishes, three-piece cardboard litho advertising poster with graphics of young black boy seeing his reflection in auto trunk, 37½" x 46", VG $2,100.00 (B).

Du Pont Car Polish, cardboard window display with graphics of young woman in shiny vintage convertible, 35" x 34½", EX . . . .$675.00 (B)

Du Pont Denatured Alcohol... Anti Rust Anti-Freeze, painted metal thermometer with scale in vertical arrow, messages at top and bottom, 8" x 38½", black, orange, and red, EX . . . .$95.00 (D)

Du Pont Generations, self-framed tin advertising sign with hunting scene of bird dogs in the field and different generations teaching and learning about hunting, by Edmund H. Osthaus, 23" x 33", EX . . . . . .$1,700.00 (B)

Du Pont Gun Powder, self-framed tin litho with graphics of father and son in field with bird dogs, 23" x 32½", NM . . . .$2,000.00 (C)

Du Pont paint, sign with hanging arm, light-up sign, 15" x 11½", EX . . . .$240.00 (B)

Du Pont, paper calendar with original metal strips with artwork of hunters with dogs, for DuPont Powder, partial calendar pad, 1907, 15" x 29¼", EX . . . .$633.00 (B)

Du Pont, paper litho advertising poster with graphics of young boys in a snowy field hunting, 14½" x 20¼", 1909, EX . . . .$625.00 (B)

Du Pont, paper litho poster advertising Du Pont Sporting Powders with image of older man and young boy resting from hunting on snow-covered log, 17" x 25⅜", EX . . . .$850.00 (B)

Du Pont Powders, cardboard advertising litho, part 2 of a six-piece set, graphics of general store scene, 13" x 8", 1909, EX . . . .$70.00 (B)

Du Pont Smokeless, celluloid pinback showing hunting dogs, "The Champion's Powder," 1¼" dia., NM $95.00 (C)

Du Pont Smokeless Shotgun Powder, titled The end of a good day, featuring artwork of hunting scene, framed, 1911, 18" x 27", EX . . . .$650.00 (B)

Du Pont Smokeless Shotgun, shell box with graphics by American Litho, 3½" x 3½", 1910, EX . . . . . .$100.00 (B)

Du Pont Sterling Spoon, with image of trap shooting in spoon bowl, marked Tiffany & Co., EX . . . . . .$75.00 (C)

Du Pont, stickpin of setter bird dog, rare item, 1880s, EX . . . .$225.00 (C)

Drummond Tobacco Co., Enterprise Mfg. Co., Philadelphia, Pat. April 13, 1875, EX, **$135.00 (D).** *Courtesy of Chief Paduke Antique Mall*

Dr. Wells, menu board, single-sided tin, "The Cooler Doctor," 18½" x 27", VG, **$35.00 (B).**

Dr. Wells The Cooler Doctor, self-framing embossed tin advertising sign, 31" x 11½", VG, **$95.00 (B).**

Du Pont Zerex, anti-freeze, cardboard die cut easel back countertop advertising sign with image of service man holding large can of product, 25½" x 32½", 1940s, EX . . . .**$150.00 (C)**

Duquesne Brewing Company... Duke Beer, metal back curved front glass advertising light-up clock, 16" x 16", EX . . . .**$55.00 (D)**

Duquesne Pilsner, metal and glass light-up sign, 24" x 6", EX . . . .**$125.00 (C)**

Duquesne Pilsner... The Finest Beer in Town, framed print, signed by Walt Otto, Duquesne Brewing Co., Pittsburgh, Pa., 1934, 29" x 32", G . . . .**$125.00 (D)**

Duquesne... The Finest BEER in Town, light-up advertising clock with reverse painted face, 24½" x 5½" x 18½", VG . . . .**$425.00 (B)**

Dutch Boy, full figure papier-mache advertising statue holding a pail of Dutch White, 9" x 8½" x 28", EX . .**$650.00 (B)**

Dutch Boy White Lead, advertising litho on cloth featuring Dutch Boy and painter, 26½" x 50", 1933, NM . .**$275.00 (C)**

Dutch Cleanser, decal on transom glass with trademark cleaning woman on both sides, 35½" x 14½", VG . . . . . .**$35.00 (B)**

Dutch Girl Coffee... Roasted and Packed by The Eureka Coffee Co., Buffalo, NY, cardboard can with tin top and bottom, with artwork of Dutch girl on front, 3" x 6½" x 4¼", EX . . . .**$130.00 (B)**

Dutch Java Blend Coffee, die cut cardboard litho with artwork of young boy holding basket, 6¾" x 8½", EX . . . . .**$190.00 (B)**

Dutch Java Coffee, pocket mirror, "Secret of Happiness" message on back, 2" dia., EX . . . .**$55.00 (B)**

Dutch Masters Cigars, self-framed tin litho hanging sign with image of Dutch pilgrims, 11" x 9", EX . . .**$66.00 (B)**

Dutch Master, paint, single-sided porcelain advertising sign with graphics of trademark Dutchman in center, 26" dia., EX . . . .**$325.00 (B)**

D-X, metal reflective license plate add-on, 5½" x 4", EX . . . .**$25.00 (D)**

Du Bois Budweiser, single-sided embossed tin advertising sign, graphics of product bottle, 13½" x 19½", G, **$65.00 (B).**

Duke's Mixture, hard-to-find porcelain door push, "the roll of fame," with graphics of tobacco pouring from bag into man's hand, 5¼" x 8", EX, **$425.00 (B).** *Courtesy of Buffalo Bay Auction Co.*

Duke's Mixture, sign with graphics of blacks in a vehicle out of control going down a hill, 17" x 14", EX, **$145.00 (B).** *Courtesy of Buffalo Bay Auction Co.*

Dunlop Tire, porcelain advertising clock, 39" dia., VG, **$210.00 (B).** *Courtesy of Collectors Auction Services*

Du Pont Auto Polishes, three-piece cardboard litho advertising poster with graphics of young black boy seeing his reflection in auto trunk, 37½" x 46", VG, **$2,100.00 (B).** *Courtesy of Collectors Auction Services*

Du Pont Car Polish, cardboard window display with graphics of young woman in shiny vintage convertible, 35" x 34½", EX, **$675.00 (B).** *Courtesy of Wm. Morford Investment Grade Collectibles*

Du Pont Explosives Dept., three months at a glance calendar, graphics of bird dog and short artist bio, 1960, 15" x 31", EX, **$25.00 (B).**

Du Pont Generations, self-framed tin advertising sign with hunting scene of bird dogs in the field and different generations teaching and learning about hunting, by Edmund H. Osthaus, 23" x 33", EX, **$1,700.00 (B).** *Courtesy of Past Tyme Pleasures*

Du Pont Smokeless Shotgun Powder, titled
The end of a good day, featuring artwork of
hunting scene, framed, 1911, 18" x 27", EX,
$650.00 **(B).** *Courtesy of Muddy River Trading Co./Gary Metz*

**Duquesne Pilsener...The Finest Beer in
Town,** framed print, signed by Walt Otto,
Duquesne Brewing Co., Pittsburgh, Pa.,
1934, 29" x 32", EX, **$140.00 (D).**

Dutch Boy Paint, single-sided embossed tin advertising sign,
EX, $250.00 (C).

Duty Calls, WWI paper advertisement
showing "doughboy" leaving home for war,
1917, G, $200.00 (C).

Edelweiss Beer, litho metal serving tray, 1913, 13½" dia., G, **$150.00 (B).**

Edgeworth Smoking Tobacco, Extra High Grade, heavily embossed tin sign, 27" x 11", EX, **$475.00 (B).** *Courtesy of Muddy River Trading Co./Gary Metz*

Edgeworth Smoking Tobacco, tin over cardboard sign with pipe image, 11" x 9", 1930s, VG, **$225.00 (B).**

Courtesy of Muddy River Trading Co./Gary Metz

Edison Mazda playhouse, from General Electric, designed to have Christmas lights placed inside for the illusion of interior lighting, 8" x 5½" x 9½", 1930s, EX, **$65.00 (B).** *Courtesy of Buffalo Bay Auction Co.*

Eagle Lye, pot scraper, VG . . . .**$90.00 (B)**

Early Times, great dimensional advertising sign of bridge with product name and log cabin across creek, Brown Foreman Distilling, Louisville, KY, 15½" x 12", 1939, EX . . . .**$325.00 (B)**

Eastern Briar Pipe Co., Whiz Mfg. Co., cardboard litho store display board with 12 Bakelite cigar holders, NOS, 9" x 10¼", EX . . . .**$65.00 (B)**

Ebbert Wagons, self-framing tin litho advertising sign, "In The Shade Of The Old Apple Tree," with graphics of horse-drawn wagon being filled with fruit, 37½" x 25½", EX . . . .**$2,900.00 (B)**

Ecco rolled oats, tin with graphics of bare foot boy with hands at mouth to yell, EX . . . .**$85.00 (C)**

Edelweiss Beer, metal litho serving tray with pretty woman and graphics for Schoenhofen Brewing Co., 13" dia., 1913, EX . . . .**$140.00 (B)**

Edgeworth Smoking Tobacco, Extra High Grade, heavily embossed tin sign, 27" x 11", EX . . . .**$475.00 (B)**

Edgeworth Extra High Grade Smoking Tobacco, advertising tin sign deeply embossed with graphics of a couple of older gents, 27¼" x 11¼", VG . . . .**$175.00 (C)**

Edgeworth Smoking Tobacco, tin over cardboard sign with pipe image, 11" x 9", 1930s, VG . . . .**$225.00 (B)**

Edison Mazda, calendar advertising light bulbs, 1926, 18" x 30", EX . . . .**$1,300.00 (C)**

Eisenhower Cigarettes, pack, unopened, with graphics of President Eisenhower on front label, 1950s, EX, $75.00 (C). *Courtesy of Buffalo Bay Auction Co.*

Egg-O-See Cereal, paper sign with image of youngster and pets, "Dere ain't goner be no leavins," 16" x 10", EX, $1,100.00 (C). *Courtesy of Buffallo Bay Auction Co.*

EIS Parts Brake Fluid, single-sided metal sign, 15" x 15", VG, $15.00 (B).

Ell-Ell Whiskey, self-framed tin litho advertising sign with graphics of ship at dock about to be loaded with the product, from Lemle Levy Co., San Francisco, an H.D. Beach litho, 28" x 22", EX, $1,450.00 (B). *Courtesy of Buffalo Bay Auction Co.*

Edison Mazda Lamps, cardboard calendar with Parrish-style litho of young girl in chair reading, with full calendar pad, 1917, 4" x 9", EX . . . .$175.00 (C)

Edison-Mazda...Name your car...I'll light it, service station counter display box with great artwork of woman holding box of bulbs, EX . . . .$695.00 (D)

Edison Mazda, playhouse from General Electric designed to have Christmas lights placed inside to give the illusion of interior lighting, 8" x 5½" x 9½", 1930s, EX .$65.00 (B)

Edison Phonograph, advertising sign featuring litho of woman listening, 20¾" x 28", EX . . . .$3,100.00 (B)

Edison Star metal polish, tin container, 2" dia. x 5½" h, VG . . . .$20.00 (B)

Effecto Auto Finishes, color display in the shape of wood-rimmed wheel with message in center, 25" dia., EX . . . .$595.00 (C)

E.F. Young Jr. Pressing Oil can, hair dressing oil to be used when pressing hair to keep hair from catching fire, graphics of young black woman, EX . . . .$55.00 (D)

Egg-O-See cereal, paper sign with image of youngster and pets, "Dere ain't goner be no leavins," 16" x 10", EX . . . .$1,100.00 (C)

Eichberg foot wear, die cut cardboard advertising calendar, graphics of young children, 7¾" x 14½", 1910, VG . . . .$125.00 (C)

Emerson Television and Radio, light-up advertising clock, 14" x 10¼", EX, **$350.00 (B).**

Ellwood Whiskey, oil on wood advertisement, out of Louisville, Ky., 1909, 26¼" x 32⅛", VG, **$575.00 (C).**

Empire Tobacco, cutter, EX, **$95.00 (D).** *Courtesy of Chief Paduke Antiques Mall*

Empire Oil Works, framed oil painting, from Reno, PA, 23½" x 18¾", VG, **$210.00 (B).**

Eisenhower Cigarettes, pack, unopened with graphics of President Eisenhower on front label, 1950s, EX . .**$75.00 (C)**

Eisenlohr's Cinco 5¢ Cigar, painted metal sign, 24" x 12", G . . . .**$65.00 (D)**

Eisman & May, die cut embossed advertisement for fashionable shoes with graphics of horse-drawn sleigh, 10" x 7½", EX . . . .**$165.00 (C)**

Electric Appliance Company...San Francisco...Electric Supplies...Automotive Equipment, wood advertising thermometer, 3" x 11½", EX . . . .**$40.00 (B)**

Electric Face Massage, heavy paper litho in old gesso frame, "sure death to all wrinkles and blackheads...35¢," with graphics of well-attired young man, 24½" x 28½", EX . . . .**$95.00 (B)**

El Gallo cigars, art plate with graphics of rooster, 1905, 10" dia., EX . . . .**$610.00 (B)**

Elgin Nat. Road Races, Aug. 29 – 30, 1913, felt cloth pennant with graphics of old vintage race car, 29½ x 11½", G . . . .**$350.00 (B)**

Empson's Ketchup, die cut cardboard advertisment, framed, 14" x 10", VG, **$145.00 (B).** *Courtesy of Collectors Auction Services*

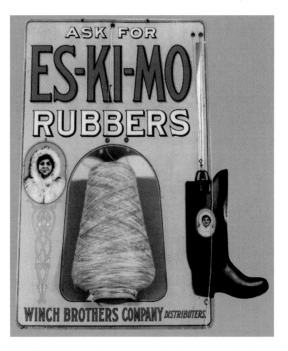

ES-KI-MO Rubbers, steel litho string holder, double-sided, 17¼" x 19¾", EX, **$4,000.00 (B).** *Courtesy of Richard Opfer Auctioneering, Inc.*

Esso "World's First Choice," canvas banner, 36" x 83", G, **$120.00 (B).**

Esso, dealer advertising calendar with full monthly peel, "P.P. Cassetty, Difficult, Tennessee," 9¾" x 16", NOS, NM, **$30.00 (B).**

Elgin Watcher, advertising sign with reverse painted glass in frame with the trademark "Full Ruby Jeweled," 23" x 29½", VG . . . .**$475.00 (B)**

Elgin Watches... Arthur J. Nyman and Sons Jewelers, round light-up advertising clock with message in center, number positions occupied by silver points, red, white, and cream, EX . . . .**$350.00 (D)**

Elgin Watches, neon advertising clock with metal body and reverse painted face, from Glo-Dial Clock Sales, 580 Fifth Ave., New York, N.Y., 22" dia., VG . . . . .**$225.00 (B)**

Eljer, Pam clock with glass face and metal back, "Eljer, fine plumbing fixtures," 15½" x 15½", 1963, EX . . .**$45.00 (B)**

Elkins Brewing Co., pint beer mug with advertising for the Elkins W. Va. Brewery on the front, 3¾" x 4¼", EX . .**$55.00 (C)**

Eureka Harness Oil, embossed tin sign, 20¼" x 5¼", G, $140.00 (B).

Esso Oil Drop Lady, single-sided die cut tin sign, 5¼" x 15¾", G, $275.00 (B).

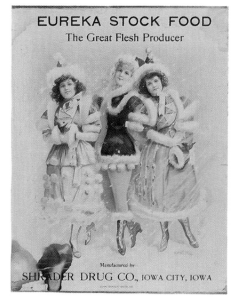

Eureka Stock Food, Shrader Drug Co., Iowa City, Iowa, paper advertisement, 15⅜" x 20¼", G, $80.00 (B).

Evening Star, paper single-sided embossed tin advertising sign, 13¾" x 9¾", VG, $65.00 (B).

Ell-Ell Whiskey, self-framed tin litho advertising sign with graphics of ship at dock about to be loaded with the product, from Lemle Levy Co., San Francisco, an H.D. Beach litho, 28" x 22", EX . . . .$1,450.00 (B)

Ellison's Flour, cardboard easel back store countertop advertising sign with graphics of swan in center between product packages, 24" x 13", EX . . . .$130.00 (B)

El Macco Cigars self-framing tin litho advertising sign with simulated wood grain surrounding center cameo of couple sitting together, 20¼" x 24", EX . . . . .$550.00 (B)

El Moriso Guaranteed Hi-Grade Cigar, cardboard advertising sign, 13½" x 10¼", EX . . . .$50.00 (C)

El-Myra Cigarettes, paper litho store advertising sign, "for goodness sake smoke...10 for 5¢," 13½" x 10", EX . . . .$150.00 (C)

Elreco Special, Gasoline, globe, "The El Dorado Refining Co.," wide glass body with two glass lenses, 13½" dia., G . . . .$200.00 (B)

El Regit Long Filled 5¢ Cigar, Alabama, felt pennant with graphics of tiger in tropics scene, 26" long, EX . .$135.00 (C)

Elsie Borden's Milk, double-sided cardboard advertising sign with graphics of Elsie home for the holidays, 25" x 30", EX . . . .$25.00 (B)

Elsie cookie jar with Elsie figural head on lid, 12" T, 1940, EX . . . .$190.00 (B)

Elsie the cow in the familiar flower collar, light-up clock, 17½" x 17½", VG . . . .$190.00 (B)

El Teano cigar, Liberty tin container, 6¼" x 4" x 5½", VG . . . .$75.00 (D)

Eveready Battery, display, extra long life flashlight batteries, metal with glass front, 9" W x 14" H x 10½" D, VG, $85.00 (C).

Eveready Flashlight Batteries, paper litho advertising poster, 22¼" x 32½", VG, $175.00 (B).

El Tino, store counter cigar cutter, reverse painting on glass, 8¼" x 6¾" x 5", VG . . . .$300.00 (C)

El Verso cigar, tip tray, graphics of man relaxing at home enjoying a cigar, 6½" x 4½", EX . . . .$145.00 (C)

El Verso... The Sweet & Mellow Cigar, metal tip tray with great graphics of man in easy chair enjoying product, 6⅝" long, EX . . . .$75.00 (B)

Emerson's Ginger Gum, in full store countertop display, 4¼" x 1" x 6", 1928, NM . . . .$450.00 (B)

Emila Garcia 5¢ Cigar, reverse glass and tin litho cigar holder that slips over a 50-count cigar tin, EX .$77.00 (B)

Emmerlings Beer, tin litho advertising sign with graphics of vintage German couple enjoying the product, 28" x 19½", EX . . . .$400.00 (B)

Empire Cream Separator Company... Fisher Building, Chicago, Ill., paper calendar top with artwork of mother and daughter, 1902, 12" x 20", EX . . . .$137.00 (B)

Empire Cream Separator, pinback, celluloid over metal with graphics of product in center, 1¼" dia., VG . . . .$40.00 (B)

Empire Milker advertising sign, "used on this farm," with graphics of milker, 19" x 13½", EX . . . .$120.00 (B)

Empire State Building... New York City, cast aluminum license plate attachment with shape of Empire State Building in left corner, 11" x 5¾", EX . . . . . .$155.00 (C)

Empire Tobacco, cutter, EX . . . .$95.00 (D)

Empress coffee, tin pail with wire metal handle, from Duluth, MN, 7½" x 9", VG . . . .$95.00 (C)

Empress Toilet Powder... Empress Powder Co., New York, NY, tin litho sample size can, 1⅝" x 2⅜" x ⅞", EX . . . .$450.00 (B)

Empson's Ketchup, die cut cardboard advertisement, framed, 14" x 10", VG . . . .$145.00 (B)

Enameline Stove Polish, advertising litho of young girl with puppy in front of advertising sign for the product, 13" x 23", EX . . . .$275.00 (B)

Enarco C-1 Motor Oil, embossed tin sign with image of Enarco boy at bottom with chalkboard, 10" x 36¼", EX . . . .$210.00 (B)

Eveready Radio Batteries, paper litho advertising poster, 1930s, 24" x 32", VG, **$220.00 (B).**

Ever-Ready Safety Razor, countertop display, tin litho with glass and wood, still contains early razor blades, 9½" x 11½", EX, **$1,100.00 (B).**

Evinrude Parts & Service, double-bubble light-up advertising clock, metal and glass, 15" dia., **$950.00 (B).**

Enarco Motor Oil, painted tin advertising scale-type thermometer with graphics of Enarco Boy with chalkboard at top of scale, NOS, 8" x 38¾", EX . . . .**$325.00 (B)**

Energee True Gasoline...The Pure Oil Co., metal flange advertising sign, 17½" x 20", EX . . . .**$475.00 (C)**

Enrico Projetti & Sons, Italian and American Grocery, advertising calendar with graphics of family and Santa Claus around the Christmas tree, full tear sheet, 14" x 20", 1915, EX . . . .**$255.00 (B)**

Enterprise Brewery, litho sign by Meek & Beach Litho, graphics of old cavalier seated in pub, 17" x 24", 1901, EX . . . .**$975.00 (C)**

Enterprise Salesman Sample Stove No/115, with gold raised lettering, 4" x 2¾", 1870s, VG . . . .**$25.00 (B)**

Erlanger Beer... Classic 1893, 13" x 10½", EX .**$15.00 (D)**

E. Robinsons Pilsner Beer tin litho serving tray with graphics of factory scene, 13⅛" dia., VG . . . .**$230.00 (B)**

Excelsior Brewing Co., tin litho metal serving tray, graphics of pretty young lady with glass of the product, 16¾" x 13¾", G, **$360.00 (B).**

Ex-Lax, porcelain thermometer with unusual horizontal scale, "Keep regular with Ex-Lax, the chocolated laxative," great graphics, 10" x 36" x 1", EX, **$550.00 (B).**

Courtesy of Muddy River Trading Co./Gary Metz

Ex-Lax, push and pull door signs, 4" x 8", VG, **$245.00 (B).**

Eskimo Pie, porcelain advertising strip sign, rare item, 36" x 6½", EX . . . .**$275.00 (C)**

ES-KI-MO Rubbers, steel litho string holder, double-sided, 17¼" x 19¾", EX . . . . **$4,000.00 (B)**

Esser's Paint, light-up advertising clock with graphics of painter in center, Pam Clock Co., 15" dia., VG . .**$150.00 (B)**

Essex Rubber Co., advertising clock, "Now is the time for magic rubber heels and soles," 14½" sq., VG . .**$180.00 (B)**

Esso, die cut tin litho advertising sign of Esso girl waving, 5¼" x 16", EX . . . .**$130.00 (B)**

Esso, double-sided porcelain advertising sign with graphics of company logo in center, 22" x 22", 1939, EX . . . .**$175.00 (B)**

Esso Elephant Kerosene, one-sided porcelain pump sign with graphics of elephant, 12" x 24", VG . . . .**$600.00 (B)**

Esso, "Fat Man," plastic bank, NOS, 5" tall, NM .**$100.00 (B)**

Essolene Gas globe, high profile metal body with glass lens, 15" dia., VG . . . .**$325.00 (B)**

Esso, plastic figure bank with product name on front, 6½" tall, red, EX . . . .**$95.00 (C)**

Esso...Put a tiger in your tank, plastic service station advertising banner, with artwork of Esso tiger, 42" x 83", EX . . . .$135.00 **(D)**

Esso...watch your savings grow, square embossed glass advertising block, EX . . . .$55.00 **(D)**

Estabrook & Eatons, Key West Cigar porcelain advertising ashtray, 4" x ¾", VG . . . .$45.00 **(C)**

Estey Organ Work, paper advertisement showing the factory, with gesso frame, from Ottmann Lith. Co., Puck Building, NY, 17" x 21", VG . . . .$110.00 **(B)**

Ethyl Gasoline, gas globe, wide hull body, 13½", G .$425.00**(B)**

Evans' Pastilles, single-sided porcelain advertising sign, "for all infections of the throat," 24" x 11", VG . . . .$350.00 **(B)**

Eveready and Mazda Lamps, product cabinet with graphics of batteries being placed in flashlight, 11" x 9" x 11½", EX . . . .$195.00 **(B)**

Eveready battery display, extra long life flashlight batteries, metal with glass front, 9"W x 14"H x 10½"D, G . .$75.00 **(B)**

Eveready Mazda Automobile Lamp Kit, metal case with spare lamps, product graphics on both sides, NOS, EX . . . .$30.00 **(D)**

Eveready Prestone, gallon metal can with original paper information sheet for car and radiator tag, 1-gal., EX . . . .$175.00 **(D)**

Eveready Prestone, tin container with graphics of vintage automobile and thermometer, 1 gal., EX . . . .$110.00 **(B)**

Everhart Confections, self-framing tin litho advertising sign with graphics of young girl, 13" x 19", EX $350.00 **(B)**

Ever-Ready Safety Razor, countertop display, tin litho with glass and wood, still contains early razor blades, 9½" x 11½", F . . . .$325.00 **(D)**

Eversweet, pin tray vintage accessory for lady's dresser with graphics of pretty young lady, 3½" x 5", VG . . . .$231.00 **(B)**

Evervess Sparkling Water...for your table at every meal, celluloid sign, a Pepsi-Cola product, 9" dia., EX . . .$250.00 **(B)**

Evervess...Yes, Yes!...Thank You...Evervess Sparkling Water, metal tip tray with artwork of Evervess bird with top hat and cane, EX . . . .$50.00 **(B)**

Everybody's Handsoap, paper ad with graphics of product can, 20" x 8", EX . . . .$95.00 **(B)**

Evinrude...first in outboards, painted metal double-sided flange sign, 26¼" x 15¾", EX . . . .$850.00 **(B)**

Evinrude...rowboat and canoe motors..., round metal tip tray "On The Crest Of The Wave," with graphics of product in action, 4" dia., EX . . . .$250.00 **(B)**

Exide Batteries, tin painted tacker sign, NOS, 19¾" x 9¼", NM . . . .$125.00 **(C)**

Exide Battery, metal double-sided flange advertising sign, die cut to battery image, 14" x 14", 1953, EX . .$275.00 **(C)**

Ex-Lax, porcelain door push with graphics of product package in center, 4" x 8", F . . . .$125.00 **(C)**

Ex-Lax, porcelain thermometer, "the chocolate laxative millions prefer," 8⅛" x 36⅛", EX . . . .$175.00 **(D)**

Ex-Lax, porcelain thermometer with unusual horizontal scale, "Keep regular with Ex-Lax, the chocolated laxative," great graphics, 10" x 36" x 1", G . . . . .$275.00 **(C)**

Ex-Lax...the chocolate laxative...millions prefer..., porcelain thermometer with vertical scale in center, EX . .$135.00 **(D)**

Ex-Lax...the chocolate laxative, porcelain advertising thermometer with small scale in center of sign, 8" x 36" x 1¼", EX . . . .$195.00 **(C)**

Eye-Fix...The Great Eye Remedy, round metal tip tray with artwork of woman being attended by angel image, 4⅛" dia., EX . . . .$250.00 **(B)**

Eze-grape drink, string hanger featuring graphics of bundle of grapes and bottle of product, 7½" x 9¾", EX . .$45.00 **(D)**

Fairway golf balls, store display for floor use, with graphics of young black caddy pulling the flag, United States Rubber Co., 25" x 48", 1920s, EX, **$550.00 (B).**

Courtesy of Buffalo Bay Auction Co.

Falstaff Beer, an old friend!, paper advertising sign, VG, **$55.00 (D).** *Courtesy of Pleasant Hill Antique Mall & Tea Room/Bob Johnson*

Fashion Cut Plug Tobacco, lunch pail with top handle, graphics of smartly dressed couple walking, 7½" x 5" x 4½", EX, **$350.00 (B).** *Courtesy of Buffalo Bay Auction Co.*

Fairbanks Gold Dust Washing Powder, wooden crate, "The N.K. Fairbank Company...Chicago St. Louis New Orleans New York Montreal," 27½" x 19½" x 12", VG . . .**$65.00(D)**

Fairbanks-Morse Illuminated Motion display advertising sign for sales & service, 15½" dia. x 5" D, EX . . .**$550.00 (B)**

Fairbanks Morse Pumping Machinery, single-sided porcelain sign with graphics of weight in hand in center of message, 20" dia., VG . . . .**$60.00 (B)**

Fairbanks Morse Sales and Service, light-up advertising sign with reverse painted face and metal housing, colors rotate in background, 15½" dia., EX . . . .**$775.00 (D)**

Fairbanks Soap, die cut plate calendar with graphics of fairy by artisit Paul Moran, Litho by American, NY, 9½" dia., 1903, EX . . . .**$30.00 (B)**

Fairbanks Soap, trade cards, set of eight cards from N.K. Fairbanks with the Gold Dust twins, 3¼" x 5", 1885, EX . . . .**$313.00 (B)**

Fairway coffee, tin litho key-wound container with graphics of young children on front, 1-lb., EX . . . .**$300.00 (B)**

Fairway golf balls, store display for floor use, with graphics of young black caddy pulling the flag, United States Rubber Co., 25" x 48", 1920s, EX . . . .**$550.00 (B)**

Fairy..."Have You a Little Fairy in Your Home," die cut cardboard easel back ad sign with fairy on bar of soap, 19" x 23½", NM . . . .**$1,850.00 (B)**

Fairy Soap, advertising sign, paper on cardboard with graphics of young mother and daughter at dressing table, 32½" x 43", 1919, G . . . .**$355.00 (B)**

Fairy Soap... Have You a Little Fairy In Your Home?, round metal tip tray with artwork of little girl sitting on bar of product, 4⅛" dia., EX . . . .**$65.00 (B)**

Falls City Beer, cardboard advertising sign with graphics of majorette with a glass of the product, 34" x 46", 1940s, EX . . . .**$110.00 (B)**

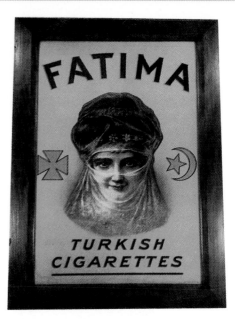

Fatima...Turkish Cigarettes, artwork of veiled woman in center of message, in original frame, 27" x 26½", EX, **$200.00 (D).**

Courtesy of Creatures of Habit

Fatima Cigarette, The Turkish Blend, embossed tin advertising sign, 20⅛" x 20⅛", G, **$230.00 (B).** *Courtesy of Collectors Auction Services*

Faust on Draught, one-piece advertising globe, 8" dia., EX, **$220.00 (B).** *Courtesy of Collectors Auction Services*

Falls City Beer, It's pasteurized, it's bitter free, paper 6-pack take-out bag with handles, 7¾" x 9¾", EX .....$10.00 (D)

Falstaff Beer...An old Friend, horizontal painted metal sign featuring artwork of medieval man with stein being served by waitress, 17½" x 15", G ....$100.00 (D)

Falstaff Beer, an old friend!, paper advertising sign, G ....$45.00 (D)

Falstaff, die cut metal advertising litho of trademark Falstaff man with product in a sitting position, from the Wm. J. Lemp Brewing Co., St. Louis, U.S.A., 7" x 18", 1900s, EX ....$1,200.00 (D)

Falstaff...Enjoy Beer, two-piece painted metal sign, 17½" x 15", EX ....$105.00 (D)

Fanny Farmer, candy container, tin litho in cylinder shape, graphics of Uncle Sam, 1944, 3" x 10", EX ....$120.00 (B)

Fan Tan Gum, tray with Oriental scene on front, 13¼" x 10½", EX ....$250.00 (B)

Farmer's Hybrid, painted tin die cut advertising license plate attachment, 9⅞" x 5⅝", NM ....$105.00 (C)

Farmers Pride Brand Steel Cut Coffee, tin coffee can with paper label of small child and man with cup of coffee, 4⅛" x 6", EX ....$300.00 (B)

Fashion cut plug tobacco, lunch pail with top handle, graphics of smartly dressed couple walking, 7½" x 5" x 4½", EX ....$350.00 (B)

Favorite Straight Cut Cigarettes, featuring artwork of hunting dog, double-sided tin, flange side, 18" x 9" EX, $2,100.00 (B).

Courtesy of Muddy River Trading Co./Gary Metz

Fayette's Ice Cream, double-sided porcelain die-cut advertising sign, 28" x 20", VG, $315.00 (B).

Federal Cartridges, tri-fold store counter advertising sign with scene of birds in field and flight, EX, $595.00 (B). *Courtesy of Buffalo Bay Auction Co.*

Fatima Turkish Cigarettes, advertising sign in wood frame with graphics of veiled woman in center of sign, 27" x 26½", 1909, EX . . . .$275.00 (D)

Fatima...Turkish Cigarettes, artwork of veiled woman in center of message, in original frame, 27" x 26½", EX . . . .$200.00 (D)

Favorite Straight Cut Cigarettes, featuring artwork of hunting dog, double-sided tin flange side, 18" x 9" EX . . . .$2,100.00 (B)

Federal Cartridges, tri-fold store counter advertising sign with scene of birds in field and flight, EX . . . .$595.00 (B)

Federal Monark Target Load, shotgun shell box, G . .$10.00 (D)

Federal Sporting Ammunition, cardboard counter top advertising sign with graphics of Monark Shell, EX . . . .$55.00 (C)

Federal Trucks, calendar with bottom tear sheets and colorful image of young lady in very short dress standing in front of fleet of trucks, 16" x 34", 1942, EX . . .$60.00 (B)

Feen-a-Mint...for constipation, porcelain sign with artwork of product blocks tumbling out of package, 29¼" x 7", F . . . .$65.00 (C)

Feen-a-Mint for constipation, single-sided porcelain advertising sign with graphics of package of product, 29½" x 7", EX . . . .$650.00 (B)

Feen-a-Mint laxative, dispenser with graphics of woman poised to take the product, mirror at top on tin construction with wood back, 7½" x 5½" x 16¼", EX . .$125.00(D)

Feen-a-Mint, porcelain advertising sign, graphics of product box at right of sign, 29¼" x 7", EX . . . .$95.00 (D)

Feen-a-Mint...The Chewing Laxative, Chew It Like Gum, advertising store display holder with artwork of woman on front holding product, EX . . . .$395.00 (C)

Fehr's Malt, self-framing metal advertising sign with pretty young lady, scantily clad, surrounded by cherubs with bottle on table beside her, 22" x 28", EX . . . .$950.00 (B)

Fehr's Famous F.F.X.L. Beer, tin litho tray from
Louisville, Ky., 1910, 13" dia., EX, $410.00 (B).

Fehr's Malt, self-framing metal advertising sign
with pretty young lady, scantily clad, surrounded
by cherubs with bottle on table beside her, 22"
x 28", EX, $950.00 (B). *Courtesy of Buffalo Bay Auction Co.*

Ferndell-Remus Tea, tin
with tranquil graphics of
bridge over stream, 3⅛" x
3⅛", VG, $25.00 (B).

Fellow Society of American Florists, light-up advertising
globe, high metal profile body with two glass lenses, 16½"
dia., EX . . . .$390.00 (B)

Ferndell, counter display bin with painted graphics and
wooden rear doors, 25¼" x 11½" x 12", VG . .$275.00 (C)

Fern Glen Rye, self-framing tin advertising sign with
graphics of black man with watermelon and hen with a
bottle of the product on the road in front of him, 23" x
33", F . . . .$975.00 (C)

Feronia Cigars, glass paperweight, 4¼" x 2½" x ¾",
EX . . . .$40.00 (B)

Ferris Corset, tin litho self-framing advertising sign, artwork of two girls, 16½" x 22½", VG . . . . . .$1,200.00 (D)

Ferro-Phos. Co., Pottstown, PA...Drink Ferro-Phos...The
Favorite Beverage, Five cents, non-narcotic, non-alco-
holic, round tip tray with artwork of product in tray center, 4⅛", EX . . . .$200.00 (B)

Ferry's Seeds, framed advertising poster, "A word to the
wise...The best that grow," 27" x 36", EX . . . .$425.00 (B)

F.F. Lewis, Cash Dealer Groceries and General Merchandise, Mansville, N.Y., with graphics of small boy standing
in boat wearing a blue coat, 5¾" x 8½", EX . . .$25.00 (B)

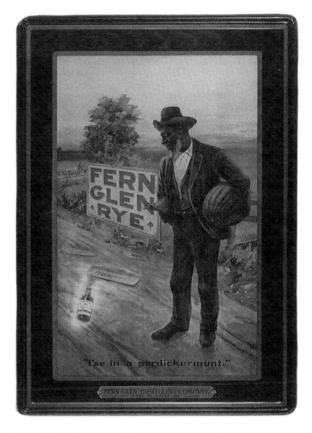

Ferris Corset, tin litho self-framing advertising sign, artwork of two girls, 16½" x 22½", NM, $2,300.00 (B). *Courtesy of Wm. Morford Investment Grade Collectibles*

Fern Glen Rye, self-framing tin advertising sign with graphics of black man with watermelon and hen with a bottle of the product on the road in front of him, 23" x 33", EX, $3,000.00 (B). *Courtesy of Collectors Auction Services*

Fidelity-Phenix Insurance, tin advertising sign, 23¼" x 11¾", VG . . . .$125.00 (C)

Fiendoil Tin, "The enemy of corrosion," litho container, cleans and protects firearms, EX . . . .$46.00 (B)

Fifth Avenue Coffee, tin litho container, Cleveland, O., 4" x 6", EX . . . .$60.00 (B)

Finast Rolled Oats, container with graphics of grocer on front label, Boston, MA, EX . . . .$85.00 (C)

Finck's Detroit-Special Overalls, celluloid advertising pocket mirror, "Wear Like a Pig's Nose," 2¾" x 1¾", EX . . . .$350.00 (B)

Finotti Beverage calendar, graphics of girl with globe, 16" x 33⅓", 1961, EX . . . .$39.00 (D)

Finotti, paper calendar with tear sheets at bottom with artwork of pretty girl sitting next to globe with message in center, 1961, EX . . . .$35.00 (C)

Fire Brigade Cigar, box with the inner lid litho from the Courier Litho Co., NY, with graphics of fire being fought by comical brigade, 50-ct., EX . . . .$1,200.00 (C)

Fire Chief Gasoline advertising sign, "Localized for you," 16" x 18¼", VG . . . .$75.00 (B)

Firestone, countertop advertising promotional statue of man tapping rubber tree, made of molded rubber, 3" x 5¾", EX . . . .$50.00 (B)

Firestone Cycle Tires...For Sale here, painted metal sign, 22" x 11½", EX . . . .$225.00 (C)

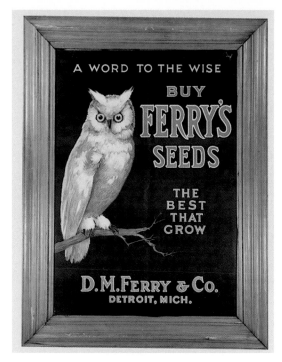

Field & Stream Outdoor Clothing, die cut cardboard, 3-D counter sign, 15¾" x 11¾", EX, $75.00 (B).

Ferry's Seeds, framed advertising poster, "A word to the wise...The best that grow," 27" x 36", NM, $455.00 (D).

Fireman's Fund Insurance Co., cardboard advertising poster showing perils of the road, 22½" x 12½", VG, $500.00 (B).

Firestone, tin advertising sign with embossed surround, 15¾" x 71½", 1947, EX . . . .$575.00 (C)

Firestone...Tires, Batteries, Spark Plugs, Brake Lining and Accessories, square advertising clock with lettering in center, 15¼" x 15¼", orange, white, and dark blue, G . . . .$155.00 (D)

Firestone Tires, advertising desk accessory, molded rubber, black man beside a rubber plant, "Firestone, Liberia," 3" dia. x 5¾", EX . . . .$375.00 (D)

Firestone Tires...Most miles per dollar...Butternut Valley Hdwe. Co...Gilbertsville, N.Y., painted tin sign, 35½" x 11½", EX . . . .$125.00 (D)

Firestone Tires, one-sided self-framing porcelain advertising sign, 72" x 23½", G . . . .$325.00 (B)

Firestone Tires, paper calendar with bottom tear sheets, great graphics of early touring car on winding road in forest, 1928, EX . . . .$175.00 (D)

Firestone...Universal Sales Co....Tire Service, one-sided porcelain advertising sign, 60" x 30", G . . . . .$200.00 (B)

First Aid Syrup bottle, die cut cover, 13" x 6", EX . .$55.00 (C)

First National Bank, reverse painted glass sign, in wood frame with metal corners, 24" x 24", VG . . . .$495.00 (B)

Fisher Peanuts, vendor case with curved front glass and advertising reverse painted on glass, EX . . . .$225.00 (B)

Fishers Peanut, lithographed tin container with graphics of peanuts all around canister, 12½" x 20¼", G $35.00 (D)

Fire Prevention Week, framed paper poster, 18¾" x 23¾", G, $95.00 (B).

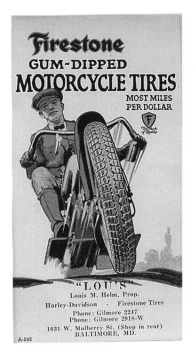

Firestone Gum-Dipped Motorcycle Tires, heavy paper blotter, graphics of motorcycle and rider, 3⅛" x 6", VG, $100.00 (B).

Fisk Balloon Tires, advertising calendar, framed die cut familiar boy in P.J.s, 3¼" x 5½", VG, $65.00 (B).

Firestone, one-sided self-framing tin advertising sign, 25" x 10", G, $20.00 (B).

Fisk...Red Tops, paper advertisement showing older model touring car with kids looking at product on car, 12½" x 17", EX . . . .$85.00 (D)

Fisk...Time to Re-tire...Tires, double-sided die cut metal sign with graphics of boy with tire and candle ready for bed, 36" x 29", VG . . . .$400.00 (B)

Fisk Tire, cardboard advertising sign with Fisk boy holding a tire and candle with mounting panel for price of tire, 24" x 11", EX . . . .$145.00 (C)

Fisk Tires...Gasoline...Auto Supplies, double-sided porcelain flange sign, "Ingram Richardson Beaver Falls, Pa.," 24" x 18", G . . . .$175.00 (B)

Fisk Tires Radiator, front cardboard advertising sign with image of Fisk Boy with candle and tire, 21¼" x 11", 1926, VG . . . .$225.00 (C)

Fisk Tires, tin litho advertising sign with logo youngster and tire, 6¾" dia., EX . . . .$95.00 (D)

Fitch's standard heart chewing gum, die cut cardboard advertising with graphics of young girl in Victorian dress and hat, 8" x 10", 1910, EX . . . .$165.00 (D)

Five Brothers Plug Tobacco, tin litho over cardboard, 16" x 16", EX . . . .$975.00 (C)

Five Brothers Plug Tobacco, sign tin litho over cardboard, 16" x 16", EX, **$975.00 (C).** *Courtesy of Wm. Morford Investment Grade Collectibles*

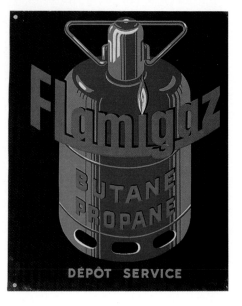

Flamigaz Depot Service, double-sided porcelain ad sign with graphics of gas container, foreign origin, 14¼" x 18⅛", G, **$110.00 (B).** *Courtesy of Collectors Auction Services*

Fleckenstein Brewing Co., beveled edge tin over cardboard sign from Fairbault, MN brewery with graphics of men enjoying the product, "choicest malt and hops," 13¼" x 19", EX . . . .$600.00 (B)

Fleet Motor Oil-Grease, painted tin sign with graphics of airplane and auto, 23" x 11¼", NM . . . .$325.00 (B)

Fleet-Wing gas globe, plastic body with glass lens, 13½" dia., VG . . . .$375.00 (B)

Fleischmann's Yeast, reverse glass advertising item, "The Only Genuine – Beware of Imitation," 21¼" x 27¾", G . . . .$100.00 (B)

Flexo chocolate and vanilla flavored confection, National Licorice Co., two-piece box with art of men in rowboat off tropical beach, 12" x 8" x 3½", EX . . . . $55.00 (B)

Floress Lipstick and Nail Lacquers, die cut cardboard litho store display, 40" x 30", VG . . . .$30.00 (B)

Florida souvenir spoon depicting a black boy and an alligator, back of handle has boy's head and palm branches, 4¼", VG . . . .$90.00 (B)

Florist Telegraph Delivery...Interflora-worldwide, with FTD runner in center of message, light-up advertising clock, metal back with curved glass front, 16" x 16", EX . . . .$125.00 (D)

Florsheim Shoe...for the man who cares, Shoes For Men, neon store display with pair of men's shoes over neon, Art Deco style, NM . . . .$395.00 (D)

Flying A Associated Gasoline, advertising sign with the "chicken wing" logo, hard-to-find item, 27¾" dia., EX . . .$750.00 (B)

Flying Red Horse, first aid kit by Mobilgas-Mobiloil, 3¼" x ¾" x 2¾", G . . . .$150.00 (D)

Foley Kidney Pills, porcelain oval door push plate, EX . . . .$330.00 (B)

Foley's coffee, in tin litho can with key-wound lid, St. Paul MN, 1-lb., VG . . . .$75.00 (C)

Folger's Coffee, pull-string cardboard container that holds free puzzle, "Free when you buy Folger's Vacuum or Flaked Coffee," ship graphics on front, 2¾" x 3½", NM . . . .$25.00 (D)

Folger's Golden Gate Steel Cut Coffee, tin can with paper label with artwork of ships in San Francisco Bay, hard-to-find-item, 2½-lb., 6" x 6", EX . . . .$90.00 (B)

Folger's, store advertising mirror with colorful graphics, J.A. Folger & Co., 13" x 9", EX . . . .$50.00 (B)

Forbe's Golden Cup Coffee, tin with several scenes around container with small lid, 3-lb., EX . . . .$75.00 (C)

Florsheim Shoe...for the man who cares, Shoes For Men, neon store display with pair of men's shoes over neon, Art Deco style, NM, **$395.00 (D).** *Courtesy of Rare Bird Antique Mall/Jon & Joan Wright*

Florsheim Shoe for the man who cares, reverse painted glass sign with easel back, 5⅜" x 7½", G, **$155.00 (C).**

Flying A Associated Gasoline, advertising sign with the "chicken wing" logo, hard-to-find item, 27¾" dia., EX, **$750.00 (B).** *Courtesy of Autopia Advertising Auctions*

Ford, fold-out advertising brochure with the new models of that year, graphics of front end of 1941 Ford, 8½" x 11", 1941, EX . . . .$45.00 (C)

Ford...Genuine...Parts, two-sided oval porcelain advertising sign, 24" x 16½", VG . . . .$450.00 (C)

Ford...Genuine...parts used here, one-sided porcelain sign, 26" x 9¾", VG . . . .$360.00 (B)

Ford Sales/Service, wood advertising thermometer with image of Fordson tractor, 4" x 14¼", VG . . . .$250.00 (C)

Ford...Service Station...Sales Agency, heavy tin tacker style advertising sign, 35½" x 11⅝", EX . . . . .$775.00 (C)

Foremost Milk, metal die cut single-sided advertising sign in shape of milk carton, 11" x 22", EX . . . . .$120.00 (B)

Forest & Stream, pocket tobacco tin, graphics of goose taking flight, EX . . . .$105.00 (C)

Forest & Stream, litho pocket tin, featuring artwork of two men fishing out of a canoe, EX . . . .$600.00 (B)

Forest & Stream Tobacco, lithographed tin container with graphics of man fishing in stream, G . . . .$100.00 (B)

Forest & Stream Tobacco, tin litho slip-lid canister with graphics of man fishing in stream in cameo on front, EX . . . .$146.00 (B)

Flying Red Horse, first aid kit by Mobilgas-Mobiloil, 3¼" x ¾" x 2¾", VG, **$165.00 (C).**

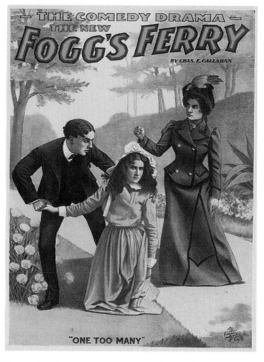

Fogg's Ferry, paper litho advertising poster, 21" x 28", VG, **$225.00 (C).**

Forest Flower Tobacco, hinged tobacco tin box with graphics of girl swinging in the forest from the S.F. Hess Co., Rochester N.Y., 6" x 4" x 2", EX . . . .**$375.00 (B)**

Fort Bedford P-Nuts 5¢...Does the party on the other side want..., advertising pocket mirror with artwork of box of product on cover, 1¾" dia., EX . . . . .**$300.00 (B)**

Fort Pitt, advertising clock, metal body with glass front and face, Telechron Inc., Ashland, Mass., 15" dia., EX .**$95.00 (B)**

Fort Pitt Beer, embossed painted metal sign in wood frame with graphics of couple sitting at table with bottle of product, 26" x 22¾", VG . . . .**$900.00 (B)**

Fort Pitt, light-up advertising clock with tin face and housing, and reverse painted advertising strip on top, 25" x 16", VG . . . .**$100.00 (B)**

Fort Pitt Special Beer, cardboard litho advertising sign with ball player artwork, 26" x 18", NM . . . . .**$875.00 (B)**

Fort Pitt Special Beer, light-up advertising sign, metal with glass face, can be counter or wall displayed, 14½" dia., EX . . . .**$300.00 (B)**

Fortune Ethyl Gasoline, one-sided painted advertising sign with likeness of Mercury, 12" x 9", G . . .**$500.00 (B)**

Fountain Tobacco, tin, strong colors on litho of fountain, 6¼" H, EX . . . .**$375.00 (B)**

Four Roses, painted advertising tin sign, self-framed, with graphics of a couple of guys playing cards while the chickens drink the Four Roses, 20" x 24", 1912, EX . . . .**$575.00 (C)**

Foursome Mixture, tobacco tin, graphics of men golfing, 4¼" x 3¼" x 1", EX . . . .**$275.00 (C)**

Fowler's Cherry Smash, ceramic advertising dispenser with metal top pump, 9½" x 15", EX . . . . . .**$2,300.00 (B)**

Fox Bread, calendar with graphics of young boy and girl with flowers, partial tear sheet, 1913, EX . . .**$110.00 (B)**

Fox Deluxe Beer, serving tray, featuring artwork of hunter with horn, G . . . .**$40.00 (D)**

Francisco Auto Heater...Summer Here All the Year, with great graphics of people in cut-away touring car on snow-covered roads at night, self-framing, 40" x 18", EX . .**$575.00 (D)**

Franklin Baker Company (Inc.), Snowdrift Coconut..., sweetened fancy shred, round tin container with paper label, 12" x 14½", EX . . . .**$35.00 (D)**

Ford Colvin Motor Sales, one-sided embossed tin dealer sign, 27¾" x 9¾", VG, $180.00 (B).

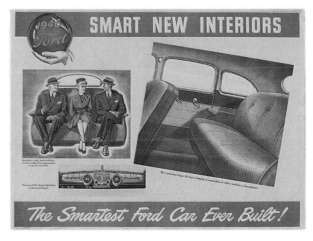

Forest & Stream, litho pocket tin, featuring artwork of two men fishing out of a canoe, EX, $600.00 (B). *Courtesy of Wm. Morford Investment Grade Collectibles*

Ford, Smart New Interiors, paper poster, 46" x 35", G, $80.00 (B).

Forest & Stream Tobacco, tin with graphics of men fishing, 3" x 4¼" x ¾", VG, $350.00 (B).

Franklin Glass & Mirror, advertising pocket mirror, 3½" dia., EX . . . .$25.00 (C)

Frank's Choice Cigar, sign, embossed tin with moveable hands to signal store hours, Freeport, Ill., 6½" sq., 1900s, EX . . . .$190.00 (B)

Frank's Dhooge, embossed die cut calendar with full calendar pad with graphics of youngster, from Milwaukee, Wisconsin grocer, 13" x 17", 1908, EX . . . . . .$140.00 (B)

Frederick's Premium Beer...Brewed with pure artesian well water, round metal serving tray with artwork of bottle in center, 13¼" dia., EX . . . .$85.00 (D)

Fred Krug Brewing Co., 50th Anniversary plate, with artwork of factory on one side and artwork of Mr. Krug on other side, 1909, NM . . . .$85.00 (B)

Freedom Perfect Motor Oil, double-sided porcelain advertising sign, 23½" dia., G . . . .$250.00 (B)

Fountain Tobacco, tin, strong colors on litho of fountain, 6¼" H, EX, **$375.00 (B).** *Courtesy of Richard Opfer Auctioneering, Inc.*

Fowler's Cherry Smash, ceramic advertising dispenser with metal top pump, 9½" x 15", EX, **$2,300.00 (B).**
Courtesy of Wm. Morford Investment Grade Collectibles

Free Land Overalls, heavy porcelain advertising sign, 30" x 10", EX, **$475.00 (B).** *Courtesy of Wm. Morford Investment Grade Collectibles*

Free Lance...Smoke a...and be Convinced, cardboard cigar sign, 11" x 9½", EX . . . .**$71.00 (B)**

Free Land Overalls, heavy porcelain advertising sign, 30" x 10", VG . . . .**$395.00 (C)**

Freeman...Headbolt Engine Heater, painted metal thermometer with messages to right of vertical scale, rolled edges, 6" x 15", G . . . .**$95.00 (D)**

Freeman...shoes for men, metal and glass light-up advertising sign, 20" x 9", EX . . . .**$80.00 (B)**

Freihofer's Cake counter display unit, tin litho sides and glass front, "A cake for every taste...pound, sponge, fruit," 14¾" x 17" x 22", EX . . . .**$895.00 (C)**

Freihofer's Cakes, store counter display rack with glass front, 14¾" x 27½", VG . . . .**$600.00 (B)**

French Bauer Ice Cream, light-up advertising glass globe, 13½" dia., EX . . . .**$425.00 (B)**

French Champaign, stone litho advertising cardboard sign with graphics of young lady at table being served, 41½" x 57", NM . . . .**$360.00 (B)**

French Marker Coffee and Chicory, tin litho key-wound container, 1-lb., EX . . . .**$25.00 (B)**

French Wine of Coca, tin sidewalk advertising sign with original legs and frame, 20" x 28", 1880s, VG .**$3,000.00 (C)**

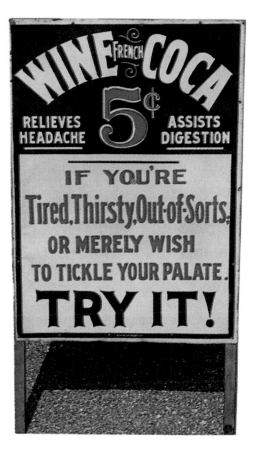

French Wine of Coca, tin sidewalk advertising sign with original legs and frame, 20" x 28", 1880s, NM, **$10,000.00 (B).**

Courtesy of Muddy River Trading Co./Gary Metz

Frictionless Metal Co., single-sided self-framing tin advertising sign, 16" x 22¼", VG, **$275.00 (B).**

Frigidaire, porcelain advertising sign promoting its line of dairy milk coolers, with graphics of cow, 19½" x 13¾", EX . . . .$175.00 **(C)**

Froehlich's Sausage Hams & Bacon, tin over cardboard advertising sign with colorful graphics of the products, designed to be string hung, 19" x 13", NM . . .$325.00 **(C)**

Frontier Rarin' to Go, gasoline globe on gill body, NM . . . .$2,200.00 **(C)**

Frostie Root Beer...the smooth one, painted metal thermometer with Frostie at top over the vertical scale, EX . . . .$45.00 **(D)**

Fruit Bowl... Drink, Nectar for a Nickel, embossed tin sign with tilted bottle under product message, 6¼" x 19½", EX . . . .$65.00 **(B)**

Fruit Bowl, painted metal flange advertising sign, "Drink Fruit Bowl," 18½" x 14", 1950s, EX . . . .$75.00 **(C)**

Fry's Chocolate, single-sided porcelain advertising sign, probably foreign, with graphics of young boy crying until he gets his Fry's Chocolate, 36" x 30", VG . . .$790.00 **(B)**

Fry's Hot Chocolate dispenser, tin litho with the product logo, 6½" x 7", EX . . . .$175.00 **(C)**

Fry's Pure Breakfast Cocoa, single-sided porcelain advertising sign with graphics of product can in center, 18" x 24", VG . . . .$170.00 **(B)**

Fuller Morrison Co., handmade tin container with logo on front, 25-ct., 3¾" x 5½", G . . . .$55.00 **(C)**

Fulton County Fair, advertising cardboard litho promoting the fair in Jamestown, NY, on Sept. 5, 6, 7, 8, 1904, 15" x 29", VG . . . .$100.00 **(B)**

Fun-To-Wash Washing Powder, in unopened box with "Mammy" on front, EX . . . .$82.00 **(B)**

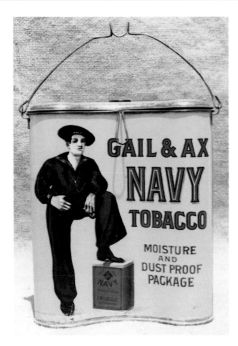

Gail & Ax Navy Tobacco, rare kidney-shaped pail, with bail handle and great graphics, 7" x 8½", EX, $2,300.00 (B). *Courtesy of Morford Auctions*

Galt House Coffee, paper label tin container, roasted and packed by Norton & Curd Co., 1-lb., 1908, EX, $450.00 (B). *Courtesy of Past Tyme Pleasures*

Gainer Feeds, "More Gains Per Dollar," single-sided painted sign with rolled edges, 20" x 20", EX, $100.00 (B). *Courtesy of Collectors Auction Services*

Gail & Ax Navy Tobacco, rare kidney-shaped pail, with bail handle and great graphics, 7" x 8½", EX . . . . .$2,300.00 (B)

Galiker's Ice Cream, metal advertising sign over cardboard with flavor holders at bottom, 9½" x 24", EX . .$55.00 (C)

Gallagher & Burton Fine Whiskey, tin litho tip tray with graphics of the product bottle in center, 4½" dia., EX . . . .$85.00 (C)

Gallagher & Burton, small tin litho tip tray with graphics of bottle of whiskey in center, 4½" dia., EX . .$135.00 (C)

Gallagher & Burton, tin litho ashtray with graphics of bottle of product in center, 4½" dia., EX . . . . .$55.00 (C)

Gallagher & Burton Whiskey, round metal tip tray with artwork of older gentleman with bottle of product, 4¼" dia., EX . . . .$35.00 (B)

Gallagher & Burton Whiskey, tip tray, "I am well preserved you see, many thanks to G & B," 4½" dia., NM . .$40.00 (B)

Gallaher's Honeydew Tobacco, tin with striker on side, 3¼" x 2" x ¾", EX . . . .$50.00 (B)

Galt House Coffee, paper label tin container, roasted and packed by Norton & Curd Co., 1-lb., 1908, EX . .$450.00 (B)

Galva Creamery Co., Galva, Ill., Kansas City, Mo., St. Paul, Minn., cardboard advertising sign for Peterson's Butter, 20¼" x 13", VG . . . .$40.00 (B)

Game Fine Cut, Jno. J. Bagley & Co., metal store cabinet with great litho images, EX, $425.00 (B).

Courtesy of Buffalo Bay Auction Co.

Garcia Grande Cigars, die cut paper on cardboard easel back store sign, featuring woman with box of product, 30" x 35", EX, $247.00 (B).

Garcia Grande, countertop display and cigar lighter with paper litho advertising on box, 8¾" x 9¼", G, $110.00 (B).

Gardner Salted Peanuts, glass store jar, "Always in Good Taste, Gardner Salted Peanuts, 5¢," 7" x 7¾", VG, $75.00 (C).

Gamble's Super Quality Coffee, glass jar, Gamble Stores, Minneapolis, 1-lb., EX . . . .$15.00 (D)

Gambrinus Cincinnati Beer, reverse painted glass advertising sign, "in Bottle & Keg" with graphics of king on throne, 16⅝" x 8", EX . . . .$235.00 (C)

Game Finecut, counter tobacco tin with graphics of grouse in field scene, 11½" x 8" x 6½", VG . .$325.00 (D)

Game Fine Cut, Jno. J. Bagley & Co., metal store cabinet with great litho images, EX . . . .$425.00 (B)

Game Finecut, store counter tobacco bin with graphics of birds in cover, Jno. Bagley & Co., Detroit, Mich, 11½" x 8" x 7", EX . . . .$525.00 (B)

Game Finecut Tobacco, tin with bird scene, manufactured by "Jno J. Bagley E. Co., Detroit, Mich.," 11½" x 6½" x 8", EX . . . .$255.00 (C)

Garcia Grande Cigar, rectangular metal tip tray with graphics of joker on stool to right of message, 6⅛" L, EX . . . .$75.00 (B)

GE Mazda, paper advertising calendar for National Lamp Works by Hayden Hayden, 1927, 8½" x 20¼", EX, **$255.00 (B)**. *Courtesy of Collectors Auction Services*

General Electric Lamps, They stay brighter longer, general store lamp tester, with original early lamps, with message on reverse painted glass, G, **$550.00 (E)**. *Courtesy of B.J. Summers*

Genesee Plating Works...Compliments of..., Rochester, NY, earlier cast iron figural match safe with hinged lid over match pocket, 4⅜" x 8½", VG, **$575.00 (C)**.

Garcia Grande Cigars, die cut paper on cardboard easel back store sign, featuring woman with box of product, 30" x 35", EX . . . .$247.00 (B)

Garden Rolled Oats, container from John Price & Co., Philadelphia, Pa., with graphics of house and garden scene, EX . . . .$185.00 (C)

Garland Stoves and Ranges, cardboard litho advertising sign featuring artwork of boy and dog, 10¼" x 14", EX . . . .$925.00 (B)

Gasoline Globe, one-piece glass globe with etched and painted lettering, 12" x 5" x 12½", VG . . . .$1,250.00 (B)

Gates Wintersafe Tire, one-sided advertising sign with graphics of tire going through the snow, 15" x 10¼", VG . . . .$20.00 (B)

Gelfands Mayonnaise, die cut cardboard sign, 10" x 13½", EX . . . .$30.00 (B)

G-E Mazda Lamps...Avoid Bulbsnatching, three-dimensional cardboard store display with original real bulb, 8½" x 12¾", G . . . .$35.00 (D)

GE Mazda Lamps, store countertop display unit with tin litho front display with various sizes of light bulbs, 27½" x 25½" x 22½", VG . . . .$475.00 (B)

Gem, tin on cardboard advertising sign promoting pantaloons and overalls, 13¼" x 9¼", EX . . . .$115.00 (B)

General Arthur Cigar, reverse painted advertising sign, graphics of bust of man in black jacket, 27" x 34½", EX . . . .$255.00 (C)

General Electric Lamps, They stay brighter longer, general store lamp tester, with original early lamps, with message on reverse painted glass, G . . . .$550.00 (E)

General Miles Cigar, Chicago, reverse chipped lettering on beveled glass, framed, 22" x 12", NM . . . . .$355.00 (B)

General Motor Fuel globe, low profile metal body with two glass lens, 15" dia., VG . . . .$1,000.00 (B)

General Petroleum Corporation, oil can, rare item, 1-gal., 10" tall, VG . . . .$275.00 (C)

General Violet Ray Anti-Knock Gasoline, double-sided porcelain advertising sign, 30" dia., VG . . . . .$425.00 (B)

Geo. Evans Honey Boy, paper litho minstrel poster, 1912, 38½" x 77", G, $1,700.00 (B).

Geo. Weidemann Brewing Co., hard-to-find tin die cut easel back advertising sign depicting man reading the newspaper while a young girl and boy look on and a bottle of beer on the table beside the man, Meek and Beach Litho, 9¾" x 13¾", 1901, EX, $1,450.00 (B).

Courtesy of Buffalo Bay Auction Co.

Genesee Beer, tin on cardboard ad sign with two people sitting on product box, 14½" x 7", EX ...... $50.00 (B)

Genesee Beer, tin over cardboard advertising sign, 14⅝" x 7⅛", 1960s, EX .... $55.00 (C)

Genesee Plating Works...Compliments of..., Rochester, NY, earlier cast iron figural match safe with hinged lid over match pocket, 4⅜" x 8½", EX .... $625.00 (B)

Geneva on the Lake, O, painted metal ashtray with stand-up, black boy smoking a cigar, made in Japan, 4¼" H, VG .... $300.00 (B)

Gen. Steedman 5¢ Cigar, embossed cardboard advertising sign with girl climbing out of coach, Hettermann Bros. Co....Makers...Louisville, KY, in old gesso frame, 13" x 16½", EX .... $400.00 (B)

Genuine Ford Parts, double-sided top-hung porcelain sign, 24" x 17", 1930s, EX .... $1,800.00 (C)

Geo. E. Sawyer's Electric Cough Drops, tin litho display box which originally held 5¢ packages, 8½" x 7¼" x 4¼", EX .... $375.00 (B)

George Benz liquors, photo sign of couple having a cocktail, 21" x 17", 1910s, EX .... $235.00 (C)

George H. Goodman Company, Incorporated, 1-gal. whiskey crock, with message in outline box on front, cream, EX .... $155.00 (C)

George Potter Cigars, advertising photogravure of George Potter smoking a cigar with a box of the product in background, 20½" x 24½", EX .... $40.00 (B)

George Washington Cut Plug, tobacco pail with side wire bail handles, good graphics on front of container, G ...$85.00 (D)

Geo. Weidemann Brewing Co., hard-to-find tin die cut easel back advertising sign depicting man reading the newspaper while a young girl and boy look on and a bottle of beer on the table beside the man, Meek and Beach Litho, 9¾" x 13¾", 1901, G .... $450.00 (C)

Gibbs Barber Shop, die-cut porcelain double-sided flange sign, 24⅛" x 12", VG, $170.00 (B).

Gillette Blue Blades, single-sided die-cut tin advertising sign, foreign, 5¾" x 7" x 4¼", scarce, $50.00 (B).

Gilbarco, clock face pump restored as an Esso pump, great example of the Art Deco influence, NM, $2,650.00 (D). *Courtesy of Riverview Antique Mall*

German Fire Insurance Company...Pittsburgh, Pa., cardboard calendar with patriotic theme, 1905, 10½" x 13½", EX . . . .$45.00 (B)

German Insurance Co., six-page advertising calendar with different scenes, 10¼" x 13¼", 1902, EX . . . . .$40.00 (B)

German Syrup, double-sided die cut cardboard litho with black boy holding sign with advertising on hat, 9" x 17", VG . . . .$450.00 (B)

Germantown Dye Works, painted cardboard sign with graphics of factory, 14" x 11", 1920s, EX . . . . .$55.00 (B)

Gerst Brewing Co., leather and celluloid notebook with 1897 calendar and graphics of William Gerst, Nashville, Tenn., 2¾" x 5¼", 1897, EX . . . .$175.00 (C)

Getty, cloth sleeve patch, 4½" x 2⅞", G . . . . .$10.00 (C)

Gevelot Ammunition, one-sided tin advertising sign with rolled edges, with graphics of man holding game taken using the product, 17" x 22½", VG . . . .$50.00 (B)

Ghostley Pearl...Our Choice...the...Assured Poultry Profits, one-sided tin embossed advertising sign, 18" x 12", VG . . . .$160.00 (B)

Gibbons Beer Ale, Bakelite electric advertising clock, 14⅝" dia., NM . . . .$135.00 (C)

Gibbs, flange die cut porcelain shop sign with die cut of barber pole, 20" x 24", VG . . . .$425.00 (B)

Gibson Girl Cigarette, tin with graphics of young lady on front, 3¼" x 3" x ⅝", EX . . . .$250.00 (B)

Gibson Girl, vertical pocket tin with graphics of Gibson Girl on front, 3¾" x 3¾" x ¾", EX . . . .$225.00 (B)

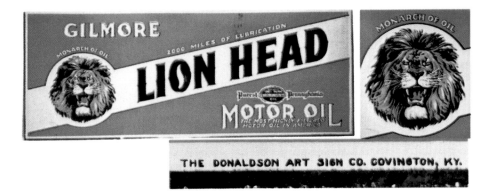

THE DONALDSON ART SIGN CO. COVINGTON, KY.

Gilmore Lion Head Motor Oil, embossed single-sided tin advertising sign, 29½" x 11½", VG, $2,500.00, (B).

Gin Seng, The Beverage of Purity, rectangular metal serving tray, VG, $100.00 (C).

Gladiator Coffee, large store bin for Brewster, Crittenden & Co., 13¼" x 21½" x 13¼", EX, **$395.00 (C).** *Courtesy of Wm. Morford Investment Grade Collectibles*

Gibson Straight Rye Whiskey, advertising glass paperweight complete with five "liars' dice" inside, 3" x 3" x 1', EX . . . .$65.00 (C)

Gilbarco, clock-face pump restored as an Esso pump, great example of the Art Deco influence, NM . . . .$2,650.00 (D)

Gilbert Rae Aerated Waters, embossed tin litho self-framed advertising sign with graphics of bottles and the factory, 19¾" x 28", EX . . . .$675.00 (B)

Gillette Blue Blades 10 for 50¢, metal coin-operated dispenser, works only with solid 50¢ pieces, 1950s, NM . . . .$125.00 (D)

Gillette, die cut porcelain double-sided flange advertising sign with graphics of razor and package of blades, 21½" x 19½", VG . . . .$3,350.00 (B)

Gillette Safety Razor, celluloid advertising pocket mirror with artwork of baby using razor, with 1909 calendar around outside of artwork, 2¼" dia., EX . . . .$160.00 (B)

Gillette Safety Razor…No Stropping! No Honing!, advertising pocket mirror with 1913 mirror, 2⅛" dia., EX . . .$140.00 (B)

Gill Mortuary/ Emergency Ambulance tin over cardboard advertising calendar with calendar number cards at bottom and graphics of Pierce-Arrow automobile, 13" x 19", G . . . .$350.00 (C)

Gill's Hotel Special Coffee and Chicory, key-wound tin litho container, 1-lb., EX . . . .$37.00 (B)

Gilmer Moulded Rubber, store countertop display unit with graphics of vintage man on front, back is open and has four shelves for storage, 16½" x 25" x 21½", G . . . . .$110.00 (B)

GMC Trucks Sales Service, neon advertising clock, metal and glass, G, $800.00 (B).

Gold Dust, die cut cardboard store display with twins on both sides of box, 14¼" x 3⅞" x 12¾", 1890s, VG, $1,690.00 (B). *Courtesy of Collectors Auction Services*

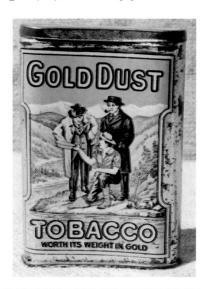

Gold Dust Tobacco, pocket tin, with great graphics, EX, $2,650.00 (B). *Courtesy of Morford Auctions*

Gilmer, super-service molded rubber fan belt, cardboard product box, EX . . . .$425.00 (C)

Gilmore, paper advertising calendar with graphics of young lady with Scottie dogs on leash tangled around her legs, 7" x 15¼", EX . . . .$45.00 (C)

Gin Seng, The Beverage of Purity, rectangular metal serving tray, EX . . . .$125.00 (C)

Ginta Cigar, advertising sign with graphics of product box that has a pretty woman on the lid, G . . . .$55.00 (B)

Gladiator Coffee, large store bin for Brewster, Crittenden & Co., 13¼" x 21½" x 13¼", EX . . . .$395.00 (C)

Glendale Fresh Daily, reverse painted on glass advertising sign with graphics of farmyard scene, product container in scene lights up, 15¼" x 11¼", EX . . . .$175.00 (C)

Glendora Coffee, embossed tin sign, NOS, 20" x 6½", NM . . . .$375.00 (C)

Glendora Coffee, tin litho container from the Glendora Products Co., Warren, Pa., 6⅝" x 8", EX . . . . .$55.00 (C)

GLF Quality gas globe, wide glass body with two lenses, 13½" dia., VG . . . .$250.00 (B)

Globe Evaporated Milk, trade card with graphics of Uncle Sam barometer, 3½" x 6", EX . . . .$40.00 (B)

Gold Dust Washing Powder, round string-hung double-sided cardboard advertising sign, 6½" dia., EX, **$120.00 (B).** *Courtesy of Muddy River Trading Co./Gary Metz*

Gold Dust Twins, embossed tin advertising sign depicting twins in tub, 27½" x 40", VG, **$2,100.00 (B).** *Courtesy of Collectors Auction Services*

Golden Bear Oil Co...Petroleum...Products, one-sided porcelain pump sign with graphics of bear in center, 15" dia., VG, **$1,900.00 (B).** *Courtesy of Collectors Auction Services*

Globe Tobacco Co., tin container advertising Hand Made Tobacco, with small lid featuring graphics of hand with plug of tobacco, 5" x 6½", EX . . . .**$390.00 (B)**

Globe Wernicke, metal litho tip tray with graphics of couple in front of bookcase at home scene, 4¼" dia., VG . . . .**$70.00 (B)**

Globe White Seal Motor Oil, tin litho double-sided flange sign with graphics of early metal oil can, 12" x 19½", VG . . . .**$1,100.00 (B)**

Gloco gas globe, plastic body with glass lens, 13½" dia., VG . . . .**$385.00 (B)**

G. Marconi, double-sided die cut porcelain advertising sign with graphics of the world in center of sign, 16" x 15", VG . . . .**$300.00 (B)**

GMC Trucks...Sales & Service, double-sided porcelain dealer sign, 42" dia., EX . . . .**$950.00 (B)**

GMC Trucks, two-sided porcelain sign, 48" x 24", VG . . . .**$520.00 (B)**

Goblin Soap cardboard container with graphics of elf-like figure on front, 2½" x 1½" x 4", EX . . . .**$85.00 (C)**

Goebel Bantam Beer...Enjoy, die cut cardboard rooster "tootin" his own horn, 9" x 11", EX . . . .**$30.00 (B)**

Golden Girl Cola, die-cut embossed tin bottle-cap shape sign, 33" dia., EX, **$175.00 (C).**

Goldenrod Ice Cream, light-up reverse painted on glass advertising clock, 15" dia., VG, **$185.00 (B).**

Courtesy of Autopia Advertising Auctions

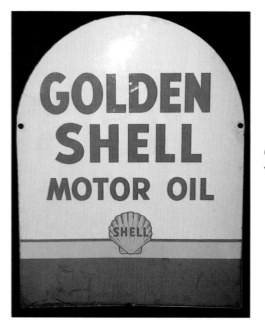

Golden Shell Motor Oil, double-sided driveway sign, 26½" x 34½", VG, **$375.00 (C).**

Goebel Private Stock Beer, advertising calendar with graphics of Civil War-era baseball game, 18" x 27¼", 1951, NM . . . .**$150.00 (C)**

Goebel 22 Beer, advertising calendar with 1887 baseball image, 18" x 27¼", 1953, EX . . . .**$135.00 (C)**

Gold Bell, gift stamps advertising store sign, painted metal, 19½" x 28", G . . . .**$165.00 (D)**

Gold Cross Talc, tin litho foot powder container, 4½" x 2½", EX . . . .**$180.00 (B)**

Gold Dust, cardboard box with litho of Gold Dust Twins cleaning, 10" x 18" x 12", VG . . . .**$110.00 (B)**

Gold Dust, die cut cardboard store display with twins on both sides of box, 14¼" x 3⅞" x 12¾", 1890s, VG . . . .**$1,690.00 (B)**

Gold Dust...For Spring House Cleaning, trolley car sign with artwork of house cleaning in progress, 26" x 10½", NM . . . .**$1,200.00 (B)**

Gold Dust, sheet music for "Twins Rag," graphics of twins at piano and dancing, EX . . . .**$25.00 (B)**

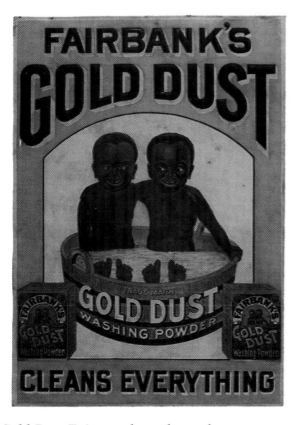

Gold Dust Twins, embossed tin advertising sign depicting twins in tub, 27½" x 40", VG, $2,100.00 (B). *Courtesy of Collectors Auction Services*

Gold Dust Washing Powder, round string-hung double-sided cardboard advertising sign, 6½" dia., EX, $120.00 (B). *Courtesy of Muddy River Trading Co./Gary Metz*

Golden Bear Oil Co...Petroleum...Products, one-sided porcelain pump sign with graphics of bear in center, 15" dia., VG, $1,900.00 (B). *Courtesy of Collectors Auction Services*

Globe Tobacco Co., tin container advertising Hand Made Tobacco, with small lid featuring graphics of hand with plug of tobacco, 5" x 6½", EX . . . .$390.00 (B)

Globe Wernicke, metal litho tip tray with graphics of couple in front of bookcase at home scene, 4¼" dia., VG . . . .$70.00 (B)

Globe White Seal Motor Oil, tin litho double-sided flange sign with graphics of early metal oil can, 12" x 19½", VG . . . .$1,100.00 (B)

Gloco gas globe, plastic body with glass lens, 13½" dia., VG . . . .$385.00 (B)

G. Marconi, double-sided die cut porcelain advertising sign with graphics of the world in center of sign, 16" x 15", VG . . . .$300.00 (B)

GMC Trucks...Sales & Service, double-sided porcelain dealer sign, 42" dia., EX . . . .$950.00 (B)

GMC Trucks, two-sided porcelain sign, 48" x 24", VG . . . .$520.00 (B)

Goblin Soap cardboard container with graphics of elf-like figure on front, 2½" x 1½" x 4", EX . . . .$85.00 (C)

Goebel Bantam Beer...Enjoy, die cut cardboard rooster "tootin" his own horn, 9" x 11", EX . . . .$30.00 (B)

Golden Girl Cola, die-cut embossed tin bottle-cap shape sign, 33" dia., EX, **$175.00 (C).**

Goldenrod Ice Cream, light-up reverse painted on glass advertising clock, 15" dia., VG, **$185.00 (B).**

Courtesy of Autopia Advertising Auctions

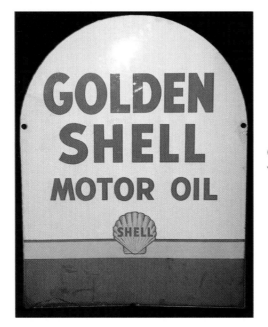

Golden Shell Motor Oil, double-sided driveway sign, 26½" x 34½", VG, **$375.00 (C).**

Goebel Private Stock Beer, advertising calendar with graphics of Civil War-era baseball game, 18" x 27¼", 1951, NM . . . .**$150.00 (C)**

Goebel 22 Beer, advertising calendar with 1887 baseball image, 18" x 27¼", 1953, EX . . . .**$135.00 (C)**

Gold Bell, gift stamps advertising store sign, painted metal, 19½" x 28", G . . . .**$165.00 (D)**

Gold Cross Talc, tin litho foot powder container, 4½" x 2½", EX . . . .**$180.00 (B)**

Gold Dust, cardboard box with litho of Gold Dust Twins cleaning, 10" x 18" x 12", VG . . . .**$110.00 (B)**

Gold Dust, die cut cardboard store display with twins on both sides of box, 14¼" x 3⅞" x 12¾", 1890s, VG . . . .**$1,690.00 (B)**

Gold Dust...For Spring House Cleaning, trolley car sign with artwork of house cleaning in progress, 26" x 10½", NM . . . .**$1,200.00 (B)**

Gold Dust, sheet music for "Twins Rag," graphics of twins at piano and dancing, EX . . . .**$25.00 (B)**

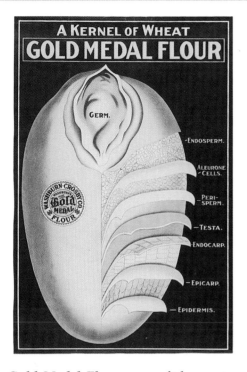

Gold Medal Flour, paper litho poster, graphics of a kernel of wheat, 28" x 42", G, $140.00 (B).

Gold Seal Boots and Overshoes, double-sided tin litho advertising sign, featuring artwork of boots and shoes, 18¼" L, G, $170.00 (B). *Courtesy of Richard Opfer Auctionering, Inc.*

Gold Seal Champagne, tip tray, manufactured by American Artworks, Coshocton, Ohio, 4½" x 6½", NM, $70.00 (C).

Gold Dust Tobacco, pocket tin, with great graphics, EX . . . .$2,650.00 (B)

Gold Dust Twins, alarm clock, wind-up with cardboard face, metal body, and plastic front with graphics of washing powder box, 3¼" dia., EX . . . .$550.00 (B)

Gold Dust Twins, can, cardboard with tin top and bottom, paper label with artwork of twins, 3" dia. x 4¾", VG . . . .$70.00 (C)

Gold Dust Twins, cloth banner with graphics of washing powder box and message, "GOLD DUST cleans everything," 58" x 24½", VG . . . .$1,000.00 (D)

Gold Dust Twins, double-sided cardboard banner advertising with graphics of twins and washing powder boxes, "...The Table and Ticket Co., Chicago & New York," 71½" x 17", EX . . . .$3,800.00 (B)

Gold Dust Twins, double-sided cardboard litho store counter advertising sign, graphics of twins doing various chores, 14" x 14", VG . . . .$2,450.00 (B)

Gold Dust Twins, embossed tin advertising sign depicting twins in tub, 27½" x 40", NM . . . .$3,000.00 (C)

Gold Dust Twins, powder box, cardboard with graphics of twins, 4¾" x 8¾", VG . . . .$35.00 (D)

Gold Dust Twins, self-framing tin advertising sign from Meek & Beach Co., Coshocton, O., with graphics of twins doing a variety of chores, "Let the GOLD DUST twins do your work," 25½" x 38", VG . . . .$7,500.00 (C)

Gold Dust Twins, washing powder advertising sign with graphics of cooking utensil on counter, "Quickly Clean with GOLD DUST," 22" x 12", EX . . . .$150.00 (B)

Gollam's Lebanon Ice Cream, We Serve, painted metal double-sided sidewalk sign, 1940s, EX, $250.00 (B). *Courtesy of Muddy River Trading Co./Gary Metz*

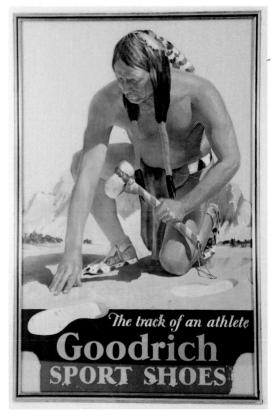

Goodrich Sport Shoes, advertising die cut cardboard poster featuring artwork of Indian, framed, 26" x 41", EX, $260.00 (B).

Goodrich Tires, supplies, porcelain flange sign, 18" dia., white lettering on blue background, VG, $295.00 (C). *Courtesy of Riverview Antique Mall*

Gold Dust Washing Powder, cardboard litho depicting twins and box of product, "Let the Gold Dust Twins Do Your Work," 13¾" x 21¼", VG . . . .$600.00 (B)

Gold Dust Washing Powder, cardboard trade cards with images of twins in washtub, 3" x 3¾", NM . . . .$71.00 (B)

Gold Dust Washing Powder, round string-hung double-sided cardboard advertising sign, 6½" dia., EX . . . . . .$120.00 (B)

Golden Bear Oil Co...Petroleum...Products, one-sided porcelain pump sign with graphics of bear in center, 15" dia., VG . . . .$1,900.00 (B)

Golden Burst popcorn, three tier countertop display with tin litho marquee, 7½" x 18" x 16", EX . . . . .$225.00 (C)

Golden Eagle, one-sided porcelain pump sign with graphics of eagle, 13" x 13", VG . . . .$350.00 (B)

Goodyear Camelback and Repair Materials, advertising clock, 7½" x 7½", G, $35.00 (B).

Gordon's Potato Chips, can with Gordon's delivery truck at top, metal, 7½" x 11½", red and cream, VG, $65.00 (C). *Courtesy of B.J. Summers*

Grand Old Party...1856 to 1908, round tip tray with artwork of Taft & Sherman in center of tray under graphics of White House, great strong graphics, 4⅛" dia., EX, $85.00 (B).

Graf's Zep, die-cut wood sign in shape of zeppelin, 48" x 13½", G, $325.00 (B).

Golden Grain Smoking Tobacco, bag, Brown & Williamson with Raleigh wrapping papers on back, G . . . .$25.00 (D)

Goldenmoon Buckeye Root Beer, syrup can, 5½" x 10" x 4½", VG . . . .$20.00 (B)

Golden Pheasant coffee, tin litho with great graphics of bird on blue background, 1-lb., EX . . . . . .$1,500.00 (C)

Golden Rail Beer, advertising sign, curved porcelain with graphics of old steam locomotive, only 50 produced, 24" x 18", EX . . . .$80.00 (B)

Goldenrod Ice Cream, light-up reverse painted on glass advertising clock, 15" dia., VG . . . .$185.00 (B)

Golden-Rod oats, tin with slip lid, Chicago, IL, EX . . . .$125.00 (C)

Golden Shell Motor Oil, double-sided driveway sign, 26½" x 34½", G . . . .$325.00 (D)

Golden Spring Beverages, celluloid over metal, chain-hanging advertising sign promoting Golden Spring Sarsaparilla, Smith Co., New Bedford, Mass., with graphics of bottle pouring into glass, 11" x 8", EX . . . . .$325.00 (B)

Golden Tip Gasoline, porcelain single-sided advertising sign, 60" x 38", VG . . . .$700.00 (B)

Golden Wedding Coffee, key-wound vaccum pack can, 1-lb., G . . . .$35.00 (D)

Grape Dee-Light, Gee but it's good, Jacob Onuschak, Northampton, PA, with great graphics, cardboard hang-up sign, 1920s, 10½" x 14", EX, $45.00 (B).
Courtesy of Muddy River Trading Co./Gary Metz

Grapette Soda, porcelain sign, urging readers to "Enjoy," 27" x 16", NM, $650.00 (B).

Golden West Brewing Co., Oakland, California, advertising Bull's Eye Beer on porcelain single-sided sign, 18" x 18", EX . . . .$320.00 (B)

Golden West Coffee Clossett & Devers, Portland and Seattle, 5-lb, EX . . . .$125.00 (B)

Gold Medal, celluloid and metal watch fob, 1½" dia., VG . . . .$50.00 (B)

Gold Medal Flour, paper on cloth advertising sign with a kernel of wheat dissected and named, 28" x 42", EX . . . .$95.00 (B)

Gold-Pak, Crown Rubber Co., Akron, OH, litho condom tin...3 for $1.00, 1½" x 2", EX . . . .$400.00 (B)

Gold Seal Boots and Overshoes, double-sided tin litho advertising sign, featuring artwork of boots and shoes, 18¼" L, EX . . . .$250.00 (C)

Gold Seal Champagne, tip tray, manufactured by American Artworks, Coshocton, Ohio, 4½" x 6½", EX . . . .$50.00 (D)

Gold Star Coffee, David G. Evans Coffee Co., St. Louis, glass jar, 3-lb., G . . . .$35.00 (D)

Gold Tip Gum...Peppermint, Sterling Mint Co., Inc., New York, cardboard gum package, EX . . . .$20.00 (D)

Golf Girl Talcum Powder, paper label container with graphics of vintage woman golfing, 2½" x 5½", EX . .$625.00 (B)

Gollam's Ice Cream, double-sided porcelain sidewalk sign in frame with graphics of youngster carrying a large cone, EX . . . .$415.00 (B)

Gollam's Lebanon Ice Cream, We Serve, painted metal double-sided sidewalk sign, 1940s, VG . . . . .$200.00 (D)

Good Gulf Gasoline globe, one-piece etched construction, 16", G . . . .$375.00 (B)

Goodrich...Batteries, Tires, Accessories, porcelain advertising sign, self-framing, 60" x 20½", EX . . . .$175.00 (D)

Goodrich Safety Tires, one-sided porcelain sign, probably Canadian, with graphics of Canadian Mountie, 18¼" x 62¾", VG . . . .$6,000.00 (B)

Goodrich Silvertowns Are Durable, die cut cardboard litho advertising with graphics of cars and ocean, 50" x 36", VG . . . .$425.00 (B)

Grape-Nuts...To school well fed on...There's a reason, self-framing tin sign with little girl walking with St. Bernard, 20¼" x 30¼", EX, **$1,350.00 (D)**. *Courtesy of Antiques Cards & Collectibles/Ray Pelley*

Grape Smash, Better Than Straight Grape Juice, tin sign, 13½" x 9½", EX, **$325.00 (B)**. *Courtesy of Muddy River Trading Co./Gary Metz*

Goodrich Silvertowns, die cut porcelain double-sided flange sign, 23½" x 19", G . . . .$210.00 (B)

Goodrich Silvertowns, one-sided porcelain advertising sign, 72" x 24", VG . . . .$325.00 (C)

Goodrich Sport Shoes, advertising die cut cardboard poster featuring artwork of Indian, framed, 26" x 41", EX . . . .$260.00 (B)

Goodrich Sport Shoes, cardboard die cut easelback display sign in likeness of vintage boy running with tie blowing in the breeze, 16½" x 23¼", NM . . . .$195.00 (C)

Goodrich Tires Slow Down...Safety First, single-sided porcelain advertising sign, 26" dia., EX . . . . .$325.00 (C)

Goodrich Tires, supplies, porcelain flange sign, 18" dia., white lettering on blue background, G . . . . .$265.00 (D)

Goodrich... You'll get more and quicker heat with this ..hot water heater, paper advertising with artwork of early model auto heater, 57" x 34", EX . . . .$25.00 (D)

Goodstock Shirts, tin litho advertising sign with applied glitter, 20" x 14", 1900s, EX . . . .$275.00 (C)

Goodyear Batteries, one-sided porcelain advertising sign, 47" x 26½", G . . . .$165.00 (B)

Good Year Bicycle Tire, paper litho advertising sign with graphics of vintage bicycle, 13" x 21", EX . . .$275.00 (D)

Goodyear, die cut porcelain advertising sign in shape of winged foot, 46" x 16" x 1", 1940s, EX . . . . . .$240.00 (B)

Goodyear #1 in Tires, die cut metal sign in shape of blimp, 39" x 17½", VG . . . .$2,500.00 (C)

Goodyear Service Station, one-sided porcelain sign with graphics circled by a Firestone tire, 71½" x 24", G . . . .$250.00 (B)

Goodyear...Tires, metal, framed glass front light-up sign with fleet foot at top center, G . . . .$65.00 (D)

Goodyear Tires, one-sided porcelain advertising sign with graphics of fleet foot in center, 72" x 24", G . .$275.00 (C)

Great Majestic Ranges, gesso bas-relief advertising sign with graphics of woman cooking on product, great details, 1915, 37" x 49" x 4¼", EX, $3,000.00 (B).

Great Western Line, advertising sign, metal over cardboard, Smith Manufacturing Co., Chicago, IL, 27½" x 19", G, $1,200.00 (B). *Courtesy of Collectors Auction Services*

Green River, cardboard counter stand-up sign advertising "first for thirst...Green River," with original bottle and cap, EX, $60.00 (B). *Courtesy of Buffalo Bay Auction Co.*

Goodyear Tires...Scranton, PA, painted tin directional arrow dealer sign, 35¼" x 11⅜", NM ......$195.00 (C)

Goodyear Tires, wooden painted thermometer with tire surrounding the earth at top, dealer message at bottom, vertical scale, 3¼" x 11½", G ....$65.00 (D)

Googh's Sarsaparilla, paper advertising, "Endorsed by the Best Chemists and Physicians in the United States," graphics of young girl angel, 11" x 14", EX ....$95.00 (D)

Googh's Sarsaparilla...Take for all blood diseases, framed paper advertisement showing small girl angel, 11" x 14", EX ....$125.00 (D)

Gordon's Fresh Foods, Truck Serving The Best, clear glass store jar with original metal lid, 7½" dia., EX ..$130.00 (C)

Gordon's Fresh Potato Chips, round metal potato chip can with artwork of old panel delivery truck over message, 11¼" tall, EX ....$65.00 (C)

Gordon's Potato Chips, can with delivery panel truck at top of container, 1-lb., 11¼" T, VG ....$65.00 (D)

Gordon's Potato Chips, can with Gordon's delivery truck at top, metal, 7½" x 11½", red and cream, EX .$85.00 (C)

Gorton's Codfish...Eat...in cans ready to use, porcelain door push, 6" x 3½", EX ....$525.00 (B)

Goudy & Kent's Biscuit, tin with paper label on tin container with pry lid, graphics of seaman at ship's wheel, 3" x 4½", EX ....$45.00 (B)

Grape Ola, tin sign with graphics of delicious looking bunch of grapes, 20" x 14", NM, $500.00 (B).

Green-Wheeler Shoes, tin on cardboard advertising sign promoting "For Ladies, None Better," with graphics of woman in vintage dress by stone wall, by American artworks, 11¾" x 14¼", 1911, EX, $600.00 (B). *Courtesy of Buffalo Bay Auction Co.*

Greenwich Insurance Co., paper advertising calendar, 8" x 12½", VG, $20.00. (B). *Courtesy of Collectors Auction Services*

Gowan Drug Co., plastic advertising sign in the shape of morter & pestal, 37" x 24" x 18", G . . . .$80.00 (B)

Grafs Beverages, "The Best What Gives," with spotlighted Graf man to left of message, tin litho advertising sign, 29½" x 11½", EX . . . .$150.00 (B)

Graham, four-page foldout advertising brochure for their automobile with graphics of car front on the cover sheet, 11" x 8½", 1938, VG . . . .$55.00 (C)

Graham's ice cream, box, waxed cardboard with graphics of old delivery truck, 3½" x 2¾", EX . . . .$55.00 (C)

Grain Belt Brewing Co., litho on canvas depicting wilderness scene of hunters, horses, wolves, and deer, Minneapolis, 31" x 26", NM . . . .$65.00 (B)

Grains of Gold, Scientifically Prepared Breakfast Cereal, cardboard box with graphics of wheat grains on box, 1929, 20-oz., EX . . . .$10.00 (D)

Grand Old Party...1856 to 1908, round tip tray with artwork of Taft & Sherman in center of tray under graphics of White House, great strong graphics, 4⅛" dia., EX . . . . .$85.00 (B)

Grand Order Cigars, "Mild and Excellent," tin litho self-framing advertising sign with top mounting bracket, 37½" x 13", EX . . . .$115.00 (B)

Grand Prize Beer, advertising clock, wood and metal, from the Texas Brewery, 12½" x 3½" x 14½", EX . . . .$240.00 (B)

Grand Republic 5¢ cigar, pocket cutter, 1" x 2", VG . . . .$50.00 (B)

Greyhound, paper advertising calendar, "Biscayne Key, Miami, Florida," only one monthly pad, 19½" x 32", EX, $85.00 (C).

Griffith & Boyd Co. Fertilizers, paper litho, framed advertisement with graphics of pretty young woman, 19¾" x 24¼", G, **$275.00 (B).**
Courtesy of Collectors Auction Services

Grand Union Coffee, key-wound tin litho container, 1-lb., EX . . . .$60.00 (B)

Grand Union Tea Company, baking powder tin container with paper litho label with graphics of two children, 3¼" x 5¼", VG . . . .$75.00 (C)

Grand Union Tea Company calendar with graphics of young girl on front, 13" x 29", 1903, EX . . . . .$525.00 (C)

Grand Union Tea Company, trade card, with artwork of Mrs. Cleveland, Lady of the White House, and WI product locations on reverse side, 7" x 13½", EX . . . . .$60.00 (B)

Grandy & Hoge, stenciled leather tire cover from Oakland-Pontiac-Paris Idaho, EX . . . .$25.00 (B)

Granger Pipe Tobacco, cardboard advertising sign with graphics of master sgt. lighting up a pipe, 16¼" x 11½", EX . . . .$75.00 (C)

Granger Pipe Tobacco, round tin, back side has a message explaining why this tobacco is cooler to smoke, G . . . .$26.00 (D)

Granger, rough cut tobacco sign, cardboard with graphics of old gentleman with horse and buggy, 15" x 20¼", EX . . . .$85.00 (C)

Grant Batteries Service... Recharging, double-sided metal flange advertising sign, NOS, 18" x 14", EX . .$275.00 (C)

Grape Crush, glass dispenser with metal pump, 6½" dia. x 12½", VG . . . .$3,000.00 (B)

Grape Dee-Light, Gee but it's good, Jacob Onuschak, Northampton, PA, with great graphics, cardboard hang-up sign, 1920s, 10½" x 14", EX . . . .$45.00 (B)

Grape-Nuts, Postum Cereal Company, cereal tin, 5½" H, EX . . . .$140.00 (B)

Grape-Nuts, tin advertising sign with self-contained frame, graphics of young girl carrying a basket of flowers, "To school well fed on Grape-Nuts...There's a reason," 20¼" x 30¼", EX . . . .$1,595.00 (C)

Grape-Nuts... To school well fed on...There's a reason, self-framing tin sign with little girl walking with St. Bernard, 20¼" x 30¼", EX . . . .$1,350.00 (D)

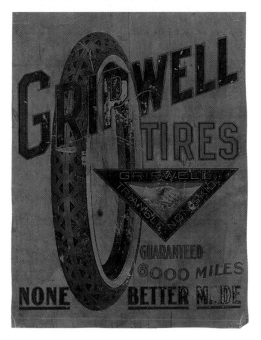

Gripwell Tires, wooden advertising sign,
12" x 16", G, **$425.00 (B).**

Gruen, advertising clock, plastic
body with glass face, 17" dia., VG,
$55.00 (B).

Gulf gas station, full color, matted and
framed photo, 41" x 22¾", NM,
$145.00 (B).

Grape Smash, Better Than Straight Grape Juice, tin sign,
13½" x 9½", G . . . .**$150.00 (C)**

Grape Sparkle, tin litho over cardboard advertising sign
with graphics of young woman enjoying a bottle of the
product, 13⅜" x 6", EX . . . .**$155.00 (C)**

Grapette... Enjoy...Soda, oval painted metal sign,
F . . . .**$125.00 (C)**

Grapette Soda, self-framing embossed tin advertising sign
with strong colors, 24" x 11½", EX . . . .**$110.00 (B)**

Great Majestic Ranges, gesso bas-relief advertising sign
with graphics of woman cooking on product, great details,
1915, 37" x 49" x 4¼", EX . . . .**$3,000.00 (B)**

Great Northern Railway, advertising calendar with
graphics of "Lazy Boy," a Blackfeet Medicine Man, Glaci-
er National Park, MT, "Route of the Empire Builder,"
with both top and bottom metal bands, 16" x 33", 1948,
NM . . . .**$145.00 (C)**

Great Northwestern Railroad, calendar with graphics of
Indian in full headdress, metal strip at top and bottom
with full tear sheet, 15½" x 33", 1944, EX . . .**$305.00 (B)**

Great Slice Plug, country store countertop tobacco cutter,
16" x 6", EX . . . .**$135.00 (D)**

Greenfield Gasoline Service, light-up pump, globe with
glass inserts in metal band, 18" x 19", EX . . .**$425.00 (C)**

Gulf, Heating Oils, three-dimensional sign on hanging arm, good graphics with sign in flames, NM, $325.00 (C).

Gulflex, self-framing embossed tin sign, 48" x 24", VG, $240.00 (B).

Gurd's Distilled Water, single-sided embossed tin sign, 21½" x 6", VG, $350.00 (B).

Green River, cardboard counter stand-up sign advertising "first for thirst...Green River," with original bottle and cap, EX . . . .$60.00 (B)

Green River, countertop resin statue of old black man and horse, 13¾" x 3½" x 9½", VG . . . .$210.00 (B)

Green River, store countertop display with bottle, "The favorite of millions 5¢ a bottle," 7½" x 11¼", EX . .$65.00 (B)

Green River...The Whiskey Without a Headache, ink blotter with graphics of old black man and sway-backed horse with jug of product on saddle, 9¼" x 4", EX . . .$71.00 (B)

Green River Whiskey, ashtray with match holder at top, 5" x 5" x 4½", EX . . . .$60.00 (B)

Green River Whiskey, blotter, "Blots out all your troubles," 9½" x 4", 1890s, NM . . . .$45.00 (D)

Green River Whiskey, embossed metal token, 1¼" dia., EX . . . .$75.00 (D)

Green River Whiskey, full-figure back bar statue of elderly black man and sway-backed horse carrying whiskey, 14" x 10½" x 4", NM . . . .$485.00 (B)

Green River Whiskey, good luck token with the trademark black man and mule, "the Whiskey without regrets," "It's lucky to Drink Green River Whiskey," EX . . . . .$30.00 (B)

Green River Whiskey, paper litho advertising with graphics of old man and horse, copyright 1889, J.W. McCulloch Owensboro, Kentucky, 22⅝" x 18¾", VG . . . .$150.00 (B)

Green River Whiskey, tin litho in wood frame, trademark advertising of old man, horse, and Green River Whiskey jug, "Chas. Shonk Co., Litho Chicago No. C. 1203," 41" x 31", EX . . . .$550.00 (B)

Green River Whiskey, tin litho serving tray with the black man and horse with jug scene, litho by Chas. Shonk, 12" dia., EX . . . .$605.00 (B)

Green River Whiskey, watch fob with the usual logo on front and product info on back, 1½", EX . . . . .$85.00 (B)

Green River Wines Liquors, sign in likeness of label, graphics of trademark Green River Jug, old black man, and horse, 19" x 7", VG . . . .$130.00 (B)

Greensmith's Derby Dog Biscuits, cardboard string-hung advertising sign with graphics of dogs doing tricks for a clown, 24" x 19", 1920s, NM . . . .$195.00 (C)

Gypsy Hosiery...George H. Buschmann, Owensville, Mo., round metal tip tray with gypsy camp scene and gypsy woman inset in center, 6" dia., EX, $210.00 (B).

Green Spot, cardboard advertising sign with graphics of orange halves and bottles of product, 21" x 11", 1936, EX . . . .$85.00 (C)

Green Spot Orange Drink, one-sided embossed chalk board with graphics of glasses having the product poured, 17¼" x 27¼", VG . . . .$45.00 (B)

Green Spot, tin litho embossed sign promoting orange-ade with tilted bottle in center, 20" x 12", EX . . . .$145.00 (D)

Green-Wheeler Shoes, tin on cardboard advertising sign, promoting "For Ladies, None Better," with graphics of woman in vintage dress by stone wall, by American artworks, 11¾" x 14¼", 1911, EX . . . .$600.00 (B)

Green Whiskey Whiske, charger, tin litho of trademark horse, old man, and jug, 24" dia., EX . . . .$425.00 (B)

Greyhound, light-up wall advertising clock, EX . .$145.00 (D)

Greyhound Lines, calendar with graphics of horse and woman and bus in background, partial tear sheet, 20" x 30", 1938, EX . . . .$175.00 (C)

Greyhound Lines, porcelain station sign with artwork of running dog in center, 36" x 20½", EX . . . . .$250.00 (D)

Greyhound...Super Motor Fuel, two-sided porcelain sign with graphics of racing greyhound, 58" x 34", G . . . .$650.00 (B)

Griesedieck Bros...Premium Light...Beer...It's De-Bitterized, round metal frame advertising clock with message in center of face, 15" dia., G . . . .$135.00 (D)

Griffon Safety Razor, tin litho container, 1⅜" x 2¼", EX . . . .$220.00 (B)

Griffon Safety Razor, tin with artwork of man shaving with product, 1¾" x 2¼" x 1⅛", EX . . . .$600.00 (B)

Grisdale Coffee, screw-top container, 4" x 6", VG . .$40.00 (C)

Grit, framed advertising calendar on heavy stock paper, "America's Greatest Family Newspaper," 1904, VG . . . .$120.00 (B)

Grizzly Brake Lining, plastic and metal light-up advertising sign with images of bears, 25¼" x 10¼" x 4¼", EX . . . .$325.00 (C)

Grohman's Drug Store, wood scale-type advertising thermometer, "prescription druggist," 4" x 15⅛", G . .$110.00 (B)

Groub's Belle Coffee, tin litho container with graphics of young woman in center cameo with screw lid from the John C. Groub Co., NY, NY, litho by the Passaic Metal Co., 1-lb., VG . . . .$300.00 (B)

Groub's Belle Oats, slip-lid tin with graphics of young woman in flower bonnet, EX . . . .$275.00 (C)

Gruen Watch Time... Post's Jewelry Store, light-up advertising clock, with local message on bottom, ad on plate, EX . . . .$425.00 (C)

Gruen, wooden watch display case with gold lettering at top of case, 8¾" x 15", VG . . . .$135.00 (C)

GSU Power Center, sign with Reddy Kilowatt figure in center, one-sided porcelain, 44" x 33", G . . . . .$50.00 (B)

Gulf, cloth sleeve patch, 2½" x 2¼", G . . . .$12.00 (C)

Gulf...dieselect Fuel, porcelain pump plate, rare sign, 10½", NM . . . .$435.00 (B)

Gulf, Heating Oils, three-dimensional sign on hanging arm, good graphics with sign in flames, EX . .$295.00 (D)

Gulflex Lubrication, paper poster for posting Sept. 1-15, 1940, 27¾" x 42", VG . . . .$65.00 (B)

Gulf, "Look How They've Stepped Up No-Nox!...Better try this Better Fuel," with graphics of built-up muscle man, 27¾" x 42", VG . . . .$110.00 (B)

Gulflube... The High Mileage Motor Oil Multi-Sol Processed, self-framing embossed tin advertising sign, 48" x 24", 1948, EX . . . .$350.00 (C)

Gulf Marine, porcelain pump sign, 11⅜" x 8½", NM **$215.00 (B)**

Gulf Marine, white gasoline globe, small wide glass body with glass lens, 12½" dia., VG . . . .$700.00 (B)

Gulf Marine, white gasoline porcelain pump sign, 10½" dia., EX . . . .$350.00 (B)

Gulf, paper poster, "Fill up with Stepped Up No-Nox," 27¾" x 42", VG . . . .$60.00 (B)

Gulf, plastic letters on metal strip, blue, EX .$115.00 (C)

Gulfpride, paper poster with graphics of cat, "Change to...Here!," 27¾" x 42", VG . . . .$150.00 (B)

Gulf, round plastic light-up sign with lettering across center, 31" dia., EX . . . .$165.00 (D)

Gulf, salesman sample of outdoor lighted sign for service stations, 7¼" x 21½", 1940s, EX . . . .$395.00 (C)

Gulf, service station attendant's summer hat, NOS, Brokfield Uniforms, 6¾", NM . . . .$95.00 (D)

Gulf Service Station, gasoline price rack with panels for Gulftane, No-Nox, and Good Gulf, 43" x 57" x 62", VG . . . .$350.00 (B)

Gulf, "Singing with sweeter power...New No-Nox...New Good Gulf," 27¾" x 42", VG . . . .$90.00 (B)

Gulf Supreme Motor Oil... Slow, porcelain single-sided dealer sign, Courtesy of Gulf Refining Co., 14" x 45", G . . . .$400.00 (B)

Gulf... That Good...Gasoline...At the sign of the orange disc...Gulf Refining Co., one-sided porcelain sign with graphics of touring car on road, 27½" x 60", VG . . .$2,400.00 (B)

Gulf... That Good Gasoline, At the sign of the orange disc, with artwork of early touring car driving up hill, porcelain sign, 27½" x 60", F . . . .$750.00 (C)

Gulf Valvetop Oil Display, service station metal rack for oil, 10¾" x 4" x 25½", EX . . . .$85.00 (B)

G. Washington coffee, store counter display case, painted tin with glass front, three shelves for product display, 11½" x 13", VG . . . .$95.00 (D)

Gypsy Hosiery... George H. Buschmann, Owensville, Mo., round metal tip tray with gypsy camp scene and gypsy woman inset in center, 6" dia., F . . . .$55.00 (D)

Gypsy Wine, celluloid over cardboard advertising sign promoting "E & K Gypsy Grape Wine," with graphics of pretty red-haired woman, 10" x 7", EX . . . . .$180.00 (B)

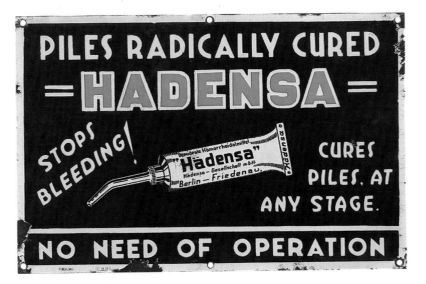

Hadensa, "Piles Radically Cured," one-sided porcelain sign, 18" x 22", EX, $195.00 (B).

Hail Insurance on growing crops...C. Douglas Bell, embossed tin sign, 15½" x 22½", VG, $65.00 (B). *Courtesy of Collectors Auction Services*

Hair Bobbing, Ladies & Children Our Specialty, porcelain advertising sign, 24" x 12", VG, $395.00 (C).

Ha Dees, auto heater, die cut cardboard counter top display sign with easel back and great graphics of female "devil" with vintage auto, NOS, 1930s, EX . . . .$175.00(C)

Ha Dees, heated tin license plate attachment with graphics of the devil in the center, 5⅞" T, EX . . . . .$250.00 (C)

Hair Bobbing, Ladies & Children Our Specialty, porcelain advertising sign, 24" x 12", G . . . .$350.00 (B)

Half and Half, Burley and Bright Pipe Tobacco, glass jar with cardboard lid, 1-lb., EX . . . .$55.00 (C)

Half and Half, Burley and Bright Tobacco, tin, 3" x 4¼" x 1", EX . . . .$9.00 (D)

Hambone, cloth tobacco pouch with graphics of black man chewing on hambone, 2" x 3" x 1", 1917, EX . . .$55.00 (C)

Hamilton Brown Shoe Co...Agency, Keep the quality up, painted metal die cut flange sign, 19½" x 14", F . .$45.00 (D)

Hamilton Brown Shoe Co...American Lady Show, American Gentleman Shoe, paper poster with couple in period dress, 29¾" x 39¾", EX . . . .$250.00 (C)

Hamilton Brown Shoe Co., paper advertising with artwork of George and Martha Washington with shoe company emblem between them, 29¾" x 39¾", EX . . . .$275.00 (C)

Half and Half, Burley and Bright Pipe Tobacco, glass jar with cardboard lid, 1-lb., EX, **$55.00 (C).** *Courtesy of B.J. Summers*

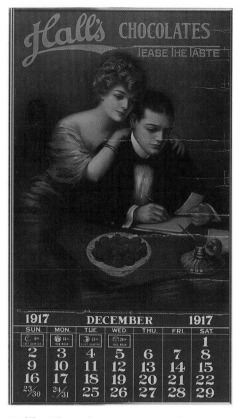

Hall's Chocolates, paper advertising calendar, partial pad, framed, 16¾" x 30", G, **$110.00 (B).**

Hamm's Beer, Born in the land of sky blue waters, metal and plastic motion light-up sign, great graphics, 31" x 18", EX, **$275.00 (D).** *Courtesy of Affordable Antiques*

Hamilton Brown Shoe Company, painted metal flange sign, two-sided, 19½" x 14", G . . . .**$125.00 (C)**

Hamilton Brown Shoe Co., paper litho advertisement, "The Prettiest Woman in America," 22" x 31", G . . . .**$275.00 (B)**

Hamm Brewing Co., B.P.O.E. guest, pinback, 2¼" x 1", 1897, NM . . . .**$95.00 (C)**

Hamm's Beer, Born in the land of sky blue waters, metal and plastic motion light-up sign, great graphics, 31" x 18", EX . . . .**$275.00 (D)**

Hamm's Beer, in cans, window paper advertising sign, 17¾" x 5½", 1930s, NM . . . .**$125.00 (C)**

Hamm's, electric motion advertising sign with flip-type advertising panels, 9" x 6" x 6½", EX . . . . . .**$110.00 (B)**

Hancock Gasoline, porcelain pump sign, 12" dia., EX . . . .**$1,200.00 (C)**

Hancocks Ale, porcelain advertising sign, "...the sign of Hospitality," 31½" x 41¾", VG . . . .**$220.00 (B)**

Hand Made Flake Cut, Globe Tobacco Co., Detroit, Mich., small top tin litho tobacco canister, 4⅞" x 6¼", EX . . . .**$525.00 (B)**

Hanlen Bros...Harrisburg, PA...The Old Reliable Liquor Dealers, round metal tip tray with artwork of horse's head in tray center, 4⅛" dia., EX . . . .**$130.00 (B)**

Hannum's Prevento, radiator and gas engine compound tin litho container with nice graphics of vintage auto on front, 3⅝" x 4½" x 2⅛", EX . . . .**$275.00 (B)**

Harrison's Heart O' Orange sold here, round embossed tin sign, 14¼" dia., EX, $250.00 (C).

Hartford Fire Insurance Company, advertising with artwork of deer in center, painted metal flange sign, 1950s, 18" x 28", VG, $350.00 (C).

Harvester Cigar, Heart of Havana, painted tin self-contained framed oval sign, "A.C. Co 71-A" at bottom, 9" x 13", EX, $125.00 (C).

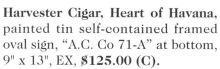

Hansen Hardware, light-up metal advertising clock on top of message, light-up strip, 26" x 18½", VG . . .$350.00 (B)

Hanson's Drug Store, advertising cardboard die cut calendar for Hanson's Headache Powders, with artwork of young woman in Panama straw hat, 1903, 7¼" x 13", NM . . . .$75.00 (B)

Happy Home Rolled Oats, container with home scene on cover, from St. Louis, MO, 1-lb. 4-oz., EX . . .$135.00 (C)

Happy Hotpoint, cardboard easel back die cut advertising figure, 9¼" x 13¼", 1920s, NM . . . .$65.00 (C)

Happy Hotpoint, die cut cardboard countertop store display with easel back, likeness of "Happy," 9¼" x 13¼", 20-30s, EX . . . .$95.00 (C)

Happy Hour Coffee, tin litho with graphics of hot steaming cup of coffee on front label, 1-lb., EX . . . .$125.00(C)

Hard A Port, tobacco tin with graphics of main at ship's wheel from Moore & Calvi, New York, 3¼" x 3¼", EX . . . .$180.00 (B)

Harding Cream Co...Cash For Cream, double-sided die cut porcelain flange sign shaped like old milk can, 15" x 27", EX . . . .$1,700.00 (B)

Hastings Piston Rings, glass sign, 18½" x 5½", VG, $90.00 (B).

Harvilla's...Have Handy, die-cut cardboard counter display designed to hold a 7 oz. bottle, G, $40.00 (B).

Haverly's United Mastodon Minstrels, paper litho advertising poster, 42" x 32½", VG, $500.00 (B).

Havoline Motor Oil, double-sided metal sign, 21½" x 18½", VG, $250.00 (B).

Harley-Davidson Motorcycle, light-up advertising clock with metal body and glass face and cover, 15¼" sq., EX . . . .$700.00 (B)

Harley-Davidson, one-day war alarm clock with advertising promoting war bonds, with original cardboard box, "Compliments of Harley Davidson Motor Co.," 1940s, EX . . . .$220.00 (B)

Harley-Davidson, Rider's Handbook, 4¾" x 6¾", 1929, VG . . . .$55.00 (B)

Harley-Davidson, 75th anniversary bullet pencil, 1978, EX . . . .$50.00 (C)

Harness Soap, paper litho advertising with graphics of man cleaning a harness, by International Food Co., Minneapolis, Minn., USA, 26¾" x 33½", VG . . . . .$975.00 (D)

Harold's Club or bust...Reno, Nevada, license plate attachment, die cut metal in likeness of covered wagon, 14" x 8", EX . . . .$135.00 (C)

Harrington & Richardson, advertising calendar with graphics of young woman dressed to shoot with dog and shotgun, with both top and bottom metal strips, 14" x 26", 1905, NM . . . .$325.00 (C)

Harrington & Richardson Arms Co., paper calendar with graphics of hunter in snow scene with full calendar pad and top and bottom metal strips, 14" x 27", 1907, NM . . . .$275.00 (C)

Harrington & Richardson, with bottom tear sheets, graphics of woman, gun, and dog in hunting scene, full calendar pad, 14" x 26", 1905, NM . . . .$575.00 (D)

Hazard Powder Co., paper advertising calendar titled "Return Of The Hunters" with graphics of young hunter returning from the hunt with game, 3½" x 6¼", 1903, EX, $450.00 (B). *Courtesy of Past Tyme Pleasures*

Hazle Club...Finer Flavor Drink, embossed tin door push, EX, $90.00 (B). *Courtesy of Muddy River Trading Co./Gary Metz*

Hazle Club Tru-Orange, painted metal flange sign, 14" x 20", EX, $130.00 (C).

Harrison's Heart O' Orange sold here, round embossed tin sign, 14¼" dia., EX . . . .$250.00 (C)

Hart Brand Canned Foods, beveled tin litho over cardboard, string-hung advertising sign with artwork of product cans, 13" x 9", EX . . . .$850.00 (B)

Hartford Fire Insurance Company, advertising with artwork of deer in center, painted metal flange sign, 1950s, 18" x 28", G . . . .$325.00 (B)

Harvard Ale, beer porter tin litho advertising sign, 23¼" x 23¾", F . . . .$115.00 (C)

Harvard Ale, reverse on glass advertising sign with cardboard backing and easel back for countertop display, graphics of product bottle and glass, 19" x 13", EX . .$145.00 (C)

Harvard Beer, metal serving tray manufactured by the H.D Beach Co. with graphics of couple at table being served beer, 12" dia., VG . . . .$170.00 (B)

Harvard Brewing Co., tin litho sign featuring artwork of woman enjoying cocktail in room overlooking garden courtyard, 36" x 45", EX . . . .$1,750.00 (B)

Harvester Cigar, Heart of Havana, self-framing tin litho advertising sign with graphics of young lady, 9" x 13", EX . . . .$165.00 (B)

Harvester Cigar, Heart of Havana, painted tin self-contained framed oval sign, "A.C. Co 71-A" at bottom, 9" x 13", EX . . . .$125.00 (C)

Harvest Queen Coffee, key-wound tin litho container with graphics of crown on front, 1-lb., EX . . . .$37.00 (B)

Harvey's Coffee, glass restaurant sign, "Serving Harvey's Coffee," 11" x 6", NM . . . .$45.00 (D)

Hatchway Union Suits, cardboard box with graphics of man walking in product with robe over arm, 1915, 10" X 15" x 1½", EX . . . .$30.00 (B)

Havana Blossom, cardboard sign with graphics of man promoting product, from P. Lorillard Co., 1910, 12" x 18", NM . . . .$185.00 (B)

Havana Plantation, metal figural paperweight, 4" x 1½", EX . . . .$75.00 (B)

Headlight Overalls, porcelain store advertising sign, featuring train with light, "Agency for...," 32" x 10", VG, **$350.00 (C).** *Courtesy of John and Vicki Mahan*

Heinz 57 Varieties, die cut string holder, double-sided, hard-to-find item, 17" x 14" x 7", EX, **$5,400.00 (B).** *Courtesy of Buffalo Bay Auction Co.*

Heinz Home-Style Soups, single-sided tin litho with rolled edges, 27½" x 10½", VG, **$275.00 (B).**

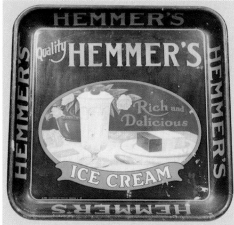

Hemmer's Ice Cream, "Rich and Delicious," serving tray, with artwork of ice cream products in center of tray, 1920s, 13" x 13", G, **$170.00 (B).** *Courtesy of Muddy River Trading Co./Gary Metz*

Have a Pepsi, self-framed tin menu board, with bottle cap logo, 19½" x 30", 1950s, VG . . . .**$110.00 (B)**

Have Some Junket, round metal tip tray with small girl with a bowl of product, 4¼" dia., EX . . . .**$90.00 (B)**

Havoline Marine Oil...it makes a difference...Havoline Oil Company, New York City, tin litho paperweight made to resemble a 1-gal. oil can, filled with sand, 1½" x 2½" x 1", EX . . . .**$1,550.00 (B)**

Hawken...Everything Musical...Pianos, vintage thin tin sign with graphics of Nipper listening to his master's voice, 28" x 19½", VG . . . .**$240.00 (B)**

Hazard Powder Co., paper advertising calendar titled "Return Of The Hunters" with graphics of young hunter returning from the hunt with game, 3½" x 6¼", 1903, EX . . . .**$450.00 (B)**

Hazle Club...Finer Flavor Drink, embossed tin door push, EX . . . .**$90.00 (B)**

Hazle Club Tru-Orange, painted metal flange sign, 14" x 20", EX . . . .**$130.00 (C)**

H.B Franklin & Co., Chicago, Ill., Each Cigar Is A Perfect Smoke And Extra Value, cigar box, G . . . .**$25.00 (D)**

H.C. Carpenter Barber Shop, paper advertising with graphics of young girls feeding a pony, 12¼" x 16¼", 1922, EX . . . .**$75.00 (B)**

Headlight Overalls, porcelain store advertising sign, featuring train with light, "Agency for...," 32" x 10", G . . . .**$300.00 (C)**

Hendlers Ice Cream, paper litho advertising sign, framed, 20" x 29", F, $625.00 (B).

Hercules Powder Company, calendar, featuring artwork of boy and dog, 1941, 13" x 29½", EX, $85.00 (C).

Hero Puts Out Fires Instantly, fire extinguisher kit in original cardboard box, 5" x 8¼" x 2⅞", VG, $15.00 (B).

Headlight Shrunk Overalls, cardboard advertising sign with tin surround, graphics of standard train headlight beam, "A New Pair Free If They Shrink," 20¾" x 10", G . . . .$175.00 (C)

Headlight work clothes, embossed metal advertising sign with original wooden frame, 60" x 8", EX . . . .$325.00 (D)

Heaney, magician, paperboard advertising sign, 14" x 20", 1915, EX . . . .$195.00 (D)

Heath & Milligan...Sunshine Finishes, tip tray with graphics of two children and dog on floor, 4¼" dia., G . . . .$55.00 (B)

Heide's Colored Coons, candy box, 10¼" x 6¾" x 1¾", EX . . . .$325.00 (C)

Heide's Mints, advertising trade card with graphics of red-haired child advertising the product on the front and a testimonial on the back by Sarah Bernhardt, made for the Pan American Exposition, 3½" x 5½", 1901, EX . . . .$70.00 (B)

Heineken Beer, sign, one-sided porcelain sign with caricature of beer glass man, 16" x 23½", VG . . . . .$250.00 (B)

Heineken Beer, wooden tapper handle, G . . . .$10.00 (C)

Heineken's Holland Beer, wooden shoe, EX . .$25.00 (C)

Hershey's Krackel Milk Chocolate, case box that held 24 bars, 1-lb. 5-oz., NM, $10.00 (D).

The Hickman-Ebbert Co., one-sided tin litho, self-framing tin sign, 34½" x 23⅜", VG, $800.00 (B).

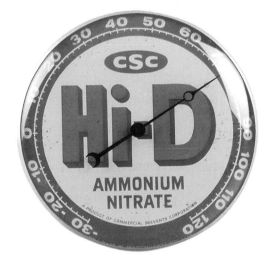

Hi-D Ammonium Nitrate, glass and tin advertising thermometer, 12" dia., VG, $80.00 (B).

Heineken's Imported Holland Beer, tin litho over cardboard, with Holland graphics in left lower corner, 1950s, EX . . . .$45.00 (B)

Heinsohn Bros. Dairy, calendar, paper calendar with full month pad and original metal strips on top and bottom, artwork of baby in highchair, 1927, 15" x 19½", EX . .$30.00 (B)

Heinz Bros., early glass catsup bottle with paper label, graphics of large tomato in center of label, 2¼" x 8¼", VG . . . .$140.00 (B)

Heinz 57 Tomato Catsup, trolley car advertising sign with graphics of catsup bottle and a 1908 date on the bottle, 21" x 11", 1908, EX . . . .$130.00 (B)

Heinz 57 Varieties, die cut string holder, double-sided, hard-to-find item, 17" x 14" x 7", EX . . . . . .$5,400.00 (B)

Heinz, tin litho delivery truck with working lights and original box, 12" x 3½" x 5", EX . . . .$550.00 (B)

Hello World Coffee, paper label over tin container with graphics of globe on center, 1-lb., EX . . . .$150.00 (B)

Helmar, rectangular metal tip tray with graphics of Turkish scenes, 6" L, EX . . . .$55.00 (B)

Helmar Turkish Cigarettes, cardboard advertising sign in wood frame, 21⅝" x 3⅝", EX . . . .$25.00 (C)

Helmar Turkish Cigarettes, framed paper advertising sign with graphics of young woman in western attire, 33" x 42½", G . . . .$670.00 (B)

Helmar...Turkish Cigarettes...Quality Superb, cardboard sign on wood, 3½" x 21½", G . . . .$15.00 (D)

Hemmer's Ice Cream, serving tray, "Rich and Delicious," with artwork of ice cream products in center of tray, 1920s, 13" x 13", EX . . . .$235.00 (C)

Hendlers Ice Cream, die cut window display with graphics of ice cream cones with message inside, 1950s, 36" x 23", NM . . . .$45.00 (B)

Hills Bros. puzzle, framed under glass with original box, 14" x 16", 1933, VG, $90.00 (B).

Hills Bros. Coffee, automated advertising sign with black youngster sitting on top of message box pouring and drinking a cup of the product, 21" x 18" x 41", VG, $2,750.00 (B).

Courtesy of Collectors Auction Services

Hiram's General Store, punch board, 12½" x 15", VG, $95.00 (C).

Hendlers Ice Cream, paper litho advertising sign, framed, 20" x 29", F . . . .$625.00 (B)

Henkel's, pot scraper, tin litho scraper advertising Henkel's Flour, 3¼" x 3", red, blue, and white, EX . . . . .$300.00 (B)

Henkes' Beer, sign, "Taste The True Juniper Flavor," self-framed porcelain advertising sign with artwork of product bottles, 12½" x 19", VG . . . .$450.00 (C)

Henry Weilersbacher, paperweight, advertising beer, carbonated drinks and fountain & bar supplies, 4" dia., EX . . . .$100.00 (B)

Hep...Get...for yourself, tin double-sided flange advertising sign with graphics of product bottle, NOS, 17⅝" X 13¼", NM . . . .$325.00 (C)

Heptol Splits...For Health's Sake...Laxative, round metal tip tray with graphics of cowboy riding bucking bronc, 4⅛" dia., G . . . .$170.00 (B)

Hires...Drink Hires, oval self-framing tray with litho of two pretty women enjoying the product, great graphics, rare item and hard to find, 23½" x 19½", VG, $1,000.00 (B). *Courtesy of Collectors Auction Services*

Hires, Drink in Bottles, cardboard ad sign featuring the artwork of Haskell Coffin on the girl and flare glass, 1910s, 15" x 21", EX, $575.00 (B).

Herbert Tareyton Cigarettes, 100-piece flat tin, F . . . .$42.00 (D)

Hercules, advertising poster with graphics of hunting scene with two men and a dog, 15½" x 24½", EX . . .$825.00 (B)

Hercules Coffee, container with small top, graphics of Hercules in cameo on front, 1-lb., VG . . . .$40.00 (B)

Hercules, condom tin, with tin litho image of Hercules holding the globe, 2⅛" x 1⅝" X ¼", EX . . . . .$125.00 (D)

Hercules Gunpowder, paper advertising poster with graphics of black youngster and older black gentleman in snowy field loading a muzzle loader, 13½" x 19", 1924, VG . . . .$85.00 (B)

Hercules Gunpowder, poster with graphics of black man and youngster hunting in the snow with dog, complete with top and bottom metal strips, 15½" x 25⅛", EX . . . .$395.00 (D)

Hercules Powder, Black Sporting, paper litho label on tin container with artwork of Hercules on front cover, 1-lb., EX . . . .$60.00 (B)

Hercules Powder Co., advertising paper litho with graphics of pheasant in field setting, 20¼" x 23¼", VG . .$700.00 (B)

Hercules Powder Company, calendar, featuring artwork of boy and dog, 1941, 13" x 29½", EX . . . .$85.00 (C)

Herny Heeren, farm machinery dealer, die cut calendar, 5¾" x 11½", 1907, EX . . . .$145.00 (C)

Hershey's Gum, 6 sticks for 5¢ cents, cardboard blotter, 5⅜" x 2⅞", EX . . . .$475.00 (B)

Hershey's Ice Cream, menu board with top litho advertising message, EX . . . .$85.00 (B)

Hershey's Krackel Milk Chocolate, case box that held 24 bars, 1-lb. 5-oz., EX . . . .$7.00 (D)

Hershey's Mint Flavor Chewing Gum, cardboard counter-top display box, 5¼" x 5⅞" x 4⅛", EX . . . . .$1,200.00 (B)

H.H. Marvin, die cut calendar that was a give-away from Oregon, WI, hardware merchant, 7" x 13", EX .$125.00 (B)

Hiawatha Airway, shot shells box, G . . . .$8.00 (D)

Hires... Drink, It hits the spot, Try a bottle and you'll buy a case, embossed tin sign with artwork of man holding bottle, 15¾" x 9¾", EX, $225.00 (B). *Courtesy of Muddy River Trading Co./Gary Metz*

Hires Root Beer...Fountain Service, double-sided tin sign with top mounting holes, rare R-J disc logo in center, "We Serve With Real Juices," 16" x 14⅝", VG, $475.00 (B). *Courtesy of Autopia Advertising Auctions*

Hires Root Beer, Finer Flavor because of Real Root Juices, tin door push with beveled edges, EX, $150.00 (B). *Courtesy of Muddy River Trading Co./Gary Metz*

Hiawatha Oil, tin can, Hiawatha Harvester Oil from Fairwell Ozmun Kirk & Co., St. Paul, MN, 3" x 7½", EX .$110.00 (B)

Hickman's Silver Birch Chewing Gum, cardboard store display complete with unopened gum packs, artwork of bird on birch limb, 6¼" x 5¼" x 4¼", EX .$1,200.00 (B)

Hickman's Silver Birch Chewing Gum, 5¢, full store countertop display package, 4½" x 6½" x 1", EX ....$625.00 (B)

Hickory Garters, countertop die cut litho on wood, display with image of children under advertising umbrella, 13" x 19½", NM ......$1,025.00 (B)

Hicks Capudine... Its Liquid-effects immediately...10¢, 25¢, and 50¢ cents a bottle, round metal tip tray with graphics of product in tray center, 6" dia., EX ....$160.00 (B)

Hi Energee, gasoline globe, plastic body with two glass lenses, 13½" dia., VG ....$190.00 (B)

High Admiral cigarette, pinback featuring yellow kid, 1¼", 1890s, EX ....$75.00 (C)

High Ball Ginger Ale, tin litho advertising sign with graphics of bottle in center, 9" x 9", EX .....$145.00 (B)

Highest Grade, tobacco tin, good strong graphics, 4½" x 3" x 2", EX ....$55.00 (C)

High Grade Sausage, from P.E. Rathjens & Sons, string-hung metal advertising sign, 9⅜" x 6⅜", NM .$125.00 (C)

Highland Evaporated Cream, metal tip tray with graphics of cream can in center of tray, 3⅝" dia., EX ..$120.00 (B)

Hires Root Beer, heavy cardboard die cut advertising sign with graphics of woman entertaining, "The Right Note for Home Refreshment," matted and framed, 34½" x 38½", VG, $475.00 (B). *Courtesy of Autopia Advertising Auctions*

Hires Root Beer, reverse painted glass, chain-hanging sign, 7¼" x 8¼", NM, $2,100.00 (C).

Hires Root Beer, tray "Quenches any thirst up to a mile long...just what the doctor ordered," Josh Slinger tray, 1914, EX, $1,750.00 (B).

Courtesy of Buffalo Bay Auction Co.

Hilbrich's Coffee, pail handle, from Hilbrich & Bastgen Co., Chicago, Ill., 7½" x 9", EX . . . .$125.00 (C)

Hills Bros. Coffee, automated advertising sign with black boy sitting on top of message box pouring and drinking a cup of the product, 21" x 18" x 41", VG   . . .$2,750.00 (B)

Hills Bros. Coffee...Coffee hungry folks prefer..., roll down paper over cloth sign with artwork of early scene in cabin around table with product, 61½" x 42", EX . . .$375.00 (B)

Hills Bros. Coffee, Drip Grind Coffee, tin container with artwork of Hills man drinking product on front, 20-lb., 9½" x 9½" x 13", EX . . . .$30.00 (D)

Hills Bros. Coffee, glass jar, 1-lb., EX . . . .$15.00 (D)

Himalaya Bouquet, porcelain flange sign, 14" x 9", VG . . . .$270.00 (B)

Hires....Say, oval sign, framed, with artwork of Hires child holding early Hires mug, 1900s, 20" x 24", EX, $600.00 (B). *Courtesy of Muddy River Trading Co./Gary Metz*

H L Black Indian Cigar Store, Indian with product message at bottom, carved wood, 20" x 20" x 73", G, $13,000.00 (B). *Courtesy of Collectors Auction Services*

Hinz's Eagle Brand Coffee, paper label on tin container with slip lid, 1-lb., NM . . . .$30.00 (B)

Hi-Plane, litho vertical pocket tobacco tin with double prop plane, EX . . . .$115.00 (B)

Hi-Plane Smooth Cut Tobacco, for pipe and cigarettes, die cut cardboard with graphics of airplane in flight, 23" x 22", G . . . .$66.00 (B)

Hi-Plane Tobacco, embossed tin, sign with artwork of package of product, 35" x 11¾", EX . . . .$75.00 (B)

Hi-Plane, tobacco pocket tin with graphics of airplane on front label, EX . . . .$55.00 (C)

Hiram's General Store, punch board, 12½" x 15", G . . . .$70.00 (B)

Hires...and it's always pure...in bottles, embossed tin advertising sign, framed, 21¾" x 16", VG . . . .$395.00 (C)

Hires, bottle thermometer, die cut embossed tin with scale in neck of bottle, 7⅝" x 28½", NM . . . . .$185.00 (B)

Hires, cardboard advertising sign with artwork of girl and paper label bottle, 22" x 12", EX . . . .$200.00 (B)

Hires, cork fasteners, cardboard store display for bottle tops, these were used for Hires home-brewed root beer, 11" x 9", G . . . .$350.00 (B)

Hires, dial-type thermometer with graphics of root beer mug in center of piece, 12" dia., EX . . . .$135.00 (C)

Hires, die cut tin embossed bottle sign, 15½" x 57", VG . . . .$325.00 (B)

H.M. Pentz, Glen Hope, Penn. Milling Specialist, paper die cut calendar of young lady with large hat, full monthly pad, 1913, 14" x 23", NM, **$363.00 (B).** *Courtesy of Buffalo Bay Auction Co.*

Hoffman House Cigar, paper litho in wood frame with graphics of famous men smoking their cigars, 1901, 37½" x 24", G, **$695.00 (C).**

Hires...Drink, embossed tin advertising sign with image of Hires bottle, 32" x 11", NM . . . .**$155.00 (B)**

Hires...Drink Hires, oval self-framing tray with litho of two pretty women enjoying the product, great graphics, rare item and hard to find, 23½" x 19½", VG . . .**$1,000.00 (B)**

Hires, Drink in Bottles, cardboard ad sign featuring the artwork of Haskell Coffin on the girl and flare glass, 1910s, 15" x 21", EX . . . .**$575.00 (B)**

Hires... Drink, It hits the spot, Try a bottle and you'll buy a case, embossed tin sign with artwork of man holding bottle, 15¾" x 9¾", VG . . . .**$175.00 (C)**

Hires...Drink...it is pure, china dispenser with metal pump, in the shape of an hourglass, 7½" dia. x 13½", VG . . . .**$450.00 (B)**

Hires...Drink, menu board with bottle image and message at top of blackboard, 16" x 29", EX . . . .**$68.00 (B)**

Hires...Drink, one-sided tin embossed advertising sign with bottle to right side of message, 32" x 11", G . .**$110.00 (B)**

Hires ...Enjoy...Healthful...Delicious, embossed "tacker" type sign with image of product bottle, 9½" x 27½", 1930s, EX . . . .**$150.00 (B)**

Hires...In Bottles, painted metal sign ,with artwork of tilted bottle at right of message, 27" x 10", EX . . . . .**$95.00 (D)**

Hires...In Bottles, tin advertising sign with embossed lettering and graphics of bottle, 27¾" x 9¾", VG . . . . . .**$140.00 (B)**

Hires, Made With Roots-Barks-Herbs, So Refreshing double-sided tin flange advertising sign, rare item, 14" x 12", NM . . . .**$325.00 (B)**

Hires, menu board, glass, cardboard, and paper advertising item in chrome frame with graphics of Hires bottle at top of menu strips, 12" x 24", EX . . . .**$225.00 (B)**

Hires, painted metal door push, "It's high time for Hires...Root Beer," graphics of bottle cap to left of message, 29½" x 4", G . . . .**$55.00 (B)**

Hires, paper advertising sign featuring graphics of soda jerk with product, 11¼" x 7", 1914, EX . . . . .**$375.00 (D)**

Hires R-J Root Beer...A Toast To Good Taste...Enjoyable In Bottles, embossed tin advertising sign, R-J disc logo in center, NOS, 35¼" x 11¼", NM . . . .**$275.00 (B)**

Hires R-J Root Beer, glass and metal counter dispenser, 22" tall, EX . . . .**$225.00 (C)**

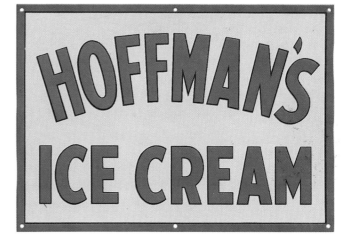

Hoffman's Ice Cream, double-sided painted metal advertising sign, 28" x 20", G, $80.00 (B).

Hoffmann's Old Time Roasted Coffee, grinder with litho tin front with wood frame on cast iron, 13½" H, EX, $1,200.00 (B). *Courtesy of Richard Opfer Auctioneering, Inc.*

Hollywoodglo...For screen star loveliness use, tri-fold cardboard advertising with early motion picture cameras and actress, G, $65.00 (D). *Courtesy of Illinois Antique Center/Kim & Dan Phillips*

Hires R-J Root Beer, stamped and embossed round type sign, 14" dia., EX . . . .$155.00 (B)

Hires R-J Root Beer, with real root juices, round tin embossed sign, 12" dia., EX . . . .$150.00 (B)

Hires Root Beer, barrel, wood and metal with claw feet and metal spouts, with Hires decal and advertising message on front and back, 21" x 31", EX . . . .$500.00 (B)

Hires Root Beer, die cut bottle thermometer, 1950s, 28" tall, EX . . . .$165.00 (B)

Hire's Root Beer, dispenser with paper label on front glass, 22" T, EX . . . .$275.00 (C)

Hires Root Beer, Finer Flavor because of Real Root Juices, tin door push with beveled edges, EX . . . .$150.00 (B)

Hires Root Beer...Fountain Service, double-sided tin sign with top mounting holes, rare R-J disc logo in center, "We Serve With Real Juices," 16" x 14⅝", VG . . . .$475.00 (B)

Hires Root Beer, German-made mug, 5" tall, EX . .$210.00 (B)

Hires Root Beer, heavy cardboard die cut advertising sign with graphics of woman entertaining, "The Right Note for Home Refreshment," matted and framed, 34½" x 38½", VG . . . .$475.00 (B)

Hires Root Beer, heavy paper poster with image of woman enjoying a glass of the product, "So Good With Food," 59" x 35½", NM . . . .$400.00 (B)

Hires Root Beer...in bottles-ice cold, embossed tin advertising sign, 27¼" x 19⅜", F . . . .$60.00 (B)

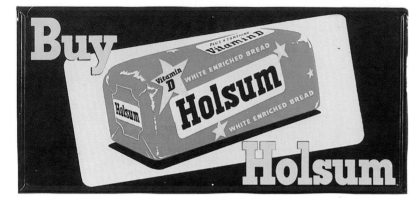

Holsum Bread, single-sided self-framed tin advertising sign, 7½" x 13", VG, $200.00 (B).

Houdaille Shock Absorber Service, double-sided tin flange sign, 26" x 19¾", $275.00 (B). *Courtesy of Autopia Advertising Auctions*

Hires Root Beer, pocket advertising mirror featuring the "ugly kid," G . . . .$275.00 (C)

Hires Root Beer, reverse painted glass, chain-hanging sign, 7¼" x 8¼", EX . . . .$1,700.00 (C)

Hires Root Beer, self-framing tin litho oval advertising sign with graphics of two young women enjoying the product from glasses with straws, made by Stelad Signs, 23¾" x 19¾", 1915, VG . . . .$250.00 (B)

Hires Root Beer, self-framing tin oval sign with graphics of the classic "ugly" kid holding a mug of the product and smiling, copyright date of May 21, 1903, by Beach Art Display, 1909, 20" x 24", 1900s, G . . . .$850.00 (B)

Hires Root Beer, tin advertising thermometer with image of Hires bottle at bottom of scale, 8¼" x 27", NM . .$325.00 (B)

Hires Root Beer, tin embossed advertising sign with image of bottle, "For Pleasure and Thirst," 55¾" x 17¾", NM . . . .$450.00 (C)

Hires Root Beer, tray "Quenches any thirst up to a mile long...just what the doctor ordered," Josh Slinger tray, 1914, EX . . . .$1,750.00 (B)

Hires Root Beer, with Roots, Barks, Herbs, stainless steel drugstore dispenser sign, EX . . . .$95.00 (B)

Hires....Say, oval sign, framed, with artwork of Hires child holding early Hires mug, 1900s, 20" x 24", VG$450.00 (C)

Hires...So Refreshing, double-sided tin flange sign, EX . . . .$200.00 (B)

Hires...So refreshing, made with roots, barks, herbs, painted metal sign, AAA Sign Co., Cottsville, Ohio, 13½" x 11½", EX . . . .$95.00 (D)

Hires, tin litho advertising charger with the familiar Hires Boy holding a mug of Root Beer, 20" x 24", 1907, VG . . . .$1,400.00 (B)

Hires, tin menu board with Hires tilted bottle at top, 15½" x 29½", EX . . . .$65.00 (B)

Honest Scrap Tobacco, advertising sign in original frame with graphics of dog and cat on both sides of product package, 30" x 22½", EX, $1,800.00 (B).
Courtesy of Buffalo Bay Auction Co.

Honey-Fruit Gum, "Nothing Like It, Delightful Flavor," tin over cardboard advertising sign, manufactured by Franklin-Caro Company in Richmond, Va., 16¼" x 9", EX, $1,300.00 (B). *Courtesy of Muddy River Trading Co./Gary Metz*

Honey Moon Tobacco, one-sided tin litho advertising sign from Penn Tobacco Co., featuring couple sitting on quarter moon, 9¾" H, EX, $525.00 (B). *Courtesy of Richard Opfer Auctioneering, Inc.*

Hires, Ugly Kid mug by Mettlach, 4¼" T, EX .$220.00 (B)

Hitchner Cookie Store, bin cover, metal and glass, 10¼" x 10½", F . . . .$15.00 (B)

Hite's, pain remedy wood, metal and glass advertising scale thermometer, from Roanoke, VA, 5⅛" x 24¼", VG . . . .$80.00 (B)

Hit Parade Cigarettes, flip-top box, G . . . .$8.00 (D)

H L Black Indian Cigar Store, Indian with product message at bottom, carved wood, 20" x 20" x 73", G .$13,000.00 (B)

H.M. Pentz, Glen Hope, Penn. Milling Specialist, paper die cut calendar of young lady with large hat, full monthly pad, 1913, 14" x 23", NM . . . .$363.00 (B)

Hoffman's House Cigar, advertising sign with graphics of young patriotic dressed girl with marching soldiers in background, 15½" x 25½", 1898, VG . . . . .$ 380.00 (B)

Hoffman's Ice Cream, double-sided hanging porcelain sign, "First choice," 25¾" x 22", EX . . . .$225.00 (D)

187

Hood's Ice Cream, double-sided painted metal advertising sign with graphics of trademark cow's head in center, 19" dia., G, **$1,200.00 (B)**. *Courtesy of Collectors Auction Services*

Hoodsies Ice Cream, die cut cardboard advertising sign with graphics of young couple on swing, 12¼" x 18½", EX, **$2,000.00 (B)**. *Courtesy of Collectors Auction Services*

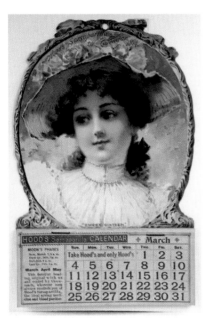

Hood's Sarsaparilla, calendar, die cut with artwork of pretty girl in bonnet, 1894, 5½" x 8¾", EX, **$55.00 (C)**.

Hoffman's Ice Cream...First Choice...Sealtest Approved, die cut porcelain outdoor advertising sign on original metal hanging arm, 25¾" x 22", G . . . .**$175.00 (D)**

Hoffmann's Old Time Coffee, early tin litho container with pry lid and graphics of "granny" in center cameo, 1-lb., EX . . . .**$150.00 (B)**

Hoffmann's Old Time Coffee, tin with great graphics on front, 4¼" H, EX . . . .**$75.00 (D)**

Hoffmann's Old Time Roasted Coffee, grinder with litho tin front with wood frame on cast iron, 13½" H, F . . . .**$250.00 (D)**

Hofnar Cigar, self-framing porcelain advertising sign, foreign, 23" x 61", G . . . .**$185.00 (B)**

Holiday Regular 94 Octane gas, light-up globe, narrow glass body, metal base with two lenses, 13½" dia., VG . . . .**$600.00 (B)**

Hood's Sarsaparilla, calendar featuring girl wearing a flowery bonnet, 1886, 7¼" x 14¾", EX, $50.00 (C).

Hopkins & Allen Arms Co., "Prairie Girl," paper litho advertising poster, good graphics and difficult to locate, 10" x 26¾", 1910s, EX, $2,500.00 (C). *Courtesy of Autopia Advertising Auctions*

Horton's Ice Cream, single-sided porcelain advertising sign, "The Premier Ice Cream of America," 20" x 28", VG, $275.00 (B). *Courtesy of Collectors Auction Services*

Holland House Coffee, key-wound tin litho container, 1-lb., EX . . . .$25.00 (B)

Hollywoodglo...For screen star loveliness use, tri-fold cardboard advertising with early motion picture cameras and actress, EX . . . .$95.00 (D)

Hollywoodglo, tri-fold counter advertising sign, 18" x 12", EX . . . .$75.00 (C)

Holman's Trailing Arbutus Face Powder, tin litho container designed to be used as trinket box after product is used, 1915, EX . . . .$50.00 (D)

Holsum Bread, yard-long advertising sign with metal strips at both top and bottom, graphics of man and woman reading, 11¾" x 35", EX . . . .$95.00 (B)

Home Lighting and Cooking Plant...The Incandescent Light and Stove Co., Cincinnati, OH, round metal tip tray with graphics of early kitchen scene, 4⅛" dia., EX . . .$260.00 (B)

Honest Long Cut Tobacco, unopened package with honest character on front and back, an early Duke Bros. piece, VG . . . .$175.00 (C)

Honest Scrap, porcelain advertising sign with graphics of arm with hammer, 9" x 12", EX . . . .$130.00 (B)

Honest Scrap Tobacco, advertising sign in original frame with graphics of dog and cat on both sides of product package, 30" x 22½", EX . . . .$1,800.00 (B)

Honest Scrap tobacco, tin sign with graphics of trademark forearm and hand with hammer, 6¾" x 8¾", VG . .$185.00 (B)

Household Match Striker, tin litho wall hung match striker "Your credit is good...The Household," by Kaufmann & Strauss Lithographers, 4¾" x 7¾", 1915s, EX, $130.00 (B).

Courtesy of Buffalo Bay Auction Co.

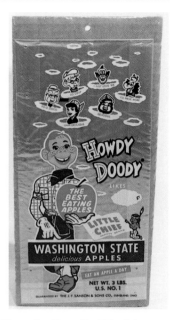

Howdy Doody Washington Apples, plastic bag, NOS, with graphics of Howdy Doody and friends on front, 3-lb., NM, $18.00 (D). *Courtesy of Rare Bird Antique Mall/Jon & Joan Wright*

Hot Ball, chewing and smoking tobacco, embossed tin litho advertising sign with jester holding package, rare piece, G, $900.00 (B). *Courtesy of Richard Opfer Auctioneering, Inc.*

Hrobak's Beverages, embossed single-sided tin sign, 20" x 9¼", VG, $50.00 (B).

Honest Tobacco, advertising cardboard sign in wood frame, "Honest Long Cut Tobacco," 1890s, G . . . .$850.00 (C)

Honest Tobacco...Long cut...smoking...chewing, cardboard advertising in frame featuring man at table in hat, 1890s, G . . . .$1,150.00 (C)

Honest Tobacco, unopened pack from American Tobacco Co., Factory #1, "Long Cut...smoking and chewing," NM . . . .$50.00 (B)

Honest...Wear-u-well...shoes, porcelain over metal double-sided flange advertising sign, 26¼" x 17½", VG . .$145.00 (B)

Honey Bee Snuff, embossed framed tin advertising sign with graphics of can of product prominently displayed, 13½" x 19¼", EX . . . .$60.00 (B)

Honey-Fruit Gum...Nothing Like It...Delightful Flavor, tin litho over cardboard, American Artworks, 9⅛" x 6¼", EX . . . .$2,500.00 (B)

Honey-Fruit Gum, "Nothing Like It, Delightful Flavor," tin over cardboard advertising sign, manufactured by Franklin-Caro Company in Richmond, Va., 16¼" x 9", F . . . .$300.00 (C)

Honeymoon Keen Cut Breakfast Coffee, key-wound tin litho container with graphics of loving couple sitting on crescent moon, 1-lb., EX . . . .$71.00 (B)

Honey Moon Tobacco, one-sided tin litho advertising sign from Penn Tobacco Co., featuring couple sitting on quarter moon, 9¾" H, F . . . .$100.00 (C)

Hully-Gee Pepsin Gum, wrapper from the Buckeye Gum Co., Salem, Ohio, featuring the famous Yellow Kid in a cameo at left of message, 3½", EX, **$575.00 (B).** *Courtesy of Buffalo Bay Auction Co*

Hudepohl Beer and Ale, cardboard advertisement with graphics of old man and dog, 29½" x 38", G, **$325.00 (B).**

Humphreys' Remedies, store display wooden cabinet with metal front, 18" W x 21" H x7¼" D, EX, **$295.00 (D).**

Honey Moon Tobacco, vertical pocket tin, litho container with graphics of man and woman sitting on crescent moon, rare variation, 3" x ⅞" x 4½", EX . . . .**$1,950.00 (B)**

Honeymoon, vertical pocket tobacco tin with graphics of trademark man on the moon, 1910s, G . . . . .**$130.00 (B)**

Hood's, advertising calendar with die cut image of young pretty girl with full unused monthly tear sheets, 4¾" x 7", 1897, NM . . . .**$210.00 (B)**

Hood's, advertising calendar with full tear sheet pad graphics of young boy and girl in front of world globe, 6" x 8½", 1893, EX . . . .**$200.00 (B)**

Hood's, advertising calendar with graphics of pretty young girl with bow in hair, 7" x 7½", 1910, VG . . . .**$175.00 (B)**

Hood's, advertising calendar with graphics of two young children playing with kittens, 7" x 8", 1913, EX . . . .**$175.00 (B)**

Hood's, advertising calendar with graphics of young girl with animals, full calendar pad, "Four Friends," 4½" x 15½", 1903, EX . . . .**$220.00 (B)**

Hood's, advertising calendar with graphics of young woman with fur hat, 5½" x 9¾", 1889, EX . . .**$120.00 (B)**

Hood's, die cut cardboard advertising calendar with full pad of tear sheets and information sheets, in likeness of young woman in bonnet, 4¾" x 8", 1888, EX .**$165.00 (B)**

Hood's Ice Cream, double-sided painted metal advertising sign with graphics of trademark cow's head in center, 19" dia., G . . . .**$1,200.00 (B)**

Huntley Palmers Biscuits, single-sided litho, foreign, 24" x 28½", F, **$425.00 (B)**.

Husemann's Soda, Clear and Sparkling, embossed painted tin sign, from Red Bud, Ill., 19½" x 13½", VG, **$75.00 (C)**.

Husky, two-piece die cut porcelain dog with Husky base, difficult item to find, NM, **$3,000.00 (C)**. *Courtesy of Autopia Advertising Auctions*

Hood's Ice Cream, tin litho embossed sign from Donaldson Art Sign, "The flavor's there," 20" x 28", EX . . **$335.00 (C)**

Hoodsies Ice Cream, die cut cardboard advertising sign with graphics of young couple on swing, 12¼" x 18½", EX . . . .**$2,000.00 (B)**

Hood's Sarsaparilla, advertising calendar with full calendar pad, with image of pretty woman titled "Donna Inez, The Spanish Beauty," 1912, NM . . . .**$50.00 (B)**

Hood's Sarsaparilla, calendar, die cut cardboard with unused calendar pad with artwork of young girls on front, NM . . . .**$95.00 (B)**

Hood's Sarsaparilla, calendar, die cut with artwork of pretty girl in bonnet, 1894, 5½" x 8¾", EX . . .**$55.00 (C)**

Hood's Sarsaparilla, calendar featuring girl wearing a flowery bonnet, 1886, 7¼" x 14¾", EX . . . .**$50.00 (C)**

Hood's Sarsaparilla, calendar with full calendar pad, 7" sq., 1892, EX . . . .**$55.00 (B)**

Hood's Sarsaparilla, die cut calendar with graphics of pretty girl and roses with full calendar pad, 1904, EX . .**$75.00 (B)**

Hood's Sarsaparilla, round calendar, "The Sewing Circle," with artwork of children sewing, 1892, NM . .**$121.00 (B)**

Hood Tire Dealer, die cut tin litho in image of the Hood Man, 11" x 35½", VG . . . .**$1,125.00 (C)**

Hood Tires, wooden thermometer with Hood man with stop flag at top center over vertical scale, Hood Tires message in circle at bottom, 4" x 15", orange, white, and black, G . . . .**$325.00 (C)**

Hudson Essex Service, double-sided porcelain sign, 30" x 16", EX, **$400.00 (B)**. *Courtesy of Autopia Advertising Auctions*

Hy-Quality Coffee, die cut cardboard store sign with young girl in swing with cup of product, 16" x 37", EX, **$1,290.00 (B).**

Courtesy of Buffalo Bay Auction Co.

Husky Gasoline, lighter, NOS, etched, painted advertising detail, 1¾" tall, M, **$110.00 (B).** *Courtesy of Autopia Advertising Auctions*

Hopalong Cassidy, popcorn container with graphics of Hoppy on front, 10-oz., EX . . . .$255.00 (C)

Hopalong Cassidy, wrist watch in original advertising box, VG . . . .$70.00 (B)

Hopkins & Allen Arms Co., "Prairie Girl," paper litho advertising poster, good graphics and difficult to locate, 10" x 26¾", 1910s, EX . . . .$2,500.00 (C)

Horlacher Brewing Company, advertising calendar with graphics of pretty woman and a penguin, 16" x 33½", EX . . . .$125.00 (C)

Horlick's...for strength and energy, drink advertising sign with graphics of bottle, 18½" x 28½", VG . . . .$170.00 (B)

Horlick's Malted Milk, advertising pocket mirror with graphics of young girl with calf, 2" dia., EX . . .$85.00 (B)

Horlick's Malted Milk, die cut dimensional stand-up trade card in shape of pretty lady and cow, 4" x 5" x ¾", EX . . . .$70.00 (B)

Horlick's Malted Milk, tin litho with small canister top lid, graphics of cow on front, #10 can, EX . . . .$45.00 (B)

Horrigan Supply Co., advertising calendar with graphics of pretty young woman, 15" x 20", 1906, EX .$235.00 (B)

Horseshoeing, wheelwrighting, and painting, painted and carved trade sign for F. Poitras & Co., 14" x 6", EX . . . .$1,500.00 (B)

Horse Shoe Tobacco...We Sell, porcelain flange advertising sign, 18" x 8", G . . . .$200.00 (B)

Horton's Ice Cream, single-sided porcelain advertising sign, "The Premier Ice Cream of America," 20" x 28", VG . . . .$275.00 (B)

Hostess, holiday fruit cake tin litho container, 63½" x 3¼" x 3", VG . . . .$40.00 (B)

Hot Ball, chewing and smoking tobacco, embossed tin litho advertising sign with jester holding package, rare piece, G . . . .$900.00 (B)

Hotel McAlpin Coffee, tin litho container with small canister-type lid on top, graphics of hotel scene, 1910, 6" x 11", EX . . . .$55.00 (B)

Hot Springs, Arkansas, souvenir spoon depicting black boy eating a watermelon, marked "Sterling," 5" l, VG . . . .$300.00 (B)

Housatonic Inn, wood ad sign from an inn on the Housatonic River in Conn., 42" x 28", 1900, VG . . . .$600.00 (B)

Household match striker, tin litho wall-hung match striker "Your credit is good...The Household," by Kaufmann & Strauss Lithographers, 4¾" x 7¾", 1915s, EX . .$130.00 (B)

Houstonia Liniment, advertising, die cut cardboard sign, EX . . . .$110.00 (B)

Howard Co. Fair...Aug 31 – Sept. 1-2-3...Horse Races, embossed tin license plate attachment with graphics of sulky racing at top of attachment, 5¾" x 6¼", NM . . . .$115.00 (C)

Howard Johnson's, dairy bar and soda fountain, neat toy still in original box, EX . . . .$35.00 (B)

Howdy, die cut cardboard bottle topper with graphics of sandwich in hand, 6½" x 10½", NM . . . .$75.00 (C)

Howdy Doody, ice cream box, unused with graphics of Howdy on lid, 12-oz., 1950s, EX . . . .$55.00 (C)

Howdy Doody, Washington apples, plastic bag, NOS, with graphics of Howdy Doody and friends on front, 3-lb., EX . . . .$15.00 (D)

Howdy...The Nose Knows, embossed tin "tacker" style sign with graphics of bottle and boy, NOS, 19½" x 9¼", NM . . . .$350.00 (B)

Howel's Orange Julep, ceramic dispenser with base, 9" x 15", VG . . . .$1,600.00 (B)

Howel's Orange Julep, pedestal glass, 1920s, EX .$120.00 (B)

Howel's Root Beer, embossed tin die cut bottle sign, 8⅜" x 29½", EX . . . .$275.00 (C)

Howertown Sanitary Dairy, metal serving tray, 13¼" sq., VG . . . .$65.00 (B)

Hoyt & Co., Buffalo Peanut Butter, tin litho pail with wire bail handle, 3¾" x 3¼", EX . . . .$325.00 (B)

H. Sandmeyer & Co., tin litho match holder, Peoria, Ill., Golden Anniversary Hardware, 5" H, G . . . . .$110.00 (B)

Hubig's Pie Co., tin litho tip tray with graphics of factory and horse-drawn delivery wagon, "A guarantee against cellar made pies," 3⅝" dia., 1906, EX . . . .$240.00 (B)

Hudson, auto catalog with graphics of new cars on front cover, 11" x 6", 1938, EX . . . .$40.00 (B)

Hudson...Rambler...Sales...Service, porcelain advertising sign, 1940s, 42" x 30", EX . . . .$500.00 (C)

Hudson's Bay Co., calendar with graphics of men at lake with canoe by artist Phillip R. Goodwin, 11½" x 6½", 1928, NM . . . .$425.00 (B)

Hudson Terraplane Authorized Service, single-sided porcelain dealer sign, 42" dia., EX . . . . . .$1,100.00 (C)

Hully-Gee Pepsin Gum, wrapper from the Buckeye Gum Co., Salem, Ohio, featuring the famous Yellow Kid in a cameo at left of message, 3½", EX . . . .$575.00 (B)

Humble, continuously improved single-sided porcelain pump sign, 10¾" x 18", G . . . .$80.00 (B)

Humble Gasoline, celluloid advertising knife sharpening stone with product message on back, 1⅝" x 2⅞", EX . . . .$110.00 (B)

Humphreys' Remedies, store display wooden cabinet with metal front, 18" W x 21" H x 7¼" D, EX . . . . .$295.00 (D)

Humphreys Specifics, medicine countertop product cabinet, with tin advertising front, back has drawers that hold product, complete with original product, 21¾" x 8" x 28¼", EX . . . .$900.00 (B)

Hunter Red Dog Shells, empty 12 gauge shotgun shell box with graphics of dog on front, 4⅛" x 4⅛" x 2½", NM . . . .$75.00 (C)

Hupmobile, paper advertising calendar with sailboat scene, full calendar pad, 14¼" x 31", 1926, EX . . . . . .$275.00 (C)

Hurtz, 100% pure black salve, painted tin sign featuring a black man in center, 22" x 22", VG . . . .$200.00 (B)

Husemann's Soda, Clear and Sparkling, embossed painted tin sign, from Red Bud, Ill., 19½" x 13½", G . . .$65.00 (D)

Husky Hi Power, one-sided porcelain pump sign with graphics of husky dog, 12" x 12", G . . . .$375.00 (B)

Husky, two-piece die cut porcelain dog with Husky base, difficult item to find, NM . . . .$3,000.00 (C)

Huyler's Candies, flange porcelain advertising sign, double-sided, "made to eat...not to keep," 20¼" x 7", VG . .$225.00 (D)

Hyde Propellers Sales and Service, one-sided porcelain sign with graphics of large propeller in center, 18" x 26", G . . . .$900.00 (B)

Hygienic Kalsomine...Germ proof your walls, cardboard hanging store sign featuring images of housewife and painter, 1909, 11" x 15", EX . . . .$47.00 (B)

Hygrade Products Co., New York, NY, fuel pump rebuild kits, metal with lift-front door, with original parts inside, 12¾" x 15" x 12¾", EX . . . .$195.00 (D)

Hy-Quality Coffee, die cut cardboard store sign with young girl in swing with cup of product, 16" x 37", P . . . .$125.00 (D)

Hy-Quality Coffee, die cut paper litho on cardboard, hanging sign of woman in swing drinking coffee, 36½" H, EX . . . .$900.00 (B)

Hyroler Whiskey...Louis J. Adler & Co., round metal tip tray with artwork of man in dress attire and top hat, 4¼" dia., EX . . . .$45.00 (B)

Hyroler Whiskey, tin litho tip tray with graphics of gentleman with top hat and cane, Louis J. Alder & Co., 4¼" dia., EX . . . .$48.00 (B)

Ideal...Quality chekd Dairy Products, plastic light-up advertising clock, 15½" dia., VG, **$135.00 (C).** *Courtesy of B.J. Summers*

Ideal Smokeless Shotgun Shells, box with paper litho, 4¼" x 4¼" x 2⅝", VG, $110.00 (B).

Ice Service...Clean Courteous...Careful cardboard advertising sign with graphics of service man carrying block ice on shoulder, 30½" x 20½", 1948, EX . . . .$125.00 (C)

Idaho Power Company, tin sign with graphics of Reddy Kilowatt, 40" x 24", NM . . . .$195.00 (C)

Ideal Bread, rack sign, painted metal, "Ideal for every meal," 40" x 17½", F . . . .$195.00 (D)

Ideal Coffee, tin litho container with screw-on lid and graphics of silver serving coffee pot , 4" x 6", EX $130.00 (B)

Ideal...Quality chekd Dairy Products, plastic light-up advertising clock, 15½" dia., G . . . .$95.00 (C)

IGA Deluxe Coffee, key-wound tin litho container with eagle graphics on front, 1-lb., EX . . . .$25.00 (B)

Illinois, metal and plastic display watch, 11" x 15" x 35", G, $895.00 (C).

Illinois Valley...Ice Cream, metal and plastic light-up sign, NM, $165.00 (D). *Courtesy of Pleasant Hill Antique Mall & Tea Room/Bob Johnson*

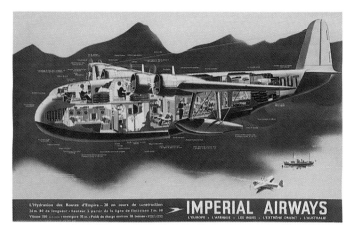

Imperial Airways, paper litho poster, graphics of cut-away of seaplane, 43" x 28", EX, $725.00 (B).

Imperial Airways, paper litho advertising poster, 28" x 43", VG, $800.00 (B).

Illinois Bell Telephone Company...American Telephone & Telegraph Co., double-sided porcelain flange, 12" x 11", NM . . . .$159.00 (B)

Illinois Farm Bureau, Illinois Agricultural Mutual Insurance Co., porcelain license plate attachment, 3¾" x 4½", EX . . . .$85.00 (C)

Illinois Valley...Ice Cream, metal and plastic light-up sign, EX . . . .$155.00 (D)

Illinois Watch, advertising photo of factory and early cars, 24⅜" x 16½", G . . . .$55.00 (C)

Illinois Watch Company, framed print showing factory scene, 24½" x 16½", EX . . . .$75.00 (D)

Imperial Cigar, embossed tin litho sign promoting Club cigars for 5¢, "The Best For The Money," 13¾" x 10", EX . . . .$135.00 (D)

Imperial Club 5¢ Cigar, embossed tin litho advertising sign with image of full box of the product, 13¾" x 10", EX . . . .$125.00 (C)

Imperial Club 5¢ Cigar, painted embossed tin sign, Wolf & Co. Selling Agents, 13½" x 10", EX . . . .$150.00 (C)

Imperial Club 5¢ Cigar, painted embossed tin sign, Wolf & Co. Selling Agents, 13½" x 10", G, $75.00 (C).

Independent Gasoline, gas globe, metal high profile body with two glass lenses, hard-to-find item, 15" dia., VG, $5,000.00 (B). *Courtesy of Collectors Auction Services*

Independent Local and Long Distance Telephone, double-sided porcelain flange sign, 17" x 18", NM, $550.00 (B). *Courtesy of Autopia Advertising Auctions*

Imperial Dry Ginger Ale, rectangular metal tip tray with graphics of product bottle at right of message, 6⅛" L, NM ....$45.00 (B)

Imperial Egg Food, litho on paper with graphics of black workers gathering eggs, from Kellogg & Bulkeley Co., Hartford CT, 29" x 35", NM ....$929.00 (B)

Imperial Egg Food, paper litho advertising with artwork of men feeding chickens while other men catch the eggs and load them on a train, 29" x 35", EX .....$875.00 (B)

Imperiales Cigarettes, framed advertisement, manufactured by The John Bollman Co., San Francisco, Calif., 16" x 20", EX ....$225.00 (C)

Imperial, no lead gas globe, plastic body with two glass lenses, 13½" dia., G ....$300.00 (B)

Inca Maidens, reel cut coffee, with scene of Inca Maiden and village in background, pail with wire handle, Bloomington, IL, 7½" x 7½", EX ....$295.00 (C)

Independent Gasoline, gas globe, metal high profile body with two glass lenses, hard to find item, 15" dia., VG $5,000.00 (B)

Independent...Gasoline...Motor oil, two-sided porcelain sign, 29½" dia., G ....$385.00 (B)

Independent Local and Long Distance Telephone, double-sided porcelain flange sign, 17" x 18", G ....$135.00 (C)

Independent Local and Long Distance Telephone...Pay Station, double-sided porcelain sign from Ing-Rich Beaver Falls, Pa., 100 Wm. St. NY, 18" x 18", EX ....$300.00 (B)

Indianapolis Speedway Limited Edition leather jacket, #33/50, XL, NM, $1,300.00 (B).

Indian Rock Ginger Ale, 5¢, syrup dispenser with Indian scenes on both sides, complete with ball pump, 12" tall, EX, $2,250.00 (B).

Indianapolis Speedway pennant, single-sided cloth, 29" x 10½", VG, $100.00 (B).

Independent Radio and TV Service, round light-up clock with message in center of clock face, 16" dia., EX . . . . . .$75.00 (D)

Independent Stove Co., Owosso, Mich., cast iron enameled advertising paperweight in shape of alligator, 5½" L, NM . . . .$118.00 (B)

Indianapolis Brewing Co., brass pocket match safe with embossing on both sides, 1½" x 3", VG . . . . .$175.00 (C)

Indianapolis Brewing Co., notebook, celluloid cover with 1903 calendar, by Whitehead & Hoag, 2½" x 4¾", 1903, VG . . . .$95.00 (C)

Indianapolis Speedway, silk checkered flag, 17" x 17", EX . . . .$85.00 (C)

Indian Crown, 10¢ Cigar, McCoy & Co. Makers, New York, embossed tin litho advertising sign with artwork of Indian in full headdress at left of info., 20¾" x 15", EX . . . .$975.00 (B)

Indian Gas globe, narrow glass body with glass lens, 13½" dia., VG . . . .$800.00 (B)

Indian Gas...Indian Refining Co., Incorporated, die cut hanging sign, held by metal brackets over round extension arm, double-sided, 45" x 36", G . . . .$575.00 (C)

Indian Gasoline, porcelain advertising sign, with artwork of Indian, gas logo at top of message, Indian Refining Co., New York, New York, 1940s, 12" x 18", G . . . .$165.00 (C)

Indian Head Overalls, porcelain advertising sign with graphics of Indian in cameo, 14" x 10", VG . .$850.00 (B)

Indian Motorcycle, cigar cutter, Hendel Manufacturing Co., Springfield, Mass., J.E. Mercot Co. Newark, N.J., 2½" x 1", EX . . . .$400.00 (B)

Ingersoll Watches, metal store display case, brown metal with woodgrain look, manufactured by the H.D. Beach Co., Coshocton, Ohio, U.S.A., 9½" W x 14¼" H x 6" D, VG, **$120.00 (C)**.

Interlux Marine Paint, single-sided porcelain ad sign, graphics of boats being painted, 24" x 14", G, **$400.00 (B)**.

International Motor Trucks, single-sided embossed tin sign, 27½" x 10⅛", G, **$45.00 (B)**.

Indian Rock Ginger Ale, embossed tin litho advertising sign with image of bottle on both sides, 35½" x 11½", EX . . . .**$325.00 (C)**

Indian Rock Ginger Ale, 5¢, syrup dispenser with Indian scenes on both sides, complete with ball pump, 12" tall, F . . . .**$1,100.00 (D)**

India Tires, single-sided porcelain advertising sign with graphics of owl , 60" x 18", G . . . .**$275.00 (B)**

Industrial Supplies Corp., advertising calendar with graphics of young woman on beach in swim suit, full pad, 16" x 33½", 1953, EX . . . .**$30.00 (B)**

Infallible Shotgun, smokeless, celluloid advertising pinback, 1¼" dia., G . . . .**$50.00 (B)**

Ingersoll Watches, metal store display case, brown metal with woodgrain look, manufactured by the H.D. Beach Co., Coshocton, Ohio, U.S.A., 9½" W x 14¼" H x 6" D, G . . . .**$100.00 (B)**

Ingram Perfumed Talcum Powder, tin litho container with graphics of woman in center cameo, 2" x 4⅞", EX . . . .**$190.00 (B)**

International Harvester, light-up advertising clock, metal body and glass face and cover, Pam Clock Co., 15½" sq., VG . . . .**$325.00 (B)**

International Harvester, neon advertising clock, metal body with tin face and glass cover, with the IH symbol in center, 15½" x 15½", EX . . . .**$650.00 (B)**

Interwoven Socks, advertising sign of elderly lady in chair with sewing basket, Norman Rockwell signature, 28" x 38", EX . . . .**$275.00 (C)**

Interwoven Socks, cardboard litho die cut ad sign, stand-up with man in front of street light, 18" x 36", 1935, VG . . . .**$55.00 (B)**

Interwoven Socks, cardboard litho die cut ad sign with 3-D effect, stand-up with easel back, has Santa in Christmas tree, 14" x 21", VG . . . .**$455.00 (B)**

Interwoven Socks, paper-linen advertising featuring artwork of woman in overstuffed chair knitting, by Norman Rockwell, 28" x 38", EX . . . .**$95.00 (C)**

Invincible Motor Insurance, painted tin advertising sign with graphics of spotlight on vintage auto, NOS, 20" x 9½", EX . . . .**$375.00 (C)**

Iroquois Beer, double-bubble, light-up advertising sign with graphics of Indian in full headdress on woodgrain look face, 15" dia., EX, **$800.00 (B).** *Courtesy of Collectors Auction Services*

Iroquois Indian Head Beer, tin litho serving tray, graphics of Indian, Buffalo, NY, 12" dia., G, **$55.00 (B).**

Ithaca Featherweight Repeaters, die cut cardboard advertising sign, graphics of pheasant in flight, 21" x 14", G, **$105.00 (B).**

Iris Brand Majoram, spice tin with great graphics of wind-blown flowers, 2¼" x 3¼" x 1", EX .... $110.00 (B)

Iris Coffee, in tin litho container with key-wound lid from Los Angeles, CA, 1-lb., EX .... $55.00 (C)

Iroquois Beer-Ale, light-up advertising clock with graphics of Indian head outlined by arrowhead, 17" dia., EX . $400.00 (B)

Iroquois, double-bubble, light-up advertising sign with graphics of Indian in full headdress on woodgrain look face, 15" dia., F .... $100.00 (C)

Iroquois, tip tray, lithographed Indian head in center, 4½" dia., VG .... $65.00 (B)

Irvin Ethyl Gasoline, globe, high profile body with two glass lenses, 15" dia., G .... $350.00 (B)

Isbrandtsen Red Label, key-wound tin litho container with graphics of large ship on front, 1-lb., EX . $75.00 (B)

Ithaca Featherweight Repeaters, die cut cardboard advertising wall-hanging sign with graphics of goose in flight, 15" x 17" x 1", VG .... $275.00 (B)

Ithaca Gun Catalog, with graphics of shotgun on cover, 11" x 8½", 1936, EX .... $140.00 (B)

Ithaca Gun Co., cardboard die cut advertising display with graphics of goose in flight, 16½" x 14½", VG . $190.00 (B)

Ivory Soap, early cardboard die cut advertising string hanger with cherub holding a bar of Ivory overhead, probably having to do with early advertising that Ivory was the soap so pure it floats, 6" x 11", 1870s, EX . $1,050.00 (B)

Ivory Soap, paper litho advertising in gesso frame, "A Busy Day," 20" x 22½", VG .... $235.00 (B)

I.W. Harper, vitrolite advertising sign with graphics of hunting dog and hunting gear inside warm cabin with a bottle of the product prominently displayed, 17" x 23", EX, **$870.00 (B).**
Courtesy of Buffalo Bay Auction Co.

Ivory Soap, early cardboard die cut advertising string hanger with cherub holding a bar of Ivory overhead, probably having to do with early advertising that Ivory was the soap so pure it floats, 6" x 11", 1870s, EX, **$1,050.00 (B).** *Courtesy of*
Wm. Morford Investment Grade Collectibles

Imperial Egg Food, paper litho with graphics of workers catching eggs and gathering hens and loading railroad freight cars, 29" x 35", EX, **$930.00 (B).** *Courtesy of Buffalo Bay Auction Co.*

Ivory Soap, porcelain advertising sign, 21" x 3¼", EX . . . .**$155.00 (C)**

I.W. Harper Oleograph, wood and canvas with graphics of honeymoon scene, from Bernheim Distilling Company, Inc., 46" x 34½", 1912, EX . . . .**$1,225.00 (B)**

I.W. Harper, reverse glass in wooden frame, with graphics of older gentleman watching young girl, 23½" x 35½", 1900s, EX . . . .**$6,500.00 (B)**

I.W. Harper, vitrolite advertising sign with graphics of hunting dog and hunting gear inside warm cabin with a bottle of the product prominently displayed, 17" x 23", G . . . .**$450.00 (D)**

J A Cigars, die cut easel back advertising sign with graphics of man in suit enjoying a cigar, 17½" x 29½", EX, **$235.00 (C).**

Courtesy of Buffalo Bay Auction Co.

Jackson Restaurant China Co., salesman's sample plate with the salesman's name C.W. Young incorporated into the message on the plate center with images of various serving pieces around the border, 3¾" dia., EX, **$300.00 (B).**

Courtesy of Wm. Morford Investment Grade Collectibles

J.A. Johnston & Co., tin sign, successors to C.D. Daniel, 29⅝" x 11¾", VG, **$115.00 (B).**

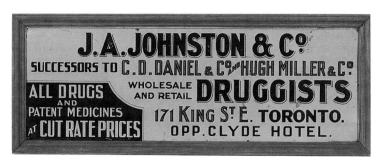

I.W. Harper Whiskey, framed print featuring bird dog in front of log cabin with hunting gear on front porch, good, strong sign, 24" x 30", NM . . . .$1,000.00 (B)

J A Cigars, die cut easel back advertising sign with graphics of man in suit enjoying a cigar, 17½" x 29½", EX$235.00 (C)

Jack Frost Baking Powder, tin container with paper label and graphics of snow and cabin scene, 3" x 5½", EX . .$350.00 (B)

Jackie Coogan Salted Nut Meal, tin litho container from Dixie Peanut Products with graphics of Coogan on elephant, 8" x 10", EX . . . .$210.00 (B)

Jack Sanitary Barber Shop, litho on paper with image of a scantily dressed woman, great strong colors, 1890s, 14" x 20", NM . . . .$325.00 (B)

Jackson Restaurant China Co., salesman's sample plate with the salesman's name C.W. Young incorporated into the message on the plate center with images of various serving pieces around the border, 3¾" dia., EX . . . .$300.00 (B)

Jackson's Best Chewing Tobacco, paper advertising sign, C.A. Jackson & Co., Petersburg, VA, 12" x 14½", EX . .$100.00 (B)

Jackson's Best Chewing Tobacco, paper litho advertising with graphics of boy sneaking a bite of a chaw, VG . . .$325.00 (C)

Jackson's Best Sweet Navy Chewing Tobacco... "Tole You Chilon," cardboard trade card, from Petersburg, Va., with graphics of old black man, 1890s, 3¼" x 5", NM .$55.00 (B)

Jacob Hoffman Brewing Co., paper litho showing image of flowers and a glass of the product, J. Ottmann Litho Co. Puck Building, N.Y., 25" x 32", VG . . . .$100.00 (B)

Jam-Boy Coffee, tin can with screw lid and graphics of young boy with toast and jam at breakfast table, from Jameson-Boyce, Binghampton, NY, 1-lb., EX, $305.00 (B). *Courtesy of Buffalo Bay Auction Co.*

James Buchanan & Co. Ltd. Scotch Whisky Distillers, Black & White Scotch Whisky, featuring dogs in field, note spelling of "whisky," 23" x 24½", EX, $225.00 (D).

Japp's Hair Rejuvenator, self-framing metal and cardboard advertisement store card, 13¼" x 9¼", EX, $45.00 (B).

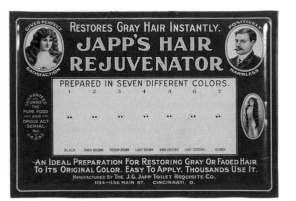

Jacob Ruppert Beer Ale, metal litho serving tray with graphics of two beer mugs with a full head of the product, 14½" x 10¾", 1939, EX . . . .$35.00 (B)

Jacob Ruppert, oval serving tray, 1930s, 10¾" x 14½", G . . . .$85.00 (C)

Jam-Boy Coffee, tin can with screw lid and graphics of young boy with toast and jam at breakfast table, from Jameson-Boyce, Binghampton, NY, 1-lb., EX .$305.00 (B)

Jam-Boy Coffee, tin litho pry-type lid with graphics of young man at table with cup of product, 1-lb., EX . . . .$352.00 (B)

James Buchanan & Co. Ltd., Scotch Whisky Distillers, Black & White Scotch Whisky, featuring dogs in field, note spelling of "whisky," 23" x 24½", G . . . .$175.00 (D)

J & P Coats...Spool Cotton...Best Six Cord...For hand & machine, painted hardboard, framed, 18" x 30", F . . . .$325.00 (D)

J & P Coats, wood sign with wood frame and gold embossed lettering and artwork of spool cotton in center, 18" x 30", EX . . . .$425.00 (C)

Janney Best Paints...authorized dealer metal light-up advertising clock with graphics of paint can , 26" x 18½", VG . . . .$350.00 (B)

Janney Best paints, electric light-up clock with metal body and reverse glass decaled front, 15½" sq., EX . .$80.00 (B)

Japalag Wood Finish, cloth banner, The Glidden Varnish Co., 61½" x 24", VG . . . .$275.00 (B)

Jesse James, paper litho advertising poster, "The Sensational Western Life Drama" with graphics of black couple, 30" x 44", G, **$1,700.00 (B).** *Courtesy of Collectors Auction Services*

Jewelry Watch Repairing, double-sided porcelain sign with iron holder, 11¼" x 16½", G, **$910.00 (B).**

Jap Rose Soap...Kirk's...Toilet, Bath, Shampoo, cobalt porcelain advertising thermometer, scarce, 1915, EX . . . .$260.00 (B)

Jap Rose Soap, metal litho tip tray with graphics of youngsters and Chinese lantern, 4¼" dia., EX . . . . .$190.00 (B)

Jap Rose Soap, metal tip tray with graphics of a couple of kids bathing a doll, 4¼" dia., EX . . . .$95.00 (D)

Jap Rose Talcum Powder, sample size tin litho with graphics of Japanese girl on front, EX . . . . . .$59.00 (B)

Jaw Teasers Bubble Gum, tin litho pail with handle and graphics of gumball on sides, 5" x 7½", EX . . . .$54.00 (B)

Jaxon Soap, cast iron advertising item in shape of rendering kettle with hole in bottom used for string holder, with embossed product lettering, 4½" x 4½", EX . . .$75.00 (B)

Jayne's Hair Tonic, paper on cardboard store sign with graphics of women admiring their hair and product message, 1880s, 12" x 15", EX . . . .$147.00 (B)

J. B. Barnaby Co., Providence, advertising pocket mirror promoting Collegian cut clothing, 1¾" dia., EX .$425.00 (B)

J.B. Lewis, Shoemaker, advertising sign, single-sided tin litho with graphics of cobbler at work at his bench, 13½" x 19½", VG . . . .$375.00 (B)

J. Devar & Sons Whiskey, advertising cardboard print in wood frame that appears to be original, 31¼" x 22¼", EX . . . .$35.00 (D)

J.D. Mahoney, paper advertising line of clothes, 5¼" x 7¼", EX . . . .$75.00 (C)

Jell-O, paper advertising sign for the product dessert mix, 15" x 40¼", EX . . . .$135.00 (D)

Jenne Lind Cigars, cardboard sign from the National Cigar Co., Bristol, Indiana, center of stamped sign has inside cigar box label, 14½" x 8¼", EX . . . . . .$120.00 (B)

Jennessy Ginger Ale, cardboard advertising sign , 11" x 14", 1940s, EX . . . .$65.00 (B)

J

J.G. Hoffman & Sons Co., paper advertisement of their buildings, manufacturer of "Star-Oak-Harness Leather," 48½" x 36", G, $405.00 (B).

Johnnie Walker Red, back bar statue, F, $45.00 (C). *Courtesy of B.J. Summers*

John Ruskin Best and Biggest, single-sided embossed tin advertising sign, 29½" x 9⅜", VG, $100.00 (B).

Jenny Gasoline, linen-finish playing cards with artwork of early service station and car on each card with original box, full deck, EX . . . .$130.00 (B)

Jenny Super Aero Gasoline, globe, narrow hull body with two glass lenses, 13½" dia., G . . . .$500.00 (B)

Jergens, Crushed Violet Talcum Powder, tin litho container, with graphics of flower on front, EX . . . .$40.00 (B)

Jergens, Violet Miss Dainty Talcum tin container with graphics of Miss Dainty around the label, 2½" x 1¼" x 4½", EX . . . .$55.00 (C)

Jersey-Creme, At Founts, The Perfect Drink, In Bottles, tin tray, nice litho with girl in period dress, 12" dia., EX . . . .$300.00 (B)

Jersey-Creme, die cut string-hung cardboard ad sign of two girls in swing reading product ad, EX . . .$425.00 (C)

Jersey-Creme, serving tray with graphics of pretty young lady, 12" dia., VG . . . .$155.00 (B)

Jersey-Creme, tin litho serving tray with graphics of young lady in pretty hat, 12½" dia., EX . . . . .$180.00 (B)

Jersey Ice Cream, double-sided porcelain advertising sign with graphics of product sandwich on saucer, 20" x 28", EX . . . .$120.00 (B)

Jersey Lane Ice Cream, double-sided porcelain hanging advertising sign, 28" x 20", VG . . . .$325.00 (B)

Jesse James, paper litho advertising poster, "The Sensational Western Life Drama" with graphics of black couple, 30" x 44", P . . . .$225.00 (C)

Jesse James, stone litho playbill with artwork of cowboys, 19" x 29", EX . . . .$460.00 (B)

Johnson's Log Cabin, tin litho store bin, resembles log cabin, 24" x 18" x 28", EX, $2,750.00 (B).

Johnson's Powder Wax, can, wax for dance floors, 14-oz., G, $20.00 (B).

Jesse Oakley's Transparent Toilet soap, one-sided tin advertising sign, 13¾" x 9¾", EX . . . .$80.00 (B)

Jetrol 100+ Octane Premium, single-sided porcelain pump sign, Canadian item, 12" sq., VG . . . . .$225.00 (B)

Jewett White Lead Paint, calendar with graphics of the Dutch Boy, 14¾" x 38", 1917, VG . . . .$425.00 (C)

J.G. Dill's Best Cut Plug, tobacco tin, G . . . . .$20.00 (C)

Jim Hogg, paper cigar sign promoting "New Governor Size," with image of James Stephen Hogg, 20" x 9", NM . .$30.00 (B)

Jno T. Barbee and Co., Louisville, Ky., tin litho advertising beer sign with graphics of log cabin scene, 16½" x 13½", EX . . . .$160.00 (B)

Jockey underwear, countertop composition display for Coopers, Kenosha, WI, EX . . . .$80.00 (B)

Joe Anderson Havana Cigars...Peace Time, advertising match dispenser...The Universal Match Corporation, with graphics of Joe Anderson on front, 9" dia. x 14½", VG . . . .$800.00 (B)

Joe Lewis, World Champion, electric advertising clock, electric "United Self Starting," molded copper, 12" H, EX . . . .$500.00 (B)

Joe Palooka lunch box, good, strong graphics, 1946, EX . . . .$50.00 (B)

John Bull Tyres, one-sided porcelain advertising foreign sign, "made for the man who will have the best," 48" x 15½", VG . . . .$300.00 (B)

John Deere...Farm Implements, double-sided porcelain hanging advertising sign with artwork of JD logo at center top, 72" x 23¾", EX . . . .$950.00 (D)

John Deere, paper sign of deer pulling a John Deere buckboard, "Deere vehicles are allright," in original wooden frame, 31½" x 23½", EX . . . .$1,610.00 (B)

John Dewar & Sons, Old World scene cardboard ad in original oak frame, 31¼" x 22¼", EX . . . .$25.00(D)

John D. Jr., hand soap, tin container, 3-lb., G .$20.00 (D)

John Drew, tin litho advertising sign with graphics of man in center, "Berdan the Mark of a Good Cigar," 18½" dia., VG . . . .$400.00 (B)

John Finzer & Bros., Louisville, Ky., tobacco cutter, EX . . . .$160.00 (D)

John Gessert Shoes, light metal "tacker" style advertising sign with graphics of man examining vintage shoe, "Rubber & Leather Goods Store," 19¾" x 13½", EX . . .$250.00 (C)

John G. Watts, meat market advertising calendar from Albion, NY, with full calendar pad and graphics of women shopping at meat market, 14" x 18", 1900, EX . .$165.00 (B)

John Hauck, embossed metal pocket match safe, 1½" x 3", VG . . . .$175.00 (C)

John M. Miller & Sons, Wholesale Confectioners, countertop store display jar with great paper label of elephant and advertising peanuts for 5¢, 5⅝" x 5⅝" x 9¼", 1915, EX . . . .$110.00 (B)

Johnnie Walker Red, back bar statue, G . . . . .$55.00 (C)

John Ruskin Best and Biggest Cigars, embossed tin sign with graphics of cigar, NOS, 29⅝" x 9⅜", NM . .$200.00 (C)

John Ruskin...Best and Biggest, single-sided embossed tin advertising sign with graphics of lit cigar, 29¾" x 9½", VG . . . .$160.00 (B)

John Ruskin, tin litho cigar container with image of John Ruskin on front, 3½" x 3½" x 5", EX . . . .$155.00 (C)

Johnson & Johnson...Baby Needs..., molded pressboard with message stenciled and decal of J & J baby in center, 32" x 6", EX . . . .$50.00 (B)

Johnson & Johnson...For Babies, cardboard advertising sign, featuring graphics of baby in diaper under moonlit sky with product box, 14½" x 22", G . . . .$95.00 (D)

Johnson and Melaa's Dry Goods, Stoughton, WI, tip tray with graphics of young black child eating watermelon, 2½" x 3¼", EX . . . .$165.00 (B)

Johnson Bros. Funeral Directors...Call Our Ambulance Phone 45, Boaz, Ky., painted metal thermometer with vertical scale between messages, 1910 – 1920s, 8½" x 38½", white on blue, F . . . .$85.00 (C)

Johnson Halter Store, advertising sign, papier-maché horse head equipped with product message embossed in halter, 23" x 21" x 10", EX . . . .$425.00 (B)

Johnson's Cold Fudge Syrup, soda fountain jar, 8½" T, 1950s, EX . . . .$45.00 (B)

Johnson's Log Cabin, tin litho store bin, resembles log cabin, 24" x 18" x 28", EX . . . .$2,750.00 (B)

Johnson's Nuts Vendor, porcelain and glass countertop display unit, "eat the best," 24" x 14" x 15", EX . .$445.00 (B)

Johnson's Peacemaker Coffee, die cut cardboard in image of store bin, 13½" x 14", EX . . . .$455.00 (B)

Johnston Milwaukee, Charm, Soda Crackers, cardboard box, 1-lb., EX . . . .$15.00 (D)

Johnston's Instant Hot Fudge, soda fountain fixture with hinged lid, lettering on band around center of item, VG . . . .$155.00 (C)

John Weisert Tobacco Co., St. Louis, U.S.A., cardboard container box, with artwork of mule on front, EX . . .$12.00 (D)

Jolly Pops, painted metal sucker dispenser with graphics of two suckers on front, 9½" x 20", VG . . . . .$125.00 (C)

Jolly Pops, Those Good Suckers 1¢, metal dispenser with artwork of sunburst on front, 9½" x 20", green panel on red background, EX . . . .$105.00 (D)

Jones Dairy Farm Sausage, tin over cardboard advertising sign with graphics of product farm building and snow-covered tree, 12" x 8", EX . . . .$86.00 (B)

Josephine Baker Follies, tray, 12" dia., G . . . .$500.00(B)

J.S. Brown Mercantile Co., Denver, Colo., advertising on both sides for Mount Cross Coffee, 5½" x 9½", VG . . . .$120.00 (B)

J.T. and Drummond Natural Leaf Chewing Tobacco, paper litho advertising piece in wood frame, "Compliments of Drummond Tobacco Co., St. Louis, MO, manufactures of Horse Shoe J.T. and Drummond Natural Leaf Chewing Tobacco, copyright 1894," 28" x 33", 1890s, VG . . . .$160.00 (B)

Juicy Fruit, advertising match holder, "The Man Juicy Fruit Made Famous," 3¼" x 4¾" x 1¼", EX . .$140.00 (B)

June Kola...Now in quarts...6 full glasses, embossed vertical tin sign, with graphics of bottle, 23" x 35¼", 1953, EX . . . .$155.00 (B)

June Kola...Now in quarts...6 full glasses, single-sided tin sign, 23½" x 11½", 1936, VG . . . .$65.00 (B)

June Kola... "Now in Quarts...6 Full Glasses," tin advertising sign with graphics of bottle of the product, 23" x 11½", VG . . . .$75.00 (D)

Junket Pot Scraper, metal, litho with advertising for Junket dessert powder, 3¼" x 2⅝", EX . . . .$135.00 (C)

Just Born Nuts Brazil & Almonds, framed glass display case with original front display papers, 7¼" x 7½" x 11", VG . . . .$175.00 (B)

Just Suits cut plug, metal tobacco pail, Buchanan & Lyall of New York, N.Y., U.S.A., G . . . .$75.00 (D)

Just Suits tobacco, lunch pail with wire handle, Buchanan & Lyall, New York, 7¾" x 5" x 4¼", EX . . . . . .$175.00 (C)

Kayo Tops in Taste, single-sided embossed tin sign, 13⅞" x 27⅜", VG, **$230.00 (B)**.

K-O your thirst with Kayo, single-sided tin sign with boy boxer graphics, 25" x 9", VG, **$125.00 (B)**.

Keen Kutter...Safety Razor, cardboard ad with artwork of man shaving, "Always Ready To Shave...The Razor That Fits The Face," good graphics, 20¾" x 10¾", EX, **$75.00 (D)**. *Courtesy of Chief Paduke Antiques Mall*

Kaffee Hag Coffee, metal vacuum pack tin with key-wound lid, 1-lb., G . . . .$40.00 (D)

Kaffee Hag Coffee, tin litho key-wound, unopened container, 1-lb., EX . . . .$37.00 (B)

Kaier's Special Beer, cardboard die cut advertising sign with graphics of horse, foreign, 19½" x 16½", VG . . . .$90.00 (B)

Kaiser Approved Service, porcelain double-sided dealer advertising sign, 57" x 42", VG . . . .$200.00 (B)

Kamo Rolled Oats, container with paper label with graphics of duck on front, from Paxton & Gallagher, Omaha, Nebraska, 3-lb., VG . . . .$190.00 (B)

Kanotex, gas globe, wide body with two glass lenses, 13½" dia., VG . . . .$500.00 (B)

Kayo, Tops In Taste...It's Real Chocolate, embossed tin advertising sign with graphics of Kayo boy holding a large bottle of the product, 14" x 27⅜", EX . . . . . .$175.00 (C)

Keck's Sparkling Beverages...Enjoy, self-framing menu board, 17" x 23½", VG . . . .$75.00 (B)

Keen Kutter, cardboard advertising sign, "Always ready to shave, the razor that knows the face," graphics of man shaving, 20¾" X 10¾", VG . . . .$65.00 (C)

Keen Kutter, dealer calendar in die cut axe shape with bottom tear sheets, all sheets present, 12" x 16½", 1935, EX . . . .$95.00 (D)

Keen Kutter, die cut cardboard advertising sign, 10¼" x 13", EX . . . .$75.00 (C)

Keen Kutter, die cut dealer advertising calendar in the shape of an axehead with graphics of mountain stream, 12" x 16½", 1935, NM . . . .$95.00 (C)

Keen Kutter...E.C. Simmons...Cutlery, Tools, die cut cardboard ad in shape of Keen Kutter logo, 10¼" x 13", EX . . . .$35.00 (C)

Keen Kutter, embossed tin advertising sign with an unusual configuration with the saw and ax, "Keen Kutter Tools," 21" x 7½", NM . . . .$225.00 (C)

Keen Kutter...Safety Razor, cardboard ad with artwork of man shaving, "Always Ready To Shave...The Razor That Fits The Face," good graphics, 20¾" x 10¾", NM . . .$135.00 (D)

Kellogg's, All-Bran, cloth roll-down advertising sign with metal strips at top and bottom with graphics of young woman displaying different products on the sign, 10" x 40½", 1920s, VG, **$2,300.00 (B).** *Courtesy of Wm. Morford Investment Grade Collectibles*

Kellogg's, paper litho advertising sign promoting Kellogg's Corn Flakes featuring Camp Fire Girl with a bowl of the product, 23" x 28", 1920s, EX, **$725.00 (B).** *Courtesy of Wm. Morford Investment Grade Collectibles*

Kellogg's puzzle, framed and matted, young boy on scooter with running dog, 6" x 8", VG, **$65.00 (B).**

Keen Kutter Tools, embossed tin sign, but with an unusual look, instead of the usual dealer banner this one has crossed saw and axe image, 21" x 7½", EX .. **$195.00 (D)**

Keen Kutter Tools...Hank Bros., Paducah, Ky., painted embossed metal sign with logo at left of message, 27" x 10", EX .... **$125.00 (C)**

Kellogg's, All-Bran, cloth roll-down advertising sign with metal strips at top and bottom with graphics of young woman displaying different products on the sign, 10" x 40½", 1920s, F .... **$895.00 (D)**

Kellogg's, cardboard jigsaw puzzle with graphics of boy throwing a baseball, NOS, 6" x 8", NM ...... **$75.00 (C)**

Kellogg's cereal, countertop display unit for display of individual cereal boxes, aluminum, 20½" x 27" x 6", EX .... **$395.00 (C)**

Kellogg's Corn Flakes, cardboard war-time box with small identification of three fighter planes, "let's go USA keep 'em flying," 1940s, 11-oz., EX .... **$95.00 (D)**

Kellogg's Corn Flakes, metal watch fob, in the shape of a box of the product, 1¼" x 1½", EX .... **$60.00 (B)**

Kellogg's Corn Flakes, three-piece paper litho window advertising sign, when displayed they show images of two women in a cornfield and a product writer with "Kellogg's, The original toasted corn flakes," 12" x 39½" each, 1917, VG .... **$435.00 (B)**

Kellogg's, Toasted Corn Flakes, double-sided sheet steel flange sign, with great graphics of small girl in basket, 13½" x 19½", EX, $3,400.00 (B).

Courtesy of Richard Opfer Auctioneering, Inc.

Kellogg's, Toasted Corn Flakes...Fine With Berries, Peaches or Bananas, cardboard store sign, featuring artwork of young girl with product box, 1915, 11" x 20", NM, $550.00 (B).

Kellogg's, Toasted Corn Flakes, hanging cardboard advertising sign, "A Hit and A Miss" featuring artwork of girl eating cereal, Look for this Signature, W.K. Kellogg, 1915, 10½" x 15½", G, $250.00 (B). *Courtesy of Muddy River Trading Co./Gary Metz*

Kellogg's, paper doll cut-out of "Daddy Bear" holding cereal box, uncut, 1925, NM . . . .$82.00 (B)

Kellogg's, paper litho advertising sign promoting Kellogg's Corn Flakes featuring Camp Fire Girl with a bowl of the product, 23" x 28", 1920s, EX . . . . $725.00 (B)

Kellogg's, paper litho advertising sign promoting Kellogg's Corn Flakes with graphics of young woman by lake and a bowl of cereal, 23" x 28", EX . . . . $1,150.00 (B)

Kellogg's Rice Krispies...Snap Crackle Pop, cardboard box with graphics of three Krispie creatures, 1948, 5½ oz., EX . . . . $50.00 (B)

Kellogg's Supreme Quality Coffee, tin litho key-wound container, 1-lb., EX . . . . $28.00 (B)

Kellogg's Toasted Corn Flakes, double-sided sheet steel flange sign, with great graphics of small girl in basket, 13½" x 19½", G . . . .$1,200.00 (C)

Kellogg's Toasted Corn Flakes...Fine With Berries, Peaches or Bananas, cardboard store sign, featuring artwork of young girl with product box, 1915, 11" x 20", NM . . . .$550.00 (B)

Kellogg's Toasted Corn Flakes, hanging cardboard advertising sign, "A Hit and A Miss" featuring artwork of girl eating cereal, Look for this Signature, W.K. Kellogg, 1915, 10½" x 15½", NM . . . .$500.00 (C)

Kelly Tires, painted metal flange sign, with the Kelly girl waving from older model touring car, 24" dia., EX . . . . $1,850.00 (C)

Kemps Nits, countertop dispenser with glass front, lights up and display rotates, unit also keep product warm, 32" x 21½" X 21", EX . . . . $95.00 (C)

Kendall De-Luxe, gas globe, plastic body with two glass lenses, 13½" dia., VG . . . .$350.00 (B)

Kendall Motor Oils, advertising light-up wall clock, plastic with fired-on lettering, 10½" dia., EX . . . . . . $195.00 (B)

Kendall Motor Oils, painted metal double-sided advertising sign, NOS, 23¾" dia., EX . . . . $110.00 (B)

Kendall Motor Oil...The Dealer Sign of Quality, vertical embossed painted metal sign, with logo at top of message, G . . . .$95.00 (C)

Kelly Builds Quality, Quality Builds Kelly, single-sided metal sign, 8"
H, G, $315.00 (B).

Kelly Tires, painted metal flange sign, with the
Kelly girl waving from older model touring car,
24" dia., VG, $1,700.00 (C).

Kendall the 2000 Mile Oil, neon spinner
advertising clock, 20" dia., EX, $1,000.00 (B).

Kendall outboard motor oil, tin double-sided flange
advertising sign, 18" x 13", EX . . . . $275.00 (C)

Kendall, tin self-framing vertical strip advertising sign
with bottom insert with graphics of oil can in hand, 12" x
72", VG . . . .$950.00 (B)

Ken-L-Ration Dog Food, tin die cut advertising sign
with graphics of dog's bust, "licking his chops," 14" x
21", NM . . . .$85.00 (C)

Kenny's Maid coffee, C.D. Kenny Co., Baltimore, MD, tin
pail, with wire pail handle, 7½" x 8", 4-lb., EX . . $525.00 (C)

Kenny's Teas & Coffees, metal litho tip tray with graphics
of the three "no evil" monkeys, 4¼" dia., VG $240.00 (B)

Kenny's Teas & Coffees, tin litho tip tray with graphics of
pretty young woman, 4¼" dia., EX . . . . $160.00 (B)

Kent Cigarettes, painted tin sign, 30" x 12", EX . $15.00 (D)

Kentucky Cardinal, 1¢ match dispenser, with paper label of
two birds, in working order, 6" x 13" x 5", EX . . $375.00 (D)

Kentucky Club, pipe and cigarette tobacco tin,
G . . . .$15.00 (D)

Kern's Bread, tin litho advertising thermometer, "Take it
Home," 5¾" x 13½", EX . . . . $110.00 (B)

Kerr-View's Milk, porcelain bottle-shaped advertising sign,
"From our own herd," 19" x 48", EX . . . . . . $2,050.00 (C)

Kentucky Power Co., one-sided porcelain sign, Redi-Kilowatt graphics, 48" x 36", G, **$230.00 (B)**.

Kern's Bread, porcelain door push bar, "Take Home...," 27" x 3", NM, **$175.00 (C)**. *Courtesy of Riverview Antique Mall*

Kerr-View's Milk, porcelain bottle-shaped advertising sign, "From our own herd," 19" x 48", G, **$1,850.00 (D)**. *Courtesy of Riverview Antique Mall*

King Cole Tea, Coffee, porcelain door push, 31½" x 3", VG, **$105.00 (B)**.

Kessler, football advertising back bar statue, rubber composition, 18" x 46", VG . . . .**$350.00 (B)**

Keystone Ice Cream, outdoor hanging porcelain advertising sign with original extension arm, 28" x 20", EX . . . . **$155.00 (C)**

Keystone Ice Cream, porcelain advertising sign with original iron hanger, with graphics of logo in center, 28" x 20", EX . . . . **$225.00 (D)**

Keystone Powerfuel Ethyl, porcelain pump sign, 12" x 14", EX . . . . **$275.00 (B)**

Kingan's Butterine, tin litho sign with man being served product with meal, 1920s, EX . . . . **$33.00 (B)**

King Arthur Flour, container with graphics of King Arthur in armor on horseback, 10" x 21", G . . . .**$97.00 (B)**

King Arthur Flour...Minnesota, double-sided heavy porcelain sign with artwork of the king on his horse, 17⅞" x 17⅞", EX . . . . **$1,050.00 (B)**

King Cole Coffee, tin litho with pry-lid with graphics of king holding cup of product, 1-lb., EX . . . . . . **$484.00 (B)**

Kingman's Meat Proof, paper litho advertising promoting its meat products with graphics of its products, 42" x 28", 1920s, EX . . . . **$95.00 (C)**

King Midas Flour, pot scraper with tin litho of small girl in bonnet, "the highest priced flour in America and worth all it costs," 2⅞" x 3⅝", EX . . . . **$135.00 (D)**

King Midas Flour, tin litho advertising scoop, 1¾" x 4", VG . . . .**$150.00 (B)**

King Midas, tin litho general store string holder advertising "King Midas...The Highest Priced Flour in America," 15" x 19¾", G . . . . **$1,000.00 (D)**

Kingsbury Pale Beer, embossed tin advertising sign, graphics of bottle of beer, 27½" x 19½", G, $130.00 (B).

King Midas, tin litho general store string holder advertising "King Midas...The Highest Priced Flour in America," 15" x 19¾", EX, $2,000.00 (B). *Courtesy of Wm. Morford Investment Grade Collectibles*

Kips Bay Pure Ales and Lager Beer, one-sided porcelain advertising sign, 28" x 20¼", VG, $380.00 (B). *Courtesy of Collectors Auction Services*

King's Castle Flour, sample bag with graphics of small village, 3¼" x 5", EX . . . . $35.00 (D)

King's Court Beverage, cardboard advertising sign with image of bottle of product, 14" x 45", 1940s, VG . .$70.00 (B)

Kings Peanut Butter, tin litho pail with graphics of king with product in hand, 1-lb., EX . . . . $786.00 (B)

King's Puremalt...good, for insomnia...strengthening...heathful, oval tip tray with graphics of product bottle in tray center, 6⅛" L, EX . . . . $120.00 (B)

Kirchhoff's Bread, door push, heavy metal and adjustable, used on screen doors before the days of air conditioning, G . . . .$95.00 (C)

Kirkman's Borax Soap, die cut tin litho match holder, featuring woman doing wash in wooden tub, 7" H, G . . . .$1,800.00 (D)

Kirkman's Floating Soap, heavy paper trolley car sign with great graphics of bar of soap to left of message, 21" x 11", EX . . . . $145.00 (C)

Kirk's Pancake Flour, embossed painted tin sign, with artwork of chef carrying serving tray, 1930s, 20" x 14", VG . . . .$255.00 (C)

"Kis-Me," die cut easel back embossed cardboard advertising sign for Kis-Me Chewing Gum, hard to find, 6½" x 10½", EX . . . . $1,550.00 (B)

Kirchhoff's Bread, door push, heavy metal and adjustable, used on screen doors before the days of air conditioning, G, $95.00 (C).

Kirkman's Borax Soap, die cut tin litho match holder, featuring woman doing wash in wooden tub, 7" H, NM, $5,700.00 (B).
Courtesy of Richard Opfer Auctioneering, Inc.

Kirk's Pancake Flour, embossed painted tin sign, with artwork of chef carrying serving tray, 1930s, 20" x 14", G, $225.00 (B). *Courtesy of Muddy River Trading Co./Gary Metz*

Kis-Me Gum, folding advertising fan, litho by Feigenspan & Co., 10" dia., EX . . . .$475.00 (B)

Kis-Me, Yellow Kid, chewing gum die cut cardboard advertising sign of the Yellow Kid walking while holding a leather satchel with product name on side of case, 3" x 6½", EX . . . .$925.00 (B)

Kissel's Garage, paper advertising calendar with graphics of vintage wrecker on front that boasts of "towing and lifting capacity 25 tons," 16¾" x 21¼", VG . . . . . .$55.00 (B)

Kist Beverages, double-sided metal "Enjoy," 21¾" x 17½", EX . . . .$295.00 (C)

Kist Beverages, double-sided tin flange sign, 22" x 17½", EX . . . .$225.00 (B)

Kist Beverages, Drink, embossed and flat tin over cardboard advertising sign with graphics of product bottle, 6" x 13¼", NM . . . .$225.00 (C)

Kist Beverages, store countertop advertising sign with graphics of woman at ship's wheel, 13" x 18½", EX . . . . .$275.00 (B)

Kist, menu board, self-framing tin litho with message at top and menu lines below, 8¾" x 19½", EX . . . $65.00 (B)

Kist, Orange and Other Flavors, die cut cardboard dimensional advertising sign with likeness of pretty woman with bottle of the product, easelback, 12" x 9" x 5", NM . . . . .$155.00 (C)

Kist...The Drinks With Real Flavor, embossed tin sign with image of bottle cap, 14¾" dia., 1959, EX . . . . . .$170.00 (B)

KKK, Adlake lantern, with embossed red glass KKK, VG . . . .$400.00 (B)

KKK, chalkware statue with uniformed man with arms crossed, 8" H, VG . . . .$235.00 (B)

KKK, etched drinking glass, 2½" dia. x 3½", NM . .$50.00 (B)

"Kis-Me," die cut easel back embossed cardboard advertising sign for Kis-Me Chewing Gum, hard to find, 6½" x 10½", EX, **$1,550.00 (B).** *Courtesy of Wm. Morford Investment Grade Collectibles*

Kist Beverage, paper litho, graphics of pretty girl with product bottle, 13½" x 17½", VG, **$210.00 (B).**

Kist Root Beer, single-sided cardboard advertising sign, graphics of product bottle, G, **$25.00 (B).**

KKK, fez-type hat with tassel, EX .... $190.00 (B)

KKK, imprinting stamp, "Women of the Ku Klu Klan...," cast iron, 8½" H, VG .... $200.00 (B)

KKK, "Kigy" plaster statue with removable arm supposedly for beginning and ending meetings, 16¼" H, VG $275.00 (B)

KKK, light-up frosted glass figurine with tin base, in shape of uniformed man, 6" H, EX .... $150.00 (B)

KKK, Loyal Order..., knife, ivory, with advertisement, 3¼" L, VG .... $140.00 (B)

KKK, plate depicting rider holding a burning cross, 10" dia., 1910s, VG .... $500.00 (C)

KKK, plate, Knowles China Co., artwork of burning cross in center of plate, 6¼" dia., VG .... $75.00 (B)

KKK, plate, unmarked on back, "God give us men," 6¼" dia., VG .... $80.00 (B)

KKK, plate, "Vitreous Edwin M. Knowles China Co.," "Made by A.C. Blair Klan Plate Co., Chester, W.VA" with "Stone Mountain" at top and artwork of cross atop the mountain, 6¼" dia., 1915, VG .... $80.00 (B)

KKK, plate with graphics of horse, rider and a burning cross, "1865 Yesterday To-Day and Forever," Knowles China Co., 6¼" dia., VG .... $75.00 (B)

Kodak, metal countertop film display case with graphics of Ed Sullivan, 12½" x 7½", VG, $50.00 (B).

Knox Gelatine, die cut cardboard litho of children standing on slanted platform with trademark cow and holding a plate of gelatin, 14" x 10" x 16", EX, $3,500.00 (D). *Courtesy of Collectors Auction Services*

Kodak, life-size die-cut cardboard display of pretty woman, "Stop Here for...Kodak Verichrome Film," 21" x 64", G, $105.00 (B).

Kleinert's Dress Shield Guimpe, advertising pocket mirror with artwork of product on back side, 2" dia., EX . . . . $44.00 (B)

Klondike Fizz drink, advertising paperboard sign and matching trade card with graphics of man and dog sled at North Pole, 10½" x 7", 1890s, EX . . . . $155.00 (B)

Knapsack Matches, tin box, one-cent, wood, metal and glass dispenser, 10" x 10½", EX . . . . $675.00 (C)

Knox Gelatine, canvas litho sign, Harry Roseland, 1901, with graphics of little girl with mammy, 29¾" x 22¾", VG . . . .$2,000.00 (B)

Knox Gelatine, cardboard box with trademark cow, from the "Charles B. Knox Gelatine Co., Inc, Johnstown, N.Y., Camden N.J., U.S.A.," 3½" x 2¾" x 5", VG . . .$100.00 (B)

Knox Gelatine, die cut cardboard litho of children standing on slanted platform with trademark cow and holding a plate of gelatin, 14" x 10" x 16", G . . . . $900.00 (D)

Knox Gelatine, die cut litho with advertising on all four sides, countertop display with children holding product and graphics of cow in center at top, hard-to-find item, 14" x 10" x 16", EX . . . . $750.00 (B)

Knox Gelatine, litho on canvas advertising sign of nanny and young girl working on a dessert, 20" x 16", EX . . . . $430.00 (B)

Knox Gelatine, litho with great detail, images of older black woman with young girl working on dessert at table, double matted and framed, 1901, 26" x 20", NM . . . .$1,250.00 (B)

Kodak All Supplies, round porcelain advertising sign, 20" dia., EX . . . . $475.00 (C)

Kodak, Developing & Printing, double-sided porcelain advertising sign with graphics of roll of product, 20" x 14", EX . . . . $425.00 (C)

Kodak...Developing...Printing...Enlarging, double-sided die cut metal advertising sign with likeness of box of film at bottom, 17" x 17", G . . . .$300.00 (B)

Koken Shop, advertising porcelain barber sign, originally held light bulbs on the outside of sign, rare find, 31" dia., G, **$1,800.00 (B).**

Kool Cigarettes, double-sided metal flange advertising thermometer, 4" x 12", EX, **$120.00 (B).**

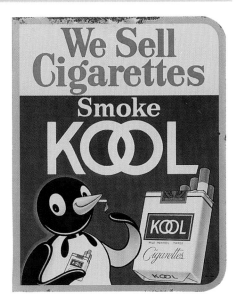

Kool Cigarettes...Mild Menthol, Cork Tipped, die cut cardboard of girl in scarf holding mask, 32" x 47", EX, **$175.00 (D).**

Courtesy of Riverview Antique Mall

Kodak film, double-sided die cut tin advertising sign in shape of box of the product with hanging arm, 17" x 6½", 1914, EX . . . . **$455.00 (C)**

Kodak, light-up advertising clock with graphics of package of film under number 12, 15¼" x 15¼", EX . **$120.00 (B)**

Kodak, light-up advertising clock with older plastic body, "America's Storyteller," 19" dia., VG . . . .**$45.00 (B)**

Kodak, metal flange double-sided advertising sign, 21½" x 25½", EX . . . . **$55.00 (C)**

Kodak's, double-sided porcelain die cut advertising sign with different image angles on each side, top hung, 26" x 22½", EX . . . . **$215.00 (C)**

Kodak, self-framing single-sided porcelain sign, foreign, 11" x 71", VG . . . .**$500.00 (B)**

Kodak, Verichrome, double-sided porcelain sign, shaped in likeness of a box of film, 21¼" x 12½", EX . . . **$225.00 (B)**

Kodak... Verichrome, safety film, heavy porcelain sign in shape of box of film, 24½" x 12½", EX . . . . . **$250.00 (C)**

Koehler, salesman sample bath tub, porcelain and iron, 11" x 5" x 3¼", VG . . . .**$95.00 (B)**

Koken, Barber Pole, porcelain and glass construction with paper cylinder, 14" x 28", G . . . .**$325.00 (B)**

Kool Cigarettes S & P, featuring Millie & Willie, promotional items, 3¼" H, VG, $50.00 (B).

Korbel Sec California Champagne, painted metal sign, 19" x 13", EX, **$175.00 (D).**

Kotex, store countertop display with litho of nurse on both ends holding product package, 8½" x 13½" x 14", VG, **$305.00 (B).**

Koken Shop, advertising porcelain barber sign, originally held light bulbs on the outside of sign, rare find, 31" dia., EX . . . .$2,200.00 (C)

KOOL Cigarettes, advertising fan, images of penguins skating around product package, EX . . . . $35.00 (B)

Kool Cigarettes, cardboard die cut easel back advertising "Willie" playing the trumpet, 9¼" x 12.675", 1940s – 1950s, NM . . . .$135.00 (C)

Kool Cigarettes, die cut cardboard of "Willie" standing playing a trumpet in front of a package of Kopol cigarettes, 9" x 13", 1940 – 1950s, EX . . . . $135.00 (D)

Kool Cigarettes...Mild Menthol, Cork Tipped, die cut cardboard of girl in scarf holding mask, 32" x 47", EX . . . . $175.00 (D)

Kool, menthol magic...Smoke Kool, metal cigarette holder with artwork of Kool penguin and product pack, EX . . . . $45.00 (D)

Koolmotor, "Refill with...The Perfect Pennsylvania Oil" on the front side and "Refill with Cities Service Oils" on reverse side, double-sided tin sign with top mounting holes, 20¾" x 12", EX . . . . $375.00 (B)

Koolmotor...The Perfect Pennsylvania Oil, die cut double-sided porcelain sign, 23¾" x 23¾", EX . . . . . $325.00 (B)

Kool...Smoke...We Sell Cigarettes, horizontal embossed painted metal sign with Kool penguin to left of message, 25" x 10½", EX . . . . $59.00 (D)

Korbel Sec California Champagne, painted metal sign, 19" x 13", NM . . . .$200.00 (C)

Korbel Sec Champagne, beveled edge tin over cardboard, self-framing, with artwork of woman with grapes and product bottle at right of artwork, 19" x 13", NM . .$365.00 (B)

Kraft Pex, die cut embossed painted metal sign in shape of chicken, 14¼" x 19½", EX . . . . $110.00 (B)

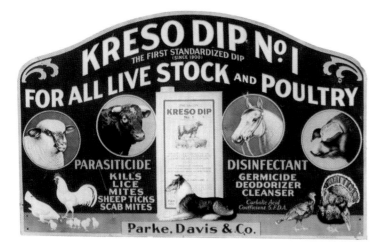

Kreso Dip No. 1, tin litho veterinary advertising sign with graphics of different animals and the medicines for each, Parke, Davis & Co., 28" x 18", EX, **$1,350.00 (B).** *Courtesy of Wm.*
Morford Investment Grade Collectibles

Kreso Disinfectant Kills Germs Everywhere, one-sided embossed tin advertising sign, 23" x 12", G, **$35.00 (B).**

Kuhn's Climatized Paints, die cut double-sided porcelain advertising sign with image of raccoon on limb with can of the product, 18" x 24", NM, **$1,500.00 (C).** *Courtesy of*
Autopia Advertising Auctions

Krantz Brewing Corp., pinback with bar scene, advertising Old Dutch Beer, 1¼" dia., NM . . . .$75.00 (C)

Kreger's Bakery and Ice Cream Parlor, calendar with artwork of two young girls on burro being led by young boy, paper litho, 1907, 15" x 20", EX . . . . $75.00 (C)

Kreso Dip No. 1, tin litho veterinary advertising sign with graphics of different animals and the medicines for each, Parke, Davis & Co., 28" x 18", G . . . . $500.00 (C)

Krout's Baking Powder, paper on cardboard with pry lid from Albert Krout Co., Philadelphia, 3" x 6", EX $425.00 (C)

Krueger Beer & Ale, in bottles and keg-lined cans, 10" x 15", EX . . . . $150.00 (B)

Krug, advertising plate celebrating the fiftieth anniversary of the brewery, photo of founder on front and brewery on reverse, 10" dia., 1909, EX . . . . $125.00 (C)

Kuhn's Climatized Paints, die cut double-sided porcelain advertising sign with image of raccoon on limb with can of the product, 18" x 24", G . . . . $500.00 (C)

Kum-Seald, handkerchief, wood and glass display with glass front, back opens for refilling, 22" W x 12" H x 8" D, EX . . . . $140.00 (D)

Kurfees Paint, double-sided porcelain flange sign with graphics of product can in center "Saves the Surface," 18¼" x 13¼", VG . . . .$395.00 (D)

Kynoch's Sporting & Military Cartridge Board, with graphics of cartridges, 18½" x 27", 1897, EX . . . . $875.00 (B)

Lance, glass store jar with crossed lances on front & back with hard-to-find metal Lance bottom, 1940s, EX, $175.00 (D). *Courtesy of Rare Bird Antique Mall/Jon & Joan Wright*

La Preferencia Seconds, My! This IS a Mild Cigar, 5¢ Straight, framed paper advertisement, 23¼" x 19¼", NM, $55.00 (C).

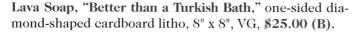

Lava Soap, "Better than a Turkish Bath," one-sided diamond-shaped cardboard litho, 8" x 8", VG, $25.00 (B).

Labatt's, porcelain serving tray, 16" x 12", EX .$65.00 (D)

LaBelle Creole Cigarettes, cardboard litho advertising poster with graphics of mammy and children at fence, 22¼" x 17¼", VG . . . .$2,000.00 (C)

LaBelle Creole Cigarettes, stamped and embossed paper advertising sign with graphics of black kids trying to hide from mammy, S. Hernsheim Bros. & Co., New Orleans, 1890s, EX . . . .$850.00 (B)

La Corna Cigar, tin, round, with 1932 tax stamp, "Havana Cigar & Tobacco Factories Ltd. Grown in Cuba Blended in Havana, Rolled and Packed in the United States of America," 2¼" dia. x 5¼", VG . . . .$35.00 (B)

Lacquerwax...Lasts Twice As Long, embossed tin advertising sign with image of product can and vintage car, 19½" x 13½", VG . . . .$195.00 (C)

Ladies' Home Journal, double-sided porcelain sign advertising LHJ pattern, 18" x 7½", EX . . . .$350.00 (B)

Ladies' Home Journal...for spring fashion read..., framed cloth banner with artwork of Irene Bordoni at left of message, 46" x 34", EX . . . .$325.00 (D)

Lady Hellen Coffee, paper label with pry lid and graphics of woman on front, 1-lb., EX . . . .$175.00 (C)

Lady Hellen Coffee, pry lid paper label on tin container, 1-lb., EX . . . .$110.00 (B)

Laflin & Rand Orange Extra Sporting Powder, tin container, with paper label, 3½" x 4" x 1", EX . . . .$55.00 (C)

Laflin & Rand Powder Co, can with litho of flying flag, "Orange...extra...sporting," 4" x 6" x 1¼", 1900s, EX . . . .$85.00 (B)

Leaf Spearmint Chewing Gum, tin litho single-sided advertising sign, 25⅛" x 8⅞", G, $80.00 (B).

Lay or Bust Feeds, Fresh Eggs, price chalkboard, 20" x 26", VG, $350.00 (B).

Leak-Proof Piston Rings, light-up advertising clock by Telechron, 15" dia., NM, $495.00 (C). *Courtesy of Autopia Advertising Auctions*

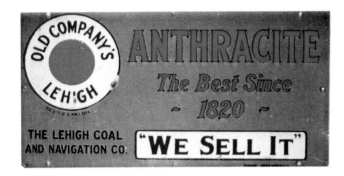

Lehigh Anthracite, single-sided porcelain sign, 21" x 11", VG, $300.00 (B). *Courtesy of Collectors Auction Services*

Lakeside Grape Juice, from selected grapes, The Beverage of Quality, metal serving tray, with great graphics of grapes and bottle, 13½" dia., EX . . . .$110.00 (B)

Lance...From the House of Lance, clear glass store jar, Lance embossed on both sides of handle on top and on bottom of jar, 7" x 8½", EX . . . .$85.00 (C)

Lance, glass store jar with crossed lances on front & back with hard-to-find metal Lance bottom, 1940s, F . . . . . .$95.00 (C)

Lance, our 75th anniversary, store jar with original glass lid, EX . . . .$100.00 (D)

L&M cigarette, advertising thermometer, self-framing embossed, with scale-type indicator, 5¾" x 13¼", EX . . . .$110.00 (B)

Land O Lakes, key-wound powdered milk tin, graphics of Indian maiden, 4¼" x 4", 1940s, EX . . . .$95.00 (C)

Land O Lakes, tin litho advertising thermometer promoting sweet cream butter with trademark Indian at bottom, 8" x 27", EX . . . .$235.00 (B)

Land O Lakes, tin litho thermometer, graphics of Indian maid at bottom of vertical scale, 1960s, NM . . .$90.00 (B)

Lane Cedar Chest, die cut easel back cardboard store sign, with graphics of moth in clothes drawer, 19" x 29¾", EX . . . .$47.00 (B)

La Palina, cigar counter display jar with embossed lettering on jar, 6½" x 8" EX . . . .$130.00 (C)

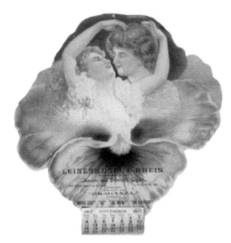

Leinenkugel & Rheim Cigar, die cut embossed cardboard advertising calendar, 19" x 20", 1917, EX, $275.00 (B). *Courtesy of Past Tyme Pleasures*

Lemon-Kola, tin over cardboard sign, featuring artwork of girl with flared glass with straw, rare, 6¼" x 9¼", EX, $400.00 (B). *Courtesy of Muddy River Trading Co./Gary Metz*

Libby's, Rolled Ox Tongues, paper litho under glass, framed, EX, $425.00 (B). *Courtesy of Richard Opfer Auctioneering, Inc.*

Lenox Soap, porcelain advertising sign, 10" x 6", G, $120.00 (B). *Courtesy of Muddy River Trading Co./Gary Metz*

La Preferencia Seconds, My! This IS a Mild Cigar, 5¢ Straight, framed paper advertisement, 23¼" x 19¼", EX . . . .$35.00 (C)

Lash's Orangeade, metal dispenser, 21½" T, VG .$500.00 (B)

Lash's Syrup, dispenser, round green depression glass, 7" x 8", EX . . . .$75.00 (B)

Lasico Medicinal, embossed tin advertising sign, advertising a cure for "nervous debility and sexual weakness," 7" x 10", EX . . . .$250.00 (B)

Lauenstrin wines and liquor, die cut advertising sign with graphics of man with sandwich board promoting Old Kentucky Whiskey, 8½" x 14½", VG . . . .$55.00 (C)

Lava Soap, cardboard fan pull, double-sided with artwork of product in center, 11" sq., EX . . . .$60.00 (B)

Lavine laundry soap, advertising sign with graphics of woman at table with box of product, from the Hartford Chemical Company, 13" x 28½", 1890s, EX . .$335.00 (C)

Lawrence Barrett Cigar, porcelain advertising sign with graphics of founder in center oval, 21" x 31", EX . . . . .$700.00 (B)

Lawrence Tiger Brand Paints & Varnishes, cardboard advertising sign in metal frame, 30" x 42", VG . . . .$160.00 (B)

Lax-ets...candy, bowel laxative, celluloid sign, 17" x 14", EX . . . .$400.00 (B)

Laxol...Castor Oil...Like Honey, round metal tip tray with artwork of product bottle, 4¼" dia., EX . . . . . .$65.00 (B)

L.B. Silver Co., Cleveland, Ohio, celluloid over metal pinback, 2" dia., VG . . . .$25.00 (B)

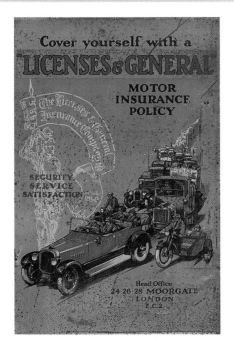

Licenses & General Motor Insurance Policy, foreign single-sided sign, 19" x 29¼", F, **$200.00 (B).**

Lift Beverage...Drink, It's Good For You, painted tin sign, 12" x 24", EX, **$175.00 (C).**

Lift Beverage...It's Good for You, single-sided embossed tin advertising sign, bottle graphics, 7" x 12", VG, **$115.00 (B).**

L.C. Smith Gun, glass advertising paperweight with graphics of breech-loading gun, 4" x 2½" x ¾", EX ....**$125.00 (C)**

Leader, Rolled Tip Spark Plugs, store countertop display with graphics of spark plug on front of unit, 15" x 4" x 10¼", G ....**$350.00 (B)**

Leadway Rolled Oats, container with graphics of bowl of hot oats, 3-lb., EX ....**$65.00 (C)**

Leaf Leafmint Gum, store counter display package with unopened packages of gum, 6⅛" x 4¼" x 3", 1930s, EX ....**$400.00 (B)**

Leak-Proof Piston Rings, light-up advertising clock by Telechron, 15" dia., G ....**$195.00 (C)**

Lee, authentic western wear cloth banner, EX **$145.00 (C)**

Lee, country store display overalls, 4' x 12', EX ..**$160.00 (B)**

Lee Jeans, neon sign, 36" x 24", EX ....**$375.00 (B)**

Lee, Overalls, die cut cardboard store advertising sign, with graphics of young boy in overalls holding hammer, 10" T, EX ....**$90.00 (B)**

Lee, Riders, double-sided sign with man riding on bucking bronc, 17½" dia., EX ....**$200.00 (B)**

Lee Tires, embossed tin, self-framing advertising sign, 72" x 17½", VG ....**$195.00 (B)**

Lee Tires, metal framed glass front light-up sign, 32" x 7½", EX ....**$165.00 (D)**

L.E. Graybill, paper three-dimensional calendar with die cut scene of animals in background with tear sheets at bottom, 1923, 15" x 15", EX ....**$25.00 (D)**

Lehnert's Beer...Drink...Made in Catasauqua, Pa., round metal tip tray with graphics of large dog sporting eyeglasses and smoking a cigar, 4¼" dia., EX ....**$300.00 (B)**

Leinenkugel & Rheim Cigar, die cut embossed cardboard advertising calendar, 19" x 20", 1917, F ......**$75.00 (C)**

Leinenkugel's Beer, double-bubble advertising clock with graphics of Indian head, 15" dia., VG ......**$485.00 (B)**

Leland McNamee's Ministrels, paper on cardboard advertising poster with graphics of black man's head, 41" x 80", VG ....**$300.00 (B)**

Lilly's, gas globe, gill body with glass lens, graphics of lilies at bottom of face, 13½" dia., VG, $1,800.00 (B). *Courtesy of Collectors Auction Services*

Lime Cola...Drink, round celluloid sign, 1950s, 9" dia., EX, $130.00 (B). *Courtesy of Muddy River Trading Co./Gary Metz*

Lily White Flour, sign, curved embossed tin sign in likeness of product can, made by Sentenne & Green, 19" x 35½", 1890s, EX, $4,800.00 (B). *Courtesy of Buffalo Bay Auction Co.*

Lemon Dry Beverages, tin litho door push, 4" x 10", EX . . . .$155.00 (B)

Lemon Kola, tin litho tip tray, 4¼" dia., EX . .$180.00 (B)

Lemon-Kola, tin over cardboard sign, featuring artwork of girl with flared glass with straw, rare, 6¼" x 9¼", VG . . . .$325.00 (C)

Lenox Soap, porcelain advertising sign, 10" x 6", EX . . . .$175.00 (C)

Leopold: The Clothier, Miffinburg, PA, round metal tip tray with scolloped edges and artwork of three white horses in tray center, 4¼" dia., EX . . . .$175.00 (D)

Levenson Hair Shop, celluloid pocket advertising mirror with artwork of red-haired woman on front, 1¾" x 2¾", EX . . . .$250.00 (B)

Levering's Coffee, paper litho on cardboard with advertising message and product image on back and a checker board on reverse side, 1910s, 4¾" x 9½", EX . .$75.00 (C)

Levis, advertising poster showing cowboy lore, 25" x 36½", 1933, EX . . . .$355.00 (C)

Levis, embossed molded plastic advertising sign with graphics of man carrying saddle, 16" x 32", 1960s, EX . . . .$925.00 (B)

Lincoln-Zephyr V 12, three-page advertising brochure, 11" x 8½", 1939, NM, $75.00 (C). *Courtesy of Past Tyme Pleasures*

Lion Coffee, store bin featuring lion pulling chariot on lift-top lid, 32¼" H, NM, $500.00 (D). *Courtesy of Richard Opfer Auctioneering, Inc.*

Lions International, porcelain sign, 30" dia., VG, $75.00 (C).

Levy's Bread, paper litho advertising poster with a young black man eating a sandwich made with Levy's bread, "You don't have to be Jewish to love Levy's...real Jewish rye," 29½" x 45¼", VG . . . .$550.00 (B)

L.F.S. Cigars, paper advertising poster with graphics of young girl and flowers, from L.F. Stander, Greencastle, Ind., 15" x 19", 1900s, NM . . . .$135.00 (B)

Libby's, rolled ox tongues, paper litho under glass, framed, G . . . .$275.00 (C)

Liberty Beer...In Bottles Only, American Brewing Co., round metal tip tray with Indian logo in center of tray, 4⅛", EX . . . .$160.00 (B)

Liberty Ice Cream...Superior, Improved, rectangular hard plastic serving tray, EX . . . .$18.00 (D)

Lictonic, embossed tin litho sign with graphics of cow eating at left and dealer strip at bottom, 20" x 9", EX . .$165.00 (C)

Lieber's Gold Medal Beer, tip tray, featuring graphics of product bottle in center of tray, 5" dia., EX . . .$55.00 (B)

Lifebuoy Soap, trolley car framed advertisment showing youngsters in school scene, 22¼" x 12¼", EX . .$120.00 (B)

Life Savers, display tin litho unit, 18½" x 24" x 11", G . . . .$55.00 (D)

Life Saver...Drive Safely, die cut tin license plate attachment with jewel-type reflector attached to center of unit, 5" x 6½", EX . . . .$250.00 (C)

Life Savers, counter display, made of polished aluminum with three tiers for merchandise display, 9¼" x 12" x 9", EX . . . .$125.00 (C)

Life Savers, tin litho counter display unit with two shelves holding the product, 3" x 6½" x 7", VG . . . .$85.00 (C)

Lipton's Tea...Always Satisfactory, double-sided die cut tin litho store string dispenser, 13¾" x 19½", EX, **$1,512.00 (B)**.

Lively Limes, metagolio mirror, 18⅛" x 12", VG, **$135.00 (C)**.

Lolita Talcum Powder, tin oval container with artwork of "Lolita" on front, 4¼" x 7" x 9", VG, **$115.00 (C)**.

Long's Ox-Heart Chocolates, double-sided cardboard advertising poster, 11⅓" dia., G, **$20.00 (B)**.

Life Savers, tin litho three-tier store display rack, would display 9 different flavors, 1920s, 15½" x 14" x 10", EX . . . .$600.00 (B)

Lift Beverage...Drink, It's Good For You, painted tin sign, 12" x 24", G . . . .$85.00 (C)

Lift...Drink, It's good for you, Three Star Bottling Works, porcelain advertising sign with product bottle image, 12" x 24", NM . . . .$200.00 (B)

Liggett & Meyers Star Brand Tobacco, unopened wooden box with 1910 Federal Stamp, 13" x 7" x 3", 1910s, EX . . . .$85.00 (C)

Liggett & Meyers Tobacco Co., Sweet Cuba...fine, cut...the kind that suits, store tin with artwork of ocean and lighthouse, F . . . .$45.00 (D)

Liggett & Meyers Tobacco Co., tin tobacco pail with wire bail handle, product information in oval on front, G . .$25.00 (D)

Liggett & Meyers Tobacco Co., Velvet Pipe & Cigarette Tobacco, round tin container with press on lid, EX . . . . .$15.00 (D)

Liggett's Coffee, promoting Java coffee, small top, 5¼" x 9½", EX . . . .$275.00 (C)

Light Horse Squadron...The Aristocrat of 10¢ Cigars, metal tip tray with camp scene in center, 6⅝" L, EX . . .$95.00 (B)

Lilly's, gas globe, gill body with glass lens, graphics of lilies at bottom of face, 13½" dia., F . . . .$500.00 (C)

Lily...A Beverage...Rock Island Brewing Co., Rock Island, Ill., metal tip tray featuring graphics of product bottle in center with sandwich and glass of product, 6½" L, EX . . . .$110.00 (B)

Look Better, Feel Better, porcelain barber pole, 7½" x 48", red, white & blue, VG, $395.00 (C).

Lowe Brothers Paint, neon advertising sign, metal and glass, 30" x 11", G, $280.00 (B).

Lowe Brothers Paints for all purposes, porcelain advertising store sign, 27¾" x 19¾", VG, $55.00 (C).

Löwenbräu, lion, back bar statue with bottle, EX, $125.00 (C). *Courtesy of B.J. Summers*

Lily Brand Compound Talcum Powder, tin by American Can, 2⅛" x 5", EX . . . .$75.00 (C)

Lily White...Bias Fold Tape...Extra Fine Quality, metal store counter display, 15" x 8¼" x 8", G . . . . .$35.00 (D)

Lily White Flour, sign, curved embossed tin sign in likeness of product can, made by Sentenne & Green, 19" x 35½", 1890s, G . . . .$1,000.00 (C)

Lily White, metal counter display unit advertising "Bias Fold Tape," 15" x 8" x 8¼", VG . . . .$75.00 (C)

Lime Cola, celluloid over cardboard disc string-hung advertising sign, 9" dia., NM . . . .$150.00 (C)

Lime Cola...Drink, embossed tin strip sign, 24" x 8", NM . . . .$110.00 (B)

Lime Cola...Drink, round celluloid sign, 1950s, 9" dia., VG . . . .$110.00 (C)

Lime Cola, painted tin menu board, "We Serve...It's Definitely Good," NOS, 14" x 20", NM . . . .$160.00 (B)

Lime-Crush...Drink, embossed tin "tacker" style sign, 19½" x 14", EX . . . .$210.00 (B)

Lime-Julep, cardboard string hanger with a couple enjoying a bottle of the product with two straws, 8" x 11", 1940s, EX . . . .$155.00 (B)

Lincoln Cab Co., wood thermometer with graphics of vintage cab at top, 4" x 15", G . . . .$80.00 (B)

Lucke's Telescopes, wood cigar box, 100-count with litho of man at telescope, 1880s, NM, $405.00 (B). *Courtesy of Buffalo Bay Auction Co.*

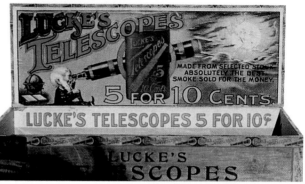

Lowney's Chocolate Bars and Cracker Jack, porcelain advertising thermometer, 8" x 30¼", VG, $235.00 (B). *Courtesy of Collectors Auction Services*

Lucky Strike Cigarettes, die cut cardboard 3-D advertising sign, 1920s, EX, $435.00 (B).

Lucky Strike, die cut easel-back cardboard countertop Santa Claus display, 8¼" x 13¼", VG, $140.00 (B).

Lincoln Flour, paper advertising sign with image of Abraham Lincoln in center, with metal top and bottom strips, "Ask Your Grocer," "Traders Meat Market, Polaski, Iowa and Standard, St. Paul," 16" x 22½", EX ....$210.00 (B)

Lincoln Steel Cut Coffee, tin container with paper label containing graphics of Abraham Lincoln, has pry-lid, from Capitol Grocery Co., Springfield, IL, EX ....$135.00 (D)

Lincoln-Zephyr V 12, three-page advertising brochure, 11" x 8½", 1939, NM ....$75.00 (C)

Linco Motor Oil, paper advertising calendar with graphics of plane sky-writing about product, 19½" x 26½", 1936, VG ....$45.00 (B)

Lion Coffee, store bin featuring lion pulling chariot on lift-top lid, 32¼" H, EX ....$450.00 (B)

Lion Naturalube...The New Type Motor Oil, embossed painted license plate attachment with die cut trademark lion at top, 6" x 6¼", VG ....$125.00 (C)

Lions International, porcelain sign, 30" dia., G $20.00 (B)

Lions International, porcelain sign with lions' heads on both sides of message, 30" dia., EX ....$150.00 (D)

Lipton's Tea...Always Satisfactory, double-sided die cut tin litho store string dispenser, 13¾" x 19½", EX ..$1,512.00 (B)

Lipton's Teas, Ceylon, stone litho on paper of young girl at table with the product ready to serve, 1899, VG ..$675.00 (B)

Lipton's Teas...Will You Have Some?, paper litho of young lady with tea tray in front, strong colors and great depth, 1899, NM ....$1,324.00 (B)

Lucky Strike, heavy easel back cardboard litho advertising "Luckies – a light smoke...it's toasted" with graphics of man and woman at ship porthole enjoying a smoke of the product, 27½" x 36", 1940s, VG, $155.00 (B).

Courtesy of Collectors Auction Services

Lucky Strike, pin-up girl, painted tin sign, 15" x 21", EX, $250.00 (B). *Courtesy of Muddy River Trading Co./Gary Metz*

Lucky Strike, pocket mirror similar to package, 2" x 3", 1938, EX, $135.00 (C).

Litchfield Ice Cream, metal-framed plastic front advertising sign, G . . . .$145.00 (D)

Little Beauties, cigar box, good strong graphics of kids dressed as adults, 50-ct., EX . . . .$225.00 (C)

Little Giant Elevators, farm equipment, painted metal sign with artwork of giant holding ball with farm equipment, EX . . . .$85.00 (C)

Little's, tin litho typewriter tin advertising a "Satin finish" with trademark image of young black child on lid, 2½" x 2½" x ¾", EX . . . .$140.00 (B)

Live-Well Pure Cocoa, cardboard container, Joyce-Laughlin Co., Peoria, Ill., 2-lb., P . . . .$40.00 (D)

Lockwood Taylor Hardware Co., metal litho tip tray, with graphics of pretty woman in center and advertising "incandescent mantles," 4¼" dia., VG . . . .$40.00 (B)

Loft Brand Midget Candy Sticks, tin litho with artwork of children feeding candy stick to squirrel, 6" x 4¾", EX . . . .$300.00 (B)

Log Cabin Cigar Box, wood in shape of log cabin with paper litho inside lid showing family dancing and smoking, 8½" x 5" x 5½", VG . . . .$775.00 (D)

Log Cabin Cigar Box, wood with paper litho scene of wagon, in shape of log cabin, 8½" x 5" x 5½", VG . . . . .$750.00 (D)

Log Cabin Coffee, Shaffer Stores, Altoona, PA, tin litho key-wound coffee can showing great graphics of cabin in clearing in woods, 1-lb., 4" x 5", EX . . . . .$1,550.00 (B)

Log Cabin Frontier Inn, with graphics of people on front porch with horse tied to rail, 5-lb., NM . . . . .$207.00 (B)

Log Cabin, Frontier Jail, tin litho syrup container, NM . . . .$141.00 (B)

Log Cabin, Stockade School, tin litho syrup container with graphics of children playing in front of school, NM . . . .$187.00 (B)

Log Cabin Syrup, quart-size syrup container with boy at door in blue and hat, tin litho, 1914, EX . . . . .$75.00 (B)

Log Cabin Syrup, cardboard shipping box with great graphics of young girl holding a syrup tin, 16½" x 11" x 10½", 1918, EX . . . .$375.00 (C)

Log Cabin Syrup, table-sized tin litho container with graphics of boy in black at door, 1914, EX . . . .$75.00 (B)

Log Cabin Syrup, tin litho container with graphics of boy in blue with hat, table size, 1914, EX . . . .$70.00 (B)

Luden's Chewing Gum, change receiver, featuring artwork of gum packages in center, 1920s, 11" dia., G, **$180.00 (B).** *Courtesy of Muddy River Trading Co./Gary Metz*

Lydia E. Pinkham's Vegetable Compound, framed advertising calendar, full monthly pad, short bio, 15" x 22¾", G, **$110.00 (B).**

Lykens Dairy Milk and Cream, one-sided tin sign, 30" x 14", VG, **$70.00 (B).**

Log Cabin Syrup, tin litho table-sized container, frontier house bank, EX . . . .$88.00 (B)

Log Cabin, wooden cigar box with inside label featuring graphics of black family entertaining themselves beside a log cabin, 100-ct., EX . . . .$165.00 (B)

Lohrey's Silver Star, advertising glass sign designed for each company's logo in blank at top of sign, "Silver Star sausage, ham and bacon," 13" x 19", EX . . . . .$85.00 (C)

Lolita Talcum Powder, tin oval container with artwork of "Lolita" on front, 4¼" x 7" x 9", EX . . . .$145.00 (D)

London House Coffee, Silver Banner, tin litho container, key-wound container, 1-lb., EX . . . .$44.00 (B)

Lone Jack...smoke the...seg-ars, etched stained glass advertising sign, 4" x 9¾", EX . . . .$900.00 (B)

Lone Star Beer, mechanical advertising monkey, 25" dia. x 39" H, VG . . . .$1,225.00 (B)

Look Out Cut Plug Tobacco, flat pocket tin with artwork of lighthouse from J.C. Dill's, Richmond, VA, 4½" x 2" x 1", EX . . . .$80.00 (B)

Look Better, Feel Better, porcelain barber pole, 7½" x 48", red, white & blue, G . . . .$350.00 (D)

Lorain Creamery, double-sided porcelain advertising sign, Jersey Lane Ice Cream, 28" x 20", VG . . . . . .$325.00 (B)

Lord Grasby, wooden cigar box with graphics of Indians with tobacco leaves, 100-ct, 1915, EX . . . .$40.00 (B)

Lord Tennyson Puritanos Cigars, Canadian tin litho container, 5" x 5⅛", EX . . . .$110.00 (B)

Lorillards "49" Cut Plug Tobacco, trade card with graphics of miners at water plume panning for gold, litho by Grocer & Canner, SF, 4½" x 3¼", EX . . . .$230.00 (B)

Love Nest Coffee, key-wound container with graphics of cozy home scene, 1-lb., EX . . . .$210.00 (B)

Lowe Brothers Paints, for all purposes, porcelain advertising store sign, 27¾" x 19¾", G . . . .$45.00 (B)

Löwenbräu, lion, back bar statue with bottle, F . . . . .$45.00 (C)

Lowney's Cocoa, sample tin litho can with graphics of Victorian woman on front, 1⅝" x 1⅜" x 1", EX . . .$250.00 (B)

Lowney's Cocoa, tin with graphics of children eating the product, 3" x 4¾" x 2⅛", EX . . . .$55.00 (C)

L.P. Thomas & Son Co., High Grade Fertilizer, paper framed calendar, Hiawatha's Wedding Journey, with theme graphics, 16" x 25½", VG . . . .$160.00 (B)

L.S. DuBois, Son & Co., Wholesale Druggist, Paducah, Ky., crock jug with block advertising on front, brown top with cream bottom, EX . . . .$135.00 (C)

Lubri-Gas...Tractor-Diesel-Aviation or Marine Fuel, self-framing tin, embossed advertising sign, 56" x 32", VG . . . .$300.00 (B)

Lubrite Motor Oil, Socony-Vacuum Oil Company, Inc., double-sided painted metal advertising sign, 20" x 11", F . . . .$70.00 (B)

Lucke's Telescopes, wood cigar box, 100-count with litho of man at telescope, 1880s, NM . . . .$405.00 (B)

Lucke's Telescopes, wooden cigar box with graphics on inside label of telescope looking to the heavens, 100-ct., 1883, EX . . . .$140.00 (B)

Luck Ghost, paper litho movie advertising poster starring Mantan Moreland and F.E. Miller, 28½" x 40½", EX . . . .$125.00 (D)

Lucky B, cigar box shaped like a book with "Works of Nietzsche and Kuhn" on spine, 50-ct., EX . . . .$75.00 (C)

Lucky Cup Coffee, tin key-wound top with graphics of steaming cup of coffee with horseshoe, 1-lb., EX $33.00 (B)

Lucky Strike, Filter 100s, green carton, never been opened, EX . . . .$45.00 (D)

Lucky Strike, flat fifties cigarettes, hinged cigarette tin, Lucky Strike...It's toasted, 5½" x 4½", EX . . . .$20.00 (C)

Lucky Strike, girl in spotlight, tin sign, signed by "Bazz," 1950s, 17" x 24", EX . . . .$300.00 (B)

Lucky Strike, Harry Heilmann, Detroit Tigers...World's Leading Batter, "I smoke Luckies because they are the best," paper trolley car sign, 21" x 11", EX . .$1,250.00 (C)

Lucky Strike, heavy easel back cardboard litho advertising "Luckies-a light smoke...it's toasted" with graphics of man and woman at ship porthole enjoying a smoke of the product, 27½" x 36", 1940s, EX . . . .$175.00 (C)

Lucky Strike, pin-up girl, painted tin sign, 15" x 21", G . . . .$175.00 (D)

Lucky Strike, pocket mirror similar to package, 2" x 3", 1938, F . . . .$65.00 (D)

Lucky Strike, tin litho vertical pocket container with graphics of the white Lucky package, 3" x 1" x 4¼", EX . . . .$225.00 (D)

Lucky Tiger, Dandruff, tin with paper label and screw-top on lid, 1-qt., VG . . . .$40.00 (B)

Lucky Tiger, For Hair and Scalp...with oil or without, cardboard easel back advertising sign featuring graphics of pretty woman with tiger bust, 22" x 33½", NM . . . . .$235.00 (C)

Luden's Chewing Gum, change receiver, featuring artwork of gum packages in center, 1920s, 11" dia., EX . . . .$215.00 (C)

Luden's Cough Drops...Give Instant Relief, Reading, Penna., round metal tip tray with graphics of early cough drop box, 3½" dia., EX . . . .$900.00 (B)

Luden's Cough Drop, tip tray with graphics of product package in center of tray, 3½" dia., VG . . . . .$360.00 (B

Ludwig Pianos...New York, round, metal tip tray with artwork of pretty woman, 4¼" dia., EX . . . .$45.00 (B)

Lunch Ice Cream Soda, die cut porcelain sign, EX . $280.00 (C)

Lush'us Rolled Oats, cardboard container with graphics of product being served, 3-lb., VG . . . .$180.00 (B)

Luter's Pure Lard, tin litho pail, "The Smithfield Packing Company, Inc., Smithfield, Virginia," 10" dia. x 11¾", VG . . . .$175.00 (C)

Luxury Tobacco, store counter cardboard easel back advertising sign with graphics of man enjoying a pipe, 9" x x 11", EX . . . .$325.00 (C)

Luxus Cigars, tin advertising sign with graphics of ostrich in center from F. Tuchfarber Co., Cincinnati, OH, 13½" x 9¾", 1890, EX . . . .$125.00 (B)

Lyons' Tea, porcelain advertising sign, 36" x 12", EX . . . .$225.00 (C)

Mac Cigars, single-sided tin advertising sign, 14" x 10", G, $80.00 (B).

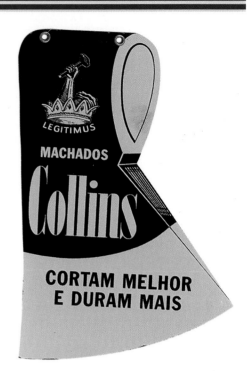

Machados Collins, double-sided porcelain die cut advertising sign, foreign, 11½" x 18", EX, $50.00 (B).

Madison Cigar, paper store advertising sign with graphics of risque Indian maiden, by Hayes Litho Co., Buffalo, NY, 15" x 30", 1906, EX, $1,200.00 (B).

Courtesy of Buffalo Bay Auction Co.

Mack...Leading Gasoline Truck of America, celluloid pocket mirror, 2½" x 3⅛", EX . . . .$550.00 (B)

Macmillian, Ring Free Motor Oil, die cut embossed tin advertising sign with graphics of hand holding a can of the product, 27¼" x 34", EX . . . .$135.00 (C)

Macmillan, Ring Free Motor Oil...Saves Fuel...Saves Wear, double-sided tin advertising sign with image of Scotsman pinching a penny, 11" x 11¾", EX . . . .$75.00 (C)

Madison Cigar, paper store advertising sign with graphics of risque Indian maiden, by Hayes Litho Co., Buffalo, NY, 15" x 30", 1906, F . . . .$300.00 (D)

Magic Chef, countertop display figure, composition man with wand and one hand with card slot, 11½" x 9" x 28", EX . . . .$100.00 (B)

Magic Leather Belt...No Binding-No Pressure, die cut tin litho on wood store bin, with graphics of man with belt, 1915, 15" x 14¼" x 4", EX . . . .$200.00 (B)

Maestro, die cut cardboard litho, 14" x 17", NOS, EX, $75.00 (B).

Magic Rust Eraser, cardboard counter display with rubber erasers, 13⅞" x 16¼", VG, $35.00 (B).

Mail Pouch Chew Tobacco, treat yourself to the best, painted embossed metal thermometer, 1950s, 3" x 9", EX, $350.00 (B).

Mail Pouch Chew Smoke, embossed tin advertising sign, 14" x 3⅜", G, $90.00 (B).

Magic...Use...Gasoline, one-sided embossed tin sign with graphics of gasoline globe, "Ellwood Myers Co., Springfield, O.," 18" x 24", F . . . .$100.00 (B)

Magic Yeast, cardboard advertising sign, stone litho with graphics of young man in turban, 10" x 15", 1906, EX . . . .$225.00 (C)

Magic Yeast, die cut cardboard advertising counter sign with graphics of black person with dog, 5" x 10", EX . .$95.00 (C)

Magic Yeast, paper stone litho advertising sign of ladies by the fireplace, 20" x 15", 1909, EX . . . .$725.00 (C)

Magnolia Brand Condensed Milk, Bordon's Condensed Milk Co., N.Y., wooden box with embossed block printed letters, 19" x 7" x 13", EX . . . .$35.00 (C)

Magnolia Brand Condensed Milk, wooden shipping box with painted debossed lettering, 19" x 7" x 13", EX . . . .$55.00 (C)

Magnolia Metal Company, celluloid over metal pocket advertising mirror, 3½", VG . . . .$60.00 (B)

Magnolia Petroleum Company...Private Road...Unauthorized Personnel...Keep Out, one-sided porcelain sign with graphics of Pegasus each side of top, 15" x 8", G . . . .$160.00 (B)

Magnus Root Beer, ceramic dispenser with top-mounted metal pump in the shape of a barrel, label on front and back, 14½" tall, 1915, NM . . . .$825.00 (B)

Maier Brewing Co., Los Angeles, CA, tin litho sign advertising California's finest 102 beer, 27" x 17", EX . . . . .$235.00 (C)

Mail Pouch, chew tobacco, treat yourself to the best, painted embossed metal thermometer, 1950s, 3" x 9", F . . . .$55.00 (C)

Mail Pouch, porcelain advertising thermometer, "treat yourself to the best," 8" x 38½", VG . . . .$210.00 (B)

Mail Pouch, porcelain sign, "chew and smoke," 42" x 12", EX . . . .$175.00 (D)

Mail Pouch, "The Real Man's Choice," single-sided cardboard advertising sign with graphics of men looking for Davy Jones's locker, 14½" x 21", VG . . . .$75.00 (C)

Malt-Nutrine, one-sided cardboard litho over tin, "A Hurry Call," 12½" x 7¾", VG, $75.00 (B).

Mansfield's Pepsin Gum, automatic clerk dispenser with advertising tag on top, 6½" W x ½" D x 11½" H, EX, $400.00 (B). *Courtesy of Muddy River Trading Co./Gary Metz*

Marie Tempest Cigars, stone litho paper advertising poster featuring graphics of young maiden, 16" x 22", 1900s, NM, $1,900.00 (B). *Courtesy of Buffalo Bay Auction Co.*

Mail Pouch Tobacco, porcelain advertising thermometer, 8" x 38¼", EX . . . .$235.00 (D)

Mail Pouch...treat yourself to the best...chew...tobacco, porcelain thermometer with messages at top and bottom, vertical scale, 8" x 38¾", blue, orange, and white, G . . . .$145.00 (D)

Maine Sardine Council, 4th Boy Scout Jamboree Special, tin litho container, 1957, 4-oz., EX . . . .$130.00 (B)

Majestic Batteries...Sales and Service, embossed painted tin advertising sign, 19½" x 26", NM . . . .$350.00 (C)

Majestic Bottling Company, seltzer bottle, Lynchburg, VA, EX . . . .$15.00 (B)

Mamma's Choice Rolled Oats, container from Samuel Mahon, Ottumwa & Ft. Madison, IA with graphics of young red-haired girl on front cover, 1-lb., EX . . . . .$325.00 (C)

Mamma's Choice rolled oats, paper label cardboard container, 4¼" x 7⅝", EX . . . .$65.00 (C)

Mammoth Salted Peanuts, Kelly Co., store tin with graphics of wooly mammoth on front, 10-lb., EX . . . .$165.00 (C)

Mammy Brand Salted Peanuts, tin litho with graphics of mammy on front, "Prepared & Packed By Murray-Roll Co. Pittsburgh, PA," 8" dia. x 9¾", VG . . . . . .$1,500.00 (D)

Mammy's Favorite, coffee from C.D. Kenny, Baltimore, Md. with image of black mammy on front and back, 4-lb., EX . . . .$275.00 (B)

Mammy's Favorite Coffee, tin litho container with metal handle, "C.D. Kenny Co., Baltimore, MD," 6¼" dia. x 10½", VG . . . .$220.00 (B)

Manbru Coffee, Schreiber Products Corporation, Buffalo, NY, tin litho with screw lid, 1-lb., EX . . . .$25.00 (B)

Marigold Dairy Products, double-bubble, light-up advertising sign, VG, $600.00 (B).

Hamlin's Wizard Oil, embossed tin sign with graphics of large bottle of product "Great for Pain," 12" x 6½", EX, $230.00 (B). *Courtesy of Autopia Advertising Auctions*

Marquette Club Ginger Ale, die cut easel back sign, man has attached glass eyes, 1940s, 8" x 11", EX, $140.00 (B). *Courtesy of Muddy River Trading Co./Gary Metz*

MIXES BEST FOR YOUR GUESTS

Mandeville and King Co., Rochester NY, advertising sign with graphics of large bouquet of flowers, 15¾" x 27½", VG . . . .$100.00 (D)

Mandeville and King Co,. Superior Flower Seeds, paper litho with signature Raphael Beck, Rochester, N.Y., graphics of young woman and windmill, 23" x 35½", VG .$275.00 (B)

M & S Soda, beveled edge tin over cardboard with image of bottle at right of message, 13" x 9", NM . . . .$33.00 (B)

M & S, "The Best" gas globe, low profile metal body with two glass lenses, 15" dia.., G . . . .$200.00 (B)

Manhattan Gasoline, double-sided porcelain advertising sign, 30" dia., EX . . . .$1,775.00 (C)

Manru and Nilo Beer, self-framed tin litho advertising sign, A. Schrriber Brewing Co., Buffalo, N.Y., with image of young woman with a glass of the product, "King and Queen of Bottled Beer," 20½" x 24", G . . . . .$130.00 (B)

Mansco Perfume Talc, tin litho container with strong graphics of baby in cameo in center, 2⅛" x 1¼" x 5⅞", EX . . . .$180.00 (B)

Mansfield's Pepsin Gum, automatic clerk dispenser with advertising tag on top, 6½"W x ½"D x 11½"H, EX . . . . . .$400.00 (B)

Marsh Wheeling Stogies, Pam light-up advertising clock, 15¼" x 15¼", VG, $275.00 (B).

Marvels, The Cigarette of Quality, tin scale-type advertising thermometer, 4" x 12", EX, $120.00 (B).

Marx Old Style Bread, Famous for Flavor, features artwork of bread wagon being pulled by oxen, 36" x 24", EX, $450.00 (B). *Courtesy of Riverview Antique Mall*

Mansfield Tires...Becker Texaco Service, plastic round light-up advertising clock with metal ring around glass clock face, EX . . . .$225.00 (D)

"Mantan Morehead, Come On Cowboy," paper litho poster with graphics of cowboy character on horseback, all-star cast, with Mauryne Brent, Johnny Lee, and F.E. Miller, 28" x 40½", VG . . . .$50.00 (B)

Manuel Silvia, die cut calendar from Newport, RI, Boot, Shoe and Rubbers retailer with great artwork of woman and two young girls, 1905, 12½" x 18", NM . .$325.00 (B)

Mapco Genuine Ignition Parts, embossed tin advertising sign, 36" x 10", 1949, NM . . . .$250.00 (D)

Mapco Speedway Coils, embossed tin advertising sign with graphics of vintage auto and graphics of product, 9⅛" x 13⅛", NM . . . .$475.00 (C)

Maquoketa Cuban Hand Made Cigars, advertising pinback, celluloid over metal with graphics of vintage automobile, 1¾" dia., VG . . . .$75.00 (B)

Marathon...Disarm Winter, graphics of snow figure with rifle, painted pressed board sign, 48" x 48", G . .$25.00 (B)

Marathon Motor Oil...For Good Running, double-sided tin flange sign with image of the Marathon runner, hard-to-find item, 13½" x 23½", EX . . . .$975.00 (C)

Marathon Motor Oil, hand-soldered can, Transcontinental Oil Co., with tin litho of logo marathon flame runner, 8½" x 6" x 5½", EX . . . .$125.00 (C)

Marathon Oil Co., advertising scale thermometer with runner at top, 5" x 16", EX . . . .$215.00 (C)

Marathon Oil Co., pocket knife, EX . . . .$20.00 (C)

Ma's Cola, single-sided embossed tin advertising sign featuring graphics of product bottle, 22½" x 31", VG, $60.00 (B).

Mason's Old Fashioned Root Beer...Everybody's Favorite, cardboard bottle rack sign with beach scene, 10" x 10", NM, $110.00 (C).

Mason's Root Beer, glass and metal advertising thermometer, 12" dia., EX, $185.00 (B).

Marburg Bros., Louisiana Perique tobacco tin, "grown in St. James Parish, La.," 3½" x 2" x 1¾", EX . . . .$75.00 (B)

Marburg Brothers, tobacco canister with small lid, good, strong graphics of two women and "seal of North Carolina, plug cut," 5" x 6", EX . . . .$225.00 (C)

Marguerite Cigar Sign, cardboard with paper litho in center cameo, Havan Cigar, 12" x 15", VG . . . .$57.00 (B)

Marie Tempest Cigars...B. Newmark & Co., New York, litho on paper of pretty woman with head scarf, 1900s, 16" x 22", NM . . . .$968.00 (B)

Marie Tempest Cigars, stone litho paper advertising poster featuring graphics of young maiden, 16" x 22", 1900s, NM . . . .$1,900.00 (B)

Marigold Dairy Products, double-bubble light-up clock with metal body with glass cover and face, 15½" dia., EX . . . .$450.00 (B)

Marine Band, large hanging store harmonica, made of high quality cardboard, 24" x 5" x 7", EX . . . .$300.00 (C)

Market Coffee, from San Francisco, CA, tin litho with key-wound lid, 1-lb., EX . . . .$55.00 (C)

Marks Bros. Dramatic Co., "The Canadian Kings of Repertoire" paper litho advertising poster with artwork of the cast, 40" x 27", 1905, EX . . . .$180.00 (B)

Marlin Blades, in original box, G . . . .$9.00 (D)

Marlin Razor Blade Display, with all blade packages present, 9" x 13½", EX . . . .$75.00 (D)

Marlin Rifle and Shotgun, cloth vertical banner, 20" x 29", VG . . . .$55.00 (B)

Marquette Club Ginger Ale, cardboard advertising sign, 14" x 3" x 15", EX . . . .$25.00 (B)

Marquette Club Ginger Ale, die cut easel back sign, man has attached glass eyes, 1940s, 8" x 11", EX . .$140.00 (B)

Martin Cigar, advertising shoe horn, give-away item, 4¼", EX . . . .$55.00 (C)

Martin Diesel, No. 1 H.I. globe, plastic body with glass lens, 13½" dia., VG . . . .$275.00 (B)

Marvel Brand Coffee and Food Products, display case decal with great graphics of product in front of window scene, 1925, 8½" x 11", EX . . . .$80.00 (B)

Marvells...the cigarette of quality, painted metal thermometer with artwork of product package at top of vertical scale, message at bottom, blue background, F . . . .$45.00 (C)

Marvel Oats, early cardboard box with great strong graphics of mountains and waterfall scene, from the Webster Grocery Co., Danville, IL, 5⅜" x 9½", EX . . . .$120.00 (B)

Ma's Root Beer, tin single-sided die cut bottle sign, 6" x 9¾", G, $125.00 (B).

Mass & Steffer Inc. Furs, paper litho poster, 17" x 23½", G, $90.00 (B).

Massasoit Coffee, presentation sign with the trademark Indian Chief, "Fine Aroma, Delicious Flavors," 27" x 34", EX, $825.00 (B). *Courtesy of Collectors Auction Services*

Marvels Mild Cigarettes, carton, G ....$40.00 (D)

Marx Old Style Bread, Famous for Flavor, features artwork of bread wagon being pulled by oxen, 36" x 24", EX ....$450.00 (B)

Mascot Tobacco, metal tip tray with scene of animals at water, 5" L, EX ....$50.00 (B)

Mason and Hamlin Piano, sign, embossed tin sign with graphics of baby grand piano in center, 32" x 24", VG ....$175.00 (B)

Mason & Stout, city bill posters reverse painted glass in wood frame, 23½" x 19½", EX ....$135.00 (C)

Mason & Stout, reverse painted glass advertising sign with wood frame, "Bill posters...orders left at wood's exchange promptly executed," 23½" x 19.33", EX .....$225.00 (C)

Mason's Blacking Box, wood box with paper litho advertising on inside lid and front of box, graphics of boot shiner , 11¾" x 9" x 3", G ....$145.00 (B)

Mason's Old Fashioned Root Beer...Everybody's Favorite, cardboard bottle rack sign with beach scene, 10" x 10", EX ....$95.00 (C)

Mason's Root Beer, chalkboard menu, G ....$50.00 (D)

Mason's Root Beer, embossed tin, tilted bottle advertising thermometer, 10¼" x 25", 1960s, EX ....$90.00 (B)

Massasoit Coffee, presentation sign with the trademark Indian chief, "Fine Aroma, Delicious Flavors," 27" x 34", F ....$300.00 (C)

Massey Ferguson...World Famous Farm Equipment, self-framing metal advertising sign, 40" x 20", G ..$140.00 (B)

Master Feeds, We sell ..., oval porcelain store sign, 26½" x 16", EX ....$75.00 (B)

Master is Good Bread, embossed tin double-sided door push bar, 3" x 29½", EX ....$80.00 (B)

Master Locks, display, Strength Security Padlock, metal, 5½" dia.., G ....$25.00 (D)

Master Mason Plug Smoking Tobacco, tin, It's good tobacco, Quebec, 3-lb., G ....$65.00 (D)

Master Trucks Inc., Chicago, USA, cast iron ink well with embossed lettering, 7" x 5½" x 2¾", EX .....$210.00 (B)

Mastercraft, pipe display item, oversized papier-mache advertising pipe, 10" x 37" x 12", G, **$895.00 (C)**.

Master Feeds, We sell ..., oval porcelain store sign, 26½" x 16", EX, **$135.00 (D)**.

Masterpiece Fertilizers, single-sided embossed tin advertising sign, 20" x 13½", G, **$155.00 (B)**.

Maxwell House High Grade Coffee, cardboard advertising sign with graphics of container and cup with "the last drop," NOS, 11" x 8¾", 1921, NM, **$275.00 (C)**. *Courtesy of Autopia Advertising Auctions*

Masury Paints-Varnishes...Masury is Good Paint, artwork of English-style soldier in spotlight at lower left of message, painted metal, 36" x 24", G . . . .**$35.00 (D)**

Masury Paints-Varnishes, painted metal flange sign, 36" x 24", EX . . . .**$55.00 (C)**

Mavis...Real chocolate flavor, double-sided tin litho flange advertising sign with graphics of bottle of product, by the American artworks, 12½" x 9½", EX . . . .**$180.00 (B)**

Maxine Shoes Sign, die cut tin litho of woman in high top shoes, 13¼" x 19½", EX . . . .**$275.00 (B)**

Maxwell House Coffee, cardboard string-hung ad sign with 1920s coffee container artwork, 1920s, EX . . .**$325.00 (B)**

Maxwell House Coffee, factory cafeteria cup and saucer with graphics of cup in front of factory, EX . .**$110.00 (B)**

Maxwell House Coffee...good to the Last Drop, celluloid advertising sign with graphics of upturned coffee cup, 12" x 6", EX . . . .**$125.00 (B)**

Maxwell House Coffee, good to the Last Drop, heavy paper sample cup with artwork of tilted coffee cup on front, 2½" x 2½", EX . . . .**$3.00 (D)**

Maxwell House Coffee...since 1892, oval metal serving tray, 15" x 12½", EX . . . .**$20.00 (D)**

Maxwell House High Grade Coffee, cardboard advertising sign with graphics of container and cup with "the last drop," 11" x 8¾", 1921, F . . . .**$75.00 (C)**

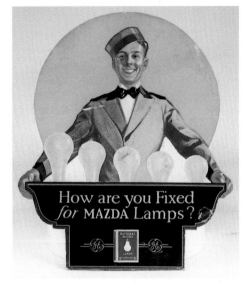

Maytag, Newton, Iowa, single-sided porcelain advertising sign, 9" x 12", EX, **$275.00 (B).** *Courtesy of Collectors Auction Services*

Mazda Lamps, cardboard store display, "How are you fixed for Mazda lamps?," featuring artwork of display being held by bellman, F, **$135.00 (C).**

Mayo's Plug, porcelain sign with rooster standing on plugs of tobacco, "Smoking cock o' the walk," 1910s, 6½" x 13", NM, **$2,300.00 (B).** *Courtesy of Muddy River Trading Co./Gary Metz*

Mazda Lamps, store display, "How are you fixed for lamps?," with artwork of box of National Mazda Lamps over message, VG, **$95.00 (C).**

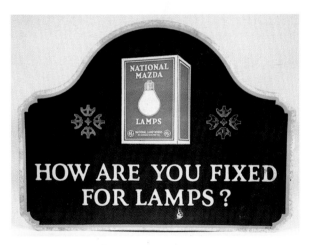

May-Day Coffee...You'll Like The Flavor, tin litho container, key-wound, unopened, 1-lb., NM . . . .$34.00 (B)

Mayo's Cut Plug "Brownie," tin litho with graphics of mammy smoking a pipe with product in dress pocket, 6" dia. x 7¼" h, VG . . . .$400.00 (B)

Mayo's Cut Plug, smoking and chewing tobacco, tin pail with wire, G . . . .$48.00 (D)

Mayo's Mammy, roly-poly tin litho container of black mammy, G . . . .$250.00 (B)

Mayo's Plug, porcelain sign with rooster standing on plugs of tobacco, "Smoking cock o' the walk," 1910s, 6½" x 13", G . . . .$900.00 (C)

Mayo's Plug Smoking Tobacco, with graphics of rooster crowing, canvas poster, 60" x 24", EX . . . . . .$155.00 (B)

Mayo's Plug Tobacco, cardboard advertising with graphics of rooster crowing about the product, advertising both "light and dark," 18½" x 31", VG . . . .$200.00 (B)

Mazawattee Tea Tin, litho depicting 3 boys with empty cups, 8½" x 5½" x 6", VG . . . .$500.00 (B)

Mazda Lamps, cardboard store display, "How are you fixed for Mazda lamps?," featuring artwork of display being held by bellman, EX . . . .$255.00 (C)

McCulloch Chain Saws, embossed tin ad sign with graphics of goose in flight, 47" dia., G, **$125.00 (D).**

McCormick-Deering Service, double-sided porcelain sign on original hanger arm, 2" x 24", G, **$80.00 (B).**

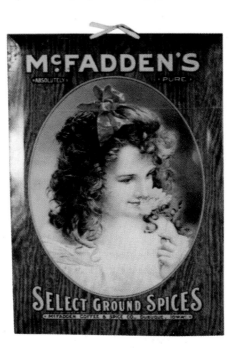

McFadden's Spice & Coffee Co., Dubuque, Iowa, vintage tin litho over cardboard advertising sign with graphics of child with a flower, "Select Ground Spices," 13⅜" x 19", EX, **$1,450.00 (B).** *Courtesy of Wm. Morford Investment Grade Collectibles*

Meadow Gold Ice Cream, Please Pay When Served, masonite display board, manufactured by Kay Displays, 11" x 16", NM, **$75.00 (D).**

Mazda Lamps, store display, "How are you fixed for lamps?", with artwork of box of National Mazda Lamps over message, G . . . .$65.00 (D)

McAvoys Malt Marrow Beer, tin litho serving tray with graphics of boy with a bottle of product and a dog, 12" dia., G . . . .$220.00 (B)

McCormick Bee Brand...teas, spices, extracts, drugs..., celluloid pocket advertising mirror, 1¾" x 2⅞", EX . . .$800.00 (B)

McCormick, calendar with full pad of tear sheets at bottom of calendar with graphics of young women with children in front of Dutch windmill, 1933, EX . . .$175.00 (C)

McCormick Deering, calendar with full calendar pad and graphics of young boy playing a horn, 13" x 20", 1942, EX . . . .$40.00 (B)

McCormick-Deering, Farm Machines, painted tin sign, from Baldwinsville Farm Supply, Baldwinsville, N.Y., 27½" x 10", EX . . . .$75.00 (B)

McCormick-Deering, Farm Machines, painted tin sign, 27½" x 10", EX . . . .$95.00 (C)

McCormick-Deering, "We Use Only Genuine Parts," self-framing tin embossed advertising sign, 16" x 12", VG . . . .$210.00 (B)

Meadow Gold Milk, wood and masonite advertising sign, 13" x 12", G, **$85.00 (C).**

Mennen, tin litho flange advertising sign, with great graphics of young child holding Mennen's product, 22¾" W x 14¼" H, EX, **$1,250.00 (B).** *Courtesy of Richard Opfer Auctioneering, Inc.*

Mentholatum, A.A. Hyde, die cut cardboard advertising display with nurse showing the many uses for the product, 31" x 43", NM, **$190.00 (B).** *Courtesy of Muddy River Trading Co./Gary Metz*

McCormick Harvester, advertising paper litho depicting a field scene showing the new product, 33¼" x 27½", 1831, VG . . . .**$750.00 (B)**

McCormick Harvesting machines, paper, advertising sign depicting the Battle of Atlanta, July 28, 1864, 28" x 27", VG . . . .**$490.00 (B)**

McCulloch Chain Saws, dial-type thermometer, reverse on bubble glass, 1950s, 14" dia., NM . . . .**$100.00 (B)**

McFadden's Spice & Coffee Co., Dubuque, Iowa, vintage tin litho over cardboard advertising sign with graphics of child with a flower, "Select Ground Spices," 13⅜" x 19", EX . . . .**$1,450.00 (B)**

McFadden's Spices, sign, beveled edge tin on cardboard advertising sign with graphics of young girl with flower, 13¼" x 19", 1904, G . . . .**$500.00 (C)**

McLaughlin Bros., game board "Parlor Football Game" with graphics of vintage football game in progress, 19¾" x 10½" x 1", 1900s, EX . . . .**$1,150.00 (B)**

McLaughlin's Coffee, store bin with slant top and graphics of cup and saucer, 16¾" x 13" x 19¼", EX . . .**$275.00 (C)**

McLaughlin's Columbian Coffee, tin litho container with graphics of sailing ship on side, pry-type lid, 1-lb., EX . . . .**$74.00 (B)**

Mentholatum, cardboard tri-fold drugstore window display, great graphics and strong colors, 48" x 35", EX, $625.00 (B). *Courtesy of Wm. Morford Investment Grade Collectibles*

Merrick...Six Cord Soft Finish Spool Cotton, wood and glass cabinet, with product message on front glass, VG, $1,875.00 (C).

McLaughlin's Manor House Coffee, tin with key-wound lid, 1-lb., F . . . .$8.00 (D)

McNish, Johnson and Slavins Refined Minstrels, paper litho advertising poster with graphics of two men on front, 1920s, 30½" x 42", EX . . . .$425.00 (B)

Meadow Gold Ice Cream, Please Pay When Served, masonite display board, manufactured by Kay Displays, 11" x 16", EX . . . .$55.00 (B)

Meadow Gold Products, self-framing porcelain advertising sign, 30" x 26", VG . . . .$175.00 (C)

Meadow Gold...Vanilla Ice Cream, round half-gallon ice cream tin, EX . . . .$15.00 (D)

Mecca Flake Cut Plug Tobacco, tin litho container by the Daniel Scotten Co., 4½" x 3¼" x 1½", EX . . . . .$50.00 (C)

Meiers Ice Cream, double-sided porcelain advertising sign, "We Serve... Meiers Ice Cream...Waukesha," 35¾" x 24", VG . . . .$325.00 (B)

Melachrino Cigarette, cardboard advertising sign, "The one cigarette sold the world over," 28" x 4", EX . . . .$55.00 (D)

Melachrino...The Cigarette Elect of all Nations, tin on cardboard advertising sign with graphics of young woman with the product, by the New York Metal Ceiling Co., 11¼" dia., EX . . . .$110.00 (B)

Melachrino...The one cigarette sold the world over, cardboard sign with wooden frame, 28" x 4", EX . .$45.00 (D)

Mellor & Rittenhouse Licorice, tin graphics of White House on lid, 5" x 5" x 6¾", 1880s, VG . . . . . .$95.00 (C)

Melox Dog Food, porcelain advertising sign with graphics of dog on large ball, 18" x 26", EX . . . .$875.00 (D)

Melox Dog Food...The Foods that Nourish, porcelain sign with artwork of dog on Melox ball, 18" x 26", EX . .$525.00 (C)

Mennen's, advertising sign, paper, framed, promoting toilet powder, 9½" x 13¼", EX . . . .$85.00 (C)

Mennen's, Violet Tiolet Powder, tin litho talc can with graphics of vintage era man on front, 2½" x 4⅝" x 1⅜", VG . . . .$300.00 (B)

Michelin, die cut cardboard easel back stand-up advertisement, foreign, 14¾" x 17½", G, **$900.00 (B).**

Michelin man on motorcycle, one-sided tin sign, foreign, 14½" x 20", G, **$430.00 (B).**

Michigan Propellers, metal and glass advertising thermometer, 12" dia., VG, **$350.00 (B).**

Michigan Bell Telephone, porcelain flange sign, 11¾" x 11", NM, **$295.00 (C).**

Mennen, tin litho flange advertising sign, with great graphics of young child holding Mennen's product, 22¾" W x 14¼" H, F . . . .$350.00 (C)

Mentholatum, A.A. Hyde, die cut cardboard advertising display with nurse showing the many uses for the product, 31" x 43", NM . . . .$190.00 (B)

Mentholatum, cardboard tri-fold drugstore window display, great graphics and strong colors, 48" x 35", EX . .$625.00 (B)

Mercantile, die cut advertising calendar from Eilers & Bolton, Monticello, IA, with full pad and graphics of young girls in boat, 10¼" x 18"x, 1900, EX . . . .$280.00 (B)

Mercurochrome, cardboard die cut counter advertising sign with graphics of man doctoring arm with product, 15" x 22", VG . . . .$95.00 (C)

Meriden Fire Arms Co., Conn., empty two-piece cardboard box advertising "Pointer Loaded Shells," 4" x 4" x 2½", NM . . . .$200.00 (C)

Merion, Hair Net, metal store display box of bobbed hair woman with mirror on lid, G . . . .$95.00 (D)

Merita Bread, self-framing embossed advertising sign with graphics of the Lone Ranger, 24" x 36", G . . .$375.00 (B)

Merriam Bulldog Segars, cast metal advertising figure, 3" x 2" x 1½", EX . . . .$85.00 (B)

Merrick...Six Cord Soft Finish Spool Cotton, wood and glass cabinet, with product message on front glass, F . . . .$900.00 (D)

Midwest Ice Cream, porcelain store advertising sign, featuring a bonnet-clad lady with a serving tray, 20" x 30", VG, $265.00 (C).

Midwest Milk, light-up clock, metal body with reverse painted glass front cover, 15½" x 15½", white and red, EX, $175.00 (C).
Courtesy of B.J. Summers

Mil-Kay...Drink...The Vitamin Drink...Large Bottle 5¢, metal advertising sign with artwork of black man with serving tray with product, scarce, 1941, 55" x 31½", G, $825.00 (D). *Courtesy of Rare Bird Antiques Mall/Jon & Joan Wright*

Merrill...Transport Company, dial-type thermometer with the outside resembling a tire, 15" dia., EX . . .$250.00 (D)

Messeroll Cough Drops, vintage glass advertising store jar with embossed lettering, 5⅛" x 5⅛" x 8¼", EX $170.00 (B)

Metz Beer, "The Old Reliable," tin litho face with square tin frame graphics of beer bottle on left side of face, 15" sq., VG . . . .$175.00 (B)

Meyer Brewing Co., Compliments of...Bloomington, Ill., round tip tray with image of young woman, same image as found on Old Reliable Coffee tip tray, 4¼" dia., EX . . . .$201.00 (B)

Meyers Pumps, paper sign with graphics of complete line of pumps and products, metal bottom and top strips with calendar tear sheets in center of paper, limited issue due to WWII, 17" x 51", 1944, EX . . . .$275.00 (B)

MH & M, die cut tin embossed sign, cut-out of hand with finger pointing to the right direction, 28" x 6½", VG . . . .$275.00 (C)

MH & M shoes, embossed tin sign die cut in the shape of an arm and hand, 28" x 6½", black on yellow, EX . . . .$225.00 (C)

M. Hohner Harmonica, wooden fold-out counter display with paper label on lid, VG . . . .$85.00 (C)

Miami Beach...World's Playground, cast aluminum license plate attachment with die cut images of palm trees and fish, 12" x 4¾", EX . . . .$95.00 (C)

Mica Wheel Grease, cardboard countertop display sign, 11" x 14¾", EX . . . .$135.00 (C)

Mil-Kay Soda, die cut cardboard advertising sign featuring graphics of black waiter with a tray holding a bottle and a glass of the product, 28" x 17", EX, **$135.00 (B).**

Milking Shorthorns, embossed tin license plate attachment, "The Breed that Fills Every Need," VG, 10¼" x 5¼", **$50.00 (B).**

Miller High Life, light-up advertising sign, "Buy it now" with bottle and can on either side of message, VG, **$75.00 (C).**

Courtesy of B.J. Summers

Miller Genuine Draft, light-up, three-dimensional advertising of bottle in ice block, NM, **$70.00 (D).** *Courtesy of Pleasant Hill Antique Mall & Tea Room/Bob Johnson*

Michael-Leonard Seed Co., salesman sample, tin thermometer, featuring three different Indian images, with original box, 9" dia., 1930s, NM . . . .**$325.00 (C)**

Michelin Man, molded ashtray, with Michelin Man standing in ashtray, 1940s, 6" x 4¾", EX . . . .**$85.00 (C)**

Michelin Man, with tire, one-sided porcelain advertising sign, NOS, 27" x 31½", EX . . . .**$300.00 (B)**

Michelin, one-sided porcelain advertising sign with graphics of motorcycle tire, 38" x 57½", G . . . .**$950.00 (B)**

Michelob, Classic Dark, tapper handle, EX . . .**$15.00 (D)**

Michelob, Light, tapper handle, with skier on top, EX . . . .**$20.00 (D)**

Michigan Ammonia Works, round tin container with graphics advertising Excelsior Carbonate of Ammonia, with small snap lid, 5-lb., 7⅞" x 4½" dia., EX . .**$25.00 (C)**

Michigan Bell Telephone, porcelain flange sign, 11¾" x 11", EX . . . .**$250.00 (B)**

Michigan Stove Co., "Michigan Stove Co. Stoves are the best," cast iron match holder, 4" x 7", EX . . .**$215.00 (B)**

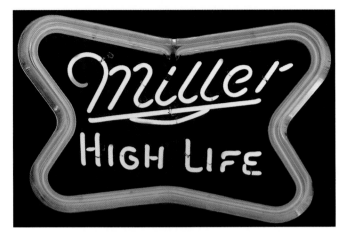

Miller High Life, neon, new, NM, $135.00 (C).

Miller's Finer, Flavor-Rich Milk, Delicious Ice Cream, reverse painted glass sign front, G, $55.00 (D). *Courtesy of Chief Paduke Antiques Mall*

Milwaukee Crane, single-sided porcelain sign, 18" x 18", VG, $200.00 (B).

Milwaukee Harvesting Machines, Always Reliable, tin litho match holder, great graphics of worker with bandana and wide brimmed hat, 5½" H, EX, $350.00 (B). *Courtesy of Richard Opfer Auctioneering, Inc.*

Mickey Mouse Cookies, from Nabisco, cardboard box with string carrier, graphics of Mickey Mouse on side, 1940s, 6" x 3" x 2", EX . . . .$165.00 (B)

Midwest Ice Cream, porcelain store advertising sign, featuring a bonnet-clad lady with a serving tray, 20" x 30", G . . . .$245.00 (D)

Midwest Milk, light-up clock, metal body with reverse painted glass front cover, 15½" x 15½", white and red, EX . . . .$175.00 (C)

Mi Favorita Cigars... "A Solace For Busy Minds"...Clear Havana, metal tip tray, 1⅛" L, EX . . . .$130.00 (B)

Milcor Steel Company, paper advertising cardboard sign with graphics of products, from Canton, Ohio, 22" x 28", 1931, NM . . . .$285.00 (C)

Mil-Kay...Drink...The Vitamin Drink...Large Bottle 5¢, metal advertising sign with artwork of black man with serving tray with product, scarce, 1941, 55" x 31½", EX . . . .$1,295.00 (C)

Mil-Kay Soda, die cut cardboard advertising sign featuring graphics of black waiter with a tray holding a bottle and a glass of the product, 28" x 17", EX . . . .$135.00 (B)

Mil K Botl, die cut cardboard countertop display "Double Size 5¢", 8½" x 10", EX . . . .$55.00 (B)

Millar's Home Blend Coffee, key-wound tin litho container, 1-lb., NM . . . .$37.00 (B)

Millar's Magnet Cocoa, tin litho container with graphics of harvesting of cocoa on each side, 3¼" x 3¼" x 6", EX . . . .$65.00 (C)

Mit-Che Ice Cold, embossed tin sign, 23½" x 15½", VG, **$52.00 (B).** *Courtesy of Collectors Auction Services*

Mobil Car-Care, at all temperatures, metal with curved glass face, advertising thermometer, 11¾" dia., VG, **$295.00 (B).**

Mission Orange, painted metal advertising bottle sign, 8¾" x 25", VG, **$90.00 (C).** *Courtesy of Patrick's Collectibles*

Mobil-flame Pegasus, bottled gas service, double-sided porcelain sign on metal arm, 32½" x 40½", G, **$1,600.00 (B).** *Courtesy of Collectors Auction Services*

Millar's Magnet Coffee, F.B. Millar & Co, Chicago, Denver, 1-lb., G . . . .$25.00 (D)

Millar's Mountain Brand Coffee, tin container with paper label graphics of Turkish tent scene, 2-lb., EX . .$210.00 (B)

Millar's, nut brown coffee tin with paper label, 3-lb., EX . . . .$125.00 (C)

Miller Genuine Draft, light-up, three-dimensional advertising of bottle in ice block, EX . . . .$55.00 (D)

Miller High Life, light-up advertising sign, "Buy it now" with bottle and can on either side of message, G . . . . .$55.00 (C)

Miller High Life, neon, new, EX . . . .$125.00 (C)

Miller High Life...The champagne of bottled beer, with lady on crescent moon, round metal serving tray, 12" dia., EX . . . .$50.00 (D)

Miller's Beer, pinback pin with graphics of Miller Girl on crescent moon, Whitehead & Hoag, ¾" dia., VG . . . .$35.00 (C)

Miller's Crown Dressing, die cut cardboard trade card in shape of woman's shoe, 7½" x 5", NM . . . .$50.00 (B)

Millers Falls...The safest name in tools, metal framed plastic front light-up sign, 25" x 8", G . . . .$55.00 (C)

Miller's, Finer, Flavor-Rich Milk, Delicious Ice Cream, reverse painted glass sign front, F . . . .$45.00 (D)

Mobil Oil, one-sided cardboard advertisement, 43" x 22", VG, **$15.00 (B)**.

Mobil Gas, double-sided porcelain shield sign with iron hanger at top, 48" x 48", EX, **$1,000.00 (B).** *Collectors Auction Services*

Mobil Oil...Pegasus, die cut porcelain horse, 36" tall, red, NM, **$1,500.00 (C).**

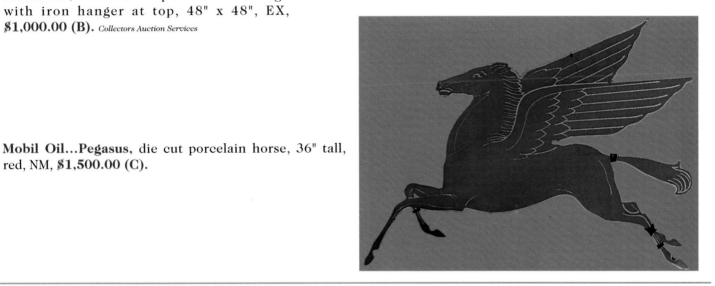

Mills Bros., 27th annual tour, three-ring circus advertising poster with graphics of trapeze act and horsemanship, 14" x 41", EX . . . .**$20.00 (B)**

Milwaukee Harvesting Machines, Always Reliable, tin litho match holder, great graphics of worker with bandana and wide-brimmed hat, 5½" H, EX . . . .**$350.00 (B)**

Milwaukee Journal, 1923 Tour Club, die cut etched brass radiator grill attachment in the shape of arrowhead with graphics of frog-faced driver with "Gatsby" type hat and glasses, 4" x 5½", NM . . . .**$500.00 (C)**

Minneapolis Underwear, cardboard die cut advertising piece with likeness of "Baby Mary," "Knit Underwear for All the Kiddies," 7" x 10", EX . . . .**$275.00 (D)**

Minneapolis Universal, celluloid pocket advertising mirror with graphics of early farm tractor on reverse side, 2⅛" dia., EX . . . .**$135.00 (C)**

Minstrels, McNish, Johnson and Slavins, paper litho advertising poster, 30½" x 42", EX . . . .**$425.00 (B)**

Miss Detroit Broad Leaf Cigars, cardboard store display box with graphics of Miss Detroit on front, 8¼" x 9½" x 9¼", EX . . . .**$700.00 (B)**

Mission Orange, countertop dispenser, cooler no. 9672 California Crushed Fruit Corporation, Los Angeles, California, 13½" x 25½", VG . . . .**$225.00 (B)**

Mission Orange, painted metal advertising bottle sign, 8¾" x 25", G . . . .**$75.00 (D)**

Mobil Tire, advertising clock, foreign, 4"
dia., $210.00 (B).

Modox Drink, Indian Herbs, tin litho die cut tip
tray with strong colors, 5⅝" x 5", EX, $500.00 (B).
Courtesy of Richard Opfer Auctioneering, Inc.

Mogul Egyptian Cigarettes, self-framing tin litho
featuring a Mogul with a cigarette and a temple, 20"
x 24", EX, $2,200.00 (B). *Courtesy of Buffalo Bay Auction Co.*

Mission Orange, tin litho self-framing advertising sign
with bottle in center, 10" x 25½", EX . . . .$225.00 (C)

Mississippi Pacific Lines, calendar with metal back and
tear sheets at bottom under graphics of speeding locomotive at top, 13" x 19", EX . . . .$85.00 (B)

Miss Minneapolis, Highest Quality Flour, die cut menu
board shows girl holding blackboard, 1918, 19" x 28",
EX . . . .$45.00 (B)

Missouri Pacific Lines, paper railroad calendar with tear
sheets at bottom, featuring artwork of steam engine moving on tracks, no year, only daily sheets, G . .$135.00 (C)

Missouri Smoking Pipes, blister pack from country store
with full sheet of pipes, NOS, EX . . . .$50.00 (D)

Miss Princine Baking Powder, cup with paper label showing graphics of Miss Princine in the center of the can, 3½"
x 3⅞", VG . . . .$45.00 (D)

Mister Donut, Exclusive Blend Coffee tin litho container with
graphics of Mr. Donut, key-wound lid, 1-lb., EX . .$250.00 (B)

M.K. Goetz Brewing Co., tin litho advertising sign,
"Jerry's Smile"with graphics of black man smiling
and enjoying a glass of beer, self-framing, 22½" x
28", EX . . . .$4,400.00 (B)

Mojud Supp-hose, three-dimensional store advertising with woman in yellow outfit sitting in ladder-back chair, plastic, EX, $175.00 (D). *Courtesy of Creatures of Habit*

Montgomery Ward, Red Head, two-piece paper litho over cardboard shell box with image of geese, 4⅛" x 4⅛" x 2½", F, $30.00 (B).

MoPar...Parts...Accessories, neon lighted advertising clock, 18¼" x 18¼", EX, $975.00 (C). *Courtesy of Autopia Advertising Auctions*

Morton's Salt, It Pours, single-sided embossed tin sign, very good, 27½" x 9¾", VG, $45.00 (C).

Mobil Attendant Display, life-size painted wood in likeness of station attendant with easel back, 21" x 72", VG . . . .$650.00 (B)

Mobil, attendant's summer hat, all original, EX . .$175.00 (C)

Mobil, cloth sleeve patch, 3⅛" x 1¼", G . . . . .$10.00 (C)

Mobil, dial advertising thermometer, 12" dia., VG .$400.00 (B)

Mobil, playing cards with original leather carrying case, NM . . . .$20.00 (C)

Mobil-flame Pegasus, bottled gas service, double-sided porcelain sign on metal arm, 32½" x 40½", G . . . . .$1,600.00 (B)

Mobil Freezone, painted tin advertising scale-type thermometer with image of Pegasus at top of scale, 8" x 36", NM . . . .$825.00 (B)

Mobilfuel Diesel, globe, low profile metal body with glass lens with Pegasus trademark, 16½" dia., VG .$800.00 (B)

Mobilgas, enameled cloisonné uniform badge with Pegasus over name, screw-on attachment, ⅝" x 1⅝", EX . .$375.00 (B)

Mobilgas Ethyl, square gas globe, metal body with 4 lenses, 22½" x 22½" x 16", VG . . . .$750.00 (B)

Mobilgas...Friendly Service, porcelain thermometer with Pegasus at top center, vertical scale, 4¼" x 34½", EX . . .$250.00 (C)

Motor Club Coffee, can with great paper label with strong graphics of couple in vintage touring car, for Beiderman Bros., Chicago, pry-lid, 1-lb., EX, **$1,350.00 (B).** *Courtesy of Wm. Morford*

Investment Grade Collectibles

Movie Guide, display, painted wood, die cut, slug, plate, "Philadelphia Enameling Works, 25¢ N. 13th St., Phila, PA," 13½" x 58½" x 23", G, **$1,350.00 (C).**

Motoroma, Boston, Mass., felt pennant, 28¼" x 12", G, **$50.00 (B).**

Mobilgas Marine Gasoline, globe with Pegasus, on wide body glass body, 13½" dia., NM . . . .$1,200.00 (C)

Mobilgas, Pegasus light-up advertising clock with the winged horse in the trademark Mobil shield, manufactured by the Pam Clock Co., 15" dia., EX . . . .$650.00 (B)

Mobilgas, porcelain advertising truck topper sign with image of Pegasus, 24" x 10", EX . . . .$875.00 (B)

Mobilgas, porcelain die cut restroom pledge sign in shape of shield, 7⅝" x 8", NM . . . .$475.00 (C)

Mobilgas, Special Gasoline, porcelain pump sign with graphics of Pegasus, sign is outlined in black, hard-to-find, 11½" x 12", EX . . . .$275.00 (C)

Mobilgas...Special, porcelain die cut gas pump sign with artwork of Pegasus at top of message, 1947, 12" x 12", EX . . . .$115.00 (C)

Mobilgas, Super Speed gas globe with graphics of greyhound racing dog on lens, low profile metal body with two glass lenses, 15" dia., G . . . .$500.00 (B)

Mobilgas, tin toy Ford tanker truck, 1940s, 2½" x 9", red & white, G . . . .$225.00 (C)

Mobiloil Authorized Service, oil bottle rack, 21" x 30" x 24½", VG . . . .$1,100.00 (B)

Mobiloil, Curb Sign, two-sided die cut porcelain advertising sign with graphics of Pegasus in center on heavy cast base, "Property of Socony Vacuum Oil Company, Inc." on base, 30½" x 64", VG . . . .$700.00 (B)

Mobil Oil...follow the magnolia trail, large shop calendar with fishing scene on front in center of message, 1933, EX . . . .$95.00 (C)

Moxie, die cut tin litho match holder, resembling Moxie drink bottle, 7" H, EX, **$500.00 (B)**. *Courtesy of Richard Opfer Auctioneering, Inc.*

Moxie, fan with young cowboy on rocking horse and Frank Archer on reverse side, EX, **$200.00 (B)**.

Moxie...I just love...don't you, round metal tip tray with litho of woman with glass of product and leaf border, 6" dia., EX, **$235.00 (B)**.

Mobil Oil...Gargoyle, double-sided porcelain curb sign with cast iron base, 30" x 63", EX . . . .$375.00 (B)

Mobiloil, Magnolia trail calendar with great graphics of ocean scene at sunset in center of message, 1933, EX . . . .$95.00 (C)

Mobil Oil...Pegasus, die cut porcelain horse, 36" tall, red, EX . . . .$900.00 (C)

Mobil Oil, porcelain curb sign with cast iron base with graphics of Pegasus, 36½" x 65", EX . . . .$350.00 (C)

Mobiloil...Vacuum Oil Company, porcelain thermometer with vertical scale, Pegasus at top in shield, 8" x 23", white, red, and blue, EX . . . .$225.00 (C)

Mobil, Pegasus die cut embossed plastic sign with red neon, 53" l, VG . . . .$600.00 (B)

Mobil, Pegasus die cut embossed tin license plate attachment, 4½" x 6¼", VG . . . .$75.00 (C)

Mobil, Pegasus die cut tin embossed license plate attachment promoting "California World's Fair," 5½" x 6¼", NM . . . .$175.00 (C)

Mobil, Pegasus porcelain die cut sign in likeness of the trademark winged horse, 44" L, G . . . .$1,100.00 (B)

Mobil, porcelain single-sided dealer advertising sign with graphics of Pegasus at bottom of sign, 81" x 39", VG . . . .$280.00 (B)

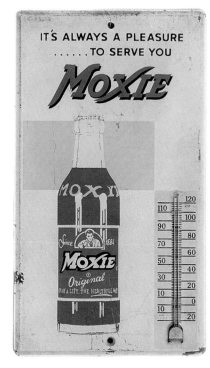

Moxie, It's Always A Pleasure to Serve You, metal scale-type advertising thermometer, 6¾" x 12⅛", G, $170.00 (B).

Moxie, tin litho advertising sign featuring graphics of the girl on the white horse in the touring car with a Moxie billboard in background, 24" x 13", 1933, EX, $575.00 (C).
Courtesy of Buffalo Bay Auction Co.

Moxie, tin litho over cardboard advertising string-hanger sign, also has easel back for countertop applications, 10" x 2⅝", NM, $150.00 (B). *Courtesy of WM. Morford Investment Grade Collectibles*

Mobil, Radiator Flush, metal rack with cardboard advertising, 25" x 40", G . . . .$80.00 (B)

Mobil, restroom porcelain sign with key outline, NOS, 8¾" x 3½", NM . . . .$500.00 (C)

Mobil Service, advertising shop clock with Pegasus in center of face, 13" dia., EX . . . .$165.00 (C)

Model, smoking tobacco for pipe or cigarette, with artwork of Model man on front, key-lift lid, with 1926 tobacco stamp on lid, G . . . .$20.00 (D)

Model, 10¢ Tobacco, tin litho advertising sign featuring artwork of cigar store Indian, 6" x 15", NM . .$127.00 (B)

Model, tin litho free sample pocket tobacco tin, 3" x 4¼" x ⅞, EX . . . .$400.00 (C)

Model Tobacco, tin litho advertising sign with graphics of Model logo man in cigar store Indian attire, 6" x 15", EX . . . .$65.00 (B)

Modern Girl...Beautiful Stockings, box with artwork of woman pulling on stockings, 7½" x 9¾" x 1½", EX .$20.00 (D)

Modern Home Series...Peaslee-Gaulbert Co...Louisville, Ky., oval metal tip tray with graphics of room setting in tray center, 6¼", G . . . .$40.00 (B)

Modox Drink, Indian Herbs, tin litho die cut tip tray with strong colors, 5⅝" x 5", EX . . . .$500.00 (B)

Mogul Egyptian Cigarettes, self-framing tin litho featuring a Mogul with a cigarette and a temple, 20" x 24", EX . . . .$2,200.00 (B)

Mohawk Gasoline, pocket lighter with die cut Indian head, 1¼" x 2¼" x ⅜", NM . . . .$300.00 (C)

Mohawk Tool Works, brass sign with raised detail featuring Indian bust, NOS, 10" x 16", NM . . . .$650.00 (C)

Mohican Coffee, tin litho container with slip-lid and artwork of Indian in full headdress on front, 1-lb., G . . . .$40.00 (D)

Mohican, sage spice tin container with graphics of Indian head in war bonnet on front label, 2-oz., EX . .$95.00 (C)

Moxie, tin litho thermometer, great graphics on this piece, 1920s, 12" x 9½", EX, $1,500.00 (B). *Courtesy of Muddy River Trading Co./Gary Metz*

Mr. Cola, single-sided tin embossed advertising sign, 18" x 18", EX, $60.00 (B).

Mojud Supp-hose, three-dimensional store advertising with woman in yellow outfit sitting in ladder-back chair, plastic, G . . . .$125.00 (D)

Mojud...Thigh-Mold, stretch top garter belt store display, 11" x 11½", EX . . . .$100.00 (D)

Mokaine Liqueurs, tin litho tip tray with graphics of old gent at cafe table, 3¾" x 4" x ½", EX . . . .$51.00 (B)

Monadnock Coffee, tin with screw-lid and graphics of mountain lake scene, from Keene, NH, 1-lb., EX . . . . .$200.00 (B)

Monadnock Peanut Butter, tin litho pail with wire handles on side, graphics of lake scene in center, 1-lb., EX . . . .$236.00 (B)

Monarch coffee, tin, Chicago, L.A. & Boston, 1-lb., EX . . . .$55.00 (C)

Monarch...green tea, tin with lid, artwork of tea pot on front, EX . . . .$12.00 (D)

Monarch Toffies, tin, key-wound lid, 1-lb., EX$125.00 (C)

Monastic, back bar ceramic advertising decanter with graphics of monks testing the product, has a metal spigot at base, 9" x 13" x 13", EX . . . .$700.00 (B)

Monogram Coffee Tin, from F.W. Wagner & Co., Charleston S.C., good paper label with great strong colors, small top, 5½" x 7½", EX . . . .$275.00 (C)

Monogram High Grade Coffee, tin shaped like a milk can with side handle bail and paper label, 2-lb., EX .$135.00 (C)

Monogram Motor Oil Stands Up, cardboard advertising sign with graphics of marching soldiers, 35½" x 11¼", VG . . . .$135.00 (C)

Monogram Uniform Quality Motor Lubricants, double-sided porcelain advertising sign, 18" dia., EX . .$375.00 (B)

Monroe Beer, round metal tip tray with banner across the globe, 4⅛" dia., EX . . . .$40.00 (B)

Monroe-Matic Shock Absorbers...Load Levelers, double-bubble advertising clock, metal body with glass face and front, NOS, 16" dia., EX . . . .$500.00 (D)

Monroe...the ultimate in shock absorbers...America rides...Monroe, light-up advertising clock, G . .$115.00 (D)

Montana Frank, Western show advertising paper litho with scene of Indians attacking a home, 20¼" x 27½", 1929, EX . . . .$625.00 (C)

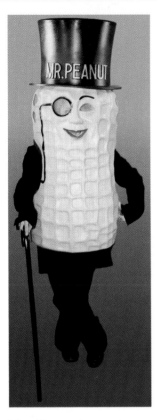

Mr. Peanut, costume, EX, $500.00 (B).

Muchlebach's, die cut tin litho match holder, shaped like bottle, "special brew," 7" H, EX, $195.00 (C). *Courtesy of Richard Opfer Auctioneering, Inc.*

Munsing Wear, easel back cardboard store advertising display, featuring artwork of small red-haired girl, "Miss Particular," 1910, 8½" x 11", NM, $65.00 (B).

Courtesy of Muddy River Trading Co./Gary Metz

Montgomery Ward, Java & Arabian coffee tin with large lid, 7" x 9", 3-lb., 1900s, EX . . . .$175.00 (C)

Monticello Special Reserve..It's All Whiskey, oval metal tip tray with graphics of Monticello along with men on horseback, 6¼", EX . . . .$65.00 (B)

Moore's Supreme Ethyl, pump sign, single-sided porcelain, NOS, 10" x 15", EX . . . .$350.00 (B)

Moose Beer..."Better Than Ever," painted wooden sign, 15" x 6⅞", G . . . .$95.00 (C)

Moose Beer, embossed wood advertising sign, 15" x 6⅛", EX . . . .$125.00 (C)

Moosehead Beer, tin advertising sign, EX . . . .$25.00 (D)

Moosehead...Imported on tap, neon wall sign with facsimile of moose in neon, EX . . . .$175.00 (D)

MoPar...Parts...Accessories, neon lighted advertising clock, 18¼" x 18¼", EX . . . .$975.00 (C)

MoPar Parts, double-sided porcelain flange sign, 26" x 18¼", G . . . .$1,100.00 (B)

Morgan & Wright Tire, advertising paper sign with graphics of young boy in yellow trench coat, 15" x 20", EX . .$150.00 (B)

Morning Glow Coffee, tin litho coffee can featuring artwork of ship, 5" x 4", EX . . . .$170.00 (B)

Morning Joy Pure Coffee, key-wound tin litho can with artwork of singing bird in front of sunrise, 5" x 3½", EX . . . .$250.00 (B)

Morrell's Boiled Ham, string-hung double-sided litho with image of ham being lifted out of cauldron being watched by sad pig, 1900s, 10¼" x 11¼", NM . . . .$333.00 (B)

Morrell's Pride Meats, pocket advertising mirror, 2" dia., EX . . . .$40.00 (B)

Morris Evans Remedies, litho on cardboard advertising store sign, 10¼" x 14¾", NM . . . .$58.00 (B)

Morris Supreme Peanut Butter, tin litho pail with scene of children at beach, 12-oz., EX . . . .$75.00 (B)

Morse's, candy tin, graphics of young lady with wide brim hat, screw-on lid, 4½" sq. x 9", EX . . . .$125.00 (C)

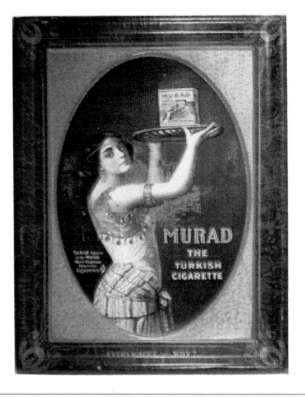

My-Cola, embossed tin door kick plate, "The Best Ever 5¢ Founts and Bottles," early imitator of Coca-Cola, 36" x 12", 1908, VG, $700.00 (B).

Murad...The Turkish Cigarette, self-framing tin advertising sign with simulated wood frame, 28" x 39", 1906, EX, $550.00 (B). *Courtesy of Buffalo Bay Auction Co.*

Morton House Coffee, tin litho screw-lid container, 1-lb., EX . . . .$61.00 (B)

Morton Salt, "Miniatures," tin wall mount dispenser with graphics of the Morton girl at top, 3" x 19½" x 2", NM . . . .$135.00 (D)

Mo-Sam Coffee, paper label tin, Morton Coffee Co., Baltimore, MD, with graphics of Egyptian scene on front label, 1-lb., EX . . . .$250.00 (C)

Mo-Sam Coffee, tin litho container with pry-lid, image of pyramid on both sides, 1-lb., EX . . . .$975.00 (B)

Mother's Oats, "Our Boy," paper litho advertising sign with graphics of young boy, 16" x 22", 1906, EX . . .$180.00 (B)

Mother's Worm Syrup, wall match holder, tin litho with good, strong colors of mother giving youngster medicine, 2¼" x 6¾", EX . . . .$975.00 (C)

Motor Club Coffee, can with great paper label with strong graphics of couple in vintage touring car, fro Beiderman Bros, Chicago, pry-lid, 1-lb., EX . . . .$1,350.00 (B)

Motorola, Auto Radio Drive Safety embossed tin license plate attachment, 4⅝" x 4¾", EX . . . .$95.00 (C)

Motorola, light-up spinner advertising clock with metal body, tin face and white neon light, 21" dia., VG . . . . .$650.00 (B)

Motorola, Radio...For Home or Car, neon spinner advertising clock, reverse painted glass face, 21½" dia., EX . . . .$675.00 (C)

Motorola, Service...Car Radio, painted metal sign, G . . . .$135.00 (D)

Mount Cross Coffee, tin litho with embossed tin lid, 5½" x 9½", VG . . . .$120.00 (B)

Moxie, advertising thermometer with graphics of girl at top and man at bottom, "The H.D. Beach Co., Coshocton, O," 9" x 26½", VG . . . .$235.00 (B)

Moxie, die cut advertising sign with Moxie girl in center of circle, "I like it," 6¼" dia., EX . . . .$325.00 (C)

Moxie, die cut tin advertising sign, graphics of girl with glass of Moxie, "I like it" message at bottom, 6" dia., EX . . . .$725.00 (B)

Moxie, die cut tin litho match holder, resembling Moxie drink bottle, 7" H, EX . . . .$500.00 (B)

Moxie...Drink, ashtray with Frank Archer promoting product, EX . . . .$70.00 (B)

Moxie...Drink, double-sided tin litho flange advertising sign, 18" x 9", EX . . . .$225.00 (B)

Moxie...Drink, embossed tin sign, 1938, 27" x 19", white on red with yellow outline, EX . . . .$125.00 (B)

Moxie...Drink...Very Healthful, round metal tip tray with product message in center of tray, 6" dia., EX .$40.00 (B)

Moxie, FDR die cut advertising, promoting benefits of Moxie as proclaimed by FDR, good, full image of FDR, 12" x 4", EX . . . .$305.00 (B)

Moxie...I Just Love...Don't You, round metal tip tray with great graphics of leaf border and woman with glass of product in center, 6" dia., EX . . . .$120.00 (B)

Moxie..."I like it," round tip tray with graphics of woman with glass of product, 6" dia., EX . . . .$170.00 (B)

Moxie...Learn to Drink...Very Healthful, cardboard die cut easel back advertising sign with likeness of Frank Archer promoting product, sitting on product box, 19" x 40", EX . . . .$790.00 (B)

Moxie, Lowell bottle, nerve food, EX . . . .$65.00 (C)

Moxie...makes you eat, sleep, and feel better, round metal tip tray, 6" dia., EX . . . .$45.00 (B)

Moxie, match holder, die cut litho in shape of bottle of product, 2½" x 7⅛", EX . . . .$500.00 (B)

Moxie...the National Health Beverage, round metal tip tray, 3½" dia., EX . . . .$195.00 (B)

Moxie, tin litho advertising sign featuring graphics of the girl on the white horse in the touring car with a Moxie billboard in background, 24" x 13", 1933, EX . . . .$575.00 (C)

Mr. Peanut, ashtray with image of Mr. Peanut standing behind ashtray shell, bisque composition, 4½" x 3", NM . . . .$40.00 (B)

Mr. Peanut, plastic figural peanut butter maker, complete with box, 12½" tall, EX . . . .$45.00 (C)

Mr. Peanut, plastic head display store jar, 7½" x 12", EX . . . .$65.00 (D)

Mr. Thomas, 5¢ Cigar...None Better, round metal tip tray with graphics of "tom" cat on tray, 4⅛" dia., EX . . . . . .$650.00 (B)

M. Stachelberg & Co's, die cut cardboard advertising promoting their Raphael Clear Havana Cigarettes, 17¼" x 21", VG . . . .$115.00 (B)

M. Stachelberg & Co.'s, Raphael Clear Havana Cigarettes die cut advertising sign with graphics of pretty woman, 17¼" x 21", VG . . . .$115.00 (B)

Mt. Cabin...Just Sweet Enough...Just Tart Enough, embossed tin sign with image of man in uniform with message sign, 11⅞" x 17⅞", NM . . . .$205.00 (B)

Mt. Rushmore...See, tin die cut license plate attachment in shape of the four presidents, 11¼" x 5½", NM . .$195.00 (C)

Muchlebach's, die cut tin litho match holder, shaped like bottle, "special brew," 7" H, G . . . .$180.00 (B)

Munsing Wear...Ask for...Fashion Books Take One, store counter display container, with artwork of woman and child, 12" x 14", EX . . . .$800.00 (B)

Munsing Wear, cardboard easel back store advertising sign with image of woman at table with flowers, 20" x 30", EX . . . .$82.00 (B)

Munsing Wear...Perfect Fitting...Union Suits, die cut tin litho with graphics of children playing with mother, EX . . . .$3,100.00 (B)

Munyon's Homeopathic Home Remedy, tin litho store cabinet with 10 drawers, artwork of product salesman on top, EX . . . .$506.00 (B)

Murad Cigarette, embossed paperboard sign with graphics of product box, 21" x 3", EX . . . .$70.00 (B)

Murad...The Turkish Cigarette, self-framing tin advertising sign with simulated wood frame, 28" x 39", 1906, G . . . .$325.00 (D)

Murdoch's Mustard, tin, paper label, 2-oz., EX $75.00 (C)

Muriel Tobacco, round tin litho container with graphics of woman wearing a veil, 5¾" x 6", G . . . .$30.00 (B)

Musgo Gasoline...Michigan's Mile Maker, two-sided porcelain advertising sign with graphics of Indian in full headdress in center of sign, 48" dia., EX . . . . . .$6,500.00 (B)

My Baby's Talc...Sears Roebuck and Co., tin litho powder container with good, strong colors with artwork of cherub on both sides, 2¼" x 6" x 1¼", EX . . . .$400.00 (B)

My-Cola, embossed tin door kick plate, "The Best Ever 5¢ Founts and Bottles," early imitator of Coca-Cola, 36" x 12", 1908, VG . . . .$700.00 (B)

Nanty-Glo, sign advertising Edelstein's for clothing, arrow-shaped painted arrow, 5" x 20", VG, **$55.00 (D).** *Courtesy of Riverview Antique Mall*

Nabisco National Biscuit Company, store bin cover, gold metal frame with glass cover, "Patented March 13, 1923" embossed on side, NM, **$45.00 (C).**

Napoleon Flour, sign with graphics of Napoleon on front, 18" x 35", EX, **$510.00 (B).** *Courtesy of Buffalo Bay Auction Co.*

Narragansett Lager & Ale, tin litho serving tray, graphics of Indian with tray of product, 12" dia., G, **$105.00 (B).**

Nabisco, Christmas sign featuring graphics of Santa Claus delivering Nabisco products, 24½" x 17", 1940s, EX . . . .$295.00 (C)

Nabisco, die cut letter opener, tin litho with graphics of Uneeda boy on handle, 1½" x 8", EX . . . .$165.00 (C)

Nabisco, die cut porcelain advertising sign in shape of Nabisco TM, 48" x 33¼", EX . . . .$600.00 (C)

Nabisco, National Biscuit Company, store bin cover, gold metal frame with glass cover, "Patented March 13, 1923" embossed on side, EX . . . .$25.00 (B)

Nabisco, Shredded Wheat, biscuit box with presidential offer on front, cardboard, 1949, 12-oz., 12-biscuit, EX . . . .$25.00 (B)

Nabob Baking Powder, tin litho from Vancouver, BC, 5" x 8¾", EX . . . .$85.00 (C)

Nabob Brand Baking Powder, tin litho with graphics of freshly cut cake on front, 5" x 7½", VG . . . . . .$35.00 (C)

Nachtegall & Veit, bar room fixtures and furniture reverse painted glass door push, hard-to-find item, 3" x 10", EX . . . .$375.00 (C)

N.A. Jordon Sporting Goods, house advertising calendar promoting their line of gambling goods, 10" x 14", 1905, EX . . . .$95.00 (C)

Nanty-Glo, sign advertising Edelstein's for clothing, arrow-shaped painted arrow, 5" x 20", EX . . . .$65.00 (D)

Naples Velvet Finish...Adams & Elting Co., paper on cardboard advertising sign, artwork of rabbit with pointer showing off different colors, 1920s, 16" x 9", EX . . . .$110.00 (B)

Napoleon Flour, sign with graphics of Napoleon on front, 18" x 35", G . . . .$275.00 (C)

National Biscuit Co., advertisement, graphics of young boy in yellow rain coat, 1901, 13¼" x 16¾", VG, $85.00 (B).

National Eagle Whiskey, papier-mache bar advertising statue, 16½ x 33½", VG, $150.00 (C).

National Fire Insurance Company of Hartford, one-sided tin sign, framed, 21" x 12", VG, $80.00 (B).

Nehi...Drink Beverages, metal self-framing painted sign with bottle to right of message, Robertson 1504, 17¾" x 53½", red, white, and gray, EX, $325.00 (D). *Courtesy of Patrick's Collectibles*

Napoleon's, litho condom tin with artwork of crossed swords, complete with original products, 1⅞" x 1⅝" x ⅜", EX . . . .$300.00 (B)

Napoleon, tobacco clippings package, unopened with graphics of Napoleon on front, EX . . . . $175.00 (C)

Nash Authorized Service, double-sided hanging sign, 22" x 36", EX . . . .$2,500.00 (C)

Nash...Authorized service, porcelain advertising sign, 42" x 42", EX . . . .$500.00 (C)

Nash, automobile advertising catalog with great graphics of the new Nash on the cover, 12" x 10", 1938, EX . .$40.00 (B)

Nash, Bonded Select Used Cars, double-sided porcelain advertising sign, 42" dia., VG . . . .$775.00 (C)

Nash...P.K. Williams, plastic dial-type thermometer with calendar tear sheet receptacle at bottom, no sheets, 7½" x 15", EX . . . .$15.00 (C)

Nash's, drip grind coffee tin pail with wire pail handle, 7½" x 8", 1920s, EX . . . .$125.00 (C)

National Ales, Brew'g Co., Syracuse, NY, heavy enamel porcelain match striker, 4" x 6", EX . . . .$500.00 (B)

National Beer...The Best in the West, round metal tip tray with artwork of cowboy riding horse with bottle of product, 4½" dia., EX . . . .$625.00 (B)

National Biscuit Company...does my baking, framed paper litho advertising sign featuring silent film star Diana Allen, 20" x 27", 1920s, VG . . . .$1,500.00 (B)

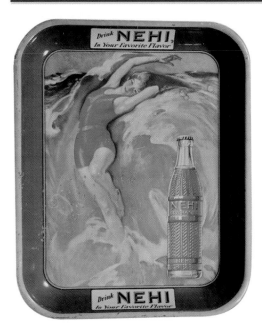

Nehi, Drink... In Your Favorite Flavor, serving tray featuring girl on wave with bottle of Nehi in foreground, G, $160.00 (B). *Courtesy of Muddy River Trading Co./Gary Metz*

Nehi, paper litho advertising, graphics of pretty lady with hat holding Nehi bottle, 16⅞" x 23⅝", VG, $60.00 (B).

Neitzey & Ballenger, Fresh and Salt Fish, early advertising litho, framed and matted, 14⅝" x 19¾", G, $375.00 (B).

National Brand Cocoa, Geo. Rashmussen Co., tin litho container with artwork of Capitol building and kids at table, 2½" x 2½" x 4⅞", EX . . . .$275.00 (B)

National Brewing Co., San Francisco, celluloid stamp holder with graphics of cowboy on horseback with a bottle of the product, 1½" x 2½", VG . . . .$100.00 (B)

National Cash Register Co., receipt holder, pressed metal, 3¼" x 6½", EX . . . .$145.00 (B)

National Cigar Stands...Our Brands, round metal tip tray with artwork of lady with early off-the-shoulder dress, 6" dia., EX . . . .$45.00 (B)

National Cigar Store, light fixture shaped like cigar store with leaded glass dome, 23" x 22½" x 11", EX .$2,700.00 (B)

National Dairy Council, paper advertment extolling the virtues of dairy products, American Litho Co., N.Y., 20" x 31", EX . . . .$325.00 (B)

National Oats Co., paper label cardboard box with Donald Duck on front promoting Donald Duck Oats, 3-lb., VG . . . .$275.00 (B)

National Premium, gas globe, one-piece, fired-on lettering with decal for company, diamond-shaped globe, foreign, 22½" x 19", G . . . .$425.00 (B)

Nesbitt's California Orange, litho cardboard poster with graphics of family outing, 36" x 25", EX, $140.00 (B).

Nesbitt's...a soft drink made from real oranges, metal thermometer displaying spotlighted bottle under message and at top of scale, not an easy piece to find, 7" x 23", yellow and orange on blue, G, $160.00 (D). *Courtesy of Patrick's Collectibles*

Nevada Bell Telephone Co., porcelain logo sign promoting both "Local & Long Distance Telephone," 12" x 18", EX, $2,200.00 (C).

National Royal, gas globe, wide glass body with glass lens, 13½" dia., G . . . .$235.00 (B

National Tobacco Co., National Specialty Mfg. Co., Philadelphia, Pa., cutter, EX . . . .$90.00 (D)

National White Rose Ethyl, gas globe, wide glass body with two glass lenses, 13½" dia., VG . . . .$375.00 (B)

National White Rose, gas globe, wide glass hull body with two lenses, 13½" dia., G . . . .$325.00 (C)

Nationwide Food Stores, die cut porcelain single-sided advertising sign, 32" x 36", VG . . . .$110.00 (B)

Nature's Remedies, menu board, self-framed and embossed, litho by H.D. Beach, 17" x 22", EX . . . .$245.00 (C)

Nature's Remedy, wood wall Gilbert clock with paper advertising sign under glass door, 15" x 4½" x 33", EX . . . .$610.00 (B)

Navy, recruiting poster featuring a girl in naval uniform, "I want you for the Navy," cloth backed, rare, and signed by Howard Chandler Christy, 1917, 26½" x 41", 1917, EX . . . . .$100.00 (B)

Neato Wintergreen Pepsin Gum, litho advertisement with graphics of two different size glass counter jars, 6¼" x 4¼", NM . . . .$95.00 (C)

New Era Dairy, Velvet Rich, Ice Cream, plastic front light-up clock, has metal back, VG, $125.00 (C). *Courtesy of B.J. Summers*

New Era... Ice Cream, neon light-up store sign, 24¾" x 14¾", VG, $400.00 (C).

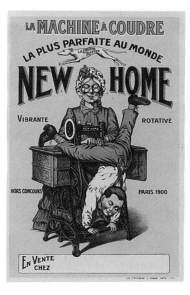

New Home, paper litho advertising poster, foreign, 1900s, 17½" x 25", G, $110.00 (B).

New York Coach Oil, metal can from Marshall Oil Company, image of coach, 3" x 3¼" x 6¾", VG, $95.00 (B).

Nectar Tea, die cut porcelain ad sign in shape of cup of product, foreign item, 21" x 12½", VG . . . . . .$160.00 (B)

Nehi, advertising sign with bottle in oval in right side portion of sign, painted tin, 45" x 18", EX . . . . .$125.00 (D)

Nehi Beverages, Drink...Ice Cold, die cut double-sided tin flange advertising sign with die cut product bottle, 18" x 13½", NM . . . .$525.00 (C)

Nehi...Curb Service...Sold Here Ice Cold, embossed tin advertising sign, NOS, 19⅝" x 27¾", NM . . . . .$80.00 (B)

Nehi...Drink...Beverages, embossed tin tacker style advertising sign with product bottle at right of message, 29½" x 11¾", 1932, EX . . . .$240.00 (B)

Nehi...Drink, painted tin sign with bottle in spotlight at right of message, 45" x 18", EX . . . .$85.00 (D)

Nehi Orange, advertising clock, "Drink...and other Nehi flavors," glass and metal, 15" dia., EX . . . . .$325.00 (B)

Nehi Orange...Drink...and other Nehi flavors, paper advertising sign, 7¼" x 12", EX . . . .$30.00 (B)

Nesbitt's...a soft drink made from real oranges, in spotlight, painted metal sign, 32" x 32", white orange, black on yellow, P . . . .$50.00 (D)

Nesbitt's California Orange, tin advertising sign, embossed lettering and bottle, 27¼" x 11", 1938, EX . . .$115.00 (C)

Nesbitt's California Orange, tin advertising sign with embossed lettering and bottle, 27¼" x 11", 1938, P . . . .$20.00 (B)

Nesbitt's, painted metal thermometer with logo at top of vertical scale and bottle to left of scale, rolled sides and corners, orange & white, EX . . . .$95.00 (C)

Niagara Shoes, store advertising sign, tin over cardboard, "for youthful feet," featuring artwork of Niagara Falls, 9" x 19", EX, $100.00 (B).

Nichol Kola...America's taste sensation 5¢, painted metal sign, The Parker Metal Dec. Co., Baltimore, Ohio, 27½" x 11¼", white, orange, and black, EX, $95.00 (D).
Courtesy of Patrick's Collectibles

Nickel King Cigars, single-sided cardboard advertising sign, 18" x 6", G, $25.00 (B).

Nesbitt's...the finest soft drink ever made...Don't say orange say..., painted metal thermometer with vertical scale, EX . . . .$55.00 (D)

Neuweiler's Beer...Watch the place awhile..., cardboard advertising sign with artwork of two men in bar, 17¼" x 13¾", EX . . . .$45.00 (C)

Neva Myss Flour, cloth sack with graphics of bird dogs flushing birds, 6-lb., EX . . . .$25.00 (B)

New Bachelor Cigar, tin with graphics of man on front, 4¼" x 5⅜" x 2¼", EX . . . .$75.00 (C)

New Century & Mushroom, 5¢ Cigars, advertising knife and corkscrew, 3¾" x 1" x ¼", VG . . . .$45.00 (C)

New Chief Ammunition, framed paper litho advertising poster with graphics of man getting ready to go hunting and wife reminding him to take the product with him, 17" x 22", EX . . . .$600.00 (B)

New Era Coffee, tin litho from G. Thealheimer, Syracuse NY, slip-on lid, good, strong colors, 3½" x 6" x 3½", 1900s, EX . . . .$155.00 (C)

New Era Dairy...Velvet Rich...Ice Cream, light-up ad clock with metal body, plastic face with message panel to right of clock face, 1960s, 24¾" x 11¾", EX . .$225.00 (C)

New Era Dairy, Velvet Rich, Ice Cream, plastic front light-up clock, has metal back, F . . . .$95.00 (C)

New Era... Ice Cream, neon light-up store sign, 24¾" x 14¾", G . . . .$375.00 (D)

New Era, Potato Chip, round tin container, 1-lb., EX . . . .$50.00 (D)

Newly Wed...Sugar Stick Candy, pennant with image of young man and woman eating candy, while a young child watches, 25" L, NM . . . .$122.00 (B)

Newport Gasoline Oils, globe, one-piece etched globe that hangs instead of sitting, 16½" dia., G . . . .$770.00 (B)

New Pullman Cigars, die cut cardboard advertising sign with graphics of pretty young woman, 10" x 15", EX . .$75.00 (B)

Newsboy Tobacco, card with early stage actress Agnes Reily likeness on front, 6" x 9", 1893, EX . . . . .$35.00 (B)

Nine O'Clock Washing Tea, embossed tin litho advertising sign, made by Tuscarora Company, Coshocton, Ohio, 13½" x 13", 1895, EX, $1,800.00 (B). *Courtesy of Buffalo Bay Auction Co.*

None Such, clock, pumpkin-shaped, paper litho, embossed in pie tin, 9½" H, EX, $925.00 (B). *Courtesy of Richard Opfer Auctioneering, Inc.*

Notary Public, celluloid over metal sign bonded by Hartford Accident and Indemnity Company with artwork of the Hartford deer in lower center, 8¾" x 4½", VG, $45.00 (C).

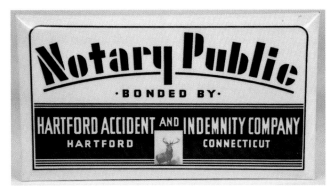

New Sharon...Iowa's City of Roses, painted tin license plate attachment with graphics of roses, 10" x 5½", EX . . . .$110.00 (C)

New York Central-Hudson Type, locomotive, printed in the U.S.A, H.O. Bailey Studios, 1934, 29" x 14", G . .$110.00 (B)

New York Stineware Co., pottery jug with floral design, 13" T, EX . . . .$195.00 (C)

Niagara Fire Insurance Company, reverse painted on glass with image of Niagara Falls, 33¼" x 25¼", EX . .$340.00 (B)

Niagara Punch...Drink, painted tin sign with product bottle at left of message, 20" x 9", EX . . . .$110.00 (C)

Niagara Punch, tin litho advertising sign with graphics of product bottle, 19½" x 9¼", EX . . . .$225.00 (C)

Niagara Shoes, self-framing tin advertising sign over wood, "Niagara Shoes for Youthful Feet," image of the falls over message, 8⅝" x 19", EX . . . .$120.00 (B)

Niagara Shoes, store advertising sign, tin over cardboard, "for youthful feet," featuring artwork of Niagara Falls, 9" x 19", EX . . . .$100.00 (B)

Niagara Shoes, tin over cardboard, self-framing, with artwork of Niagara Falls, from "The American artworks, Coshocton, Ohio," 9" x 19", VG . . . .$190.00 (B)

Nichol Kola...Drink...America's taste sensation, with embossed bottle in center of sign, 8" x 24", EX $95.00 (D)

Nichol Kola...Drink...Vitamin B1 added...America's taste sensation, with marching soldier at lower left, painted metal sign, 20" x 28", EX . . . .$95.00 (D)

Noxie Kola, embossed single-sided tin strip sign, 13¾" x 3⅛", G, $65.00 (B).

NuGrape, Drink...A Flavor You Can't Forget, serving tray with great graphics of woman and child in front of fountain and pool, VG, $275.00 (B). *Courtesy of Muddy River Trading Co./Gary Metz*

NuGrape, A Flavor You Can't Forget, rectangular metal serving tray, featuring artwork of girl with bottle, EX, $120.00 (B). *Courtesy of Muddy River Trading Co./Gary Metz*

Nigger Baby Oranges, paper litho for shipping crate, 24" x 10", 1930s, NM . . . .$90.00 (B)

Nigger Hair Tobacco, litho tin with graphics of black man with ring in nose and ear, 5½" x 6½"h, VG . . .$800.00 (B)

Nigger Head Oysters, can with paper label of black man holding an oyster, strong colors, unopened, 4-oz., NM . .$92.00 (B)

Nigger Head Oysters, label, early version and envelope from company with hard-to-find 1933 Chicago Century of Progress stamp, 8" x 2¾", 1930s, EX . . . . . .$135.00 (B)

Nigger Head Oysters, die cut paper litho of clown holding a wooden looking sign promoting Baltimore Fresh Oysters from the Aughinbaugh Canning Co., 11" x 12½", EX . .$675.00 (B)

Nikolai, back bar bottle stand with dancing Kossack, 12" x 12", EX . . . .$65.00 (C)

Nine O'Clock Washing Tea, embossed tin advertisement in wood frame, 15¼" x 15", VG . . . .$950.00 (B)

Nitro Club, Loaded Paper Shells, empty cardboard box with graphics of mallard on front, 4" x 4" x 2½", NM . .$100.00 (C)

Ni-Tro Ethyl, gas globe, high profile metal body with two glass lenses, 16½" dia., G . . . .$800.00 (B)

Nobel's, Empire Smokeless Sporting Powder, lithographed tin container, 3½" x 6" x 1½", EX . . . .$240.00 (B)

None Such, clock, pumpkin-shaped, paper litho, embossed in pie tin, 9½" H, EX . . . .$925.00 (B)

None Such, Mince Meat, die cut cardboard sign promoting the product with graphics of woman holding a freshly prepared pie, 8¾" x 11", EX . . . .$195.00 (C)

Noonan's, Hair Petrole for falling hair, double-sided porcelain flange sign, Zepp's Hair Dressing advertised on other side, 16" x 12", EX . . . .$400.00 (B)

Norco Feeds, single-sided tin sign with graphics of pig sharpening a knife, 24" x 12", VG . . . .$220.00 (B)

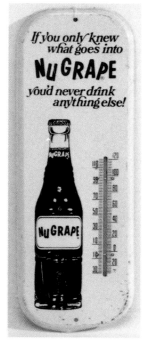

NuGrape, metal thermometer with artwork of bottle at left of scale, 6" x 16¼", yellow, grape, and white, EX, $100.00 (D).

NuGrape Soda, light-up advertising clock, featuring convex glass front, by Swihart, 1940s, 13" X 14", VG, $195.00 (C). *Courtesy of B.J. Summers*

NuGrape Soda, metal advertising thermometer, with graphics of marching bottles, 6¾" x 16", G, $90.00 (B).

Norfolk, food of strength, paper litho with graphics of young child's development, 33½" x 23½", 1900s, EX . . . .$355.00 (C)

Normans Ink, single-sided porcelain ad sign with artwork of bulldog, 21" x 37½", EX . . . .$900.00 (B)

North American Savings Company, embossed cardboard calendar with graphics of Indian bust, 14" x 19", EX . . . .$95.00 (B)

Northampton Brewing Co...Lager Beer, round metal tip tray with artwork of hand holding 3 bottles of product, 4⅛" dia., EX . . . .$140.00 (B)

Northern Navigation Division, Ticket and Information sign, Canadian National Route, graphics of steamship at dock, celluloid over metal, 8" x 9", EX . . . . . .$650.00 (B)

Northland Oils...Lubes, painted tin sign, 24" x 24", EX . . . .$175.00 (C)

North Pole Tobacco, lunch pail with topwire bail handle, 6" x 4" x 6", EX . . . .$350.00 (B)

North Star tobacco, pocket flat tin with litho of goddess in clouds, EX . . . .$750.00 (B)

Northwestern National Bank...Portland Trust Co. of Oregon, oval tip tray with artwork of bank building in center of tray, 6⅛" L, EX . . . .$95.00 (B)

North Woods, egg coffee in tin litho can with key-wound lid, 1-lb., EX . . . .$50.00 (C)

Nor'way Antifreeze, thermometer and chalk board with graphics of Nor'way man at bottom, 15¼" x 22¼", VG . . . .$120.00 (B)

Nourse Motor Oil, double-sided metal lubster sign with graphics of Nourse warrior, 6½" x 8½", G . . .$300.00 (C)

Nugget, shoe polish store advertising sign, porcelain, 1920 – 1930s, 42" x 17", G . . . .$900.00 (C)

NuGrape, advertising clock with bottle in center, 1940 – 1950s, 13¼" x 16", EX . . . .$175.00 (C)

NuGrape Soda, painted aluminum door push bar, reverse side says, "Thank You Call Again," 30" x 4½", EX, **$300.00 (B)**. *Courtesy of Autopia Advertising Auctions*

Nutriola Blood & Nerve Food, early cardboard sign with great graphics, 14" x 18", EX, **$975.00 (B)**. *Courtesy of Morford Auctions*

NuGrape, A Flavor You Can't Forget, rectangular metal serving tray, featuring artwork of girl with bottle, G .**$75.00 (D)**

NuGrape...If you only knew what goes into...you'd never drink anything else!, light-up advertising clock with message panel to right of clock face, EX . . . .**$275.00 (C)**

NuGrape, metal thermometer with artwork of bottle at left of scale, 6" x 16¼", yellow, grape, and white, G .**$55.00 (D)**

NuGrape...More Fun With Soda, round painted metal sign with likeness of bottle cap, EX . . . .**$110.00 (C)**

NuGrape Soda...A Flavor You Can't Forget, die cut tin double-sided flange advertising sign with image of bottle in hand, 19½" x 13½", VG . . . .**$350.00 (B)**

NuGrape Soda, light-up advertising clock, featuring convex glass front, by Swihart, 1940s, 13" x 14", G . . .**$175.00 (C)**

NuGrape Soda, painted aluminum door push bar, reverse side says, "Thank You Call Again," 30" x 4½", VG . . . .**$225.00 (C)**

Nutmeg...Ice Cold Club Beverages, painted tin advertising sign, with artwork of bottle at left, 28" x 10", EX . . . .**$100.00 (D)**

Nutriola Blood & Nerve Food, early cardboard sign with great graphics, 14" x 18", EX . . . .**$975.00 (B)**

Nuvana Cigar, door push, aluminum door push with embossed lettering, 2" x 6", VG . . . .**$80.00 (B)**

N.V. Van Melle's Toffee, store counter bin, great bright graphics, 9½" x 8" x 10", EX . . . .**$1,495.00 (C)**

Nyal Service Drugstore, oval single-sided porcelain advertising sign, 36" x 23½", EX . . . .**$150.00 (B)**

NY Central, advertising sign for the "Twentieth Century Limited," titled As Centuries Past In The Night, 1923, VG . . . .**$75.00 (B)**

Nylotis Baby Powder, tin litho container with artwork of three babies on front, unopened, NM . . . .**$169.00 (B)**

O-Cedar, store display rack, metal with woodgrain look, featuring advertisement from 1925, 1920s, 14"W x 40½"H x 11½"D, VG, **$135.00 (C).**

Odin 5¢ Cigar, embossed tin advertising sign, 19½" x 27½", VG, **$380.00 (B).**

Ohio Rake Co., Dayton, vintage paper litho with graphics of Statue of Liberty and patriotic farming type scenes, 34½" x 28½", EX, **$2,100.00 (B).** *Wm. Morford Investment Grade Collectibles*

Oakland Pontiac, Sales-Service, double-sided porcelain advertising sign, 35½" x 23¾", EX .... $375.00 (C)

O & F Star, pure spices, tin litho general store counter dispenser with graphics of large star between O & F, 7" x 7" X 8", EX .... $100.00 (B)

O-Baby, cardboard countertop display box with pop-up die cut marquee with image of young girl holding an O-Baby candy bar, 6¾" x 4½" x 8¼", EX ...... $400.00 (B)

Obermeyer & Leibmann's...Bottled Beer, beer push cart with big iron wheels and product message on sides, 43" tall, EX .... $1,500.00 (B)

Obermeyer & Leibmann's, bottled beer vendor's cart, wood with metal handle and wheels, 16" x 43", EX ... $2,500.00 (C)

O'Brien's Candies, die cut cardboard advertising sign with graphics of young boy and girl at fence gate and the girl is holding a package of the product, from Omaha, NE, 6½" x 9", NM .... $100.00 (B)

OCB...Roll Your Own with...Cigarette Papers, tin paper holder with product message on front, yellow lettering on black, EX .... $30.00 (D)

Oceanic Oysters...in Season, tin over cardboard advertising sign, 9¼" x 13¼", yellow lettering on green, EX .. $75.00 (B)

Ohio Valley Fire & Marine Insurance, advertising sign, solid brass with embossed lettering and copper flashing on front, from Paducah, Kentucky, framed and restored, 24" x 9", EX, **$425.00 (C).** *Courtesy of B.J. Summers*

Old Judge Coffee, store paper sample cup with graphics of product can on front, 2½" x 2½", NOS NM, **$5.00 (D).** *Courtesy of Rare Bird Antique Mall/Jon & Joan Wright*

Old Judson, tin litho match holder, J.C. Stevens, 518 Delaware St., Kansas City, MO, USA, 5" H, EX, **$200.00 (B).** *Courtesy of Richard Opfer Auctioneering, Inc.*

O Jayco Paints, sign with graphics of large paint can and painter beside can, metal construction, 17" x 20", VG, **$95.00 (C).** *Courtesy of Autopia Advertising Auctions*

O-Cedar Mops...cleans as it polishes, die cut tin litho store display, 20¼" x 18½" x 4¼", EX . . . .$375.00 (B)

O-Cedar, store display rack, metal with woodgrain look, featuring advertisement from 1925, 1920s, 14"W x 40½"H x 11½"D, G . . . . $120.00 (B)

O'day Pep, gas globe, high profile metal body with two glass lenses, 15" dia., G . . . . $1,200.00 (C)

O.F. C., cardboard advertising sign with graphics of black waiter with a tray of the product, litho by Stecher Litho Co., Rochester, N.Y., 15" x 26", EX . . . . $200.00 (B)

O.F.C. Rye, framed paper advertising with graphics of black butler with product on tray "Massa's Favorite," 26" x 30¼", EX . . . . $110.00 (B)

Official National Automobile Club, double-sided hanging porcelain sign, 18" x 21", EX . . . .$225.00 (C)

Offutt & Pierce, die cut advertising souvenir calendar from "the Reliable Home Furnishers, Lowell, Mass.," promoting Household Ranges with graphics of young girl and her pet, missing calendar pad, 9½" x 14½", EX . . . . . .$120.00 (B)

Ogburn, Hill & Co. Tobacco, cardboard advertising sign with graphics of Indian maiden in canoe that's full of flowers, "rich and waxy tobacco," 10¾" x 14", EX . . . . .$160.00 (B)

Oh Boy, 1¢ Gum, tin litho advertising sign with graphics of young boy holding samples of the product, 7¼" x 15¼", 1920s, EX . . . .$425.00 (B)

Old Reliable Coffee, always good, single-sided embossed tin sign with raised lettering, 13¾" x 6½", G, $80.00 (B).

Old Reliable, pocket mirror, graphics of old logo, gentleman in center, celluloid back, 2" dia., EX, $175.00 (C). *Courtesy of Buffalo Bay Auction Co.*

Old Reliable Coffee...Always good, tin sign, 1910s, 6½" x 9", EX, $350.00 (B).
Courtesy of Muddy River Trading Co./Gary Metz

Ohio Rake Co., Dayton, vintage paper litho with graphics of Statue of Liberty and patriotic farming type scenes, 34½" x 28½", F ....$425.00 (C)

Ohio Valley Fire & Marine Insurance, advertising sign, solid brass with embossed lettering and copper flashing on front, from Paducah, Kentucky, framed and restored, 24" x 9", VG ....$375.00 (C)

Oilzum, "America's finest choice," porcelain double-sided advertising sign with the Oilzum man in the upper part of this sign, 19¾" x 27½", G ....$290.00 (B)

Oilzum...America's Finest Oil, double-sided painted tin sign with artwork of Oilzum Man at lower left, 60" x 36", G ....$1,800.00 (C)

Oilzum, double-sided flange, painted advertising sign promoting Oilzum Motor Oil, 20" x 14", 1950s, EX ....$625.00 (B)

Oilzum Motor Oil...Choice of Champions, light-up advertising clock with Oilzum Man in center, 14½" dia., EX ....$1,100.00 (C)

Oilzum Motor Oil...Choice of Champions, square advertising clock, 16" sq., EX ....$175.00 (D)

Oilzum Motor Oil, die cut tin flange advertising sign, graphics of the Oilzum Man, 15¾" x 17", EX ..$275.00 (C)

Oilzum Motor Oil, two-sided metal advertising sign with graphics of the Oilzum Man, "If motors could speak we wouldn't need to advertise," 20" x 10", VG ..$1,600.00 (B)

Oilzum, service station leather attendant cap with Oilzum Man on both sides, , EX ....$50.00 (B)

Oilzum...The Choice of Champion Race Drivers, painted tin thermometer, artwork of Oilzum Man to left of vertical scale, message at top & bottom, 7½" x 15", EX ......$450.00 (C)

Oilzum, tin litho advertising sign, "Choice of Champions," 72" x 36", EX ....$325.00 (B)

Oilzum, tin litho advertising sign with Oilzum Man in upper left corner, "If motors could speak we wouldn't need to advertise," 72" x 32", EX ....$950.00 (B)

Oldsmobile Service, double-sided porcelain advertising dealer sign with "coat of arms" in center, 42" dia., EX, $975.00 (C).

Old Southern Coffee, Larkin Co., Buffalo, NY, tin litho container with slip-lid, features artwork of woman in chair with cup of product, 1-lb., EX, $75.00 (D).

Courtesy of Rare Bird Antique Mall/Jon & Joan Wright

Old Sport Tobacco, framed advertising print, 10½" x 10½", EX, $75.00 (C). *Courtesy of Collectors Auction Services*

Oilzum, tin oil container with graphics of the Oilzum Man, 1-gal., EX . . . .$75.00 (C)

Oilzum, vertical painted tin sign with Oilzum Man inside the O in the name, 10¾" x 43½", NM . . . . . .$575.00 (B)

Oklahoma Vinegar, etched advertising glass from Fort Smith, Arkansas, 5" H, G . . . . $35.00 (B)

"OK," porcelain neon for Chevrolet Used Cars, 24" dia. x 8" d, NM . . . .$1,500.00 (C)

OK Tire, die cut tin litho saluting man advertising sign, 34" x 60", EX . . . .$235.00 (C)

OK Used Cars and Trucks, Chevy truck advertising sign, painted one-sided metal sign, 48" x 36", G . .$350.00 (B)

Old Abe, Chewing Tobacco tin, with litho of Abe and slaves, "Manufactured By B. Leidersdorf & Co. Milwaukee, Wis.," 8" dia., VG . . . .$750.00 (B)

Old Barbee, Vienna Art Plate, graphics of old man pouring product and women conversing beside log house, Louisville distillery, 1908, 10" dia., NM . . . . .$594.00 (B)

Old Boone Whiskey...Thixton, Millett & Co., Louisville, Ky., round metal tip tray with graphics of log cabin distillery, 4⅛" dia., EX . . . .$210.00 (B)

Old Colony, gas globe, wide glass body with glass lens, graphics of bee hive on face, 13½" dia., G . . . $550.00 (B)

Old Colony, tin litho advertising sign with center hanger with graphics of colonist, 15½" x 5", EX . . . . .$85.00 (C)

Old Company's Lehigh...anthracite...It lasts longer!, single-sided die cut porcelain advertising sign, 12" x 12", VG . . . .$200.00 (B)

Old Crow, composition advertising figural back bar display, 3½" x 11½", EX . . . .$75.00 (D)

Old Crow, figural whiskey decanter complete with cane and spats, EX . . . .$40.00 (C)

Old Dutch Beer, embossed die cut store advertising sign with man holding mug of product, EX . . . .$55.00 (B)

Old Dutch Beer, pinback by Bastian Bros., "The good, Beer," 1¼" dia., VG . . . .$55.00 (C)

Old Dutch Cleanser, double-sided tin litho advertising sign, good, strong colors, 12¾" L, NM . . . . . .$160.00 (B)

Old Dutch Cleanser, "for Healthful Cleanliness," tin over cardboard sign with graphics of old "Dutch" cleaning woman, 18" x 9¼", EX . . . .$275.00 (C)

Old Virginia Cheroots, cardboard advertising sign matted, framed, and under glass, 1900s, 6½" x 10½", EX, **$350.00 (B).** *Courtesy of Muddy River Trading Co./Gary Metz*

Oliver Chilled Plows, self-framed embossed tin litho advertising sign with graphics of youngster on horseback and the products in foreground, 27¼" x 36½", 1890, EX, **$1,000.00 (B).** *Courtesy of Buffalo Bay Auction Co.*

Old Dutch Cleanser, tin over cardboard ad sign with hands shown scrubbing pan and product container in lower right, EX . . . .$450.00 (B)

Old English, Curve Cut, "A Slice to a Pipeful, It Fits the Pocket," store bin with slanted front with graphics of product on all sides, 13" x 10¼" x 8½", G . . . $125.00 (B)

Olde Philadephia, coffee tin with key-wound lid, graphics of Philadelphia landmarks, 5" x 3½", EX . . . . .$75.00 (D)

Old Faithful, lighter fluid can with graphics of the geiser on the front, 4-oz., NM . . . .$135.00 (C)

Oldfield Tires, double-sided porcelain flange sign, 21¼" x 16½", VG . . . . $800.00 (B)

Old Fitzgerald, motion advertising lamp, 14" H, EX . .$80.00 (B)

Old Fort Feeds, one-sided die cut porcelain advertising sign, with graphics of wagon wheel, 40" x 47½", VG . $425.00 (B)

Old Fort Feeds, one-sided porcelain advertising sign with graphics of wagon wheel, from Marion, Ohio, and Harrisburg, PA, 40" x 47½", EX . . . .$420.00 (B)

Old Gold Cigarette, self-framed embossed tin litho with image of cigarette packages, 33" x 14", EX . . .$125.00 (B)

Old Gold Cigarettes, flat tin, F . . . .$33.00 (D)

Old Gold Cigarettes, horizontal porcelain sign, 36" x 12", F . . . .$25.00 (D)

Old Gold Cigarettes, Not a cough in a carload, porcelain sign, 36" x 11", G . . . .$225.00 (D)

Old Gold Cigarettes...Not a Cough in a Carload, self-framing single-sided porcelain advertising sign, 36" x 12", VG . . . .$325.00 (B)

Old Gold Cigarettes, paper on cardboard, easel back ad sign with artwork of Dick Powell promoting product, 10½" x 13½", EX . . . .$18.00 (B)

Old Gold Cigarettes, porcelain advertising sign, 36" x 12", VG . . . .$95.00 (C)

Old Gold Cigarettes, the treasure of them all, round vacuum pack tin, 50-count, F . . . .$55.00 (D)

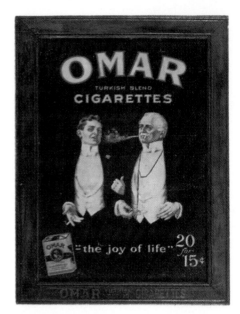

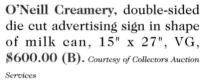

Omar Turkish Cigarette, framed paper litho with graphics of father and son enjoying a smoke, engraving on frame bottom, "American Tobacco Co., Omar Turkish Blend Cigarettes," 18½" x 25", VG, $405.00 (B). *Courtesy of Collectors Auction Services*

O'Neill Creamery, double-sided die cut advertising sign in shape of milk can, 15" x 27", VG, $600.00 (B). *Courtesy of Collectors Auction Services*

Onondaga Brand Glass, flange painted metal advertising sign, featuring artwork of Indian in center, 18½" x 13½", EX, $200.00 (B).

Old Gold, die cut easel back cigarette girl with product vendor tray, 14" x 32", EX . . . .$140.00 (B)

Old Gold Special Cigarettes, cardboard litho advertisng with street car scene, 29" x 41", G . . . . $250.00 (B)

Old Grandad Whiskey, canvas litho with graphics of old man in chair beside table with bottle of Old Grand Dad on table, 29½" x 23½", EX . . . .$295.00 (B)

Old Green River Tobacco, stoneware container in shape of whiskey jug with paper label with information about Old Green River Tobacco, top comes off jug for product access, 6" dia. x 8¼" h, EX . . . .$400.00 (B)

Old Harvest Corn Whiskey, tin litho advertising sign, graphics of man holding child reaching for glass, 19½" x 13", VG . . . .$750.00 (B)

Old Hickory Distillers Co., thermometer with artwork of bottle of product next to dial-type thermometer face, 8⅞" dia., VG . . . . $40.00 (B)

Old Hickory Distillery...Madisonville, Ky., advertising crock jug, 1-gal., EX . . . .$150.00 (C)

Old Hickory, shoe lace advertising store bin for product, 12½" x 6" x 11", EX . . . .$175.00 (C)

Old Hickory, typewriter tin litho ribbon container with image of black man resting under tree, 2½" x 2½", EX ..$170.00 (B)

Old Home Brand Candies, pail, wood bucket with paper label, "Manufactured Expressly for Ridenour-Baker Grocery Co., Kansas City, Mo." with graphics of man cooking over a fire with cabin and mammy in background, 35-lb., VG . . . .$250.00 (D)

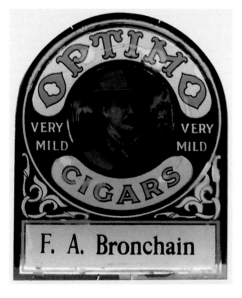

Optimo Cigars, Very Mild, F. A. Bronchain, reverse imaging under beveled glass sign, 11¼" H, EX, **$170.00 (B).**
Courtesy of Richard Opfer Auctioneering, Inc.

Orange Crush, counter dispenser, stainless steel with porcelain sign sides, 11" x 17" x 20", EX, **$2,100.00 (B).** *Courtesy of Muddy River Trading Co./Gary Metz*

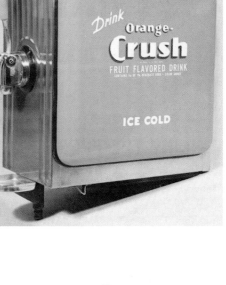

Orange-Crush...Drink, The National Fountain Drink, Color Added, tin over cardboard sign with artwork of girl with glass of Orange Crush, 1920s, 6¼" x 9¼", G, **$500.00 (B).**
Courtesy of Muddy River Trading Co./Gary Metz

Orange Crush, embossed metal sign, self-framing with bottle in center, 17" x 53¼", NM, **$495.00 (C).**

Old Judge Coffee, store paper sample cup with graphics of product can on front, 2½" x 2½", EX ......**$4.00 (D)**

Old Judge Rye, carved wood statue with yarn hair, man is holding a cane and bottle of the product, 9½" x 12" x 47½", VG ....**$1,000.00 (B)**

Old Judson, tin litho match holder, J.C. Stevens, 518 Delaware St., Kansas City, MO, USA, 5" H, F ....**$75.00 (C)**

Old Judson, tin litho match holder, 3" x 5" x 1¼", G ....**$125.00 (D)**

Orange Crush, painted metal menu board with message and bottle at top, 19" x 27¼", VG, **$145.00 (C)**.

Orange Crush, Enjoy The Fresh Taste, single-sided embossed tin sign with rolled lip edge, 35¼" x 34¼", G, **$100.00 (B)**.

Orange Crush, single-sided metal advertising sign with bottle graphics, 31½" x 11¾", VG, **$90.00 (B)**.

Orange Crush, tin flange sign with Crushy at the bottom of the diamond, 1930s, 18" x 18", EX, **$450.00 (B)**. *Courtesy of Muddy River Trading Co./Gary Metz*

Old Judson Whiskey, tin litho advertising hanging match holder with graphics of man pulling on coat in front of roaring fire, 3½" x 5", EX . . . .**$230.00 (B)**

Old Kentucky's Boss, whiskey bottle with paper label, G . . . .**$10.00 (D)**

Old King Cole, smoking mixture, paper label pocket tin with artwork by Maxfield Parrish, rare and hard-to-find, 3½" x 1½" x 4½", EX . . . .**$575.00 (C)**

Old Manse Syrup, tin with graphics of snow scene of house in winter, 6" x 3½" x 11", EX . . . .**$135.00 (C)**

Old Master Coffee, container with graphics of the old master on the front, 5½" x 9½", EX . . . .**$75.00 (C)**

Old Mr. Boston, embossed advertising clock in shape of flask, made by Gilbert at Winstead, Conn., 10" x 5½" x 21¼", VG . . . .**$125.00 (B)**

Old North State Tobacco, canvas barn sign with graphics of product package on blue background, framed in quarter-sawn oak frame, 30" x 20", EX . . . .**$120.00 (B)**

Old Overholt, oleograph, graphic of old gentleman in stream fly fishing and pouring whiskey from a bottle into a container, signed R. Bohunck, 27½" x 38½", 1913, EX . . . .**$575.00 (C)**

Old Overholt Rye, tin litho advertising sign in original wood frame with scene of hunters in field with dog, 37" x 28", EX . . . .**$745.00 (B)**

Orange-Julep, cardboard hang-up sign, featuring artwork of man and woman drinking from a single bottle with two straws, 1930s, 7¾" x 11", EX, $140.00 (B). *Courtesy of Muddy River Trading Co./Gary Metz*

Orange-Julep... Drink, It's JULEP Time, bottle topper, EX, $65.00 (B). *Courtesy of Muddy River Trading Co./Gary Metz*

Orange Julius, A Devilish Good Drink, with artwork of devil figure in center, rare, 1920s, 24" x 35", G, $800.00 (B). *Courtesy of Muddy River Trading Co./Gary Metz*

Old Overholt Whiskey, oleograph canvas in wood frame with artwork of man with bottle of product and a fishing rod, 1913, 27½" x 38½", EX . . . .$350.00 (D)

Old Plantation Steel Cut Coffee, heavy paper bag with graphics of black man with sack of product in front of paddle wheeler, 1-lb., EX . . . .$15.00 (B)

Old Reading Beer...Traditionally Pennsylvania Dutch, round metal serving tray, 12" dia., EX . . . .$35.00 (D)

Old Reliable Coffee, Always Good...Go to G.M. Law's General Merchandise embossed tin litho advertising sign, 6½" x 13¾", EX . . . .$40.00 (B)

Old Reliable Coffee...Always good, tin sign, 1910s, 6½" x 9", F . . . .$95.00 (C)

Old Reliable Coffee...A Real Breakfast, Always The Same, Always Good, with graphics of breakfast scene and product box, trolley car sign, cardboard, 21" x 11", NM . .$97.00 (B)

Old Reliable Coffee...Guaranteed Pure, round metal tip tray with artwork of Russian man and package of product, 4¼" dia., EX . . . .$100.00 (B)

Old Reliable Coffee, metal tip, tray with image of pretty woman with flower in hair, 4¼" dia., NM . . . .$143.00 (B)

Old Reliable Coffee, paper litho with trademark old Russian and package of product "Always the same...Always good," 11½" x 21½", VG . . . .$95.00 (B)

Old Reliable Coffee, sign with graphics of the logo gentleman, litho by H.D. Beach Co., 6¼" x 9¼", EX . .$425.00 (C)

Old Reliable Coffee, tin litho tip tray with graphics of the old Cossack man, 4¼" dia., EX . . . .$155.00 (B)

Old Reliable Coffee...Welcome as April showers, trolley car sign with artwork of man with cup of coffee, 21" x 11", EX . . . .$175.00 (D)

Old Reliable Peanut Butter, tin litho pail with wire side-mounted bail, 1-lb., EX . . . .$75.00 (C)

Old Reliable, pocket mirror, graphics of old logo gentleman in center, celluloid back, 2" dia., G . . . .$100.00 (C)

Old Seneca Stogies, tin litho container with graphics of Indian bust on front, 4" dia. x 5½", EX . . . . .$240.00 (B)

Oregon Winter Sports Association, embossed tin advertising license plate attachment with graphics of ski jumper in action, 12" x 5", 1942, EX, $275.00 (C). *Courtesy of Autopia Advertising Auctions*

Ortlieb's Laeger Beer – Ale, tin litho self-framing ad sign, 14" dia., VG, $100.00 (B).

Oshkosh R.R. Suits, Union Made, reverse painted glass in wood frame, featuring good graphics of oil worker at left side of sign, 48¼" x 18½", EX, $3,800.00 (B). *Courtesy of Richard Opfer Auctioneering, Inc.*

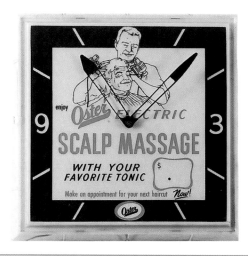

Oster Electric Scalp Massage, light-up plastic advertising clock, 16" x 16" x 3¾", G, $80.00 (B).

Oldsmobile, light-up electric advertising clock, Pam Clock Co., 15½" sq., VG . . . . $475.00 (B)

Oldsmobile Service, double-sided porcelain advertising dealer sign with "coat of arms" in center, 42" dia., G . . . . $425.00 (C)

Oldsmobile Service, neon clock, neon circle on outside, 21" x 6", VG . . . . $600.00 (B)

Oldsmobile Service, one-sided porcelain advertising sign, 42" dia., VG . . . . $875.00 (C)

Old Southern Coffee, Larkin Co., Buffalo, NY, tin litho container with slip-lid, features artwork of woman in chair with cup of product, 1-lb., G . . . . $55.00 (D)

Old Southern Molasses, can, litho label on tin, "Packed by J. Stromeyer Co., Philadelphia, Pa.," 9" x 9" x 15", VG . . . . $100.00 (B)

Old Squire tobacco, pocket tin from Tuckett Tobacco Co., Canada, 3⅛" x 4½" x .775, EX . . . . $700.00 (B)

Old Style...Brewed with water from when the earth was pure, plastic light-up sign, 15" x 10¼", EX . . . . $25.00 (D)

Old Style Lager, cigarette wooden back bar point of sale vendor, "We don't aim to make the most beer: just the best," 21½" x 4" x 12¾", EX . . . . $55.00 (B)

Old Style, tin litho die cut advertising thermometer in the likeness of musketeer holding a mug of the product, 6" x 13¼", EX . . . . $725.00 (B)

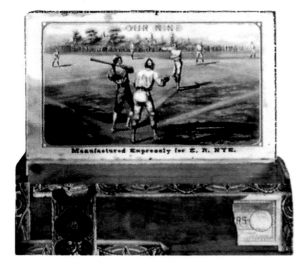

Our Game, cigar box, with great graphics of vintage baseball game, scarce item, 1900s, VG, $600.00 (B). *Courtesy of Buffalo Bay Auction Co.*

Overland Motor Car, single-sided tin ad sign, 13¾" x 9¾", VG, $170.00 (B).

Owl Cigars, cardboard double-sided die cut string hanger, 7" x 9½", EX, $300.00 (B). *Courtesy of Wm. Morford Investment Grade Collectibles*

Ozonite, The Complete Detergent, paper advertisement, 22¾" x 19¾", VG, $40.00 (B).

Old Virginia Catsup, cardboard give-away Halloween mask of Mammy with products information on reverse, 9" x 10¼", EX . . . .$225.00 (B)

Old Virginia Cheroots, cardboard advertising sign matted, framed, and under glass, 1900s, 6½" x 10½", G . . . .$125.00 (D)

Old Virginia Cheroots, cardboard litho advertising with artwork of couple greeting each other, 20½" x 20½", VG . . . .$150.00 (B)

Old Virginia Cheroots, tin litho advertising sign with cigar box image on front, 8½" sq., VG . . . .$185.00 (D)

Olin Winchester, flashlight and battery store counter display, 34" T, VG . . . .$75.00 (C)

Oliver Chilled Plows, self-framed embossed tin litho advertising sign with graphics of youngster on horseback and the products in foreground, 27¼" x 36½", 1890, F . . . .$250.00 (C)

Oliver Implements, "Plowmakers for the world," flange tin sign with artwork of globe in center, 18" x 18", EX . . . .$160.00 (B)

Oliver Implements...plowmakers for the world, painted die cut tin flange sign, with artwork of the earth in center, 18" x 18", EX . . . .$225.00 (C)

Olixir...Feel the Difference, tin advertising sign with image of vintage auto moving up a hill, "JB Clark Oil Co., Buffalo, NY, 17⅝" x 18", G . . . .$140.00 (B)

Ology Quality Cigar, cardboard die cut easel back sign with graphics of man with golf club, 1930s, 25" x 37", EX . . . .$145.00 (B)

Ols English, curve cut pipe tobacco, slant top country store countertop bin with colorful graphics of country gentleman enjoying a smoke from the product, 13" x 10¼" x 8", EX . . . .$370.00 (B)

Olympian Coffee, tin litho pry-lid container, 1-lb., EX . . . .$88.00 (B)

Omar Baking Co., Indianapolis, "Fresh at your door every day," 6½" x 8", EX . . . .$525.00 (B)

Omar Cigarette, sign, cardboard in original frame, featuring artwork of two older gentlemen enjoying a smoke, 18¼" x 25", EX . . . .$575.00 (C)

Omar Turkish Cigarette, framed paper litho with graphics of father and son enjoying a smoke, engraving on frame bottom, "American Tobacco Co., Omar Turkish Blend Cigarettes," 18½" x 25", F . . . .$110.00 (D)

One Eleven American cigarette, full pack with graphics of Indian bust in full headdress, 2" x 2¾", NM . . .$80.00 (B)

O'Neill Creamery, double-sided die cut advertising sign in shape of milk can, 15" x 27", F . . . .$125.00 (D)

Onondaga Brand Glass, flange painted metal advertising sign, featuring artwork of Indian in center, 18½" x 13½", G . . . .$125.00 (C)

On the Stroke of Twelve, paper litho advertising poster with graphics of two men getting ready to box, 24½" x 32½", VG . . . .$185.00 (B)

On Time Gum, stenciled chewing gum tin with top-mounted wire handle, 7¾" x 5¼" X 2", EX . . .$900.00 (B)

Onyx, gas globe, plastic body with glass lens, 13½" dia., VG . . . .$160.00 (B)

Opex Lacquers...enamels, porcelain flange sign with the Sherman Williams Paint logo at top left and right, 22" x 16", EX . . . .$225.00 (D)

Opex Paints, two-sided porcelain flange sign, "Sherman Williams, The Modern Automobile Lacquer Finish," 22" x 16", EX . . . .$200.00 (B)

Optimo Cigars, Very Mild, F. A. Bronchain, reverse imaging under beveled glass sign, 11¼" H, F . . . .$75.00 (D)

Orange Crush, Carbonated Beverages, embossed tin advertising sign with graphics of "Crushy" at bottom, diamond-shaped, 21¼" x 21¼", 1938, EX . . . . .$275.00 (B)

Orange Crush, cast brass street marker, "National Safety Eng. Bham, ALA" on back side, 3¾" dia., EX .$325.00 (B)

Orange Crush, counter dispenser, stainless steel with porcelain sign sides, 11" x 17" x 20", F . . . . . .$500.00 (D)

Orange-Crush...Drink, The National Fountain Drink, Color Added, tin over cardboard sign with artwork of girl with glass of Orange Crush, 1920s, 6¼" x 9¼", G . . $500.00 (B)

Orange Crush...Drink, with bottle in snow at outer edge of sign, 17½" x 11½", NM . . . .$75.00 (D)

Orange Crush, electric advertising clock with tin litho face and wooden body, 15½" sq., 1940s, VG . $425.00 (C)

Orange Crush, embossed metal sign, self-framing with bottle in center, 17" x 53¼", EX . . . .$460.00 (D)

Orange Crush, embossed tin menu board with "Crushy" figure at top, 19¼" x 27", EX . . . .$280.00 (B)

Orange Crush, glass, Art Deco style, made of Bakelite and frosted glass, rare, EX . . . .$450.00 (C)

Orange Crush, glass, with flared top and etched syrup line, NM . . . .$195.00 (C)

Orange Crush, painted metal advertising thermometer with bottle cap at top of scale, 5¾" x 16", NM . .$120.00 (B)

Orange Crush, painted metal menu board with message and bottle at top, 19" x 27¼", G . . . .$125.00 (D)

Orange Crush, paper on cardboard advertising sign with graphics of woman and dog, 13½" x 19¼", EX .$150.00 (B)

Orange-Crush, PELCO 510-E, electric drink box, other versions of this box were made for other drinks, most were embossed, 1940 – 1950s, 10-case, orange, NM . . . .$2,995.00 (D)

Orange Crush, soda tin die cut embossed tin bottle thermometer, 7" x 28¾", 1950s, NM . . . .$300.00 (B)

Orange Crush...Taste, metal and glass dial thermometer, 12" dia., VG . . . .$120.00 (B)

Orange Crush...Taste, plastic light-up advertising clock, 15" sq., EX . . . .$125.00 (C)

Orange Crush, tin flange sign with Crushy at the bottom of the diamond, 1930s, 18" X 18", F . . . .$125.00 (C)

Orange Crush, Ward's Orange Crush, Lemon Crush, and Lime Crush, single-sided metal advertising sign with embossed lettering and bottles, 19¾" x 9¼", VG . $375.00 (B)

Orange Drink, wooden advertising barrel with painted on lettering, 14" x 20", G . . . .$75.00 (B)

Orange-Julep, cardboard hang-up sign, featuring artwork of man and woman drinking from a single bottle with two straws, 1930s, 7¾" x 11", G . . . .$95.00 (C)

Orange-Julep... Drink, It's JULEP Time, bottle topper, G . . . .$55.00 (D)

Orange-Julep, Drink, metal serving tray, featuring girl at beach with umbrella, and holding a glass of Orange-Julep, G . . . .$130.00 (B)

Orange Julius, A Devilish Good Drink, with artwork of devil figure in center, rare, 1920s, 24" x 35", F . . . . .$300.00 (C)

Orange Kist, metal and tin cooler, "Drink Orange Kist," 31" x 22" x 31", VG . . . .$350.00 (B)

Orcico, cigar tin litho container with graphics of Indian on front, advertising 2 for 5¢, 6" x 5½" x 4", 1919, EX . . . .$350.00 (B)

Oregon Association of Nurserymen, double-sided porcelain member sign, 18½" x 15¼", NM . . . .$145.00 (B)

Oregon Winter Sports Association, embossed tin advertising license plate attachment with graphics of ski jumper in action, 12" x 5", 1942, F . . . .$100.00 (D)

Original Hoffman House Rye, stone litho paper advertising sign with graphics of nudes cavorting around Satyr, in original stamped wood frame, "Buckeye Distillery Co.," 24½" x 32½", EX . . . .$1,025.00 (B)

Oshkosh R.R. Suits, Union Made, reverse painted glass in wood frame, featuring good graphics of oil worker at left side of sign, 48¼" x 18½", P . . . .$100.00 (C)

Oshkosh Work Clothes, octagonal neon clock, 1930s, EX . . . .$375.00 (B)

Our Advertiser Smoking Tobacco, bag with OCB papers, G . . . .$8.00 (D)

Our Game, cigar box, with great graphics of vintage baseball game, scarce item, 1900s, EX . . . . $750.00 (C)

Our Hobby Sliced Plug, Taylor & Co., Burlington, VT, early tin litho pocket tin, rare, 4⅝" x 2¾" x ⅞", EX . .$300.00 (B)

Our Jewel Roasted Coffee, Ericsson's Mills, New York, tin litho with knob handle top, graphics of young child in cameo on front, scarce, 1-lb., G . . . . $159.00 (B)

Our Mutual Friends, cigar box, wood box with paper litho labels that shows 3 young boys, 8¼" x 4¾" x 2¼", VG . . . .$170.00 (B)

Ovaltine, tin litho advertising sign, "For Health Strength and Energy," 12" x 18", G . . . .$300.00 (B)

Overholt Whiskey, advertising tin in wood frame with a metal slug plate that says "It's Old Overholt" with graphics of field scene with folks and dog, 36½" x 27¼", VG . . . .$1,000.00 (B)

Overland Co. Garage, painted tin service sign, 23½" x 12", EX . . . .$175.00 (D)

Owl Cigars, cardboard double-sided die cut string hanger, 7" x 9½", F . . . .$125.00 (D)

Ox-Heart Cocoa, porcelain push plate promoting Dutch Process Cocoa, 4" x 6½", EX . . . .$175.00 (D)

Ozark Mountain Spring Water...Drink Million Smiles, embossed tin "tacker" style sign, 20" x 9", G . $95.00 (C)

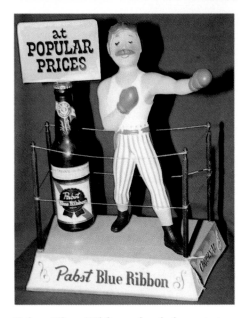

Pabst Blue Ribbon, back bar statue featuring boxer in ring with bottle, NM, **$145.00 (C).** *Courtesy of Pleasant Hill Antique Mall & Tea Room/Bob Johnson*

Pabst Blue Ribbon Beer, advertising cardboard poster, framed, waiter in uniform carrying a tray of beer and glasses, older version, 26½" x 36", EX, **$675.00 (C).**

Pabst Blue Ribbon Beer, menu board, new, NM, **$45.00 (C).** *Courtesy of B.J. Summers*

Pabst Beer, die cut cardboard sign in shape of beer bottle, easel back, 9½" x 32", EX . . . .**$25.00 (B)**

Pabst Beer, sign with artwork of Spanish-American war heroes around table celebrating with product, 1899, EX . . . .**$610.00 (B)**

Pabst Blue Ribbon, back bar statue featuring boxer in ring with bottle, EX . . . .**$125.00 (D)**

Pabst Blue Ribbon Beer, advertising cardboard poster, framed, waiter in uniform carrying a tray of beer and glasses, older version, 26½" x 36", G . . . .**$225.00 (C)**

Pabst Blue Ribbon Beer, advertising tin sign, "at popular prices...6 for...," with graphics of PBR can at bottom, 26" x 60", EX . . . .**$75.00 (C)**

Pabst Blue Ribbon Beer...at popular prices, painted tin sign with artwork of beer can with message at top, 26" x 60", EX . . . .**$95.00 (C)**

Pabst Blue Ribbon Beer, cardboard advertising sign with graphics of black waiter with tray, 24" x 33¼", 1931, EX . . . .**$375.00 (C)**

Pabst Blue Ribbon beer, cardboard litho advertising sign with graphics of black waiter, 30" x 39½", 1938, VG . .**$275.00 (B)**

Pabst Blue Ribbon Beer, menu board, new, EX . .**$35.00 (D)**

Pabst Blue Ribbon Beer, molded plastic advertising light-up clock, 17" dia., VG . . . .**$80.00 (B)**

Pabst Blue Ribbon...Old Time Beer Flavor, light-up motion train, EX . . . .**$275.00 (C)**

Pabst Blue Ribbon, serving tray, Pabst Brewing Company, Milwaukee, Wisc., EX . . . .**$12.00 (D)**

Pabst Blue Ribbon, tin litho advertising sign with graphics of Rip Van Winkle "The Beer that brings back Memories," 17½" x 11½", EX . . . .**$200.00 (D)**

Pabst Brewing Co., match safe, metal with embossing on both sides of advertising, 1½" x 2⁹⁄₁₀", VG . . .**$225.00 (C)**

Pabst Brewing Co., paper litho pre-Prohibition advertising sign with graphics of worker elves tapping into a barrel of the product in the factory storage cellar, 34¾" x 26¾", G . . . .**$1,100.00 (C)**

Pabst Blue Ribbon...Old Time Beer
Flavor, light-up motion train, G,
$155.00 (C). *Courtesy of B.J. Summers*

Pabst Brewing Co., paper litho pre-Prohibition advertising
sign with graphics of worker elves tapping into a barrel of the
product in the factory storage cellar, 34¾" x 26¾", EX,
$2,700.00 (B). *Courtesy of Wm. Morford Investment Grade Collectibles*

Pabst's, Okay Specific Medicinal Remedy, embossed tin
sign, 6" x 9", EX, $85.00 (B). *Courtesy of Muddy River Trading Co./Gary Metz*

Pabst, display, plaster composition of young lady with a
bonnet with inset for bottle of product, 9½" x 4" x 11½",
VG . . . .$90.00 (B)

Pabst Extract, cardboard and paper calendar with
graphics of woman with yellow scarf, 1917, 7¼" x 36",
NM . . . .$380.00 (B)

Pabst Extract, yard-long American Girl, in long dress
with top strip, bottom strip missing, 1914, 35½" L,
EX . . . .$100.00 (B)

Pabst, neon window sign, 21" x 19", EX . . . . .$80.00 (B)

Pabst's, Okay Specific Medicinal Remedy, embossed tin
sign, 6" x 9", F . . . .$35.00 (C)

Pacific Coast Steamship Co., round metal tip tray with
company flag in tray center, 3⅝" dia., EX . . . .$75.00 (B)

Pacific Inter-Mountain Express, advertising calendar, tin
over cardboard with tear sheets at bottom and artwork of
truck at top, 12½" x 19", G . . . .$130.00 (B)

Page Baby Talc, tin litho container with graphics of woman
holding baby on front label, 4½" T, EX . . . . . .$375.00 (C)

Pall Mall, Menthol 100s, in green, unopened pack, 20-count, EX, $8.00 (D). *Courtesy of Chief Paduke Antiques Mall*

Pall Mall, wooden countertop display rack, with debossed message on each side, dovetailed joints, EX, $115.00 (D). *Courtesy of Chief Paduke Antiques Mall*

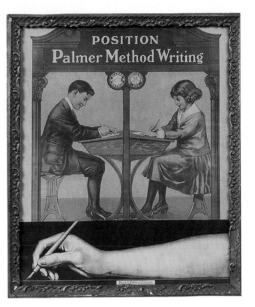

Palmer Method Writing Position, paper litho featuring two children at their desks, 17¾" x 21⅝", VG, $155.00 (B).

Pan-Am Ink Blotters, "Keep Pace with Pan-Am Gasoline," 6¼" x 3", EX, $160.00 (B).

Patterson Sargent Paint, die cut porcelain advertising sign "For Better Results," 33" x 24", NM, $75.00 (B).

Page Borated Baby Talc, tin litho container with graphics of woman with baby, 2½" x 1¼" x 4½", EX ...$45.00 (C)

Palace Brand Coffee, tin litho, slip-lid container with graphics of Winter Carnival Ice Palace, from Atwood & Co., Minneapolis, 3-lb., G ....$236.00 (B)

Pal Ade, tin door push, EX ....$75.00 (B)

Paladin, lunch box with graphics of Paladin on horseback, 1960s, EX ....$65.00 (B)

Palethorpes Royal Cambridge sausage, single-sided porcelain, foreign advertising sign, 36" x 24", EX ..$325.00 (B)

Pallas Peanut Butter, pail, tin litho with wire bail handle, Kansas City, MO, with slip-lid, EX ....$95.00 (C)

Pall Mall Cigarette, tin sign with pin-up girl, same set-up used in Lucky Strike advertisement, 1950s, 15" x 21", EX ....$230.00 (B)

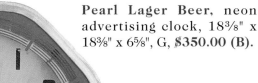

Pearl Lager Beer, neon advertising clock, 18⅜" x 18⅜" x 6⅝", G, $350.00 (B).

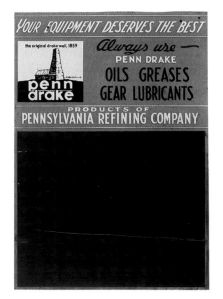

Penn Drake, one-sided tin chalkboard, 19⅜" x 27½", G, $130.00 (B).

Pennsylvania Rubber Co., Jeannette, PA, non-skid with CV logo, ashtray in vaseline glass, NM, $145.00 (D). *Courtesy of Antiques, Cards & Collectibles/Ray Pelley*

Pennsylvania Rubber Company, Jeannette, PA, paper litho advertising their oil-proof tires with artwork of pretty woman with hat, "Euphemia" under artwork, 25¼" x 35½", VG, $400.00 (B). *Courtesy of Collectors Auction Services*

Pall Mall Cigars, paper litho advertising poster by Currier & Ives featuring artwork of two black sailors dancing on a vintage sailboat, "The Pall Mall Yacht Club-On the Winning Tac," 19¼" x 17¼", 1885, G . . . .$325.00 (D)

Pall Mall Cigars, paper litho advertising sign by Currier & Ives of the Pall Mall Yacht Club "The Cup Secure," 15" x 11½", 1885, VG . . . .$245.00 (B)

Pall Mall, Menthol 100s, in green, unopened pack, 20-count, EX . . . .$8.00 (D)

Pall Mall, wooden countertop display rack, with debossed message on each side, dovetailed joints, EX . . . .$115.00 (D)

Pall Mall, wooden countertop display store rack, with paper message at top, Streamlined for better smoking...A Cooler Smoother Smoke, debossed sides, EX . .$95.00 (D)

Palm Cigars, embossed tin advertising sign from the De Nobili Cigar Company, Long Island City, N.Y., 19" x 6", EX . . . .$35.00 (C)

Palmer House Key West Cigars, round glass paperweight, graphics of crown in center, 3" x 1½", EX . . . .$50.00 (B)

Palmer's Root Beer, barrel sign, NOS, 19" x 14", NM . . . .$375.00 (C)

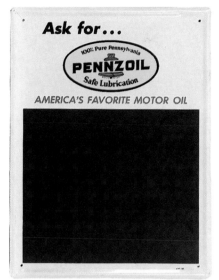

Pennzoil Lubrication, chalkboard, self-framing tin, 17½" x 24", EX, $125.00 (B).

Pennzoil...Safe Lubrication, with early brown bell in center, metal lollipop sign with original heavy embossed stand, 1920s, G, $675.00 (D). *Courtesy of Illinois Antique Center/Kim & Dan Phillips*

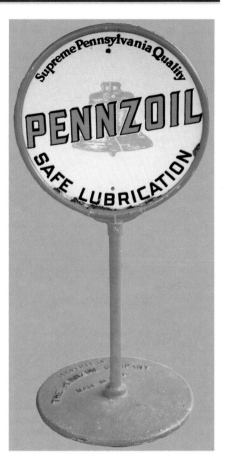

Pepsi...Be Sociable...Serve, cardboard poster with woman in hat holding six-pack in palm with bottle cap logo at left, double-sided, 36" x 24¾", VG, $145.00 (C).

Palmer Tires, advertising sign with graphics of pretty woman in bonnet, 19¾" x 28", VG ....$525.00 (C)

Pan American Airlines, advertising table lighter, EX ....$100.00 (C)

Pan-American Airlines, hat box with artwork of airplanes on all sides, 11½" x 14" x 6¾", EX ....$175.00 (B)

Pan American Exposition, clock by C.F. Chouffer, Jeweler Buffalo, NY, with graphics of scantily clad young ladies, in shape of frying pan, 6" x 11½", EX ....$145.00 (B)

Pan-Am Motor Oils, one-sided porcelain pump sign, 15" dia., VG ....$425.00 (B)

Panhandle, gas globe, low profile body with two glass lenses, 15" dia., VG ....$1,100.00 (B)

Pan-Handle Scrap Tobacco, tin litho from Currier & Ives with graphics of black rolling the dice while the cops wait to make a bust, 1890s, EX ....$490.00 (B)

Paraland, gas globe, plastic body with two glass lenses, 16½" x 5½" x 12½", VG ....$300.00 (B)

Park Brewing Co., advertising charger sign with image of game birds and products in foreground on table, 24" dia., EX ....$751.00 (B)

Parke Davis Wormwood Drug, tin with turn-of-the-century drug house graphics on all four sides, 1900s, 4½" x 4" x 9", EX ....$77.00 (B)

Parker Bros., picture puzzle, "The Darktown Fancy Ball" with graphics of black people in horse-drawn sleigh, 9⅜" x 7¾" x 1¼", 1890s, EX ....$575.00 (B)

Parker Brothers, Inc., Touring...Improved Edition, automobile card game, in original package, complete, G . .$15.00 (D)

Parker Pen, light-up display, wood and glass with original key, 20½" x 9" x 9", EX ....$85.00 (B)

Parker's Foot Powder, tin litho on container with graphics of foot on front, 2-oz., EX ....$35.00 (C)

Pepsi-Cola...Buy...Here, oval tin double-sided flange metal advertising sign, 16" x 12", VG, **$550.00 (B).** *Courtesy of Autopia Advertising Auctions*

Pepsi-Cola, Bigger Better, painted tin advertising thermometer with graphics of double dot bottle at right of scale, 6¼" x 15¾", NM, **$475.00 (B).** *Courtesy of Autopia Advertising Auctions*

Pepsi-Cola, Double Size, store display featuring a die cut cardboard stand that holds a paper label 12-oz. Pepsi bottle, NOS, 6½" x 13½", EX, **$380.00 (B).** *Courtesy of Autopia Advertising Auctions*

Pepsi-Cola, chain-hung reverse glass mirror with cap logo, 1950s, 9½" dia., G, **$130.00 (B).** *Courtesy of Muddy River Trading Co./Gary Metz*

Parke's Newport Coffee, tin litho can with graphics of factory scene on front cameo, with pry-lid, 1-lb., EX . . .**$130.00 (B)**

Parrot & Monkey Baking Powder, cardboard container with tin top and bottom with paper label with graphics of trademark monkey and parrot, 2½" x 5", EX .**$215.00 (B)**

Par-t-pak...full flavor...Beverages, self-framing metal advertising sign, 52" x 34", VG . . . .**$95.00 (C)**

Pastum...J. Sarubi, hair dressing, double-sided tin litho flange sign, 18½" x 7", EX . . . .**$83.00 (B)**

Pate Challenge, pump sign, single-sided porcelain, with graphics of shield, 12" x 15", VG . . . .**$450.00 (B)**

Patterson Sargent Paint, die cut porcelain advertising sign "For Better Results," 33" x 24", EX . . . .**$65.00 (C)**

Patterson's Recut Tobacco, 10¢ value for 5 cents, paper sign with product image on both sides of message in center, 36" x 18", NM . . . .**$55.00 (B)**

Paul Jones & Co. Whiskey, rolled tin sign, "The Temptation of St. Anthony," with graphics of woman with a watermelon and a man holding a bottle of the product, 19½" x 13½", VG . . . .**$550.00 (B)**

Paul Jones Havana Cigars, tin litho, wood grained, self-framing with cameo of Paul Jones in center, also self-framed, this type sign is difficult to find, 20" x 24", EX . . . .**$725.00 (B)**

Paul Jones, paper litho on wood advertising sign with black woman with watermelon and older gentleman with bottle, VG . . . .**$275.00 (B)**

Pepsi-Cola, die cut bottle sign, 1930s, 12" x 45", EX, **$625.00 (B).** *Courtesy of Muddy River Trading Co./Gary Metz*

Pepsi-Cola, die cut cardboard advertising sign with graphics of couple enjoying the product, 16¾" x 22½", EX, **$200.00 (B).** *Courtesy of Autopia Advertising Auctions*

Pepsi-Cola, die cut cardboard sign, 1930s, 21" x 15", EX, **$375.00 (B).**
Courtesy of Muddy River Trading Co./Gary Metz

Paul Jones Pure Gin, tin litho advertising sign with graphics of young boys at a split rail fence, 13¼" x 19½", 1905, EX . . . .**$550.00 (B)**

Paul Jones whiskey, litho by H.D. Beach, a big name in early advertising, featuring old gent with bottle and glass, "Comrades for 81 years," 1903, EX . . . .**$525.00 (C)**

Paul Jones, wooden advertising sign promoting Rye Whiskey with graphics of black family, 20" x 13¾", 1900s, EX . . . .**$475.00 (C)**

Pay Car Scrap Tobacco, Chew...the best flavor, tin litho advertising sign with graphics of product package in center, 13¾" x 17¾", EX . . . .**$225.00 (D)**

Peachy, vertical pocket tin with graphics of peach in bloom, VG . . . .**$160.00 (B)**

Peacock Condom, tin litho container with artwork of peacock in full feathers, 1⅝" x ⅝", EX . . . .**$250.00 (B)**

Peacock Condom, tin with graphics of peacock with his tail feathers spread, 1½" dia. x ¾", EX . . . .**$65.00 (C)**

Peacock Ice Cream, Cleveland Indians tin license plate attachment with graphics of Indian on attachment, 9⅞" x 4¾", EX . . . .**$155.00 (C)**

Peak Coffee, packed for Independent Grocers Alliance Dist. Co., Chicago, Ill., EX . . . .**$35.00 (D)**

Pearless Majestic...American Brewing Co., Phil., round metal tip tray with see, hear, and speak no evil monkeys artwork, 4¼" dia., EX . . . .**$185.00 (B)**

Pearl Oil...We Sell...Heat and Light, string-hung advertising sign with graphics of family in warm well-lit house, 10⅜" x 14", EX . . . .**$135.00 (C)**

Pepsi-Cola, Drink...Delicious Heathful, script hat pin on emblem for employee, EX, $50.00 (D). *Courtesy of Antiques, Cards & Collectibles/Ray Pelley*

Pepsi-Cola, door pull handle, 2¾" x 12", EX, $210.00 (B). *Courtesy of Muddy River Trading Co./Gary Metz*

Pepsi-Cola...Drink, Double Size 5¢, double-sided hand-stenciled canvas banner, rare piece, 1930s, G, $275.00 (B). *Courtesy of Muddy River Trading Co./Gary Metz*

Pepsi-Cola...Drink, fan, 1912, 8" x 9", G, $1,000.00 (B). *Courtesy of Muddy River Trading Co./Gary Metz*

Pear's Soap, advertising framed paper sign with graphics of young child sitting on towel, 9½" x 14", 1910s, EX . . . .$85.00 (C)

Pear's Soap, center magazine plate, with graphics of youngster in countertop bathing tub, 15½" x 10¼", 1909, EX . . . .$50.00 (B)

Pear's Soap, paper die cut sign of woman scrubbing child's ear, 5½" x 9½", EX . . . .$141.00 (B)

Pear's Soap, paper die cut sign of young child trying to climb out of wash tub, 10" x 6¼", EX . . . . . .$135.00 (C)

Pedro Smoking Tobacco Cut Plug, tin pail, Wm. S. Kimball & Co., The American Tobacco Co., F . . . .$35.00 (D)

Pedro Tobacco, cut plug tobacco bag with graphics on both sides, full opened bags, 2¾" x 4¼" x ⅞", G . . . .$230.00 (B)

Peerless Tobacco, canister, tin litho pail with wire handles, factory scene on front, NM . . . .$110.00 (B)

Peerless Weighing Machine Co., curved porcelain penny scale sign, "Did you weigh yourself today," 5½" x 9", G . . . .$170.00 (B)

Pepsi-Cola...Drink Iced, self-framed painted tin sign, 55" x 17½", NM, $850.00 (C).

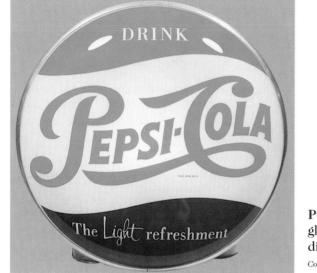

Pepsi-Cola, 5¢, embossed painted tin sign...America's Biggest Nickel's Worth, 40" x 12", VG, $600.00 (B). *Courtesy of Collectors Auction Services*

Pepsi-Cola, Drink...The Light Refreshment, glass light-up sign with convex glass, 1950S, 16" dia., NM, $1,350.00 (B). *Courtesy of Muddy River Trading Co./Gary Metz*

Peerless Weighing Machine Co., curved porcelain sign off penny scale, "Did you weigh yourself today," 5½" x 9", EX . . . .$230.00 (B)

Pegasus, light-up advertising clock with artwork of the flying horse on the clock face, metal body with glass face and front, 15" dia., EX . . . .$500.00 (B)

Pegasus, die cut one-sided porcelain sign in shape of the winged horse, 44" L, G . . . .$1,100.00 (B)

Peg Top...The Old Reliable, porcelain advertising door push with graphics of cigar, 4" x 12½", EX . . .$135.00 (D)

Peg Top, The Old Reliable, metal door push, 4" x 12½", EX . . . .$150.00 (C)

Peidmont Cigarettes, porcelain advertising sign with graphics of cigarette pack in center of sign, 30" x 49", VG . . . .$155.00 (C)

Peidmont Cigarettes, tin litho advertising sign with scene of George Washington at Mount Vernon, from Liggett & Myer Co., 30" x 24", 1911, EX . . . .$1,000.00 (B)

Penn City Motor Oil, can with graphics of the old Quaker on the front, 2-gal., EX . . . .$175.00 (C)

Penn-Drake Motor Oil, embossed tin sign with image of well tower at left of message, 27¾" x 9¾", NM $280.00 (B)

Pennsey Select Beer, tin litho tip tray with graphics of young serving woman with bottle, 4¼" dia. VG . . . . .$125.00 (C)

Penn's Spells Quality, tin box, metal with hinged lid, 6½" W x 2½"H x 6½"D, G . . . .$330.00 (B)

Pennsylvania Motor Oil...100% Pure, early tin container, 8-qt., EX . . . .$110.00 (B)

Pennsylvania Railroad, "convoy yard" graphics at top with tear sheets at bottom, 28½" x 28½", 1958, EX . .$35.00 (C)

Pennsylvania Railroad...Conway Yard, paper calendar with 3-month tear sheets at bottom with artwork of rail-yards at top, 1958, G . . . .$55.00 (C)

Pennsylvania Railroad...Dynamic Progress, paper calendar, no pad, artwork at top of modern train passing piggy-back freight traffic, 1956, G . . . .$25.00 (C)

Pepsi-Cola, Hot Dogs Hamburgers, Ice Cold Bigger – Better, 5¢, embossed tin sidewalk sign, 1930s, 20" x 28", G, $325.00 (B).

Courtesy of Muddy River Trading Co./Gary Metz

Pepsi-Cola...Ice Cold...Hits The Spot, metal salesman sample box cooler with embossed bottle caps on lid & sides, logo on front, rare item, NM, $3,200.00 (D). *Courtesy of Rare Bird Antique Mall/Jon & Joan Wright*

Pennsylvania Railroad...Mass Transportation, paper calendar with 3-month tear sheets at bottom of artwork, 1955, EX . . . .$55.00 (C)

Pennsylvania Railroad...Vital Lines To The World..., paper calendar with 3-month tear sheets at bottom, artwork of ship/rail loading facility, 1957, G . . . . .$45.00 (C)

Pennsylvania Rubber Co., Jeannette, PA, non-skid with CV logo, ashtray in vaseline glass, EX . . . . . .$125.00 (D)

Pennsylvania Rubber Company, Jeannette, Pa., paper litho advertising their oil-proof tires with artwork of pretty woman with hat, "Euphemia" under artwork, 25¼" x 35½", F . . . .$210.00 (D)

Penn Tobacco Co., tin litho pocket tin advertising Honey Moon Tobacco, 3" x 4½" x ⅞", EX . . . .$1,950.00 (B)

Penny Post Cut Plug, tin pail with wire handle, good bright colors, EX . . . .$275.00 (C)

Pennzip, gas globe, wide body, 13½" , G . . . .$500.00 (B)

Pennzoil, five-quart tin with the airplane graphics, 5-qt, EX . . . .$125.00 (B)

Pennzoil...Get Protection Reserve...Motor Oil, dial-type thermometer, with message in center, metal body, glass front, 12" dia., EX . . . .$145.00 (C)

Pennzoil, metal lubster sign, 9½" x 3⅞", VG . .$175.00 (C)

Pennzoil...Safe Lubrication, oval porcelain sign with bell in center, 62" x 35", black & orange on yellow, G . .$155.00 (C)

Pennzoil...safe lubrication, porcelain double-sided flange sign, still in original crate, 26½" x 26", VG .$2,500.00 (B)

Pennzoil...Safe Lubrication, with early brown bell in center, metal lollipop sign with original heavy embossed stand, 1920s, G . . . .$675.00 (D)

Pennzoil...Sound Your Z, vertical painted metal sign with logo at bottom, G . . . .$105.00 (D)

Pennzoil, tin oil can with graphics of logo owls and airplane, 1-qt., EX . . . .$80.00 (B)

Pensupreme Ice Cream, single-sided porcelain advertising sign with graphics of old Quaker at bottom, 24" x 13", G . . . .$300.00 (B)

Pep Boys, Handy Bulb Kit Tin, with graphics of the boys on the front, 4" x 2¼" x 2½", EX . . . .$45.00 (C)

Pepsi...Be sociable...Serve, cardboard poster with woman in hat holding six-pack in palm with bottle cap logo at left, double-sided, 36" x 24¾", G . . . .$125.00 (D)

Pepsi Cola Ice Cold, single-sided embossed tin advertising sign, 30½" x 27", G, $205.00 (B).

Pepsi-Cola, mechanical advertising display with image of monkey with can of Pepsi that spins when plugged in, 26" dia. x 37", VG, **$1,100.00 (B).** *Courtesy of Collectors Auction Services*

Pepsi-Cola, metal and glass light-up clock, with bottle cap in center, good strong colors, 9¼" x 12½", red, white, blue cap on yellow, VG, $145.00 (C).

Pepsi, cardboard ad in wood frame, hard-to-find piece even in less than perfect condition, 25" x 32", P . . . .$250.00 (C)

Pepsi-Cola, advertising 45 rpm record in original paper cover, with original mailing package, "Your Man In Service," EX . . . .$55.00 (D)

Pepsi-Cola...A nickel drink worth a dime, featuring artwork of early Pepsi bottle, fiberboard sign, 1930s, 12¾" x 14¾", G . . . .$140.00 (B)

Pepsi-Cola, animated cardboard boy and girl, EX . .$675.00 (C)

Pepsi-Cola, base for patrol boy, cast iron, 1950s, 24" dia., G . . . .$150.00 (B)

Pepsi-Cola, Bigger Better, painted metal door pull, 2¾" x 12", EX . . . .$190.00 (B)

Pepsi-Cola, Bigger Better, painted tin advertising thermometer with graphics of double dot bottle at right of scale, 6¼" x 15¾", VG . . . .$225.00 (C)

Pepsi-Cola...Bigger, Better, tin thermometer, 6¼" x 15¾", G . . . .$175.00 (D)

Pepsi-Cola, bottle radio, "Have a Pepsi," Bakelite construction, 24" T, 1940s, VG . . . .$135.00 (C)

Pepsi-Cola, bottle radio, resembles older paper label bottle, 24", 1940s, VG . . . .$425.00 (C)

Pepsi-Cola...Buy...Here, oval tin double-sided flange metal advertising sign, 16" x 12", VG . . . .$550.00 (B)

Pepsi-Cola...Buy Here, round cardboard sign, 21" dia., G . . . .$95.00 (C)

Pepsi-Cola, metal serving tray, 13¾" x 10⅜", G, $90.00 (B).

Pepsi-Cola, mileage chart, measuring mileage from Paducah, Ky., to various parts of the country, metal and plastic, 1950s, 7" x 31", yellow, white, and black, EX, $45.00 (C). *Courtesy of B.J. Summers*

Pepsi-Cola, self-framed cardboard sign featuring girl with lace hat and an early bottle of Pepsi-Cola, 1930s, 30" x 20", EX, $800.00 (B).

Courtesy of Muddy River Trading Co./Gary Metz

Pepsi-Cola, More Bounce to the Ounce, one-sided embossed tin, 57" x 33", G, $150.00 (B).

Pepsi-Cola...Buy...Here, round double-sided tin advertising flange sign, 17" x 16", EX . . . .$575.00 (B).

Pepsi-Cola, chain-hung reverse glass mirror with cap logo, 1950s, 9½" dia., EX . . . .$250.00 (D).

Pepsi-Cola, Coast to Coast, Bigger and Better, metal serving tray with artwork of United States map with Pepsi bottle, EX . . . .$410.00 (B).

Pepsi-Cola, cooler radio, 1950s, EX . . . .$350.00 (C).

Pepsi-Cola, cooler, slider in original Pepsi colors with logo on left side of front, 31" x 20" x 32", VG . . . . .$200.00 (B).

Pepsi-Cola, die cut bottle sign, 1930s, 12" x 45", F . . . .$125.00 (D).

Pepsi-Cola, die cut cardboard advertising sign with graphics of couple enjoying the product, 16¾" x 22½", G . . . .$135.00 (C).

Pepsi-Cola, die cut cardboard sign, older cardboard 6-pack, 1930s, 21" x 15", VG . . . .$275.00 (D).

Pepsi-Cola, die cut tin embossed bottle cap advertising sign, in double dot style, 13¼" x 17⅞", EX . . .$325.00 (C).

Pepsi-Cola, door pull handle, 2¾" x 12", VG . .$175.00 (C).

Pepsi-Cola, double dot light-up advertising clock, by Telechron, 15" dia., 1940s, NM . . . .$425.00 (C).

Pepsi-Cola, double-sided porcelain advertising sign, "Hit the spot," 56" x 23", G . . . .$700.00 (B).

Pepsi-Cola, double-sided wood advertising sign with "Drink...," 23¼" x 18½", VG . . . .$30.00 (B).

Pepsi-Cola...Drink, bottle cap button sign, embossed tin, Stout Sign Co., St. Louis, Mo., Made In U.S.A., M-104, 30" dia., G . . . .$250.00 (B).

Pepsi-Cola ...think young, Say Pepsi please, glass under glass light-up clock, 1955, EX, $800.00 (B). *Courtesy of Muddy River Trading Co./Gary Metz*

Pepsi-Cola, syrup dispenser, rare and hard-to-find, 1900s, EX, $3,700.00 (B). *Courtesy of Muddy River Trading Co./Gary Metz*

Pepsi. . . Have a. . ., double-sided porcelain advertising sign, 28" x 25½", G, $140.00 (B).

Pepsi-Cola, Drink, countertop light-up sign, 1950s, 14" dia., EX . . . .$175.00 (B)

Pepsi-Cola, Drink...Delicious Delightful, embossed tin sign, 1910s, 3½" x 9¾", EX . . . .$275.00 (B)

Pepsi-Cola, Drink...Delicious Heathful, script hat pin on emblem for employee, VG . . . .$40.00 (D)

Pepsi-Cola...Drink, Double Size 5¢, double-sided hand-stenciled canvas banner, rare piece, 1930s, P . $75.00 (C)

Pepsi-Cola...Drink, fan, 1912, 8" x 9", EX .$2,000.00 (C)

Pepsi-Cola...Drink...5¢, embossed painted metal sign, self-framing, 58½" x 36", G . . . .$125.00 (D)

Pepsi-Cola, Drink...Ice-Cold, plastic bottle cap light-up sign, 1950s, 16" dia., EX . . . .$500.00 (B)

Pepsi-Cola, Drink Iced, porcelain store sign, 60" x 36", G . . . .$475.00 (C)

Pepsi-Cola...Drink Iced, self-framed painted tin sign, 55" x 17½", EX . . . .$750.00 (C)

Pepsi-Cola, Drink, metal self-framing sign, with the price 5¢, 1950s, 40" x 34", F . . . .$330.00 (D)

Pepsi-Cola...Drink, self-framing painted tin sign with bottle cap graphics in center of sign, G . . . .$1,150.00 (D)

Pepsi-Cola, Drink...The Light Refreshment, glass light-up sign with convex glass, 1950S, 16" dia., EX $1,250.00 (B)

Pepsi-Cola, embossed tin advertising sign, "Drink...5¢," 58½" x 36", EX . . . .$195.00 (D)

Pepsi-Cola, embossed tin advertising sign in shape of bottle cap, 19¼" dia., NM . . . .$200.00 (B)

Pepsi-Cola, embossed tin die cut bottle sign in double dot pattern, NOS, 8" x 29½", NM . . . .$475.00 (C)

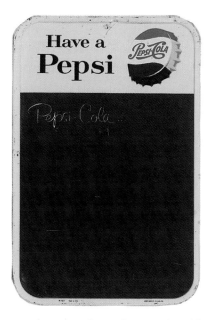

Pepsi menu board, metal self-framing with bottle top, graphics at top, 20" x 30", G, **$85.00 (B).**

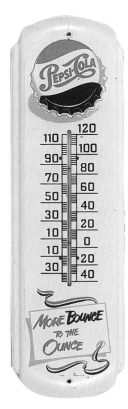

Pepsi, painted metal advertising thermometer, "More Bounce to the Ounce," 8" x 27", VG, **$250.00 (B).**

Pepsi, painted metal sidewalk or curb sign with original metal base, Stout Sign Co., St. Louis, MO, 24" x 50½", VG, **$450.00 (B).** *Courtesy of Collectors Auction Services*

Pepsi-Cola, embossed tin litho advertising sign, "Drink...Delicious Delightful," 1910, NM . . . .**$395.00 (C)**

Pepsi-Cola, embossed tin sign, 1950s, 3½" x 4", EX . . . .**$100.00 (B)**

Pepsi-Cola, figural bottle opener, metal, "America's biggest Nickel's Worth," 2¾" L, 1930s, G . . . . .**$40.00 (B)**

Pepsi-Cola, 5¢ embossed painted tin sign...America's Biggest Nickel's Worth, 40" x 12", VG . . . .**$600.00 (B)**

Pepsi-Cola, fountain dispenser radio, 1950s, EX . .**$675.00 (C)**

Pepsi-Cola, glass with syrup line and double dot, NM . . . .**$25.00 (C)**

Pepsi-Cola, glass with syrup line, "Hits The Spot," NM . . . .**$55.00 (C)**

Pepsi-Cola...Have a Pepsi, plastic and metal fountain counter dispenser, EX . . . .**$250.00 (D)**

Pepsi-Cola, hits the spot, calendar, complete with full pad, featuring girl with bottle, 1941, 15" x 23", NM . .**$340.00 (B)**

Pepsi-Cola, Hot Dogs Hamburgers Ice Cold Bigger Better, 5¢, embossed tin sidewalk sign, 1930s, 20" x 28", EX .**$475.00 (C)**

Pepsi-Cola, Hot Popcorn, foil-backed sign, G .**$95.00 (B)**

Pepsi-Cola...Ice Cold...Hits The Spot, metal salesman sample box cooler with embossed bottle caps on lid & sides, logo on front, rare item, EX . . . .**$2,500.00 (D)**

Pepsi-Cola, Ice Cold, salesman sample cooler, rare and hard-to-find, G . . . .**$1,200.00 (C)**

Pepsi-Cola, Ice Cold, Sold Here, celluloid sign, 9" dia., EX . . . .**$250.00 (B)**

Pepsi-Cola, light-up advertising clock, metal and glass Telechron, 15½" dia., EX . . . .**$505.00 (B)**

Pepsi, "The light refreshment," light-up plastic clock, 1950s, NM, $600.00 (B). *Courtesy of Muddy River Trading Co./Gary Metz*

Pepsodent, die cut cardboard litho of Andy holding tube of product, "Um! Um! Ain't dis sumpin," 22½" x 62", 1930s, VG, $925.00 (B). *Courtesy of Collectors Auction Services*

Permit to smoke, a good cigar, framed litho advertisement, 1910s, 25" x 31½", EX, $250.00 (B)

Pepsi-Cola, light-up bottle cap, 16" dia., EX . $575.00 (C)

Pepsi-Cola, light-up clock with bottle cap in the center and yellow face, 1970s, EX . . . .$325.00 (B)

Pepsi-Cola, mechanical advertising display with image of monkey with can of Pepsi that spins when plugged in, 26" dia. x 37", F . . . .$325.00 (C)

Pepsi-Cola, mechanical seal distributor display unit, seal moves as if balancing the Pepsi-colored ball on his nose, 37" x 39" x 40", VG . . . .$1,675.00 (B)

Pepsi-Cola, menu board, tin litho with self-framing sides, 19½" x 30", 1930s, EX . . . .$250.00 (C)

Pepsi-Cola, metal and glass light-up clock, with bottle cap in center, good strong colors, 9¼" x 12½", red, white, blue cap on yellow, EX . . . .$160.00 (D)

Pepsi Cola, metal body light-up advertising clock with glass face and cover, "Say Pepsi please," with gold outside ring and white face, 16" sq., VG . . . .$190.00 (B)

Pepsi-Cola, mileage chart, measuring mileage from Paducah, Ky., to various parts of the country, metal and plastic, 1950s, 7" x 31", yellow, white, and black, VG . .$35.00 (C)

Pepsi-Cola, More Bounce to the Ounce, celluloid sign, 9" dia., EX . . . .$225.00 (B)

Pepsi-Cola...More Bounce to the Ounce, painted tin sign with bottle breaking through sign beside bottle cap logo to right of message, unusual and hard-to-find, 36" x 14", G . . . .$195.00 (C)

Pepsi-Cola, round tip tray, "The Pepsin Drink," 6" round, VG . . . .$140.00 (D)

Perry's Quality Beverages, triple filtered, nothing finer, tin door push, EX, $55.00 (B). *Courtesy of Muddy River Trading Co./Gary Metz*

Peters Cartridge, wooden case with black debossed lettering, 8½" x 14½" x 7⅛", G, $65.00 (B).

Peter Pan Ice Cream, embossed tin sign, 23½" x 32", G, $350.00 (B).

Peters Diamond Brand Shoes, embossed single-sided tin sign, 23½" x 12", G, $25.00 (B).

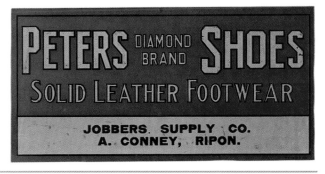

Pepsi-Cola...say Pepsi please, double-bubble light-up advertising clock, made by Advertising Products, 15" dia., NM . . . .$825.00 (C)

Pepsi-Cola... say Pepsi please, plastic and metal light-up clock, 16" x 16", G . . . .$125.00 (C)

Pepsi-Cola...say please, with facsimile of glass of Pepsi in snow, 1970s, EX . . . .$65.00 (B)

Pepsi-Cola, self-framed cardboard sign featuring girl with lace hat and an early bottle of Pepsi-Cola, 1930s, 30" x 20", G . . . .$300.00 (D)

Pepsi-Cola, serving tray, featuring girl with glass of Pepsi, 1908, EX . . . .$2,900.00 (C)

Pepsi-Cola, serving tray featuring tilted bottle over a map of the US, rectangular, 1939, EX . . . .$425.00 (C)

Pepsi-Cola, serving tray, 12" dia., G . . . .$150.00 (C)

Pepsi-Cola, single case countertop store rack, 1930s, EX . . . .$500.00 (B)

Pepsi-Cola, small milk glass tray, about the correct size for a tip tray, 4¼" x 3¼", EX . . . .$200.00 (B)

Pepsi-Cola, stand-up cardboard advertising of girl with product, easel back, 1940s, 20" x 15", EX . . .$775.00 (C)

Pepsi-Cola, store countertop display with Pepsi and Pete and early bottle, 12" x 13½", EX . . . .$290.00 (B)

Pepsi-Cola, straws in original unopened box with graphics of 5¢ bottle, NM . . . .$540.00 (B)

Pepsi-Cola, syrup dispenser, rare, and hard-to-find, 1900s, EX . . . .$3,700.00 (B)

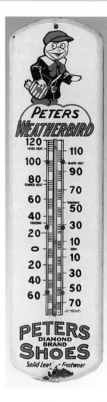

Peters Weatherbird Shoes, procelain thermometer, 1915, 7" x 27", VG, $160.00 (B).

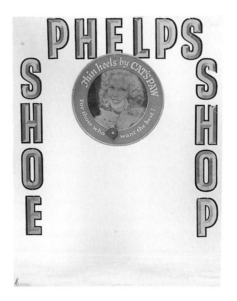

Phelps Shoe Shop, glass window sign, graphics of pretty lady with cats, for Cat's Paw Heels, 27¼" x 35¼", G, $175.00 (C).

Philco, die cut cardboard standup advertising sign, featuring Don McNeill of the "Breakfast Club" showing all the features of the refrigerator, 1940s, 32" x 64", G, $35.00 (C).

Pepsi-Cola, "The Light Refreshment," metal and glass light-up advertising sign, 19" x 9" x 6½", 1950s, EX . .$195.00 (D)

Pepsi-Cola...the Light Refreshment, scale thermometer with graphics of bottle cap at top of scale, embossed lettering, 7¼" x 27¼", EX . . . .$195.00 (C)

Pepsi-Cola ...think young, Say Pepsi please, glass under glass light-up clock, 1955, G . . . .$400.00 (C)

Pepsi-Cola, tip tray featuring Gipson Girl at soda fountain with glass of Pepsi, 1909, VG . . . .$1,200.00 (B)

Pepsi-Cola, tip tray featuring woman with glass of Pepsi, 9½" x 9¾", 1908, NM . . . .$3,000.00 (C)

Pepsi-Cola, trolley car sign, featuring boy and girl with early bottles of Pepsi, 28" x 11", EX . . . .$240.00 (B)

Pepsi-Cola, upright vending machine radio, 1960s, G . . . .$300.00 (C)

Pepsi...Enjoy, porcelain advertising sign with graphics of bottle cap at right, 29¼" x 12¼", NM . . . . . .$400.00 (B)

Pepsi...Enjoy, tin embossed menu board, 19¼" x 27¼", EX . . . .$165.00 (B)

Pepsi...it's got a lot to give, horizontal litho on cardboard with graphics of young couple enjoying a bottle of Pepsi, in original metal Pepsi frame, 37¼" x 25½", EX . .$110.00 (B)

Pepsi, painted metal sidewalk or curb sign with original metal base, Stout Sign Co., St. Louis, MO, 24" x 50½", VG . . . .$450.00 (B)

Pepsi...say "Pepsi" please, metal menu board, EX . .$45.00 (D)

Pepsi...Say...Please, tin easel back advertising sign with graphics of bottle of the product, 8½" x 12", EX .$110.00 (B)

Pepsi...say...please, vertical scale thermometer with message at top and logo at bottom, painted tin, red, white, yellow, and blue, EX . . . .$55.00 (C)

Pepsi, self-framing tin sign with graphics of bottle and cap, 17" x 47", VG . . . .$210.00 (B)

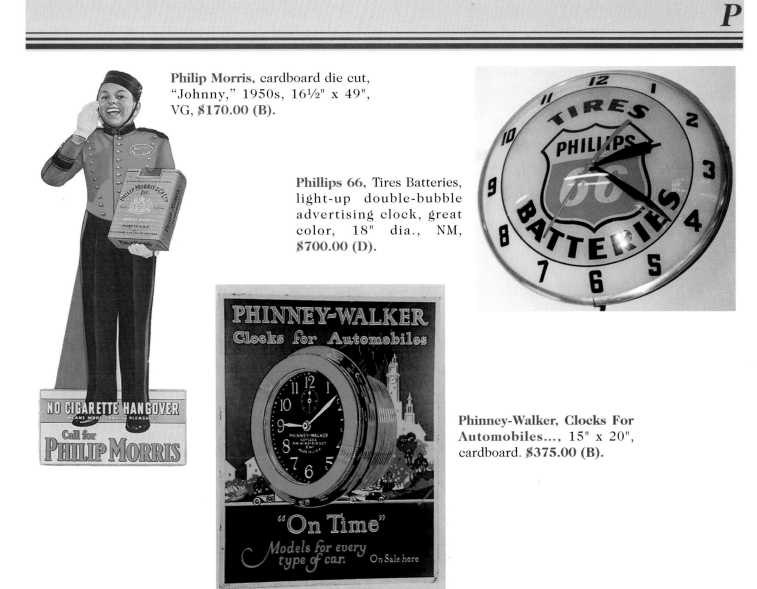

Philip Morris, cardboard die cut, "Johnny," 1950s, 16½" x 49", VG, $170.00 (B).

Phillips 66, Tires Batteries, light-up double-bubble advertising clock, great color, 18" dia., NM, $700.00 (D).

Phinney-Walker, Clocks For Automobiles..., 15" x 20", cardboard. $375.00 (B).

Pepsi, single-sided porcelain advertising sign, "enjoy" on bottle cap graphics in sign center, 29" x 12½", VG . .$125.00 (B)

Pepsi, single-sided self-framed metal advertising sign, "say Pepsi please" with graphics of bottle cap, 31" x 11½", VG . . . .$110.00 (B)

Pepsi, "The light refreshment," light-up plastic clock, 1950s, G . . . .$350.00 (C)

Pepsi...The light refreshment, tin advertising thermometer with embossed bottle cap at top of scale, 7" x 27", G . . . . .$40.00 (B)

Pepsi, tin litho self-framing advertising thermometer, "say Pepsi please" with scale-type bar, 7¼" x 28", VG .$90.00 (B)

Pepsodent, die cut cardboard litho of Andy holding tube of product, "Um! Um! Ain't dis sumpin," 22½" x 62", 1930s, EX . . . .$975.00 (C)

Pepto-Bismol, die cut cardboard bottle sign, 10⅞" x 27¼", EX . . . .$65.00 (D)

Pepto-Bismol, die cut cardboard in the shape of a bottle, 10⅞" x 27¼", EX . . . .$75.00 (C)

Pepto-Bismol, die cut cardboard store display with graphics of young boy and dog, 31" x 31½", VG . . . . . .$110.00 (B)

Perfect Circle Piston Rings...Home of...The Doctor Of Motors, double-sided tin, hanging advertising sign with graphics of mechanic in center, complete with wrought iron hanging arm, NOS, 24" x 24", NM . . . . . .$650.00 (C)

Perfection Dyes...For Silk, Woolen, Cotton and Feathers, embossed tin dye cabinet front door sign, 10" x 14", EX . . . .$115.00 (B)

Permit to smoke, a good cigar, framed litho advertisement, 1910s, 25" x 31½", F . . . .$95.00 (D)

Pickwick Ale, advertising, painted tin over cardboard, Copyright Hoffenreffer & Co., Inc., 23" x 6½", G, **$65.00 (C)**.

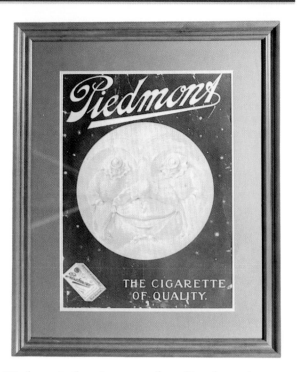

Piedmont, the cigarette of quality, featuring artwork of man in moon, framed, matted, and under glass, 1907, 14" x 20", EX, **$425.00 (B)**.
Courtesy of Muddy River Trading Co./Gary Metz

Piedmont, the cigarette of quality, featuring artwork of woman with big hat and fancy hair style, 1910s, 19" x 25", EX, **$350.00 (C)**. *Courtesy of Muddy River Trading Co./Gary Metz*

Perry's Quality Beverages, triple-filtered, nothing finer, tin door push, G . . . .**$40.00 (C)**

Pet Cigarettes are the Best, Allen & Ginter, hanging cardboard sign with graphics of young girl at well, 4" x 9½", EX . . . .**$77.00 (B)**

Pet cigarettes...are the best, die cut easel back store sign with graphics of young girl sitting on tree limb swinging her straw hat, 1905, EX . . . .**$155.00 (B)**

Peter Bold's "Prudencia," wood cigar advertising sign in likeness of product, 4½" x ¾" x ¾", EX . . . . .**$75.00 (B)**

Peter Doelger...Bottled Beer, round metal tip tray with eagle image in center, 4⅛" dia., EX . . . .**$160.00 (B)**

Peter Pan Bread, broom holder, tin front is stenciled with product message, wooden top has holes for brooms, EX . . . .**$350.00 (B)**

Peter Pan Cottage, cardboard item that came with variety of products, all products listed on reverse side, 10½" x 12" x 9", EX . . . .**$70.00 (B)**

Peter Rabbit Peanut Butter, tin litho pail with wire side-mounted handles, 1-lb., EX . . . .**$484.00 (B)**

Peters ammunition, easel back countertop advertising sign with elk in sight, 13" x 9", EX . . . .**$85.00 (D)**

Peters Cartridge Co., paper calendar with artwork of hunting dogs in field, 1909, 13¾" x 27", G . . .**$165.00 (B)**

Peters Cartridges, celluloid pinback with graphics of bullet and capital letter P, ⅞" dia., NM . . . .**$75.00 (C)**

Peters Cartridges, postage cover with graphics of hunter taking aim, 6½" x 3½", 1904, VG . . . .**$85.00 (B)**

Piedmont, The Virginia Cigarette, double-sided, porcelain back wooden folding chair, VG, $125.00 (B).

Piel's Beer, dispenser, die cast bar top straw and napkin dispenser with a couple of elves getting beer from a keg, 6½" x 7" x 6", EX, $30.00 (B). *Courtesy of Buffalo Bay Auction Co.*

Pinkerton's, caution sign, reflective metal, 12" x 14", VG, $55.00 (B).

Pippins 5¢ Cigar, tin litho tip tray, 5½" L, EX, $210.00 (B). *Courtesy of Richard Opfer Auctioneering, Inc.*

Peter Schuyler...Get a heck of a cigar, with silhouette of man's head smoking a cigar at top center, porcelain advertising sign, 36" x 12", EX . . . .$125.00 (C)

Peter Schuyler Perfecto Cigars, round tip tray with graphics of Peter Schuyler in tray center, 6" dia., EX . . . .$200.00 (B)

Peters, die cut countertop stand-up with graphics of the new belted bullet and a charging bear, "The New 50 Caliber Belted Bullet," 17" x 18", EX . . . .$145.00 (C)

Peters High Velocity, shotgun shell box for .410 gauge with graphics of duck leaving water, 25 shell size, EX . . . .$60.00 (B)

Peters No. 12, target celluloid pinback in likeness of shell brass, ⅞" dia., EX . . . .$155.00 (B)

Peterson's Rose Butter, cardboard litho with easel back, plastic coating, 20¼" x 13", VG . . . .$40.00 (B)

Peters...Packs the Power, "Know your game," paper ad chart, with top and bottom metal strips, 24" x 35", EX . . . .$176.00 (B)

Peters Rustless Metallic ammunition, cardboard die cut easel back advertising sign with graphics of moose and package of the product, 13½" x 9", EX . . . .$95.00 (C)

Peters Weatherbird Shoes, porcelain advertising thermometer, "Pat. March 16, 1915, Mfg. by Beach, Coshocton, O," 7" x 27", EX . . . .$375.00 (C)

Petter, Use the Petter blue book, double-bubble electric clock, great graphics, 1950s, 15" dia., F . . . . .$100.00 (C)

Pittston Gazette, porcelain advertising sign, manufactured by Ing-Rich, Beaver Falls, Pa., "Bright, Clean, Newsy," 16" x 8", VG, $85.00 (C).

Pirelli Tire, single-sided embossed tin sign, 19¼" x 27¼", EX, $3,200.00 (B).

Planters Peanut, container, shaped to resemble a peanut, 11" long, VG, $45.00 (C).

Planters Peanut, glass barrel jar, with original lid featuring peanut-shaped handle, EX, $200.00 (B). *Courtesy of Muddy River Trading Co./Gary Metz*

Pexwear clothing, die cut paper on wood easel back advertising sign with likeness of man in lab coat, 17" x 40", EX . . . .$60.00 (B)

Phelax Rain Resisting Coat, single-sided porcelain ad sign with graphics of a man shooting a gun, 16¾" x 60", VG . . . .$675.00 (B)

Philco, die cut cardboard stand-up advertising sign, featuring Don McNeill of the "Breakfast Club" showing all the features of the refrigerator, 1940s, 32" x 64", EX . . . .$95.00 (C)

Philip Morris Cigarette, self-framed embossed tin litho with image of Johnny, 27" x 14½", EX . . . . . .$150.00 (B)

Philip Morris, painted metal sign featuring the Philip Morris boy holding a metal cigarette pack, 1940s, 27" x 15", G . . . .$195.00 (D)

Philip Morris, porcelain strip sign promoting "do you inhale-Is call for Philip Morris...smoking pleasure with smoking penalties," 22½" x 3¼", EX . . . . . .$725.00 (B)

Philip Olin & Co., Whol. Grocers (sp. on cutter), Sheffield, Anniston, Ala., EX . . . .$95.00 (D)

Phillies Cigar, rolled edge embossed tin advertising sign, "America's No. 1 cigar," with graphics of cigar, 20¼" x 13", VG . . . .$65.00 (B)

Phillips Ethyl, porcelain double-sided shield-shaped advertising sign, 29" x 29", G . . . .$700.00 (B)

Phillips 66, Agricultural Ammonia, tin litho menu board with application information and price lines, 30" x 20", G . . . .$15.00 (B)

Planters Peanuts, wax-coated box, VG, $55.00 (D).

Courtesy of Muddy River Trading Co./Gary Metz

Pay Car Scrap Tobacco, Chew...the best flavor, tin litho advertising sign with graphics of product package in center, 13¾" x 17¾", VG, $200.00 (B).

Courtesy of Buffalo Bay Auction Co.

P. Lorillard & Co. Tobacco, store display cabinet, wood with etched glass and brass lettering, great piece, 43" H, EX, $6,000.00 (B). *Courtesy of Richard Opfer Auctioneering, Inc.*

Phillips 66, die cut embossed porcelain neon shield sign, "Federal Electric Co.," 46" x 48", VG .....$1,600.00 (B)

Phillips 66, map rack with rotating base that holds 48 assorted maps with Phillips 66 shield at top, 12" x 10" x 22", VG ....$650.00 (B)

Phillips 66, motor oil...our finest quality...100% paraffin base, double-sided painted metal sign, 22" x 11", F ...$240.00 (B)

Phillips 66...Phillips Petroleum Co., Chicago Division, silver anniversary pocket mirror, 1955, 3½" dia., EX ..$130.00 (C)

Phillips 66, service station attendants hat, cloth top with embroidered patch, this is the type that comes without the vinyl bill and has snap for attaching the bill, VG ....$210.00 (B)

Phillips 66, Tires Batteries, light-up double-bubble advertising clock, great color, 18" dia., NM ......$700.00 (D)

Phillips 66...Tires...Batteries, metal and glass light-up double-bubble advertising clock with trademark shield in center of clock face, 15" x 4", VG ....$900.00 (B)

Phinney-Walker...Clocks for automobiles..."On Time," models for every type of car, with great graphics of clock in front of city scene, cardboard, 15" x 20", EX ..$395.00 (C)

Phoenix, match safe from St. Louis Brewery, metal body with embossing on sides, 1¾" x 3", EX .....$275.00 (C)

Phurnod Smokeless Coal, single-sided porcelain advertising sign, "For all Types of Hot-Water Boilers," 15" x 22½", EX ....$160.00 (B)

Polar Bear Tobacco, store counter display bin with graphics of large polar bear with product package, 18" x 14" x 12", VG, **$900.00 (B).**

Polarine and Gasoline, painted tin litho advertising sign with graphics of two vintage automobiles and young ladies at the wheel, 19¼" x 27½", 1913, EX, **$7,000.00 (B).**

Courtesy of Collectors Auction Services

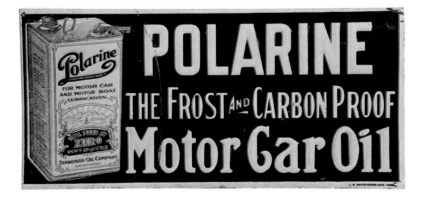

Polarine Motor Car Oil, embossed tin advertising sign with image of vintage Polarine can, 19⅝" x 9¼", EX, **$475.00 (B).** *Courtesy of Autopia Advertising Auctions*

Picaninny Freeze, advertising paper on cardboard sign, 14" x 11", VG . . . .$135.00 (D)

Pickaninny Peanut Butter, tin litho pail with graphics of black girl sitting on front with slip-lid and side-mounted pail handles, 1-lb., EX . . . .$214.00 (B)

Pickwick Ale, "Ale that is Ale," round serving tray, Copyright Hoffenreffer & Co., Inc., artwork of ale barrels being drawn by team of horses, 12" dia., EX . . . . . .$100.00 (C)

Pickwick Coffee, tin litho coffee can with artwork of Mr. Pickwick on front, 3-lb., EX . . . .$90.00 (B)

Piedmont...For cigarettes Virginia Tobacco is the best, porcelain sign with product package in center of message, 30" x 49", EX . . . .$125.00 (D)

Piedmont, the cigarette of quality, featuring artwork of woman with big hat and fancy hair style, 1910s, 19" x 25", EX . . . .$350.00 (C)

Piels Real Lager Beer, on Draught, Made in America, self-framing porcelain advertising sign, 24" x 12", EX .$185.00 (B)

Piel's Real Lager Beer, on draught, porcelain advertising sign, 24" x 12", EX . . . .$135.00 (C)

Pierce Oil Corporation, Pennant Oils, one-sided porcelain advertising sign, 14½" dia., G . . . .$450.00 (B)

Piff's beverages, tin litho embossed advertising sign "The Perfect Refreshment In Bottles," 30" x 14", EX . .$155.00 (C)

Polaroid Land Camera, light-up display sign with clock in left side of display, 1960s, VG, $140.00 (D).
Courtesy of Creatures of Habit

Poll-Parrot, revolving store shoe display, motorized so parrot and shoes revolve, 20" x 33", EX, $145.00 (B).

Polaris Sno-Traveler, self-framing single-sided tin advertising sign, 28" x 35", G, $485.00 (B).

Poll-Parrot, advertising radio, "Poll-Parrot Shoes for Boys and Girls," plastic and composition, 3¾' x 11", VG, $95.00 (B).

Pigmeat Almo Markham, House Rent Party, paper litho advertising poster by Ted Toddy Pictures, 28½" x 43", VG . . . .$325.00 (B)

Pilot Cigarette, tobacco litho tin container with graphics of airplane, by W.C. McDonald, Montreal, 4½" x 4½", EX . . . .$50.00 (B)

Pilot Knob Coffee, container with bail handle from Bowers Bros., Richmond VA, 5-lb., EX . . . .$275.00 (B)

Pinch Hit Chewing Tobacco, sign, embossed painted tin, 14" x 9", P . . . .$200.00 (C)

Pinkerton's National Detective Agency, porcelain advertising sign, 7¼" x 3⅜", EX . . . .$85.00 (D)

Pioneer Auto Service Co., Official Service Station, two-piece double-sided porcelain sign with vintage iron hanging bracket, 18" x 24½", NM . . . .$775.00 (C)

Pioneer Club...Downtown Las Vegas, Nevada, aluminum license plate attachment with die cut image oif cowboy, 10⅝" x 7⅜", EX . . . .$250.00 (C)

Pioneer Glass & Paint Co., calendar with artwork of Indian maiden in canoe, partial months pad, 1923, 10" x 14", EX . . . .$30.00 (B)

Piper Heidsieck Champagne advertising sign, clay coat litho, graphics of dogs chasing a rat, John Osborn & Sons, NY, 29" x 20", EX . . . .$350.00 (C)

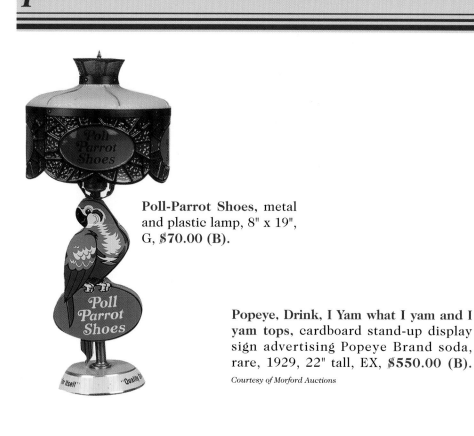

Poll-Parrot Shoes, metal and plastic lamp, 8" x 19", G, $70.00 (B).

Popeye, Drink, I Yam what I yam and I yam tops, cardboard stand-up display sign advertising Popeye Brand soda, rare, 1929, 22" tall, EX, $550.00 (B).

Courtesy of Morford Auctions

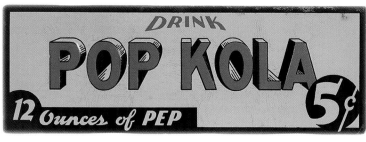

Pop Kola, 12 ounces of Pep, one-sided embossed tin sign, 14" x 15", VG, $110.00 (B).

Pippins Cigar, tin litho advertising sign, 21" L, G ..$250.00 (B)

Pittsburgh Brewing Company, cardboard construction with logo in upper right hand corner, 40½" x 22", VG ..$75.00 (C)

Pittsburgh Paint...Satisfaction in service since 1855, tin self-framed ad sign with graphics of product container, 38" x 27", NM ....$390.00 (B)

Pittsburgh Paints, light-up motion clock, 15½" dia., VG ....$600.00 (C)

Plano Harvesting Machines, calendar with artwork of Indian and full calendar pad, 1905, 13" x 19", NM ....$165.00 (B)

Planters, jar with tin litho lid and paper lady label on each side, 9¼" x 5" x 7¾", 1937, EX ....$225.00 (C)

Planters, Jumbo Block wax cardboard countertop advertising die cut display, 8" x 10¾" x 7", EX ....$350.00 (C)

Planters Novola Peanut Oil, with litho image and message on sides, metal container, 5-gal., EX ....$175.00 (D)

Planters Peanut Butter, pail with litho of Mr. Peanut, 3½" x 3⅞", EX ....$900.00 (B)

Planters Peanut, container, shaped to resemble a peanut, 11" long, G ....$35.00 (B)

Planters Peanut, 5 cent Jar, embossed lettering and Peanut man, 9" x 9" x 12", G ....$110.00 (B)

Planters Peanut, glass barrel jar, with original lid featuring peanut-shaped handle, G ....$95.00 (C)

Planters Peanut, parade costume shaped like a peanut, made from a composition material, 24" x 48", 1950s, EX ....$2,300.00 (B)

Planters Peanut, tin early key-wound top with Mr. Peanut on front, 4¼" x 4¾", G ....$95.00 (C)

Postal Telegraph, double-sided porcelain flange sign, "The International System," 29½" x 16", EX, $325.00 (D). *Courtesy of Riverview Antique Mall*

Post-Standard Branch, metal double-sided flange sign, 13" x 9¾", VG, $125.00 (B).

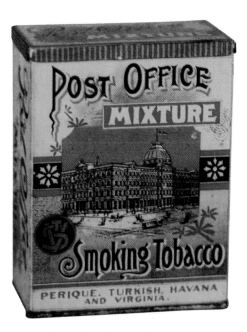

Post Office Smoking Tobacco, tin litho tin container with graphics of large building in center cameo, 3½" x 4¾" x 2", EX, $2,200.00 (B). *Courtesy of Wm. Morford Investment Grade Collectibles*

Post Toasties String Dispenser, self-framing tin sign with metal string holder, 11½" dia., 1916, VG, $645.00 (B).

Planters Peanut, waxy two-piece container with scarce globe version, 7¼" x 5¾" x 3⅜", 1930s, VG . .$1,400.00 (B)

Planters Peanuts, barrel store jar with etched lid and embossed Mr. Peanut running around jar, 1935, NM . . . .$286.00 (B)

Planters Peanuts, die cut cardboard sign of Mr. Peanut and small child in cowboy attire, easel back, 6½" x 14", NM . . . .$215.00 (B)

Planters Peanuts, fish bowl store jar with decal of fish, product message on fish body, hard-to-find item, 1929, NM . . . .$220.00 (B)

Planters Peanuts, football glass store jar, embossed "Planters Salted Peanuts" on both sides, 1930, NM . . . . . .$302.00 (B)

Planters Peanuts, glass store container with metal lid which has graphics of Mr. Peanut, 5¼" x 10" x 8½", VG . . . .$275.00 (B)

Planters Peanuts, leap-year glass store jar with paper label, 1940, NM . . . .$150.00 (B)

Planters Peanuts, seven-sided embossed store jar with paper label, 1926, EX . . . .$225.00 (B)

Prairie Farmer, paper litho subscription form, 32¼" x 24½", G, **$110.00 (B)**.

Prairie Farms, Milk, Ice Cream, round light-up clock, plastic front cover on plastic base, VG, **$135.00 (C)**. *Courtesy of B.J. Summers*

Prairie Rose Coffee, rare tin litho key-wound can from E-H-B Coffee, Kansas City with graphics of young girl in center cameo, 1-lb., EX, **$850.00 (B)**.
Courtesy of Wm. Morford Investment Grade Collectibles

Pratt & Lambert Paint, double-sided porcelain sign, 36" x 24", VG, **$65.00 (C)**.

Planters Peanuts, six-sided store jar with Mr. Peanut decals on all sides, etched glass lid, 1936, NM . . . .**$160.00 (B)**

Planters Peanuts, streamlined glass store jar with yellow metal lid, 1937, NM . . . .**$155.00 (B)**

Planters Peanuts, wax-coated box, G . . . .**$40.00 (B)**

Planters, plastic clip-on earrings, in original gift box, ⅞" x 1¼", EX . . . .**$70.00 (B)**

Planters Salted Peanuts, waxy cardboard airplane container, 6" x 9" x 3", 1944, EX . . . .**$375.00 (B)**

Planters, tin litho countertop display unit, 14" x 4¾" x 7¾", EX . . . .**$595.00 (C)**

Player's Weights Cigarettes, cardboard advertising sign in original wood frame with the "Players" name stamped on the bottom of the frame, graphics of clown with musical instrument, 18¼" x 22¾", NM . . . .**$500.00 (B)**

P. Lorillard & Co. Tobacco, store display cabinet, wood with etched glass and brass lettering, great piece, 43" H, G . . . .**$1,500.00 (C)**

Plow Boy Chewing and Smoking Tobacco, pail, with side-mounted wire bail handle and paper label, G . . .**$95.00 (D)**

Pratts Poultry Food, A Guaranteed Egg Producer, framed paper litho, 21" x 28", EX, $675.00 (B). *Courtesy of Morford Auctions*

Primley's California Fruit and Pepsin Chewing Gum, display case with oak framing and etched glass, 18¼ ", EX, $525.00 (B). *Courtesy of Richard Opfer Auctioneering, Inc.*

Primley's Gum, die cut cardboard bear promoting California Fruit Gum, 6½" x 2¾", EX, $305.00 (B). *Courtesy of Buffalo Bay Auction Co.*

Prince Albert Crimp Cut, framed paper advertisement, 1927, 29" x 15", EX, $105.00 (B).

Plow Boy, counter store bin with image of tobacco package on front and sides, 8" x 10½" x 10½", EX . . . .$1,200.00 (C)

Plymouth Binder Twine, cloth litho advertising banner, "Insures a successful harvest," 28" x 7", 1920, VG . . . .$95.00 (C)

Plymouth Dry Gin...Coates...Original, with artwork of monk with product bottle, 4⅛" dia., EX . . . . .$40.00 (B)

Poehler, quick rolled oats from Poehler Mercantile, Lawrence, Topeka, Emporia & McPherson Kansas, EX . . . .$575.00 (C)

Polar Bear Tobacco, store counter display bin with graphics of large polar bear with product package, 18" x 14" x 12", VG . . . .$900.00 (B)

Polarine Gasoline, painted tin litho advertising sign with graphics of two vintage automobiles and young ladies at the wheel, 19¼" x 27½", 1913, G . . . .$1,800.00 (C)

Polaroid Land Camera, light-up display sign with clock in left side of display, 1960s, G . . . .$125.00 (D)

Poll Parrot, advertising thermometer, dial-type thermometer with advertising and Poll Parrot sitting below it on a trapeze, rare item, 10" x 24", EX . . . . . .$325.00 (B)

Poll Parrot, chalkware parrot on trapeze with name strip below parrot, 19" H, EX . . . .$400.00 (B)

Poll Parrot, neon advertising store sign, EX . .$1,250.00 (C)

Prince Albert, Crimp Cut Tobacco,
jar with paper label and original lid,
rare, EX, $80.00 (D). *Courtesy of Chief*
Paduke Antiques Mall

Procter & Gamble Co., die cut advertising
sign for "Crisco...Better than Butter," produced by Baltimore Enamel Nov. Co., 14"
x 20", EX, $4,500.00 (B).

Providence Washington Insurance Company, tin
advertising sign with wood frame, 20½" x 26¼", EX,
$330.00 (B).

Poll Parrot, neon over porcelain sign with die cut bird sitting on perch at top of sign, EX . . . .$1,350.00 (D)

Poll Parrot Shoes...for Boys, for Girls, die cut metal
advertising sign with cut-out of parrot at top, rare and
hard-to-find, double-sided, EX . . . .$1,250.00 (D)

Poll Parrot Shoes, reverse painted glass advertisement in
wood frame, 14½" x 25", VG . . . .$560.00 (B)

Polly Prim Cleaner, old cardboard litho with graphics of
woman with cleaning to do and the product in hand,. N.K.
Fairbank Company, 20½" x 28½", G . . . . . .$185.00 (B)

Ponoco Cayenne Pepper, tin, Grand Union Co., New York
City, graphics of Indian head with full war bonnet on
label, 2½-oz., EX . . . .$165.00 (C)

P.O.N., reverse painted glass for Pride of Newark quality
brews, 16" x 13", EX . . . .$135.00 (C)

Pontiac...Authorized Service, porcelain sign with Indian
head logo in center of sign, 41½" dia., EX . . .$325.00 (C)

Pontiac, die cut embossed porcelain Indian head sign, 25"
x 18", EX . . . .$1,100.00 (C)

Public Telephone, The Lincoln Telephone and Telegraph Company, porcelain flange sign, 16" dia., NM, $375.00 (C). *Courtesy of Riverview Antique Mall*

Pulver's Cocoa, metal tip tray, 4½", VG, $125.00 (B).

Pulver's Kola-Pepsin Chewing Gum, two-piece cardboard box with great graphics of vending machine on both sides, 6⅞" x 5¼ x 5" x 1⅜", G, $3,000.00 (B).

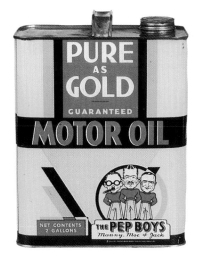

Pure as Gold Motor Oil, two-gallon tin can with graphics of the Pep Boys, Manny, Moe & Jack, 1933, $100.00 (B).

Pony Brand Marshmallow, Canadian tin with ponies and flags all around top of tin, 12" x 5", EX . . . .$85.00 (B)

Popel-Giller Co. Inc., High Grade Bottled Beer, round metal tip tray with artwork of woman with glass of product and bouquet of flowers, 4¼" dia., EX . . . . .$90.00 (B)

Popeye, Drink, I Yam what I Yam and I Yam tops, cardboard stand-up display sign advertising Popeye Brand soda, rare, 1929, 22" tall, G . . . .$225.00 (C)

Popper's Ace Tobacco, store counter display case with glass front lid, 6" x 7" x 8¾", VG . . . .$675.00 (D)

Popper's Eight Center, cigar tin embossed advertising sign with graphics of spotlight from cigar on eight-ball, 35¼" x 11¼", EX . . . .$175.00 (C)

Popsicle, embossed tin litho "Everybody Loves Popsicle" sign, 27½" x 10", NM . . . .$150.00 (C)

Portuondo Cigars, vintage wooden advertising thermometer with graphics of product at bottom of thermometer, 5" x 21", VG . . . .$325.00 (B)

Possum Cigar, tin with graphics of possum on front, 50-ct, EX . . . .$175.00 (C)

Possum, 3 for 5¢ Cigar, canister with graphics of white opossum on front, 5" x 5", EX . . . .$360.00 (B)

Postal Telegraph, double-sided porcelain flange sign, "The International System," 29½" x 16", F . . . .$95.00 (D)

Putnam Dyes, wooden store display box featuring General Putnam litho on outside cover, also litho on inside cover, strong colors, with original dye packages, EX, $350.00 **(B).**
Courtesy of Richard Opfer Auctioneering, Inc.

Pur-ox, Syrups, Beverages, wooden thermometer, 5" x 21", EX, $400.00 **(B).** *Courtesy of Muddy River Trading Co./Gary Metz*

Pyrene, die cut cardboard advertisement depicting father putting out auto fire while mother and child wait, "Pyrene kills auto fires," 21" x 31½", VG, $750.00 **(B).** *Courtesy of Collectors Auction Services*

Post Cereals, advertising calendar with graphics of youngster enjoying a bowl of the product, 8" x 12", 1924, VG . . . .$70.00 **(B)**

Postmaster Cigar, tin container with graphics of postmaster smoking a cigar, 5¼" x 5", VG . . . .$55.00 **(D)**

Post Office Smoking Tobacco, tin litho tin container with graphics of large building in center cameo, 3½" x 4¾" x 2", F . . . .$825.00 **(B)**

Post Toasties...with peaches and cream, paper advertising showing milk being poured on bowl of cereal, framed, 15¼" x 12¼", EX . . . .$135.00 **(D)**

Postum...Drink...There's a Reason...Health First, round tin string holder with message in center, EX .$280.00 **(B)**

Poth's Beer, pinback by Whitehead & Hoag advertising Poth's Beer, 1¼", NM . . . .$65.00 **(C)**

Power House...Bigger, two-piece 24-count candy box with artwork of product bar on front, 9" x 5" x 2", EX $5.00 **(B)**

Powerlube Motor Oil, two-sided porcelain sign with graphics of tiger, 59½" x 36", G . . . .$950.00 **(B)**

Prairie Farms...Milk...Ice Cream, round plastic body and cover light-up advertising clock, 16" dia., G .$135.00 **(D)**

Prairie Rose Coffee, rare tin litho key-wound can from E-H-B Coffee, Kansas City with graphics of young girl in center cameo, 1-lb., F . . . .$175.00 (D)

Pralines, Genuine Creole, litho cardboard product box with silhouette couple in lower corner and mammy in other corner, 1-lb., EX . . . .$75.00 (C)

Pratt & Lambert Paint, double-sided porcelain sign, 36" x 24", EX . . . .$125.00 (C)

Pratts Poultry Food, A Guaranteed Egg Producer, framed paper litho, 21" x 28", P . . . .$75.00 (D)

Prescriptions, reverse painted glass sign with wood frame, 17¼" x 11¼", VG . . . .$275.00 (B)

President Suspenders... Absolute Comfort...J.H. Beamer, round metal tip tray with artwork of pretty woman in tray center, 4⅛" dia., EX . . . .$25.00 (B)

Prestone Anti-Freeze, dial-type advertising thermometer, 10" dia., EX . . . .$225.00 (C)

Prestone Anti-Freeze, early wooden advertising thermometer promoting "the perfect anti-freeze," 7¾" x 39½", 1930s, EX . . . .$275.00 (B)

Price's Milk, glo-dial neon advertising clock, in chrome case, 14½" dia., NM . . . .$575.00 (C)

Pride of Aden, coffee canister with small lid, refund for return of tin, The Ginter Grocery Co., 6¾" x 9", 4-lb., 1906, EX . . . .$185.00 (C)

Pride of Virginia, sliced plug, rectangular tobacco tin with cameo on front cover, G . . . .$15.00 (D)

Primley's California Fruit and Pepsin Chewing Gum, display case with oak framing and etched glass, 18¼", G . . . .$325.00 (D)

Primley's California Fruit Chewing Gum...sweeter than honey, cardboard die cut easel back stand-up advertising sign with bear holding product package, 13⅞" x 10½", EX . . . .$4,000.00 (B)

Prince Albert, Crimp Cut Tobacco, jar with paper label and original lid, rare, NM . . . .$95.00 (C)

Prince Albert... The National Joy Smoke, cloth banner, promoting both pipe and roll your own uses for the product, 95" x 43", 1941, NM . . . .$375.00 (C)

Prince Albert tobacco, sign with artwork of Chief Joseph Nez Perce, tin litho from American Art Works, 19" x 25½", EX . . . .$5,500.00 (C)

Princine Baking Powder, tin litho container with side handle and graphics of woman and product, 3" x 3", 1916, EX . . . .$135.00 (B)

Principe Alfonso Cigar, tin litho advertising sign, "5 in bundle 25¢," 13½" x 10", NM . . . .$250.00 (B)

Priscilla Crayons... High Quality Brilliant Colors, tin litho container with brilliant colors on artwork of crayons in hand, 1937, NM . . . .$70.00 (B)

Procter & Gamble Co., die cut advertising sign for "Crisco...Better than Butter," produced by Baltimore Enamel Nov. Co., 14" x 20", G . . . .$1,200.00 (D)

Prosper Lambert Automobiles, oval metal serving tray with scalloped edges, graphics of man in early auto, product message on reverse side, 5", G . . . .$500.00 (B)

Pro-To-Co Tank Car Gasoline, globe, high profile metal body with glass lenses, from "The Standard Oil Co. of New York," 16½" H, VG . . . .$500.00 (B)

Providence Washington Insurance Co., tin litho with artwork of George Washington, 18" x 24", EX . . .$300.00 (B)

Public Telephone, Bell System Connections, double-sided porcelain flange sign, white on blue, P . . . . . .$295.00 (D)

Public Telephone, die cut porcelain flange sign with older model 202 phone in center of message, 16" x 16", EX . . . .$375.00 (C)

Public Telephone, The Lincoln Telephone and Telegraph Company, porcelain flange sign, 16" dia., EX .$345.00 (D)

Pulver, gum dispenser, green porcelain construction with glass window at payout with traffic cop graphics, 8½" x 20", EX . . . .$775.00 (C)

Pulver's Kola-Pepsin Chewing Gum, two-piece cardboard box with great graphics of vending machine on both sides, 6⅞" x 5¼" x 1⅜", F . . . .$1,200.00 (D)

Punch Baking Powder, tin container with paper label, 2½" x 5", VG . . . .$125.00 (B)

Pure-Pep... Be Sure With Pure, porcelain pump sign, 10" x 12", EX . . . .$90.00 (B)

Puritan, crushed plug mixture, tin litho vertical pocket tobacco tin, 3" x 4⅜" x ⅞", EX . . . .$275.00 (B)

Purity Butter Pretzels, die cut cardboard stand-up advertising sign with image of young boy and a giant pretzel, 12½" x 22", VG . . . .$135.00 (B)

Purolator, oil rack complete with top sign, 1950s, G . . . .$125.00 (C)

Purol Gasoline, one-sided porcelain sign with graphics of arrow in center of face, 14" dia., G . . . .$175.00 (B)

Pur-ox, Syrups, Beverages, wooden thermometer, 5" x 21", G . . . .$95.00 (C)

Putnam Dyes, metal cabinet with front graphics of Gen. Putnam charging on his horse, 1940s, G . . . .$150.00 (B)

Putnam Dyes, wooden store display box featuring General Putnam litho on outside cover, also litho on inside cover, strong colors, with original dye packages, G . .$165.00 (D)

Putnam Fadeless Dyes, tin store display box with artwork of woman admiring clothing, 16½" x 8" x 11¼", EX . . . .$135.00 (D)

Pyrene, die cut cardboard advertisement depicting father putting out auto fire while mother and child wait, "Pyrene kills auto fires," 21" x 31½", EX . . . .$825.00 (C)

Quadriga Cloth...The girl who sews has better clothes, wooden die cut advertising sign with logo at left of message, 20" x 6½", EX . . . .$75.00 (D)

Quaker Crackels, cardboard store sample dispenser with artwork of Quaker on front, would dispense sample by moving lever on side, 21" x 22" x 5½", EX . . .$225.00 (B)

Quaker Maid...First In Quality...Milk, die cut porcelain advertising sign with graphics of woman in maid attire, 41" x 24", NM . . . .$575.00 (C)

Quaker Maid Milk, porcelain die cut advertising sign with graphics of Quaker woman in center, "First In Quality," 41¼" x 23¾", EX . . . .$575.00 (C)

Quaker Maid Petroleum Products, dial-type advertising thermometer, 12" dia., EX . . . .$225.00 (C)

Quaker Oats, cardboard wood framed advertising sign with artwork of Silhouette Quaker Man and sunset, 21" x 11", EX . . . .$50.00 (B)

Quaker Oats Dionne Quints, die cut cardboard floor display unit, 60" x 30", EX . . . .$120.00 (B)

Quaker State, light-up advertising clock with trademark clover leaf on face, metal body with glass face and cover, 15" dia., VG . . . .$425.00 (B)

Quaker State...Lubrication Service, tin advertising sign with wood frame, single-sided, 63½" x 33", VG . . . . .$325.00 (B)

Quaker State Motor Oil...ask for, plastic construction, 16" sq., VG . . . .$80.00 (B)

Quaker State Motor Oil...Certified Guaranteed, round top double-sided porcelain driveway sign with logo at top of sign, 26½" x 29", G . . . .$95.00 (D)

Quaker State Motor Oil, metal double-sided advertising sign with original metal frame, 28¼" x 29¾", EX . . .$110.00 (B)

Quality Inn Coffee, tin key-wound litho, can with good graphics of horseback travelers arriving at inn, 1-lb., 5" x 4", EX . . . .$250.00 (B)

Quasar...Pete's Discount...Whirlpool, painted metal thermometer with dealer information in bottom panel, G . . . .$25.00 (C)

Quick Meal, oval porcelain advertising sign with graphics of chick emerging from an egg shell in grass, 44¾" x 33⅛", EX . . . .$275.00 (D)

Quick Meal, oval porcelain sign with artwork of egg, and chick chasing insect, 44¾" x 33½", EX . . . . .$215.00 (C)

Quaker State Duplex Outboard Oil, double-sided tin advertising sign, 24" x 12", VG, **$55.00 (B).**

Queen Cola, painted tin advertising sign, 7" x 19⅞", G, **$95.00 (B).**

Quaker State, Summer Oil, banner, 57" x 33¾", VG, **$65.00 (B).** *Courtesy of Collectors Auction Services*

Quiky, Tart, Tangy, Terrific, metal advertising thermometer, 8" x 16½", G, **$150.00 (B).**

Quickure Mfg. Co., metal stand-up counter display sign for radiator leak cure, 9¾" x 11¼", EX, **$485.00 (B).** *Courtesy of Collectors Auction Services*

Quick Meal Steel Ranges, ten-page booklet, featuring Buster Brown and Tige on front and back with product information inside, 1910, NM . . . .$100.00 (B)

Quincey Brewing Co., pocketknife with embossing "Compliments of Dick & Bros." on back, has corkscrew, 3¼". VG . . . .$75.00 (C)

Radiola, double-sided porcelain flange advertising sign, 19" x 17¾", EX, $100.00 (B).

Railway Express Agency, self-framing tin over cardboard ad sign, 19¼" x 13¼", very good, $925.00 (B).

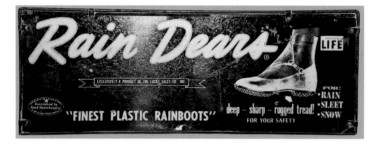

Rain Dears, self-framed painted metal sign, "Finest Plastic Rainboots," 25" x 9½", EX, $45.00 (D). *Courtesy of Riverview Antique Mall*

Raleigh Cigarettes, easel back cardboard advertising poster with image of Douglas Fairbanks, Jr., 20" x 30", VG, $50.00 (B).

Radiant Coffee, tin with key-wound lid, Chris Hoerr & Sons, Peoria, Ill., 1-lb., F . . . .$20.00 (D)

Ragtime Jubilee, advertising cardboard poster, 15" x 22½", EX . . . .$35.00 (B)

Ragtime Jubilee, cardboard advertising window card, directed by Max Presnell featuring a caricature of a large well-dressed black man, 15" x 22¾", VG . . . .$200.00 (D)

Railway Express Agency, one-sided porcelain strip advertising sign, 120" x 5", NM . . . .$325.00 (B)

Railway Express Agency, single-sided porcelain advertising diamond-shaped sign, 8" x 8", EX . . . . . .$120.00 (B)

Rainbo...is good bread, steel advertising door push and pull handle, NOS, 26½" x 8½", NM . . . .$300.00 (C)

Rainbow Dyes, countertop wood display cabinet, "one dye for all fabrics," paper label and complete with product packages, 6" x 12½" x 16¾", G . . . .$750.00 (B)

Rainbow Dyes, wooden cabinet with tin insert on door, "One Dye for All Fabrics," 11½" x 5" x 19", G . .$225.00 (B)

Rain Dears, self-framed painted metal sign, "Finest Plastic Rainboots," 25" x 9½", EX . . . .$45.00 (D)

Rainier Ale & Beer, die cut embossed metal advertising sign, 13" x 8⅜", 1940s, NM . . . .$135.00 (C)

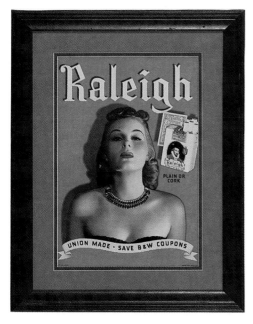

Raleigh Cigarettes, paper litho, framed advertisement, 16½" x 21½", EX, $70.00 (B).

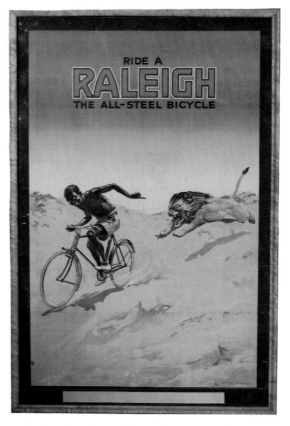

Raleigh, the all-steel bicycle, paper advertising poster, 40" x 60", VG, $3,500.00 (C).

Rainier Beer, metal and plastic barometer, 9⅝" x 12½", G . . . .$55.00 (C)

Rainier Brewing Company, metal serving tray, 12" dia., G . . . .$75.00 (C)

Rainier Pale Beer, serving tray, "Compliments of the season" with graphics of snow scene on front, pre-Prohibition item, 9¼" dia., EX . . . .$150.00 (C)

Raleigh, change receiver, graphics of product package under glass on wood base, 7¾" x 7½" x 2½", EX . . . . . .$45.00 (B)

Raleigh Cigarette, cardboard sign featuring advertising of free playing cards with Raleigh coupons, framed, 13½" x 19½", EX . . . .$35.00 (C)

Raleigh Cigarette, framed paper advertising, 14½" x 17½", G . . . .$20.00 (B)

Raleigh Tobacco, sign advertising cigarettes with filter tip, 28" x 14½", EX . . . .$45.00 (D)

Rambler, light-up advertising clock from the Pam Clock Co., New Rochelle, N.Y., "Rambler Time," 16" sq., EX . . . .$425.00 (C)

Ramer's Chocolates, self-framing tin ad sign with graphics of products on table, 19" x 13", G . . . .$61.00 (B)

Ramon's Brownie Pills, painted wood thermometer with the little doctor at right of the scale, 9" x 21", EX . .$425.00 (B)

Ramon's Brownie Pills...The Little Doctor Brings Happy Days, with artwork of the doctor at right of scale, tin litho in cream color, 9" x 21", NM . . . .$332.00 (B)

R.A. Patterson Tobacco Co... Lucky Strike Tobacco Clock, wood case with brass and glass door, with eight-day wind-up mechanism, 12¼" x 19", VG . . . . . .$600.00 (B)

Rat Bis-Kit, die cut easel back display for rat bait, NOS, artwork of rat eating product, 8¾" x 12", EX .$300.00 (B)

Rambler, light-up advertising clock from the Pam Clock Co., New Rochelle, N.Y., "Rambler Time," 16" sq., VG, $350.00 (B).
Courtesy of Collectors Auction Services

Red Indian Motor Oils, porcelain sign with graphics of Indian in full headdress, with back mounting bracket, 17" x 24", EX, $2,000.00 (C). *Courtesy of Autopia Advertising Auctions*

R. Brand & Co....Fine Whiskies and Wines...Toledo, O, tin litho advertising sign with graphics of pretty young woman, in original period frame, 17" x 23", 1880s, EX, $3,700.00 (B). *Courtesy of Buffalo Bay Auction Co.*

Rawleigh's Baking Powder, sample size, free sample, 1" x 1½", EX . . . .$175.00 (C)

Rawleigh's Cocoa, tin, sample size, "Free Sample," 1¾", EX . . . .$125.00 (C)

Rawleigh's Good Health Cocoa...packed by The W.T. Rawleigh Co., Freeport, Ill., USA, sample tin with great litho of Mr. Rawleigh and outdoor scene, 1¼" x 1¾" x ⅝", EX . . . .$180.00 (B)

Rawleigh's Good Health Products and Service, double-sided tin flange dealer sign, 18" x 15¼", EX . .$325.00 (C)

Rawleigh's talcum, tin litho container with graphics of clown on unicycle, 7½" T, EX . . . .$55.00 (C)

Raybestos Brake Service, double-sided metal flange sign with graphics of hand pulling early "on the floor" emergency brake lever, 18½" x 14", G . . . .$425.00 (B)

RCA, His Master's Voice, double-sided porcelain, foreign advertising sign, very rare sign, 16" x 18", VG, $3,000.00 (C).

RCA, His Master's Voice, single-sided porcelain advertising sign, 27" x 21½", G, $700.00 (B).

RCA, presentation watch fob, sterling silver with cloisonne enameled image of Nipper at the horn, 1⅜" x 1½", EX, $1,050.00 (B).

Courtesy of Wm. Morford Investment Grade Collectibles

Raybestos Fan Belt...Avoid Breakdowns, tin advertising sign with graphics of service man holding a belt, 21" x 11⅞", EX . . . .$175.00 (C)

Ray Cotton Company, Franklin, Mass., Agents Cotton Mills Waste Association, cast iron inkwell with heavily embossed lettering, 8" x 3¾" x 3", EX . . . .$95.00 (C)

Ray's Standard Oil...Gas...Mt.Vernon, LA, tin painted license plate attachment, 10" x 2½", EX . . . . .$95.00 (C)

Raytheon Radio Service, flange double-sided metal advertising sign promoting Raytheon radio tubes, 18" x 14", EX . . . .$135.00 (C)

Razzle Dazzle Tobacco, store barrel with paper label showing mule kicking off shoe at black man, 15" x 21", EX . . . .$350.00 (B)

Razzle Dazzle, wood barrel with paper label advertising depicting mule kicking shoe off, 16" dia. x 21½", VG . . . .$995.00 (C)

R. Brand & Co....Fine Whiskies and Wines...Toledo, O, tin litho advertising sign with graphics of pretty young woman, in original period frame, 17" x 23", 1880s, F . . . .$900.00 (D)

RCA, "His Master's Voice" porcelain advertising sign with the familiar Nipper at the gramophone, 23" x 17", EX . .$375.00 (C)

RCA...His Master's Voice...Radio, single-sided porcelain advertising sign with graphics of trademark Nipper, 24" x 15", NM . . . .$500.00 (B)

RCA, Nipper, bank made of pot metal, covered by felt, marked Radio Corporation of American, 6", NM . . . .$185.00 (B)

RCA, Radiola Dealer, porcelain scroll advertising sign, 14½" x 19", F, **$125.00 (C)**.

RCA, Victor Records, oleograph, pictures early Nipper at phonograph, "His Master's Voice," framed, 30" x 24", EX, **$550.00 (B)**.

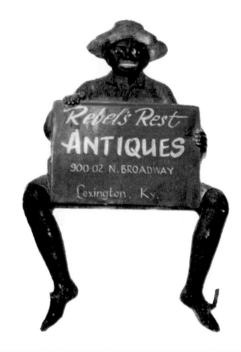

Rebel's Rest Antiques, die cut tin litho of black man holding a sign advertising an antique business, item is probably older than the advertiser, 35" x 56", 1915, VG, **$475.00 (B)**. *Courtesy of Buffalo Bay Auction Co.*

RCA, Nipper papier-mache advertising dog, 5" x 11¼", 1920s, VG . . . .**$195.00 (D)**

RCA, placemat, with Donald Duck and Nipper dog logo, G . . . .**$15.00 (C)**

RCA, watch fob, sterling silver with image of Nipper at the horn, 1⅜" x 1½", EX . . . .**$125.00 (D)**

RCA, Radiola Dealer, porcelain scroll advertising sign, 14½" x 19", EX . . . .**$225.00 (D)**

RCA, Victor Records, oleograph, pictures early Nipper at phonograph, "His Master's Voice," framed, 30" x 24", G . . . .**$195.00 (C)**

RC...Royal Crown Cola, painted metal thermometer with vertical scale under message, EX . . . .**$55.00 (C)**

Record's Ale, light-up globe with metal body and glass lenses, 15½", VG, **$1,000.00 (B).**
Courtesy of Collectors Auction Services

Red Crown Gasoline, circular porcelain sign with crown logo in center, 42" dia., NM, **$950.00 (D).**

Red Goose Shoes, Telechron light-up clock with goose in center, 1930s, EX, **$400.00 (B).** *Courtesy of Muddy River Trading Co./Gary Metz*

Rebel's Rest Antiques, die cut tin litho of black man holding a sign advertising an antique business, item is probably older than the advertiser, 35" x 56", 1915, EX ......$550.00 (C)

Recommended Hotel, AAA, porcelain neon, double-sided, hanging sign, 48" x 31½", red, white & blue, EX .$425.00 (C)

Record's Ale, light-up globe with metal body and glass lenses, 15½", F ....$325.00 (C)

Recruit Little Cigars, die cut store tri-fold sign featuring scenes on each fold of places to enjoy product, 39" x 29", EX ....$225.00 (B)

Red & White Corn Flakes, cardboard box with #2 Davy Crockett edition, graphics of bowl of cereal on front, 13-oz., EX ....$60.00 (B)

Red Belt, vertical pocket tin with likeness of belt and buckle from John J. Bagley & Co., 3" x 3" x 1", EX .....$90.00 (B)

Red Bird Rolled Oats, from Highland Grocery Co. of Ohio with graphics of red bird on front, EX .....$175.00 (C)

Red Bird, rolled oats from Midland Groceries, Ohio with image of red bird on front, 20-oz., VG ......$70.00 (B)

Red Indian Gasoline, globe with graphics of Indian in full headdress with screw-on glass body, 13½" dia., EX, **$1,300.00 (B).** *Courtesy of Autopia Advertising Auctions*

Red Man, wax wrapped paper litho advertisement, 20½" x 10½", VG, **$60.00 (B).**

Red Rock Co., advertising tin embossed sign promoting their flavors, 19½" x 27½", G, **$95.00 (B).**

Red Rock Cola, door opener, 24" x 3", VG, **$95.00 (B).**

Red Cap, At Your Service Everywhere 5¢, 24-count two-piece cardboard candy box with graphics of red-capped man carrying vendor box of product, 7" x 10" x 2½", EX ....**$36.00 (B)**

Red Crest tobacco, lunch box with artwork of rooster on front label, leather with strap closure, hard-to-find, 8" x 5" x 4", VG ....**$275.00 (C)**

Red Cross Coffee, container with paper label from C.A. Cross Co., Fitchburg, MA, 1-lb., EX ....**$50.00 (B)**

Red Cross Shoes, neon sign manufactured by Lackner, Cin. O, 21" x 7", VG ....**$185.00 (B)**

Red Crown Ethyl, gas globe, one-piece glass globe in shape of crown with embossed lettering at bottom band, 17½" dia., VG ....**$1,100.00 (B)**

Red Crown Gasoline, circular porcelain sign with crown logo in center, 42" dia., EX ....**$875.00 (C)**

Red Crown Gasoline, double-sided porcelain advertising sign with image of crown trademark in center, 30" dia., 1929, EX ....**$485.00 (B)**

Red Crown Gasoline, globe, high profile metal body with glass lenses with painted lettering and image of crown, 15" dia., VG ....**$575.00 (B)**

Red Crown tobacco, lunch pail with wire bail handle on lid, 6½" x 5" x 4¼", VG ....**$225.00 (C)**

Red Crown...You Can't Beat...for Mileage, paper poster, 27¾" x 44", 1938, VG ....**$60.00 (B)**

Reddi-Kilowatt, mechanical pencil, EX ......**$10.00 (C)**

Red Seal, automotive ignition battery advertising sign, tin over cardboard, strong colors, 27" x 19", EX, $1,500.00 (B). *Courtesy of Wm. Morford Investment Grade Collectibles*

Reed Manufacturing Co., tin over cardboard ad sign with image of bench vise, 19¼" x 13¼", G, $155.00 (B).

Rees, A.F., single-sided embossed tin sign, "We pay for dead stock," G, $160.00 (B).

Rehkopf's Special, Straight Kentucky Whiskey, Paducah, Ky., 1-qt. stone jug, EX, $325.00 (C). *Courtesy of B.J. Summers*

Red Dot Cigars, double-sided cardboard fan pull, 6½" x 8½", EX . . . .$85.00 (D)

Red Dot Cigars, painted cardboard sign with lady in red dot and image of product in lower left corner, 9" x 12½", EX . . . .$95.00 (C)

Red Earl Cigars... 5¢ in price 10¢ in price, round tip tray with graphics of the Red Earl in tray center, 3⅝" dia., EX . . . .$80.00 (B)

Red Gate Mocha and Java Coffee, cardboard advertising sign, framed, EX . . . .$101.00 (B)

Red Goose...Ask for a Golden Egg, egg machine-made of papier-maché and cardboard, eggs contain prizes, EX . . . .$325.00 (B)

Red Goose Paper, advertising poster featuring the Red Goose with the golden egg, 28" x 9", EX . . . . .$65.00 (C)

Red Goose Shoes, metal neon advertising clock with face graphics of logo Red Goose in center, 18" x 18", 1930s, EX . . . .$495.00 (D)

Red Goose Shoes, cardboard counter display with easel back with young girl and Red Goose, 7" x 10", EX . . . . .$25.00 (C)

Red Goose Shoes, cardboard easel back poster with the admonition to watch the Red Goose lay a golden egg every time you buy Red Goose shoes, 11" x 13, EX . .$45.00 (C)

Red Goose Shoes, composition display in shape of goose, 5½" x 11½", VG . . . .$285.00 (B)

Remington, UMC, Sportsmen's Headquarters, Firearms & Ammunition, double-sided die cut flange sign featuring the Remington bears, 7" x 8", EX, **$2,200.00 (B).** *Courtesy of Morford Auctions*

Rexall Foot Bath Tablets, for Foot Comfort, framed litho sign, 22" x 47¼", VG, **$310.00 (B).**

Rexall, (McFarlin), double-sided porcelain arm-hung advertising sign, 72" x 30" x 4¼", VG, **$400.00 (B).**

Red Goose Shoes, die cut porcelain neon advertising sign with the trademark Red Goose, 20" x 36", VG . . **$405.00 (B)**

Red Goose Shoes, light-up advertising clock, plastic and wood construction with trademark Red Goose in center of face, 19½" x 18", VG . . . .**$130.00 (B)**

Red Goose Shoes, round metal body glass front light-up advertising clock with Red Goose in center with message over goose, EX . . . .**$575.00 (D)**

Red Goose Shoes, store entry carpet with graphics of two Red Goose images, "Half The Fun of Having Feet," 59" x 27", G . . . .**$525.00 (B)**

Red Goose Shoes, Telechron light-up clock with goose in center, 1930s, G . . . .**$275.00 (D)**

Red Hawks, wooden cigar box with inside lid graphics of Indian, 50-ct., 1895, VG . . . .**$40.00 (B)**

Red Head Bottle Caps, resealable bottle caps on blister pack from country store, NOS, 1940s, EX . . . .**$40.00 (D)**

Red Head, Hi-Octane Gasoline globe, glass wide body with two glass lenses, 13½" dia., G . . . .**$1,100.00 (B)**

Red Indian Gasoline, globe with graphics of Indian in full headdress, screw-on glass body, 13½" dia., G . . .**$675.00 (C)**

Red Man ...The mild mellow chew, hard-to-find porcelain advertising sign with graphics of arrow through product package, 22" x 10½", EX . . . .**$825.00 (B)**

Rex Flintkote Roofing, "For all roofs," tin litho match holder, great graphics of barn with message on roof, 5" H, G, $350.00 (B). *Courtesy of Richard Opfer Auctioneering, Inc.*

Richfield, dealer advertising calendar, paper, never used, 7⅜" x 7½", NM, $125.00 (B).

Richlube Motor Oil, double-sided metal sign, 24" dia., EX, $1,300.00 (B). *Courtesy of Collectors Auction Services*

Red Crown Ethyl Gasoline, double-sided porcelain sign with very strong colors, 30" dia., EX, $425.00 (B). *Courtesy of Autopia Advertising Auctions*

Red Man, The mild mellow chew, porcelain sign, 22" x 10½", G . . . .$295.00 (D)

Redmen Archery...Shoot, painted wooden advertising sign with artwork of Indian head in center of message, 24" x 34", EX . . . .$250.00 (C)

Redmen Archery, wood advertising sign with graphics of Indian in center, 24" x 34", VG . . . .$475.00 (D)

Red Mill, rolled oats tin, Winona, MN, EX . . .$175.00 (C)

Red-Ola Cigars...Edward D. Depew & Co., New York, round metal tip tray with artwork of pretty woman in center of tray, 4¼" dia., EX . . . .$175.00 (B)

Red Raven, "Ask the Man," round metal tip tray, with graphics of woman with red raven, 4" dia., NM . . . . .$376.00 (B)

Red Raven ...For Headache...For Indigestion, rectangular metal tip tray with graphics of red raven and woman on tray center, 6⅛" L, EX . . . .$170.00 (B)

Ridenour-Johnson Hardware Co., advertisement, framed cardboard litho, copyright 1922, 1920s, 16" x 26½", VG, $95.00 (D).

Rit Dye, medicine tin cabinet with six product drawers in back, 10" x 16¼", G, $135.00 (B).

Red Man "Mellow Chew," scarce porcelain sign with pack and arrow, 22" x 10½", EX, $500.00 (B). *Courtesy of Autopia Advertising Auctions*

Ritz Crackers, cardboard advertising poster, 26" x 14", G, $40.00 (B).

"Red Raven Splits...Ask the man," porcelain advertising ashtray, 6" x 3½", EX ....$110.00 (B)

Red Raven Splits, metal advertising tip tray, "For high livers' livers," with red raven and bottle in center, 12" dia., EX ....$440.00 (B)

Red Raven Splits, tin lithographed serving tray, "Ask the man," 13¾" x 10½", VG ....$235.00 (B)

Red Raven, tin litho tip tray with artwork of young girl hugging an oversized version of the logo bird, 4¼" dia., EX ....$350.00 (B)

Red Raven, tip tray, good graphics, 4¼", EX ..$300.00 (C)

Red Rock Ginger Ale, paper litho under glass with link chain frame with graphics of woman with product, 6" x 8", 1920s, EX ....$185.00 (B)

Red Seal, automotive ignition battery advertising sign, tin over cardboard, strong colors, 27" x 19", EX ..$1,500.00 (B)

Red Seal Battery...A battery for every use, flange painted metal sign in likeness of dry seal battery, G ..$135.00 (D)

Red Seal Battery, die cut curved porcelain advertising sign shaped in the image of the product, 14½" x 34¼", EX ....$575.00 (C)

Red Seal Battery, double-sided die cut porcelain advertising sign in image of the product, 13" x 24½", EX ..$925.00 (C)

Red Seal Bottlers Extracts, litho on heavy paper with artwork of woman wearing red hat and red dress, St. Louis, Mo., business, 11½" x 16½", G ....$125.00 (B)

Red Seal Peanut Butter, tin litho container with artwork of three fiddlers, 12-oz., EX ....$196.00 (B)

Roadfinder Cycle Tyres, one-sided porcelain advertising sign, 24" x 8", VG, **$125.00 (B).**

Roanoke Rye, Thompson, Wilson & Co., Distillers, Paducah, Ky., framed paper litho, still has good colors, professionally restored, in original frame, 1900s, 14" x 19", EX, **$1,500.00 (C).** *Courtesy of B.J. Summers*

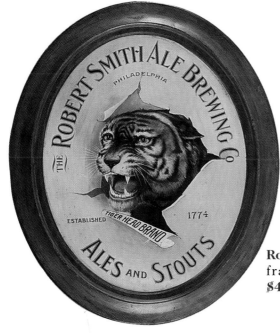

Robert Smith Ale Brewing Co., tin litho, self-framing serving tray, 19" x 23½", EX, **$4,500.00 (C).**

Red Seal, porcelain advertisir   mometer with graphics of battery at top and me: The guarantee protects you," 7¼" x 27¼", EX . . . .$170.00 (B)

Red Spot Coffee, embossed i door push bar, 19¾" x 2¾", NM . . . .$60.00 (B)

Red Star cleaning powder, paper label cardboard box with early family scene, 5" x 3½" x 1¼", 1880s, VG **$95.00 (D)**

Red Top, steel posts, painted metal sign, 18" x 24", G . . . .$85.00 (D)

Red Wing, pot scraper, advertising Red Wing Flour, with artwork of flour bag on front, tin litho, 3" x 2½", EX . . . .$1,050.00 (B)

Red Wolf Steel Cut Coffee, tin litho container with wire handle, graphics of wolf in oval on front, 6-lb., EX . .$200.00 (B)

Refiners, gas globe, high profile metal body with two glass lenses, 16½" dia., G . . . .$650.00 (B)

Rehkopf's Special, Straight Kentucky Whiskey, Paducah, Ky., 1-qt. stone jug, G . . . .$150.00 (C)

Reids Special Ice Cream, double-sided die cut porcelain sign, top hanger, 30" dia., VG . . . .$375.00 (B)

Reliance Advertising Co., single-sided advertising sign promoting their porcelain enameled advertising signs, 24" x 13¼", VG . . . .$170.00 (B)

Reliance Baking Powder, tin litho match holder, graphics of woman working in kitchen, 5¾" H, G . . . .$425.00 (B)

Remer's Tea Store, cardboard advertising die cut sign featuring cup on edge with cat drinking from saucer, 10" x 6¼", EX . . . .$35.00 (D)

Roe Feeds, painted metal sign, 7" x 12", VG, $75.00 (C).

Rogers Bros. Silverplate, paper litho advertising poster, 31" x 45", VG, $100.00 (B).

Rose Valley Whiskey, self-framing tin advertising sign, 1905, 28¾" x 22¼", G, $425.00 (B).

Remer's Tea Store, die cut cardboard of cat in cup, 10" x 6¼", EX . . . .$25.00 (B)

Remington, advertising calendar with top graphics of "Old Mike" in boat ready for waterfowl hunting, 15" x 29", 1924, NM . . . .$475.00 (C)

Remington Ammunition, sign with graphics of animals, 20" x 27", EX . . . .$60.00 (B)

Remington, cardboard window sign, advertising .22 rifle, 20½" x 18½", G . . . .$135.00 (D)

Remington, Household Knives, "At last I've found a knife that cuts," cardboard ad sign with graphics of woman at kitchen table with product, 12" x 18", G . . . . .$98.00 (B)

Remington, idea poster with graphics of different long guns and the game for each, 13" x 25", VG . .$155.00 (C)

Remington...Let 'er rain, with hunter in boat, 1925, 15" x 28½", EX . . . .$560.00 (B)

Remington, light-up advertising sign, featuring artwork of muzzle loader with powder horn, "the most famous name in shooting," metal and plastic, 25" x 12", G . .$85.00 (D)

Remington, Nitro Express...Long Range Game Loads, cardboard shell box with Remington UMC spotlight at top of message, full box, EX . . . .$95.00 (B)

Remington, Sporting Cartridges, wall-hanging sign, cardboard with graphics of cartridges and their sizes. 13" x 20", EX . . . .$70.00 (B)

Roszell's Sealtest... Homogenized Milk, plastic and neon sign, EX, **$175.00 (D)**.

Ross, Jesse L., & Co., Druggists, metal litho serving tray, 13¾" x 16¾", VG, **$225.00 (B)**.

Royal Crown Cola, heavily embossed bottle sign, 15½" x 58½", EX, **$165.00 (D)**. *Courtesy of Riverview Antique Mall*

Royal Crown Cola, cardboard poster with Shirley Temple, 29½" x 12¼", G, **$225.00 (B)**.

Remington, UMC Nitro club, cardboard shotgun shell box with graphics of goose on front, 4" x 4" x 2½", NM .**$95.00 (C)**

Remington, UMC, Sportsmen's Headquarters, Firearms & Ammunition, double-sided die cut flange sign featuring the Remington bears, 7" x 8", EX ....**$2,200.00 (B)**

Resinol Soap & Ointment...For All Skin Diseases...At All Drug Stores, round metal tip tray with artwork of red-haired woman in center of tray, 4¼" dia., EX . .**$170.00 (B)**

Return of Mandy's Husband, paper litho advertising poster starring Mantan Morehead and Flourney E. Miller, 26½" x 40½", G ....**$125.00 (C)**

Rev-O-Noc, tin litho over cardboard advertising sign promoting firearms, sporting goods, fishing tackle, 19¼" x 13¼", 1915, EX ....**$1,100.00 (C)**

Rexall...Compare the price and save on..., light-up clock with message to left of clock face, EX ....**$85.00 (C)**

Rexall...From the ...store, clear glass store bowl with heavily embossed lettering, 4¼" x 4¾", EX . . .**$35.00 (D)**

Rexall, tin litho baby talc container with artwork of young baby in cameo shot in center, 2½" x 4½" x 1⅜", EX ....**$300.00 (B)**

Royal Crown Cola, light-up advertising clock by Pam Clock Co., 14½" dia., $190.00 (B).

Royal Crown Cola, light-up advertising clock, cardboard body with glass face and cover, Telechron Inc., Ashland, Mass., U.S.A. C.A.P., 15" dia., VG, $275.00 (B). *Courtesy of Collectors Auction Services*

Royal Crown Cola, miniature bottle, 1936, 3" tall, G, $50.00 (D). *Courtesy of Antiques, Cards & Collectibles/Ray Pelley*

Royal Crown Cola, one-sided cardboard poster with graphics of girl on phone, 28" x 11", EX, $75.00 (B).

Rex Flintkote Roofing, "For all roofs," tin litho match holder, great graphics of barn with message on roof, 5" H, EX . . . .$475.00 (C)

Rex King's, framed cardboard sign advertising belladonna, porous and kidney plasters, 16" x 25", VG . . .$115.00 (C)

R.G. Sullivan Co., light-up advertising sign, reverse painted glass for 7-20-4 cigar, 24" x 8" x 3¾", EX . . . .$355.00 (B)

R.G. Sullivan's, Quality 10¢ Cigar, single-sided porcelain advertising sign, 30" x 12", VG . . . .$170.00 (B)

Rhinelander Butter, tin over cardboard advertising sign with graphics of products and bottom of sign, 13¼" x 9¼", NM . . . .$165.00 (C)

Rice Oil Co, Johnstown, O., gas globe, high profile metal body with two glass lenses, 15" dia., VG . . .$1,200.00 (B)

Rice Shoes, cardboard die cut shoe, compliments of C.W. Rice, Baldwinsville, N.Y., 9¼" x 6", EX . . . .$35.00 (C)

Rice's Seeds, stone litho paper poster with graphics of a man lifting a very large turnip, 20½ x 28¼", 1890s, EX . . . .$805.00 (B)

Richardson Root Beer, electric animated bear and glass mug, papier-mache bear turns and spins on base simulating ice skating, 16½" x 16½" x 25", NM . . . .$425.00 (B)

Richardson Root Beer...Rich in Flavor, tin litho ad sign, 1950s, 14" x 10", red, white, and black, NM . . .$57.00 (B)

Richelieu Coffee, Sprague, Warner & Company, Chicago, Ill., U.S.A., with screw-on lid, 1-lb., G . . . .$35.00 (D)

Richfield Gasoline...Just Ahead, embossed tin advertising sign with graphics of eagle in center, 70" x 56", EX . . . .$795.00 (C)

Royal Crown Cola, self-framing embossed metal advertising sign, NOS, 31½" x 12", EX, $80.00 (B).

Royal Crown Cola, Tastes Best, paper on board advertising poster with graphics of 20th Century Fox star Linda Darnell serving the product to two service men, 43" x 31", VG, $150.00 (B). *Courtesy of Collectors Auction Services*

Royal Crown Cola, Drink... Best By Taste Test, mirrored thermometer and barometer, rare piece, 12" x 24", G, $250.00 (B). *Courtesy of Muddy River Trading Co./Gary Metz*

Royal Crown Cola...the fresher refresher, metal thermometer, 10" x 26", white, red, and blue, G, $120.00 (D). *Courtesy of Patrick's Collectibles*

Richfield...here soon, paper poster with artwork of man in early model race car, 39½" x 54½", G .....$225.00 (C)

Richfield, Hi-Octane, gas globe with Richfield bird in center, low profile metal body with two glass lenses, 15" dia., VG ....$350.00 (B)

Richfield, Oil Company, game reserve embossed tin sign, "No Hunting In This Closed Area," 13¾" x 9¾", NM ....$150.00 (B)

Richfield...The gasoline of power, two-sided die cut porcelain shield-shaped sign, 48" x 48", G .....$1,200.00 (B)

Richlube, All-Weather Motor Oil...30¢ per quart, double-sided metal rack sign, 16" x 12", 1938, EX ...$255.00 (C)

Richlube Motor Oil, double-sided porcelain advertising sign, 24" dia., F ....$275.00 (C)

Richlube Motor Oil, pole sign, die cut metal in shape of oil can, 9" x 15", VG ....$130.00 (B)

Ridenour-Johnson Hardware Co., advertisement, framed cardboard litho, copyright 1922, 1920s, 16" x 26½", G ....$70.00 (B)

Rienzi Beer...In Bottles Only...Bartholomay Brewery.. Rochester, NY, round tip tray with artwork of man on white horse with product bottle, 4⅛" dia., EX .....$130.00 (B)

Right-Cut Chewing Tobacco, tin litho wall dispenser with graphics of old gent, 4¼" x 10¼" x 2¼", EX ...$55.00 (C)

Royal Scot Feeds, single-sided embossed tin advertising sign, 16" x 23½", VG, **$125.00 (B).**
Courtesy of Collectors Auction Services

Ryzon, The Perfect Baking Powder, double-sided tin sign with artwork of baking powder can, arm-hung, 1940s, 12" x 16", EX, **$475.00 (B).** *Courtesy of Muddy River Trading Co./Gary Metz*

Right Food Company, Moorman Mfg. Co. Quincy, Ill., hog watch fob in gold wash, EX . . . .$65.00 (C)

Riley Bros., That's oil, tin litho advertising sign, 13½" x 5½", EX . . . .$65.00 (C)

Ringling Bros. and Barnum & Bailey, paper advertising poster for "May Wirth, the greatest bareback rider of all time," 16¾" x 24½", VG . . . .$100.00 (B)

Ringling Bros. and Barnum Bailey Circus, paper litho advertising poster with graphics of leopard head, 29" x 43½", EX . . . .$110.00 (B)

Rinso...Soak the clothes – that's all...saves coal every wash-day, one-sided porcelain advertising sign, 24" x 18", VG . . . .$650.00 (B)

Rising Sun, stove polish, store advertising sign, 8¾" x 6", EX . . . .$325.00 (C)

Rival Stove, by J & E Stevens Co., Cromwell CT, nickel-plated sample item, 5½" x 7½" x 15½", 1895, EX . . . . .$1,500.00 (C)

River Front Coffee, container with paper label, cardboard sides and metal top and bottom, with waterport scene, from Reeves, Parvin & Co., Philadelphia, 1-lb., EX . . .$155.00 (C)

R-KAO Coffee, For Lovers of True Flavor, tin litho container with slip-lid, scarce item, 1-lb., EX . . . .$85.00 (B)

Roanoke Rye, Thompson, Wilson & Co., Distillers, Paducah, Ky., framed paper litho, still has good colors, professionally restored, in original frame, 1900s, 14" x 19", VG . . . .$1,000.00 (C)

Robin Hood, Tread Straight, reverse painted advertising, 15" x 4", VG . . . .$110.00 (B)

Robinson's Pilsner Beer, tin litho serving tray with graphics of folks enjoying beer in canoes on lake at a dock, 12", EX . . . .$288.00 (B)

Rochester percolator, paper litho advertising with graphics of woman enjoying the "new" product, 27" x 21", EX . . . .$40.00 (B)

Rochester Root Beer, dispenser with front tap with Rochester decals on back and side panels, made by Multiplex Faucet Co., St. Louis, MO, 16½" x 16½" x 25", G . . . .$90.00 (B)

Rockford High Grade Watches, Oscar Holmes, Cambridge, Minn., metal tip tray with artwork of woman sitting beside tree, 4⅞" L, G . . . .$45.00 (B)

Rock Spring ...Sparkling water...ginger ale, kola, round metal serving tray, 12" dia., EX . . . .$15.00 (D)

Rocky Ford...A new high in two for five cigars, 50-count cigar box with graphics of Indian looking with hand over eyes, EX . . . .$25.00 (B)

Rocky Mountain Honey Co., embossed tin advertising sign, graphics depict child eating breakfast, 16" x 12", VG . . . .$550.00 (B)

Rogers Drugs, light-up advertising sign, leaded glass, 63" x 27", VG . . . .$600.00 (B)

Roi-Tan, die cut cardboard cigarette girl sign, countertop size, easel back, NOS, 7" x 19", 1930s, EX . . .$375.00 (C)

Roi-Tan, great advertising tin litho automobile, "Take a ride with Sophie Tucker and Roi-Tan" with double-sided marquee, 4¼" x 1½" x 4½", EX . . . .$475.00 (C)

Roi-Tan...Man to Man...A Real Fine Cigar, reverse glass sign in original brass frame, 13" x 21¼", NM . .$687.00 (B)

Rolling Rock, Extra Pale Beer, painted metal advertising thermometer, 8¼" x 27", EX . . . .$55.00 (B)

Rolling Rock, The Premium Beer, advertising glass sign, easel back, cobalt, EX . . . .$125.00 (C)

Rose Exterminator Co., die cut oval porcelain advertising sign with image of owl and "Wise Protection...Since 1860," 18¾" x 11¼", NM . . . .$175.00 (C)

Rose Exterminators, die cut "spraying man" advertising figural sign, 10¾" x 10¾", NM . . . .$275.00 (C)

Rosemary Foods...the highest standard of purity and excellence, metal wagon with rubber tires, 15" x 14" x 34", G . . . .$75.00 (C)

Rose-O-Cuba Cigar, tin litho container with graphics of roses and senorita on front and back, 5½" x 5¼", EX . . . .$75.00 (B)

Round Oak Stove, calendar with Indian graphics, 10½" x 20½", 1926, NM . . . .$410.00 (B)

Round Oak Stoves, Ranges & Furnaces, metal pocket match safe, with celluloid advertising on sides, 1½" x 3" x ⅜", EX . . . .$325.00 (B)

Round Up Coffee, glass jar with paper label manufactured by the Round Up grocery Co., Spokane, WA, with cowboy riding a bucking horse in center cameo, 4" x 6", EX . . . .$110.00 (B)

Rowntree's Toffee, tin with slip-on lid, 6½" x 4" x 8¼", EX . . . .$95.00 (C)

Royal Baking Powder, wooden shipping box with good advertising on ends and sides, debossed and painted lettering, 14¾" x 8½" x 7¾", EX . . . .$75.00 (C)

Royal Beer...Ale cardboard advertising sign, 21" x 11", G . . . .$55.00 (C)

Royal Blend High Grade Roasted Coffee, Granger & Co., Buffalo, NY, paper litho on cardboard with crown graphics on lid and front, trolley on reverse, 1-lb., EX . .$45.00 (B)

Royal Crown Cola, die cut painted metal bottle sign of 1936 bottle, 15¾" x 59¾", EX . . . .$395.00 (D)

Royal Crown Cola...Drink, metal menu board with message and logo at top, 19¾" x 28", red, blue, black, and white, EX . . . .$95.00 (D)

Royal Crown Cola, heavily embossed bottle sign, 15½" x 58½", NM . . . .$225.00 (D)

Royal Crown Cola, heavy paper advertising sign with graphics of Jeanette MacDonald enjoying the product with three service men, 40" x 28½", VG . . . .$150.00 (B)

Royal Crown Cola, light-up advertising clock, cardboard body with glass face and cover, Telechron Inc., Ashland, Mass., U.S.A. C.A.P., 15" dia., NM . . . .$450.00 (D)

Royal Crown Cola, miniature bottle, 1936, 3" tall, EX . . . .$75.00 (C)

Royal Crown Cola, "RC tastes best!" says Barbara Stanwyck, with artwork of actress holding a bottle of RC, trolley car sign, 28" x 11", G . . . .$140.00 (B)

Royal Crown Cola, stenciled on tin double-sided bracket-hung advertising sign with graphics of 6-pack and message "Six Big Bottles 25¢," strong colors, 23¾" x 15¾", EX . . . .$525.00 (B)

Royal Crown Cola, Tastes Best, paper on board advertising poster with graphics of 20th Century Fox star Linda Darnell serving the product to two service men, 43" x 31", EX . . . .$195.00 (C)

Royal Crown Cola...the fresher refresher, metal thermometer, 10" x 26", white, red, and blue, EX .$175.00 (D)

Royal Crown, Drink... Cola Best By Taste Test, mirrored thermometer/barometer, rare piece, 12" x 24", EX . . . .$395.00 (D)

Royal Crown, "Relax and Enjoy," Art Deco style metal advertising sign with tilted bottle in spotlight in center, 23¾" x 16", EX . . . .$435.00 (D)

Royal Daylight Lamp Oil...Best American Lamp Oils, single-sided porcelain advertising sign with graphics of horse-drawn oil wagon, 21" x 14½", VG . . . .$800.00 (B)

Royal Portable Typewriter, paper litho advertisment from the Continental Litho Corp., Cleveland O., with graphics of typewriter with a card that reads "Merry Christmas to The Family," 21½" x 27½", VG . . . .$100.00 (B)

Royal Princess, cigar box, with artwork of Indian princess on inside lid and front label, 50-ct., 1930, EX . . . . .$95.00 (C)

Royal Rose Talcum Powder, tin litho container with graphics of rose, by the National Drug Co., 2¼" x 6" x 1¼", EX . . . .$130.00 (B)

Royalty Club Whiskey....A. Friedman Co...Sole Distributers, framed painted glass, 31" x 21", EX . . . .$55.00 (D)

Roza De Luzon cigars, stone litho sign, by Kurz & Allison, Chicago, depicting the Battle of Chattanooga, 34¼" x 27¼", 1888, EX . . . .$975.00 (C)

RPM Motor Oil...A Knockout For Winter, painted tin sign with image of Donald Duck and a snowman, 23⅝" dia., 1940s, NM . . . .$2,250.00 (B)

Ruhstaller's Lager...Best Beer Brew...Sacramento, Cal., round metal tip tray with serving maid carrying steins of product, 4¼" dia., EX . . . .$170.00 (B)

Runkel Brothers Breakfast Cocoa, tin litho with small top, 2½" x 2½" x 4¾", EX . . . .$75.00 (C)

Runkel's, "Essence of chocolate," tin, screw-on lid, 6" x 6" x 9", EX . . . .$375.00 (C)

Rusco Fan Belts, countertop display unit, 12½" x 22" x 16¾", VG . . . .$175.00 (B)

Rush Park Seeds, shipping and countertop display box with colorful paper labels, 31" x 16" x 5½", EX $95.00 (B)

Ryan's Jet, Regular, heavy milk glass gas globe, NOS, still in original shipping box, 16½", NM . . . .$350.00 (B)

Ryzon, The Perfect Baking Powder, double-sided tin sign with artwork of baking powder can, arm-hung, 1940s, 12" x 16", F . . . .$95.00 (C)

Saboroso Cigar Store, celluloid advertising tape measure, 1¾" x ½", EX . . . .$40.00 (B)

Safety First...Compliments of the Atlanta Coca-Cola Bottling Company, school tablet with graphics of crossing guard, 8½" x 11", EX . . . .$9.00 (D)

Salada Coffee, die cut single-sided advertising sign in shape of can of coffee, 12" x 12", EX . . . .$450.00 (B)

Salada Tea...Delicious Flavor, porcelain door push, 34" x 3½", G . . . .$65.00 (D)

Salem...Change To, rubber change pad with astro turf, 10" x 10", G . . . .$12.00 (D)

Salinas Brewing Co., give-away advertising plate with graphics of horse head in center, by the Sterling China Co., 9" dia., 1904, EX . . . .$50.00 (B)

Salisbury's, new car rental, cardboard advertising sign with post-war auto, 23" x 12½", NM . . . .$155.00 (C)

Sally Clover Coffee, tin litho screw-lid container, 1-lb., NM . . . .$45.00 (B)

Sambo, counter store display, featuring likeness of Smoking Sambo standing enjoying a cigar, "Smoking Sambos Fine Cigars, Euclid, OH," 8½" x 16", 1930s, EX . . . . .$85.00 (B)

Sambo, drink advertisment with black bell man, made by Carvin Bottle Cap Corporation, Brooklyn, N.Y., tin litho, 13¾" x 19⅝", VG . . . .$300.00 (B)

Sambo's Fine Cigars, advertising clock with tin litho face and wooden frame, with graphics of smoking Sambo in center of clock face, 15¼" x 15¼", 1930s, EX . . . .$190.00 (B)

San Alto Cigar, cardboard ad sign with graphics of black servant serving product, 14" x 30", EX . . . . . .$230.00 (B)

S & H Green Stamps, advertising clock, "We Give S & H green stamps," 15¼" x 22¾", EX . . . .$125.00 (C)

S & H Green Stamps, porcelain, double-sided hanging sign, EX . . . .$210.00 (D)

Salada Tea, single-sided porcelain sign, out of Canada, 14⅞" x 6¾", G, $450.00 (C).

San Antonio Brewing Assoc., paper advertisement, "The Famous Judge Roy Bean Horse Thief Trail," 1945, 26" x 21¼", G, $110.00 (B).

San Diego Bus Stop, one-sided porcelain sign, 16" x 12½", VG, $325.00 (B).

Sandusky Gold Bread, Radiant Baked, tin log holder, 36½" x 13½" x 3½", G, $95.00 (B).

San Felice Cigar, cardboard advertisement with graphics of man and woman critiquing a painting, "for gentlemen of good taste," 18¼" x 23¾", VG . . . .$170.00 (B)

Sanford's Inks, advertising embossed tin litho sign with graphics of products in jars and bottles, by the Tuscarora Advertising Co., Coshocton, OH, 19½" x 13½", 1890s, P . . . .$300.00 (D)

Sanita Malt Coffee, paper litho ad sign with art of two small girls at table, 10" x 15", EX . . . .$44.00 (B)

Sanitary Ice Cream and Milk, light-up advertising clock, metal body with glass face and lenses, 15" dia., F . . . . . .$130.00 (B)

San Marto Coffee, tin litho with screw-on lid, graphics of horseback warrior, 1-lb., 1923, EX . . . .$225.00 (C)

Santa Fe Pure Ground Mustard, spice tin with paper label with strong graphics of Indian beside trademark, 3¼" x 2⅛ x 1¼", EX . . . .$55.00 (C)

Santovin, veterinary remedy tin litho advertising sign with graphics of animals and sunrise, 20⅛" x 27⅛", NM . . . .$195.00 (C)

Sapolio Soap, sign, paper trolley sign with graphics of man and woman shown using the product, 21" x 11", EX . . . .$165.00 (B)

Satin Luminall...one coat, painted metal thermometer with vertical scale in center with product messages at top and bottom, 8½" x 38½", EX . . . .$55.00 (D)

Satin Skin Cream & Powder, die cut countertop cardboard advertising sign with likeness of woman and cherub, 18" x 18", 1911, F . . . .$75.00 (D)

Satin...Turkish Cigarettes, 20 for 15¢, round metal serving tray, 13¾" dia., EX . . . .$35.00 (D)

Sauer's, flavoring and extracts, wood case clock with reverse painting and lettering, 42½" H, VG . . . .$1,200.00 (D)

Sanford's Inks, advertising embossed tin litho sign with graphics of products in jars and bottles, by the Tuscarora Advertising Co., Coshocton, OH, 19½" x 13½", 1890s, EX, **$3,000.00 (B).** *Courtesy of Buffalo Bay Auction Co.*

Satin Skin Cream & Powder, die cut counter-top cardboard advertising sign with likeness of woman and cherub, 18" x 18", 1911, EX, **$440.00 (B).** *Courtesy of Buffalo Bay Auction Co.*

Savage Arms, firearms catalog with graphics of Indian with firearm, 28 pages, 1935, VG . . . .**$185.00 (B)**

Savage Stevens Fox Shotguns, cardboard advertising poster with geese in flight, 16" x 12", NM . . . . .**$75.00 (C)**

Sav-More System, regular gas globe, plastic body with glass lenses, 13½" dia., VG . . . .**$325.00 (B)**

Sayman's Soap, store box with lid that folds into display unit containing 12 full bars of vegetable soap, 7" x 6½" x 2½", EX . . . .**$145.00 (C)**

Schell's Carbonated Mead, Prohibition advertising sign for August Schell Brewing Co., New Ulm, Mn., great artwork of woman with peacock, 16¼" x 33", NM . . . . .**$1,350.00 (B)**

Schell's Mead, stone litho from the August Schell Brewery in New Ulm, MN, featuring graphics of woman and peacock, very colorful, 16" x 32", 1910, G . . . . .**$575.00 (C)**

Schepps Cake, box litho embossed tin container with vintage family scene, 13" x 13" x 14", VG . . . . .**$165.00 (B)**

Schlaich Locks, tin litho store counter display box for the Boyce MotoMeter, 13" x 2 x 8¾", VG . . . . . .**$325.00 (C)**

Schlitz Beer, sign, great litho from Chas. Shonk Co., with graphics of logo man in center, 13½" x 19", EX . .**$2,030.00 (B)**

Schlitz Hotel & Palm Garden, complimentary pocket knife with image of clown in center, "Milwaukee Carnival Knife," EX . . . .**$70.00 (B)**

Schlitz, match and stamp safe, metal with embossed sides and two separate compartments, 1½" x 3", EX . .**$195.00 (C)**

Schlitz, neon sign in original wood crate, three-color, red, blue, and green, 1930s, 17" x 29", NM . . . . .**$490.00 (B)**

Schmauss Garden Cafe...Milwaukee, Wis., round metal tip tray with very colorful graphics of restaurant interior scene, 6" dia., EX . . . .**$65.00 (B)**

Schmidt's, bronze bartender with embossed lettering, 7¾" H, EX . . . .**$175.00 (C)**

Scholl's Axle Grease, tin litho pail with metal handle with graphics of runaway wagon, "Independent Oil Co., Mansfield, Ohio," 6" x 9½", EX . . . .**$80.00 (B)**

School Boy Peanut Butter, tin litho pail with side-mounted wire bail, 2-lb., EX . . . .**$88.00 (B)**

Schroeder, advertising calendar promoting horseshoeing, blacksmithing, and general repairing with graphics of young girl in bonnet, 14½" x 20", EX . . . . . .**$450.00 (C)**

Schulteiss Beer, porcelain sign, German spelling of "bier," 24" x 47½", VG . . . .**$95.00 (B)**

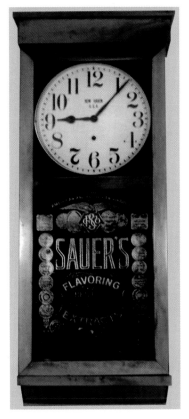

Sauer's, Flavoring and Extracts, wood case clock with reverse painting and lettering, 42½" H, EX, **$1,550.00 (B).** *Courtesy of Richard Opfer Auctioneering, Inc.*

Sauer's Flavoring Extracts, wood advertising thermometer, 7¾" x 23½", G, **$175.00 (B).**

Schell's Carbonated Mead, Prohibition advertising sign for August Schell Brewing Co., New Ulm, Mn., great artwork of woman with peacock, 16¼" x 33", EX, **$1,200.00 (C).**

Scotten Dillon Company, Detroit, Mich., Ojibwa Tobacco, tin litho store bin, originally had 48 five-cent packages, 8½" x 11¼", G . . . .**$325.00 (B)**

Scudder's, Brownie Brand Confection Butter Maple Flavor, featuring Brownie characters, 1½-lb., EX . . . . .**$240.00 (B)**

Scull's Coffee, tin store bin, featuring great stenciled and litho graphics, 21½" H, EX . . . .**$925.00 (B)**

Seagram's Seven, Crown advertising clock, metal housing with pressed form front with images of horses on front, 16" x 14½", VG . . . .**$80.00 (B)**

Sea Gull Baking Powder, tin container with paper litho of sea gull in flight, unopened, 2⅛" x 3¼", EX . .**$275.00 (B)**

Sealed Power Piston Rings, double-sided light-up advertising dealer sign, 34" x 14" x 6", VG . . . .**$275.00 (C)**

Seal of Kentucky Mustard, Covington, Ky., paper litho on cardboard, with graphics of seal of Kentucky on front, 1½-oz., NM . . . .**$223.00 (B)**

Seal of North Carolina, paper litho advertising sign with graphics of woman lying on a day bed with a bird on a swing over the bed, inset of product in upper right corner, 12" x 7½", NM . . . .**$255.00 (C)**

Seal of North Carolina, paper litho advertising, six black men and a dog, 21¼" x 24¼", VG . . . .**$1,500.00 (D)**

Sealtest...Dairy Products, square plastic light-up advertising clock, 15¼" sq., G . . . .**$1,115.00 (C)**

Sealtest Ice Cream, embossed tin self-framing advertising sign, "Sealtest Ice Cream," 30" x 14", G . . . . . .**$40.00 (B)**

Schlitz, bottle flashlight, VG, $45.00 (D). *Courtesy of Pleasant Hill Antique Mall & Tea Room/Bob Johnson*

Schlitz, salt & pepper set, VG, $15.00 (D). *Courtesy of Pleasant Hill Antique Mall & Tea Room/Bob Johnson*

Schmidt's, bronze bartender with embossed lettering, 7¾" H, NM, $195.00 (C).

Scudder's, Brownie Brand Confection Butter Maple Flavor, can featuring Brownie characters, 1½-lb., EX, $240.00 (B). *Courtesy of Morford Auctions*

Sealtest Ice Cream, menu board, tin with product name over nine message panels, 9¾" x 25⅝", G . . .$100.00 (B)

Sealy Mattress, four-piece die cut cardboard litho advertising with easel backs, life-size characters, man with cotton basket on his shoulder, a couple of black children and scene of slaves picking cotton in field, VG . . .$650.00 (C)

Search Light, match box holder, with litho of instruction on front and original box, NM . . . .$150.00 (B)

Sears, Rivera coffee pail with small lid, 7¼" x 10½", EX . . . .$295.00 (C)

Sears, Roebuck and Co., Chicago, oval metal tip tray with factory scene and Lady Justice, 6", EX . . . . . .$75.00 (B)

Sears, Roebuck and Co., Sun-Kist tin litho tobacco canister, 4¼" x 5", EX . . . .$135.00 (C)

Selmer Band Instruments, light-up advertising clock with graphics of band member in various poses for hour positions, 16" dia., EX . . . .$750.00 (B)

Seminola Cigar, embossed celluloid advertising sign with graphics of Indian bust, 9" x 6", NM . . . .$100.00 (C)

Seneca Red Top Socks, cardboard box with artwork of Indian in center of arrowhead with kids ice skating, 5" x 14" x 2", NM . . . .$58.00 (B)

Senn & Ackerman Brewing Co., Elk Carnival advertising pocket mirror, with graphics of elk head in center, "Elks Carnival... Oct-1899," 2" dia., 1899, EX . . . . .$95.00 (C)

Senora Cubana, embossed die cut metal sign advertising Perecoy & Moore's Cigars with lady in fur jacket, 7¼" x 13", EX . . . .$135.00 (C)

Serv-us Brand Coffee, tin litho with screw-on lid, graphics of steaming cup of product, 1-lb., EX . . . .$80.00 (B)

Seven-Up, die cut embossed bottle sign, 13" x 44½", 1962, EX . . . .$350.00 (C)

Scull's Coffee, tin store bin, featuring great stenciled and litho graphics, 21½" H, EX, $925.00 (B). *Courtesy of Richard Opfer Auctioneering, Inc.*

Seagram's, Canadian Hunter, paper advertising poster in wood frame, 34½" x 78¼", VG, $80.00 (B).

Seagram's, Queen's & King's Plate Winners, paper advertisement, 1905, 49½" x 35", G, $250.00 (C).

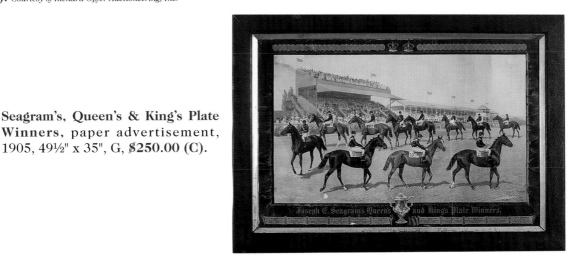

Seven-Up, display lamp with one-quart bottle base and Seven-Up advertising shade from the San Diego, Calif. bottling company, 15" x 24", 1950s, VG . . . .$190.00 (B)

Seven-Up, embossed tin advertising sign, 13¾" x 18", 1947, EX . . . .$190.00 (B)

Seven-Up, embossed tin advertising sign with graphics of bottle neck and "Fresh Up with," 27" x 19", NM .$370.00 (B)

Seven-Up, embossed tin octagon advertising sign "it likes you," 14" x 13¾", G . . . .$225.00 (C)

Seven-Up, embossed tin sign with a mesh wire frame, 28" x 50", VG . . . .$150.00 (B)

Seven-Up, Fresh Up bottle image tin thermometer, NOS, 6" x 15", NM . . . .$225.00 (C)

Seven-Up, Fresh Up embossed tin advertising sign, NOS, made by Stout Sign Co., 6¾" x 13¼", 1960, NM . .$125.00 (C)

Seven-Up, light-up advertising clock with graphics of the 7up with bubbles in center, 15" x 15", VG . . .$120.00 (B)

Seven-Up Likes You, double-sided metal flange advertising sign, 12½" x 10", 1946, EX . . . .$275.00 (C)

Seven-Up, porcelain door push, "Fresh Up...Seven Up," 31" x 3", VG . . . .$135.00 (B)

Seven-Up, porcelain thermometer, G . . . .$70.00 (C)

Sealy Mattress, advertising set, includes print with black workers picking cotton, and three die cut black figures working in cotton, unusual to find the die cut items, EX, **$1,550.00 (B)**. *Courtesy of Buffalo Bay Auction Co.*

Seiberling Air-Cooled Tires, double-sided porcelain sign, 30" x 17½", VG, **$375.00 (B)**.

Seven-Up, embossed tin advertising sign, 13¾" x 18", 1947, EX, **$190.00 (B)**. *Courtesy of Buffalo Bay Auction Co.*

Seven-Up...Slow School Zone curb side sign with graphics of policeman, 34" x 61½", EX . . . .$1,500.00 (C)

Seven-Up, tin bag rack sign, "You Like It...It Likes You" with metal wire slots for placing bags, 38½" x 17½", EX . . . .$275.00 (C)

Seven Up, You Like It...It Likes You, square light-up advertising clock, plastic face and wood frame, 15" x 15", NM . . . .$135.00 (C)

Shaker and New Tariff Ranges, trade card with graphics of Lt. Greenley with Eskimos at North Pole, 10" x 6", NM . . . .$130.00 (B)

Shaler Rislone...The Oil Alloy, painted metal thermometer, vertical scale with artwork of product can to left of scale, 9½" x 25", EX . . . .$45.00 (C)

Shamrock Coffee, tin litho container with pry-lid and graphics of cloverleaf in back of steaming coffee cup, 4" x 5", EX . . . .$75.00 (D)

Shamrock, Trail Master Regular, single-sided porcelain pump sign with graphics of shamrock, 10½" x 10½", VG . . . .$240.00 (B)

Sharpleigh Hardware Co., tin over cardboard advertising sign, "Hope Inspires...Work Wins...Success Rewards," St. Louis, U.S.A., 9¼" x 6¼", EX . . . .$40.00 (B)

Sharples, embossed tin sign advertising their tubular cream separator, 10" x 14", EX . . . .$315.00 (B)

Sharples, The Pet of the Dairy, match holder, with image of mother and daughter, great graphics, 2" x 7", EX . . . .$150.00 (B)

Seven-Up Likes You, dial-type aluminum advertising thermometer, 10" dia., NM, **$225.00 (C)**. *Courtesy of Autopia Advertising Auctions*

Seven-Up...Slow School Zone, curb side sign with graphics of policeman, 34" x 61½", VG, **$1,000.00 (B)**.

Courtesy of Collectors Auction Services

Seven-Up, vintage tin sign "anti-acid...Lithiated Lemon Soda," 9" x 20", 20s, G, **$325.00 (C)**. *Courtesy of Autopia Advertising Auctions*

Sharples, tin match safe with litho of woman operating the product, 2" x 6¾", EX . . . .$285.00 (B)

Shasta Sparkling Beverages, tin advertising sign with graphics of snow-covered mountains, 23½" x 11½", NM . . . .$180.00 (B)

Shave Master, Electric Shaver, countertop display unit for Sunbeam shavers, 10" x 10" x 16", G . . . . . .$105.00 (D)

Shaw & Truesdell Scratch & Chick Foods, cardboard advertising sign, farmyard scene, 21" x 31", F .$310.00 (C)

Shaw Piano, die cut advertising easel back sign of young girl with her dogs, 6¼" x 8¼", 1892, EX . . . . . .$45.00 (B)

Sheboygan Natural Mineral Water, Better Than Imported, tin litho of graphics of Indian being served by black waiters, 1910, 10" x 14", EX . . . .$660.00 (B)

Shell, Air Meter, double-sided die cut clam sign, 11¾" x 11⅛", VG . . . .$850.00 (B)

Shell, cloth flag with early company logo in center, mfg. by Emerson Mfg., S.F., Cal., NOS, 70" x 47", 1920s, NM . . . .$350.00 (B)

Shell, gas globe, one-piece milk glass clam-shaped globe, 18½" h, VG . . . .$450.00 (B)

Shell Gasoline & Motor Oil advertising calendar with graphics of pretty woman titled Roxana, from Lockport, Illinois, with full monthly pad, 10¼" x 17", 1929, EX . . . .$135.00 (C)

Shell Gasoline, porcelain paddle-type sign in shape of shell clam, 15" x 12", EX . . . .$700.00 (B)

Shell Gasoline, porcelain scale-type thermometer proomoting both gasoline and motor oil, 7¼" x 27", VG . . . .$1,800.00 (B)

Shell, light-up double-bubble advertising clock from the Pam Clock Co., New Rochelle, NY, great graphics of clam shell sign in center of clock face, hard-to-find this variation, 15½" sq., EX . . . .$250.00 (B)

Seven-Up, You Like It. . . It Likes You, glass, wood, and metal light-up advertising clock, 16" x 16" x 4", G, $110.00 (B).

Sharples Pot Scraper, with graphics of woman at separator, "The 1909 tubulars are better than ever," 1909, EX, $280.00 (B). *Courtesy of Buffalo Bay Auction Co.*

Sharples Separator, advertising sign with graphics of cherub and lady operating separator, self-framing metal composition, EX, $2,900.00 (C).

Courtesy of Buffalo Bay Auction Co.

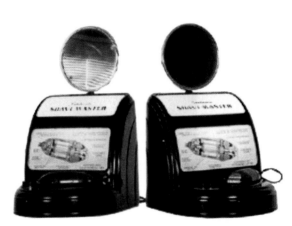

Shave Master, Electric Shaver, countertop display unit for Sunbeam shavers, 10" x 10" x 16", EX, $215.00 (B).

Shell Motor Oil, die cut double-sided porcelain sign with graphics of clam shell in center, in likeness of oil can, 15¾" x 20", G . . . .$600.00 (B)

Shell Oil Company...Private Road, one-sided porcelain sign, 14¹⁴⁄₁₆" x 11", VG . . . .$750.00 (B)

Shell, porcelain one-sided service station letter set, 15" H, VG . . . .$195.00 (B)

Shell, Premium Gasoline, die cut porcelain pump sign in classic clam shell shape, 12" x 12¼", NM . . . .$975.00 (B)

Shell, "Protected by...fly control program," one-sided metal sign with graphics of clam shell logo, 18" x 15", G . . . .$160.00 (B)

Shell Station, architectural porcelain sign in shape of trademark clam shell, 23" x 24" x 7½", EX . . .$800.00 (C)

Shaw & Truesdell Scratch & Chick Foods, cardboard advertising sign with farmyard scene, 21" x 31", VG, **$925.00 (B).** *Courtesy of Past Tyme Pleasures*

Shell, die cut metal, one-sided sign of scantily clad girl, rare item, probably foreign, 6½" x 15½", EX, **$1,100.00 (B).**

Shell, radiator cover, double-sided, cardboard, 18" x 13½", VG, **$40.00 (B).**

Shell, X-100 pump spinner in original box promoting motor oil, NOS, 14½" x 8" x 17", EX . . . .**$275.00 (B)**

Sherbrooke Pure Milk Co., double-sided tin advertising sign with graphics of ice cream cone, 20" x 28", VG . .**$80.00 (B)**

Sheridan Sugar Co., celluloid advertising pocket mirror with artwork of factory, 2¾" x 1¾", EX . . . . . .**$95.00 (C)**

Sherwin-Williams Paints and Varnishes, Sold Here, porcelain advertising sign with image of "Covers The Earth" logo at left, top mounting holes, 22" x 16", NM . . . .**$325.00 (C)**

Sherwin Williams Paints, porcelain advertising sign, with graphics of paint covering the world, 48" x 36", EX . . . .**$275.00 (C)**

Sherwin-Williams Paints-Varnishes-Enamels, double-sided porcelain hanging advertising sign with bracket, 12" x 8", VG . . . .**$275.00 (C)**

Sherwin-Williams, single-sided porcelain die cut advertising sign in the likeness of product pouring over the world, 35½" x 63", VG . . . .**$255.00 (C)**

Sherwood's Confectionery and Grocery, advertising calendar with scene of Indians hunting buffalo, 7" x 9½", 1925, NM . . . .**$100.00 (B)**

Shipmate Cigarettes, pocket advertising mirror with graphics of two sailors on front, 2" dia., VG . .**$185.00 (B)**

Showanda Cigar, tin with paper label on round tin with likeness of Indian on front, 25-ct, EX . . . .**$185.00 (B)**

Shredded Wheat, paper litho framed ad with graphics of box of product and bowl of cereal, 16" x 10½", VG . . .**$60.00 (B)**

Shryack Rolled Oats, container from Missouri, 3-lb., VG . . . .**$55.00 (C)**

Sidney Dillon Cigar, self-framing tin litho advertising sign with graphics of horse, 22¼" x 17", EX . . . . .**$450.00 (B)**

Sierra Ice Cream, metal serving tray, 16¼" x 12¾", NM . . . .**$235.00 (B)**

Signal Gasoline, porcelain pump sign with trademark signal light in center, 11⅞" dia., VG . . . .**$400.00 (C)**

Join the
Share-the-Road
Club *here*

Shell, Share-the-Road Club, paper litho poster, 39¼" x 56", EX, $155.00 (B).

Sherwin-Williams Paints, Cover the Earth, painted metal sign, G, $225.00 (C).

Silk Hosiery, advertising mirror, acid-etched figural hanging sign, 13" H, G, $625.00 (B). *Courtesy of Richard Opfer Auctioneering, Inc.*

Sherwin-Williams Paints-Varnishes-Enamels, double-sided porcelain hanging advertising sign with bracket, 12" x 8", NM, $575.00 (C).

Signal Lubrication Chek-Chart System, double-sided porcelain top-hung sign, 30" x 24", EX . . . . . .$400.00 (B)

Silencer, Stops Knocks, gas globe, low profile metal body with two glass lenses, "Made by Burford Oil Company," 15" dia., VG . . . .$1,300.00 (B)

Silk Hosiery, advertising mirror, acid-etched figural hanging sign, 13" H, G . . . .$625.00 (B)

Silver Birch Chewing Gum, store counter display box with unopened packages of gum, 6¼" x 5½" x 4¼", EX . . . .$1,500.00 (B)

Silver Flash, gas globe, one-piece glass body , 15" x 6" x 16¼", F . . . .$1,625.00 (C)

Silver Spring Brewery Ltd., paper litho advertising showing graphics of fireman with a glass of the product, 16¼" dia., VG . . . .$70.00 (B)

Silver Star, condom litho tin with artwork of streaking star, Silver Star Rubber Co., New York, NY USA, 2¼" x 1⅝" x ¼", G . . . .$825.00 (B)

Silverwoods Deluxe Ice Cream, double-sided tin advertising sign, "Dairy Products Advertising, Weston, Ontario," 23¼" x 35", VG . . . .$80.00 (B)

Simonds, Circular Saws, tin over cardboard advertising thermometer, 7" x 19", EX . . . .$135.00 (C)

Silver Birch Chewing Gum, store counter display box with unopened packages of gum, 6¼" x 5½" x 4¼", EX, $1,500.00 (B). *Courtesy of Wm Morford Investment Grade Collectibles*

Silver Flash, gas globe, one-piece glass body, 15" x 6" x 16¼", VG, $3,500.00 (B). *Courtesy of Collectors Auction Services*

Simoniz...Gives Lasting Beauty and Saves Finish, too!, cardboard store display with metal can in center with artwork of man and woman polishing table and car, EX . . . $135.00 (D)

Simon's Roosevelt Havana Cigars, rounded corner tin litho container with FDR's picture in cameo, 5" x 3½" x 1½", EX . . . . $95.00 (C)

Sinclair Dino Gasoline, globe with plastic body and two glass lenses featuring the trademark Dino dinosaur, 13½" dia., EX . . . . $190.00 (B)

Sinclair Gasoline, advertising calendar with graphics of pretty woman with jump rope by artist Earl Moran, 16" x 33½", 1946, NM . . . . $165.00 (C)

Sinclair, illuminated metal & glass clock with Dino, 1950s, EX . . . . $500.00 (D)

Sinclair, Marx, toy tanker truck, 18½" long, red & white on green, EX . . . . $675.00 (C)

Sinclair Oil, hand-soldered gallon can with tin litho image of early race car, "Opaline Motor Oil... Sinclair Refining Company...Chicago," 10½" x 8" x 3", EX . . . . . $395.00 (C)

Sinclair, pennant gas globe, narrow hull body with two glass lenses, 13½" dia., EX . . . . $900.00 (B)

Sinclair, porcelain pump sign with graphics of Dino, 7" x 5", EX . . . . $375.00 (C)

Singer Mfg. Co...Sewing Machine Makers for the World, heavily embossed calendar with artwork of young girl, 1898, 9" x 12", EX . . . . $53.00 (B)

Sir Walter Raleigh Smoking Tobacco, porcelain sign with graphics of pocket tin, 1920s, 36" x 12", EX . . $825.00 (B)

Sir Walter Raleigh...Union Made, paper advertising for smoking tobacco for pipe and cigarettes, 19¾" x 24", VG . . . . $25.00 (B)

S.J. Tuft...178 Genesee St.,...Utica, N.Y., Dealers in ladies furnishing goods, die cut cardboard dust pan, 9½" x 9", EX . . . . $45.00 (C)

Skelly Gasoline, advertising calendar with graphics of Earl Moran flag girl, 16" x 32½", 1946, EX . . . . . . $145.00 (C)

Simplex, one-sided embossed tin sign, 20" x 9", G, $220.00 (B).

Sinclair Opaline Motor Oil, single-sided porcelain sign, 15" x 60", VG, $275.00 (B).

Sinclair Coal Co., advertising thermometer, "Parade of the Finest," strong graphics, 8¼" x 38⅝", G, $375.00 (B).

Sir Walter Raleigh Smoking Tobacco, porcelain sign with graphics of pocket tin, 1920s, 36" x 12", EX, $825.00 (B). *Courtesy of Muddy River Trading Co./Gary Metz*

Skelly-Hood, snow dome, plastic and glass advertising dome for Skelly and Hood tires with advertising billboard inside dome, 4" x 3" x 3", EX . . . .$130.00 (B)

Ski...drink, one-sided tin advertising sign with graphics of bottle water skiing, 31¾" x 11¾", G . . . .$160.00 (B)

Ski-Hi, round cigar tin with paper label with artwork of plane flying over city scene, 5¼" x 5", EX . .$3,000.00 (B)

Skiles Electric Bread, celluloid spinner in shape of hand with finger pointing to "Who Pays," with graphics of "Electric Bread," 2½" x 1¼", NM . . . .$65.00 (C)

Skylark Ethyl Gasoline, globe, narrow glass body with glass lenses, 13½" dia., G . . . .$850.00 (C)

Slade's Spices and Baking Powder, advertising litho paper sign with likeness of small girl with flowers, 20" x 25¾", EX . . . .$575.00 (D)

Sleepyeye Beckstrand Imp. Co., tin die cut license attachment, 9¾" x 3", EX . . . .$100.00 (B)

Sleepy Eye Flour and Cereal Products, embossed tin litho advertising sign with graphics of Old Sleepy Eye, rare sign and hard-to-find, 19" x 27½", VG . . . . .$760.00 (B)

Slade's Spices and Baking Powder, advertising litho paper sign with likeness of small girl with flowers, 20" x 25¾", G, **$475.00 (B)**. *Courtesy of Richard Opfer Auctioneering, Inc.*

S.M. Hess & Brother, advertising calendar, by Hayes Litho Co., "manufacturers of rich grade fertilizers," 1907, 15" x 22¼", F, **$140.00 (B)**.

Smile, easel back tripod tin sign with Smile man serving at counter, 1920s, 27" x 41", G, **$1,000.00 (B)**. *Courtesy of Muddy River Trading Co./Gary Metz*

Sleepy Eye Flour, beveled edge tin on cardboard by New York Metal Sign Works Co. with image of Old Sleepy Eye himself in center cameo, VG . . . .$2,300.00 (B)

Slicker Pipe & Tool Company, oil and gas well supplies with great litho at top of tear sheets of fishing scene, 1927, EX . . . .$45.00 (D)

S.M. Hess & Brother, advertising calendar, by Hayes Litho Co., "manufacturers of rich grade fertilizers," 1907, 15" x 22¼", VG . . . .$195.00 (D)

Smile, easel back tripod tin sign with Smile man serving at counter, 1920s, 27" x 41", EX . . . .$1,800.00 (C)

Smile Orange Drink, die cut paper advertising sign holding a Smile sign with graphics of Smile figures, 22" x 28¾", NM . . . .$150.00 (B)

Smilin' Sam, peanut vendor from General Merchandise Co. made of cast aluminum in the shape of a man's head, 10" x 11" x 13½", 1931, VG . . . .$2,050.00 (B)

Smith Bros....Black...Cough Drops, cloth advertising banner, graphics of brothers, 27" x 14", EX . . . .$95.00 (B)

Smith Bros. Chewing Gum and cough drops, blotter with graphics of the Smith Bros. and product packages, 9½" x 4", EX . . . .$50.00 (B)

Smith Bros., cough drop advertising, paperboard sign with both brothers asking the public to be kind and not cough in public by buying their product, 24" x 16", EX . .$98.00 (B)

Smith Brothers, advertising blotter promoting their chewing gum, with graphics of both men on front, hard-to-find item, 9½" x 4", 1915s, EX . . . .$95.00 (D)

Smith's Ice Cream..., "It's Pleasingly Different," one-sided metal advertising sign, NOS, 31½" x 19½", NM . .$275.00 (B)

Smiths' Overalls, advertising sign, 7" x 2½", 1930s, NM . . . .$225.00 (B)

Smith-Wolf Oil Co., die cut metal embossed arrow advertising sign, 19½" x 4¾", NM . . . .$95.00 (C)

Smoke "BIJOU" cigars, stone litho of young girl with ocean scene in background, 15½" x 20", 1900s, EX . . .$450.00 (B)

Snow King Baking Powder, die cut countertop display in the likeness of Santa Claus in sleigh being pulled by reindeer, 29" x 17", EX, $750.00 (B). *Courtesy of Buffalo Bay Auction Co.*

Solo, Drink...High in Quality, 6 fruity flavors, painted tin litho, 15" x 30", G, $50.00 (C).

Southern Bell Telephone and Telegraph Co./American Telephone & Telegraph Co., milk glass globe, at one time these hung at Bell business offices, getting to be a hard item to find, blue lettering and bell on white, NM, $1,000.00 (C). *Courtesy of B.J. Summers*

Smoke Hignett's Mixture, embossed tin litho advertising sign with graphics of vintage touring car out for a drive in the country, 19½" x 13½", VG . . . .$500.00 (B)

Smoker's Dream, cardboard advertising sign promoting Big John, Granulated 54, and Orphan Boy tobacco, with graphics of all three products, 13½" x 19", NM . . . .$107.00 (B)

Smooth Sailin', two-part candy box with sailboats on both sides, Hollywood Brands, Centralia, Ill., 10" x 8" x 2", NM . . . .$28.00 (B)

Snag Proof Boots, from Lambertville Rubber Co., calendar, artwork of "L" girl in cameo surrounded by brownies with products, 1910s, 8" x 12", EX . . . .$116.00 (B)

Snapshot Black Sporting Powder, tin with litho of geese on front, 3½" x 4¼" x 1", NM . . . .$85.00 (C)

Snider's Catsup, embossed tin die cut sign featuring image of the product bottle, 11" x 17", 1930s, NM . .$475.00 (B)

Sno-King...peanuts, caramel, nougat, candy bar store box with great graphics of snow scenes on front, 10" x 7¾" x 2", EX . . . .$35.00 (D)

Snow Bird Cigar, wood advertising thermometer, EX . . . .$250.00 (B)

Snowdrift...Perfect Shortening, single-sided porcelain ad sign with artwork of product container on center, 26" sq., G . . . .$140.00 (B)

Southwestern Bell Telephone Co., porcelain double-sided flange advertising sign, 11" x 11⅞", 1950s, EX, $180.00 (B).

Spear Head Plug Chew Tobacco, tin sign with heavy relief and embossing, 28" x 10", EX, $500.00 (B). *Courtesy of Muddy River Trading Co./Gary Metz*

Sparkeeta UP Soda...California's flavorite, framed cardboard advertising sign with graphics of pretty red-haired woman with bottle of product, 25¾" x 31½", NM, $325.00 (C). *Courtesy of Autopia Advertising Auctions*

Snow King Baking Powder, die cut countertop display in the likeness of Santa Claus in sleigh being pulled by reindeer, 29" x 17", F . . . .$225.00 (D)

Socony Aircraft Oil, No. 2 Heavy Medium, two-sided porcelain lubster sign, 8" x 12", G . . . .$115.00 (B)

Socony Air-Craft Oils... Standard Oil of New York, porcelain advertising sign with image of vintage airplane, very sought-after item, 30" x 20", EX . . . .$1,050.00 (B)

Socony Motor Oil, single-sided porcelain pump sign, 13½" x 15", F . . . .$110.00 (B)

Socony Polarine oil, watch fob with trademark polar bear, 1⅜" x 1⅝", VG . . . .$75.00 (C)

SOC, Super, gas globe, plastic body with glass lenses, 13½" dia., G . . . .$130.00 (B)

Softex Shampoo, countertop display, consisting of wooden box that folds out for three-level display and product container, 10" T, EX . . . .$55.00 (C)

Solace Tobacco, paper advertising sign with graphics of young girl on ladder, 12½" x 29", 1884, EX . .$2,000.00 (D)

Solene No-Nox Gasoline, gas globe, wide body glass with double lenses, 13½" dia., G . . . .$800.00 (B)

Solo, Drink...High in Quality, 6 fruity flavors, painted tin litho, 15" x 30", G . . . .$50.00 (C)

Sooner Select Oats, container from Lawton, OK, with graphics of oxen wagon and horseback rider, 1-lb., VG . . . .$305.00 (B)

South Bend Watches... Sold By W.F. Sellers & Co., tin litho retailers sign, 19" x 13", EX . . . .$192.00 (B)

Southern Bell Telephone and Telegraph Co./American Telephone & Telegraph Co., milk glass globe, at one time these hung at Bell business offices, getting to be a hard item to find, blue lettering and bell on white, G . . . .$425.00 (C)

Spearmint Toothpaste, W.W. Wrigley, heavy cardboard advertising sign, 24" x 18", F, $45.00 (D). *Courtesy of Courtesy of Chief Paduke Antiques Mall*

Speedboat mixture, tobacco tin, featuring artwork of 1930s-style boat, 5¾" x 3¼", G, $200.00 (C).

Sparrows Chocolate, metal litho tray, graphics of little girl climbing onto table for candy, 6¼" x 8⅛", G, $70.00 (D).

Spiffy, A Swell Cola Drink, painted metal flange sign, 12½" x 10", F, $75.00 (C).

Southern Brand, Pure White Lead paint sign with Dutch boy sitting on ledge with brush, double-sided metal flange, 14¼" x 21", EX . . . .$875.00 (C)

Southern Rose Hair Dressing, advertising calendar with graphics of fishing couple at top and bottle of product on each side of bottom tear sheet, 17" x 35", 1950, EX . . . .$110.00 (B)

Southwestern Associated Telephone Company, double-sided porcelain sign with graphics of "toll line" pole in center, 30" dia., VG . . . .$425.00 (B)

Southwestern Bell Telephone Co., porcelain double-sided flange advertising sign, 11" x 11⅞", 1950s, EX . . .$180.00 (B)

Sozodont Tooth Powder, tin litho container with graphics of vintage era man brushing his teeth, with original box, 1¾" x 3¹⁴⁄₁₆", 1900s, EX . . . .$475.00 (B)

Spalding...athletic goods...for sale here, double-sided porcelain over metal flange advertising sign, 19½" x 19", EX . . . .$1,600.00 (B)

Sparkeeta UP Soda...California's flavorite, framed cardboard advertising sign with graphics of pretty red-haired woman with bottle of product, 25¾" x 31½", G . . . .$135.00 (D)

Sparrow Chocolates, small metal serving tray with litho of young girl standing in a chair to climb onto a table after the product, 6½" x 8", EX . . . .$350.00 (C)

Squeeze...Drink...that distinctive carbonated beverage, with graphics of young cartoon figures on bench in front of a full moon, 28" x 10", EX, $235.00 (B). *Courtesy of Past Tyme Pleasures*

Squire's Hams, "John P. Squire & Company, Boston," embossed self-framing tin sign, artwork of sitting pig in center of sign, 1906, 20" x 24", EX, $300.00 (B). *Courtesy of Muddy River Trading Co./Gary Metz*

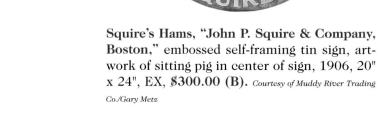

Squirt, light-up advertising clock with large size boy and product bottle, 15" dia., 1946, NM, $575.00 (C).

Sparrows Chocolate, tin litho advertising tray with graphics of young girl in a chair reaching for the candy, 6½" x 8", EX . . . .$130.00 (B)

Spartan Ethyl, gas globe, high profile metal body with two glass lenses, 15" dia., VG . . . .$250.00 (B)

Spear Head Plug Chew Tobacco, tin sign with heavy relief and embossing, 28" x 10", G . . . .$175.00 (C)

Spearhead Plug Tobacco, embossed double-sided tin hanging sign, diamond-shaped, 6" sq., EX . . . .$80.00 (B)

Spearior Saws, tin litho advertising sign with graphics of wood-handled hand saw, 27" x 9", VG . . . . .$210.00 (B)

Spears Inspected...Approved...Station & Rest Rooms porcelain double-sided advertising sign, 30" dia., G .$175.00 (B)

Special Combination Coffee, from Sears Roebuck & Co., Chicago, Illinois, tin litho container with wire bail handle, 10-lb., black on green background, EX . . . . . .$80.00 (B)

Spectacles, reverse painting on glass, advertising eye glasses and glass eyes, 20" x 8", NM . . . .$550.00 (C)

Speedboat mixture, tobacco tin, featuring artwork of 1930s-style boat, 5¾" x 3¼", EX . . . .$275.00 (C)

Speedwell Motor Oil, double-sided porcelain flange sign with graphics of young black boy being chased by a tiger, 23½" x 16", VG . . . .$1,900.00 (B)

Spiffy, A Swell Cola Drink, painted metal flange sign, 12½" x 10", EX . . . .$150.00 (C)

Spur, Drink Canada Dry... Ice Cold, It's A Finer Cola, embossed tin sign, 13½" x 30", G . . . .$75.00 (B)

Squirt, Switch to, painted metal ad sign, graphics of Squirt boy, 27¼" x 9¼", EX, **$180.00 (B)**.

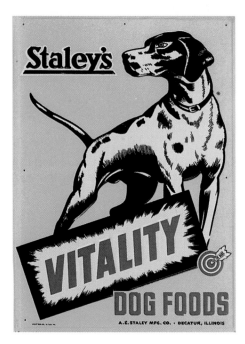

Squirt, tin litho serving tray, "Squirt, The Drink with the Happy Taste," 11½" x 14½", G, **$255.00 (B)**.

Staley's Vitality Dog Foods, self-framing embossed tin advertising sign, 19⅛" x 27⅛", G, **$120.00 (B)**.

Standard Ale, framed cardboard advertisment, with artwork of delivery truck, Standard Brewing Co., Inc., Rochester, N. Y., 16" x 12½", VG, **$75.00 (C)**.

Squadron Leader, tin litho tobacco container with graphics of bi-plane on cover, NM . . . .**$120.00 (B)**

Square Deal Coffee, tin litho container with artwork of hands shaking in agreement, 4" x 6", G . . . . .**$375.00 (B)**

Squeeze, easel back cardboard advertising sign with image of bathing girl with large brim hat, 15" x 20", VG . . . .**$275.00 (B)**

Squeeze, easel back cardboard advertising sign with scenes of sandlot baseball, 15" x 20", EX . . . .**$425.00 (B)**

Squeeze, embossed tin litho advertising sign with graphics of couple on a bench, "Drink...all flavors," 28½" x 10", VG . . . .**$180.00 (B)**

Squeeze Orange Drink...That distinctive...embossed tin litho of boy and girl looking at the moon, 27" x 19½", VG . . . .**$275.00 (C)**

Squirrel Brand, die cut cardboard advertising sign with cut-out of squirrel on top of sign, 11" x 12", EX . . .**$380.00 (B)**

Squirrel Brand Peanut Butter, tin litho with pry-lid, graphics of squirrel on front, 3-lb., EX . . . . .**$225.00 (B)**

Squirrel Brand Salted Peanuts, die cut cardboard counter-top display, 12" x 11", EX . . . .**$130.00 (B)**

Squirt, embossed tin advertising thermometer with image of bottle at right of scale, 5¾" x 13½", NM . . .**$350.00 (B)**

Standard Heating Oils, die cut porcelain advertising sign, 24" x 15", EX, $275.00 (C). *Courtesy of Autopia Advertising Auctions*

Standard Oil Co., Superla Cream Separator Oil, metal can litho of cows and cream separator, 5" x 9½", VG, $70.00 (A).

Standard Oil, Credit Cards Good Here, die cut tin double-sided flange advertising sign, NOS, first Standard Oil card sign, 23¾" x 25½", 1932, EX, $600.00 (B). *Courtesy of Autopia Advertising Auctions*

Standard Oil Products, porcelain sign, 30" x 20", white on blue, VG, $255.00 (C). *Courtesy of Riverview Antique Mall*

Squirt, embossed tin chalk menu board, 19½" x 27½", 1950s, EX . . . .$225.00 (C)

Squirt...enjoy...never an after thirst, painted metal thermometer with artwork of Squirt to right of vertical scale, EX . . . .$45.00 (C)

Squirt, Glass with Squirt Boy, 4¼", 1948, EX . .$70.00 (B)

Squirt, It's Tart Sweet, tin double-sided flange advertising sign, 18⅜" x 14", 1941, NM . . . .$225.00 (C)

Squirt, light-up advertising clock, "Switch to..." with graphics of Squirt Boy and product bottle, 15" dia., EX . . . .$375.00 (C)

Squirt, tin litho delivery truck with friction movement, "Advertising in Reader's Digest," 8" L, EX . . .$175.00 (B)

Stay Cool Oil...Keeps The Motor Cool, tin oil can with product label on front and back, 1-gal., EX . . .$35.00 (C)

Stag tobacco, tin litho container with graphics of large buck and men on horseback, 4½" x 4" x 4", EX . . . . . .$95.00 (C)

Stanley Garage Door Holders, tin litho advertising sign with great graphics of vintage garage door, "Hold Your Garage Doors Open," 34" x 26¼", 1910s, EX, **$1,000.00 (C).** *Courtesy of Autopia Advertising Auctions*

Star Brand Shoes Are Better, store wall mirror, 15½" x 21½", VG, **$100.00 (B).**

Standard Ale, framed cardboard advertisment, with artwork of delivery truck, Standard Brewing Co., Inc., Rochester, N. Y., 16" x 12½", EX . . . .**$100.00 (C)**

Standard Brewing Co., self-framing tin litho advertisng sign with grisly graphics of execution of 38 Sioux Indians while soldiers sit on the porch enjoying their beer, 26" x 18", VG . . . .**$2,800.00 (B)**

Standard Gasoline...Polarine Motor Oil, double-sided porcelain advertising sign, 30" dia., G . . . . .**$325.00 (B)**

Standard Gasoline...Unsurpassed, cardboard advertising with graphics of Mickey Mouse on skis, 17" x 14", EX . . . .**$525.00 (C)**

Standard Heating Oils, die cut porcelain advertising sign, 24" x 15", G . . . .**$125.00 (C)**

Standard Mixed Paint of America...Goes Farthest...Locks Best...Wears Longest, round metal tip tray with artwork of product can in center of tray, 4⅛" dia., EX . . .**$15.00 (B)**

Standard Oil Company of N.Y...Polarine oil and greases for motors, porcelain sign, 12" x 22", G . . . . .**$275.00 (C)**

Standard Oil, Credit Cards Good Here, die cut tin double-sided flange advertising sign, first Standard Oil card sign, 23¾" x 25½", 1932, G . . . .**$175.00 (C)**

Standard Oil, metal mailbox for letters to Santa Claus, "letters mailed here will be postmarked with the famous Santa Claus, Ind., postmark," 12½" x 17" x 7¾", VG . . . .**$230.00 (B)**

Standard Sewing Machine, stone litho on paper advertising sign with image of small child with cats, 12" x 22", VG . . . .**$255.00 (B)**

Standby Tomato Juice, porcelain button ad sign with graphics of product can in center, 35½" dia., VG . . . .**$275.00 (B)**

Stanley Garage Door Holders, tin litho advertising sign with great graphics of vintage garage door, "Hold Your Garage Doors Open," 34" x 26¼", 1910s, G . . . .**$425.00 (C)**

Star Brand Shoes, embossed tin advertising sign with graphics of young black boy shining shoes, produced by the Grimm Metal Sign Corp., St. Louis, "Yes sah !...Star Brand Shoes are better...sold at the best stores," 23" x 18", EX . . . .**$500.00 (B)**

Star Cup Coffee, key-wound tin litho coffee can with great graphics of a king drinking a cup of coffee, 1-lb., EX . . . .**$190.00 (B)**

Star Razor, tin, complete with original safety razor and blades, litho on all sides, 2¼" x 1¼" x 1½", EX . .**$135.00 (B)**

Star Soap, Extra Large, Extra Good, one-sided porcelain, 20" x 28", G, $390.00 (B).

St. Bruno Tobacco, sign, 3-D die cut cardboard stand-up advertising sign from the Imperial Tobacco Co. of Great Britian, graphics depict blacks packing tobacco leaves, 20" x 14½", 1915s, EX, $850.00 (B). *Courtesy of Buffalo Bay Auction Co.*

"Steamro" Red Hots, porcelain advertising sign, 17¼" x 2¼", VG, $195.00 (C).

Star Tobacco, porcelain advertising sign, "Star Tobacco Sold Here," 24" x 12", G . . . . $55.00 (C)

Star Tobacco, single-sided porcelain advertising sign with graphics of star over tobacco plug, 24" x 12", VG . . . . $160.00 (B)

State Automobile Mutual Insurance Company, one-sided porcelain advertising sign, graphics of colorful castle over message, 27½" x 60", EX . . . . $305.00 (B)

State Fair Rolled Oats, Sedalia, Mo., container with slip-lid, graphics of fair building on front, 1-lb., 4-oz., EX . . . . $130.00 (B)

State House Coffee, paper on cardboard container with graphics of Indian bust on back and State House on front, from Waterloo IA, all on bright yellow background, 1-lb., EX . . . . $460.00 (B)

St. Bruno Flake, cardboard stand-up with scene of slaves in fields by the Imperial Tobacco Company, 22½" x 18½", VG . . . . $1,275.00 (D)

St. Bruno Tobacco, sign, 3-D die cut cardboard stand-up advertising sign from the Imperial Tobacco Co. of Great Britian, graphics depict blacks packing tobacco leaves, 20" x 14½", 1915s, NM . . . . $1,000.00 (C)

Steamer City of Erie...Record 22¾ miles per hour...Daily Between Cleveland & Buffalo, rectangular metal tip tray with graphics of ship at sea, 6⅝" L, EX . . . . $250.00 (B)

Steamro Red Hots, porcelain advertising sign with graphics of hot dogs, for use on hot dog vendor cart, 19" x 3¾", EX . . . . $200.00 (C)

Stegmaier Brewing Co., tin litho match holder, 5" H, G . . . . $110.00 (B)

Stegmaier Brewing Co...Wilkes Barre, Pa., round metal tip tray with artwork of hand holding 4 bottles of product, 4⅛" dia., EX . . . . $150.00 (B)

Sterling Motor Oil, embossed tin advertising sign, 27½" x 13¾", VG, $600.00 (B).

Sterling Beer...Mellow, metal figural bell that rings when her hands are squeezed together, 4¾" x 14¾", VG, $95.00 (C).

Sterling, porcelain and brass advertising thermometer, rare item, 9½" x 12¼", EX, $1,000.00 (B).

Stegmaier's...We Serve...Gold Metal Beer, tin litho ad sign featuring cone-top can and short neck bottle of product, EX . . . .$72.00 (B)

Stegner Lager Beer, sign, glass with neon framing , 13½" x 6", EX . . . .$230.00 (B)

Stephens Inks...for all temperatures, advertising thermometer, porcelain over wood, 12" x 61", VG .$350.00 (B)

Stephenson Union Suits, porcelain advertising thermometer with graphics of man holding the product, "Stephenson Union Suits for all seasons," made by Beech Enamel of Coshocton, Ohio, 8" x 39", 1915, EX . . . . .$275.00 (C)

Sterling Beer, advertising mirror, with Sterling logo on back, 14" x 10", EX . . . .$75.00 (D)

Sterling Beer, sign, beveled edge tin on cardboard advertising sign, with graphics of food tray with glass of product, 19" x 13¾", EX . . . .$399.00 (B)

Sterling Beer, tin litho on cardboard advertising sign from an original painting "A Night At The Circus" from the Evansville, Ind. brewery, 20½" x 27", 1938, VG . . . . .$325.00 (B)

Sterling Cinnamon Gum, advertising package, 3" x ¾" x ½", EX . . . .$65.00 (B)

Stickney & Poor's, Mustards, Spices, and Extracts, paper litho advertising sign, framed and matted, 19½" x 24½", VG, $150.00 (B).

Studebaker Authorized Sales & Service, double-sided porcelain dealer sign, 48" dia., 1940s, EX, $725.00 (B). *Courtesy of Muddy River Trading Co./Gary Metz*

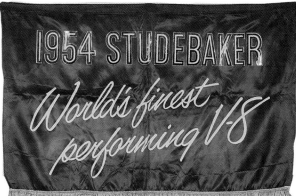

Studebaker, 1954, World's Finest Performing V-8, silk wallhanging, 40" x 27½", $80.00 (B).

Sterling Gasoline...A Quaker State Product, single-sided porcelain pump sign with the ethyl sign in center, 11½" x 10", EX . . . .$550.00 (B)

Sterling Motor Oil, metal double-sided advertising "tombstone" sign, 26½" x 29", 1930s, G . . . .$160.00 (B)

Sterling Spark Plugs, tin litho advertising display featuring graphics of product, 11¼" x 14" x 5¾", VG . .$1,150.00 (B)

Sterling Tobacco, counter canister, with small twist lid, 8¼" x 7", EX . . . .$155.00 (C)

Stevens Firearms, premium sewing kit with graphics of crossed rifles on front, 1" x 2¾", 1900s, EX . .$150.00 (B)

St. Joseph Aspirin, electric light-up clock, metal body with glass face, 15" dia., EX . . . .$395.00 (D)

Stoeckers...It's got the pep...Old-fashioned lemon soda, painted embossed tin sign with artwork of lemon leaf in center of message, G . . . .$55.00 (C)

Stollwerck Chocolat and Cocoa, advertising tip tray, painted metal, 5⅛" dia., VG . . . .$45.00 (D)

Stone's Peanut Butter, tin pail with wire bail handle, pry-lid, Duluth, MN, 5-lb., EX . . . .$85.00 (C)

Stone's, Regular, gas globe, plastic body with glass lenses, 13½" dia., EX . . . .$335.00 (B)

Studebaker, single-sided tin sign, "The Sun Always Shines on the Studebaker," graphics of product wagon, 29½" x 24", F, **$300.00 (B)**.

Sunbeam Bread, self-framing tin sign with graphics of young girl eating a slice of bread, 19" x 55", EX, **$750.00 (B)**. *Courtesy of Collectors Auction Services*

Sunbeam Bread, door push with bread loaf cut-out in center of door bar, used on screen doors before air conditioning to protect screens, 1950s, 30" x 15", EX, **$275.00 (B)**.

Storz, Bitter Free Beer, advertising dial-type thermometer, 12½" dia., EX . . . .$95.00 (C)

Stowman Brother Oysters, tin, Maurice River, N.J., 6¾" x 7¼", EX . . . .$95.00 (C)

Straight...Smoke Inside...Cheroots, Baron & Co. Cigar Manufacturers, Baltimore, Md., die cut cardboard of young woman framed by anchor, 1900, 10" x 14", NM . . . .$230.00 (B)

Stratford Regency, The Dependable Pen, three-dimensional cardboard store display with original pen, 1945, G . . . .$33.00 (D)

Stride Rite, light-up advertising sign, metal body with glass face, 20" x 9", EX . . . .$125.00 (B)

Strong Heart Coffee, round coffee tin can with paper label bearing artwork of colorful Indian, 5¼" x 4¼", EX . . . .$300.00 (B)

Strong Heart Coffee, tin litho can with screw-on lid, graphics of Indian in center on front, 1-lb., EX . . . . .$467.00 (B)

Strong Heart, coffee tin litho, with graphics of Indian in oval cameo on front and back, Charles Hewitt & Sons Co., 1-lb., EX . . . .$550.00 (C)

Sunbeam Bread, with a Bonus, wooden screen door with metal embossed door, push bar, and pull handle, 34" x 82", NM, $425.00 (B).

Sun Crest Beverages, Swihart light-up clock with convex front glass, great graphics, 15" x 18", NM, $285.00 (D).

Courtesy of Affordable Antiques

Sun Crest...Drink, refreshes you best, metal thermometer with artwork of bottle to right of scale, 6" x 16½", blue, orange, and white, F, $115.00 (C).

Studebaker Authorized Sales & Service, double-sided porcelain dealer sign, 48" dia., 1940s, NM .$1,000.00 (C)

Studebaker Batteries, light-up clock, metal body with glass front, logo at top center with message at lower center, 15¼" sq., EX . . . .$175.00 (C)

Stud Smoking Tobacco, cardboard countertop display box with product packages, 9½" x 5½" x 4", EX . . . .$75.00 (C)

Sultana Coffee Fan, die cut cardboard in shape of a pet with bonnet-style hat holding a cup of product, from Great Atlantic and Pacific Tea Company, with advertising on back of fan, 6¼" x 13", 1892, EX . . . .$30.00 (B)

Sultana Peanut Butter, pail, "Atlanta and Pacific Tea Company...New York, NY...Distributors," 1-lb., VG . .$55.00 (C)

Summer Girl, coffee tin litho in can with key-wound lid, 1-lb., EX . . . .$55.00 (C)

Summer-Time Tobacco, paper litho container with pry-lid, NM . . . .$140.00 (B)

Summit Shirt, pennant with graphics of young man in the process of putting on French cuffs, 25" L, EX . . .$99.00 (B)

Sunbeam Bread, door push with bread loaf cut-out in center of door bar, used on screen doors before air conditioning to protect screens, 1950s, 30" x 15", G . . . . .$125.00 (D)

Sunbeam Bread, metal and glass dial-type advertising thermometer with trademark Miss Sunbeam in center, 12" dia., 1957, G . . . .$375.00 (B)

Sunbeam Bread, money clip, metal and plastic, with graphics of the Sunbeam Bread girl in plastic center, 1¾" x 1⅜", EX . . . .$125.00 (C)

Sunbeam Bread, self-framing tin sign with graphics of young girl eating a slice of bread, 19" x 55", G . . . . . .$175.00 (C)

Sun Crest, glass and metal advertising thermometer, VG, $190.00 (B).

Sun Crest, metal and glass advertising light-up clock, graphics of bottle in center, Telechron, 15¼" dia., VG, $300.00 (B).

Sun Crest, Tingle-ated, cardboard party poster, 22" x 17", G, $25.00 (B).

Sun-drop Cola, single-sided self-framing embossed tin sign, 28" x 12", VG, $160.00 (B).

Sunbeam Bread, store employee tie with charm type emblem at bottom of tie with image of Miss Sunbeam, NM . . . .$135.00 (C)

Sunbeam...White Stroehmann, door push bar with die cut likeness of loaf of bread with Sunbeam girl, EX . .$165.00 (D)

Sun Crest Beverages, Swihart light-up clock with convex front glass, great graphics, 15" x 18", VG . . . .$195.00 (D)

Sun Crest, die cut metal bottle thermometer with vertical scale at bottom of bottle, EX . . . .$75.00 (C)

Sun Crest...Drink, refreshes you best, metal thermometer with artwork of bottle to right of scale, 6" x 16½", blue, orange, and white, G . . . .$135.00 (D)

Sun Crest, self-framed embossed painted tin sign, 41" x 23", EX . . . .$325.00 (B)

Sun Crest, Telechron electric light-up clock with bottle in center in green spotlight, good strong graphics, 1940s, EX . . . .$350.00 (B)

Sundown Coffee, tin container with paper label with graphics of Egyptian pyramid desert scene, from Wm. Scotten Coffee Co., St. Louis, MO, 1-lb., EX . .$95.00 (D)

Sun Drop...Have you had your lemonade today, made with pure lemon juice, sold only in bottles, self-framing metal sign, scarce, 40" x 22¼", orange, blue, and white, EX . . . .$450.00 (D)

Sun Flower Brand, Steel Cut Coffee, tin litho coffee can with pry-type lid, artwork of large sunflower on front, 1-lb., 5¼" x 3¾", EX . . . .$1,100.00 (B)

Sun Insurance Office Agency, porcelain advertising sign with graphics of sun in upper right corner, 20" x 11", EX . . . .$325.00 (B)

Sun-drop, dial-type advertising thermometer, 12¼" dia., VG, $45.00 (B).

Sun-drop, Gold-en Girl Cola, die cut tin bottle sign, 16" x 60", VG, $485.00 (B).

Sun Drop...Have you had your lemonade today, made with pure lemon juice, sold only in bottles, self-framing metal sign, scarce, 40" x 22¼", orange, blue, and white, G, $325.00 (D). *Courtesy of Patrick's Collectibles*

Sunkist Orange Juice, I'll tell you a secret...Every day, artwork of girl with a glass, litho by Forbes, 1920s, 28" x 42", F . . . .$145.00 (D)

Sunlight Soap, die cut litho advertisng sign from Lever Bros., 8½" x 10¾", 1900s, G . . . .$100.00 (C)

Sunny Brook, light-up advertising clock, "Time to come over on the Sunny Brook," metal body with glass front, 17½" x 10¼" x 3¼", EX . . . .$130.00 (B)

Sunny Brook, Pure Rye Bourbon, advertising tin litho match holder featuring artwork of whiskey bottle, good, graphics, 5"H, G . . . .$130.00 (B)

Sunny Brook, tin litho match holder with graphics of bottle in center, souvenir of 1904 World's Fair, 3⅜" x 4⅞", 1904, EX . . . .$400.00 (B)

Sunoco & Disney Blotter, "there's only one" with graphics of Mickey and Minnie, 7¼" x 4", NM . . . . .$150.00 (C)

Sunoco, blotter with Donald Duck in car being pushed by a billy goat, "A quick start," VG . . . .$135.00 (B)

Sunoco, Sun Heat Furnace Oil, Disney theme blotter with graphics of Mickey Mouse asleep in chair, 6" x 3¼", 1939, G . . . .$125.00 (C)

Sunray Cigar, paper sign "pleasing to all, mild and fragrant," 15" x 8½", EX . . . .$165.00 (C)

Sunray Natural Power Oils, one-sided porcelain sign, 25" x 25", VG . . . .$850.00 (B)

Sunset Corn Flakes, distributed by Montgomery Ward & Co., cereal box, very scarce item due to limited production, G . . . .$95.00 (C)

Sunset Trail Cigars, tin with strong colors on artwork of cowboys on horseback, 6⅛" x 4⅛", EX . . . . .$475.00 (B)

Sunshine Andy Gump Biscuits, die cut paper window advertising sign for Loose-Wiles Biscuit Co., 11" x 12", EX . . . .$350.00 (B)

Sunshine Biscuit, Inc, self-framing brass building plate, 21" x 21", VG . . . .$475.00 (B)

Sunkist orange juice, I'll tell you a secret...Every day, artwork of girl with a glass, litho by Forbes, 1920s, 28" x 42", EX, $600.00 (B). *Courtesy of Muddy River Trading Co./Gary Metz*

Sunlight Soap, die cut litho advertising sign from Lever Bros., 8½" x 10¾", 1900s, EX, $400.00 (B). *Courtesy of Buffalo Bay Auction Co.*

Sunny Brook Pure Rye, tin match holder with great litho of rye bottle, 5" H, VG, $125.00 (C). *Courtesy of Richard Opfer Auctioneering, Inc.*

Sunshine Biscuits, metalcraft battery operated advertising truck, Metalcraft Corp. St. Louis, Made in U.S.A., with Goodrich Silvertown tires, 12" L, G . . . .$160.00 (B)

Sunshine Cigarettes, painted tin advertising sign with graphics of cigarette package, "Twenty for 15¢," 14" x 18", F . . . .$175.00 (B)

Sunshine Peanut Butter, tin litho metal pail with wire handles, 1-lb., EX . . . .$91.00 (B)

Sun Spot...Drink bottled sunshine, round painted metal flange sign, EX . . . .$185.00 (C)

Sun Spot, Orange Drink, "Drink America's favorite," tin store advertising sign, 26" x 8", G . . . .$125.00 (C)

Sun Spot, tin litho sign with embossed lettering, graphics show a tilted bottle in upper left corner, 11½" x 14½", 1940s, VG . . . .$135.00 (D)

Superior Flower Seeds, paper framed advertisement with graphics of large bouquet of flowers, 15¾" x 27½", VG . . . .$100.00 (B)

Super Kant-Nock Gasoline, globe, wide hull body with two lenses, 13½", VG . . . .$425.00 (B)

Super-Shell, "Saves on Stop and Go Driving," paper poster with graphics of car and trolley, 57½" x 33", F . . . .$45.00 (D)

Sunoco Motor Oil, cloth banner, 60" x 36", VG, $330.00 (B).

Sunoco, Sun-Heat Furnace Oil, Disney, theme blotter with graphics of Mickey Mouse asleep in chair, 6" x 3¼", 1939, EX, $225.00 (C). *Courtesy of Autopia Advertising Auctions*

Sunset Corn Flakes, Distributed by Montgomery Ward & Co., cereal box, very scarce item due to limited production, EX, $135.00 (B). *Courtesy of Buffalo Bay Auction Co.*

Sun Spot, Drink America's Favorite...made with real orange juice, embossed tin sign, 1940s, 11½" x 14½", EX, $70.00 (B). *Courtesy of Muddy River Trading Co./Gary Metz*

Super-x...Steel oil ring...Dry As A Bone, papier-maché likeness of bone with product message on front, rare piece, 24" long, EX ....$225.00 (C)

Surburg's Tobacco, tin, with dome top, "High grade smoking tobacco," 7" x 4¼" x 5¼", VG ....$255.00 (C)

Sure Shot...Chewing Tobacco..It Touches The Spot, rectangular store tin with artwork of Indian with bow and arrow, metal lid, NM ....$650.00 (C)

Sure Shot, hinged lid store countertop tobacco tin with continuing graphics and message around container sides, 15" x 6½" x 10¼", G ....$475.00 (B)

Sutherland & McMillian Co., Columbia Spice tin litho container, 2-oz., VG ....$275.00 (B)

Swansdown Coffee, tin can with graphics of swan in center cameo, 4¼" x 6¼", EX ....$125.00 (C)

Sweet Caporal Cigarettes, die cut advertising fan, 6¾" x 9", EX ....$35.00 (B)

Sweet Caporal Cigarettes, paper advertising sign with graphics of toga-clad woman, 14" x 23", 1900s, NM ....$395.00 (B)

Sweet Cuba, slant front store counter bin, "The Kind that Suits," from Spaulding & Merrick, Chicago, 8" x 8" x 9½", EX ....$155.00 (B)

Sweet Cuba, store counter bin with "Sweet Cuba Tobacco" advertisement on front, 11" x 8¼", G ...$125.00 (C)

Superior Northwestern Mixed Paint, canvas advertising poster with graphics of German shepherd with paint can, 1920s, 48" x 36", VG, **$80.00 (B).**

Super-Shell, paper litho poster, 57½" x 33⅜", EX, **$70.00 (B).**

Sweet Cuba, fine cut tobacco, metal canister, 8" x 8" x 10", G, **$115.00 (C).**

Sweetheart Pure Peanut Butter, tin litho pail with wire handles with slip-lid, 9¼" x 10½", EX . . . .**$82.00 (B)**

Sweetheart Sugar Cones, litho tin container with graphics of ice cream cones on front, 12½" x 15½", VG . . . .**$245.00 (B)**

Sweet Mist Chewing Tobacco, tin with paper litho label, 8" x 10" x 6½", VG . . . .**$30.00 (B)**

Sweet Mist Tobacco, cardboard store bin, from Scotten Dillon, Detroit, 8" x 6¼" x 11", EX . . . .**$130.00 (B)**

Sweet Mist Tobacco, tin litho can with graphics of three children playing in a water fountain, 8½" dia. x 11½", VG . . . .**$135.00 (B)**

Sweet Orr & Co., advertising sign, tin litho depicting the tug-o-war using the product for a rope, 26" x 19½", VG . . . .**$900.00 (B)**

Sweet-Orr...Clothes To Work In, rare round porcelain advertising sign with the usual tug-o-war in the center, 17¾" dia., VG . . . .**$700.00 (C)**

Sweet-Orr, embossed tin advertising sign, "Wear Sweet, Orr & Co.'s union made Overalls and Pants," 10" x 7¼", EX . . . .**$60.00 (B)**

Sweet-Orr...pants, shirts, overalls, porcelain sign with union made label in center of message, 24" x 10", EX . . . .**$225.00 (C)**

Sweet-Orr, Trousers Union Made, double-sided porcelain flange sign, 18" x 8", EX . . . .**$350.00 (B)**

Sweet Rose, countertop cast iron advertising cigar cutter and lighter with light, 7" x 10¼" x 12", EX . . .**$475.00 (C)**

Swell Blend Coffee, container with graphics of steam ship on front, key-wound lid, 1-lb., EX . . . .**$90.00 (B)**

Swell Magic Colors Bubble Gum, cardboard store display with original bubble gum cigarette packages, priced per package, 1960s, EX . . . .**$3.00 (D)**

Swift's Arrow, Borax American's Best, die cut cardboard, double-sided arrow sign with product box in center, EX . . . .$75.00 (B)

Swift's Ice Cream, light-up advertising clock, metal body with message at top of clock face, EX . . . . .$235.00 (C)

Swift's Peanut Butter, tin litho container, "Swift's Premium Quality," 10½" x 10⅛", VG . . . .$30.00 (B)

Swift's Pride, Soap and Washing Powder, cardboard fan with wood handle featuring artwork of woman with wash basket, 1910s, 9½" dia., EX . . . .$165.00 (B)

Swift's Pride Soap, stone litho on cardboard with graphics of winged delivery boy delivering a box of soap, 9¼" x 13½", 1900s, EX . . . .$375.00 (C)

Syke's, comfort powder, tin litho container with graphics of pair of small girls, 4½", EX . . . .$275.00 (C)

Sylcraft...Undergarments of Quality, cardboard box with artwork of pretty woman on box top, 11¼" x 11½" x 1½", EX . . . .$30.00 (D)

Sylvania Halo Light, neon window sign, 20" x 19", EX . . . .$250.00 (D)

Sylvania Radio Service, advertising thermometer, painted metal scale type with graphics of tube at bottom of thermometer, 8¼" x 38½", G . . . .$100.00 (B)

Symphonie Powder, paper framed litho with graphics of pretty girl with a can of the product, 14½" x 20½", EX . . . .$60.00 (B)

Taft Oil Burners...authorized dealer for cook stoves...for room heaters, heavy porcelain enamel sign, 22" x 13¾", EX . . . .$350.00 (B)

Taka-Kola...Every Hour...Take No Other, round metal tip tray with woman over clock face on tray center, 4¼" dia., EX . . . .$325.00 (B)

Talbot's Ant Powder, tin store display shelf, 14½" x 10½", EX . . . .$50.00 (B)

Tansill's Punch, wooden cigar box with elf graphics on inside lid and partial tax stamp on box, 50-count, 1901, G . . . . $65.00 (C)

Target Cigarette Tobacco, canvas advertising banner with graphics of man and a large package of the product, 118" x 43", EX . . . . $175.00 (C)

Taxi Crimp Cut Tobacco, vertical pocket tin with graphics of early taxi with two men waiting on street in formal attire, F . . . .$425.00 (D)

Taylor Co. Cigars, reverse glass on foil-framed sign advertising "Tobacco & Sporting Goods," G . . . . . .$325.00 (C)

Taystee Bread...Enjoy...Famous for its freshness...today and everyday, paper advertising sign with artwork of chef holding bread, 1950s, 12" x 18", EX . . . .$40.00 (B)

T.C. Evans Advertising Agency, Boston, tin litho book marker with strong graphics promoting the company, EX . . . .$95.00 (C)

Teaberry Gum, litho tin with great graphics on all sides and on both the inside and outside of the lid, good strong colors, 6¾" L, EX . . . .$225.00 (B)

Tech Beer...None Better...Pittsburgh Brewing Co., metal tip tray with artwork of product bottle in center, 6⅝", EX . . . .$80.00 (B)

Tech Beer, Too good to forget, self-framing painted metal advertising sign, Pittsburgh Brewing Co., Pittsburgh, Pa., artwork of hunting scene, 26½" x 18½", G . .$125.00 (D)

Teddie Peanuts, John W. Leavitt Co., Boston, Mass., tin litho peanut container with center artwork of large peanut, 10-lb., 8¼" x 9⅝", EX . . . .$300.00 (B)

Teddy Brand Peanuts, tin, one-pound tin container with Jumbo Whole Salted Peanuts label on both sides, red, EX . . . .$75.00 (B)

Ted Toddy Pictures Co., paper litho advertising poster promoting "She's too Mean For Me," 26" x 39", VG . . . . $100.00 (C)

Taxi Crimp Cut Tobacco, vertical pocket tin with graphics of early taxi with two men waiting on street in formal attire, NM, $4,900.00 (B). *Courtesy of Buffalo Bay Auction Co.*

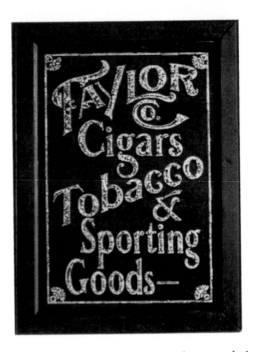

Taylor Co. Cigars, reverse glass on foil-framed sign advertising "Tobacco & Sporting Goods," NM, $575.00 (B). *Courtesy of Buffalo Bay Auction Co.*

Tech Beer, Too good to forget, self-framing painted metal advertising sign, Pittsburgh Brewing Co., Pittsburgh, Pa., artwork of hunting scene, 26½" x 18½", VG, $135.00 (C).

Teem, metal scale-type advertising thermometer with graphics of bottle beside the scale, 12" x 27¾", VG . . . .$90.00 (B)

Telephone, double-sided porcelain flange sign with "Bell System" logo in center, 16¼" x 14", VG . . . .$225.00 (C)

Telephone, double-sided porcelain sign, "American Telephone and Telegraph Co and Associated Companies," with the "Bell System" logo in center, 20" x 20", EX . . . .$395.00 (C)

Telephone, double-sided porcelain sign "The Pacific Telephone and Telegraph Co....American Telephone and Telegraph Co." with "Bell System" logo in center, 12" x 11", VG . . . .$125.00 (C)

Telephone, light-up sign for pay station booths, metal frame and plastic message, 19½" x 5¾", VG .$135.00 (C)

Telephone, porcelain flange sign advertising "Public Telephone" with graphics of very early cradle phone in center, 16" x 16", EX . . . .$575.00 (C)

Telephone, porcelain flange sign "Public Telephone," with artwork of early telephone in center, 18" x 18", EX . . . .$225.00 (C)

Tennessee Brewing Co., "51" Extra Aged Splits 10¢, painted metal advertising sign, 20¼" x 28¼", EX . $50.00 (C)

Terre Haute Brewing Co., Inc., Terre Haute, Indiana, tin litho advertising for Champagne Velvet Beer with graphics of man fishing in stream, 19½" x 14½", VG . .$160.00 (B)

Terre Haute Brewing Co., pressed board, advertising CV Beer, 16½" x 10½", EX . . . .$110.00 (B)

Telephone, light-up sign for pay station booths, metal frame and plastic message, 19½" x 5¾", EX, $165.00 (C). *Courtesy of B.J. Summers*

Telephone, porcelain, single-sided sign with graphics of hand pointing to phone, foreign, 31½" x 7⅞", G, $210.00 (B).

Texaco, restroom key tags, NOS, 3½" x 5½", EX, $40.00 (C).

The Brunswick Bakle-Collender Co., cardboard framed advertisement featuring a scene from the National Bowling Association International Tour in Madison Sq. Garden 5/24-6/12, 1909, 37" x 28", EX, $1,200.00 (B).

Terriff Talcum Powder, tin litho container with cameo graphics of man, Portland, Mich, 2⅝" x 5¾", EX $925.00 (B)

Tetley's Tea, sample tin litho container with elephant graphics on lid, 2¼" x 1¾" x ¾", EX ......$125.00 (C)

Texaco, cloth sleeve patch with star in circle at bottom of patch, lettering in black, 2¼" x 2", G ......$10.00 (C)

Texaco Diesel Chief Diesel Fuel, single-sided porcelain pump sign, "Made in U.S.A./3-11-61," 12" x 18", VG .... $140.00 (B)

Texaco...Exclusive Texaco dealer offer, motorized plastic toy tanker with original cardboard box, 5" x 26½", EX ....$200.00 (C)

Texaco Fire Chief Gasoline, porcelain sign, 18" x 12", EX ....$225.00 (C)

Texaco Fire Chief hat, promotional celluloid hat with reflective front shield, 5" x 11", EX ....$55.00 (C)

Texaco Fire Chief, plastic fireman's hat with large white shield on front with product message, 8" tall, white on red, EX ....$75.00 (C)

The Foster Hose Supporters, celluloid litho on cardboard advertising sign, featuring artwork of woman with garter belt, 17" H, NM, **$310.00 (B).** *Courtesy of Richard Opfer Auctioneering, Inc.*

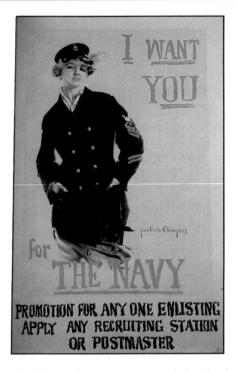

The Navy...I want you, cloth-backed recruiting poster signed by artist, Howard Chandler Christy, with artwork of girl in uniform, 1917, 26½" x 41", EX, **$325.00 (C).**

The Orange Candy Kitchen Ice Cream & Candy, framed die cut litho advertising calendar, featuring artwork of little boy and kittens, 1911, 14½" x 18½", VG, **$85.00 (D).**

Texaco Fire Chief, pump sign, one-sided porcelain with trademark fire hat, 12" x 18", VG ....$85.00 (B)

Texaco gas globe, narrow glass body with two glass globes, red star with green T, 13½" dia., VG ......$475.00 (B)

Texaco...Gasoline...Motor Oil, porcelain single-sided dealer sign, 41½" dia., G ....$140.00 (B)

Texaco..., G.T. Fowle...consignee, one-sided porcelain "keyhole" sign, 21" x 16", VG ....$250.00 (B)

Texaco, metal body, glass front dial-type thermometer with dealer info around outside face, 12" dia., EX ..$325.00 (D)

Texaco Motor Oil...Easy Pour Can...Two Quarts, double-sided painted metal flange sign with artwork of oil being poured from a vintage two-quart can, 17½" x 27⅜", G ....$2,500.00 (B)

Texaco, restroom key tags, NOS, 3½" x 5½", NM ..$50.00 (C)

Texaco, service station attendant's metal pinback badge featuring artwork of Texaco Scotties, 3¼" x 3¼", EX ....$525.00 (B)

Texaco, watch fob, embossed metal fob with Texaco star, 1¼" x 1⅜", EX ....$240.00 (B)

The Aristocrat Gums, 5¢ Cigarette Form, gum box with original contents, EX ....$20.00 (D)

The Badger Mutual Fire Insurance Co., cast metal badger paperweight, EX ....$65.00 (C)

The Bell Telephone Company of Canada...Local...Long Distance Telephone, double-sided porcelain advertising sign with trademark bell in center, 18" x 18", EX ...$125.00 (B)

The Brunswick Bakle-Collender Co., cardboard-framed advertisement featuring a scene from the National Bowling Association International Tour in Madison Sq. Garden 5/24-6/12, 1909, 37" x 28", EX ....$1,200.00 (B)

The Chimes Coffee, paper litho on cardboard container with pry-lid, with graphics of stage with curtains drawn, 1-lb., EX ....$77.00 (B)

The Columbus Brewing Co...Select Pale Beer, round metal tip tray with image of middle-aged woman in center, 4⅛" dia., EX ....$75.00 (B)

The P.J. Sorg Co., Spear Head, tobacco cutter with arrow-shaped end, EX, $150.00 (D). *Courtesy of Chief Paduke Antiques Mall*

The Royal Tailors, die cut painted tin stand-up advertising sign, great graphics, 19½" x 9", EX, $450.00 (D).

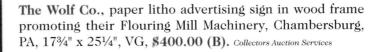

The Wolf Co., paper litho advertising sign in wood frame promoting their Flouring Mill Machinery, Chambersburg, PA, 17¾" x 25¼", VG, $400.00 (B). *Collectors Auction Services*

The Devilish Good Cigar...None Better, embossed tin advertising sign designed to hung by a chain , 13¾" x 10", VG . . . .$175.00 (C)

The "Flower" of the Family...It's William Tell Flour, round metal tip tray with artwork of red-haired woman, 4¼" dia., EX . . . .$120.00 (B)

The Foster Hose Supporters, celluloid litho on cardboard advertising sign, featuring artwork of woman with garter belt, 17" H, EX . . . . $255.00 (C)

The Franklin Life Insurance Company...Springfield, Illinois, round metal tip tray with artwork of Ben Franklin on tray, 4¼" dia., EX . . . .$20.00 (B)

"The Girl on the Barge," heavy paper window card from the Unique Theatre, 14" x 22", G . . . .$25.00 (D)

The Globe's Best...Keep Rollin' With Globe, double-sided tin advertising sign with images of oil cans, 21½" x 12", EX . . . .$550.00 (B)

The Home Insurance Co., collapsible drinking cup in leather case, EX . . . .$30.00 (C)

The Kellogg & Bulkeley Co., advertising paper litho depicting men feeding hens and other men catching the eggs and loading them onto a train, 29" x 35", VG . . . . .$875.00 (B)

The May Company...Ohio's Largest Department Store, round metal tip tray with artwork of woman with flower in hair, 4¼" dia., EX . . . .$90.00 (B)

The Meilink Mfg. Co., salesman sample, cast iron safe, 9¼" x 9¼" x 14", EX . . . .$610.00 (B)

Third Liberty Loan, paper litho advertising poster, 21" x 28", VG, $225.00 (C).

Tintex, painted tin sign, tints as you rinse, artwork of woman tinting clothes, 21¼" x 23", G, $60.00 (C).

Tobacco Girl, tin litho container with graphics of pretty young woman with a tobacco leaf, 6¼" x 4½" x 5½", VG, $1,500.00 (B). *Courtesy of Collectors Auction Services*

The Model Meat Market, paper advertising calendar with graphics of young children and a cat, 14" x 18", EX $1,906.00

The Morey Mills Mocha & Java Coffee, Denver, Colo., tin litho hinged-lid coffee can with artwork of moon and star on front, 1900s, 6" x 6¾" x 3¾", EX . . . .$170.00 (B)

The Navy...I want you, cloth-backed recruiting poster signed by artist, Howard Chandler Christy, with artwork of girl in uniform, 1917, 26½" x 41", NM . . . .$475.00 (C)

The Orange Candy Kitchen Ice Cream & Candy, framed die cut litho advertising calendar, featuring artwork of little boy and kittens, 1911, 14½" x 18½", G . . .$60.00 (B)

The Pilsener Brewing Co..., Cleveland, Ohio, round metal tip tray with bottle and glass of product, 4¼" dia., EX . . . .$90.00 (B)

The P.J. Sorg Co., Spear Head, tobacco cutter with arrow-shaped end, G . . . .$100.00 (D)

Thermo, anti-freeze can with graphics of snowman wearing a scarf, 6½" x 7¾", 1945, VG . . . .$65.00 (D)

Thermo Denatured Alcohol, tin advertising thermometer, "Protect Your Radiator With...," 16" x 72", G . .$325.00 (C)

The Royal Tailors, die cut painted tin stand-up advertising sign, great graphics, 19½" x 9", EX . . . .$450.00 (D)

The Texas Company...Petroleum and its Products, die cut paper calendar with Texaco logo at top, bottom tear sheets complete, 1922, EX . . . .$195.00 (C)

The Turkish Dyes, wooden store dye cabinet with inside dividers, sliding door has heavy waxed litho, 16½" x 11" x 28½", EX . . . .$375.00 (B)

Toledo Scales, porcelain weight sign, 17½" x 11", EX, $95.00 (B).

Tom's Toasted Peanuts, metal advertising thermometer, VG, $35.00 (C).

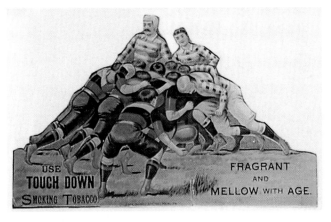

Touch Down Smoking Tobacco...Fragrant and Mellow with Age, die cut cardboard counter sign with graphics of men at goal line, 9½" x 6", EX, $407.00 (B). *Courtesy of Buffalo Bay Auction Co.*

Tracto Motor Oil, embossed painted metal sign, 35" x 11", NM, $75.00 (C).

The Wichita Construction Co., litho on canvas-type paper with artwork of Indian girl on front with full calendar pad, NM . . . .$465.00 (B)

The Wolf Co., paper litho advertising sign in wood frame promoting their Flouring Mill Machinery, Chambersburg, PA, 17¾" x 25¼", F . . . .$100.00 (D)

Thomas A. Edison, Edison-Splitdorf Corporation, spark plug in original cardboard box, G . . . .$12.00 (D)

Thomas J. Lipton, tea tin litho with graphics of slaves, factory, and cattle, 8½" x 5½" x 6", VG . . . . .$175.00 (D)

Thos. J. Scalon, tin litho over cardboard calendar top with graphics of young girl, advertising for bar supplies and hotel china, 13¼" x 19¼", 1906, VG . . .$225.00 (B)

Three Knights, Goodyear Rubber Co., NY, condom tin with litho of three knights on horseback, 2⅛" x 1⅝", EX . . . .$150.00 (B)

Thrift Regular Gas globe, three-piece glass gill body with glass lens 13½" dia., VG . . . .$500.00 (B)

Thurber Coffee, tin litho can with graphics of early company headquarters, 1-lb., 1880s, EX . . . . . .$165.00 (D)

Tidewater Associated Credit Cards Welcome, double-sided hanging metal sign, 20" x 14", EX . . . .$175.00 (C)

Tidex gas globe, low profile metal body with two glass lenses, 16½" dia., VG . . . .$375.00 (B)

Trasks Ointment, die cut cardboard advertising Magnetic Ointment for hemorrhoids and chafing, little boy and girl on front, 6¾" x 9", NM, **$150.00 (C).** *Courtesy of Buffalo Bay Auction Co.*

Tree Brand Shoes, Battreall Shoe Co., metal flange sign, double-sided, NM, **$1,000.00 (D).**
Courtesy of Riverview Antique Mall

Triple AAA Root Beer, single-sided self-framing tin advertising sign with graphics of bottle, 28" x 19½", VG, **$85.00 (B).**

Tiger Chewing Tobacco, tin container with artwork of tiger in center of lid in spotlight, 6" x 4" x 2½", EX . .**$45.00 (D)**

Times Square, smoking tobacco pocket tin with graphics of sky line at night, flip-lid, EX . . . .**$2,255.00 (D)**

Timur Coffee, tin litho pry-lid container, with graphics of Arabian-type rider on horseback, 1-lb., NM . .**$1,210.00 (B)**

Tintex, painted tin sign, tints as you rinse, artwork of woman tinting clothes, 21¼" x 23", F . . . .**$50.00 (C)**

Tip-Top Sweet Smoke and Chew Tobacco, pail with paper label and 1926 tobacco stamp on lid, G . . . . .**$95.00 (D)**

Tivioli Brewing Co...Detroit, round metal tip tray, with product bottle in center, 4⅛" dia., EX . . . . . .**$80.00 (B)**

Tobacco Girl, tin litho container with graphics of pretty young woman with a tobacco leaf, 6¼" x 4½" x 5½", F . . . .**$375.00 (D)**

Tobins' Cork Town Pipe Tobacco, rare piece, EX .**$600.00 (B)**

Toddy Pictures Company, paper litho advertising movie poster promoting "Return of Mandy's Husband" starring Mantan Morehead and F.E. Miller, 26½" x 40½", G . .**$135.00 (D)**

Tokheim Gasoline Pumps Authorized Service, one-sided porcelain sign, NOS, 19½" x 13", EX . . . .**$375.00 (B)**

Tokio Cigarettes, cardboard advertising sign in stamped wood frame, with graphics of man in turban enjoying a cigarette, good strong colors, 25" x 33", VG .**$210.00 (B)**

Trojan T Gasoline, porcelain sign, 28" X 22", VG, $450.00 (D).

True Fruit Soda, delicious, cardboard sign with artwork of grapes and berries, 1905, 9" x 16", EX, $90.00 (B). *Courtesy of Muddy River Trading Co./Gary Metz*

Triple 16 Cola, embossed tin advertising sign with graphics of product bottle, NOS, 11½" x 31½", EX, $150.00 (B).

Tomahawk Scrap Tobacco, embossed tin litho sign in original oak frame, 9¼" x 12", EX . . . .$500.00 (B)

Tom Keene Cigars, cardboard easel back store display sign with graphics of product container, NM . .$98.00 (B)

Tom's Toasted Peanuts, store jar, Tom's lid, EX . . . . .$65.00 (B)

Tom's Toasted Peanuts, tin advertising thermometer with image of bag of the product on front of thermometer, 6" x 16", NM . . . .$95.00 (C)

Topaz, roasted coffee tin container with paper label with graphics of knight on horseback, free sample container, 1⅞" x 2⅝", EX . . . .$65.00 (D)

Top Notch Soda, cardboard advertising sign with display area for list of products under advertising area, 7" x 14", VG . . . .$45.00 (B)

Topsy City Dairy, electric advertising clock with artwork of black child on face, promoting chocolate milk, 14¼" sq., EX . . . .$275.00 (B)

Torrey's Original Old Mt. Vernon Ale, round metal tip tray with graphics of product bottle in tray center, 3⅝" dia., EX . . . .$40.00 (B)

Totem Tobacco, oval pocket tin, with good strong coloring and graphics, EX . . . .$1,150.00 (B)

Touch Down Smoking Tobacco...Fragrant and Mellow with Age, die cut cardboard counter sign with graphics of men at goal line, 9½" x 6", EX . . . .$407.00 (B)

Tower Gasoline globe, wide glass body with lenses, graphics of tower on face, 13½" dia., VG . . . .$700.00 (B)

Tower Root Beer, embossed tin sign with image of product bottle, "Like Mother Used To Make," 8¾" x 19½", EX . . . .$100.00 (B)

Towle's Blacksmith Syrup Tin, tin litho with graphics of black-smith scene on front, 5" x 4¾" x 2⅞", EX . . . . .$195.00 (C)

Towle's Log Cabin Syrup, tin litho pull toy in shape of log cabin, 5¾" x 4¾" x 3¾", EX . . . .$195.00 (C)

Tubular Cream Separators match holder, The Pet of the Dairy, great image of woman with child at separator, 6¾" H, EX, $375.00 (B). *Courtesy of Richard Opfer Auctioneering, Inc.*

Tuckett's Orinoco Tobacco, tin, Canadian item with litho of old man enjoying his pipe, 4¼" x 3¾", G, $110.00 (B).

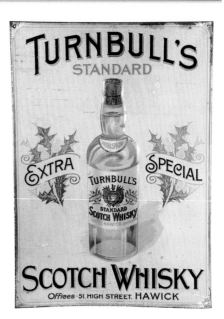

Turnbull's Standard Scotch Whisky, Offices-51 High Street, HAWICK, artwork of bottle in center, embossed painted tin, note spelling of whisky, 24½" x 18", VG, $100.00 (C).

Twang Vitamin Root Beer, embossed tin bottle, tap sign, 14¼" dia., EX, $120.00 (B).

Townsend, cream top milk, bill hook, celluloid, 2' x 2¾", EX . . . .$75.00 (C)

Trasks Ointment, die cut cardboard advertising Magnetic Ointment for hemorrhoids and chafing, little boy and girl on front, 6¾" x 9", VG . . . .$95.00 (D)

Travelers Express Money Orders, light-up advertising clock, 26" x 12" x 4¼", G . . . .$40.00 (B)

Tree Brand Shoes, Battreall Shoe Co., metal flange sign, double-sided, EX . . . .$850.00 (D)

Tricora Corset, yard-long advertising sign, 12" x 28", EX . . . .$575.00 (C)

Trico Wiper Blades, tin double-sided flange advertising sign promoting "replace your...once a year", 18" x 19¾", VG . . . .$195.00 (C)

Triple AAA Root Beer, decal featuring graphics of girl with product, advertising 5¢ root beer, 8" x 6½", EX . . . .$15.00 (C)

Triple 16 Cola...It's Bigger, It's Better, 16 ounces, embossed tin advertising sign with tilted bottle under message, 11½" x 31½", P . . . .$25.00 (D)

Trojan-Enz Condom, tin litho container with artwork of Roman helmeted man in center, 2⅛" x 1⅝" x ¼", EX . . . .$300.00 (B)

Trojan T Gasoline, porcelain sign, 28" x 22", G ..$125.00 (D)

Tropic, cigar tin liberty can with a scene from "Othello" on front, 6¼" x 4" x 5½", VG ....$85.00 (C)

Trout-Line, vertical tobacco tin with graphics of man netting a trout in a stream, EX ....$650.00 (B)

Tru Ade, Drink a better beverage, Not Carbonated, double-sided porcelain sign, 1951, 20" x 14", EX .$230.00 (B)

Tru-Ade, Drink...Naturally Delicious Orange, metal door push, 31" x 2½", orange on yellow, EX ......$25.00 (B)

Tru Ade, litho and stenciled advertising thermometer with likeness of bottle, 6" x 15", EX ....$195.00 (C)

True Fruit Soda, delicious, cardboard sign with artwork of grapes and berries, 1905, 9" x 16", VG ......$65.00 (B)

T T Bitters...Stulz Bros., Kansas City, Mo., Sole Owners, wall-hung tin litho match holder, 3⅜" x 4⅞", EX $425.00 (B)

Tube Rose...It's mild and suits your taste, painted tin sign with artwork of Scotch Snuff can at right of message, 27⅝" x 17½", EX ....$95.00 (D)

Tubular Cream Separators match holder, The Pet of the Dairy, great image of woman with child at separator, 6¾" H, G ....$125.00 (C)

Tubular Cream Separators, advertising sign, tin litho with graphics of separators, 28" x 5", EX ....$245.00 (B)

Tuckett's Old Squire, vertical pocket tin with litho of old squire in cameo, 3⅛" x 4½" x .785", EX ....$700.00 (B)

Tucketts Orinco Cut Fine Smoking Tobacco, tin container with graphics of fishing scene, from Hamilton Canada, 3½" x 2¾" x 1⅝", EX ....$55.00 (C)

Tudor Coffee, paper litho on tin container with graphics of mansion on mountain, 1-lb., EX ....$88.00 (B)

Tudor Tea, Coffee, Cocoa, vintage celluloid advertising watch fob with graphics of factory, 1¾" x 2", EX .....$400.00 (B)

Tums...Bring on your hot mince pie–all foods agree with me now, I use Tums for my Tummy, die cut easel back cardboard store sign, 9¼" x 15¼", EX ....$60.00 (B)

Tums, die cut advertising Baby Snooks toy with advertising message on the back for both Tums and the NBC Radio Show of Fanny Brice, 16" T, 1950s, EX ......$50.00 (B)

Tums...for the tummy...for acid indigestion, heartburn, painted metal vertical scale thermometer with messages at top and bottom of scale, 4" x 9", NM .....$75.00 (C)

Tums, light-up, advertising clock with reverse glass face, metal body and wood frame, 16¼" x 16¼", EX ..$80.00 (B)

Tung Sol Electron Tubes, light-up clock advertising "Radio...Television ...Service," Telechron electric clock, 15" dia., VG ....$140.00 (B)

Turf Cigarettes...Quality Wins, porcelain ad sign with Pegasus image at top, 20" x 30", NM ....$165.00 (B)

Turnbull's Standard Scotch Whisky, Offices-51 High Street, HAWICK, artwork of bottle in center, embossed painted tin, note spelling of whisky, 24½" x 18", G ....$85.00 (C)

Tuxedo, glass paper label humidor with wire-snap closure lid, 7" H, EX ....$175.00 (C)

TWA, airplane metal ashtray, plane on arm over ashtray , 10" x 6", VG ....$165.00 (D)

Twang Vitamin Root Beer...Save Caps for Premiums, embossed round tin sign, 14¼" dia., G ......$65.00 (C)

Twin, cola cardboard advertising sign, "ice cold...a new thirst chaser," 9" x 11½", EX ....$25.00 (B)

Twin Ports Coffee, container with paper label and screw-top, graphics of ocean vessel on front, 1-lb., EX ....$135.00 (C)

Two Homers Cigars, paper label advertising sign with clock hands to indicate time store owner would return to the store, advertising 2 cigars 5¢, 12" sq., EX ..$35.00 (B)

Tydol Flying A, cloth banner with Flying A giant putting wings on older model car, 79" x 34", EX ....$135.00 (C)

Tydol Flying A, one-sided porcelain pump sign, 9¾" dia., G ....$300.00 (C)

Tydol gas globe, low profile metal body with two glass lenses, 16½" dia., G ....$375.00 (B)

Tydol "Running Man," die cut embossed tin license plate attachment, 4½" x 6⅝", G ....$75.00 (C)

Tyee Tackle, paper advertising calendar with graphics of young woman in a fishing scene, 12" x 16½", 1928, EX ....$550.00 (B)

U and I Lemonade, single sided advertising cardboard sign, 22" x 19", VG, $10.00 (B).

UMC Cartridges, die cut painted tin flange sign, likeness of bull head, G, $695.00 (D).

Courtesy of Riverview Antique Mall

UMC Co., advertising calendar with graphics of mother dog and pups, 14" x 28¼", 1894, EX, $4,550.00 (B). *Courtesy of Past Tyme Pleasures*

Ubero Coffee Co., tin litho tip tray featuring graphics of coffee container in center, 4¼", VG . . . .$170.00 (B)

UMC Co., advertising calendar with graphics of mother dog and pups , 14" x 28¼", 1894, G . . . . . . $1,000.00 (C)

UMC Cartridges, die cut painted tin flange sign, likeness of bull head, EX . . . .$995.00 (C)

UMC "Club" Brass Shells, two-piece 12 ga. box, 4¼" x 4¼" x 2¼", EX . . . .$80.00 (B)

UMC-Remington, advertising poster with graphics of cowboy getting ready to go hunting, by Phillip R. Goodwin, 17" x 24½", 1910, EX . . . .$325.00 (C)

UMC Shot, advertising poster with graphics of a covey of quail in flight, 15" x 29¼", 1908, EX . . . .$160.00 (B)

UMC (Union Metallic Cartridge Co.), advertising calendar with great graphics of Teddy Roosevelt and the 1st U.S. Cavalry "Rough Riders," with both top and bottom metal bands, 13½" x 28", 1899, G . . . .$150.00 (C)

UMWA, miner's hat, salesman sample hat on wood display complete with helmet light, 15" x 17½", G . . . .$75.00 (C)

Uncle John's Syrup, five-piece paper store window display, with original envelope, measurement of Uncle John is 40" x 24", NM . . . .$600.00 (B)

Uncle John's Syrup, window display with graphics of Uncle John pouring syrup on hot cakes being held by young boy, 45" x 50", NM . . . .$875.00 (C)

Uncle Sam Shoe Polish, tin container with artwork of Uncle Sam on front and image of small boy polishing Uncle Sam's shoes on back side, 3½", EX . . . . .$40.00 (B)

Union Farmer's Gin...phone 32, Portageville, Mo., vertical scale thermometer in country scene with silhouettes in foreground, 10¼" x 8¼", VG, **$35.00 (C).**

Courtesy of B.J. Summers

Uncle Sam Stock Medicine Co., Quincy, Ill., U.S.A., heavy paper with patriotic images of Statue of Liberty and naval ships returning home, great item, 1919, 15" x 20", NM, **$225.00 (B).** *Courtesy of Buffalo Bay Auction Co.*

UMC (Union Metallic Cartridge Co.), advertising calendar with great graphics of Teddy Roosevelt and the 1st U.S. Cavalry "Rough Riders," with both top and bottom metal bands, 13½" x 28", 1899, EX, **$425.00 (C).**

Courtesy of Past Tyme Pleasures

Union Leader, smoking tobacco paperweight, EX, **$25.00 (D).**

Courtesy of Chief Paduke Antiques Mall

Uncle Sam Stock Medicine Co., Quincy, Ill., U.S.A., heavy paper with patriotic images of Statue of Liberty and naval ships returning home, great item, 1919, 15" x 20", VG . . . .$135.00 (D)

Uncle Tom's Cabin, advertising poster with graphics of exaggerated black man's head, "Jes Yo Come Along an' laff at Uncle Tom's Cabin," 41" x 89½", VG . . . . .$750.00 (B)

Uncle Tom's Cabin, cardboard litho advertising poster with graphics of black man dancing with a child, 21" x 28", 1890s, EX . . . .$275.00 (B)

Uncle Tom's Cabin, paper litho advertising poster with graphics of black man in front of cabin with young girl, Wm. M. Donaldson & Co. Pub's Cincinnati, Oh, 33½" x 27⅜", G . . . .$175.00 (B)

Uncle Tom's Cabin, paper litho framed advertising poster, "Topsy's Recreation" with graphics of Topsy in center, 45½" x 83", EX . . . .$700.00 (B)

Uncle Tom's Cabin, stone litho printers proof by Donaldson & Co., Cincinnati, features old black man seated next to a dog with a young white girl standing next to him, 33¼" x 27½", 1883, NM . . . .$350.00 (B)

Uncle Wiggily, early litho pail from the Mueller Keller Candy Co., St. Joseph, MO, containing graphics of the Lang Campbell comic strip characters, 1923, EX . .$475.00 (B)

Uneeda Biscuit...Don't Forget, string-hung cardboard sign with kid in slicker, never used, 21" x 16½", EX . .$275.00 (B)

Uneeda Biscuit, paperboard trolley advertising sign with the product bound up on top of books, EX . . . .$60.00 (B)

Uneeda Biscuit, paper litho in wood frame, according to the info this was to be displayed only in November, 21½" x 12½", VG . . . .$75.00 (B)

Uneeda Biscuit, tin litho letter opener, trademark boy in yellow slicker on handle, 1¾" x 8¾", G . . . . .$20.00 (B)

Union Metallic Cartridge Co., two-piece paper litho over cardboard box, graphics of duck in flight, 4" x 4⅛" x 25", VG, **$25.00 (B).**

Union Oil...Motorite, porcelain die cut shield flange sign, 19½" x 19¾", EX, **$425.00 (C).**
Courtesy of Autopia Advertising Auctions

Union 76, Certified Service Truck, toy truck in original box, has steerable wheels, with original decals, NOS, 24½" x 9½" x 9½", EX, **$200.00 (D).**
Courtesy of Rare Bird Antique Mall/Jon & Joan Wright

Union Diesel, Diesel Fuel, one-sided porcelain pump sign, 11½" dia., G . . . .$160.00 (B)

Union Farmer's Gin...phone 32, Portageville, Mo., vertical scale thermometer in country scene with silhouettes in foreground, 10¼" x 8¼", EX . . . .$45.00 (C)

Union Gasoline "Carigas," running board storage can, 1-gal., F . . . .$100.00 (C)

Union Leader Redi Cut Tobacco, round tin with Uncle Sam likeness smoking pipe on label, P. Lorillard Company, G . . . .$15.00 (D)

Union Leader...smoke and chew...Cut Plug, tin litho container in milkcan-style, hard-to-find, 4¾" x 9¼", EX . .$350.00 (B)

Union Leader, smoking tobacco, paperweight, NM .$35.00 (C)

Union Leader, tin litho sign advertising smoking tobacco with eagle logo in center, 10½" x 15", EX . . . . .$225.00 (C)

Union Made Overalls, one-sided curved porcelain ad sign, 16" x 14", EX . . . .$360.00 (B)

Union Oil...Motorite, porcelain die cut shield flange sign, 19½" x 19¾", EX . . . .$425.00 (C)

Union 76, brass padlock with trademark, 3" tall, EX . . . .$125.00 (C)

Union 76, Certified Service Truck, toy truck in original box, has steerable wheels, with original decals, NOS, 24½" x 9½" x 9½", G . . . .$95.00 (C)

Union 76, Regular Gasoline, one-sided porcelain pump sign, 9" x 11¾", VG . . . .$115.00 (C)

Union 76, salt & pepper set, hard-to-find, 2¾" tall, EX . . . .$200.00 (C)

Union Shop, celluloid window sign for Bakery and Confectionery Workers, 12" x 7", EX . . . .$35.00 (C)

United Motors Service, oval porcelain advertising sign with image of early auto in center, 60" x 36", 1930s, EX, $1,500.00 (B). *Courtesy of Muddy River Trading Co./Gary Metz*

United States Fur Company, paperboard poster featuring black boys trying to run an animal out of a hollow log, only to discover it's a skunk, United States Fur Co., St. Louis Mo., "Ship us your Furs," 15" x 20½", 1920s, EX, $350.00 (B). *Courtesy of Buffalo Bay Auction Co.*

Upson Processed Board, single-sided porcelain ad sign, 40" x 20", F, $50.00 (B). *Courtesy Collectors Auction Services*

United American Ship Lines, advertising sign with graphics of ship, 20½" x 26½", EX . . . .$250.00 (B)

United Motors Service, oval porcelain advertising sign with image of early auto in center, 60" x 36", 1930s, VG . . . .$775.00 (C)

United States Army Reserve, porcelain over metal double-sided advertising sign with image of Minuteman in center, 36" x 36", EX . . . .$165.00 (B)

United States Brewing, self-framed tin litho, graphics of men in boat and decal of bottles on frame portion, 19½" x 15½", EX . . . .$475.00 (C)

United States 5¢ Cigar, 250-count cigar box with stars and stripes on front and inside cover, NM . . .$150.00 (B)

United States Fur Company, paperboard poster featuring black boys trying to run an animal out of a hollow log, only to discover it's a skunk, United States Fur Co., St. Louis Mo., "Ship us your Furs," 15" x 20½", 1920s, VG . . . .$275.00 (C)

United States Fur Company, paper litho advertising with graphics of youngsters chasing a skunk out of a log, "An Unwelcome Surprise," 18½" x 24¾", G . . . . .$200.00 (B)

United States Rubbers, calendar, trifold panels show young lady, girl with dog, and a miner wearing their rubber footwear, American Litho Co., NY, 1900s, EX . .$145.00 (C)

United States Tire, cardboard advertising in shape of tire, cardboard with wood backing with graphics of types of tires, 6¾" x 12", VG . . . .$210.00 (B)

U.S. Army, I Want You, double-sided recruiting sign designed to fit in metal sidewalk frame, 25" x 38", EX, **$375.00 (C).** *Courtesy of B.J. Summers*

U.S. Quality Enameled Ware, curved glass light-up store advertising sign, featuring enamel steam pot likeness in center, 7" x 13½", EX, **$550.00 (B).** *Courtesy of Muddy River Trading Co./Gary Metz*

United Telephone Service...Long Distance, double-sided porcelain flange advertising sign, 16" x 16", NM . **$225.00 (C)**

United, unleaded globe, plastic body with two glass lenses, 13½" dia., VG . . . .**$225.00 (B)**

United Van Lines...W. Jeff Hammond Moving & Storage, light-up advertising clock with metal body and glass face, EX . . . .**$150.00 (D)**

Universal Home Wares, light-up advertising clock with glass face and cover on a pressed cardboard body, "electrical appliances," EX . . . .**$90.00 (B)**

Universal Olive Oil, tin with image of cherubs on label, 1-gal., EX . . . .**$105.00 (C)**

Universal Stoves and Ranges, advertising match holder with good strong litho on tin, 5" H, EX . . . . . **$240.00 (B)**

Universal Stoves, metal litho tip tray with graphics of globe, 4¼" dia., EX . . . .**$95.00 (B)**

Universal, tin litho container with graphics of Uncle Sam-like figure, slip-lid, 1-lb., EX . . . .**$163.00 (B)**

Unguentine cardboard litho display, graphics of sunburned woman applying the product, 22½" x 35", EX . . . . .**$100.00 (B)**

Urbana Wine Co...Gold Seal...Champagne, metal tip tray with artwork of product bottle in tray center, 6⅝", EX . . . .**$45.00 (B)**

U.S. Army, I Want You, enamel double-sided recruiting sign designed to fit in metal sidewalk frame, 25" x 38", VG . . . .**$275.00 (C)**

U.S. Cartridge Co., paper calendar with image of large grizzly bear carrying a box of cartridges while a hunter hides in a tree, 14" x 26", 1922, EX . . . .**$325.00 (C)**

U.S. Marine, Smoke or Chew, tin litho lunch pail with graphics of service man on front, EX . . . . . . **$209.00 (B)**

U.S. Quality Enameled Ware, curved glass light-up store advertising sign, featuring enamel steam pot likeness in center, 7" x 13½", VG . . . .**$425.00 (C)**

U.S. School Garden...Raised 'em myself in my..., cardboard poster with artwork of young boy with large basket full of vegetables, framed, EX . . . .**$175.00 (D)**

3V Cola, round metal sign, 29" dia., G, $85.00 (B).

V.D. Morgan, Van Services & Storage, paper advertising calendar, graphics of vintage moving van, 1950, 16⅜" x 24¼", VG, $15.00 (B).

Veedol, single-sided die cut tin litho, girl on skates, 5½" x 14¼", G, $325.00 (B).

Vacuum Harness Oil, paper litho advertising sign with graphics of trotter on front, 1890s, EX . . . . . $175.00 (B)

Vacuum Oil Company, Gargoyle Mobiloil "E" metal oil can with paper label, 1-gal. . . . . $35.00 (C)

Valentine & Co...why drive a shabby car...refinish with Valentine's Colors..., celluloid vertical thermometer, 5½" x 20", NM . . . . $145.00 (C)

Valiant Authorized Service, porcelain double-sided advertising sign, 40⅜" dia., VG . . . . $400.00 (B)

Valvoline ...motor oil...ask for, neon advertising clock, 18" x 18", VG . . . . $650.00 (D)

Valvoline Oil Company, advertising celluloid pocket mirror in shape of oil barrel, 2¾" x 1¾", EX . . . . $155.00 (C)

Valvoline Racing Oil, double-sided tin sign, 30" dia., EX . . . . $210.00 (B)

Van Dam Cigars, embossed tin litho advertising sign with graphics of trademark Van Dam and message "Java Wrapped," 27¾" x 13½", EX . . . . $160.00 (B)

Van De Kamp's Bakeries, cardboard advertising poster with graphics of sporting and camping scenes, 42" x 11", NM . . . . $75.00 (C)

Vanderbilt Premium Tread..., round light-up advertising clock with logo in center of face, 1958, 14½" dia., EX . . $135.00 (D)

Van Dyck Havana Cigars, die cut tin litho sign in shape of artist palette with artwork of "Van Dyck" in center of sign, 13½" x 9½", EX . . . . $675.00 (B)

Van Heusen Collar, tin on cardboard advertising sign, 13" x 6", EX . . . . $60.00 (B)

Van Houten's Cocoa, cardboard ad in original oak frame with artwork of woman in hat, frame etched Van Houten's Cocoa, 24¼" x 30¼", G . . . . $75.00 (D)

Van Houten's Cocoa, sign, cardboard print in original oak frame, "Van Houten's Cocoa" etched into frame, graphics of woman in straw hat, 24¼" x 30¼", EX . . . . . $95.00 (C)

Vantage...Buy a pack today, painted metal three-sided dial-type thermometer, with message at top and scale at bottom, white on blue background, EX . . . . . $35.00 (C)

Vernor's Ginger Ale, deliciously different!, with artwork of woman with bottle, cardboard sign with wood frame, 21" x 11¾", EX, $250.00 (C).

Vic's Special Beer, tin over cardboard advertising sign from the Northern Brewing Co., Superior, Wis., 11⅜" x 5⅜", EX, $60.00 (B).

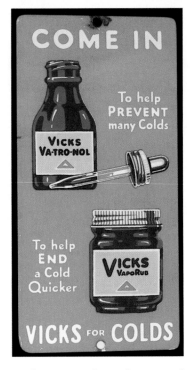

Vicks, porcelain door push plate with artwork of Va-tro-nol, and VapoRub, 3¾" x 7¾", EX, $130.00 (B). *Courtesy of Muddy River Trading Co./Gary Metz*

Vaseline, counter tin litho store display, with storage space inside and product display on front, 6¼" x 7¼" x 15¾", EX . . . .$625.00 (C)

Veedol...it's time to change to warm weather..., cloth banner, with artwork of bird on clothesline and artwork at lower right, 58" x 36", EX . . . .$135.00 (C)

Veedol Motor Oils, double-sided porcelain tombstone style curb sign, "100% Pennsylvania At Its Best", 22" x 28", NM . . . .$375.00 (B)

Velvet Ice Cream...High In Food Value, painted on canvas advertising banner, 48" x 12", EX . . . .$65.00 (B)

Velvet Ice Cream, light-up advertising clock with clock under message panel, which is reverse painted glass, G . . . .$235.00 (C)

Velvet Pipe Tobacco, porcelain sign with likeness of product package at left of message, "Aged In Wood," 39" x 12", EX . . . .$180.00 (B)

Velvet... the Best Milk & Ice Cream, light-up clock with message panel to right of clock face, EX . . . . .$95.00 (C)

Venables Chew Tobacco, cutter, Pat.1875 with 1" & 2" measurements, EX . . . .$115.00 (D)

Vermont Mutual Fire Insurance Co., tin advertising sign with indented oval center that has graphics of headquarters building, 20¼" x 24¼", EX . . . .$950.00 (B)

Vernor's Ginger Ale, deliciously different!, with artwork of woman with bottle, cardboard sign with wood frame, 21" x 11¾", G . . . .$95.00 (C)

Vernor's Ginger Ale, Ice Cold, chrome topper sign from fountain dispenser, EX . . . .$60.00 (B)

Vernor's Ginger Ale, self-framing embossed tin sign with image of elf rolling a barrel of the product, 54¼" x 18⅜", 1940s, EX . . . .$410.00 (B)

Vulcan Plow Co., die cut tin litho match strike, rare item, 2¾" x 7¾", VG, $560.00 (B).

Vuelta Seal Cigar, double-sided metal sign by Chas. Shonk, 17½" x 13½", EX, $195.00 (B).

Vernor's, menu board, tin self-framing, 19" x 25", VG . . . .$45.00 (B)

Vess...Drink, light-up metal clock with metal body, 18" dia., EX . . . .$145.00 (D)

Veteran Brand Coffee, tin litho, with graphics of old soldier, 1-lb., EX . . . .$135.00 (C)

Veteran Coffee, key-wound tin container, 1-lb., EX$65.00 (C)

Veteran Salt, cardboard container with paper label, unopened, 2-lb., EX . . . .$35.00 (B)

Viceroy Open, plastic sign with product package to right of message, 15¾" x 9", G . . . .$15.00 (D)

Vicks, porcelain door push plate with artwork of Va-tro-nol, and VapoRub, 3¾" x 7¾", G . . . .$75.00 (C)

Vic's Special Beer, advertising sign, stamped celluloid over tin, Northern Brewing Co., Superior, WI, 5¼" x 11½", VG . . . .$40.00 (B)

Victor Duck Decoys, papier-maché, hand-painted store advertising piece, 6" x 6" x 4½", EX . . . .$575.00 (B)

Virginia Dare, metal serving tray with great litho of Virginia and Paul promoting American Wines, 12" dia., EX . . . .$185.00 (B)

Virginia Dare Wine, serving tray with "Paul & Virginia" in center graphics "American Wines," 12" dia., EX . . . .$195.00 (B)

Virginia Dare Wine...The Drink of Sociability, metal serving tray with graphics of grapevines and bottle of the product in center, 12" dia., EX . . . .$150.00 (B)

Virginity Smoking Tobacco, tin litho tobacco box with hinged lid and graphics of woman on lid, 7" x 4½" x 3⅞", EX . . . . $400.00 (B)

Visa, double-sided porcelain sign with image of smoking cigarette under product message, foreign, 27½" x 19", VG . . . .$60.00 (B)

Visible Gasoline, round ball-shaped gas globe with etched lettering, 13½" dia., VG . . . .$500.00 (B)

Vision Baking Powder, container with paper label and graphics of cherubs, 3" x 7", EX . . . .$80.00 (B)

Vision Baking Powder, paper label container with graphics of young children playing, 3" x 7", VG . . . . . .$175.00 (B)

Voigt Cream Flakes, cardboard cereal box with graphics of woman and cow on front, EX . . . .$215.00 (B)

Voltaic Compound, die cut advertising calendar promoting cure rheumatism and neuralgia, 5¾" x 10", 1892, EX . . . .$155.00 (B)

Vuelta Seal Cigar, double-sided metal sign by Chas. Shonk, 17½" x 13½", EX . . . .$195.00 (B)

Vulcanized...We Repair Tubes, double-sided tin flange advertising sign, 17½" x 13½", EX . . . .$375.00 (C)

Walk-Over Shoes, single-sided tin litho promoting Wm. Archdeacon Co., Grafton, W. Va., 23½" x 11¾", VG, **$55.00 (B).**

Walk-Over Shoes, double-sided sheet steel flange sign, 13½" x 19½", EX, **$600.00 (B).**

Courtesy of Richard Opfer Auctioneering, Inc.

War Bonds, government paper poster, 1944, 20" x 27", VG, **$55.00 (B).**

Ward's Lemon-Crush, dispenser, china with metal pump in shape of lemon, embossed lettering, 9" x 12¾", EX, **$1,500.00 (B).** *Courtesy of Collectors Auction Services*

Wadham's Gas, tin advertising sign with wood frame, 18" x 83½", F . . . .$250.00 (B)

Wadham's Tempered Motor Oil, tin advertising sign with graphics of oil bottle in spotlight at top, 18" x 83½", F . . . .$250.00 (B)

Wagner Lockheed Hydraulic Brake Parts & Fluid, double-sided tin flange sign, 12½" x 9¾", EX . . . .$155.00 (C)

Wagner's Ice Cream, tin advertising sign featuring artwork of different ice cream products on a wooden serving tray, 1920s, 19½" x 13½", G . . . .$250.00 (B)

Wagon Wheel, sample pocket tin with graphics of wagon wheel and wagon train, 3" x 4½" x ⅞", EX . . .$335.00 (C)

Wak-em-up coffee, tin litho coffee can with artwork of Indian in full headdress, 7½" x 8¾", EX . . . . .$450.00 (B)

Ward's Orange-Crush...Sold Here, double-sided tin flange sign, 1920s, 11" x 9", EX, $650.00 (B). *Courtesy of Muddy River Trading Co./Gary Metz*

Ward's Orange-Crush Dispenser, in shape of large orange with top pump, 14" T, EX, $1,150.00 (B). *Courtesy of Buffalo Bay Auction Co.*

Walburn Ethyl Gasoline, globe, high profile metal body with glass lens, 15½" dia., VG . . . .$350.00 (B)

Walkers Grape Juice, enameled advertising bowl with graphics of grape clusters, 19" x 7", VG . . . . .$300.00 (B)

Walker's Talc, tin litho can with graphics of woman on front, 1¾" x 4", EX . . . .$325.00 (B)

Walk-Over Shoes, double-sided sheet steel flange sign, 13½" x 19½", VG . . . .$450.00 (C)

Walla-Walla Peppermint chewing gum, cardboard box, 4" x 6" x 1", VG . . . .$50.00 (B)

Walter A. Wood, Hoosick Falls, NY, USA, cardboard calendar for mowing and reaping machines with great graphics of horse-drawn reaper, 7½" x 8¾", NM . . . .$140.00 (B)

Walter A. Wood Implements, calendar 1892, double-sided cardboard calendar with young girls in front of rake, implements on reverse, 1892, 6" x 7", NM . . . .$50.00 (B)

Walter's Beer, double-sided porcelain advertising sign in iron frame, from Eau Claire, Wis., 60" x 37", NM . . .$425.00 (B)

Walter's Pilsner Beer...Time for, light-up advertising clock with artwork of brown bear in center spotlight, reverse painted glass, 15" dia., NM . . . .$293.00 (B)

Wampum, coffee tin with graphics of bare-breasted maiden, from Duluth MN, 5½" x 9¼", EX . . . .$225.00 (C)

Wan-Eta Cocoa, tin container with paper label that bears the image of an Indian maiden, 4⅛" x 2½" x 1½", EX . . . .$65.00 (C)

Ward's Lemon-Crush, ceramic dispenser in the shape of a lemon with metal pump at top, 13" tall, 1920s, EX . . . .$1,530.00 (B)

Ward's Lemon-Crush, dispenser, china with metal pump in shape of lemon, embossed lettering, 9" x 12¾", G . . . .$700.00 (D)

Ward's Lime-Crush Deliciously Different, cardboard advertising sign with silhouette figure drinking the product, 24" x 14½", 1920s, EX . . . .$250.00 (C)

Ward's Orange-Crush Dispenser, in shape of large orange with top pump, 14" T, G . . . .$625.00 (C)

Watertite Paints & Enamels, painted embossed metal sign, 24" x 12", VG, $145.00 (D). *Courtesy of Riverview Antique Mall*

Warren's Paints, double-sided porcleain advertising sign, 24" x 26", VG, $235.00 (B).

Weather-Bird Shoes, neon and porcelain advertising sign in the shape of a rooster weather vane, 17" x 25½", EX, $1,700.00 (D).

Ward's Orange-Crush...Sold Here, double-sided tin flange sign, 1920s, 11" x 9", G . . . .$225.00 (C)

Ward's Orange Juice....Drink, painted tin sign with artwork of bottle to left of message, 28" x 20", EX . . . . . .$125.00 (C)

Ward's Orange Juice, figural ceramic dispenser with metal pump, in shape of orange, 8" dia. x 13½", VG . . . .$1,550.00 (B)

Wareco, neon sign with waving service station attendant, 20" x 20", EX . . . .$170.00 (B)

Washburn's Ice Cream, watch fob, cloisonne enamel, EX . . . .$170.00 (B)

Waterman's Ideal Fountain Pen, store countertop display case, wood and glass with lettering on front glass, 18" x 17" x 9½", VG . . . .$700.00 (B)

Watertite Paints & Enamels, painted embossed metal sign, 24" x 12", G . . . .$135.00 (D)

Watkins Egyptian, tin litho talc container with graphics of sphinx on front and pyramid on back, EX . . .$185.00 (B)

Welch Juniors, tin advertising sign in the unusual large size, 40" x 18", 1931s, EX, $600.00 (B). *Courtesy of Buffalo Bay Auction Co.*

Welch Motor Oil, one-sided painted metal sign, 24" x 9", VG, $90.00 (B).

Wells, Richardson & Co., advertising sign, chromo-litho paper on canvas backing with embossed frame, advertising lactated foods for infants and invalids, good rare piece, 25½" x 34¾", G, $500.00 (B).

Waverly Kerosene...Lighting Heating Cooking, porcelain sign with graphics of pennant and Shell logo, 22" x 12", EX . . . .$200.00 (B)

Waverly Pure Rye, advertising, painted plaster featuring a three-man band, 25½" x 32", VG . . . .$1,500.00 (D)

Waverly Pure Rye, advertising sign from Sample & Co., 84 Front St., NY with image of three black musicians in a stone archway, 25½" x 32½" x 1¾", 1900s, EX . . . . .$953.00 (B)

Wayne Dairy Ice Cream, double-sided porcelain hanging sign, 20" x 15", EX . . . .$400.00 (B)

Wayne Feed, advertising thermometer, die cut tin with chicken on feed sack, "a better fed for every need," 3½" x 6¼", EX . . . .$315.00 (B)

Wayne Gas Pumps, paper advertising poster with graphics of pumps and other parts, 22" x 32¾", NM . . .$120.00 (C)

Waynesboro Motor Club, AAA, Spring Water, porcelain sign, 9¾" x 12", red, blue & black, G . . . .$175.00 (C)

Wear U Well, porcelain flange advertising sign, 25" x 17", VG . . . .$240.00 (B)

Weather-Bird Shoes, neon and porcelain advertising sign in the shape of a rooster weather vane, 17" x 25½", G . . . .$450.00 (C)

Web Foot cigar box, wooden with graphics of Indian maiden, 10-ct, 1920s, VG . . . .$80.00 (B)

Webster Cigars, nice reverse glass agency advertising sign with likeness of Noah Webster in center, 11½" x 15½", VG . . . .$275.00 (C)

Webster Grocery Co., cardboard container for Marvel Oats with mountain scene, 3-lb., 7-oz., EX . .$120.00 (B)

Webster's Seeds, wood store counter box with dovetailed corners and great graphics on inside paper label, 8¾" x 6" x 3", VG . . . .$135.00 (C)

Wedding Bouquet Cigar, embossed tin litho advertising sign with graphics of early Puritan wedding scene, 27½" x 19½", EX . . . .$475.00 (B)

Western Union, double-sided porcelain flange sign, 24" x 12", VG, $135.00 (B).

Western Field, Leaded Waterproof Paper Shot Shells, two-piece cardboard box with image of grouse on label, 4⅛" x 4⅛" x 25", G, $230.00 (B).

Western Union Telegrams may be telephoned from here, porcelain flange advertising sign, 22" X 12", VG, $255.00 (D). *Courtesy of Riverview Antique Mall*

Western Winchester, paper litho poster, featuring scene of men in cabin getting ready for duck hunting, G, $45.00 (C).

Wedding Breakfast Coffee, Behring-Stahl Coffee Co., St. Louis, Mo., features graphics of wedding party, 1-lb., EX . . . .$35.00 (D)

Weddles Tea Tin, with vintage automobiles on front and rear, 5" x 3" x 3¼", VG . . . .$250.00 (B)

Weed Chains, tin litho over wood hanging advertising sign with graphics of tire chain over tire, 17¼" x 23¼", EX . . . .$1,400.00 (B)

Wee Willy Beer, glass window advertising sign, 14" x 6", EX . . . .$75.00 (C)

Weideman Boy Brand Coffee, key-wound tin litho can with trademark image of Weideman Coffee, 1-lb., 5" x 4", EX . . . .$190.00 (B)

Welch Juniors...Drink a bunch of grapes, horizontal painted tin sign with artwork of product to left of message, 40" x 18", VG . . . .$375.00 (C)

Welch Juniors, Drink A Bunch Of Grapes, tin over cardboard easel back sign, 9" x 6", G . . . .$450.00 (B)

Welch Juniors Grape Juice, embossed tin sign, 1930s, 19½" x 13½", G . . . .$400.00 (B)

Western Winchester, paper litho poster, scene of men in camp with deer in background, VG, $60.00 (C).

West Hair Nets, countertop store display cabinet with graphics advertising West Hair Net and Electric Hair Curlers, 12¾" x 11¼" x 20", 1920s, EX, $2,500.00 (C).

Welch Juniors, tin advertising sign in the unusual large size, 40" x 18", 1931s, F . . . .$95.00 (C)

Welch's, "The National Drink," celluloid over tin made by Whitehead and Hoag, 10" x 10", EX . . . .$625.00 (B)

Wellington...London Mixture, tin litho container, 4⅜" x 3⅞", EX . . . .$325.00 (B)

Wells, Richardson & Co., advertising sign, chromo-litho paper on canvas backing with embossed frame, advertising lactated foods for infants and invalids, good rare piece, 25½" x 34¾", EX . . . .$1,250.00 (B)

Wells Richardson Lactated Food for Infants and Invalids, tin litho container with slip-lid, 1879, NM . . . .$77.00 (B)

Welsbach Assures Dependable Lighting Service, round metal tip tray with graphics of woman in chair with small girl in floor, 4⅛", EX . . . .$220.00 (B)

West End Brewing Co., Utica, New York, tin litho tray with graphics of Lady Liberty standing in center between beer keg and eagle, 13" dia., G . . . .$163.00 (B)

Western Ammunition, paper advertising sign titled "The Unexpected," 17" x 23", EX . . . .$675.00 (C)

Western Auto Associate Store...Home Owner, die cut embossed tin arrow sign, 33" x 9", EX . . . . .$175.00 (C)

Western Auto, light-up advertising clock, 12" dia., G . . . .$135.00 (C)

Western Cartridges with Lubaloy bullets, store counter-top advertising sign, 7¾" x 8", EX . . . .$65.00 (D)

Western Club Whiskey, pot metal bottle stand for back bar use, 4" tall, EX . . . .$25.00 (C)

Western Field Shotgun Shells, one-piece cardboard box, graphics of quail on front of box, 25-count, EX .$156.00 (B)

Western Ledger, tin litho marker with advertising on front for Western Assurance Co., 3" x 12¼", EX . . .$225.00 (D)

Western Motor Association...Approved Motor Court, double-sided porcelain advertising sign, 29" x 27½", G . . .$45.00 (B)

Westland Ice Cream, light-up advertising clock, Covington, Ky., brand, 26" x 8¼", F, $90.00 (B).

West Virginia Pilsner Beer, cardboard advertising poster, featuring artwork of woman and glass of beer, 14" x 22", VG, $100.00 (C).

Whistle, advertising clock by PAM, featuring the elf pushing a bottle of the product 14½" dia., VG, $650.00 (B).

Whistle, advertising wall-mounted cast iron figural bottle holder in the likeness of hand holding the hour-glass bottle, 10" x 3" x 2½", EX, $775.00 (D). *Courtesy of Wm. Morford Investment Grade Collectibles*

Western...Shoot...Super X & Xpert ammunition, die cut advertising cardboard sign with graphics of geese in flight and product boxes, 10" x 9¼", 1927, EX .....$80.00 (B)

Western Super X, cardboard hanging poster with graphics of cartridges arranged in shape of X, 21" x 13", EX . . . .$230.00 (B)

Western Super X shotgun shells, box, G .....$10.00 (D)

Western Super X .22 Long rifle, fold-out advertising brochure with graphics of product box on front, 6½" x 3½", EX . . . .$40.00 (B)

Western Super X, two-piece shotgun shell box, 4" x 4" x 2½", VG . . . .$30.00 (B)

Western Union, bell page with product name on front, 3½" x 5¾", EX . . . .$65.00 (C)

Western Union, flange porcelain sign with graphics of early "candlestick" phone in center, 18" x 19½", G . .$575.00 (C)

Western Union, porcelain messenger bicycle-mounted sign, 13" x 2¾", NM . . . .$225.00 (C)

Western Union, porcelain telegraph key with great blue and white colors, 3½" x 6" x 3", EX . . . .$45.00 (B)

Western Union Telegrams may be telephoned from here, porcelain flange advertising sign, 22" x 12", G . .$225.00 (D)

Whistle, die cut cardboard store advertising sign, with graphics of small elf next to product bottle, 1951, EX, $82.00 (B). *Courtesy of Buffalo Bay Auction Co.*

Whistle, cardboard die cut advertising sign in likeness of woman with Whistle bottle with straw, 15¾" x 22¾", NM, $185.00 (B). *Courtesy of Autopia Advertising Auctions*

Whistle, framed die cut paper advertisment from H. Gramse and Bro. Litho, Balto., Md., 23" x 7", VG, $75.00 (B). *Courtesy of Collectors Auction Services*

Whistle...Golden Orange...Refreshment Time, die cut pressed board electric advertising clock, 24" x 23", VG, $1,055.00 (B). *Courtesy of Collectors Auction Services*

Western Union Telegraph and Cable Office, double-sided porcelain flange sign, 24" x 12¼", VG . . . . . .$165.00 (B)

Western Union...Telegraph Here, double-sided porcelain flange sign, 25" x 17", NM . . . .$220.00 (B)

Western Union Telegraph here, porcelain advertising sign with side-mounting tab, 25" x 16¾", white and yellow on dark blue, EX . . . .$155.00 (C)

Western Union...Telephone your telegrams from here, flanged porcelain sign with artwork of candlestick phone at lower left of message, 18" x 19½", EX . . . .$195.00 (C)

Western Winchester, paper litho poster, featuring scene of men in cabin getting ready for duck hunting, G . .$45.00 (C)

Western Winchester, paper litho poster, scene of men in camp with deer in background, G . . . .$45.00 (C)

Western X, four-page fold-out advertising brochure, 3½" x 6¼", EX . . . .$45.00 (C)

Western Xpert, shotgun shell cardboard box with graphics of bird dog in field, 4" x 4" x 3", VG . . . .$85.00 (B)

Western Xpert Super Target Load, shotgun shell box, F . . . .$9.00 (D)

Westfield Steam Laundry, celluloid over metal pinback, "Compliments of Westfield Steam Laundry Westfield, Mass.," 1¾" dia., VG . . . .$10.00 (B)

Whistle, paper ad, NOS, with graphics of boy and product bottle, 1950s, NM, $25.00 (D).

Courtesy of Rare Bird Antique Mall/Jon & Joan Wright

Whistle, Sparkling Orange Goodness, one-sided self-framing embossed tin sign, 56" x 32", G, $235.00 (B).

Whistle, wood coatrack with graphics of elves on top of coathook, 35½" x 8", EX, $275.00 (B). *Courtesy of Autopia Advertising Auctions*

West Hair Nets, countertop store display cabinet with graphics advertising West Hair Net and Electric Hair Curlers, 12¾" x 11¼" x 20", 1920s, G . . . . . .$750.00 (C)

Westinghouse Mazda Automobile Lamps, metal display storage countertop cabinet, 24" t, EX . . . .$95.00 (C)

Westinghouse Mazda Lamps for Automobiles, metal store cabinet with logo on end, 1929, black on orange, EX . . . .$295.00 (D)

Westinghouse Radio, light-up advertising clock, pressed cardboard body with glass front and face cover, 15" dia., G . . . .$95.00 (B)

West Virginia Pilsner Beer, cardboard advertising poster, featuring artwork of woman and glass of beer, 14" x 22", G . . . .$75.00 (C)

Weyman's Cutty-Pipe Chewing and Smoking Tobacco, store display bin, 9" x 10" x 13½", G . . . .$400.00 (B)

Whippet...Dollar for Dollar Value...Product of Willys-Overland Company, embossed tin advertising sign, 22½" x 12", G . . . .$225.00 (B)

Whip, tin litho pocket container with horse and rider, 4½" x 3" x ¾", EX . . . .$12,350.00 (B)

Whistle, advertising wall-mounted cast iron figural bottle holder in the likeness of hand holding the hourglass bottle, 10" x 3" x 2½", G . . . .$350.00 (D)

Whistle, cardboard die cut advertising sign in likeness of woman with Whistle bottle with straw, 15¾" x 22¾", VG . . . .$125.00 (C)

Whistle, cardboard die cut bottle sign, 1936, EX .$140.00 (C)

Whistle, cardboard die cut litho, "Thirsty? Just Whistle" with a Brownie at each end of sign, 17⅜" x 4¾", VG . . . .$80.00 (B)

Whistle, die cut cardboard advertising bottle, "Litho In U.S.A.," 8" x 30½", EX . . . .$85.00 (B)

Whistle, die cut cardboard advertising bottle with Whistle Brownie at top of bottle, 2¾" x 11½", VG . . . . .$75.00 (B)

Whistle, die cut cardboard litho countertop display, "Golden Orange Refreshment," with graphics of brownies pouring from Whistle bottle, NOS, 17" x 15", EX . . . . .$250.00 (B)

Whistle, die cut cardboard store advertising sign, with graphics of small elf next to product bottle, 1951, G . . . .$55.00 (D)

White Rose, double-sided porcelain sign with iron frame, 48½" dia., VG, **$1,000.00 (B).**

Courtesy of Collectors Auction Services

White House Coffee, die cut tin litho double-sided flange advertising sign with image of hand holding a container of coffee, "None better at any price," 13½" x 8¾", NM, **$4,800.00 (B).**

Courtesy of Buffalo Bay Auction Co.

Whistle, die cut double-sided cardboard display with elf pushing a cart that holds a 7-oz. bottle of Whistle, 7" x 7⅞", EX . . . .$335.00 (C)

Whistle, die cut easel back cardboard advertising sign with graphics of elves marching and pushing a bottle of Whistle, 13⅜" x 11¾", NM . . . .$400.00 (B)

Whistle, die cut wood and masonite painted advertising clock with graphics of elf on one side of the clock and a bottle of the product on the other side, 23¾" x 23¾", NM . . . .$825.00 (B)

Whistle...Drink Certified Pure, porcelain advertising sign with scarce "certified pure" slogan, 20" x 7", NM . . . . . .$700.00 (B)

Whistle, embossed tin advertising sign with musical notes and image of bottle, 30" x 12", NM . . . .$210.00 (B)

Whistle, embossed tin litho advertising sign featuring graphics of bottle in hand, "thirsty?...just Demand the Genuine Whistle," 27¾" x 9½", EX . . . .$975.00 (B)

Whistle, embossed tin sign, "Thirsty? Just Whistle...morning-noon-night," 27½" x 12½", 1939, VG . . . .$140.00 (B)

Whistle, embossed tin sign, "Thirsty...just Whistle," 12½" x 3", 1939, VG . . . .$80.00 (B)

Whistle, framed die cut paper advertisment from H. Gramse and Bro. Litho, Balto., Md., 23" x 7", VG . . . . . .$75.00 (B)

Whistle...Golden Orange...Refreshment Time, die cut pressed board, electric advertising clock, 24" x 23", EX . . . .$1,200.00 (C)

Whistle On Ice, embossed tin advertising sign with image of bottle in hand, 8¾" x 6", NM . . . .$725.00 (B)

Whistle, orange advertising sign in new frame, 4¼" x 24", EX . . . .$170.00 (B)

Whistle, painted tin advertising thermometer with graphics of two elves holding a bottle of the product, 9" x 20", EX . . . .$850.00 (B)

Whistle, paper ad, NOS, with graphics of boy and product bottle, 1950s, VG . . . .$12.00 (C)

Whistle, paper die cut headband in shape of Indian headdress, 23½" x 5½", NM . . . .$100.00 (D)

Whistle Soda, cardboard bottle sign, NOS, 9" x 31", NM . . . .$140.00 (B)

Whistle Soda, cardboard vertical advertising sign, 1948, 2¾" x 23", NM . . . .$95.00 (B)

Whistle...Thirsty Just...Certified Pure, embossed tin advertising sign with image of bottle in center, 20" x 14", VG . . . .$170.00 (B)

White House Coffee, "The Very Highest Quality," tin litho match holder, featuring graphics of the White House, 5" H, G, $375.00 (B). *Courtesy of Richard Opfer Auctioneering, Inc.*

White Rock Beer, tin litho in wood frame with graphics of girl holding wheat with image of bottle of White Rock, The Akron Brewing Co., Akron, Ohio, 33" x 24¾", VG, $560.00 (B). *Courtesy of Collectors Auction Services*

White Rock...The World's Best Table Water, rectangular tip tray with fairy on rock over water, 6" tall, EX, $130.00 (B). *Courtesy of Richard Opfer Auctioneering Inc.*

Whistle...Thirsty? Just...Refreshing Fruit Flavor, decal, unused, in shape of bottle cap, NM . . . .$5.00 (D)

Whistle, tin advertising sign with graphics of farm scene and Brownie hauling a large bottle of Whistle on a hand cart, 26" x 30", G . . . .$300.00 (B)

Whistle, tin litho advertising arrow sign, NOS, 27" x 7", NM . . . .$175.00 (C)

Whistle, 12-oz. bottle with applied color label with elves and logos on both sides with Whistle cap, 12-oz., NM . . . .$90.00 (B)

Whistle, wood coatrack with graphics of elves on top of coathook, 35½" x 8", G . . . .$135.00 (D)

White Ash, Liberty, can, advertising "Genuine Sumatra Wrapped," 50-count, EX . . . .$55.00 (C)

White Bear Coffee, paper on cardboard container with graphics of polar bear on ice, 4½" x 3" x 6", VG . $275.00 (B)

Whitehead & Hoag, advertising calendar with advertising for their many pinbacks and badges and graphics of young woman at top, 1911, EX . . . . $40.00 (B)

White Horse Spice, cardboard container with paper label, graphics of Indian on horseback, EX . . . .$75.00 (C)

White House Coffee, die cut tin litho double-sided flange advertising sign with image of hand holding a container of coffee, "None better at any price," 13½" x 8¾", NM . . . .$4,800.00 (B)

White House Coffee, "The Very Highest Quality," tin litho match holder, featuring graphics of the White House, 5" H, EX . . . .$450.00 (C)

White Rose, Motor Gasoline, single-sided tin advertising sign, graphics of two roses, 14¼" x 10¼", NOS, EX, $810.00 (B).

Wiedemann Fine Beer, 3-D plastic sign with trumpeter swan flying over wetlands, 16" x 18", VG, $65.00 (C). *Courtesy of B.J. Summers*

Wieland, John, Extra Pale Beer, chalkware advertising figurine out of San Jose, Calif., 3" x 9", G, $40.00 (B).

Wielands Beer, serving tray, graphics of pretty lady reading, from San Francisco, CA, 1909, 10½" x 13¼", G, $155.00 (B).

White House Ginger Ale...Standard Bottling & Extract Co., Boston, round metal tip tray with bottle of product in center, 4¼" dia., EX . . . .$90.00 (B)

White King Soap, tin "tacker" type advertising sign with graphics of a box of the product pouring the granulated powder, NOS, 9⅞" x 13⅞", NM . . . .$175.00 (C)

White King...Washes Everything, tin litho with additional reverse on glass light-up clock face showing image of king in center, 1927, 24" x 17" x 6", EX . . . . . .$1,275.00 (B)

White Label Coffee, tin litho with graphics of hot cup of coffee on front label, 1-lb., EX . . . .$125.00 (C)

White Label 5¢ Cigars, embossed tin sign with graphics of box of product, 13¾" x 10", EX . . . .$198.00 (B)

White Lilac Coffee, tin litho can, Consolidated Tea Co., Inc., New York, rectangular with artwork of lilacs in bloom on front, 4¼" x 6" x 2⅞", EX . . . .$450.00 (B)

White Lion, cigar tin with graphics of lion's head on front and top, 6¼" x 5½" x 4⅛", EX . . . .$135.00 (C)

Wildroot, ask for, embossed painted metal sign featuring a barber pole at right of message, 28" x 10", VG, **$110.00 (C).** *Courtesy of Riverview Antique Mall*

Wilbur's Seed Meal, box, wood with paper litho label, 20" x 22" x 36", VG, **$7,000.00 (B).** *Courtesy of Collectors Auction Services*

Wildroot Cream Oil, cardboard easel back die cut advertising sign featuring Fearless Fosdick, "Get Wildroot Cream Oil Charlie!," 30" x 30¼", 1954, EX, **$275.00 (C).** *Courtesy of Autopia Advertising Auctions*

White Owl Cigar, advertising lighter with trademark owl, on side, 1½" x ½", EX . . . .**$130.00 (B)**

White Owl Squires, metal advertising tin with product logo in diamond-shaped outline on front, yellow background, EX . . . .**$20.00 (D)**

White Rock Beer, tin litho in wood frame with graphics of girl holding wheat with image of bottle of White Rock, The Akron Brewing Co., Akron, Ohio, 33" x 24¾", G . . . .**$325.00 (C)**

White Rock Lithia Water, self-framing embossed tin litho advertising sign with fairy at water on rock, 16½" x 19¾", EX . . . .**$875.00 (C)**

White Rock Sparkling Beverages, die cut metal sign with graphics of fairy on rock, 18" x 13", VG . . . . .**$500.00 (B)**

White Rock Sparkling Beverages, tin double-sided flange advertising sign with fairy nymph looking at water, 18" x 13¾", EX . . . .**$475.00 (C)**

White Rock...The World's Best Table Water, rectangular tip tray with fairy on rock over water, 6" tall, G . . . .**$65.00 (C)**

White Rock...The World's Best Table Water, round metal tip tray with fairy image on rock looking over water, 4¼" dia., EX . . . .**$300.00 (B)**

White Rock, tin litho tip tray with graphics of Atlantic City beach scene, Kaufman & Strauss Lithographers, 4⅜" dia., EX . . . .**$375.00 (B)**

White Rock, tip tray with graphics of fairy looking at its reflection in water from rock, 4¼" dia., VG . .**$180.00 (B)**

Wild Woodbine Cigarettes, one-sided porcelain sign, foreign, 48¼"
x 17¾", VG, $375.00 (B). *Courtesy of Collectors Auction Services*

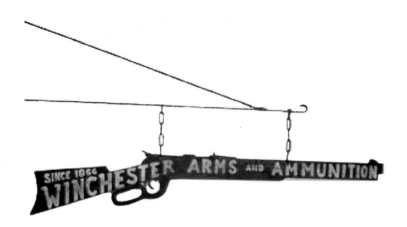

Winchester Arms & Ammunition, die cut double-sided metal
advertising sign on hanging arm, probably a fantasy item, 41¼"
x 6½", EX, $450.00 (B). *Courtesy of Buffalo Bay Auction Co.*

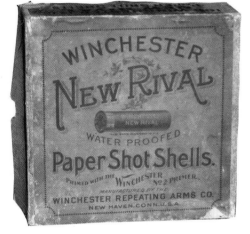

Winchester, New Rival, paper shot
shells box, 8⅛" x 8⅛" x 2¾", F,
$50.00 (B).

White Rock Water, pastel on canvas of Psyche kneeling
on rock studying her reflection in the water, the original
oil was completed for the 1893 Columbian Exposition and
adopted for use as White Rock logo in 1894, 42" x 62",
1910s, EX . . . .$3,900.00 (B)

White Rose Flour...Bakes Better Bread, painted wooden
sign, self-framing, 74" x 26", G . . . .$325.00 (D)

White Rose Flour, wooden sign with wood frame, "White
Rose Flour bakes better bread," 74" x 26", VG . .$595.00 (D)

White Rose...Gasoline...Motor Oil, one-sided porcelain
advertising sign with graphics of a white rose in center,
72" x 17", G . . . . $2,750.00 (B)

**White Rose Gasoline...Use The Best...To Get The
Best,"** one-sided self-framing embossed tin sign with
graphics of trademark Enarco boy holding sign, 40" x
26½", VG . . . .$350.00 (B)

White Rose Motor Gasoline, tin litho advertising sign
with graphics of rose, 13¾" x 9¾", EX . . . . .$525.00 (C)

White Rose No Knock, one-piece gasoline globe with
trademark boy holding black board, EX . . .$3,000.00 (C)

White Rose...Quick Starting, tin litho advertising bank
with artwork of the Enarco kid with board, 3½" x 2⅛",
EX . . . .$210.00 (B)

White Sewing Machine, paper over heavy cardboard
advertising puzzle, litho by W.J. Morgan & Co., Cleveland,
1910, EX . . . .$325.00 (C)

White's Golden Tonic for Horses, advertising, paper litho
with graphics of horse in center of message, 21½" x 28",
VG . . . .$50.00 (B)

Winchester New Rival Shells, cardboard advertising sign with graphics of box of the product, 16½" x 10", EX, **$95.00 (C).** *Courtesy of Past Tyme Pleasures*

Winchester, paper advertising calendar with graphics of hunting scene in snow and desert with top and bottom metal strips, 14¼" x 27", 1899, EX, **$1,500.00 (B).** *Courtesy of Past Tyme Pleasures*

Winchester Silvertip bullet, double-sided cardboard litho, 21" x 12¾", VG, **$85.00 (B).**

White Squadron Spice, store bin with slant front, litho contains graphics of ships and other patriotic items, 7" x 9" x 10", EX . . . .$223.00 (B)

White Swan Coffee, tin litho with graphics of swan on front, White Swan Spices & Cereals, Toronto, 1-lb., EX . . . .$235.00 (C)

White Top Champagne, round metal tip tray with product bottle artwork on tray center, 4⅛" dia., EX . . .$35.00 (B)

Whitman's Chocolates, porcelain sign "Agency Whitman's Chocolates and Confections since 1842," 39½" x 13½", VG . . . .$195.00 (C)

Whiz Bang, rim fire cartridges, cardboard countertop display box with graphics of .22 shell on front, 10" x 5" x 4½", NM . . . .$75.00 (C)

Whiz Patch Outfit, extra-heavy metal store display with artwork of man repairing tire on older model car, NM . . . .$425.00 (C)

Whiz White Rubber, coating for tires, tin sign with image of woman in vintage car, 12" x 17", EX . . . .$525.00 (C)

Wickenburg, Arizona, die cut metal license plate attachment in shape of ten-gallon hat, NOS, 6" x 5⅜", NM . . . .$150.00 (C)

Wiedemann Brewing Co., pocket plated brass match safe with embossing on both sides, 1½" x 3", EX . .$200.00 (C)

Wiedemann Fine Beer, 3-D plastic sign with trumpeter swan flying over wetlands, 16" x 18", G . . . . . .$45.00 (C)

Wigwam Brand Coffee, tin litho with pry-lid and graphics of Indian silhouette on front, 1-lb., EX . . . .$75.00 (B)

Wigwam, spice cardboard container with paper label, EX . . . .$75.00 (C)

Wigwam Sugar Corn, tin container with hand soldering, graphics of Indian with bow drawn in front of teepee, EX . . . .$350.00 (B)

Wilbur's Cocoa Glove, hook with advertising image on celluloid button, 2½", EX . . . .$50.00 (B)

Winchester Western, thermometer, "sporting ammunition sold here," shape of shotgun shell, 12" x 32", F, $55.00 (D).
Courtesy of Pleasant Hill Antique Mall & Tea Room/Bob Johnson

Winchester, window display, showing target practice scene, 48" tall, G, $350.00 (C).

Winston...tastes good...like a cigarette should!, embossed painted metal thermometer with vertical scale at top right and product package lower left, no warning label, 6" x 13½", EX, $65.00 (C).

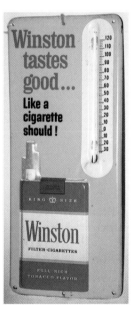

Wings Cigarettes, paper advertisement, graphics of lighted cigarette, 14" x 20", VG, $5.00 (B).

Wilbur's Cocoa, paper label container with small lid, with graphics of cherub-like figure stirring a cup of the product, 2½" x 3⅛", VG . . . .$95.00 (C)

Wilbur's Seed Meal, box, wood with paper litho label, 20" x 22" x 36", F . . . .$895.00 (C)

Wildroot, ask for, embossed painted metal sign featuring a barber pole at right of message, 28" x 10", G . .$95.00 (D)

Wildroot...Barber Shop, embossed metal self-framing advertising sign with graphics of barber pole, 39½" x 13½", NM . . . .$150.00 (B)

Wildroot Barber Shop, single-sided self-framing tin sign, 39½" x 13½", VG . . . .$140.00 (B)

Wildroot Cream Oil, cardboard easel back die cut advertising sign featuring Fearless Fosdick, "Get Wildroot Cream Oil Charlie!", 30" x 30¼", 1954, G . . . .$125.00 (D)

Wildwood...By The Sea N.J.World's Safest Beach, painted tin license plate attachment, 6" x 6¼", EX . . .$135.00 (C)

Willard Batteries, check here, dial-type advertising thermometer, 16" dia., VG . . . .$135.00 (C)

Willard Batteries, light-up advertising clock with center spotlight bearing message, 15" dia., VG . . . . .$235.00 (B)

Willard Batteries, one-sided embossed tin sign, 39½" x 12", VG . . . .$140.00 (B)

Wonder Bread, Howdy Doody, heavy paper die cut stand-up, 5½" x 13", VG, $80.00 (B).

Wisconsin Engines, embossed painted metal dealer sign, 30" x 24", VG, $255.00 (C). *Courtesy of Riverview Antique Mall*

Wonder Enriched Bread. . . Helps Build Strong Bodies 8 Ways, embossed tin sign, graphics of product loaf, 30" x 18", VG, $120.00 (B).

Williams Bread, porcelain and wrought iron door push bar, G . . . .$230.00 (B)

Williams Bread, tin advertising sign featuring image of loaf of the product, 26" x 16", NM . . . .$175.00 (C)

Will's Cigarettes, framed advertising sign, 13" x 24", VG . . . .$175.00 (C)

Will's Cigarettes...WD & Howills, framed sign showing different planes and cars, 13" x 24" . . . .$55.00 (D)

Will's Gold Flake Cigarettes...Smoke, two-piece heavy back bar advertising mirror with hand-painted lettering, 70" x 26", G . . . .$750.00 (C)

Willys-Overland Company...Dollar for Dollar Whippet Product of.., porcelain sign, 36" x 24", cream on red, G . . . .$325.00 (C)

Willys-Overland Company, embossed tin advertising sign for Whippet, 22½" x 12", G . . . .$225.00 (B)

Wilson's Certified Smoked Ham, die cut cardboard easel back ad sign with art of Uncle Sam slicing product, 29½" x 40", EX . . . .$180.00 (B)

Wilson's Peanut Butter, tin litho of the old woman in the shoe, 1-lb., EX . . . .$375.00 (C)

Winchester, advertising calendar with graphics of eagle and mountain goat, 15¼" x 30¼", 1915, EX . . . . .$1,050.00 (B)

Winchester, advertising poster, "Big Game Rifles and Ammunition" with graphics of early hunter on a mountaintop, complete with metal bands on top and bottom, 15½" x 26¼", EX . . . .$325.00 (C)

Winchester, advertising sign, litho on paperboard by H.R. Poore with original oak frame, graphics of pair of dogs, 35" x 25½", 1907, EX . . . .$350.00 (B)

Winchester After Shave Talc, tin container with great litho of hunter and his dog on front, NM . . . .$205.00 (B)

Winchester Arms & Ammunition, die cut double-sided metal advertising sign on hanging arm, probably a fantasy item, 41¼" x 6½", G . . . .$135.00 (D)

Winchester calendar, advertising calendar with graphics of bird hunter behind a couple of bird dogs in a fall hunting scene, 15¼" x 30¼", 1914, VG . . . .$480.00 (B)

Wonder Orange, Drink, embossed tin advertising sign, featuring spotlight on oranges at left of message, 1930s, 19½" x 13½", G, *$225.00* (B). *Courtesy of Muddy River Trading Co./Gary Metz*

Woodlawn Mills Shoe Lace Service Station, metal litho in the shape of a service station, EX, **$3,200.00 (B).** *Courtesy of Collectors Auction Services*

Worcester Elastic Stocking & Truss Co., celluloid advertising pocket mirror, great graphics of partially clad woman, EX, *$400.00* (B). *Courtesy of Wm. Morford Investment Grade Collectibles*

Winchester Cartridge Shop, World War Two paper motivational shop poster, "reveille for workers...taps for japs," 14" x 22", EX . . . .*$190.00* (B)

Winchester, countertop die cut cardboard easel back advertising sign with image of vintage dressed man with gun in front of product, 10" x 22", EX . . . . . .*$175.00* (D)

Winchester, die cut cardboard stand-up of C.G. Spenser, champion shot for Winchester, 10" x 22", EX . .*$155.00* (C)

Winchester, die cut cardboard stand-up with graphics of grizzly bear, "from the grizzly to the squirrel," 13" x 22", EX . . . .*$195.00* (C)

Winchester Double A, trap loads, shotgun shell box, F . . . .*$7.00* (D)

Winchester, double-sided porcelain flange advertising sign with graphics of Winchester gun with various sizes of shells and factory, 18" x 13½", EX . . . .*$1,650.00* (B)

Winchester Gun Advisor Center, tin litho shield-shaped sign on wood, 1950s, 20" x 20", NM . . . .*$100.00* (B)

Winchester Leader Waterproofed Paper Shot Shells, Winchester Repeating Arms Co., two-piece shell box with DuPont label on side, EX . . . .*$240.00* (B)

Wrigley Chewing Gum, die cut cardboard store counter display with Wrigley man and young girl, promoting 1¢ P-K Gum, 12" x 8", EX, **$425.00 (C).**
Courtesy of Buffalo Bay Auction Co.

Wrigley's Doublemint, General Store, double-sided porcelain sign, 30" x 9", F, **$2,400.00 (B).** *Courtesy of Wm. Morford Investment Grade Collectibles*

Wrigley's, In Bond, cardboard litho, advertising the famous gum and its unique packaging, 22¼" x 12¼", VG, **$45.00 (B).** *Courtesy of Collectors Auction Services*

Winchester New Rival Shells, cardboard advertising sign with graphics of box of the product, 16½" x 10", VG . . .**$75.00 (C)**

Winchester Nublack Loaded Black Powder Shells, 10-gal., two-piece box with graphics of wild fowl in flight, 25-count, EX . . . .**$140.00 (B)**

Winchester, paper advertising calendar with graphics of hunting scene in snow and desert with top and bottom metal strips, 14¼" x 27", 1899, EX . . . . . .**$1,500.00 (B)**

Winchester, paper shot shells, 32-gal., two-piece box, empty, 3" x 3" x 2½", EX . . . .**$95.00 (C)**

Winchester Ranger Mark 5, shotgun shell box, F . .**$9.00 (D)**

Winchester Ranger, shotgun shell box, F . . . . . .**$8.00 (D)**

Winchester Ranger Super Target Load, shotgun shell box, G . . . .**$10.00 (D)**

Winchester Ranger Super Trap Load, shell box with graphics of vintage shooter on front, 4¼" x 4¼" x 2½", EX . . . .**$55.00 (D)**

Winchester Ranger, two-piece shotgun shell box with graphics of geese in flight, 12-ga., 4" x 4" x 2½", G . . . .**$40.00 (B)**

Winchester Repeater Oval, 16-gauge shell box, 4" x 4' x 2½", EX . . . .**$95.00 (C)**

Winchester Salesman, sample box of shot shell, window displays, 3" x 4¼" x 1", EX . . . .**$155.00 (C)**

Winchester Shells, advertising poster in wooden frame, "Shoot them and avoid trouble," 27" x 18¾", 1900s, EX . . . .**$300.00 (B)**

Winchester Staynless Cartridges, advertising paper litho with graphics of various sizes of cartridges, 13" x 21½", EX . . . .**$120.00 (B)**

Wrigley's Spearmint, Taste the Juice of Real Mint Leaves, single-sided cardboard poster, 21" x 11", G, $130.00 (B).

Wurlitzer, bubbling display advertising sign, limited edition, great presentation piece, 1990, EX, $425.00 (B). *Courtesy of Muddy River Trading Co./Gary Metz*

Wyandotte Detergent, self-framing tin litho advertising sign from J.B. Ford Company with graphics of Indian in full headdress with hunting bow drawn, 28" x 39", NM, $4,500.00 (B). *Courtesy of Past Tyme Pleasures*

Winchester Western Silvertip CF cartridges, easel back cardboard store countertop sign, NOS, 24" x 20", NM . . . .$100.00 (C)

Winchester Western, thermometer, "sporting ammunition sold here," shape of shotgun shell, 12" x 32", VG .$135.00 (C)

Winchester, window display, 4-panel fold display, front side displays Winchester products, back side shows Winchester logo of Junior Rifle Corp., 20¼" x 48" each panel, G . . . .$500.00 (D)

Wincroft Ranges and Stoves, tradecard with graphics of Uncle Sam weather indicator, 3½" x 6", EX . . $30.00 (B)

Windsor...Supreme, figural head pitcher, EX . .$25.00 (D)

Wineberre Beverage Sold Here, embossed tin litho advertising sign, 17½" x 12", EX . . . .$55.00 (B)

Wingold Flour, cardboard cut-out, give-away in uncut condition, images of delivery truck and train by Bay State Milling Co., 12½" x 10¼", NM . . . .$65.00 (B)

Wings Regular Gasoline, single-sided porcelain pump sign with graphics of flying geese, 7" x 6", VG . .$1,700.00 (B)

Wing's, tin litho baby powder talc container with graphics of baby in center, from Frederick Ingram & Co., 1¾" x 4", EX . . . .$95.00 (C)

Winner Cut Plug, tobacco pail with racing scene on front, "J Wright Co., The American Tobacco Co., Richmond, Va.," 4" T, VG . . . .$125.00 (D)

Winston...tastes good...like a cigarette should!, embossed painted metal thermometer with vertical scale at top right and product package lower left, no warning label, 6" x 13½", VG . . . .$45.00 (D)

Winston...the taste is tops...pack or box, round dial-type painted metal thermometer with artwork of product packages on both sides of dial, EX . . . .$30.00 (D)

Wisconsin Engines, embossed painted metal dealer sign, 30" x 24", G . . . .$235.00 (D)

Wise Potato Chip, advertising painted wooden thermometer from Berwick, PA, 2⅞" x 8⅜", EX . . . .$75.00 (C)

Wishbone Coffee Tin, with graphics of wishbone on front, 7½" x 7½", EX . . . .$75.00 (C)

Wishing Well Orange, porcelain door push, "We sell Wishing Well Orange," 4" x 32½", VG . . . .$135.00 (B)

Wix Oil Filters and Filterfils, reverse glass light-up advertising sign, 16" x 8" x 6", EX . . . .$225.00 (C)

W.J. Guy Implement Dealer, embossed tin sign with farm implements in row between message lines, 28" x 10", EX . . . .$242.00 (B)

Wolf's Head Motor Oil...We sell, painted metal curb sign with logo in lower right, with original cast base with raised letters, 59" dia., red, white, and green, EX . . .$350.00 (C)

Wonder Bread, die cut metal advertising sign in shape of loaf of the product, "It's slo baked," 12" x 9", 1950s, EX . . . .$235.00 (C)

Wonder Bread, embossed painted metal door push, "We Suggest...it's fresh," 27½" x 2¾", VG . . . . . . $150.00 (B)

Wonder Bread Howdy Doody, heavy paper die cut advertising sign showing Hoody holding a loaf of Wonder Bread, NOS, 6" x 13", NM . . . .$275.00 (B)

Wondercade Illusion Spectacular, paper poster with graphics of various acts to be performed, 22" x 28", NM . . . .$25.00 (C)

Wonder Orange, drink, embossed tin advertising sign, featuring spotlight on oranges at left of message, 1930s, 19½" x 13½", EX . . . .$350.00 (C)

Woodlawn Mills Shoe Lace Service Station, metal litho in the shape of a service station, EX . . . .$3,200.00 (B)

Woods Lollacapop Mosquito Antidote, tin container with graphics of mosquito on lid, 3¼" x 1¾" x ¾", EX . .$100.00 (B)

Wood's Mowers, Walter A. Wood Mowing and Reaping Machine, cardboard ad sign depicting mowers and reapers in use, 1895, 27" x 19", G . . . .$350.00 (B)

Woodward Candy Co., metal tip tray with artwork of man and woman in early dress with product, 6¾" L, EX . . . .$190.00 (B)

Worcester Elastic Stocking & Truss Co., celluloid advertising pocket mirror, great graphics of partially clad woman, G . . . .$150.00 (C)

Workman's Friend, pocket celluloid pocket mirror, "For Removing Obstructions from Eyes and Other Uses Where Close Examinations is Required," 2½" dia., VG . .$45.00 (B)

Wrigley Chewing Gum, die cut cardboard store counter display with Wrigley man and young girl, promoting 1¢ P-K Gum, 12" x 8", G . . . .$135.00 (C)

Wright and Taylor Old Charter Distillery, tin litho serving tray with factory scene, 12" dia., VG . . . . . .$330.00 (B)

Wrigley's, cardboard counter gum display, held 20 of the 5-stick packages, with back graphics of the Wrigley arrow and pretty girl, 12½" x 9" x 6¾", NM . . . . . .$375.00 (C)

Wrigley's Doublemint, General Store, double-sided porcelain sign, 30" x 9", EX . . . .$3,900.00 (C)

Wrigley's Soap, metal tip tray with graphics of cat sitting on product bars, 3⅝" dia., EX . . . .$170.00 (B)

Wrought Iron Range, paper in wood frame advertising sign, 22½" x 16½", EX . . . .$475.00 (D)

W. Schneider...Wholesale Wine & Liquor Co., crock jug, 1- gal., brown over cream, EX . . . .$100.00 (D)

Wurlitzer, bubbling display advertising sign, limited edition, great presentation piece, 1990, G . . . . .$200.00 (C)

Wyandotte Detergent, self-framing tin litho advertising sign from J.B. Ford company with graphics of Indian in full headdress with hunting bow drawn, 28" x 39", VG . . . .$1,900.00 (C)

"X" Liquid Repairs Leaky Radiators, embossed tin advertising sign with "X man" image at vintage auto with area for current gas price at top, 19¼" x 27⅛", EX, **$475.00 (B)**. *Courtesy of Autopia Advertising Auctions*

X Powder Repairs Leaky Radiators, countertop display unit in likeness of "X boy" with packages of product, 10¾" x 15", VG, **$165.00 (B)**. *Courtesy of Collectors Auction Services*

Yacht Club, drip grind coffee tin litho can with key-wound lid, from Chicago, Ill., 1-lb., EX . . . .$135.00 (C)

Yankee Razor Blade, metal container with patriotic theme on cover from Reichard & Scheuber Mfg Co., NY, 2¼" x 1" x ¼", EX . . . .$75.00 (B)

Ybala's Spring Beverages, embossed tin sign with graphics of product bottle, NOS, 9" x 20", NM . . . . . .$115.00 (C)

Yeast Foam, framed paper litho with graphics of young girl with pancakes, 11½" x 16¼", VG . . . .$40.00 (B)

Yeast Foam, paper advertising poster featuring great graphics of young girl at table in front of a stack of "Buckwheat Cakes," 10" x 15", EX . . . .$125.00 (C)

Yeast Foam, wall dispenser, tin litho with "Eat yeast foam" on side rail, 2¾" x 27", EX . . . .$105.00 (D)

Yello-Bole Pipe, cardboard & fabric wrapped countertop display unit with graphics of pretty girl with a honeycomb, easel back, 30" x 33", NM . . . .$275.00 (C)

Yello-Bole, pipe store display stand featuring woman in green evening dress holding a sample pipe, metal, plastic, and cardboard, 1950s, G . . . .$55.00 (C)

Yellow Bonnet, coffee can tin-wound lid with graphics of woman in bonnet on front, Springfield, MO, 1-lb., EX . . . .$125.00 (C)

Yellow Cab, cigar box with great graphics of man hailing cab, "takes the right of way," 1918, VG . . . . .$80.00 (C)

Yellow Cab 5¢ Cigar...Takes The Right of Way, embossed tin litho sign with artwork of policeman at intersection with old yellow cab, 1920s, 19⅞" x 6¾", EX . . . . .$1,000.00 (B)

Yeast Foam, paper advertising poster featuring great graphics of young girl at table in front of a stack of "Buckwheat Cakes," 10" x 15", NM, $145.00 (D).

Yello-Bole, pipe store display stand featuring woman in green evening dress holding a sample pipe, metal, plastic, and cardboard, 1950s, EX, $135.00 (D).

Courtesy of Creatures of Habit

Yellow Kid, paper poster promoting the syndicated comic strip series from the *New York Sunday Journal* newspaper, 20" x 15", EX, $1,195.00 (C). *Courtesy of Wm. Morford Investment Grade Collectibles*

Yellow Kid, leather pocket match holder from the Bartholomay's Brewing Co. with logo on back and Yellow Kid on front, "match me if ye can," 2¼" x 5¼", EX . . . . $495.00 (C)

Yellow Kid, paper poster promoting the syndicated comic strip series from the *New York Sunday Journal* newspaper, 20" x 15", F . . . . $125.00 (C)

Yocum Brothers, nice cigar tin with graphics of the brothers on the front label, 50-count, 6¼" x 4¼" x 5¼", EX . . . . $115.00 (C)

Youth's Companion, fold-out calendar, 21" x 12", EX . . . . $170.00 (B)

Yuengling's...Beer, Porter and Ale, round metal tip tray with graphics of eagle with wooden keg, 4¼" dia., EX . . . . $50.00 (B)

Yuengling's Bottled Beer, tin litho tip tray with graphics of young lady in bonnet, 4¼" dia., EX . . . . . . $65.00 (D)

Yum Yum Tobacco Tin Pail, "Manufactured by the American Tobacco Successors to Aug. Beck & Co. Factory No. 26, First District of Illinois," 6½" H, VG . . . . . . $50.00 (B)

Zambora Cigar, advertising clock for the Chicago World's Fair, although in the likeness of clock this wasn't ever meant to be a timepiece, and only had one hand, from J.P. Hier, Syracuse, NY, 1893, EX, **$845.00 (B).** *Courtesy of Buffalo Bay Auction Co.*

Zipp's Cherri-O, syrup dispenser, 1920s, EX, **$1,500.00 (B).**

Zephyr Gasoline, wide body globe with two glass lenses, 13½" dia., VG, **$355.00 (B).**

Zenith, Long Distance Radio, scale-type advertising thermometer, embossed tin, 17" x 71", G, **$475.00 (B).**

Zambora Cigar, advertising clock for the Chicago World's Fair, although in the likeness of clock this wasn't ever meant to be a timepiece, and only had one hand, from J.P. Hier, Syracuse, NY, 1893, EX . . . .$845.00 (B)

Zanzibar Carbon, tin litho with paper label on front, depicting African village scene, 10½" x 6" x 8¼", VG . . . .$225.00 (C)

Zeno, countertop wood and glass three-shelf display unit, 10" x 8" x 17", EX . . . .$475.00 (B)

Zeno Gum, tin with graphics of young man reaching for package of product, 9½" x 4½" x 2½", EX . . . .$55.00 (B)

Zephyr, two-sided metal advertising sign, 59½" x 37¾", VG . . . .$200.00 (B)

Zero Flo...Pours at 35° below, paraffin base motor oil, painted tin sign, 28" x 20", white, orange & black, EX . . . .$155.00 (C)

Zig-Zag, cigarette paper dispenser with artwork of hands pulling papers at top of container, 6" T, EX . . .$75.00 (C)

Zipp's Cherri-o, syrup dispenser, 1920s, EX . .$1,500.00 (B)

Zira cigarette, cardboard advertisement for their satin wonder in each package, 16" x 13", VG . . . . . .$40.00 (B)

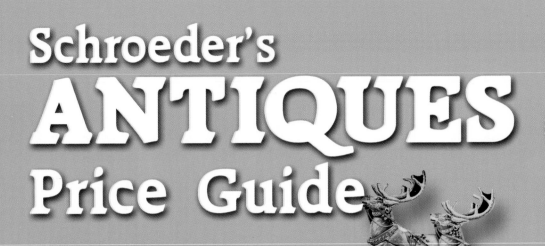
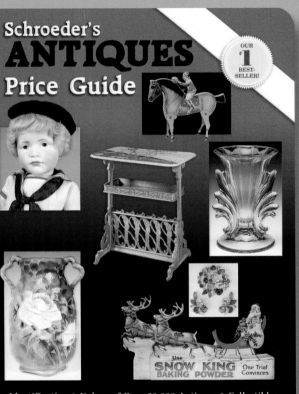

Past Tyme Pleasures

Purveyors of Fine Antiques & Collectibles
Presents Annual Spring and Fall Antique Advertising Auctions

Call / Fax / Email today to be added to our mailing list to receive future auction information.
To receive the next color catalogue and prices realized, send your check for $15 today to:

Past Tyme Pleasures

PMB #204, 2491 San Ramon Valley Blvd., #1   San Ramon, CA 94583

Ph: **925-484-6442**   FAX: **925-484-2551**   CA Bond SD 09017

email: **pasttyme@excite.com**   web site: **www.pasttyme.com**

Sales include 240+ items with a fine selection of rare signs, trays, tins, and advertising items
relating to tobacco, sporting collectibles, breweriana, soda, talc, and general store, etc.

ANTIQUE MALL

TWIN LAKES

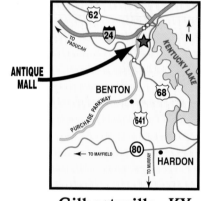

BENJ. G. CARLL
Wholesale Commission Merchant
Fancy Fruits and Vegetables
No. 137 Dock Street   PHILADELPHIA